Year	Present Value at 21%	Present Value at 22%	Present Value at 23%	Present Value at 24%	Present Value at 25%	Present Value at 26%	Present Value at 27%	Present Value at 28%	Present Value at 29%	Present Value at 30%
1	0.826446	0.819672	0.813008	0.806452	0.800000	0.793651	0.787402	0.781250	0.775194	0.769231
2	0.683013	0.671862	0.660982	0.650364	0.640000	0.629882	0.620001	0.610352	0.600925	0.591716
3	0.564474	0.550707	0.537384	0.524487	0.512000	0.499906	0.488190	0.476837	0.465834	0.455166
4	0.466507	0.451399	0.436898	0.422974	0.409600	0.396751	0.384402	0.372529	0.361111	0.350128
5	0.385543	0.369999	0.355201	0.341108	0.327680	0.314882	0.302678	0.291038	0.279931	0.269329
6	0.318631	0.303278	0.288781	0.275087	0.262144	0.249906	0.238329	0.227374	0.217001	0.207176
7	0.263331	0.248589	0.234782	0.221844	0.209715	0.198338	0.187661	0.177636	0.168218	0.159366
8	0.217629	0.203761	0.190879	0.178907	0.167772	0.157411	0.147765	0.138778	0.130401	0.122590
9	0.179859	0.167017	0.155187	0.144280	0.134218	0.124930	0.116350	0.108420	0.101086	0.094300
10	0.148644	0.136899	0.126168	0.116354	0.107374	0.099150	0.091614	0.084703	0.078362	0.072538
11	0.122846	0.112213	0.102576	0.093834	0.085899	0.078691	0.072137	0.066174	0.060745	0.055799
12	0.101526	0.091978	0.083395	0.075673	0.068719	0.062453	0.056801	0.051699	0.047089	0.042922
13	0.083905	0.075391	0.067801	0.061026	0.054976	0.049566	0.044725	0.040390	0.036503	0.033017
14	0.069343	0.061796	0.055122	0.049215	0.043980	0.039338	0.035217	0.031554	0.028297	0.025398
15	0.057309	0.050653	0.044815	0.039689	0.035184	0.031221	0.027730	0.024652	0.021936	0.019537
16	0.047362	0.041519	0.036435	0.032008	0.028147	0.024778	0.021834	0.019259	0.017005	0.015028
17	0.039142	0.034032	0.029622	0.025813	0.022518	0.019665	0.017192	0.015046	0.013182	0.011560
18	0.032349	0.027895	0.024083	0.020817	0.018014	0.015607	0.013537	0.011755	0.010218	0.008892
19	0.026735	0.022865	0.019580	0.016788	0.014412	0.012387	0.010659	0.009184	0.007921	0.006840
20	0.022095	0.018741	0.015918	0.013538	0.011529	0.009831	0.008393	0.007175	0.006141	0.005262
21	0.018260	0.015362	0.012942	0.010918	0.009223	0.007802	0.006609	0.005605	0.004760	0.004048
22	0.015091	0.012592	0.010522	0.008805	0.007379	0.006192	0.005204	0.004379	0.003690	0.003113
23	0.012472	0.010321	0.008554	0.007101	0.005903	0.004914	0.004097	0.003421	0.002860	0.002395
24	0.010307	0.008460	0.006955	0.005726	0.004722	0.003900	0.003226	0.002673	0.002217	0.001842
25	0.008519	0.006934	0.005654	0.004618	0.003778	0.003096	0.002540	0.002088	0.001719	0.001417

Year	Present Value at 31%	Present Value at 32%	Present Value at 33%	Present Value at 34%	Present Value at 35%	Present Value at 36%	Present Value at 37%	Present Value at 38%	Present Value at 39%	Present Value at 40%
1	0.763359	0.757576	0.751880	0.746269	0.740741	0.735294	0.729927	0.724638	0.719424	0.714286
2	0.582717	0.573921	0.565323	0.556917	0.548697	0.540657	0.532793	0.525100	0.517572	0.510204
3	0.444822	0.434789	0.425055	0.415610	0.406442	0.397542	0.388900	0.380507	0.372354	0.364432
4	0.339559	0.329385	0.319590	0.310156	0.301068	0.292310	0.283869	0.275730	0.267880	0.260308
5	0.259205	0.249534	0.240293	0.231460	0.223013	0.214934	0.207204	0.199804	0.192720	0.185934
6	0.197866	0.189041	0.180672	0.172731	0.165195	0.158040	0.151243	0.144786	0.138647	0.132810
7	0.151043	0.143213	0.135843	0.128904	0.122367	0.116206	0.110397	0.104917	0.099746	0.094865
8	0.115300	0.108495	0.102138	0.096197	0.090642	0.085445	0.080582	0.076027	0.071760	0.067760
9	0.088015	0.082193	0.076795	0.071789	0.067142	0.062827	0.058819	0.055092	0.051626	0.048400
10	0.067187	0.062267	0.057741	0.053574	0.049735	0.046197	0.042933	0.039922	0.037141	0.034572
11	0.051288	0.047172	0.043414	0.039980	0.036841	0.033968	0.031338	0.028929	0.026720	0.024694
12	0.039151	0.035737	0.032642	0.029836	0.027289	0.024977	0.022875	0.020963	0.019223	0.017639
13	0.029886	0.027073	0.024543	0.022266	0.020214	0.018365	0.016697	0.015190	0.013830	0.012599
14	0.022814	0.020510	0.018453	0.016616	0.014974	0.013504	0.012187	0.011008	0.009949	0.008999
15	0.017415	0.015538	0.013875	0.012400	0.011092	0.009929	0.008896	0.007977	0.007158	0.006428
16	0.013294	0.011771	0.010432	0.009254	0.008216	0.007301	0.006493	0.005780	0.005149	0.004591
17	0.010148	0.008917	0.007844	0.006906	0.006086	0.005368	0.004740	0.004188	0.003705	0.003280
18	0.007747	0.006756	0.005898	0.005154	0.004508	0.003947	0.003460	0.003035	0.002665	0.002343
19	0.005914	0.005118	0.004434	0.003846	0.003339	0.002902	0.002525	0.002199	0.001917	0.001673
20	0.004514	0.003877	0.003334	0.002870	0.002474	0.002134	0.001843	0.001594	0.001379	0.001195
21	0.003446	0.002937	0.002507	0.002142	0.001832	0.001569	0.001345	0.001155	0.000992	0.000854
22	0.002630	0.002225	0.001885	0.001598	0.001357	0.001154	0.000982	0.000837	0.000714	0.000610
23	0.002008	0.001686	0.001417	0.001193	0.001005	0.000848	0.000717	0.000606	0.000514	0.000436
24	0.001533	0.001277	0.001066	0.000890	0.000745	0.000624	0.000523	0.000439	0.000370	0.000311
25	0.001170	0.000968	0.000801	0.000664	0.000552	0.000459	0.000382	0.000318	0.000266	0.000222

PRINCIPLES

OF

CORPORATE

FINANCE

ABOUT THE AUTHOR

Ward S. Curran, chairman of the department of economics at Trinity College, is the George M. Ferris Professor of Corporation Finance and Investments. In addition to having held visiting appointments at Wesleyan and Yale universities, Professor Curran has published widely in areas ranging from the economics of regulated industries to the economics and financing of higher education. The bulk of his professional work, however, has been in finance.

The author not only is active academically but also serves as a consultant for business firms and testifies as an expert witness in lawsuits involving issues associated with concepts of valuation. He is a member of the American Economic Association, American Finance Association, Financial Management Association, and the Eastern Finance Association.

PRINCIPLES

OF

CORPORATE

FINANCE

Ward S. Curran

George M. Ferris Professor of
Corporation Finance and Investments
Trinity College

HBJ

Harcourt Brace Jovanovich, Publishers

San Diego   New York   Chicago   Austin   Washington, D.C.
London   Sydney   Toyko   Toronto

COPYRIGHTS AND ACKNOWLEDGMENTS AND ILLUSTRATION CREDITS

TABLES

3-5: Reprinted by permission of *Wall Street Journal*, © Dow Jones & Company, Inc. (1982). All rights reserved. 5-2: © First Boston Corporation (1981). Reprinted with permission. 7-4: Reprinted by permission of *Moody's Bond Survey*, © Moody's Investors Service (1983). All rights reserved. 19-2: Reprinted by permission of *Moody's Bond Survey*, © Moody's Investors Service (1985). All rights reserved.

FIGURES

17-2, 17-3, 17-4: Dillon, Read & Co., Inc., Oliver C. Hazard, Senior Vice-President. Reprinted with permission.

CARTOONS/ILLUSTRATIONS

5-A: Oliphant, Copyright 1987, Universal Press Syndicate. Reprinted with permission. All rights reserved. 8-A: Drawing by Vietor; © 1976, The New Yorker Magazine, Inc. 19-A: Reprinted by permission of Tribune Media Services. 21-A: From the *Wall Street Journal*—Permission, Cartoon Features Syndicate.

ISBN: 0-15-571550-X
Library of Congress Catalog Card Number: 87-81160
Printed in the United States of America

To Kathy
and our daughters
Andrea and Colleen

Why another book on finance? The primary motive was the author's conviction, shared by most other colleagues in the field, that the teaching of finance is too compartmentalized. Theoretical advances permit one to unify at the introductory level what to many beginning students appear to be disparate topics in portfolio theory and financial management. To accomplish this unification, at times one must substitute intuitive explanations for more formal proofs, leaving the latter for advanced courses in financial theory. However, the approach in Chapters 2 through 10 offers beginning students a basic analytical framework from which to view the more traditional topics in finance, while simultaneously preparing them for the advanced topics in portfolio theory and financial management generally included in upper-level courses.

The foregoing approach also readily lends itself to supplementary materials, such as case studies appropriate to either portfolio theory or financial management. To assist the reader, the author has included at the end of each chapter selected problems and questions designed to test understanding of the concepts developed. Answers to selected odd-numbered problems appear in Appendix H and detailed explanations of all the problems and questions appear in the Instructor's Manual.

Appendixes A through D develop more fully the basic mathematics and statistical tables underlying certain of the models employed throughout the book. Appendix E presents the fundamentals of accounting-based financial statements and key ratios; Appendix F analyzes pertinent features of the Tax Reform Act of 1986; and Appendix G covers the use of a financial calculator. Appendix I, of necessity a last-minute entry, details the startling events of Monday, October 19, 1987—the great stock-market meltdown. There follows a complete glossary of all significant financial terms (boldface in text), with definitions keyed to their use in the book. Finally, in a further attempt to aid the reader and to minimize confusion, all negative arithmetic values are italicized.

Reinforcing the primary motive is the conviction that students of finance are better served, at least initially, if they receive a general grounding in the overall discipline rather than excessive emphasis on one area. Only then will students learn whether more specialized study is necessary; if it is, the foundation has been laid.

Finally, recent theoretical and empirical developments suggest that finance and economics are becoming increasingly intertwined.[1] Although this intellectual reunion engenders mixed feelings among scholars in each discipline, it is inevitable—given advances in knowledge of financial theory and econometrics. This does not mean that the disciplines' research agendas overlap or, equally important, that their teaching objectives are coterminous. Of course, the goals of business schools, which house most finance programs, differ from those of economics departments in liberal arts colleges. Nevertheless, the latter have begun to recognize that finance is an appropriate component of an economics curriculum; the former have, for some time, included considerably more theory (some of it developed by economists) in their finance offerings. Financial economics, as with physical organic chemistry or chemical physics, is not an oxymoron but a logical outcome of the pursuit of knowledge. It is in this spirit that the author has written the book.

He could not have done so, however, without the assistance and cooperation of many people. The undergraduates and master-of-arts candidates who have studied corporate finance in the economics curriculum at Trinity College over the years are the unsung heroes and heroines—having withstood everything from illegible handwriting to computer printouts so the author might test, validate, and revise the conceptual presentations. To their numbers must be added a phalanx of undergraduates at Yale University who were subjected to similar treatment.

The opportunity to teach at Yale was made possible by Andrew G. De Rocco, president, Denison University, and Borden W. Painter, Jr., former deans of faculty at Trinity, and by Merton J. Peck and Donald J. Brown, former chairmen of the department of economics at Yale. Several years of teaching the undergraduate economics offering in portfolio theory and financial markets provided the opportunity to test further, with a different audience, much of the analytical material contained in the book. This experiment in interinstitutional cooperation reinforced my conviction that textbooks in basic corporate finance do not clarify sufficiently the degree of symmetry between portfolio decisions by investors and financial decisions by business firms. The Yale experience profoundly influenced the manner in which I have organized and integrated the material in *Principles of Corporate Finance*.

Two practitioners of finance have been extremely helpful in the writing of this book. Worth Loomis, president of Dexter Corporation, is a leader among business executives in applying modern financial theory to corporate practice. He graciously provided me with several examples from the company, some of which are incorporated in the text. Gary P. Brinson, president and chief executive officer of First Chicago Investment Advisors, is one of the pioneers in the application of Modern Portfolio Theory to pension funds. His experience in portfolio diversification, particularly as it

---

[1]For contrasting views, see Stephen A. Ross, "The Interrelations of Finance and Economics: Theoretical Perspectives" and Michael R. Gibbons, "The Interrelationships of Finance and Economics: Empirical Perspectives," *American Economic Review*, Vol. 77 (May 1987, pp. 29–41).

applies to a broader base of investments in an international context, has been especially useful to me in ascertaining the extent to which this fundamental principle of Modern Portfolio Theory functions in practice. Each practitioner, through classroom and public presentations, has shared his experience with students and faculty at both Trinity College and Yale University.

Others whose assistance has been invaluable include Marjorie V. Butcher, department of mathematics at Trinity; Kurt A. Strasser and Stephen G. Utz, University of Connecticut School of Law; Oliver C. Hazard, senior vice president, Dillon, Read & Co.; and Brian Cullinan, Price Waterhouse (Boston).

Numerous people labored diligently to prepare readable copy: Priscilla A. Davis, Erika T. Wojnarowicz, Lynn T. Casasanta, Timothy Black, and the student staff at Trinity's word-processing center under the direction of Nancy S. Sowa.

Providing valuable service in reading and correcting early drafts was my teaching assistant, Robert E. McDonald, Jr. And offering numerous useful suggestions after reading later drafts were my reviewers: William W. Damon, Vanderbilt University; Les R. Dlabay, Lake Forest College; John S. Dunkelberg, Wake Forest University; Francis L. Stubbs, University of Missouri; John M. Wachowicz, Jr., University of Tennessee; Wilbur Widicus, Oregon State University; Bruce F. Rubin, Old Dominion University; and Thomas W. Hazlett, University of California, Davis.

Finally, I owe much to Johanna McHugh and Marguerite L. Egan, my acquisitions editors at Harcourt Brace Jovanovich. Their encouragement sustained me in what was necessarily a lengthy process. It could have been lengthier had it not been for the able assistance of Robert C. Miller, who swiftly yet skillfully edited the completed manuscript. In his hands, editing is not a craft but an art. And both of us owe a special debt to our efficient production editor, Kay Kaylor. Maggie Porter, art editor, adeptly oversaw the transformation of my primitive sketches into artwork; Martha Gilman, designer, brought the book to life graphically; and Sharon Weldy, production manager, performed her scheduling magic.

As Diogenes searched in vain to find an honest man, so an author strives in vain to produce an error-free book. This author has labored diligently to come as close as possible; failure to achieve the ideal is his responsibility alone. The labor, however, has not been in vain. As the Bard observed through Falstaff: "'tis my vocation Hal. 'Tis no sin for a man to labor in his vocation."

WARD S. CURRAN

CONTENTS

PRINCIPLES
OF
CORPORATE
FINANCE

1

INTRODUCTION

AND OVERVIEW

What is finance?

   Pose the preceding question to one without formal training and you could easily receive any of the following answers. First, finance is the study of how business firms raise money. Second, finance concerns the stock market. Third, finance is what banks do when they loan money for the purchase of goods and services. None of these answers is wrong; all are, however, incomplete. Governments raise money, as do households. The stock market is a part of finance, but only the most visible part. Banks loan money for a variety of reasons and to a variety of interests. Insurance companies, among other institutions, also loan money. Because they are so pervasive, banks are simply the first to come to mind.

   A complete definition of finance, unfortunately, is not possible in a single sentence or even in a single paragraph. However, when you finish this book, you will have a more complete understanding of the nature of the subject. As a starting point, let us say that finance is the process by which households, business firms, and governments acquire and use funds. Yet for our purposes, this description is too broad. As we shall see in Chapter 2, in the aggregate households are the ultimate but primarily indirect source of funds. Federal, state, and local governments acquire funds. They do so either by taxing or by borrowing. The manner in which governments raise funds will be of oblique interest to us; what they do with the funds they raise will not. Both topics are covered in detail in treatises on public finance.

   This leaves business firms, the primary concern of this book. How they raise and use funds is central to the study of finance. One type of business firm organizes human and nonhuman resources to produce goods and services. The nonhuman resources employed consist primarily of plant and equipment. A major part of the study of finance concerns an analytical framework of how to raise funds at the lowest possible cost and invest the funds profitably in plant and equipment, with due consideration given to risk. The person responsible for this task is the **financial manager**; *the production unit is a* **nonfinancial business firm**. *The financial manager will be a central protagonist in our narrative. He or she will be supported by a management team.*

   A second type of business firm is one that invests in financial instruments issued by the nonfinancial business firm (the production unit), as well as by governments and households. These financial instruments come in various types; all, however, are issued in order to raise funds. They are the claims of those who buy them against those who issue them. The legal status of such claims at times can be exceedingly important. A part of the study of finance also concerns an analytical framework of how to maximize the profits derived from investing in financial instruments, with due consideration given to the risk involved in purchasing and holding them. The person responsible for this task is the **portfolio manager**; *the firm that invests is a* **financial intermediary**. *The portfolio manager will be the main supporting actor in our story.*

INCORPORATED AND UNINCORPORATED BUSINESS FIRMS

At the risk of being pedantic, we shall use often the nouns *firm* and *corporation* interchangeably, even though the latter is a subset of the former. A corporation is a separate legal entity that raises funds by issuing stock that represents ownership and issuing debt instruments that represent borrowing. With such funds, the financial manager and his team purchase assets, primarily plant and equipment. The incorporated financial intermediary raises funds in a similar way, but the portfolio manager (in some instances several managers) purchases primarily financial assets. In each case the corporation owns the assets. The stockholders own shares in the corporation; debtholders are creditors of the corporation. If the corporation fails to repay its creditors, the creditors' ultimate recourse is to seize, in accordance with the law, the assets of the corporation to satisfy their claims. However, creditors cannot take the personal assets of the stockholders; stockholders' liability is limited to the amount they have invested. If the assets of the corporation fail to satisfy the claims of the creditors, the stock is worthless and the creditors have no further claim. In short, the liability of stockholders is limited to the amount they have invested. Limited liability of owners of corporate shares contrasts with unlimited liability of owners of unincorporated business firms, specifically general partnerships and individual proprietorships. The distinction between the assets of the business and those of the owners—the proprietor or general partners—is not clear-cut. With certain exceptions[1], the personal assets of the owners of an unincorporated enterprise may be used to satisfy the claims of the creditors.

Another feature of the corporation, as distinct from the unincorporated

---

[1] David G. Epstein. *Debtor–Creditor Law in a Nutshell*, 3rd ed. (St. Paul, MN: West, 1985, pp. 15–19).

enterprise, is the ease with which ownership interests can be transferred. If you own 100 shares of stock in IBM and you wish to sell it, you may do so through your broker. Perhaps this is one reason why the stock market springs to mind when one is asked to define finance. Partnership interests may be more difficult to sell. Generally, other partners must agree to the sale and new articles of partnership must be drawn.

Legal ingenuity has altered somewhat the stark contrast we have drawn between the incorporated and the unincorporated enterprise, both with respect to liability and to transferability of ownership interest. Such subtleties are best left to a course in law; however, when pertinent to our discussion, we will make use of them.[2]

Of the two subsets, incorporated businesses are economically more significant, although unincorporated enterprises are more numerous. In the nonfinancial sector, by the end of 1986 unincorporated business firms had accumulated about $500 billion in plant and equipment compared with $2,800 billion for corporations.[3]

A BRIEF HISTORY OF FINANCE

Finance began as a branch of economics. Influenced by the great corporate-merger movements of the late nineteenth and early twentieth centuries, the subject evolved as a description of the means by which corporations raised funds. The treatise that dominated this approach was Arthur Stone Dewing's two-volume (in later editions) tome, *The Financial Policy of Corporations*, the first edition appearing in 1919 and the fifth and final edition in 1953. The topics Dewing discussed were influenced by the environment in which finance took place. This period encompassed the great expansion of the 1920s, the disastrous crash of the stock market in 1929, and the subsequent depression and numerous bankruptcies that accompanied it. The depression was followed by World War II and the emergence of the United States as the dominant world power. Dewing's treatment varied accordingly. However, his last edition still placed great emphasis on what concerned corporate management in the 1930s—how to stay out of bankruptcy by keeping the firm liquid and what would happen if financial failure took place. The volumes also contained an extended discussion of the types of instruments one might use to raise funds as well as the institutional environment in which such funds are raised.

As finance evolved, it became further removed from its traditional base in economics and became an integral part of the business-school curriculum. Not fully appreciated at the time but subsequently revered as a classic was John Burr Williams' 1938 treatise, the *Theory of Investment Value*. From today's perspective, we can say

---

[2] To illustrate briefly, the shares of IBM are freely transferable through a broker because they have been issued pursuant to the regulations of the Securities and Exchange Commission under the Securities Act of 1933 and the Securities Exchange Act of 1934 as amended. If you owned corporate stock that had not been issued in compliance with these regulations, you personally could sell or transfer ownership to someone else but could not use a broker to sell the stock on the open market.

[3] Board of Governors of the Federal Reserve System. *Balance Sheets for the U.S. Economy* (May 1987, pp. 20 and 25). Data are in terms of 1986 dollars.

that modern finance owes a great deal to his work—even though it was the 1950s before students of the subject began to appreciate his insights.

The contrast between Dewing and Williams is sharp. Dewing had canny insights into and deep understanding of the practice of finance, but was less concerned with an analytical framework that would explain important phenomena in the field. Modern finance, the principles of which are covered in Chapters 2–10, is the tradition that has developed since Williams published his treatise. These principles of finance also may be called principles of financial theory or principles of financial economics. The last term suggests that finance is again a part of economics. Indeed it is. As we shall see, contributions to the field have been made by economists, at least two of whom have received the Nobel prize in economics.

The tradition of Dewing, however, has not been jettisoned. The practice of finance is important in itself, and will be the lifetime occupation of many reading this book. A central motivation for writing this text is the conviction that financial theory (aided by empirical work performed on the computer) complements the practice of finance. The two are intertwined in ways that students of the subject are just beginning to appreciate.

THE PLAN OF THE BOOK

Chapter 2 covers in detail the nature of a capital market and elaborates on its role in bringing those who supply funds (households and financial intermediaries) together with those who demand funds (nonfinancial business firms). Chapter 3 discusses the central conceptual issue in finance—the determination of value. Chapter 4 develops the fundamentals of risk analysis and Chapter 5 applies them to a major building block in financial economics—Modern Portfolio Theory (MPT). The implications of Chapter 5 are far-reaching: they offer a means with which to manage a portfolio of financial instruments so as to optimize between the return from investing in them and the risk incurred in doing so. But these implications also tell us something about the way in which financial managers can minimize the cost of those funds relative to the risk involved, a subject that Chapters 6 and 7 explore. Such implications also concern the investment decisions of the nonfinancial business firm, subject matter that Chapters 8 and 9 analyze in depth.

These implications of Chapter 5, however, are not fully developed until Chapter 10, which ties together the concepts presented in earlier chapters. What emerges is a valuation model for the firm, first developed by Franco Modigliani and Merton H. Miller, in which certain key components are the same whether one views the result from the perspective of the investor or that of the financial manager. What has been compartmentalized into two separate areas of finance, portfolio management and financial management, can theoretically be unified to a degree not usually presented in the early stages of the study of finance.

Chapter 11 addresses one of the unexplained phenomena in finance—the practice of paying dividends. Here the theoretical prescription is at variance with what happens and we look to alternative explanations. As a counterpoint, Chapter 12, Financial Theory in Practice, perhaps can be viewed as a transition from the tradition of John Burr Williams to that of Arthur Stowe Dewing, but from the perspective of what is developed in Chapters 2 through 10. Our discussion then turns to what theorists believe is an accounting artifact, but which is of daily concern to financial managers—the administration of working capital. Chapter 13 examines the administration of working capital in some detail; Chapters 14 and 15 treat the components of current assets and short-term funds, or current liabilities.

Accounting artifact or not, Chapter 15 leads logically to raising funds and to capital markets, specifically markets for long-term debt securities and stock or equity. Chapters 16 and 17 concern these issues as well as the role of public policy toward securities markets. Chapter 18 takes up the special topic of financing assets through leases.

Chapter 19 discusses the concept of options, employing an analytical framework whose implications may extend beyond current application to the shares of widely traded corporations. Chapter 20 examines a relatively new application of the futures market: long the preserve of commodities, futures are now another feature of the financial process.

Chapter 21 covers mergers. Although a specialized topic, it is as old as the field of finance. Its recent context, however, is new, and the corporate landscape may be altered as fundamentally as it was at the turn of the century.

Chapter 22 deals with international finance. Although principles of finance do not stop at our nation's borders, certain facets of the finance process—foreign-currency exchange rates, for example—are unique to the context and are treated accordingly. Chapter 23 summarizes the basic themes of the text and offers an overall perspective on the field of finance.

One of the problems with the finance field is that it draws upon other disciplines—economics, accounting, statistics, mathematics, and law. Moreover, the subject has a specialized vocabulary. Although few people are equally prepared in all these subjects—including the author—you must have at least a nodding acquaintance with relevant aspects of corporate and tax law as well as some understanding of the principles of accounting and economics. In addition, you must be able to function proficiently at appropriate levels of mathematics and statistics. Consequently, the road to success in this field is at time tortuous. To aid you along the way, we include numerous illustrations, provide many problems and questions, and supply appendixes of financial mathematics and accounting as well as a glossary of financial terms. An additional incentive is simply the fact that the study of finance has both material and intellectual rewards. The former have been long recognized; the latter are comparatively recent in origin.

We began by noting that finance is difficult to define in a few brief yet substantive sentences. When you finish the book, you will know what finance is about. With that in mind, let us begin our journey.

2

FINANCE IN
THE MODERN
WORLD

There are many avenues of entry to the study of finance. From one perspective, finance can be seen as the process by which savings are channeled into investment or, more broadly, how the sources of funds find their way to the users of funds. In a Robinson Crusoe economy, there is no financial function. Crusoe decides to fish less now and use the time to construct more nets with which to catch more fish later. His decision to consume less now is a decision to save; his decision to construct more nets is a decision to invest. The nets are his stock of real capital, and will become the means through which he increases his future consumption.

In the modern world, of course, the process is more complicated: those who save are not necessarily the same as those who invest. Advanced industrial economies that rely heavily on markets to allocate resources have developed complex institutional arrangements to ensure savings are channeled into investment or funds flow from source to use. In Chapter 2 we develop the basic theory of how individuals choose to consume now or later (that is, to save), of how the business firm decides to invest in plant and equipment, and explore the role interest rates and markets for funds (financial or capital markets) play in the savings and investment process. Finally, through what is called the flow of funds process, we show briefly how funds actually move from source to use in the private sector of the economy. The chapter offers both an intellectual rationale for financial markets and the role played by interest as well as a brief description of the process by which these markets function.

SAVINGS AND CONSUMPTION

A young man or woman setting out to earn a livelihood is not generally endowed with the funds necessary to purchase a home. He or she initially may earn enough to rent an apartment, make the down payment on a new car, and purchase such basic necessities of life as food and clothing. Marriage and children lead to increased expenditures. Even with two incomes, the down payment on a home may be difficult. However, at the other end of the life cycle when the children are grown and the mortgage is reduced or even paid off, many adults reach their peak earning capacity. At this point, expenditures may be considerably less than income and the desire to save (in anticipation of retirement and a lower income) may dominate one's behavior. Exceptions, of course, exist. Very successful or otherwise wealthy people may leave trust funds for their offspring, enabling offspring to make purchases they could not afford on their income. Some people are chronically poor all their lives. A few people with adequate incomes lead a spartan, some might say miserly, existence, consuming a less than typical fraction of their lifetime earnings. No fun to live with perhaps, such people often make great ancestors. Still others display a zest for personal consumption that some might term hedonistic.

The miser and the spendthrift, however, earn their sobriquets because their saving and consumption patterns are atypical. For a large segment of the population, borrowing against future income gives way to net saving from current income as the family matures and careers reach their zenith. Let us, therefore, focus on two individuals, a young computer scientist embarking upon her career and a successful attorney in midcareer. In her early twenties, the computer scientist has sufficient income to make the down payment on a new car but insufficient income to purchase the car outright. In his early fifties, the attorney has made the final college tuition payment for his third and last child and now can increase his savings.

We can illustrate the position in which each individual finds himself or herself by examining Figure 2-1. One axis is labeled *present* (current) *income* and the other *future income*. To simplify the exposition, we leave the length of time between present and future vague, and simply say that future is a single time period removed from present. The function of line YY' is to connect present income with future

Figure 2-1 **Present and Future Income**

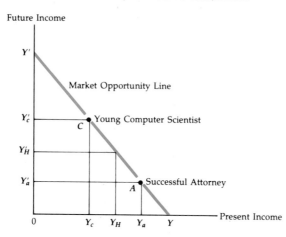

income. How that is accomplished becomes clear momentarily. YY' may be called the *market opportunity line*.

For now let us concentrate on points C and A and the perpendiculars drawn to the two axes. For our young computer scientist, current income OY_c is less than future income OY'_c. This is typical of a young person embarking on a career: earnings increase as career progresses. The attorney, on the other hand, at the peak of his earning capacity, expects his future income to be less than his present income as he approaches the end of his career and phases out his legal practice. His current income is, therefore, OY_a and his future income OY'_a, which is less than OY_a.

Given the desire to purchase goods her current income will not cover, the computer scientist, we assume, is willing (through borrowing) to increase her current consumption at the expense of her future income. The attorney, we assume, desires to decrease his current consumption and is willing to lend money today, the proceeds returning to him in the future.

Suppose the computer scientist meets the attorney by chance. Their discussions lead to an agreement whereby the attorney lends the computer scientist $Y_a Y_H$. In terms of our nomenclature, her current income (including the borrowing) rises from OY_c to OY_H. The attorney reduces his current income from OY_a to OY_H. $Y_c Y_H$, therefore, equals $Y_H Y_a$. In the next time period, our computer scientist reduces her income from OY'_c to OY'_H, as she repays the loan. The income of the attorney rises from OY'_a to OY'_H. $Y'_H Y'_c$, therefore, equals $Y'_a Y'_H$.

From the graph of Figure 2-1 we note that income $Y_H Y_a$ given up by the attorney is less than $Y'_H Y'_a$ he receives from the computer scientist in the future. Similarly, the computer scientist, in repaying $Y'_c Y'_H$ from future income, gives the attorney more than Y_cY_H she is currently borrowing. The explanation for the difference lies in the rate of interest paid on the loan.

The concept of interest is fundamental to the study of finance. Although it conjures up in the minds of some a perjorative image—due in part to the low esteem in which it was held from the time of Aristotle to the Medieval church and beyond—interest, nevertheless, performs a vital function in any modern industrial economy. In the foregoing context, the attorney wants to transfer some of his income from the present to the future and the computer scientist wants to transfer some of her income from the future to the present. In this case, interest is the price she is willing to pay to consume more now than later. Alternatively, it is the price he must receive to postpone present consumption in favor of future consumption.

Although the sensibilities of those living in modern industrial societies that have a large base of private enterprise are rarely offended by the concept of interest, vestiges of suspicion remain. It is not uncommon for people to complain that rates are too high, or that they border on usury, or are indeed usurious. Yet what economists call the **real rate of interest**, or the price for lending and borrowing money, is comparatively low; that is, generally between 1 and 3 percent.[1] How can this be, the reader might ask, when, in some years, we have seen people earning up to 15 percent interest on a variety of investments and borrowing at even higher rates to purchase cars or homes?

The answer begins with an insight first attributable years ago to Yale's famous economist, Irving Fisher.[2] Fisher postulated that the rates of interest we observe consist of the real rate that reflects the price for not consuming or spending today and the expected rate of increase in the price level. To these two factors can be added a third—a premium for risk bearing: a premium to compensate for the possibility the borrower will default in whole or in part and not pay back the total amount borrowed. If we make the plausible (some might say heroic) assumption that the debt of the U.S. government is free of risk of default, then we can say that the observed interest rates paid on U.S. government securities consist of the real rate of interest plus a premium for inflation anticipated over the life of the security. Since people have greater confidence in the accuracy of shorter- than longer-run forecasts of inflation, most researchers base their estimates of the real rate of interest on U.S.

---

[1] Whether the real interest rate is constant in the long run has been the subject of intellectual inquiry leading to some disagreements. See, for example, Eugene F. Fama, "Inflation, Uncertainty and Expected Returns on Treasury Bills," *Journal of Political Economy*, Vol. 84 (June 1976, pp. 427–48) and "Short Term Interest Rates as Predictors of Inflation," *American Economic Review*, Vol. 65 (June 1975, pp. 269–82); John A. Carlson, "Comment," Douglas Joines, "Comment," Charles R. Nelson and G. William Schwert, "Short Term Interest Rates as Predictors of Inflation: On Testing the Hypothesis that the Real Rate of Interest is Constant," and Eugene Fama, "Interest Rates and Inflation: The Message in the Entrails," all in *American Economic Review*, Vol. 67 (June 1977, pp. 469–96). See also Herbert Taylor, "Interest Rates: How Much Does Expected Inflation Matter?" *Business Review*, Federal Reserve Bank of Philadelphia (July–August 1982, pp. 3–12), for an overview of salient issues.

[2] Irving Fisher. *The Theory of Interest: As Determined by Impatience to Spend Income and Opportunity to Invest It* (New York: Macmillan, 1930). See also Fisher's earlier work, *Appreciation and Interest* (New York: Macmillan, 1896).

Treasury bills that mature from 91 days to a year. It is on the basis of such research that scholars have concluded the real rate of interest is comparatively low. Most of the observed rate paid is compensation for actual or expected inflation.[3]

For present purposes of analysis, we may neglect inflation and assume that a dollar in the future will have the same purchasing power as a dollar today. Moreover, although the future income of the computer scientist is not assured, we shall assume the risk of default on the loan is negligible. The attorney, therefore, is willing to lend her the money at a risk-free real rate of interest. Let that rate be 2 percent. In terms of Figure 2-1, if $Y_H Y_a$ is \$5,000, then $Y'_c Y'_H$ is \$5,000 + .02 × \$5,000 = \$5,100 or \$5,000(1 + .02) = \$5,100.

More generally, a sum S today will be worth S' one time period from today. Given a positive real rate of interest r, then

$$S' > S \text{ because } S(1 + r) = S' \tag{2-1}$$

Similarly

$$S = \frac{S'}{1 + r} \tag{2-2}$$

When written as Equation 2-1, we can say that a sum S is **compounded** for one time period at a rate r to equal S'. Equation 2-2 states that the value today (**present value**) of a sum S', received one time period into the future, is S. The link between present and future value is the rate of interest—in terms of Figure 2-1, the real rate of interest. The slope of the line $Y'Y$ is $1 + r$. If, for example, one were to lend the amount OY at $1 + r$, it would equal OY' in the next time period. The greater the value of r, the steeper the slope of $Y'Y$.

In Chapter 3, we develop the mathematics of *present value* more fully as we consider several future time periods in a context that more closely approximates the real world in which financial decisions are made. At this juncture, it is the concept of interest rather than the details of calculation that concerns us.

---

[3] See references cited in footnote[1]. Partly because the Federal Reserve System buys and sells U.S. government securities to influence bank credit and subsequently influences growth in the money supply, the real rate of interest can fluctuate considerably. In the 1970s, calculations made by the author suggest that at times the real rate was negative; by the early 1980s, it had risen to historically high levels of 5 to 6 percent but has since declined along with inflation. From about 1953 through 1971, however, the real rate was often above 1.5 percent and below 2.5 percent; this period was one of relatively stable changes in the price level, sandwiched between two major events. In 1951, the Federal Reserve abandoned the policy of purchasing U.S. government securities at par. This policy, a vestige of World War II, was designed to fund the war effort at low rates of interest. In 1971, President Nixon imposed wage and price controls. Thus the standard measure of inflation, the Consumer Price Index, would be disturbed. See Fama. For a more detailed survey of the literature, see Milton Friedman and Anna J. Schwartz, *Monetary Trends in the United States and the United Kingdom, Their Relation to Income Prices and Interest Rates, 1867–1975* (Chicago: University of Chicago Press, 1982), a National Bureau of Economic Research Monograph, pp. 477–588. See also Taylor, pp. 3–12, for a brief summary of factors other than inflation and monetary policy that can affect the real rate of interest—tax policy, for example.

INTEREST AND PRODUCTIVITY

Shifting spending patterns from the present to the future or from the future to the present is not the only role of interest. There are also real investment opportunities—investment in such productive assets as plant and equipment—in which the concept of interest is used in a different context. To illustrate, consider a real-world example, Apple Computers. In 1976, from an initial investment of about $1,500, Steven P. Jobs and Stephen G. Wozniak built their original computer and marketed it through a local store. Unable to keep up with demand, they used more of their own funds and obtained monies from other sources to invest in production facilities. By 1980, the market value of Wozniak's interest in the company was $88 million and that of Jobs $165 million. Although increased competition—particularly from IBM—later caused the market price of the stock to fall and ultimately led to the severance of the two founders from the company, their entrepreneurship was impressive.[4]

Success of the magnitude of Apple often results from recognizing the existence of an extensive market. Further, the market sometimes can be enlarged by technological advances that lower the costs of production. For example, microcomputers tapped a growing market. Technological advance continues to bring the price within reach of more home users.[5] In this sense, the industry resembles the early years of automobile manufacturing, when Henry Ford brought the motor car within the price range of the average citizen.[6]

In the foregoing illustration, the concept of interest plays a different role. People are willing to lend money at a rate of interest; those using the funds invest them in plant and equipment to produce a product, in this case computers. What one earns on the investment—after deduction of all expenses, wages, materials, and so forth—we shall call for now the *return on the investment*. One may, of course, use his or her own funds: abstain from present consumption in order to invest in plant and equipment. Because such an individual also has the opportunity to lend money rather than consume, the going rate of interest is, in the jargon of economics, the **opportunity cost** of funds. In a competitive economy, returns that are high in comparison with the opportunity cost of capital encourage entry of new firms. Sometimes the initial innovators retain their market position, sometimes they do

---

[4] Andrew Pollack. "Next a Computer on Every Desk," *New York Times* (August 23, 1981, Sec. 3, pp. 1 and 15). Susan G. Nozem. "The Folks Who Brought You Apple," *Fortune*, Vol. 103 (January 12, 1981, p. 68). J. Brouttal. "Behind The Fall of Steve Jobs," *Fortune*, Vol. 112 (August 5, 1985, pp. 20–24).

[5] Pollack, pp. 1 and 15.

[6] Walter Adams and James W. Brock. "The Automobile Industry," in Walter Adams, *The Structure of American Industry*, 7th ed. (New York: Macmillan, 1986, pp. 126–27). For a discussion of the computer industry, see Gerald W. Brock, "The Computer Industry," pp. 239–60.

Figure 2-2   Investment in Real Assets

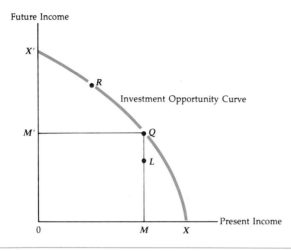

not.[7] What does happen, however, is that the rate of growth in demand declines over time, technological innovation and subsequent cost reductions may become more intermittent, and returns fall toward the opportunity cost of capital.

Although we cannot hope to capture the rich institutional detail of every case in a simple analytical model, Figure 2-2 suggests the basic framework. An entrepreneur similar to those who built Apple computer has a given amount of income OX and a set of productive opportunities represented by *investment opportunity curve XX'*. As drawn, the slope of the curve varies as the entrepreneur invests more of his or her money in plant and equipment. In the extreme case, the entrepreneur invests all present income OX in plant and equipment. The return OX' is the future income from this investment. In an intermediate case, the entrepreneur invests MX in plant equipment and consumes or spends OM. OM' is the future income from investing MX dollars in plant and equipment today.

It is apparent from the graph of Figure 2-2 that as one invests more, additional future income from the investment declines. Implicit in this formulation are the assumptions that market demand is given and technology is constant. The entrepreneur invests in plant and equipment while holding other factors constant. As a result, the return, or in economic jargon *marginal productivity of capital*, declines

---

[7] In the microcomputer market, the issue has yet to be resolved. See Michael S. Malone, "The Big Fight for Computer Sales," *New York Times* (August 1, 1982, Sec. 3, p. 4). See also "Cut-Rate Computers, Get 'Em Here," *Time*, Vol. 128 (July, 21, 1986, p. 50).

as we add more capital to a given stock of other resources.[8] Capital, as with all factors of production, experiences *diminishing returns*. For our purposes, it is not necessary to relax these assumptions; their net effect is to delay the inevitable, as depicted in Figure 2-2. More important to the study of finance is the basic relationship between MX the outlay and OM' the one-period return. Conceptually

$$MX = \frac{OM'}{1 + r}$$

In this case one solves for r, which we may call the **yield**, or **internal rate of return**, on the investment. Thus if MX is \$1,000,000 and OM' is \$1,100,000, then

$$\$1,000,000 = \frac{\$1,100,000}{1 + r}$$

$$r = 10 \text{ percent}$$

Thus an investment of \$1,000,000 has a useful life of one time period. At the end of that time period, revenues from the sale of the product return the initial outlay and a profit of \$100,000—a 10-percent yield on investment.

As in earlier illustrations, yield can be expressed in nominal or real terms. Continuing with our assumption that there is no change in the purchasing power of the dollar between time period one and time period two, we can say that 10 percent is the real rate of return on the investment.

The slope of the curve reflects the rate of return on investment in productive facilities and declines with increasing investment. Thus an outlay of \$2,000,000 may bring a future return of \$2,150,000, so that

$$\$2,000,000 = \frac{\$2,150,000}{1 + r}$$

$$r = 7.5 \text{ percent}$$

The additional \$1,000,000 results in another \$50,000, or 5 percent, return. The yield on \$2,000,000, however, is 7.5 percent.

THE OPTIMAL INVESTMENT OPPORTUNITY   In Figure 2-2, XX' defines the frontier of investment opportunities. One can invest anywhere within the boundaries of XX'. However, the most productive opportunities lie on the frontier. Although it is possible, for example, to invest MX dollars in opportunity L, a greater return is at Q. Consequently, for the same investment the entrepreneur would prefer Q to L. What about point R? Clearly, the rate of return is lower and the outlay higher

---

[8] If the entrepreneur sold the product in an imperfectly competitive market, return on the investment also would decline since marginal revenue is less than price. In this instance, more investment results in selling more at lower prices. If the market is perfectly competitive under the assumptions made, only diminishing returns to capital are responsible for the lower yields on additional investment.

at R than at Q. From the information available, we have no clear-cut answer. Recall, however, our earlier discussion of the real rate of interest. Implicit in that commentary was a market for funds, the rate being 2 percent. The computer scientist paid that rate to the attorney because she would have had to borrow at that rate in the market. Similarly, the attorney could have earned no more than 2 percent on a risk-free investment elsewhere. Thus the rate they agreed upon was the opportunity cost of capital in a world free of risk of default and with a stable price level.

What about the entrepreneur? Should he or she invest money up to the point where the yield, or return on investment, equals the opportunity cost of capital? The answer is yes. If a return of 10 percent, even 7.5 percent, is greater than the opportunity cost of funds, then the entrepreneur should invest so as to maximize the return on those funds. Investment should stop at the point where the internal rate of return equals the opportunity cost of capital: the market rate of interest.

Suppose our entrepreneur does not want to invest more than a given amount of his or her own money or suppose that he or she lacks the necessary funds. Enter now the capital markets. The function of these markets is to bring together those who want to consume or invest now with those who want to consume later, those who want to save. (In the case of the miser, later may mean leaving a large estate; for the spendthrift, later may mean leaving unpaid bills.)

In Figure 2-3, we have reproduced Figure 2-2 but have added the market opportunity line YY' from Figure 2-1. The market opportunity line still reflects the trade-off between present income and future income in capital markets. The slope of the market opportunity line is the equilibrium rate of interest, the rate at which

Figure 2-3 Entrepreneural Equilibrium Level of Present and Future Consumption

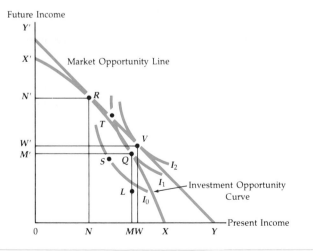

4—return and risk are positively correlated. The capital markets reward more those who accept greater risk.

Partly because of the variety of instruments through which funds are raised, specialists in the field have tended to use the term *financial markets* to encompass the entire spectrum. The term **capital markets** is usually reserved for long-term debt and equity. **Money markets** connote markets for short-term credit instruments with maturities of a year or less. The division between short and long term, however, is somewhat arbitrary.

Of importance also is the classification that divides primary from secondary markets. **Primary markets** are markets for new issues of securities; **secondary markets** are markets for existing securities. In the case of large national or multinational corporations, there are both well-developed primary markets for issuing new stock (the details of which we cover in Chapter 17) and secondary markets for trading in outstanding stock. The best known secondary market is the New York Stock Exchange. In most cases, stock, once issued, has an indefinite life. Secondary markets develop because the holding period of many investors is finite and sometimes quite short. Thus secondary markets offer liquidity.

When demand for liquidity is an important consideration of those who supply funds, secondary markets flourish; when liquidity is not in demand, secondary markets do not develop. The commercial paper market is a good example of the latter case. **Commercial paper**, one of the money market securities, represents a short-term credit instrument issued primarily by private corporations and a few states and municipalities. No secondary market exists for commercial paper. "If an investor is hard pressed, the dealer customarily will buy back the paper and hold it in inventory as a service to both issuer and investor."[11]

To present an extended discussion of the details of financial markets would carry us beyond the scope of this book.[12] In Chapters 15, 16, and 17, however, we develop more fully the details of those financial markets and instruments essential to the financing of business firms, particularly nonfinancial corporations. The nonfinancial sector of the American economy—manufacturing, construction, wholesale and retail trade, public utilities, transportation, and service industries—is a major user of funds and accounts for the bulk of real capital formation that takes place each year. How funds flow to this sector is of sufficient interest to warrant further discussion.

---

[11] Evelyn M. Hurley. "The Commercial Paper Market Since the Mid-Seventies," *Federal Reserve Bulletin*, Vol. 68 (June 1982, p. 331).

[12] See John R. Brick, H. Kent Baker, and John A. Haslem, eds. *Financial Markets Instruments and Concepts*, 2nd ed. (Richmond, VA: Robert F. Dame, Inc., 1986) for an excellent collection of readings. See also Herbert E. Dougall and Jack E. Gaumnitz, *Capital Markets and Institutions*, 5th ed. (Englewood Cliffs, NJ: Prentice-Hall, 1986); Charles N. Henning, William Pigott, and Robert Hancy Scott, *Financial Markets and the Economy*, 3rd ed. (Englewood Cliffs, NJ: Prentice-Hall, 1981); Peter S. Rose and Donald Fraser, *Financial Institutions*, 2nd ed. (Plano, TX: Business Publications, Inc., 1985).

FLOW OF FUNDS

It is helpful to portray the process by which funds flow from those who save to those who invest; we do this in Figure 2-4, which depicts the process as it pertains to the private sector of the economy. In this instance, the financial markets represent all markets in which new funds are raised; that is, they are the money and primary markets for short- and long-term funds, both debt (or credit) and equity (or stock). These markets directly or indirectly connect those who demand funds (in the private sector, primarily nonfinancial business firms) and those who supply them (households and financial intermediaries). In a highly developed country such as the United States, households supply relatively small amounts of funds directly to nonfinancial business firms; rather, they tend to do so indirectly through financial intermediaries. A financial intermediary accepts funds from households and issues its own liabilities. In turn, the funds are partially reinvested in instruments nonfinancial business firms issue in order to raise funds with which to build plants, purchase equipment, produce goods, and provide services.

To illustrate, let us suppose you are employed and deposit your paycheck in a

Figure 2-4   Abbreviated Flow of Funds in the Private Sector

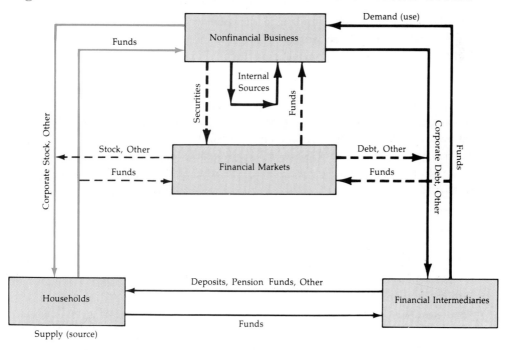

bank account. In addition, your employer puts 5 percent of your salary in a pension fund, which in turn is managed by a subsidiary of a life insurance company. Both the bank and the life insurance company are financial intermediaries. You have a deposit in the former and after a period of time a vested interest in the latter. Whether single or married, you are a household. In terms of Figure 2-4, your funds—the bank deposit and your employer's contribution to your pension fund—are in the hands of two different financial institutions, or intermediaries.

Because your deposit is available to you on demand, within a relatively short period of time, the bank probably will seek a short-term investment for those funds. One possibility is to make your deposit part of a loan to a nonfinancial business that requires funds to purchase raw materials for manufacturing products. The loan is short-term because the firm expects to manufacture the product, sell it, and convert the sale to cash within a brief period of time. The bank has placed funds directly with a nonfinancial firm that in turn has received credit from (hence has an outstanding debt) the bank. In this instance, the flow of funds is from the household through the bank to the business. There is no direct use of financial markets.

But what about the pension contribution your employer has made? Because it is not available to you until retirement, the insurance company may choose to invest the funds differently: it may not put those funds into a short-term loan; it may choose to make a long-term investment. For example, suppose a public utility, building new generating facilities, decides to issue debt instruments: borrow funds to help finance the construction of the plant. To do so, it issues a series of **bonds** that mature in 25 years. In short, it borrows funds using a specific type of debt instrument sold in a primary market for new securities. While the funds are outstanding, holders of the bonds receive an interest payment on them. Because you will not receive your pension for at least 25 years, the bonds may be viewed as a good investment for your pension fund and for other employers in the same age group. Therefore, in this instance the insurance company may buy the bonds in a primary market and channel the pension contributions to the utility in exchange for some of the bonds issued. You can trace this pattern in Figure 2-4.

Intermediation, then, is the process by which sources of funds flow to ultimate users. Financial intermediaries—all types of banks (deposit-type institutions), insurance companies, finance companies, and pension funds, among others—are the conduits through which a great part of savings and investment takes place in the modern economy. In Figure 2-4, we allow for the fact that nonfinancial business firms may raise funds directly from households or indirectly from them through primary financial markets. We emphasize again, however, that this is not the major way in which nonfinancial business firms acquire funds. (The right-hand side of Figure 2-4 dominates the left-hand side.)[13]

---

[13] As we discuss in Chapter 8, nonfinancial business firms also depend heavily upon the reinvestment of profit from and depreciation on existing plant and equipment. If a firm uses these sources as the only means of finance, it bypasses the intermediation process altogether. Again, this is shown in Figure 2-4.

As constructed, Figure 2-4 is only a partial representation of the flow of funds; it is, however, the part that concerns us in this book. A complete exposition would include the public sector—federal, state, and local governments—the fact that households borrow in particular for the purpose of buying homes, and the fact that financial intermediaries must at times raise funds. In addition, we have to recognize that the U.S. economy must be viewed in an international context.

When one aggregates the net amount raised by various sectors of the economy, we have a better picture of the total flow of funds; in Table 2-1, we summarize the results for 1985. Although the table is largely self-explanatory, a few comments may be useful. Nineteen eighty-five was a particularly devastating year for agriculture. Consequently, on balance, farms actually reduced their credit demands. In real

Table 2-1   **Net Funds Raised in the U.S. during 1985 ($ billions)**

Net Credit Market Borrowing		
Nonfinancial Sectors		
Government		
U.S.	223.7	
State and local	140.9	
Household and Farm		
Household	294.0	
Farm	*−11.9*	
Business		
Nonfarm, noncorporate	85.4	
Corporate	166.1	
Total nonfinancial sectors		898.2
Financial Sectors		
Private	92.1	
U.S. government related	101.6	
Total financial sectors		193.7
Foreign Sector		
Total foreign sector		1.5
Total		**$1,093.4**
External Equity Funds		
Nonfinancial corporations		*−81.6*
Financial corporations		5.3
Mutual funds		105.3
Foreign		4.0
Total		**$33.0**

SOURCE: Board of Governors of the Federal Reserve, *Flow of Funds*, Summary Statistics, June 3, 1986.

terms, interest rates were relatively high compared to those elsewhere in the world. As a result, net foreign borrowing in the United States was negligible (the use of foreign markets by American firms to raise funds is not included in the data). Through the process of combining (through merger) one firm with another, nonfinancial corporations liquidated more equity than they raised during the year.

Finally, 1985 data show that *mutual funds* increased their number of shares outstanding by more than $105 billion. A mutual fund is a particular type of financial intermediary that falls within a category generally known as an *investment company*. The fund buys shares of stock, bonds, and other financial instruments with funds raised from an issue of its own shares. If one buys shares in the fund, he or she indirectly owns a part of the portfolio of securities into which his or her funds have been invested. A mutual fund may issue an unlimited number of shares and invest the proceeds in additional securities. Figures for 1985 reflect the recent trend for individuals to buy securities (in this case, primarily common stock traded in the secondary market) through financial intermediaries rather than to own them directly.

Before closing this brief discussion on the flow of funds, we should note two points to keep in mind. First, it is convenient to separate sectors of the economy in order to understand the basic process by which funds flow. One must not assume, however, that financial intermediaries always are separated from nonfinancial business firms. Sears, Roebuck and Company is known for its retail trade outlets, which fit into the nonfinancial classification. However, Sears is also an insurer, a banker, a stockbroker, and a real estate broker, as well as a supplier of other financial services. To be sure, these divisions or subsidiaries may be managed separately within the corporation. Nevertheless, the conglomeration of nonfinancial and financial institutions is a fact of life in late twentieth-century America.

Second, the protean environment in which financial intermediaries have operated during the 1980s has led to a blurring of traditional lines of demarcation among some institutions. Consider, for example, the four types of deposit institutions: commercial banks, savings banks, savings and loan associations, and credit unions. Since the early nineteenth century, savings banks were designed to encourage thrift among immigrants and others whose meager savings were of scant interest to many commercial banks that specialized in business deposits and loans. Savings and loan associations (S and Ls), initially called building and loan associations, date from the mid-nineteenth century and were designed to make mortgage loans to members. S and Ls subsequently evolved into institutions that accepted deposits from the public but continued to emphasize mortgages. Credit unions, an early twentieth-century institution, were designed to provide credit to members who were employees of the same company or members of the same union.

Of the four, at one time commercial banks played a unique role as demand-deposit-creating (and therefore money-creating) institutions. This distinction has blurred as new types of accounts, such as NOW (Negotiable Order of Withdrawal) accounts issued by all deposit-type institutions, are readily accessible as a means of payment for goods and services. Moreover, restrictions on portfolios—types of investments one bank but not another can make—are also rapidly blurring.[14] In Connecticut, for example, all legal distinctions between commercial banks, savings and loan associations, and savings banks disappeared in 1987.

Although neither of these two points is highly germane to our analytical treatment, each deepens your understanding of the institutional material presented in later chapters.

SUMMARY

In Chapter 2 we introduce the notion that interest is what transforms present consumption into future consumption. Interest is the price that must be paid to motivate people to save—to abstain from present consumption in order to consume more at a later date. One might look upon interest as the price of being impatient. Those desiring to consume more today must pay the rate of interest to those willing to put off present consumption. The former reduces and the latter increases future income and hence future consumption accordingly.

Interest also plays another role, that of allocating funds to investment in real capital—plant, equipment, machinery, and so forth—which in turn is used to produce the goods and services people demand. In the latter case, the internal rate of return or yield on investment should be carried to the point where the return on the last dollar allocated to the investment equals the rate of interest.

Conceptually, the capital market is the place where those demanding funds (those willing to increase present consumption or to raise funds for investment in real capital) find those wanting to abstain from present consumption (those willing to supply the funds). The intersection of the demand and supply curves determines the equilibrium rate of interest.

Although the foregoing offers a starting point upon which to build an analytical framework for the study of finance, we emphasize it is only a beginning.

The concept of interest discussed in Chapter 2 abstracts from the risk inherent in changes in the purchasing power of money and in the uncertainty associated with the inability to predict—even in the absence of price level changes—the yield on real capital. The concept discussed is, therefore, a real rate of interest.

Real-world financial markets are highly complex, offering many variations on the basic debt (borrowing) or equity (ownership) contract. Such markets are, however, remarkably adept at ensuring that owners of financial instruments receive a yield commensurate with the risks they assume.

---

[14] Thomas F. Cargill and Gillian Garcia. *Financial Reform in the 1980's* (Palo Alto, CA: The Hoover Institution Press, 1985), particularly pp. 52–73.

3

COMPOUND INTEREST, PRESENT VALUE, AND RETURN ON INVESTMENT

In Chapter 2, we developed the concepts of return on investment and present value of future income. The trade-off between present and future income was presented in terms of a single time period. In Chapter 3, we take a more sophisticated approach. Return and present value are discussed both in terms of a fraction of one time period and more than one time period. The principles presented here are fundamental to the study of finance. So reach for your favorite beverage, find a straight-back chair, and try not to fall asleep. To help keep you alert, interested, and informed, we apply the principles to several important examples in our study of finance.

RETURN ON INVESTMENT

Recall in Chapter 2 we noted that sum S today will be worth S' one time period from today because S can be invested at positive rate of interest r, so that $S(1 + r) = S'$.

Anyone who has a savings account has experienced the practical consequences of this basic formula. The value for r is the rate of interest the bank states it will pay on an amount of money deposited with it. Assume the rate is 10 percent per year and S is $1,000 per year. Then $1,000 deposited in a savings account for a year will equal $1,000(1.10) = $1,100. $100 is the interest on $1,000 for one year. $1,000 plus interest at 10 percent is $1,100 (at the end of the year). We can also say, again recalling our discussion in Chapter 2, that the investment earns a 10 percent return, so that

$$\$1,000 = \frac{\$1,100}{1 + r}$$

$$r = 10\%$$

If reality were so simple, our discussion might end at this point; alas, this is not the case. Two complications arise. First, banks (as well as other institutions) have the audacity to break up the annual interest payments into quarterly, monthly, and even daily components. Secondly, although a year is a convenient reference point for stating the rate of interest, there is no reason why funds cannot remain in the account for a longer period of time.

COMPOUND INTEREST   The 10-percent rate of interest on the preceding account is the nominal rate paid; it is the actual rate paid, or actual return, only if the interest is paid at the end of the year. If the interest were paid quarterly and the investor allowed interest to accumulate, or *compound*, until the end of the year, the account would earn 2.5 percent per quarter (10 percent divided by four quarters). For the first quarter, $1,000(1.025) = $1,025. But this amount would earn interest, so the next quarter, $1,025(1.025) = $1,050.63. Similarly, for the third and fourth quarters we have $1,050.63(1.025) = $1,076.89 and $1,076.89(1.025) = $1,103.81, respectively Because of interest earned each quarter, $1,000 becomes $1,103.81 at the end of the year—instead of $1,100. We achieve the same result by dividing

10 percent by four quarters, adding one, raising the expression to the fourth power, and multiplying $1,000 by the result.

$$\$1,000\left(1 + \frac{.10}{4}\right)^4 = \text{value at end of year}$$

$$\$1,000(1.025)^4 = \text{value at end of year}$$

$$\$1,000(1.10381) = \text{value at end of year}$$

$$\$1,000(1.10381) = \$1,103.81$$

In this case, r equals 10.381 percent: $(1.10381 - 1)(100) = 10.381\%$.

The nominal rate of interest compounded for one year can be called the *effective rate* of interest. The smaller the increments into which the nominal rate is broken and compounded, the higher the effective rate and the greater the value at the end of the year of a given amount invested at the beginning of the year. Table 3-1 shows the effect of various compounding periods for a $1,000 investment. Many banks compound interest daily; some employ **continuous compounding**.

Continuous compounding represents the upper limit of compound interest. Inasmuch as formal proof requires a little algebra, to the delight of some and to the chagrin of others we have relegated a more formal proof to Appendix A—where it can be studied at leisure or conveniently overlooked. Our presentation here is intuitive.

As one divides the nominal rate of interest into smaller segments, the actual rate being compounded becomes miniscule. As Table 3-1 suggests, there are 8,760 hours in a year. The fraction $\frac{.10}{8,760} = .0000114155$. When we add one to the decimal, compound to the 8,760th power, subtract one, and multiply the results by 100, we have $(1.0000114155)^{8,760} = 1.105165 - 1 \times 100 = 10.5165$ percent.

When one or 100 percent is divided into tiny increments—perhaps into millionths—and compounded at that rate, we have

$$\left(1 + \frac{1}{1,000,000}\right)^{1,000,000} = (1.000001)^{1,000,000} = 2.71828$$

The result, 2.71828, is the base of natural logarithms and universally recognized by the symbol e. When e is raised to a power equal to the nominal rate of interest—in this case 10 percent—we have

$$e^{.10} = (2.71828)^{.10}$$
$$= 1.105171$$
$$= (1.105171 - 1)(100)$$
$$= 10.5171\%$$

In the parlance of financial mathematics, 10.5171 percent is the value of a nominal rate of interest of 10 percent compounded continuously. Compare

Table 3-1   **Value of $1,000 Investment at Year's End at 10-percent Interest Rate for Various Compounding Periods**

Compounding Period	Value at Beginning		$1 + r$, where $r = 10\%$		Value at End
Annually	$1,000	×	(1.10)	=	$1,100.00
Semiannually	$1,000	×	$\left(1 + \dfrac{.10}{2}\right)^2$	=	$1,102.500
Quarterly	$1,000	×	$\left(1 + \dfrac{.10}{4}\right)^4$	=	$1,103.813
Monthly	$1,000	×	$\left(1 + \dfrac{.10}{12}\right)^{12}$	=	$1,104.713
Weekly	$1,000	×	$\left(1 + \dfrac{.10}{52}\right)^{52}$	=	$1,105.065
Daily	$1,000	×	$\left(1 + \dfrac{.10}{365}\right)^{365}$	=	$1,105.156
Hourly	$1,000	×	$\left(1 + \dfrac{.10}{8760}\right)^{8,760}$	=	$1,105.165
Continuously	$1,000	×	$(2.71828)^{.10}$	=	$1,105.171

this result with 10.5165 percent when we compounded hourly. The difference, .0006 percent, would be eliminated as we moved from compounding by the hour to the minute and from the minute to the second.

We have, therefore, two ways to reach the compounding limit. We may break the nominal rate of interest into successively smaller components and compound by the divisor, as illustrated in Table 3-1. Alternatively, we may raise e to the nominal rate of interest, and arrive at the same result.

Continuous compounding, of course, provides the investor with more interest on a given sum of money. However, unless substantial sums are involved, the gain from compounding continuously rather than compounding daily is small. From Table 3-1, we learn that the difference on $1,000 at a nominal rate of 10 percent is .015 cents per year. Even those who deposit the fully insured $100,000 earn only $1.50 more in interest when 10 percent is compounded continuously than when compounded daily. Assuming your funds are in a bank that compounds interest daily, should you switch to a bank that compounds the same nominal interest rate continuously? Or is the cost in time and shoe leather not worth the benefit? The answer, as we shall see, may depend in part on how long you intend to keep your funds on deposit.

TIME PERIOD OVER WHICH INTEREST IS COMPOUNDED   In 1626, Peter Minuit paid the Manhattan Indians $24 in trinkets for Manhattan Island. If this amount had been invested and allowed to compound annually at a nominal interest rate of 5 percent from 1626 to 1986—or for 360 years—it would have been worth $24(1.05)^{360} = \$1,019,433,514$.

Compounded daily, \$24 would have been worth $24\left(1 + \dfrac{.05}{365}\right)^{365 \times 360} = \$1,573,835,502$.

Compounded continuously, \$24 would have been worth $24(2.71828)^{.05 \times 360} = \$1,575,820,180$.

We can now generalize the arithmetic and say that to find the value S' of a sum S earning a nominal rate r paid m times per year for n years, we use the following equation (see Appendix A for proofs of all equations employed):

$$S\left(1 + \frac{r}{m}\right)^{mn} = S' \tag{3-1}$$

When interest is compounded continuously, then

$$S(e)^{rn} = S' \tag{3-2}$$

Equations 3-1 and 3-2 are general. If n is a single year, the equations become

$$S\left(1 + \frac{r}{m}\right)^{m} = S' \tag{3-3}$$

$$S(e)^{r} = S' \tag{3-4}$$

We developed the results in Table 3-1 from the preceding equations.

Perhaps financier J. P. Morgan had in mind the proceeds from the sale of Manhattan Island when he was alleged to have said that compound interest was the eighth wonder of the world. More likely, however, his thoughts were on one or more of his own successful ventures. Moreover, although Morgan may not have been quite as concerned about such finer points of compound interest as the difference between daily and continuous compounding, he would have, to say the least, found the discussion *profitable*.

Of course, 360 years is a long time to compound interest on any investment. One must have not only great faith in the stability of society but also great love for several unborn generations—who may or may not revere their ancestors for the bounty bestowed upon them.

A single lifetime is a more realistic span over which to accumulate. Assume that under legislation in force at the time, an individual is eligible to invest as much as \$2,000 in an Individual Retirement Account (IRA) in any given year. As long as the individual did not withdraw funds until at least age 59-1/2 (except for death or disability), payment of taxes on the amount deposited and the interest earned is postponed. Thus, a 25-year-old person embarking upon a career has an incentive to deposit \$2,000 each year until he or she is at least 59-1/2 and may wish to continue to deposit monies until retirement. Assume such an individual does plan to invest

$2,000 each year for the next 40 years—until age 65. What will be the total amount available at that time? The equation for determining the amount is

$$S = \frac{a[(1 + r)^n - 1]}{r},$$ (3-5)

where S equals the future sum to which an amount invested each year for n years at r percent will accumulate. The amount invested each year is a dollars. Assume r equals 12 percent. Then

$$S = \$2,000 \frac{[(1.12)^{40} - 1]}{.12} = \$1,534,182.84$$

Of course, if interest rates averaged only 6 percent, S at $2,000 per year would equal $309,523.93 after 40 years. Disappointment, however, would be tempered by the fact that a lower interest rate would be indicative of lower anticipated inflation. Fewer dollars would, therefore, be necessary to maintain a given standard of living 40 years later.

Variations of the equation are possible. One that suggests an appealing degree of symmetry assumes the nominal rate of interest and annual payments are divided into m periods, so that

$$S = \frac{\frac{a}{m}\left[\left(1 + \frac{r}{m}\right)^{mn} - 1\right]}{\frac{r}{m}} = \frac{a\left[\left(1 + \frac{r}{m}\right)^{mn} - 1\right]}{r}$$ (3-6)

Results for an investment of $2,000 per year at a 12 percent nominal rate of interest for 40 years are shown in Table 3-2. Again, we observe the more frequently

Table 3-2 **Value of $2,000 Annual Investment after 40 Years at Nominal 12-percent Interest Rate for Various Compounding Periods**

Compounding Period	Value after 40 Years
Annually	$1,534,182.84
Semiannually	$1,746,599.89
Quarterly	$1,870,475.86
Monthly	$1,960,795.42
Weekly	$1,997,337.46
Daily	$2,006,906.35
Continuously	$2,008,500.42

one compounds interest the greater the total future value. However, once we compound daily, even weekly, the switch to continuous compounding at the same rate produces comparatively small gains—although in this case, they are probably worth the shoe leather and the time involved.

PRESENT VALUE

As noted in Chapter 2, the value today S, or *present value*, of a sum S' received one year into the future is illustrated by the relationship

$$S = \frac{S'}{1 + r}$$

If S' is $1,100 and r is 10 percent, then

$$S = \frac{\$1,100}{1.10}$$

$$S = \$1,000$$

Conceptually, present value is the opposite of compound interest. Thus, Equations 3-1 and 3-2 can be rewritten

$$S = \frac{S'}{\left(1 + \dfrac{r}{m}\right)^{mn}} \tag{3-7}$$

$$S = \frac{S'}{e^{rn}} \tag{3-8}$$

The same is true for Equations 3-3 and 3-4, so that

$$S = \frac{S'}{\left(1 + \dfrac{r}{m}\right)^{m}} \tag{3-9}$$

$$S = \frac{S'}{e^{r}} \tag{3-10}$$

The link between the present and the future—as the discussion in Chapter 2 clarified—is the rate of interest. Discussion in Chapter 3 simply extends the concept to allow for compounding under various assumptions.

Although compound interest is often a familiar concept to those beginning a study of finance, present value is not. Perhaps this is because we are accustomed to thinking in terms of interest earned on investment rather than present value of future income. Nevertheless, present value has several important applications in finance. We must, therefore, become accustomed to using it.

We begin with a relatively straightforward illustration and move on to more difficult terrain. Every week the U.S. Treasury auctions two series of treasury bills: one matures in 13 weeks (91 days); the second matures in 26 weeks (182 days). Every fourth week the U.S. Treasury also auctions 52-week (364-day) treasury bills. The minimum purchase for each is $10,000. When purchasing treasury bills, buyers may submit a competitive bid specifying the price they are willing to pay. Alternatively, buyers may submit a maximum $500,000 noncompetitive bid, in which they agree to pay the average price of the competitive tenders accepted by the U.S. Treasury. Large institutional investors, including commercial banks, generally submit competitive bids; smaller investors, including individuals[1], tender noncompetitive bids.

A major characteristic of treasury bills is the lack of an explicit interest payment. One receives the face value—for example, $10,000—at the end of 91, 182, or 364 days. The question those who submit tenders must answer is: What is the value today—the *present value*—of receiving $10,000 at one of the future time periods? Using the 26-week (approximately one-half year) treasury bill as an illustration, buyers may implicitly use equation 3-7 for m equals one, so that

$$S = \frac{S'}{1 + r}$$

$$S = \frac{10,000}{1 + r}$$

In this case, S is the present value of $10,000 in the future; it is also the price one is willing to pay for the treasury bill. What is critical, of course, is the value of r. Suppose there exists a 52-week treasury bill with 26 weeks remaining until maturity. Assume the treasury bill is currently selling at $9,450. Then

$$S(1 + r) = S'$$
$$\$9,450(1 + r) = \$10,000$$
$$r = .0582$$
$$r = 5.82\%$$

Given a comparable alternative investment that yields 5.82 percent over the next six months, 5.82 percent is the appropriate figure by which to discount $10,000

---

[1] Publishers caution authors that students no longer read footnotes even though footnotes often contain substantive material. To those who persevere, we shall from time to time offer *bonus footnotes* that contain helpful hints for constructing your own portfolio, or hints that help you in a career in finance or simply as a consumer. For example, you may purchase newly issued U.S. government securities—bills, notes, and bonds—directly and without commission from the Federal Reserve bank in your district. The details can be found in a booklet entitled *Buying Treasury Securities at Federal Reserve Banks*. The brochure is written by James F. Tucker, and the 11th edition was published in 1987 by the Federal Reserve Bank of Richmond. Copies may be obtained from the Bank's public relations department, P.O. Box 27622, Richmond, VA 23261. When you buy U.S. Treasury notes that mature within one to four years, minimum purchases are usually $5,000; for longer-term notes and bonds, minimum purchases are generally $1,000. See what you might have missed?

Table 3-3 **Present Value of $1,000 Received at Year's End at 10-percent Interest Rate for Various Discounting Periods**

Discounting Period	Value at End		$1 + r$, where $r = 10\%$		Present Value
Annually	$1,000	$\div$	(1.10)	$=$	$909.091
Semiannually	$1,000	$\div$	$\left(1 + \dfrac{.10}{2}\right)^2$	$=$	$907.029
Quarterly	$1,000	$\div$	$\left(1 + \dfrac{.10}{4}\right)^4$	$=$	$905.951
Monthly	$1,000	$\div$	$\left(1 + \dfrac{.10}{12}\right)^{12}$	$=$	$905.212
Weekly	$1,000	$\div$	$\left(1 + \dfrac{.10}{52}\right)^{52}$	$=$	$904.924
Daily	$1,000	$\div$	$\left(1 + \dfrac{.10}{365}\right)^{365}$	$=$	$904.850
Hourly	$1,000	$\div$	$\left(1 + \dfrac{.10}{8760}\right)^{8,760}$	$=$	$904.842
Continuously	$1,000	$\div$	$(2.71828)^{.10}$	$=$	$904.837

to be received 26 weeks into the future. The present value, hence the market pr̃᷉
of the new treasury bill is $9,450.[2]

PRESENT VALUE—DISCOUNTING WITHIN A YEAR The int̃᷉an one
on the foregoing treasury bill was the nominal rate of interest for six mon̓st can be
allow for interest payments at different points during a period? Just as end of the
compounded during the year, so the present value of a sum receive of interest at
year can be discounted to allow for the payment of the nomir᷉ is the present
various points during the year. Using Equations 3-9 and 3 ᷉al interest rate of
value of $1,000 received at the end of the year, assumin᷉ weekly, daily, and
10 percent paid annually, semiannually, quarterly,᷉est, readers may wish to
continuously? The breakdown is shown in Table 3 we established the value
   Because present value is the opposite of cor᷉ning a nominal rate of in-
compare Tables 3-1 and 3-2 with Table 3-3 ᷉ccordingly. In Table 3-3, we
at the end of one year of $1,000 invest᷉ end of one year under similar
terest spread over various periods an᷉
establish the value today of $1,00᷉of discount known as *bank discount rate*. A complete
᷉marketed as though the year consisted of 360 rather

_____

[2] 26 weeks is actually 182 days. Moreove᷉
than 365 days. They are also markete᷉
explanation is found in the append᷉

assumptions concerning the division of the nominal rate of interest and the period over which discounting takes place.

PRESENT VALUE—FROM A YEAR TO INFINITY   Let us continue with the concept of present value and extend our analysis to the more distant future. Suppose you have won $2,000,000 in the state lottery. As you savor your good fortune, you are informed you will receive a check today for $100,000; the additional $1,900,000 will be paid in $100,000 installments over the next 19 years. The second payment will be made one year from today; the third, two years from today; and so forth.

Although it may be inconsiderate to bring up the matter in front of television cameras recording your reactions for the evening news, the present value of these payments is not $1,900,000. It is a lesser sum. How much less depends upon the rate at which you can invest funds. Because the payments are guaranteed (unless the state is bankrupt), the appropriate rate would seem to be the risk-free rate approximated by U.S. government securities. Inasmuch as rates generally vary with the maturities of the instrument, to simplify calculations we use a single rate and assume it is 12 percent.[3] Moreover, because the funds are received at the end of the year, we also assume interest is paid annually. The present value ($p.v.$) of these payments is

$$p.v. = \frac{\$100,000}{1 + r} + \frac{\$100,000}{(1 + r)^2} + \cdots + \frac{\$100,000}{(1 + r)^{19}}$$

The limit of this expression is

$$p.v. = \$100,000 \frac{[1 - (1 + r)^{-n}]}{r}$$

or $r = 12$ percent and n equals 19, the present value of $100,000 per year received year is

$$p.v. = \$100,000 \frac{[1 - (1.12)^{-19}]}{.12}$$

$$p.v. = \$736.578$$

More g
discount   he present value of a dollar received n years into the future and
at a rate of interest r is given by the equation

$$p.v. = a \frac{[1 - (1 + r)^{-n}]}{r} \tag{3-11}$$

The expression within the brackets is the present value of a dollar received at the end of each year for n years and discounted at r percent. Calculators and computers readily handle this and other computations developed in this chapter. (See Appendix G for discussion of use of calculators.) Because of its importance later in the text, however, we have included in Appendix C the present value of a dollar received each year up to 25 years at various rates of interest. Examining Appendix C for r equals 12 percent and n equals 19 years, the present value of a dollar is $7.365777. Multiplying by $100,000, we have $100,000 × $7.365777 = $736,577.7 = $736,578.

Equation 3-11 is the counterpart of Equation 3-5, where we compounded a sum annually at a rate of interest r for n years into the future. To complete the comparison, Equation 3-11 can be written so as to allow for payment of the nominal rate of interest as well as the dollars to be received for m periods. Thus

$$p.v. = \frac{a}{m} \frac{\left[1 - \left(1 + \frac{r}{m}\right)^{-mn}\right]}{\frac{r}{m}} = a \frac{\left[1 - \left(1 + \frac{r}{m}\right)^{-mn}\right]}{r} \tag{3-12}$$

So Equation 3-12 is comparable to Equation 3-6 when interest is compounded. In this case, the limit of the expression $\left(1 + \frac{r}{m}\right)^{-mn}$ is $\frac{1}{e^{rm}}$ or e^{-rm}.

If the state agreed to pay your lottery win in quarterly installments rather than at the end of each year, you would find (assuming the nominal rate of interest is paid quarterly) that

$$p.v. = \$100,000 \frac{\left[1 - \left(1 + \frac{.12}{4}\right)^{-4 \times 19}\right]}{.12}$$

$$p.v. = \$745,190$$

Under these calculations you would be $8,612 richer ($745,190–$736,578) if you received $100,00 in quarterly installments rather than in a lump sum at the end of each year.

PRESENT VALUE AND RETURN APPLIED TO PREFERRED STOCK

We are now equipped to apply and to extend somewhat the concepts we have developed. We begin with a conceptually simple illustration—preferred stock. In its basic form, preferred stock represents ownership interest in a company. Dividends are paid at regular intervals, often quarterly. Unless otherwise specified in the stockholder's contract, dividends remain constant. In addition, preferred stock does not actually mature and can usually be repurchased from stockholders by the company at a specified *call* price. (If there is a market for the stock, the company can always buy the shares at the going market price.) Otherwise, the stock has no maturity date; it is, in essence, a perpetuity.[4] (Because a stockholder may, of course, sell shares at any time at the going market price, his or her holding period may not be infinite.)

Consider a real-world exmple. In 1973, AT&T issued preferred stock with an annual dividend payment of $3.64 broken into quarterly installments of $0.91. What is the present value of the payments? Using equation 3-12

$$p.v. = a\frac{\left[1 - \left(1 + \dfrac{r}{m}\right)^{-mn}\right]}{r} = 3.64\frac{\left[1 - \left(1 + \dfrac{r}{4}\right)^{-4n}\right]}{r}$$

However, two pieces of information are missing: values for n and r. If we treat the preferred stock as a perpetuity, then $n \to \infty$. Since

$$\left(1 + \frac{r}{m}\right)^{-mn} = \frac{1}{\left(1 + \dfrac{r}{m}\right)^{mn}}$$

then as $n \to \infty$

$$\frac{1}{\left(1 + \dfrac{r}{m}\right)^{mn}} \to 0$$

In this instance, Equation 3-12 becomes

$$p.v. = a\frac{1}{r} = \frac{a}{r} = \frac{\$3.64}{r}$$

Although we have simplified the mathematics, we still need a value for r. How do we find one? Opportunity cost to the rescue! Investors are continuously evaluating present value of future dividend streams relative to other investment opportunities. Their collective judgment is reflected in the market price of the stock as well as in the market price of other investments. If we substitute price p for present value, we have

$$p = \frac{a}{r} \tag{3-13}$$

$$r = \frac{a}{p} \tag{3-14}$$

---

[4] Britain has government issues outstanding known as consols; these instruments never mature and are, therefore, perpetuities. Application of present value techniques to such instruments is similar to this application to preferred stock.

YIELD TO MATURITY ON A ZERO COUPON BOND   When a debt instrument pays no interest but only face value at maturity, it is known as a zero coupon bond.[14] To calculate YTM for this type of security, again use Equation 3-15. However, because the nominal rate of interest is zero, the first term in the equation is dropped.

$$p.v. = \frac{F}{\left(1 + \dfrac{r}{m}\right)^{mn}} \tag{3-16}$$

In the spring of 1982, J. C. Penney offered the public zero coupon notes maturing November 25, 1992. From the date of issue to the date of maturity, the notes would be outstanding for approximately 10.59 years. The notes could be purchased for $25 per $100 of face value, payable at maturity. To make them comparable to ordinary coupon bonds, m must equal 2, so when issued

$$\$25 = \frac{100}{\left(1 + \dfrac{r}{2}\right)^{2 \times 10.59}}$$

$$r = 13.50\%$$

The YTM was 13.50, the rate quoted on the date of issue.[15]

Because zero coupon securities provide a single payment at maturity, they increase in value over time. Suppose, for example, that 5.6 years from the date of issue the yield to maturity on zero coupon issues of comparable quality with 5 years to maturity is 13.50 percent. The present value of the issue 5.6 years later is

$$p.v. = \frac{\$100}{\left(1 + \dfrac{.1350}{2}\right)^{5.6 \times 2}}$$

$$p.v. = \$48.11$$

If interest rates rise to 16 percent, the present value five years from the date of maturity is

$$p.v. = \frac{\$100}{\left(1 + \dfrac{.16}{2}\right)^{5 \times 2}}$$

$$p.v. = \$46.32$$

---

[14] The term **original issue discount** (OID) bond is applied to new instruments with coupons that are low relative to the going rate of interest so they may be marketed at a substantial discount from par. The zero coupon is the extreme case of such an instrument. See Solveig Jansson, "The Deep Discount Bond Fad," *The Institutional Investor*, Vol. XV (August 1981, pp. 69–75).

[15] *Moody's Bond Survey* (April 5, 1982, p. 2339).

If interest rates fall to 9 percent, the present value five years from the date of maturity is

$$p.v. = \frac{\$100}{(1.045)^{5 \times 2}}$$

$$p.v. = \$64.39$$

In all cases, the present value rises—but at different rates.

Zero coupon bonds are generally attractive to institutions and often attractive to pension funds, where current need for cash is relatively low. These instruments are a good example of one of many variations on the basic debt contract designed to appeal to a specific group of investors.[16]

COMMON STOCK

As a final example of a financial asset, let us consider application of the principles developed in this chapter to common stock. Common stock represents ownership interest in a company. Unlike preferred shares, common shares pay no stated dividend; the dividend paid today may be greater than, equal to, or less than the dividend paid in the future. Like preferred stock, there is no maturity date. We may, therefore, treat common stock as a perpetuity. And if we do, we have two alternatives. First, we may assume the dividend will remain constant. Second, we may assume the dividend will grow or decline at some rate or set of rates in the future. In the former case, the analysis parallels our discussion of preferred stock. We can use Equation 3-11 or Equation 3-12 if dividends are paid at less than annual intervals. (Dividends are usually paid quarterly.) Thus

$$p.v. = a \cdot \frac{[1 - (1 + r)^{-n}]}{r}$$

or

$$p.v. = a \cdot \frac{\left[1 - \left(1 + \dfrac{r}{m}\right)^{-mn}\right]}{r}$$

In each case, as $n \to \infty$ the equation becomes

$$p.v. = \frac{a}{r}$$

---

[16] Because the value of zero coupon bonds rises as they approach maturity, investors (for tax purposes) must impute an interest payment each year and declare it as taxable income. Pension funds, however, do not pay taxes. This is another reason why this group is attracted to these securities.

The characteristic of common stock that attracts investors is that dividends might grow as the firm grows more successful. Suppose a is the current annual dividend paid at the end of the year and is expected to grow at g rate per year beginning next year. To simplify the exposition, ignore the refinement a/m or assume m equals 1, so that

$$p.v. = \frac{a}{1+r} + \frac{a(1+g)}{(1+r)^2} + \frac{a(1+g)^2}{(1+r)^3} + \cdots + \frac{a(1+g)^{n-1}}{(1+r)^n}$$

It can be shown (see Appendix A) that this expression becomes

$$p.v. = \frac{a\left[1 - \left(\dfrac{1+g}{1+r}\right)^n\right]}{r-g} \tag{3-17}$$

For values of $r > g$, the expression $\dfrac{(1+g)^n}{(1+r)} \to 0$ as $n \to \infty$, so that

$$p.v. = \frac{a}{r-g} \tag{3-18}$$

If $r = g$, there are no solutions. If $r < g$, then as $n \to \infty$, again there are no finite solutions. Clearly, over the long run—as $n \to \infty$—the opportunity cost of capital r must be greater than the growth in dividends g.

Dividends are a function of earnings and earnings are a function of productivity of physical capital: plant and equipment. As suggested in Chapter 2, adding plant and equipment to a given level of other resources results in diminished returns and hence in diminished growth of earnings and dividends. Technological advances can lower costs and tapping new markets can increase sales. One can delay the decline, but the inevitable may not be postponed forever. Thus, in the long run $r > g$, and as $n \to \infty$, Equation 3-18 is the logical economic outcome of Equation 3-17. Of course, in the short run that $g > r$ is a distinct possibility. One might combine Equations 3-11 or 3-12 with 3-14 to determine present value of a common stock—use a short-run growth rate g' for perhaps two years, followed by a long-run growth rate g.

To illustrate, suppose a company is currently paying a dividend of $2.00 per share. Assume the dividend is paid annually at the end of the year and the dividend date has just passed. Those just buying the stock will receive nothing for one year. On the basis of an analysis of the company's earnings prospects, you expect dividends to grow at 20 percent per year for the next two years: dividends will be

$$2.00(1.2) = \$2.40 \text{ at the end of } T_1$$
$$2.40(1.2) = \$2.88 \text{ at the end of } T_2$$

Thereafter, dividends are expected to grow at 5 percent per year indefinitely. Similar investments currently earn a 15-percent return. Therefore

$$p.v. = \frac{\$2.00(1.20)}{1.15} + \frac{\$2.00(1.20)^2}{(1.15)^2} + \frac{\dfrac{\$2.00(1.20)^2}{.15 - .05}}{(1.15)^2}$$

Or combining Equations 3-17 and 3-18

$$p.v. = \frac{2.40\left[1 - \left(\dfrac{1.20}{1.15}\right)^2\right]}{.15 - .20} + \frac{\dfrac{\$2.88}{.15 - .05}}{(1.15)^2}$$

$$p.v. = \$4.26 + \$21.78$$

$$p.v. = \$26.04$$

In words, Equation 3-17 functions on the assumption that the dividend is received at the end of the year. Because you expect the dividend to grow at 20 percent annually for two years, at the end of the first year the dividend is $2.40. You also expect the long-run growth rate to become operative at the beginning of the third year, at which time the dividend paid at the end of the second year is $2.00(1.2)^2 = \$2.88$. It is this dividend ($2.88) that is discounted by the difference between what investors expect to receive (.15) and the long-run growth rate (.05). However, in the analysis using Equation 3-18, discounting does not take place until the end of the second year or beginning of the third year. Consequently, the result

$$\$28.00 = \frac{2.88}{.15 - .05}$$

must be returned to its present value by discounting it at $(1.15)^2$.

In the analysis of common stock, present value is often called **intrinsic value** or *present intrinsic value*. One finds the true value of the stock and then compares that value with the stock's current market price. Albeit somewhat naively, we can say that if the intrinsic value of the stock is less than its market price, it should be sold or, if unowned, not purchased. Alternatively, if the intrinsic value of the stock is greater than its market price, it should be purchased.

The interpretation may be naive because it implies we have information the market does not have or, stated differently, we have a better understanding of the values that constitute g, r, and n. Although this may be true, our discussion in Chapter 5 suggests that consistently superior insights into the intrinsic value of common stock are rare.[17] Nevertheless, securities analysts are paid six-figure salaries

---

[17] A similar problem occurs with respect to predicting the present value of a bond, a preferred stock, or indeed any investment. In addition, the comparatively vague terms of the common stock contract make the task more difficult. As noted, for preferred stock all we need is r for issues of comparable quality. For debt instruments, although YTM is a difficult measure to use, at least we can compare issues of similar maturity and similar coupons.

to find stocks that the market has either undervalued or overvalued. (College professors earning half their incomes or less will not deter analysts from meeting the challenge for which they were hired). Equations 3-11, 3-12, 3-14, 3-17, and 3-18 (or variations of them) are one part of the toolbox analysts employ to discharge their duties.

For example, in June 1979, IBM stock dropped several points on the strength of an executive's remarks that earnings growth would slow temporarily. The reason for the slowdown was an increase in leasing, relative to sales of the then new 4300 line of computers. Nevertheless, one analyst predicted

> If you are patient and in for the long haul, 1981 is going to be an outstanding year for I.B.M., because at that time the sales–lease ratio will have stabilized at a sustainable level and the company's high shipments against its strong backlog will produce very strong earnings.[18]

As it turned out, the analyst was wrong—but only partially wrong. At the end of the third quarter of 1981, the market price of IBM stock hit a low of 53-1/8. However, by the end of 1982, the price had risen to 96-1/4. From 1981 to 1984, profits grew at an average annual rate of 22 percent. Moreover, dividends—which had been a steady 86 cents a quarter, or $3.44 per year, since 1979—were increased in 1983 and 1984. During the mid-1980s, dividends leveled off at $4.40 per year and by the first quarter of 1986, IBM stock had risen to $161 per share. By that time, securities analysts were beginning to question whether, in light of a slowdown in growth, IBM would have to alter its strategy for seeking new products and markets.[19] By the end of 1986, the price had fallen to $120.19. By mid-1987—partly due to increased demand for personal computers, including its new line—IBM's stock was again trading in excess of $160 per share.

It is, of course, easy to criticize. Even if your timing is off, it is better to be right than wrong. Nevertheless, to paraphrase Burton G. Malkiel, there is a fundamental indeterminateness about the present intrinsic value of common stock. God Almighty may not know the appropriate values to give r and g in any given instance.[20]

HOLDING PERIOD RETURN   Securities analysts, and the rest of us, do not believe we can second-guess God. In the IBM illustration, the analyst was attempting to predict a turning point on the price of the stock. This is no mean feat (in Chapter 5 we learn why). Nevertheless, to the extent clients followed his advice and were patient, they eventually enjoyed some spectacular returns.

Suppose you decided in 1979 to wait and see if the analyst was correct and, in addition, to do some investigating on your own. You knew IBM had entered the

[18] Peter J. Shuyten. "Why the Bloom Fades From I.B.M.," *New York Times* (June 17, 1979, Sec. 3, p. 2).

[19] *Moody's Handbook of Common Stocks*, annual issues. *Wall Street Journal*, various issues. *Hartford Courant* (April 3, 1986, pp. A20 and 23). *Wall Street Journal* (January 2, 1987, Sec. 2, p. 10B).

[20] Burton G. Malkiel. *A Random Walk Down Wall Street*, 4th ed. (Newton: Norton & Company, 1985, p. 92.)

personal computer market—a new venture for a company whose marketing strategy had been primarily directed toward large systems and toward commercial, not retail, markets. It remained to be seen how successful IBM would be in this area. At the same time, you sensed a growing market demand for personal computers. As the largest firm of its kind, IBM should benefit from such growth.

For nearly 18 months you bide your time and finally, on December 31, 1981, decide to buy 100 shares of IBM at $56.375 per share. As it develops, you have gotten in on the ground floor of a major rise in the price of IBM shares, and the market in general. You hold the stock for four years, and on New Year's Eve 1985, you sell at the closing price of $155.50. As you recover from the celebration your malaise is mitigated by the fact that you have realized—before Uncle Sam takes his share in taxes—almost $100 per share in profits less transactions costs. You also received dividends during this period. Over a late breakfast, you begin to contemplate your return before taxes. One simple method of making the calculations involves *holding period return* (HPR). To calculate holding period return, let

D = dividends paid over the holding period
P_0 = market price per share at the beginning of the holding period
P_1 = market price per share at the end of the holding period

Then

$$HPR = \frac{P_1 - P_0 + D}{P_0} \tag{3-19}$$

In Table 3-4, we calculate annual holding period returns using end-of-year IBM prices for the years 1982–1985 (but beginning with the closing price in 1981). Dividends are annual dividends paid during 1982, 1983, 1984, and 1985. To average these returns over time, use a *time-weighted*, or **geometric, mean** rather than an arithmetic mean. A geometric mean is the nth root of the product of n numbers. To understand why we use a geometric rather than an arithmetic mean, consider the following case.

A person buys a rare stamp for $100. The next year the stamp increases in value to $200. The year after, however, the market price falls back to $100. The holding period returns are

Year One	*Year Two*
$\dfrac{200 - 100}{100} = 100\%$	$\dfrac{100 - 200}{200} = -50\%$

The simple-average, or arithmetic, mean is

$$\frac{100\% - 50\%}{2} = 25\%$$

Table 3-4 Holding Period Returns and Average-annual Rate of Return for IBM (1982–1986)

Year	Holding Period Return[a]
1982	$\dfrac{96.25 - 56.375 + 3.44}{56.375} = .7683 \times 100 = 76.83\%$
1983	$\dfrac{122 - 96.25 + 3.80}{96.25} = .3070 \times 100 = 30.70\%$
1984	$\dfrac{123.125 - 122 + 4.40}{122} = .0453 \times 100 = 4.53\%$
1985	$\dfrac{155.5 - 123.125 + 4.40}{123.125} = .2987 \times 100 = 29.87\%$

Average-annual, or Time-weighted Rate of Return (geometric mean)

$$\text{Geometric Mean} \equiv \sqrt[4]{(1.7683)(1.3070)(1.0453)(1.2987)} - 1$$
$$\equiv \sqrt[4]{3.13748} - 1 \equiv 1.3309 - 1 = .3309 \times 100 = 33.09\%$$

[a] Based upon closing prices, prices for each year and the annual dividends paid for the year.

SOURCE: *Wall Street Journal*, end-of-year stock prices. Calculations based upon these prices.

Yet, the individual who bought the stamp has experienced no gain. If averaged geometrically

$$\sqrt{(1 + 1)(1 - .5)} - 1 = 1 - 1 = 0$$

Because averaging geometrically reveals precisely what happened to the holding period returns for two years, we average holding period returns over time geometrically rather than arithmetically.[21]

REAL CAPITAL INVESTMENTS

Although stocks are the glamour investments, a major portion of our treatment concerns the return on investment in such real assets as plant and equipment. Details of the treatment are presented in Chapters 8 and 9; here we simply suggest how the principles of present value are applied.

---

[21] The geometric mean has a different problem: built-in reinvestment assumptions. We can think of the geometric mean in terms of compound interest. A 33.09-percent geometric mean of four disparate measures of holding period returns, when compounded annually, equals the product of those rates. Thus, $(1.3309)^4 = 3.13748$. In terms of stock price, this suggests that from 1982 through 1985, $\$56.375 \times 3.13748 = \$176.88$.

The stock, however, was sold at $155.50. The discrepancy between the two figures is partly accounted for by total dividends of 16.04, for a total of $171.54. What accounts for the $5.34 difference? Specifically, it is assumed that dividends are reinvested and not spent. Details of the *reinvestment assumption* are developed in Chapter 8.

When a nonfinancial business firm—manufacturing company, public utility, wholesale or retail business, trade or service industry—invests in real capital, it expects to get back the outlay through depreciation of the asset and also anticipates earning a profit. The sum of the after-tax profit and depreciation are called the *net cash flows* from the asset. To illustrate, suppose a manufacturing firm installs machinery that costs $300,000. From past experience, management knows the machinery will last three years. Net cash flows at the end of each of three years will be

Year	Net Cash Flow
T_1	$200,000
T_2	$250,000
T_3	$125,000

To calculate the return on this investment, solve the following equation (assume interest is compounded annually):

$$\$300,000 = \frac{\$200,000}{(1 + r)} + \frac{\$250,000}{(1 + r)^2} + \frac{\$125,000}{(1 + r)^3}$$

We cannot use Appendix C to solve the equation because the cash flows—the value of a in Equation 3-11—are not constant. Here the easiest solution is to use a preprogrammed computer or calculator that simply inputs values for r until, through trial and error, a figure is found that equates present value of future cash flows with outlay. Using this approach[22], $r = 44.38\%$.

Although the return looks impressive, how it should be interpreted is a topic we discuss in Chapter 8.

Consider another example. A company buys land upon which to build a plant. Ten years later it sells a portion of that land. For the acreage sold, the company paid $250,000; it received $545,000 for the parcel. Assuming interest is compounded annually, to calculate the return on the land solve the following equation

$$\$250,000 = \frac{\$545,000}{(1 + r)^{10}}$$

---

[22] The calculations were made using the *Hewlett-Packard 12-C*. The strokes and displays are

Keystroke	Display
f CLXREG 0.00	0.00
300,000 CHS g CF_0	– 300,000
200,000 g CF_j	200,000
250,000 g CF_j	250,000
125,000 g CF_j	125,000
f IRR	44.375808

This example is similar to Equation 3-16, which we employed to calculate return on the zero coupon bond. Here, however, we have assumed the value of m is 1, not 2. In Appendix B, one can find the present value of a dollar received at the end of n years for $m = 1$. To use the table in Appendix B, we must rearrange the equation so that

$$\$250,000 = \frac{\$545,000}{(1 + r)^{10}}$$

$$(1 + r)^{10} = \frac{\$545,000}{\$250,000}$$

and

$$\frac{1}{(1 + r)^{10}} = \frac{\$250,000}{\$545,000} = .458716$$

The table shows values for $\dfrac{1}{(1 + r)^{10}}$ for whole percentages. Thus, for $n = 10$ and $r = 8$ we find the present value of one dollar is .463193. For $r = 9$ percent, the present value is .422411. The value for r that solves the equation lies between 8 and 9 percent. We can readily establish a proportion so that

$$\frac{x}{.01} = \frac{.463193 - .458716}{.463193 - .422411}$$

$$x = .001098$$

$$.08 + .001098 = .081098 \times 100 = 8.1098 = 8.11\%$$

The interpolation is linear, not geometric. However, a preprogrammed calculator substituting values for r—using trial and error—resulted in a value of 8.104967 percent.[23]

---

[23] For those who enjoy getting as much as possible from a table, use Appendix B to approximate the value of r in the J. C. Penney example. Since n was 10.59 and m was 2, the product 21.18 is equivalent to just over 21 years for a nominal rate of interest of one-half 13.50, or 6.75 percent. Note that in the table for $n = 21$, the present value of one dollar at 6 percent is .294156. At 7 percent, it is .241513. From the original equation

$$\$25 = \frac{100}{\left(1 + \dfrac{r}{2}\right)^{mn}}$$

$$\frac{1}{\left(1 + \dfrac{r}{2}\right)^{mn}} = .25$$

Interpolating between the two percentages, we have

$$\frac{x}{.01} = \frac{.294156 - .25}{.294156 - .241513}$$

$$x = .008388$$

$$.06 + .008388 = .068388 = 6.84\% > 6.75\%$$

If there had been values for 21.18 years in the table, we could have reached as close an approximation to the solution of the equation as we did for the real-property example.

SUMMARY

Compound interest and present-value mathematics, in particular the latter, are crucial to the study of finance. Although most financial decisions occur in the present, their consequences are realized in the future. Building on the conceptual framework sketched in Chapter 2, we have intuitively developed the reasoning underlying the basic equations—leaving more formal proofs for Appendix A. By now, readers should be comfortable with the notion that compound interest and present value are mirror images, or two sides of the same coin. However, present value is operationally more significant because most decisions in finance represent outlays of cash today in order to realize benefits tomorrow.

Whether one is buying a bond, a stock, or investing in plant and equipment (real capital), the concept is the same. The details, however, differ. Hence, use Equation 3-15 to calculate the return on a bond (or any long-term debt instrument) because the annual (or nominal) rate of interest is conventionally paid in two equal installments over a year. On the other hand, because a preferred stock may be viewed as a perpetuity, employ Equation 3-14 to calculate its yield or, alternatively, its present value. The yield (or return) on a six-month treasury bill is simply the ratio of the difference between the face value of the bill and its purchase price divided by the purchase price. These words underly the mathematics

$$S = \frac{S'}{1 + r}$$

where S is the amount paid today for the treasury bill and S' is the face value to be received six months in the future.

Equations, of course, can be solved. In finance, solving for r is finding the rate that equates the present value of future benefits in dollars with the present outlay paid for those benefits. This is the yield (or return) on the investment. Alternatively, as the illustrations suggest, you can substitute a value for r—an opportunity cost— and calculate the present value of the future benefits compared to the market price of the investment.

Equations also give us a sense of precision. As noted in the discussion of common stock, however, precision may be an illusion. Unfortunately, when one expends funds today for benefits in the future, those future benefits are what the investor expects—but are only certain in a very few circumstances. Consequently, intertwined with the notion of return is the degree of risk one is willing to assume before making an investment. In turn, degree of risk implies that one has developed a definition of risk and some notion of how people might react toward risk. We undertake this exercise in Chapter 4.

APPENDIX 3-A

THE MARKET FOR TREASURY BILLS— AN OVERVIEW

As noted, U.S. Treasury bills are marketed in three different maturities: 13 weeks, 26 weeks, and 52 weeks. The bills are sold in minimum denominations of $10,000 and in multiples of $5,000 thereafter. The 13- and 26-week bills are marketed every week and the 52-week bills every four weeks. The bills pay no interest but are sold at a discount from face value. The interest payment is, therefore, implicit in the difference between the price paid for the bill and its face value.

When marketing new bills, the Treasury, through its fiscal agent, the Federal Reserve, accepts competitive bids representing prices individuals and institutions are willing to pay for a new issue. Noncompetitive bids, to a maximum of $500,000, are also accepted. Those submitting noncompetitive bids agree to pay the average price of the competitive tenders accepted by the Treasury.

Table 3-5 records the results of an auction held Monday, August 9, 1982. The first four entries are self-explanatory. The price paid and the discount rate on average-, high-, and low-price bids are based upon $100 units. Thus, the average price on 13-week bills is $97.438 . The average rate of discount is known as the *bank discount rate*. Bank discount is based on a 360-day year. The formula for determining bank discount is given in Table 3-6. Given the number of days to maturity, if one knows the price of a treasury bill, one can determine the discount. Also, given the number of days to maturity, one can determine the price if one knows the discount rate.

The last entry in Table 3-5 is labeled *coupon equivalent*. The coupon equivalent is the same as the nominal rate of interest, or yield: the interest paid at the end of the year, assuming the bill matured in 365 days. The formula for determining the coupon rate, or yield, is given in Table 3-6. The calculations of discount and yield for 13- and 26-week bills (based upon the average price for each) are also given in Table 3-6, consistent with the information contained in Table 3-5.

Table 3-5   Results of Treasury Bill Auction (August 9, 1982)[a]

	13-week Bills	26-week Bills
Applications	$12,031,405,000	$11,943,865,000
Accepted bids	85,500.725,000	5,500,435,000
Accepted at low price	61%	81%
Accepted noncompetitively	1,051,620,000	972,310,000
Average price (rate)	97.438 (10.025%)	94.469 (10.940%)
High price (rate)	97.478 (9.869%)	94.499 (10.881%)
Low price (rate)	97.422 (10.088%)	94.449 (10.980%)
Coupon equivalent	10.43%	11.74%

[a] Both issues were dated August 12, 1982. The 13-week bills matured November 12, 1982 (hence 92 rather than 91 days because of the holiday on November 11, 1982). The 26-week bills matured February 10, 1983.

SOURCE: *Wall Street Journal* (August 10, 1982, pp. 45).

Table 3-6   Discount on Treasury Bill Yields

Formula for Discount	Formula for Coupon Rate (or yield)
$$d = \frac{360}{n}\frac{(100-p)}{100}$$	$$i = \frac{365}{n}\frac{(100-p)}{p}$$

$d \equiv$ discount, $n \equiv$ days to maturity, $p \equiv$ market price, $i \equiv$ yield

Application to Treasury Bills Issued August 12, 1982

13-week	26-week	52-week
$p = 97.438$	$p = 94.469$	$p = 88.746$
$n = 92$ days	$n = 182$ days	$n = 364$ days
$d = \dfrac{360}{92}\dfrac{(100 - 97.438)}{100}$	$d = \dfrac{360}{182}\dfrac{(100 - 94.469)}{100}$	$d = \dfrac{360}{364}\dfrac{(100 - 88.746)}{100}$
$d = .10025$	$d = .10940$	$d = .1113$
$i = \dfrac{365}{92}\dfrac{(100 - 97.438)}{97.438}$	$i = \dfrac{365}{182}\dfrac{(100 - 94.469)}{94.469}$	$i = \dfrac{365}{364}\dfrac{(100 - 88.746)}{88.746}$
$i = .1043$	$i = .1174$	$i = .1268$
$i = 100 \times .1043$	$i = 100 \times .1174$	$i = 12.68\%$
$i = 10.43\%$	$i = 11.74\%$	$i = 12.68\%$

SOURCE: *Wall Street Journal* (August 10, 1982, pp. 45 and 52).

Table 3-6 also gives the discount rate and yield on a 52-week treasury bill for August 9, 1982 issued August 12, 1982. The bill (auctioned on August 5, 1982) was trading on a when-issued basis in the secondary market on August 9, 1982, the day the 13- and 26-week treasury bills were auctioned. On August 9, 1982, the 52-week bill could be purchased at a discount of .1113. Using this discount rate and the formula in Table 3-6, the price of the bill on that date was \$85.746 per \$100 face value. Employing the formula for the coupon rate, the yield shown in Table 3-6 was

---

Table 3-7   Applying the Treasury and Federal Reserve Formula to Determine Yields on Treasury Bills Maturing Between 26 and 52 Weeks

Quadratic Formula

$$i = \frac{-b \pm \sqrt{b^2 - 4ac}}{2a}$$

$b = \dfrac{r}{y}$ r = number of days from delivery date to maturity

$a = \dfrac{r - 0.25}{2y}$ y = number of days in year following date of issue

$c = \dfrac{p - 100}{p}$ p = price

Yield on a 52-week treasury bill trading on August 9, 1982, on a *when-issued basis* is calculated as follows:

$$r = 364 \qquad b = \frac{364}{365} = .99726$$

$$y = 365 \qquad a = \frac{364}{730} - 0.25 = .24863$$

$$p = 88.746 \qquad c = \frac{88.746 - 100}{88.746} = -.126811$$

$$i = \frac{-.99726 \pm \sqrt{(.99726)^2 - 4(.24863)(-.126811)}}{2(.24863)}$$

$i = 12.34\%$ and -4.13%.

The latter figure, -4.13%, can be ignored.

SOURCE: *U.S. Department of the Treasury*, "Method for Calculating Equivalent Coupon Issue Yield for Treasury Bills with a Term to Maturity of More than a Half Year and Less than a Whole Year," (Washington, D.C.: Mimeographed, U.S. Department of the Treasury).

.1268, or 12.68 percent. However, the yield quoted for the bill was .1234 or 12.34 percent.[24]

The discrepancy of 34 *basis points*—34 percentage points—is attributable to the use by the Treasury and the Federal Reserve of a formula for all bills maturing between 26 and 52 weeks. In employing the formula (actually the quadratic formula), one allows for the fact other treasury securities, notably notes and bonds, pay half the nominal annual rate of interest every six months.[25] To make treasury bills on which interest is effectively paid at maturity comparable to notes and bonds, allow for the fact that there are no interest payments at 26 weeks. Table 3-7 contains both the formula and the appropriate calculations. The results are consistent with the yield quoted on August 9, 1982: .1234, or 12.34 percent.

INTERPRETING YIELD TO MATURITY

Suppose a bond with a 10-percent nominal interest rate (coupon) is selling at par and matures in 20 years. Thus, using Equation 3-15

$$\$1,000 = \frac{\$100\left[1 - \left(1 + \frac{r}{2}\right)^{-40}\right]}{r} + \frac{\$1,000}{\left(1 + \frac{r}{2}\right)^{-40}}$$

$$r = YTM = 10\%$$

If a general rise in interest rates causes YTM to rise to 12 percent, the new market price is

$$P = (\$100)\frac{\left[1 - \left(1 + \frac{.12}{2}\right)^{-40}\right]}{.12} + \frac{\$1,000}{\left(1 + \frac{.12}{2}\right)^{40}}$$

$$P = \$849.54$$

---

[24] *A Bonus Footnote!* When banks offer a rate on a time deposit, savings, or money-market account based upon the treasury-bill rate, they are probably using the bank discount rather than the nominal yield. Moreover, if you live in a state that has a state income tax on interest, you must pay that tax. However, if you buy treasury bills directly, not only do you receive the true yield but you also avoid the state income tax. States cannot tax interest on federal securities, just as the U.S. Treasury cannot tax interest on the securities of state and local governments.

[25] For some of the complexities underlying the Treasury's formula, see William J. Landes and Frank Thompson, "Bank Discount, Coupon Equivalent and Coupon Yields," *Financial Management*, Vol. 11 (Autumn 1982, pp. 80–84). See also John D. Finerty, "Bank Discount, Coupon Equivalent, and Compound Yields: Comment," *Financial Management*, Vol. 12 (Summer 1983, pp. 40–44).

$$P = (\$100) \frac{\left[1 - \left(1 + \dfrac{.08}{2}\right)^{-40}\right]}{.08} + \frac{\$1,000}{\left(1 + \dfrac{.08}{2}\right)^{40}}$$

$$P = \$1,197.93$$

The *capital loss* from a 2-percent rise in rates is

$$\frac{\$849.54 - \$1,000}{\$1,000} = -15.05\%$$

The *capital gain* from a 2-percent fall in rates is

$$\frac{\$1,197.93 - \$1,000}{\$1,000} = 19.79\%$$

As a generalization, capital gain from an $x\%$ fall in YTM will be greater than capital loss from an $x\%$ increase in YTM. Remember that the bulk of dollar return on a bond is the repayment of principal. In this case, the principal is repaid in 20 years. Note below the effect of compound interest after 20 years of 8- and 12-percent interest rates compared to a 10-percent rate, and it becomes clear why equal but opposite changes in YTM create greater capital gains than capital losses. The difference, of course, is less spectacular the closer payment of principal is to the present. Thus

$$\frac{\$1,000}{\left(1 + \dfrac{.10}{2}\right)^{40}} = \$142.05; \qquad \frac{\$1,000}{\left(1 + \dfrac{.08}{2}\right)^{40}} = \$208.29; \qquad \frac{\$1,000}{\left(1 + \dfrac{.12}{2}\right)^{40}} = \$97.22;$$

$$\frac{\$208.29 - \$142.05}{\$142.05} = 46.6\% \qquad\qquad \frac{\$97.22 - \$142.05}{\$142.05} = -31.6\%$$

DURATION AND ELASTICITY OF A DEBT INSTRUMENT

Duration of a debt instrument is found by the following formula.

$$\text{duration} = \sum_{t=1}^{n} \frac{t\left[\dfrac{(\text{cash flow})^t}{(1 + YTM)^t}\right] + n\left[\left(\dfrac{F}{(1 + YTM)^n}\right)\right]}{\text{present value of the bond}}$$

where t = year cash flow received

where n = number of years to maturity

YTM = yield to maturity on debt instrument

F = face value of debt instrument

Duration is the average time that elapses until the cash flows of the debt instrument are received. Duration reflects the amount and timing of every cash flow rather than simply the length of time until final payment occurs. Hence, duration is considered a better measure of the term structure of a debt instrument than yield to maturity. The upper limit of duration is the maturity date. A zero-coupon bond has a maturity date n equal to its duration date. Thus

$$\text{duration} = \frac{n\left[\dfrac{F}{(1 + YTM)^n}\right]}{\text{present value of a bond}} = n\,\frac{\text{present value}}{\text{present value}} = n$$

By analogy, the higher the coupon or cash flow received relative to the face value of the debt instrument, the lower the duration.

Elasticity of a debt instrument is defined as

$$\text{Elasticity} = \frac{\%\ \text{change in price of bond}}{\%\ \text{change in } YTM}$$

Table 3-8 Duration and Elasticity of AT&T 10.375% Issue (August 31, 1982)

Cash Flow	$\dfrac{\text{Cash Flow}}{(1.12773247)^\dagger}$	× Year	=	Duration Factor
10.375	9.20	× 1	=	9.20
10.375	8.16	× 2	=	16.32
10.375	7.23	× 3	=	21.69
10.375	6.41	× 4	=	25.64
10.375	5.69	× 5	=	28.45
10.375	5.04	× 6	=	30.24
10.375	4.47	× 7	=	31.29
107.781	42.46	× 7.75	=	329.09
	$88.66 \approx 88.38$			491.90

$$\text{Duration} = \frac{491.90}{88.66} = 5.55 \text{ years}$$

$$\text{Elasticity} = 5.55\left[\frac{.12773247}{1.12773247}\right](-1.0)$$

$$\text{Elasticity} = -.63$$

Table 3-9 **Duration and Elasticity of AT&T 13.25% Issue (August 31, 1982)**

Cash Flow	$\dfrac{\text{Cash Flow}}{(1.13002531)^{\dagger}}$	×	Year	=	Duration Factor
13.25	11.73	×	1	=	11.73
13.25	10.38	×	2	=	20.76
13.25	9.18	×	3	=	27.54
13.25	8.13	×	4	=	32.50
13.25	7.19	×	5	=	35.95
13.25	6.36	×	6	=	38.16
13.25	5.63	×	7	=	39.41
13.25	4.98	×	8	=	39.84
106.63	37.73	×	8.5	=	320.71
	$101.31 \approx 101.25$				566.60

$$\text{Duration} = \frac{566.60}{101.31} = 5.59 \text{ years}$$

$$\text{Elasticity} = 5.59\left[\frac{.13002531}{1.13002531}\right](-1.0)$$

$$\text{Elasticity} = -.64$$

Because the price of a bond varies inversely with its YTM, elasticity is always <0. Elasticity is related to duration, so that[26]

$$(-1.0) \text{ elasticity} = \text{duration}\left(\frac{YTM}{1 + YTM}\right)$$

If the elasticity of a debt instrument is $-.5$, for every 1-percent increase (decrease) on YTM there is a 0.5-percent decrease (increase) in the price of the debt instrument.

For the two AT&T issues of August 31, 1982, duration and elasticity were $-.63$ and $-.64$. (See Tables 3-8 and 3-9.)

Because the elasticities and durations of the two instruments are similar, their YTMs (as calculated in the text) are also similar—but not exactly the same. Consequently, bonds of comparable quality but with different durations and elasticities have different yields to maturities.

[26] See Robert A. Hangen and Dean W. Wichem, "The Elasticity of Financial Assets," *Journal of Finance* (September 1974, pp. 1229–40). See also J. R. Hicks, *Value and Capital*, 2nd ed. (New York: Oxford University Press, 1965, p. 186). For the original concept of duration, see F. R. Macaulay, *Some Theoretical Problems Suggested by the Movement of Interest Rates, Bond Yields and Stock Prices in the United States Since 1856*, National Bureau of Economic Research (New York: Columbia University Press, 1938). For a summary of subsequent measures of duration, see Robert A. Haugen, *Modern Investment Theory* (Englewood Cliffs, NJ: Prentice-Hall, 1986, pp. 332–37).

PROBLEMS AND QUESTIONS

1. Compute the value of $1,150 received at the end of 20 years using a nominal interest rate of 8 percent compounded (a) annually, (b) quarterly, (c) daily, and (d) continuously.

2. Compute the present value of $3,500 received at the end of the year using a nominal interest rate of 12 percent compounded (a) annually, (b) semiannually, (c) weekly, and (d) continuously.

3. Compute the present value of $25,000 received at the end of four years using a nominal interest rate of 16 percent compounded (a) quarterly and (b) continuously.

4. A corporation has an employee pension fund in which it invests $3,000 per year in twelve monthly installments. The nominal rate of interest is 12 percent compounded monthly. Assuming a worker is 35 years of age when hired, what is the total value of the fund when the worker reaches age 65? What is the value of the fund if interest were compounded quarterly?

5. A company issues preferred stock rated "aa" by Moody's at $40 per share. The stock pays an annual dividend of $5.00 per share.
   a. What is the yield on the preferred stock?
   b. Another company whose preferred stock is also rated "aa" by Moody's pays an annual dividend of $3.50 per share. What should the market price of this stock be?

6. A treasury bill maturing in 182 days is marketed at a 9.851 percent discount. What is the price of and the nominal annual yield on this security? (Read Appendix 3-A before attempting the problem.)

7. Your great-grandmother died recently. She left funds that will provide you an annual annuity of $12,000 per year beginning at age 30, to cease at age 65. You are now 20 years of age. What is the present value of that annuity using a nominal interest rate of 12 percent compounded quarterly?

8. a. A bond currently selling at $84.75 carries a 10-percent coupon. The bond matures in 19 years. What is the yield to maturity (YTM) on the bond?
   b. Suppose the very next day the going YTM on new issues of bonds of comparable quality maturing in 19 years is 14 percent. What should the market price of such a bond with a 10-percent coupon be?

9. ABC corporation pays an annual dividend of $2.00 per share. Dividends are expected to grow at 5 percent per year indefinitely. The opportunity cost for investments of comparable risk is 16 percent. What is the long-run intrinsic value of a share of ABC corporation stock?

10. In problem 9, assume the current dividend of $2.00 per share grew at 10 percent

a year for five years and then at 5 percent a year indefinitely. What is the present intrinsic value of the stock?

11. XYZ corporation pays an annual dividend of $3.00 per share. The market price is $37.50 per share. What is current yield on the stock? If the long-run growth rate is 7 percent, what is the value of r?

12. The current market price of a stock is $27 per share. At the end of the year, an investor expects to receive a $1.28 dividend. She also expects to have a holding period return of 14 percent. What does she expect the market price of the stock to be at the end of the year?

13. From an investment in heavy equipment, a corporation expects to receive the following cash flows:

Year	Cash Flow
1	$75,500
2	$97,300
3	$45,800
4	$30,600

Assuming interest is compounded annually, what is the present value of these cash flows if the company has an opportunity cost of capital of 18 percent?

14. A corporation expects to spend $400,000 on a piece of equipment. It anticipates receiving $155,000 per year for four years in cash flows from the equipment. Assuming it is compounded annually, what is the yield on the investment? (HINT: If you do not have a calculator, use Appendix C and interpolate.)

15. The elasticity of a bond is $-.73$; its duration is 6.73. The elasticity of a second bond is $-.25$; its duration is 9.46. Both share the same bond rating. What is their difference in YTM? (Read Appendix 3-A before attempting this problem.)

SELECTED ADDITIONAL REFERENCES

Bauman, W. Scott. "Investment Returns and Present Values," *Financial Analysts Journal*, Vol. 25 (November–December 1969, pp. 107–18).

Ben-Shahar, H. and M. Sarnat. "Reinvestment and the Rate of Return on Common Stocks," *Journal of Finance*, Vol. XXI (December 1966, pp. 737–42).

Blume, Marshall E. "On the Assessment of Risk," *Journal of Finance*, Vol. XXVI (March 1971, pp. 1–10).

Bower, Richard S. and Dorothy H. "Risk and the Valuation of Common Stock," *Journal of Political Economy*, Vol. 77 (May–June 1969, pp. 349–62).

Brigham, Eugene F. and James L. Pappas. "Duration of Growth, Changes in Growth Rates, and Corporate Share Prices," *Financial Analysts Journal*, Vol. 22 (May–June 1966, pp. 157–62).

Butcher, Marjorie V. and Cecil J. Nesbitt. *Mathematics of Compound Interest* (Ann Arbor: Ulrich's Books, 1971).

Fama, Eugene F. "Components of Investment Performance," *Journal of Finance*, Vol. XXVII (June 1972, pp. 551–67).

———. "Multiperiod Consumption—Investment Decisions," *American Economic Review*. Vol. LX (March 1970, pp. 163–74).

Fama, Eugene F. and Merton H. Miller. *The Theory of Finance* (New York: Holt, Rinehart and Winston, 1972).

Fesher, L. "An Algorithm for Finding Exact Rates of Return," *Journal of Business*, Vol. 39, Part II (January 1966, pp. 111–18).

Finerty, John D. "Bank Discount, Coupon Equivalent, and Compound Yields: Comment," *Financial Management*, Vol. 12 (Summer 1983, pp. 40–44).

First Boston Corporation. *Handbook of Securities of the United States Government and Federal Agencies* (New York: First Boston Corporation, Biennially).

Haley, Charles W. and Lawrence D. Schall. *The Theory of Financial Decisions*, Ch. 5 (New York: McGraw-Hill, 1973).

Hirshleifer, J. *Investment, Interest and Capital* (Englewood Cliffs, NJ: Prentice-Hall, 1970).

Holt, Charles C. "The Influence of Growth Duration on Share Price," *Journal of Finance*, Vol. XVII (September 1962, pp. 465–75).

Homer, Sidney and Martin L. Liebowitz. *Inside the Yield Book* (Englewood Cliffs, NJ: Prentice Hall, 1972).

Landes, William J. and Frank Thompson. "Bank Discount, Coupon Equivalent and Coupon Yields," *Financial Management*, Vol. 11 (Autumn 1982, pp. 80–84).

Lerner, Eugene M. and Willard T. Carleton. *A Theory of Financial Analysis* (New York: Harcourt Brace Jovanovich, 1966).

Malkiel, Burton G. *A Random Walk Down Wall Street*, 4th ed. (New York: Random House, 1985).

———. "Equity Yields, Growth, and the Structure of Share Prices," *American Economic Review*, Vol. LXIII (December 1963, pp. 467–94).

———. "Expectations, Bond Price, and the Term Structure of Interest Rates," *Quarterly Journal of Economics*, Vol. 76 (May 1962, pp. 197–218).

Malkiel, Burton G. and John G. Cragg. "Expectations and the Structure of Share Prices," *American Economic Review*, Vol. XL (September 1970, pp. 601–17).

Mao, James C. T. "The Valuation of Growth Stocks: The Investment Opportunities Approach," *Journal of Finance*, Vol. XXI (March 1966, pp. 95–102).

Molodofsky, Nicholas. "Common Stock Valuation," *Financial Analysts Journal*, Vol. XXI (March–April 1965, pp. 104–23).

———. "Stock Values and Stock Prices," *Financial Analysts Journal*, Vol. XVI (July–August 1960, pp. 53–64).

————. "Valuation of Common Stocks," *Financial Analysts Journal*, Vol. XV (January–February 1959, pp. 23–44).

Mossin, Jan. *Theory of Financial Markets* (Englewood Cliffs, NJ: Prentice-Hall, 1973).

Myers, Stewart C. "A Time–State Preference Model of Security Valuation," *Journal of Financial and Quantitative Analysis*, Vol. III (March 1968, pp. 1–34).

————. "The Application of Finance Theory to Public Utility Rate Cases," *Bell Journal of Economics and Management Science*, Vol. III (Spring 1972, pp. 58–97).

Robichek, Alexander A. "Risk and the Value of Securities," *Journal of Financial and Quantitative Analysis*, Vol. IV (December 1969, pp. 513–38).

Sharpe, William F. *Portfolio Analysis and Capital Markets* (New York: McGraw-Hill, 1970).

Sloane, William R. and Arnold Beisman. "Stock Evaluation Theory: Classification, Reconciliation, and General Model," *Journal of Financial and Quantitative Analysis*, Vol. III (June 1968, pp. 171–204).

Van Horne, James C. and William F. Glassmire, Jr. "The Impact of Unanticipated Changes in Inflation on the Value of Common Stocks," *Journal of Finance*, Vol. XXVII (December 1972, pp. 1081–92).

Wendt, Paul F. "Current Growth Stock Valuation Methods," *Financial Analysts Journal*, Vol. XXX (March–April 1965, pp. 3–15).

RISK IN FINANCIAL ANALYSIS

In Chapter 2, we noted that individuals hold different attitudes about present consumption and future consumption. Their reasons vary, but we chose to emphasize an intuitively appealing argument that age and family responsibilities make a difference. In Chapter 2, however, our partial purpose was to develop a rationale for a capital market. To simplify the discussion, we chose to ignore the fact that the decision to save (or to invest) is a decision to accept a degree of risk (or uncertainty) about the outcome: about the future state of the world and its impact upon the decision. Even so-called risk-free investments, such as U.S. government securities, are subject to a major uncertainty: changes in the purchasing power of the dollar when the securities mature. This risk is greater the farther away the date of maturity.

Because investors can only minimize risk and not avoid it completely, a systematic approach to the topic is a necessary concomitant to the study of finance. In Chapter 4, we employ a general perspective and rely upon the basic tenets of probability to understand the nature of some of the risks involved in financial decision-making. We next analyze how people might behave when faced with choices involving risk or uncertainty of outcome. In later chapters we extend, and in some cases further refine, the material developed here, but in the context of specific topics in finance.

Before we begin, a word of caution: although the tools we develop can provide insights into the nature of risk-taking and the behavior of investors or financial managers in a world of uncertainty, they are far from perfect. For example, our initial discussion of probability leads to the use of what is called the **normal curve**. *The normal curve is a useful tool in understanding the consequences of risk-taking; however, the probability distribution of the outcomes of some financial decisions may not conform to this model. Modifications, or an entirely different model, may be required.*

On a philosophical level, the theory of financial decision-making assumes those responsible for decisions behave in a rational way. Setting aside for the moment a more detailed explanation of rational behavior, we merely note that a rational individual acts in a predictable way toward risk. Yet, aberrant behavior abounds in the real world. Certain departures may be better explained from the psychiatrist's couch than from the models adumbrated here. Our interest must focus on typical patterns of behavior.

PROBABILITY AND RISK

The next time you visit the gambling houses of Las Vegas, Reno, Lake Tahoe, Atlantic City, or the more sedate casinos of Monaco and other European haunts, take time out to devote a few moments to the more intellectually enticing concepts that underlie *games of chance*. Consider the comparatively simple case of a roulette wheel. Notice there are 38 numbers (in the United States at least), 1 through 36 and 0 and 00. The numbers 1 through 36 are colored either red or black. Assume you bet a dollar on red. The croupier spins the wheel and releases the ball in the opposite direction. If the ball comes to rest in the compartment of a red number (there are 18), you win a dollar; if it comes to rest in the compartment of a black number (there are also 18), you lose a dollar. Assume our roulette wheel does not have a 0 and 00.[1] If p equals the probability you will win and q equals the probability you will lose, in terms of the 36 numbers

$$p + q = 1$$
$$\frac{18}{36} + \frac{18}{36} = 1$$
$$\frac{1}{2} + \frac{1}{2} = 1$$

Suppose we could bet on two roulette wheels at once—each turned independently. The probability red will appear on either wheel is still $1/2$. However, for both wheels

$$(p + q)^2 = 1$$
$$p^2 + 2pq + q^2 = 1$$
$$\left(\frac{1}{2}\right)^2 + 2\left(\frac{1}{2}\right)\left(\frac{1}{2}\right) + \left(\frac{1}{2}\right)^2 = 1$$
$$\frac{1}{4} + \frac{1}{2} + \frac{1}{4} = 1$$

---

[1] *A Bonus Footnote!* If you actually play, you cannot assume away 0 and 00, which are neither red nor black—but green. If the ball falls into one of these compartments, both black and red lose. Who wins? The casino! It collects from all who bet on red or black (odd or even numbers). Thus the casino shades the odds to 18 out of 38, not 18 out of 36. Over the long run, you cannot win or break even at roulette.

The odds are only one in four that both numbers will be black or red but one in two that one number will be black and the other red. The reason is demonstrated qualitatively with the simple matrix

Wheel	*2, 1*	*1, 2*
1, 2	red	red
	red	black
2, 1	black	black
	red	black

Of four possible outcomes, two are a combination of red and black. It makes no difference what the order is—the black number could be on wheel one and the red number on wheel two; the red number could be on wheel one and the black number on wheel two—the outcome is the same. You win on one and lose on the other. Although the order is of no concern to you, the combination pq is.

Similarly, if three croupiers spin three roulette wheels at once, each independent of the other, we have $(p + q)^3 = 1$. Using the binomial theorem (see Appendix 4-A for further explanation), we obtain

$$p^3 \quad + \quad 3p^2q \quad + \quad 3pq^2 \quad + \quad q^3 = 1$$
$$\left(\frac{1}{2}\right)^3 + 3\left(\frac{1}{2}\right)^2\left(\frac{1}{2}\right) + 3\left(\frac{1}{2}\right)\left(\frac{1}{2}\right)^2 + \left(\frac{1}{2}\right)^3 = 1$$
$$\frac{1}{8} \quad + \quad \frac{3}{8} \quad + \quad \frac{3}{8} \quad + \quad \frac{1}{8} = 1$$

The chances are one in eight the ball for each wheel will stop on red and one in eight the ball for each wheel will stop on black. However, the chances are three in eight there will be two black numbers and one red number and three in eight there will be two red numbers and one black number. Again, we do not care on which wheel black appears or on which wheel red appears—only the combination matters.

We may continue to expand the binomial $(p + q)^n$ by adding to the number of roulette wheels. The combinations would increase algebraically so that, for example

$$(p + q)^6 = 1$$
$$p^6 \quad + \quad 6p^5q \quad + \quad 15p^4q^2 \quad + \quad 20p^3q^3 \quad + \quad 15p^2q^4 \quad + \quad 6pq^5 \quad + \quad q^6 = 1$$
$$\left(\frac{1}{2}\right)^6 + 6\left(\frac{1}{2}\right)^5\left(\frac{1}{2}\right) + 15\left(\frac{1}{2}\right)^4\left(\frac{1}{2}\right)^2 + 20\left(\frac{1}{2}\right)^3\left(\frac{1}{2}\right)^3 + 15\left(\frac{1}{2}\right)^2\left(\frac{1}{2}\right)^4 + 6\left(\frac{1}{2}\right)\left(\frac{1}{2}\right)^5 + \left(\frac{1}{2}\right)^6 = 1$$
$$\frac{1}{64} \quad + \quad \frac{6}{64} \quad + \quad \frac{15}{64} \quad + \quad \frac{20}{64} \quad + \quad \frac{15}{64} \quad + \quad \frac{6}{64} \quad + \quad \frac{1}{64} = 1$$

To put the results in a different perspective, if we were to spin six roulette wheels simultaneously 64 times, only once would all six balls stop on black numbers and only once on red numbers. The number of times various combinations of red and

Figure 4-1   **A Histogram**

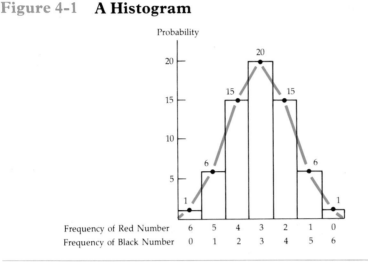

The probabilities that red or black will appear when simultaneously spinning six roulette wheels 64 times are depicted.

black would appear varies. However, as one might expect, the combination of three blacks and three reds appears more often (20 times in 64 attempts) than any other combination.

It is instructive to picture the various outcomes suggested by spinning six roulette wheels 64 times. (Because six roulette wheels are usually unavailable, try six coins, where the probability of heads p and tails q equals one-half.) The outcomes are shown in Figure 4-1. There is a tendency for results to cluster around the most likely outcome suggested by the probabilities (half red and half black) and to diverge systematically from that outcome (four reds and two blacks or four blacks and two reds), and so forth. We would expect as n becomes larger—as n approaches ∞—that gradations between probable outcomes narrow. By connecting the midpoints of the histogram in Figure 4-1, we can see the outline of what eventually will become a continuous function. The graph of the function is depicted in Figure 4-2 (the equation is in Appendix 4-A). Known as the **normal curve**, it plays a central role in applied statistics—primarily because of the tendency of so many natural phenomena to lend themselves to distributions that approximate normality.

The normal curve is completely described by two measures: the *mean* μ (shown in Figure 4-2) and the *standard deviation* σ. The mean of any probability distribution is the mathematical expectation (or expected outcome)

$$E(x) = \sum_{t=1}^{n} x_t p_t = \mu \tag{4-1}$$

Figure 4-2   The Normal Curve

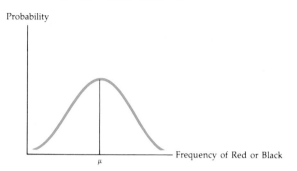

Using the example of six roulette wheels, we have (for x equals the frequency of red)

$$E(x) = 6\frac{1}{64} + 5\frac{6}{64} + 4\frac{15}{64} + 3\frac{20}{64} + 2\frac{15}{64} + 1\frac{6}{64} + 0\frac{1}{64}$$

$$= \frac{6}{64} + \frac{30}{64} + \frac{60}{64} + \frac{60}{64} + \frac{30}{64} + \frac{6}{64} + 0$$

$$E(x) = \frac{192}{64}$$

$$E(x) = 3 \text{ red}$$

The standard deviation σ is defined as

$$\sigma_x = \sqrt{\sum_{t=1}^{n} (x_t - \mu_x)^2 p_t} \tag{4-2}$$

The standard deviation is a measure of dispersion about the mean; it suggests the degree of variability in the measure of central tendency. The reason why standard deviation is widely employed is because $\mu \pm 3\sigma$s encompasses 99.74 percent of the area under the normal curve. The curve itself is asymptotic to the abscissa. All possible outcomes are never included under the curve; there is always the outside chance of an exceptionally rare event occurring—for example, 1,000,000 red (or black) numbers on 1,000,000 roulette wheels turned simultaneously. The odds of this occurring are $\left(\frac{1}{2}\right)^{1,000,000}$ —an exceptionally rare event. Using the example of six roulette wheels, we have

$$\sigma_x = \left[(6-3)^2\frac{1}{64} + (5-3)^2\frac{6}{64} + (4-3)^2\frac{15}{64} + (3-3)^2\frac{20}{64} \right.$$
$$\left. + (2-3)^2\frac{15}{64} + (1-3)^2\frac{6}{64} + (0-3)^2\frac{1}{64} \right]^{1/2}$$

$$\sigma_x = [.140625 + .375000 + .234375 + .234375 + .375000 + .140625]^{1/2}$$
$$\sigma_x = [1.500000]^{1/2}$$
$$\sigma_x = 1.224745$$

In our illustration, of course, n is 6. We know that at best the frequency of red numbers is 6 and at worse it is zero. Since $(p + q)^6$ is a binomial whose limit as $n \to \infty$ is the normal curve, we find that

$$\mu + 3\sigma s =$$
$$3 + 3(1.224745) = 6.674235$$
$$3 - 3(1.224745) = -0.674235$$

The range encompassed includes more than 6 and less than zero. As we increase n, the calculated range of $\mu \pm 3\sigma s$ would more closely conform to the extreme outcomes. For n equals 10,000, for example, the mean outcome would be 5,000 red numbers. 5,000 red numbers $\pm 3\sigma s$ would approximate 10,000 and 0.

To test and extend our understanding of the foregoing concepts, let us apply them to an example in finance. Suppose we ask a security analyst who specializes in the stock of company x to evaluate the possible returns from holding the stock for one year. Recall from Chapter 3 that holding period return is defined as

$$HPR = \frac{P_1 - P_0 + D}{P_0}$$

where

P_0 = current market price
P_1 = price a year from today
D = dividends paid during the holding period (implicitly assumed to be at the end of the year)

In this case the analyst is determining the expected $E(R_H)$, not calculating the actual holding period return. The analyst bases forecast on five scenarios about the economy and their impact upon the expected holding period return. The analyst's estimates of both the expected holding period return of 15.5 percent and the standard deviation of 2.97 percent are in Table 4-1. The probabilities, of course, are subjective: they represent the analyst's guess, based upon considerable knowledge, about the impact of various changes in the level of economic activity on the profitability of the company.

It does not necessarily follow that the expected holding period return of 15.5 percent is the mean of a finite probability distribution that would approximate a normal curve. From the analyst's estimates, it is clear a greater probability has been attached to the occurrence of a 20-percent holding period return than to a 10-percent holding period return. If the probability of the former had been .15 and the probability of the latter had also been .15 (with all other probabilities remaining the same), using the procedures outlined in Table 4-1 the expected

Table 4-1   Expected Holding Period Return and Standard Deviation on Stock Investment

Possible Yield	×	Probability of Occurrence	=	Components of Expected Holding Period Return
.10	×	.1	=	.010
.13	×	.2	=	.026
.15	×	.3	=	.045
.17	×	.2	=	.034
.20	×	.2	=	.040
$E(R_H)$			=	.155

$$R_H = \sqrt{\sum_{t=1}^{n} (R_t - ER_H)^2 p_t}$$

$$.1(.10 - .155)^2 = .000303$$
$$.2(.13 - .155)^2 = .000125$$
$$.3(.15 - .155)^2 = .000008$$
$$.2(.17 - .155)^2 = .000045$$
$$.2(.20 - .155)^2 = .000405$$
$$\sigma^2_{R_H} \qquad\qquad\quad = .000886$$

$$\sigma_{R_H} = \sqrt{.000886} = .0298$$
$$E_{R_H} = .155 \times 100 = 15.5\%$$
$$\sigma_{R_H} = .0298 \times 100 = 2.98\%$$

holding period return would have been 15.0 percent, or equal to what the analyst expects to be the most likely outcome. In this instance, the analyst's estimate is based upon a forecast more optimistic than would be suggested by a normal curve. Perhaps if the analyst could develop more definitive scenarios about the course of the economy that resulted in more estimates of possible yields, we could have a more refined estimate of expected holding period returns in closer approximation to the normal curve.

We shall proceed as though *the expected one-period holding period return is the mean of a normal distribution*, with 15.5 percent $\pm 3\sigma$s suggesting the range of possible outcomes within which the analyst expects the return to lie. Bear in mind there is an outside chance the interval will not contain the actual holding period return. With the foregoing caveats, the analyst expects the return to lie somewhere within the interval $15.5\% \pm 3 \times 2.98\%$, or from 6.56% to 24.44%.

Although the range is considerable, the analyst, nevertheless, expects the return to be positive. Whether he or she expects this stock to perform better than the stock market as a whole is a point to which we return in Chapter 5. For the present, it is sufficient to note that the normal curve is a convenient starting point[2] from which to analyze the nature of risk-taking in financial decision-making. The mean of the probability distribution, the standard deviation, and sometimes the square of the standard deviation σ^2 (known as the *variance*) are important measures in a description of the risks inherent in a particular decision.

USING THE NORMAL CURVE

Because of its importance in a basic discussion of risk in finance, we have delineated (in Appendix D) areas within (under) the normal curve. Since the normal curve is a symmetrical distribution—50 percent of the area within the curve lies either to the left or right of the mean (or expected value)—one can easily measure the probability of occurrence of a particular value in relation to the expected value. Let us see how.

Suppose one estimates the expected holding period return on a given security is 17 percent and the standard deviation is 2.5 percent. What is the probability the holding period return is less than 14.5 percent? From Appendix D, we know the expected holding period return is labeled $E(x)$ and any particular value, x, is either to the left or right of $E(x)$. Since $E(x)$ in this case is 17 percent and x is 14.5 percent, the value we seek is to the left of 17 percent—that is, it is smaller than $E(x)$. Since

---

[2] It is not necessarily a terminus. For example, some of the evidence of returns on stocks suggests they do not conform to a normal distribution. Fama, for example, found that daily returns on stocks comprising the Dow Jones Industrial Average conformed more to a leptokurtic distribution, with observations concentrated nearer the mean.

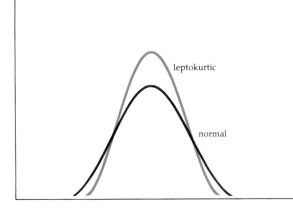

However, when weekly and monthly data were used, Blattberg and Gonedes found that returns approached a normal distribution. See Eugene Fama, "Behavior of Stock Market Prices," *Journal of Business*, Vol. 63 (January 1965, pp. 34–105) and R. Blattberg and N. Gonedes, "A Comparison of the Stable and Student Distributions as Statistical Models for Stock Prices," *Journal of Business*, Vol. 74 (April 1974, pp. 244–80).

The issue is important because many statistical tests designed to evaluate propositions and collected under the rubric *Modern Portfolio Theory* are based upon normal distributions of returns.

distance along the abscissa can be expressed in terms of standard deviations, the equation shown in Appendix D as

$$Z = \frac{x - E(x)}{\sigma}$$

(4-3)

measures the distance between x and $E(x)$ in those terms. In this instance

$$Z = \frac{14.5 - 17.0}{2.5}$$
$$Z = -1.0$$

We can interpret Z to mean that 14.5 percent lies one standard deviation below (to the left; hence the negative sign) of the expected return of 17.0 percent. If x had been 19.5 percent, then

$$Z = \frac{19.5 - 17.0}{2.5}$$
$$Z = 1.0$$

17.0 lies one standard deviation above (to the right) of the expected return of 17.0 percent.

   In the body of the table are values for Z and corresponding areas under the normal curve. Notice at $Z = 0.0$, the area to the left or right of x is .50, or 50 percent of the total area. At that point $x = E(x)$. Thus the body of the table measures the area within one-half of the normal curve.

   For $Z = 1.0$, the area to the left or to the right of x is .1587. The interpretation is that 15.87 percent of the area within the curve lies to the left in the case of 14.5 percent or to the right in the case of 19.5 percent of the expected return of 17.0 percent. In other words, the chances are 15.87 in 100 the yield will lie either below 14.5 percent or above 19.5 percent.

   What are the chances the return will be above 11.0 percent? Calculating Z, we find that

$$Z = \frac{11.0 - 17.0}{2.5}$$
$$Z = -2.40$$

At 2.40, the area below 11.0 is .0082. However, we want to know the chances that the return would lie above 11.0 percent. Since .0082 (or .82 percent) of the area is to the left of 11.0 percent, then $100.00\% - .82\% = 99.12\%$ is to the right of 11.0 percent. Stated differently, the chances are 99.12 in 100 the return will be greater than 11.0 percent.

Finally, what are the chances the return will be below 22.0 percent? Calculating Z, we obtain

$$Z = \frac{22.0 - 17.0}{2.5}$$
$$Z = 2.0$$

For $Z = 2.0$, the area above (to the right) of 22.0 percent is .0228 (or 2.28 percent) of the total area within the normal curve. Thus, the area below (to the left) of 22.0 percent is $100.00\% - 2.28\% = 97.72\%$. The chances are 97.72 in 100 the return will be below 22.0 percent.

ATTITUDE TOWARD RISK

It is one thing to develop measures of risk; it is another to develop principles of behavior toward risk. We observe that people respond differently to risk. Some refuse to fly in an airplane even though the odds of disaster are minuscule. Others take risks that seem awesome at the time. When the United States first attempted to put a man on the moon, the author overheard a person discussing the topic suggest that astronauts had an underdeveloped sense of self-preservation, a sentiment echoed by others with whom he was conversing.

Less dramatic perhaps are the subtle attitudes toward risk that comprise everyday decision-making. The New Jersey resident who mails a check for homeowner's insurance on her way to Atlantic City is behaving in an interesting way. On the one hand, even though the odds are low, she is paying a premium to protect herself from significant loss. On the other hand, she is willing to participate in games of chance actuarially unfair but that just might enhance or decrease her wealth. Our concern with risk is limited to these kinds of choices: the choices individuals make that impact their wealth. A wag once observed that economics is the discipline that relegates avarice to a science. With that quip in mind, we shall assume people always prefer more wealth to less—in other words, they are greedy. Although the marginal utility of wealth is always positive, for some it increases at a decreasing rate.

In addition, we shall assume people are rational. To behave rationally[3], an individual must know he or she prefers outcome x to outcome y and outcome y to outcome z. By rank ordering preferences, that person will make a rational decision and prefer outcome x to outcome z. If x, y, and z are levels of wealth—$250,000, $200,000, and $150,000, respectively—we see why that person prefers x to either y or z. The interesting question is whether an individual with wealth y would wager that amount to gain x whose probability is p when the individual might find himself

---

[3] For a more detailed explanation, see Eugene F. Fama and Merton H. Miller, *The Theory of Finance*, Ch. 5 (New York: Holt, Rinehart and Winston, 1972).

or herself with z whose probability is $1 - p$ or q. In short, how does one rank order preferences under conditions of risk?

THE UTILITY FUNCTION Let us illustrate the meaning of rational behavior by employing an arithmetic example and three graphs commonly used to depict three different behavior patterns under conditions of risk. Suppose each of three individuals has $800,000. Each is offered the opportunity to bet that sum on a game of chance where the odds of winning (p) are .8 and the odds of losing ($1 - p$ or q) are .2. If one loses, that person's wealth is zero dollars; if one wins, that person's wealth is $1,000,000. The expected value of this game is equal to the amount wagered: $.2(\$0) + .8(\$1,000,000) = \$800,000$.

How each individual might react to these outcomes is suggested by Figure 4-3. Rational individuals order (rank) their preferences and thereby establish their utility functions. In this context, utility is simply a number representing the degree of satisfaction gained from wealth. In general the expected utility of wealth, $E[u(w)]$, under conditions of risk is maximized so that

$$Max\ E[u(w)] = \sum_i^n p_i u(w_i) \qquad \text{(4-4)}$$

Each function is consistent with the basic assumption that more wealth is preferred to less wealth. What distinguishes each is that the function in Figure 4-3(a) rises at a decreasing rate; the function in Figure 4-3(b) rises at an increasing rate, and the function in Figure 4-3(c) rises at a constant rate.

Because the expected value of this gamble is $800,000, the utility of expected wealth $u[E(w)]$ is the utility of the amount that must be wagered, or $800,000. In Figure 4-3(a) we see that $u[E(w)]$ is .85. (The actual number is unimportant. It need only be consistent with the behavior pattern shown: diminishing marginal utility of wealth for this person.) However, the utility of the gamble, or the expected utility of wealth, $E[u(w)]$ is

$$.2u(\$0) + .8u(\$1,000,000) =$$
$$.2(0) + .8(1.0) = .8$$

Thus $u[E(w)] > E[u(w)]$. This individual is said to be *risk-averse*[4] because he or she prefers the actuarial value of this gamble—the amount that must be wagered ($800,000)—to the gamble itself.

In Figure 4-3(b), $u[E(w)]$ is .625 whereas $E[u(w)]$ is .8. Thus $u[E(w)] < E[u(w)]$.[5] This is the case for the *risk-lover* or *risk-acceptor*, who prefers the gamble to the $800,000. In other words, the risk-lover experiences increasing marginal

---

[4] See Harry Markowitz, *Portfolio Selection* (New Haven: Yale University Press, 1959) for the distinctions in behavioral pattern: risk-averse, risk-neutral, and risk-lover.

[5] We have merely assumed the utility of $1,000,000 is the same for all three individuals—the functions implicitly converge at this point. Although the assumption is not necessary, it facilitates the presentation.

Figure 4-3   Three Utility Functions of Wealth under Risk Condition

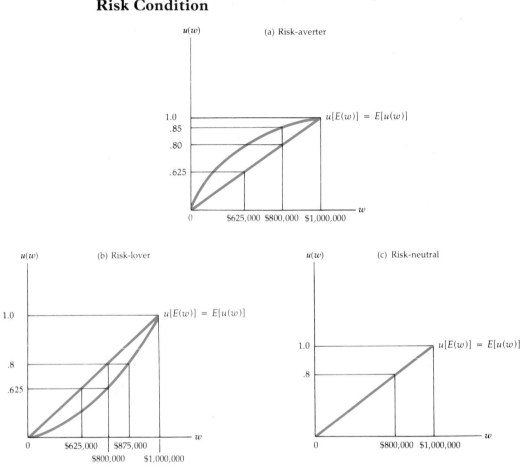

utility of wealth from assuming an actuarially fair gamble.

Finally, in the case of the *risk-neutral* individual in Figure 4-3(c), $u[E(w)] = E[u(w)] = .8$. The risk-neutral individual is indifferent to the wager ($800,000) and the gamble.

The risk-neutral individual provides a convenient behavioral pattern from which to summarize. The gamble, as we have noted, is actuarially fair. The expected outcome is equal to the amount one wagers. For the risk-neutral individual, the utility of the sum wagered equals the expected utility of the gamble; therefore, that person is indifferent to keeping the wealth or risking it. A risk-averse individual avoids all actuarially fair gambles; a risk-lover accepts all actuarially fair bets.

To relate the foregoing discussion to finance, suppose the gamble was the probable outcomes of an investment decision available to the firm. Suppose further the owner-manager was a risk-averse individual whose utility function is depicted in Figure 4-3(a). It is apparent from the graph the owner-manager would be indifferent to a sum certain of $625,000 and the actuarially fair gamble of $800,000. That is, $u[E(w)] = E[u(w)] = .8$ for a $625,000 bet with an expected outcome of $800,000.

If a market for *options* existed, the owner-manager could make the investment in the firm and sell an option on the outcome for at least $625,000. In this way the buyer of the option would accept the risk of receiving 0 or $1,000,000 and the seller (in this case, the owner-manager) would receive the $625,000 as a sum certain, regardless of the outcome. The owner-manager, therefore, was willing to pay a risk-premium of $175,000 to entice someone else to accept the risk. Since a risk-lover of the type depicted in Figure 4-3(b) would have invested $875,000 for the same probable outcomes, that person would have purchased the option for $625,000. Indeed, in a well-organized options market, there would be an equilibrium price for options on investment opportunities of the kind described. The owner-manager may not have to pay the entire risk premium: he or she may sell the option for more than $625,000.

Of course, options of the type discussed are rare; at least, there is no well-organized market for them. The concept of an option, however, is quite robust. (The kind of options we discuss in Chapter 19 pertain to company securities rather than to specific investments within the firm.) Consider a further complication of the investment decision under analysis. Suppose it was necessary to invest $800,000 in the firm to keep it competitive. In other words, the owner-manager must accept the risk (.2) that the value of the firm will be zero, or face gradual erosion of its value over time because the firm failed to keep pace with the market. Clearly, the investment must be made; equally clearly, it will not be made by the risk-averse owner-manager.

The solution to what appears to be a Hobson's choice is sale of the company. The buyer is purchasing an option on the outcome and using the resources of the firm ($800,000) to make the investment.[6] The owner-manager is willing to accept as little as $625,000 for the firm. The upper limit depends upon the buyer's utility function. For the risk-neutral individual [Figure 4-3(c)], the upper limit is $800,000; for the risk-lover [Figure 4-3(b)], the upper limit is $875,000.

SOME QUALIFICATIONS

The preceding exercise sheds some light on the nature of risk-aversion; it also suggests why people are willing to pay different prices for what may be perceived to be similar investment opportunities. Yet, we must be careful not to read too much

---

[6] We oversimplify in order to emphasize the major point: the firm may have other assets. Failure to make the investment may cause the value of the firm to erode—but not to zero. The buyer, of course, will take this into consideration when making an offer to the owner-manager. There is also the possibility of dividing the risk between the owner-manager and another individual.

into arithmetic exercises of this type. Consider that the sums involved here may seem large to most people. If the amounts were smaller and had less significant impact upon total wealth, would the risk-averter become a risk-lover or at least relatively less risk-averse? People who buy insurance against a disaster may also spend small amounts of money on lottery tickets or stand in line at an Atlantic City or Las Vegas casino to "feed" the nickel "one-arm bandits." Financial managers, too, may make small capital investments that have an outside chance for a large payoff. Portfolio managers sometimes have *slush funds* from which they risk a small amount of money on the outside chance the price of a stock will rise five or ten times above what they paid for it. In short, there may be times when such small amounts are involved that one acts as though $E[u(w)] > u[E(w)]$ and the gamble is preferred to a sum certain. If the sums involved are large, that same individual may act as though $E[u(w)] < u[E(w)]$.

Without further development of these concepts[7], we shall assume (because finance generally involves large amounts of money) that risk-aversion dominates investment behavior. Thus, we shall assume that utility functions are similar to those in Figure 4-3(a) rather than in Figures 4-3(b) and 4-3(c). Intuitively, we would expect risk-averters to prefer less variability to more.[8] Given two investment opportunities with identical expected returns but with different standard deviations, the one with the smaller standard deviation would be preferred over the one with the larger standard deviation. Thus, in Figure 4-4 the distribution labeled *a* is preferred over the distribution labeled *b* because the same expected return is accompanied by greater variability in the case of *b*.

As long as the probability distribution of returns on all assets approximates the normal curve, the choices facing risk-averse investors are straightforward. Assume investments A, B, and C all require the same outlay of funds. If investment A has an expected return of 12 percent and a standard deviation of 3 percent, it would be preferred to investment B that has an expected return of 9 percent on a standard deviation of 3 percent. However, it is not immediately clear whether investment C that has an expected return of 16 percent and a standard deviation of 4 percent is preferred to investment A. The *coefficients of variation* for both are

$$\frac{\sigma}{E(R)} = \frac{3\%}{12\%} = .25; \frac{4\%}{16\%} = .25$$

Although relative variability is the same, we intuitively expect risk-averse investors

[7] A rigorous treatment would take us beyond the scope of this text. For further analysis and an empirical test, see, for example, J. W. Pratt, "Risk Aversion in the Small and the Large," *Econometrica*, Vol. 32 (January–April 1964, pp. 122–36). See also Kenneth J. Arrow, *Essays in the Theory of Risk Bearing* (Amsterdam: North Holland Publishing Company, 1971). See also Irwin Friend and Marshall Blume, "The Demand for Risky Assets," *The American Economic Review*, Vol. 65 (December 1975, pp. 900–22).

[8] See G. Hanoch and H. Levy, "The Efficiency Analysis of Choices Involving Risk," *Review of Economic Studies*, Vol. 36 (July 1969, pp. 335–46).

Figure 4-4 Two Investments with Identical Returns but Different Standard Deviations

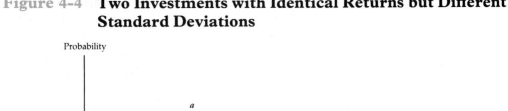

to accept greater risk only if there is a more than proportional increase in return. Consequently, investment C would not be preferred to investment A. Since there is no clear reason to prefer one over the other, we shall presume investors are indifferent to investments A and C.

Based upon the foregoing reasoning, Figure 4-5 summarizes graphically the trade-offs risk-averse investors will make on investments whose probability distribution of expected returns approximates normality. The indifference curves summarize the intuitive presentation. Indifference curve I_3 is preferred to indifference curve I_2, which in turn is preferred to indifference curve I_1. This is because one can obtain a higher expected return for the same degree of risk. This is true of investments A and B. If we introduce investment D, with an expected return of 12 percent and a standard deviation of 4 percent, D will be inferior to A because D has the same expected return as A but greater variability. Since D has the same coefficient of variation as investment B

$$\frac{\sigma}{E(R)} = \frac{0.04}{.12} = .33; \frac{.03}{.09} = .33$$

we may presume investors are indifferent between B and D. Similarly, investors are indifferent between A and C, but prefer either to investments B and D.

Thus, risk-averse investors can easily make choices among investments whose expected returns are normally distributed. In practice, we can neither assume that all investors are risk-averse nor that expected returns on all investments are normally distributed. Yet much can be learned by maintaining these assumptions. Unless otherwise noted, we shall continue to do so throughout much of this text.

Figure 4-5   Indifference Curves for a Risk-averse Investor

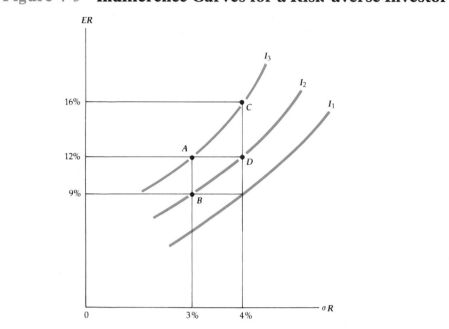

SUMMARY

Our purpose in Chapter 4 has been to explain the nature of risk and how individuals might react toward investment opportunities involving risk. Accordingly, by employing games of chance we developed finite probability distributions that approached the normal curve. Because the normal curve has long been established as useful for analyzing variability in many natural phenomena, it is an appropriate tool for introducing the nature of risk in investments, whether those investments are in financial or real assets.

The normal curve is a symmetrical probability distribution completely described by its mean, or expected value, and its standard deviation as shown in Equations 4-1 and 4-2. Equation 4-3 permits one to measure (in terms of standard deviation) the distance between any value x and its expected value, $E(x)$, assuming those values are normally distributed. Using the result of this calculation, it is possible to determine the chances outcomes will lie above or below the value of x. We applied these concepts to a probability distribution of anticipated holding period returns and standard deviation about those returns.

We then turned our attention to individual attitudes toward risk-taking and distinguished among risk-averters, risk-acceptors, and risk-neutrals. The risk-neutral individual receives the same utility from an actuarially fair gamble as from the outlay on that gamble. In other words, the utility of expected wealth, $u[E(w)]$, equals the expected utility of wealth, $E[u(w)]$. The risk-averse individual prefers keeping the outlay to accepting the actuarially fair gamble: $u[E(w)] > E[u(w)]$. For the risk- acceptor, $u[E(w)] < E[u(w)]$.

In the study of finance (given the substantial size of most outlays), it is customary to assume investors are risk-averse. Accordingly, we extended this assumption to the holding period return and its standard deviation. Thus, risk-averse investors prefer an investment with a 10 percent expected return and a 2 percent standard deviation to an investment with a 10 percent expected return and a 3 percent standard deviation. In addition, because risk-averse investors expect to be compensated for accepting an increase in the standard deviation, they will generally accept greater risk only in anticipation of greater return. Risk-averse investors could, however, be indifferent between two investments where the risk-return trade-offs are proportional. Thus, one might be indifferent between an expected return of 12 percent with a standard deviation of 3 percent and an expected return of 16 percent with a standard deviation of 4 percent. In each case, the co-efficient of variation (or the ratio of the standard deviation to its expected return) is .25, suggesting the return is commensurate with the risk undertaken.

Implicit in the preceding analysis is the assumption that investors seek to avoid variability, whether above or below expected return. Remember, there is usually joy when one receives more than expected: the outcome lies to the right of the expected return. Because standard deviation is the result of a square-root calculation, no negative sign is attached to it. Also, one can only measure sadness—returns to the left of the expected return—as being below standard deviation. Furthermore, since a holding period return and its standard deviation are percentages, they are independent of absolute magnitudes. People who might otherwise be risk-averse are risk-acceptors when the outlay or expected utility of wealth is small relative to total wealth. Finally, the assumption of normality in the probability distributions of financial variables is convenient and useful. There will be times, however—particularly in our study of options in Chapter 19—when we must forego that assumption. Fortunately, an alternative—the log normal distribution—can be employed in that instance.

THE BINOMIAL THEOREM AND THE NORMAL CURVE

The binomial $(p + q)^n$, where n equals 6, becomes

$$(p + q)^6 =$$
$$p^6 + 6p^5q + 15p^4q^2 + 20p^3q^3 + 15p^2q^4 + 6pq^5 + q^6$$

The coefficients of this expansion conform to a special operation

$$\binom{n}{r} = \frac{(n)_r}{r!}$$

where n is a total number, or universe of outcomes, and r is a subset to be selected. The exclamation point in $r!$ does not indicate excitement—although some of the applications of this principle might engender enthusiasm. Rather, $r!$ should be interpreted as: multiply the number that replaces r by every whole number below it until you reach 1. The expression $r!$ is referred to as "r factorial." The expression $(n)_r$ should be interpreted as: multiply n by every whole number below n for r numbers below n. The expression $\binom{n}{r}$ is the *binomial coefficient*, and now can be written as

$$\binom{n}{r} = \frac{n(n - 1)(n - 2) \cdots (n - r + 1)}{r!}$$

To give the expression substance, suppose you were playing a friendly game of five-card-draw poker. Cards are dealt and you find yourself with an ace, king, queen, jack, and ten of spades. As you maintain a stolid countenance so as not to give away what is an unbeatable hand, you contemplate the odds of drawing such a combination. You know 52 cards are in the deck (no jokers in this game); 52 is therefore the value of n. You do not care about the order in which you received the cards, merely the combination. Thus, when from 52 cards you received one of five cards in the royal flush, 51 cards remained in the deck that contained the other four. When you received the second card, 50 remained that contained the other three. Thus, using the binomial coefficient, we have

$$\binom{n}{r} = \frac{52_5}{5!} = \frac{52 \times 51 \times 50 \times 49 \times 48}{5 \times 4 \times 3 \times 2 \times 1} = 2{,}598{,}960$$

There are 2,598,960 different ways of selecting five cards from a deck of 52 cards; only one of those combinations is the five cards you hold. Thus, the chances of selecting a royal flush in spades (or any other suit) is 1 in 2,598,960. As you smile politely and say to the dealer, "I'll play these," when she asks how many cards you want the second time, contemplate the odds!

If poker is too plebian for your tastes, consider in bridge the odds of drawing all 13 hearts, or any other suit. They would be

$$\binom{n}{r} = \frac{52_{13}}{13!} = 635,013,559,600$$

The chances of doing so are one in more than 635 billion. Have you ever seen it happen?

In the binomial $(p + q)^6$, zero also can be employed. In so doing, we define

$$\binom{n}{0} = 1$$

Thus, the coefficients 1, 6, 15, 20, 15, 6, 1 can be formed as:

$$\binom{6}{0}\binom{6}{1}\binom{6}{2}\binom{6}{3}\binom{6}{4}\binom{6}{5}\binom{6}{6}$$

and are equal to

$$1, \frac{6}{1}, \frac{6 \cdot 5}{2 \cdot 1}, \frac{6 \cdot 5 \cdot 4}{3 \cdot 2 \cdot 1}, \frac{6 \cdot 5 \cdot 4 \cdot 3}{4 \cdot 3 \cdot 2 \cdot 1}, \frac{6 \cdot 5 \cdot 4 \cdot 3 \cdot 2}{5 \cdot 4 \cdot 3 \cdot 2 \cdot 1}, \frac{6 \cdot 5 \cdot 4 \cdot 3 \cdot 2 \cdot 1}{6 \cdot 5 \cdot 4 \cdot 3 \cdot 2 \cdot 1}$$

Because the power of p rises by one and the power of q falls by one as n increases, we can write the full binomial expansion as

$$p^n + np^{n-1}q + \frac{n(n-1)}{2 \cdot 1}p^{n-2}q^2 + \frac{n(n-1)(n-2)}{3 \cdot 2 \cdot 1}p^{n-3}q^3 +$$

$$\frac{n(n-1)(n-2)(n-3)}{4 \cdot 3 \cdot 2 \cdot 1}p^{n-4}q^4 + \cdots + q^n$$

Known as the binomial theorem, its primary function is to simplify calculations as n increases. In the case of a probability distribution, the sum of the odds must equal 1, so that $(p + q)^n = 1$. For any value of n, we can simplify the notation, so that $\binom{n}{r}p^{n-r}q^r = 1$. Suppose, however, $n \to \infty$, then

$$\int_{-\infty}^{\infty} F(x)dx = 1$$

When $p = q = \frac{1}{2}$, then as the binomial approaches a continuous function, it becomes a normal distribution such that

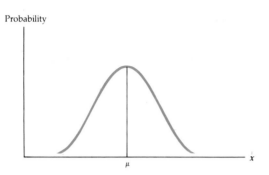

Probability

μ

x

The normal distribution is defined[9] by the equation

$$F(x) = \frac{1}{\sigma\sqrt{2\pi}} \, e^{-\left[\frac{(x-\mu)^2}{2\sigma^2}\right]}, \quad -\infty < x < \infty$$

To find the area under the curve, one integrates the function so that

$$I = \int_{-\infty}^{\infty} \frac{1}{\sigma\sqrt{2\pi}} \, e^{-\left[\frac{(x-\mu)^2}{2\sigma^2}\right] dx}$$

For μ equals 0 and σ equals 1, the expression simplifies to

$$I = \int_{-\infty}^{\infty} \frac{1}{\sqrt{2\pi}} \, e^{-x^2/2 \, dx}$$

The probabilities, of course, sum to 1. Because the distribution is asymptotic to the x axis, when employing it in practical work we can never be completely certain we have included all possible outcomes. Nevertheless, $\mu \pm 3\sigma s$ encompasses 99.74 percent of the area within the curve.

PROBLEMS AND QUESTIONS

1. Suppose you toss three coins in the air. What are the odds of heads appearing on all three coins? Of two heads and a tail? Of two tails and a head?

2. Suppose in problem 1 you are offered the opportunity to toss three coins

---

[9] For proofs of the equations, see Robert V. Hogg and Elliot A. Tanis, *Probability and Statistical Inference*, 2nd ed. (New York: Macmillan, 1983, pp. 171–73).

simultaneously a total of 32 times. The price of doing so is one dollar for each toss. Each time three heads appear, you win $4. Is this an actuarially fair bet? Explain. Suppose you win $4 each time three heads or three tails appeared. Is this an actuarially fair bet? Explain.

3. Two coins are tossed 800 times.
   a. What is the result (two heads, two tails, a head and a tail) you expect to observe most often? Explain.
   b. How many times should the result in (a) occur?
   c. What is the mean, μ, and standard deviation, σ, of the distribution of heads?
   d. Why would one calculate μ and σ? What purpose does each serve?

4. Suppose an individual is offered the opportunity of investing $3,000 in an oil drilling venture. The odds of a dry hole are one in four; with a dry hole, the investor loses all $3,000. The odds are three in four the hole contains oil and the investor will receive $4,000 for the $3,000 invested.
   a. What is the expected value of this gamble?
   b. For the individual, the utility of 0 dollars is zero; for $3,000, it is 1.2; for $4,000, it is 1.4. Will the individual make the investment? Explain.

5. Suppose for each of three people the utility of 0 dollars is zero and the utility of $1,000 is 1. All are offered the opportunity to bet $400 on the toss of a coin. The first person accepts the bet, the second person declines the bet, and the third person accepts the bet. From the information available, can you determine which people are risk-neutral? Explain.

6. Would your answer to 5 change if the wager required was $500 and the first and third persons still accepted the bet?

7. Using available geological estimates, the financial officer of a natural gas company calculated the returns and associated probabilities from making an investment in a drilling venture. The results were

Probability	Return
.1	.10
.2	.12
.4	.15
.2	.18
.1	.20

   a. Calculate the expected return, μ, and the standard deviation σ.
   b. Do you believe the financial officer was suggesting that returns would conform to a particular type of probability distribution?

8. A risk-averse investor can choose among the following investment opportunities

Investment	Expected Return	σ
A	.15	.05
B	.20	.04
C	.25	.05
D	.12	.04

Can you tell which investment the investor would prefer? Explain.

9. The expected holding period return on an investment is 13.75 percent. The standard deviation about that holding period return is 2.25 percent. Using the table in Appendix D, answer the following:

   a. What are the odds the holding period return will be above 18.25 percent?
   b. What are the odds the holding period return will be less than zero?
   c. What is the holding period return anticipated at a 1.5 standard deviation below the mean?
   d. What are the odds the holding period return will be less than 20.50 percent?
   e. What are the odds the holding period return will be greater than 9.25 percent?

SELECTED ADDITIONAL REFERENCES

Arrow, K. J. *Essays in the Theory of Risk Bearing* (Amsterdam: North Holland, 1971).

Bawa, V. J. "Optimal Rules for Ordering Uncertain Prospects," *Journal of Financial Economics*, Vol. 2 (March 1975, pp. 95–121).

Blattberg, R. and N. Gonedes. "A Comparison of the Stable and Student Distributions as Statistical Models for Stock Prices," *Journal of Business*, Vol. 74 (April 1974, pp. 244–80).

Fama, Eugene. "Behavior of Stock Market Prices," *Journal of Business*, Vol. 63 (January 1965, pp. 34–105).

Fama, Eugene F. and Merton H. Miller. *The Theory of Finance*, Ch. 5 (New York: Holt, Rinehart and Winston, 1972).

Friedman, M. and L. Savage. "The Utility Analysis of Choice Involving Risk," *The Journal of Political Economy*. Vol. 56 (August 1948, pp. 279–304).

Friend, Irwin and Marshall Blume. "The Demand for Risky Assets," *The American Economic Review*, Vol. 65 (December 1975, pp. 900–22).

Hanoch, G. and H. Levy. "The Efficiency Analysis of Choices Involving Risk," *Review of Economic Studies*, Vol. 36 (July 1969, pp. 335–46).

Herstein, I. N. and J. Milnor. "An Axiomatic Approach to Expected Utility," *Econometrica*, Vol. 21 (April 1953, pp. 291–97).

Jean, W. "Comparison of Moment and Stochastic Dominance Ranking Methods," *Journal of Financial and Quantitative Analysis*, Vol. 10 (March 1975, pp. 151–62).

Markowitz, H. *Portfolio Selection, Efficient Diversification of Investments* (New Haven: Yale University Press, 1959).

Pratt, J. W. "Risk Aversion in the Small and in the Large," *Econometrica*, Vol. 32 (January–April, pp. 122–36).

Tobin, J. "Liquidity Preference as Behavior Toward Risk," *The Review of Economic Studies*, Vol. 25 (February 1958, pp. 65–86).

Vickson, R. B. "Stochastic Dominance for Decreasing Absolute Risk Aversion," *Journal of Financial and Quantitative Analysis*, Vol. 10 (December 1975, pp. 799–812).

Vickson, R. G. and M. Altman. "On Relative Effectiveness of Stochastic Dominance Rules: Extension to Decreasing Risk-Averse Utility Functions," *Journal of Financial and Quantitative Analysis*, Vol. 12 (March 1977, pp. 73–84).

5

PRINCIPLES
OF MODERN
PORTFOLIO THEORY

In the preceding chapters, we discussed the concepts of risk and return in some detail and developed basic measures for each. In Chapter 5, we systematically employ these concepts in a discussion of the principles of Modern Portfolio Theory (MPT).

MPT is the rubric for a set of propositions initially concerned with showing how an investor could maximize return on a portfolio of investments in a manner consistent with the investor's willingness to bear risk. The path-breaking article on the subject was written by Harry Markowitz, who later expanded his work into a major book.[1] A second contributor was Nobelist James Tobin, who worked independently and from the perspective of macroeconomics.[2] Their work helped inspire others to make significant contributions to the subject. The result is a set of building blocks that comprise a theory of pricing and, ultimately, return on all capital assets.

Because MPT deals systematically with the risk–return tradeoff so fundamental to financial decision-making, its importance cannot be underestimated. Furthermore, although the theory was developed in terms of a portfolio of financial assets (specifically, debt and equity instruments), there is no reason why these concepts cannot be extended to portfolios of real assets (to plant, equipment, inventories, and the like), which make up the bulk of the assets of nonfinancial corporations. One can even make a case for including investment in the education and training of individuals—the foundation of human capital—in the portfolio.

However, we cannot get ahead of ourselves; the principles must be developed systematically. Consequently, we shall proceed step-by-step through the fundamentals, employing them initially in the context of financial assets. At the end of the chapter, we shall examine some of the criticisms of MPT and touch upon the direction of current and future research in the area.

---

[1] Harry Markowitz. "Portfolio Selection," *Journal of Finance*, Vol. 12 (March 1952, pp. 77–91); *Portfolio Selection, Efficient Diversification of Investments* (New York: John Wiley and Sons, 1959).

[2] James Tobin. "Liquidity Preference as Behaviour Towards Risk," *Review of Economic Studies*, Vol. 25 (February 1958, pp. 65–86).

EFFICIENT CAPITAL MARKETS

Much of MPT hinges upon a concept of **efficient capital markets**. To gain some insight into this notion, let us examine briefly one subset of such markets, common stock. In such advanced industrial societies as those of Western Europe, the United States, much of the British Commonwealth, Japan, and Hong Kong, where private ownership of nonlabor resources is common, the instruments reflecting this ownership—corporate shares or stock—are actively traded through a system of securities markets. Any individual can buy or sell shares of thousands of different corporations. For the shares of many companies traded in markets throughout the world, there is a going market price at any time of the day or night.

Investors, securities analysts, and other professionals—some of whom may be using the intrinsic value models developed in Chapter 3—are continually reassessing the earnings and dividend prospects of companies. Partly the result of their analyses, orders to buy and sell shares are placed. Although the market price can and will change, if all information that might affect the market price of any security is readily (costlessly) available to investors, then the current market price of that security reflects the market's consensus of its value. If what is true about information for one security is true for all securities, the securities market is said to be *efficient*. Following Fama, in efficient markets the current price of any stock equals its present intrinsic value.[3]

Let us briefly examine the implications of the definition of efficient market. In truth, information is never costless; yet much can be obtained at nominal cost. Consider the history of prices. Charts picturing the daily or weekly pattern of stock prices can be obtained from many brokerage houses or from investment services to which local libraries subscribe. Like medical personnel monitoring the vital signs of a patient undergoing surgery, market technicians follow the pattern of stock prices or a popular average of stock prices, such as the Dow Jones Industrials or Standard & Poor's 500. Their purpose is to detect a trend or pattern that may be the specific basis

---

[3] Eugene F. Fama. "Efficient Capital Markets: A Review of Theory and Empirical Work," *Journal of Finance*, Vol. XXV (May 1970, pp. 383–417).

for buying or selling a stock or the general basis for putting more or less money into the market. Such information, however, cannot be used to predict future stock prices. The historic pattern of changes in stock prices is essentially random. Consequently, the term *random walk* has been applied to characterize the movement of stock prices.[4] Needless to say, market technicians are viewed with suspicion by the academic community.

What about participants who rely on intrinsic value models? Those who employ such tools must have considerable insights into future levels of earnings, dividends, growth rates, and opportunity costs of capital and must be able to process publicly available information in unique ways.[5] The test is whether those who presumably have some insight into the future or who might have some unique way of processing information are able to earn excess returns. The evidence generally suggests that professionals—mutual funds, pension funds, and security analysts—recommending stock purchases or sales do not, as a group, outperform the market.[6] Exceptions do exist. Among mutual funds, the Templeton Growth Fund has been a superior performer (in terms of return to its owners) for several years.[7] The tantalizing question is whether such performance results from superior insight or is a random outcome—with the $\pm 3\sigma$s of the average return of all mutual funds. For those who believe in efficient markets, the performance of the Templeton Fund is similar to that of the 1 person in 64 who, upon tossing six coins in the air, finds that all six coins are heads—a result consistent with $(p + q)^6$, where $p = q = 1/2$. Moreover, for each *Templeton* there is another *fund* that undoubtedly would prefer not to be known as the consistent poor performer in the *group*: the 1 in 64 whose six coins were

---

[4] There is a large body of literature on the subject. Those interested might begin with note[3] pp. 389–404 and Paul H. Cootner, ed., *The Random Character of Stock Market Prices* (Cambridge, MA: MIT Press, 1964).

Stock prices do exhibit a long-term upward trend that reflects growth in earnings and dividends. This is expected and is reflected in the return on stocks over an extended period of time. See Roger G. Ibbotson and Rex A. Sinquefield, *Stocks, Bonds, Bills and Inflation: The Past and the Future* (Charlottesville, VA: The Financial Analysts Research Foundation, 1982, pp. 36–39). All that an efficient market hypothesis suggests is that one cannot use available information to earn excess returns. Once the trend is removed, the random pattern persists.

For successive transactions in a stock, there are also runs: a succession of upward or downward price movements (plus or minus ticks) not suggested by a random model. The process, however, is short-lived. The ordinary investor trying to trade on this type of inefficiency would find his or her profits more than offset by brokerage commissions. See Eugene Fama and Marshall Blume, "Filter Rules and Stock Market Trading Profits," *Journal of Business*, Vol. 39 (Special Supplement, January 1966, pp. 226–41).

[5] One of the early attempts was Volkert S. Whitbeck and Manown Kisor, Jr., "A New Tool in Investment Decision-Making," *Financial Analysts Journal*, Vol. XIX (May–June 1963, pp. 55–62). To the extent one can develop ways of processing public information, it is unlikely such methods can be kept secret for any length of time. Thus, one is under constant pressure to find new techniques.

[6] Again the literature is extensive. However, you might sample Irwin Friend, Marshall Blume, and Jean Crocket, *Mutual Funds and Other Institutional Investors* (New York: McGraw-Hill, 1970); Robert S. Carlson, "Aggregate Performance of Mutual Funds, 1948–1967," *Journal of Financial and Quantitative Analysis*, Vol. V (March 1970, pp. 1–32); Burton G. Malkiel and John G. Cragg, *Expectations and the Valuation of Shares* (National Bureau of Economic Research, Working Paper No. 471, April 1980). A summary of the findings is available in James H. Lorie, Peter Dodd, and Mary Hamilton Kimpton, *The Stock Market: Theories and Evidence*, 2nd ed. (Homewood, IL: Richard D. Irwin, 1985, pp. 65–73).

[7] Burton G. Malkiel. *A Random Walk Down Wall Street*, 4th ed. (New York: W. W. Norton, 1985, pp. 166–69 and 335–36).

tails. For those who doubt the efficient market hypothesis, the performance of Templeton is due to skill; the performance of the fund (that prefers to remain anonymous), is due to incompetence. Which interpretation does one accept? In either case, consistently good or bad performance relative to the group is unusual. However, it is not impossible, and one must recognize that unusual skill or the lack of it could be responsible for the outcomes observed.

Nevertheless, suppose in real-world markets that all known information affecting the market price of a stock is not generally available: *insiders* have access to facts about a company that, if generally known, would materially affect the market price of the stock. For example, assume you are a secretary taking notes at the director's meeting of Megabucks, Inc., a major conglomerate. On the agenda is discussion of a tender offer to be made by Megabucks to Softsoap, Inc., a leading manufacturer of detergents. The current market price of Softsoap is $18 per share. The directors agree to offer all stockholders $25 per share to tender their stock to Megabucks. Clearly, when the offer is made public, the market price of Softsoap will rise. When the meeting adjourns, why not place an order for several hundred shares of Softsoap and make a quick profit?

Because you are an insider with access to information that would materially affect the market price of the stock, you run the risk of a fine and perhaps spending time the guest of Uncle Sam in a federal penitentiary for violating the Securities Exchange Act of 1934.[8] Legal risks aside, the serious intellectual question is whether there is sufficient inside information to render markets inefficient. Certainly, there have been occasions when individuals have profited from inside information.[9] And there undoubtedly will be more in the future. (See Appendix 17-A for further discussion of insider trading.)

To have inside information, however, is by definition to have information that, when generally known, leads to a new market price and therefore to a new intrinsic value of the stock. Consequently, the greater the speed with which information is disseminated, the fewer the opportunities to profit from knowledge unavailable to others. Those in a position to find out relevant information will, within the framework of law, do so. In their diligence to earn excess profits, market participants eagerly seek new information that could materially affect the market price of a stock. Such efforts lead to increased flow of information. The result—as Lorie, Dodd, and Kimpton note—is a paradox. For markets to be efficient, investors must believe they

---

[8] For a discussion of the finer points of the law, see W. Scott Cooper, John J. Huber, and Benjamin M. Vandergrift, "Chiarella and Rule 14e-3: Theory and Practice," in Michael Keenan and Lawrence J. White, eds., *Mergers and Acquisitions* (Lexington, MA: D. C. Heath, 1982, pp. 113–68).

[9] Henry C. Manne. *Insider Trading and the Stock Market* (Glencoe, IL: The Free Press, 1966). John C. Gillis. "Securities Law and Regulation," *Financial Analyst Journal*, Vol. 29 (March–April 1973, pp. 8–10 and 94–95). Jeffrey Jaffee. "Special Information and Insider Trading," *Journal of Business*, Vol. 47 (July 1974, pp. 410–28). Karen Arenson. "How Wall Street Bred An Ivan Boesky," *New York Times* (November 23, 1986, Sec. 3, pp. 1 and 8). George Russell. "A Raid on Wall Street," *Time* (February 23, 1987, pp. 64–66).

'GOLDMAN, SKINNER AND LYNCH, INSIDER TRADING DIVISION.'

SOURCE: TIME (February 23, 1987, p. 66). Reprinted with permission. All rights reserved.

are not. Thus:

> Market prices will promptly and fully reflect what is knowable about the companies whose shares are traded only if investors seek to earn superior returns, make conscientious and competent efforts to learn about companies whose securities are traded, and analyze relevant information promptly and perceptively. If that effort were abandoned, the efficiency of the market would diminish rapidly.[10]

Many of the propositions of Modern Portfolio Theory are built upon the assumption that securities markets are efficient. The evidence with respect to securities, especially with respect to widely traded stocks and debt instruments, suggests that these markets are generally efficient. The current market price of the security is the best estimate of its present value. As an investor or potential investor, you should accept this conclusion, but for the sake of maintaining efficient markets, act as though you do not believe it.

---

[10] Lorie, Dodd, and Kimpton, p. 80. For a recent summary of the literature as well as exceptions to the efficient market hypothesis, see Robert A. Hauyen, *Modern Investment Theory* (Englewood Cliffs, NJ: Prentice-Hall, 1986, pp. 486–518).

THE ELEMENTS OF PORTFOLIO THEORY— EXPECTED RETURN AND STANDARD DEVIATION

When an individual—either for his or her own account or as the manager of a portfolio of securities—buys stock, that person can select from among the shares of thousands of companies. In doing so, we assume he or she will maximize the return on the portfolio of securities relative to the risk assumed.

For an individual security, we use the concept of the holding period return introduced in Chapter 3.

$$\bar{R}_{jt} = E(R_{jt}) = \frac{E(P_{jt}) - P_{jt-1} + E(D_{jt})}{P_{jt-1}} \tag{5-1}$$

where

$$\bar{R}_{jt} = E(R_{jt}) = \text{expected return on security } j \text{ at time } t$$
$$E(P_{jt}) = \text{expected price of security } j \text{ at time } t$$
$$P_{jt-1} = \text{actual price of security } j \text{ at time } t - 1$$
$$E(D_{jt}) = \text{expected dividend on security } j \text{ at time } t$$

As a measure of risk, we use the standard deviation σ_{jt}. Assuming the probability distribution of returns is normal, then (as we saw in Chapter 4) the expected return $E(R_{jt})$ and σ_{jt} provide the basic information necessary with which to select a portfolio of securities designed to minimize risk while maximizing return. For every security under consideration there is an expected return and a standard deviation. The expected return on a portfolio of securities is the sum of the expected returns on individual securities multiplied by the respective proportion of the total portfolio accounted for by each security, W_j. Thus, the expected return $E(R_{pt})$ on a portfolio of securities at time period t is

$$E(R_{pt}) = \sum_{j=1}^{n} W_{jt} E(R_{jt}) \tag{5-2}$$

The formula for the standard deviation of the portfolio with all variables at time period t is

$$\sigma_p = \sqrt{\sum_{j=1}^{n} \sum_{k=1}^{n} W_j W_k r_{jk} \sigma_j \sigma_k} \tag{5-3}$$

where

$\sigma_p \equiv$ standard deviation of the portfolio

$r_{jk} \equiv$ coefficient of correlation between returns on securities j and k

$\sigma_j\sigma_k \equiv$ product of respective standard deviations of expected returns on securities j and k

$W_jW_k \equiv$ product of respective proportions of portfolio dollars accounted for by securities j and k

In keeping with our practice of hiding the unpleasant, we have placed the derivation of this formula in Appendix 5-A to this chapter. Suffice it to say, the standard deviation of the portfolio does not depend solely on the standard deviation of the return on individual securities comprising the portfolio. The standard deviation of the portfolio depends also on how the returns on these securities change in relationship to one another: it depends on the **covariance** among the returns on securities.

To illustrate graphically the meaning of covariance, consider the respective probability distributions of securities j and k (see Figure 5-1). Assume both securities have the same expected return and the same standard deviation. As individual investments, then, they are equally risky. Suppose, however, the probabilities

Figure 5-1 Probability Distribution of Expected Returns of Two Securities

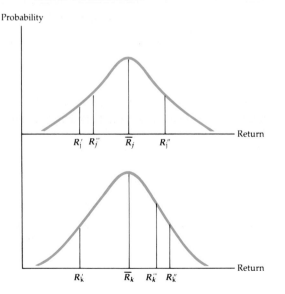

are such that when the return on security j was R'_j, the return on security k was R''_k. Similarly, when the return on security j was R''_j, the return on security k was R'_k. More generally, suppose the return on security j covaried with the return on security k, so that when the return on one fell x percent from its expected return, the return on the other rose x percent above its mean (or expected) return. Let $\bar{R}_j$ and $\bar{R}_k$ represent the expected (or mean) returns on securities j and k. As the probability distributions of j and k are identical, let us assume that one standard deviation to the left of $\bar{R}_j$ is $\bar{R}_j - x$ percent, or R'_j. If so, one standard deviation to the right of $\bar{R}_k$ is $\bar{R}_k + x$ percent, or R''_k. The two securities in this case are said to be perfectly but negatively correlated.

The coefficient of correlation in this instance is -1. This follows from the definition of coefficient of correlation between two jointly distributed variables (coefficient of correlation of bivariate distribution), which is

$$r_{jk} = \frac{\text{COV}_{jk}}{\sigma_j \sigma_k} \qquad (5\text{-}4)$$

Alternatively

$$\text{COV}_{jk} = r_{jk}\sigma_j\sigma_k \qquad (5\text{-}4a)$$

The term COV_{jk} stands for covariance between securities j and k. It can be defined as

$$\text{COV}_{jk} = \sum_{x=1}^{n} (R_{xj} - E(R_j))(R_{xk} - E(R_k))P_{xjk}$$

where

$$R_{xj}, R_{xk} \equiv x\text{th possible returns for securities } j \text{ and } k, \text{ respectively}$$
$$E(R_j), E(R_k) \equiv \text{expected returns on securities } j \text{ and } k\text{: also equivalent to } \bar{R}_j, \bar{R}_k$$
$$P_{xjk} \equiv \text{joint probability that } R_{xj} \text{ and } R_{xk} \text{ will occur simultaneously:}$$
$$\text{also called joint probability of occurrence}$$

Based upon the presentation in Chapter 4, the standard deviation σ and variance σ^2 for securities j and k are

$$\sigma_j = \sqrt{\sum_{x=1}^{n} (R_{xj} - E(R_j))^2 P_{xj}}, \qquad \sigma_k = \sqrt{\sum_{x=1}^{n} (R_{xk} - E(R_k))^2 P_{xk}}$$
$$\sigma_j^2 = \sum_{x=1}^{n} (R_{xj} - E(R_j))^2 P_{xj}, \qquad \sigma_k^2 = \sum_{x=1}^{n} (R_{xk} - E(R_k))^2 P_{xk}$$

where

$$R_{xj}, R_{xk} \equiv x\text{th possible returns for securities } j \text{ and } k, \text{ respectively}$$
$$E(R_j), E(R_k) \equiv \text{expected returns on securities } j \text{ and } k: \text{ also equivalent to } \bar{R}_j, \bar{R}_k$$
$$P_{xj} \equiv \text{probability that } R_{xj} \text{ will occur}$$
$$P_{xk} \equiv \text{probability that } R_{xk} \text{ will occur}$$

Underlying the notation is the fact that variance and covariance are comprised of $R_{xj} - E(R_j)$ and $R_{xk} - E(R_k)$. In the case of variance, one squares each expression; in the case of covariance, one expression is multiplied by the other. In Figure 5-1, we assume the deviations on one side of the expected return on one security are equally matched but move in the opposite direction to deviations from the expected return on the other security. In absolute terms, therefore, the values necessary to compute variances and covariances are such that in each instance $R_j - E(R_j) = R_k - E(R_k)$ or $R_j - \bar{R}_j = R_k - \bar{R}_k$.

In the case of variance, the square of the sum of either $(R_j - \bar{R}_j)$ or $(R_k - \bar{R}_k)$ is positive. Therefore, the standard deviation is positive $\sigma_j = \sqrt{\sigma_j^2}$. In the case of covariance, $(R_j - \bar{R}_j)$ is negative when $(R_k - \bar{R}_k)$ is positive. Alternatively, $(R_j - \bar{R}_j)$ is positive when $(R_k - \bar{R}_k)$ is negative. The product of the two is, therefore, negative. In absolute terms, however, $\sum (R_j - \bar{R}_j)(R_k - \bar{R}_k) = \sum (R_j - \bar{R}_j)^2 = \sum (R_k - \bar{R}_k)^2$. With identical probabilities $P_{xj} = P_{xk} = P_{xjk}$, then in absolute terms, $\text{COV}_{jk} = \sigma_j^2 = \sigma_k^2$. Since

$$\sigma_j^2 = \sigma_k^2$$
$$\sigma_j = \sigma_k$$

Substituting, we have

$$\sigma_j \sigma_k = \sigma_j^2 = \sigma_k^2$$
$$\text{COV}_{jk} = \sigma_j \sigma_k$$

Using the negative sign for covariance, it follows from Equation 5-4 that

$$r_{jk} = -\frac{\text{COV}_{jk}}{\sigma_j \sigma_k} = -1$$

By analogy, if the deviations from $\bar{R}_j$ had been matched by equal deviations from $\bar{R}_k$ (but in the same rather than in the opposite direction), then r_{jk} would equal $+1$.

Let us return now to Equation 5-3. Note the expression $W_j W_k r_{jk} \sigma_j \sigma_k$, which is equal to the products of the weights for security j and security k and the covariance of security j with security k (see Equation 5-4a, $\text{COV}_{jk} = r_{jk} \sigma_j \sigma_k$). The double $\sum \sum$

commands us to sum all pairs of securities in the portfolio. Assume we have a two-security portfolio. A matrix of all pairs is

	Security 1	Security 2
Security 1	σ_{11}^2	COV_{12}
Security 2	COV_{21}	σ_{22}^2

In this case, Security 1 is paired with itself once; Security 2 is paired with Security 1 twice. In other words, Security 2 covaries with Security 1 and Security 1 covaries with Security 2. Finally, Security 2 is paired with itself once. Given the weights W_1 and W_2, we can now use Equation 5-3, so that

$$\sigma_p = \sqrt{W_1^2\sigma_1^2 + 2W_1W_2COV_{12} + W_2^2\sigma_2^2}$$
$$\sigma_p = \sqrt{W_1^2\sigma_1^2 + 2W_1W_2r_{12}\sigma_1\sigma_2 + W_2^2\sigma_2^2}$$

When paired with itself, the covariance of a security is its variance, so that $r_{11}W_1W_1\sigma_1\sigma_1 = W_1^2\sigma_1^2$. The coefficient of correlation r_{11} equals 1.

To make certain you understand Equation 5-3, try these securities. The matrix in this case is

	Security 1	Security 2	Security 3
Security 1	σ_{11}^2	COV_{12}	COV_{13}
Security 2	COV_{21}	σ_{22}^2	COV_{23}
Security 3	COV_{31}	COV_{32}	σ_{33}^2

Consequently:

$$\sigma_p = \sqrt{W_{11}^2\sigma_{11}^2 + W_{22}^2\sigma_{22}^2 + W_{33}^2\sigma_{33}^2 + 2W_1W_2COV_{12} + 2W_1W_3COV_{13} + 2W_2W_3COV_{23}}$$

Try four securities, so that

	Security 1	Security 2	Security 3	Security 4
Security 1	σ_{11}^2	COV_{12}	COV_{13}	COV_{14}
Security 2	COV_{21}	σ_{22}^2	COV_{23}	COV_{24}
Security 3	COV_{31}	COV_{32}	σ_{33}^2	COV_{34}
Security 4	COV_{41}	COV_{42}	COV_{43}	σ_{44}^2

Consequently:

$$\sigma_p = [(W_{11}^2\sigma_{11}^2 + W_{22}^2\sigma_{22}^2 + W_{33}^2\sigma_{33}^2 + W_{44}^2\sigma_{44}^2 + 2W_1W_2\mathrm{COV}_{12} + 2W_1W_3\mathrm{COV}_{13}$$
$$+ 2W_1W_4\mathrm{COV}_{14} + 2W_2W_3\mathrm{COV}_{23} + 2W_2W_4\mathrm{COV}_{24} + 2W_3W_4\mathrm{COV}_{34})]^{\frac{1}{2}}$$

Clearly, one can expand the matrix further. Before we pursue the implications of doing so, it is instructive to extend our analysis of what happens to the expected return and σ_p of a portfolio when the coefficient of correlation (and hence the covariance) changes. The weights given each security, however, remain unchanged. To do so, we shall relax some of the rigid assumptions employed earlier so we may gain a sense of the significance of covariance. Suppose, as indicated in Figure 5-2, the expected returns and standard deviations on Securities 1 and 2 are

	Security 1	*Security 2*
Return	5%	10%
σ	4%	4%
Weight	50%	50%

Figure 5-2   Effect of Differences in Covariance on the Standard Deviation of a Two-security Portfolio

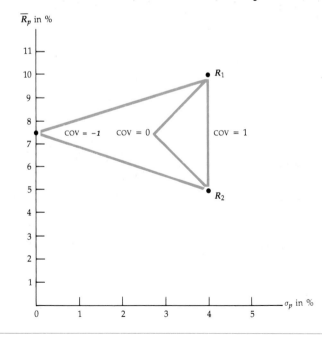

Assume the covariance is -16 percent. Hence the coefficient of correlation is (-1): $r_{12} = \dfrac{-16\%}{(4\%)(4\%)}$. The expected return $\bar{R}_p$ on this portfolio is $\bar{R}_p = (.5)(10\%) + (.5)(5\%) = 7.5\%$. However

$$\sigma_p^2 = W_1^2\sigma_1^2 + 2W_1W_2\text{COV}_{12} + W_2^2\sigma_2^2$$
$$= (.5)^2(.04)^2 + 2(.5)(.5)(-1)(.04)(.04) + (.5)^2(.04)^2$$
$$\sigma_p^2 = .0004 - .0008 + .0004$$
$$\sigma_p^2 = 0$$

If an investor is selecting only one security, obviously the security with the 10-percent return is superior because it has a higher return but the same standard deviation as the security with a 5-percent return. By combining these two securities in an equally weighted portfolio, we eliminate risk altogether and earn a 7.5-percent return. Whether this is preferable to investing in Security 1, with a 10-percent return and a 4-percent standard deviation, depends upon one's preference for risk over return. We come back to this point shortly.

Instead of -1, suppose the coefficient of correlation had been $+1$—covariance is 16 percent—then

$$\sigma_p^2 = W_1^2\sigma_1^2 + 2W_1W_2\text{COV}_{12} + W_2^2\sigma_2^2$$
$$= (.5)^2(.04)^2 + 2(.5)(.5)(+1)(.04)(.04) + (.5)^2(.04)^2$$
$$\sigma_p^2 = .0016$$
$$\sigma_p = .04 = \sigma_1 = \sigma_2$$

Suppose there was no association between security j and security k—covariance is zero; therefore, r_{jk} is also zero—then

$$\sigma_p = \sqrt{(.5)^2(.04)^2 + (.5)^2(.04)^2}$$
$$\sigma_p = \sqrt{.0008}$$
$$\sigma_p = 2.83\%$$

Thus, even with zero coefficient of correlation, in this case the σ_p is less than the standard deviation of each individual security. The arithmetic example employed also suggests a more general principle: specifically, the upper limit (see Figure 5-2) of the σ_p equals the weighted average of the standard deviations of the individual securities. This occurs when r_{jk} equals 1. As long as $r_{jk} < 1$ the σ_p is less than the weighted average of the standard deviations of each security. Of course, the actual outcome can be affected by changes in the weights, changes in standard deviations, and changes in covariances.[11]

---

[11] Suppose W_1 is .1, W_2 is .9, σ_1 is 2 percent, σ_2 is 10 percent, and r_{12} is -0.9, then

$$\sigma_p = \sqrt{(.1)^2(.02)^2 + 2(.1)(.9)(-.9)(.02)(.10) + (.9)^2(.10)^2}$$
$$\sigma_p = 8.8\%$$

The weighted average of the σs of the two securities is $(.1)(.02) + (.9)(.10) = 9.2$ percent. Although $\sigma_2 > \sigma_1$, the σ_p is still smaller than the weighted average of the standard deviation of each security.

The standard deviation of the portfolio is also affected by the number of securities. To illustrate using a simple arithmetic example, suppose instead of two securities we choose a portfolio of ten securities, each with a standard deviation of 4 percent and each representing 10 percent of the market value of the portfolio. Assume further that the covariance between each pair of securities is zero. Only the variances (the diagonals along the matrix) remain. In this instance, the weighted average of each variance is $W_j^2 \sigma_1^2 = (.1)^2(.04)^2 = .000016$. We have ten securities in the portfolio, so that

$$\sigma_p = \sqrt{10(.000016)}$$
$$\sigma_p = 1.3 \text{ percent}$$

For 50 securities, each comprising 2 percent of the portfolio

$$\sigma_p = \sqrt{50(.02)^2(.04)^2}$$
$$\sigma_p = .57\%$$

Again, we have oversimplified the arithmetic. Standard deviations vary. Some covariances are positive, others are negative. One can also intentionally vary the weights. Nevertheless, it is possible to decrease the standard deviation of a portfolio by increasing the number of securities. Moreover, the impact on the standard deviation of the portfolio declines materially as the number of securities in the portfolio rises.

In the case of 100 securities, each with a standard deviation of 4 percent and each accounting for 1 percent of the portfolio

$$\sigma_p = \sqrt{100(.01)^2(.04)^2}$$
$$\sigma_p = .40\%$$

Not only is it possible to reduce σ_p by adding securities, the number required need not be large. In an earlier instance, 50 securities resulted in a standard deviation of .57 percent. The addition of another 50 only brought the standard deviation of the portfolio to .40 percent.

No doubt by this time ennui has triumphed. Time for a break. Do 30 pushups and proceed to the next section.

EFFICIENT PORTFOLIOS

In their path-breaking work in portfolio theory, Markowitz and Tobin gave substance to what practitioners of finance had intuitively understood: specifically, a portfolio should contain securities from various industries. As Markowitz noted in his initial article "... there is a diversified portfolio which is preferable to all

Figure 5-3   Possible Portfolio Opportunities

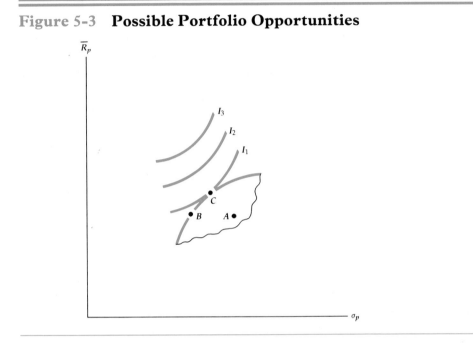

non-diversified portfolios. Diversification is both observed (in practice) and sensible..."[12]

In his book, *Portfolio Selection: Efficient Diversification of Investment*, Marko-witz developed the analytical foundation upon which other scholars and practi-tioners have subsequently built. Briefly, given the variances and covariances of all securities, it is possible to develop an opportunity set of portfolios and choose from among them the efficient portfolios of securities. Although the computational tech-niques are beyond the scope of this volume, Figure 5-3 illustrates the essence of what is involved.[13] On the y-axis, $\bar{R}_p$ represents the mean (or expected) return on the portfolio of securities. On the x-axis, σ_p represents the standard deviation of the portfolio. Both are calculated from the equations presented earlier. Figure 5-3, labeled as an opportunity set, illustrates a portion of all possible portfolios. Thus points A, B, and C represent three of many portfolio combinations possible from the securities available.

Clearly, portfolios B and C are preferred to portfolio A because they each have a higher return but a lower standard deviation. However, it is not apparent from the opportunity set that portfolio C is preferable to portfolio B; both are efficient

---

[12] Markowitz, p. 77.

[13] For the development of the procedure employed, see Philip Wolfe, "The Simplex Method for Quadratic Programming," *Econometrica*, Vol. 27 (July 1959, pp. 382–98).

portfolios. This is true because, in order to realize the higher return on portfolio C, one must accept greater risk. In other words, portfolios B and C lie on the frontier of the opportunity set; all such portfolios are efficient in this sense. To obtain a higher return, one must accept greater risk. All portfolios below the frontier are inefficient portfolios. There is always a portfolio with a higher return and the same or smaller standard deviation.

Among efficient portfolios, however, the choice depends upon one's risk preferences. Using the indifference-curve approach developed in Chapter 4, we show (in Figure 5-3) three of the many possible indifference curves representing the trade-off between risk and return. I_2 represents a higher level of total satisfaction, or utility, than I_1; I_3 represents a higher level of total utility than I_2. The opportunity set, however, does not permit the investor to realize the level of satisfaction suggested by indifference curves I_2 and I_3. The investor must, therefore, be content with portfolio C at the point of tangency between the opportunity set and the indifference curve I_1.

Before proceeding, we pause to summarize. A portfolio is efficient, in the sense Markowitz uses that term, only if one can earn a higher return on a different portfolio by accepting a greater degree of risk. Portfolios in which risk must be traded off against return lie on the efficient frontier. The ultimate choice among efficient portfolios is determined by the point of tangency between one's indifference curve and the efficient frontier. Moreover, it is not crucial to this portion of MPT that capital markets are efficient, as Fama uses that term. Covariance is the driving force behind Markowitz's insight. Covariance is possible in efficient as well as inefficient capital markets.

THE CAPITAL MARKET LINE

The opportunity set Markowitz developed contained only risky investments. Actually, there is no unique portfolio suitable to every individual—no portfolio everyone would hold. Given a choice between a portfolio of risky investments and a portfolio of risk-free investments, an investor can trade off risk against return in a broader context. Moreover, as we shall see, one and only one portfolio is appropriate to all investors—the **market portfolio**.

For our purposes, a portfolio of risk-free securities or a risk-free asset is one with a standard deviation about the expected holding period return of zero. In short, the expected return equals the actual return. Short-term U.S. Treasury bills discussed in Chapter 3 are considered by many to be the best proxy for the risk-free rate. Savings accounts and other government-insured time deposits also may be viewed as risk-free investments. Longer-term U.S. government securities are also risk-free, in the sense that the nominal return is as certain as possible (the U.S. government could conceivably collapse and its debt become worthless.) However,

Figure 5-4   The Opportunity Set and the Risk-free Rate

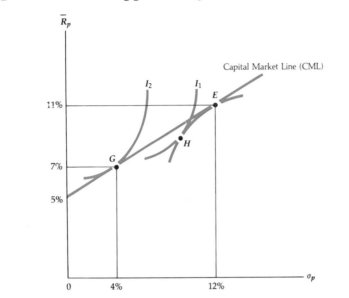

the inflation-adjusted expected real return may be higher or lower than anticipated. The effect of inflation on real returns is easier to anticipate for three-, six-, or twelve-month holding periods than for holding periods that extend several years into the future. Consequently, unless otherwise noted, we shall adopt the nominal annualized yield on short-term U.S. Treasury bills as our proxy for the risk-free rate.

To illustrate the approach, Figure 5-4 depicts a situation in which the investor's risk–return trade-off as expressed in his set of indifference curves is tangent to the opportunity set at H. Assume the risk-free rate is 5 percent. If we draw a line tangent to both the indifference curve I_2 and the opportunity set, we can obtain a different portfolio for the investor. This portfolio, E, we shall call the **market portfolio**.

At the point of tangency with indifference curve I_2 (at point G), the investor, now at a higher level of total satisfaction, is seeking a portfolio with a 7-percent return and a 4-percent standard deviation. How can this portfolio be obtained from risk-free securities and the market portfolio? Consider the slope of the line tangent to the indifference curve and the opportunity set. A linear equation of the form $y = a + bx$, where b is the slope, suggests

$$7\% = 5\% + b(4\%)$$
$$b = .5$$

Thus, if the standard deviation of portfolio E to which the line is also tangent is

12 percent, the expected return $\bar{R}_p$ is

$$\bar{R}_p = 5\% + .5(12\%)$$
$$\bar{R}_p = 11\%$$

If we let W_i equal the proportion of securities invested in the risk-free security, W_E equal the proportion invested in portfolio E, and σ_G equal the standard deviation of portfolio G, then

$$\sigma_G = \sqrt{\sigma_i^2 W_i^2 + \sigma_E^2 W_p^2 + 2W_i W_E \text{COV}_{iE}}$$
$$\sigma_G = \sqrt{0 + \sigma_E^2 W_p^2 + 0}$$

But

$$\sigma_G = \sigma_E W_p$$
$$W_p + W_i = 1$$
$$W_p = 1 - W_i$$
$$\sigma_G = \sigma_E(1 - W_i)$$
$$4\% = 12\%(1 - W_i)$$
$$W_i = \frac{2}{3}$$

Because

$$\frac{2}{3} + W_p = 1$$

$$W_p = \frac{1}{3}$$

A portfolio consisting of two-thirds of the total dollars invested in risk-free securities and one-third invested in portfolio E has a mean (or expected) return of 7 percent and a standard deviation of 4 percent, as follows:

$$\bar{R}_G = \frac{2}{3} \times 5\% + \frac{1}{3} \times 11\%$$
$$\bar{R}_G = 7\%$$
$$\sigma_G = \frac{1}{3} \times 12\%$$
$$\sigma_G = 4\%$$

Given the opportunity to invest in a portfolio of securities lying on the efficiency frontier as well as the chance to invest all monies in a risk-free portfolio, the investor can weight the portfolio in accordance with preferences expressed in his or her indifference map. The point of tangency varies from individual to individual along the line connecting the risk-free rate to the efficiency frontier of the opportunity set, known as the **Capital Market Line** (CML).

In Figure 5-4, the CML terminates at point E; it can, however, be extended beyond point E. Suppose the individual wants to invest 125 percent of her wealth in the market portfolio. To do so, assume the investor can borrow at the risk-free rate. In Figure 5-5, we depict the indifference map of a different individual than the one depicted in Figure 5-4; this individual, however, faces the same opportunity set. Investing 100 percent in the portfolio lying on the frontier, she would hold portfolio L. However, by borrowing 25 percent of her wealth and placing it in the market portfolio, she can reach a higher level of total satisfaction at K. Following our earlier discussion, the standard deviation of the portfolio is

$$\sigma_k = 1.25(\sigma_p)$$
$$\sigma_k = 1.25(12\%)$$
$$\sigma_k = (15\%)$$

However, from the expected return we must subtract the interest on the loan, so that

$$\bar{R}_k = 1.25(\bar{R}_p) - .25(i)$$
$$\bar{R}_k = 1.25(.11) - .25(.05)$$
$$\bar{R}_k = .1375 - .0125$$
$$\bar{R}_k = .1250 = 12.5\%$$

Figure 5-5 Borrowing at the Risk-free Rate

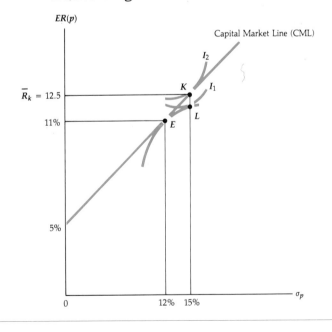

Inasmuch as an investor can allocate funds in various proportions between risk-free securities and the market portfolio, such an investor does so in a manner that maximizes his or her total satisfaction. For the investor depicted in Figure 5-4, total satisfaction was maximized at G; for the investor depicted in Figure 5-5, total satisfaction was maximized at K. Portfolios that represent less than 100 percent invested in the market portfolio are known as *lending portfolios*; those that represent more than 100 percent invested in the market portfolio are known as *borrowing portfolios*. Portfolios representing the former are lending (investing) at the risk-free rate; those representing the latter are borrowing at the risk-free rate.

Because the proxy for the risk-free rate is the return on U.S. Treasury bills, we know that in reality the federal government markets its securities at rates lower than even the most creditworthy of mortals can borrow. For the time being, however, we ignore this *institutional detail* so as to focus on the central idea. Assuming that borrowing and lending rates are the same, the portfolio purchased is the same for *all* investors. In other words, along the frontier there is only one portfolio that is the efficient portfolio for all investors. Originally holding portfolio H, the individual in Figure 5-4 maximizes total satisfaction by moving to portfolio E and allocating funds between the market and risk-free securities. For the same reason, the individual in Figure 5-5 moved from portfolio L to portfolio K. First articulated by Tobin and known as the *separation theorem*, individual preferences are independent of the portfolio of risky securities.[14] The market portfolio is the same for all investors.

In terms of Figures 5-4 and 5-5, the return for any portfolio can be expressed as[15]

$$\bar{R}_p = i + \left[\frac{\bar{R}_M - i}{\sigma_M}\right]\sigma_p \tag{5-5}$$

---

[14] Tobin, pp. 65–82. His emphasis was on lending portfolios. Once introduced, however, the concept was easily extended to borrowing portfolios.

[15] The proof for this formula is $\bar{R}_p = W_i i + W_M \bar{R}_M$, where W_i and W_M are the respective proportions of the risk-free portfolio and the market portfolio. However, $\sigma_p = \sqrt{W_i^2 \sigma_i^2 + W_M^2 \sigma_M^2 + W_i W_M \mathrm{cov}_{iM}}$. Since $\sigma_i = 0$, $\mathrm{cov}_{iM} = 0$

$$\sigma_p = \sqrt{W_M^2 \sigma_M^2} = W_M \sigma_M$$
$$W_M = \frac{\sigma_p}{\sigma_M}$$
$$W_M + W_i = 1$$
$$W_i = 1 - W_M$$

Substituting, we have

$$\bar{R}_p = i(1 - W_M) + W_M \bar{R}_M$$
$$\bar{R}_p = i\left(1 - \frac{\sigma_p}{\sigma_M}\right) + \frac{\sigma_p}{\sigma_M} \bar{R}_M$$
$$\bar{R}_p = i - i\frac{\sigma_p}{\sigma_M} + \frac{\sigma_p}{\sigma_M} \bar{R}_M$$
$$\bar{R}_p = i + \frac{\sigma_p}{\sigma_M} [\bar{R}_M - i]$$
$$\bar{R}_p = i + \left[\frac{\bar{R}_M - i}{\sigma_M}\right]\sigma_p$$

Where $\bar{R}_p \equiv$ expected return on the portfolio selected

$i \equiv$ risk-free rate

$\bar{R}_M \equiv$ mean (or expected) return on the Markowitz efficient portfolio tangent to the capital market line

$\sigma_M \equiv$ standard deviation in R_M

$\sigma_p \equiv$ standard deviation in the portfolio selected

To illustrate, let us rework the earlier example in which (see Figure 5-4) the investor's indifference curve I_2 was tangent to the capital market line with a standard deviation of 4 percent. We can use the same numbers to derive the return on the portfolio held, so that

$$\bar{R}_p = 5\% + \left[\frac{11\% - 5\%}{12\%} \right] 4\%$$

$$\bar{R}_p = 7\%$$

Similarly, from Figure 5-5 we have

$$\bar{R}_p = 5\% + \left[\frac{11\% - 5\%}{12\%} \right] 15\%$$

$$\bar{R}_p = 12.5\%$$

SYSTEMATIC AND UNSYSTEMATIC RISK

Because the market portfolio represents a fully diversified portfolio of securities, the standard deviation is—at a minimum—relative to the expected return. The emphasis is on *minimum*; risk is not completely eliminated. To completely eliminate risk, one would have to purchase only risk-free securities. The reasons for this are straightforward. The return on risky securities is affected by factors that impact upon the industry as well as by factors that generally affect the economy. For example, a restriction on the number of cars imported to the United States may increase the return (at least over a short holding period) on shares of domestic automobile companies. Although this restriction will not noticeably affect the returns on shares of furniture manufacturers or textile companies, a general decline in the level of economic activity could affect the returns on all stocks, even though some may be more adversely affected than others. As a result, the coefficient of correlation between pairs of stocks is often positive but less than one. Consequently, the standard deviation (or variance) in a diversified portfolio will not fall to zero.

It is customary to label the risk associated with specific securities as **unsystematic risk** (sometimes called unique risk, residual risk, or **diversifiable risk**). Unsystematic risk is the portion of risk that can be minimized through diversification. What remains is the undiversifiable risk, the risk that affects all securities: the risk that occurs from changes in the level of economic activity. The returns on all securities are affected differently—some more severely than others—by exceptional increases in the price level or by recession or both; it is a matter of degree. How the return on each security relates to the return on the market as a whole becomes the dominant consideration in selecting a security for a fully diversified portfolio.

The relationship between the return on a security and the return on the market portfolio is known as its **systematic risk**. (We develop a measure of systematic risk in the next section). Figure 5-6 suggests the distinction between the two components of risk as they relate to a portfolio of securities. The standard deviation of the portfolio is affected by both systematic and unsystematic risk. Increasing the number of securities in a portfolio helps reduce the standard deviation through diversification. Once a portfolio is fully diversified, the standard deviation of the portfolio is predominantly a function of systematic risk.

THE BETA COEFFICIENT   Systematic risk is measured by

$$\frac{\text{COV}_{jm}}{\sigma^2_M} = \beta_{jm} \tag{5-6}$$

The term β is the beta coefficient for stock j relative to the market portfolio. As the left-hand side of the expression suggests, β_{jm} is the ratio of the covariance of stock j and the market portfolio to the variance in the market portfolio.

Figure 5-6   Classifications of Risk in a Portfolio of Securities

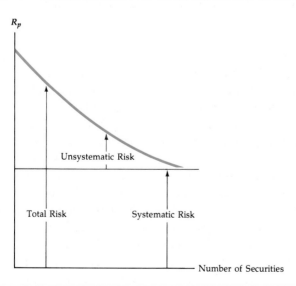

Figure 5-7   A Matrix of n Securities Representing the Market Portfolio

	Security						
	1	*2*	*3*	*4*	*5*	$\cdots$	*n*
1	σ_{11}^2	COV_{12}	COV_{13}	COV_{14}	COV_{15}	$\cdots$	COV_{1n}
2	COV_{21}	σ_{22}^2	COV_{23}	COV_{24}	COV_{25}	$\cdots$	COV_{2n}
3	COV_{31}	COV_{32}	σ_{33}^2	COV_{34}	COV_{35}	$\cdots$	COV_{3n}
4	COV_{41}	COV_{42}	COV_{43}	σ_{44}^2	COV_{45}	$\cdots$	COV_{4n}
5	COV_{51}	COV_{52}	COV_{53}	COV_{54}	σ_{55}^2	$\cdots$	COV_{5n}
$\vdots$	$\vdots$	$\vdots$	$\vdots$	$\vdots$	$\vdots$	$\vdots$	$\vdots$
n	COV_{n1}	COV_{n2}	COV_{n3}	COV_{n4}	COV_{n5}	$\cdots$	σ_{nn}^2

	1	2	3	4	5	$\bullet\bullet\bullet$	n
1	σ_{11}^2	COV_{12}	COV_{13}	COV_{14}	COV_{15}	$\bullet\bullet\bullet$	COV_{1n}
2	COV_{21}	σ_{22}^2	COV_{23}	COV_{24}	COV_{25}	$\bullet\bullet\bullet$	COV_{2n}
3	COV_{31}	COV_{32}	σ_{33}^2	COV_{34}	COV_{35}	$\bullet\bullet\bullet$	COV_{3n}
4	COV_{41}	COV_{42}	COV_{43}	σ_{44}^2	COV_{45}	$\bullet\bullet\bullet$	COV_{4n}
5	COV_{51}	COV_{52}	COV_{53}	COV_{54}	σ_{55}^2	$\bullet\bullet\bullet$	COV_{5n}
$\vdots$	$\vdots$	$\vdots$	$\vdots$	$\vdots$	$\vdots$	$\vdots$	$\vdots$
n	COV_{n1}	COV_{n2}	COV_{n3}	COV_{n4}	COV_{n5}	$\bullet\bullet\bullet$	σ_{nn}^2

To gain some insight into the beta coefficient, let us examine a matrix of the kind shown in Figure 5-7. The matrix consists of n securities (in this case, corporate stock) representing the market portfolio. Let us begin with row 1, security 1. In row 1 there is a covariance for security 1 and every other security in the matrix.

(The covariance of security 1 with security 1 is its variance.) There are n securities with which security 1 covaries. Those n securities comprise the market portfolio. There is also an average covariance for security 1 and the market portfolio of n securities. Therefore

$$\sum_{j=1}^{n} COV_{1j} = COV_{1M}$$

The left-hand side of the expression is the sum of the covariances of stocks 1 through n and is equivalent to the right-hand side of the expression, which represents the average covariance of stock 1 with the market portfolio of n stocks.

Stock 1 also accounts for a specific proportion of the total market value of all stocks: its proportion, or weight, is W_1. Similarly, stocks 2 through n account for specific proportions of the total market value of all stocks. Therefore

$$W_1 \sum_{j=1}^{n} COV_{1j} = W_1 COV_{1M}$$

The same logic applies to securities 2 through n, so that

$$W_2 \sum_{j=1}^{n} COV_{2j} = W_2 COV_{2M}$$

$$W_n \sum_{j=1}^{n} COV_{nj} = W_n COV_{nM}$$

If we sum all rows, we account for all covariances (COV_{21} and COV_{12}, and the like) so that

$$\sum_{j=1}^{n} \sum_{k=1}^{n} W_j W_k COV_{jk} = \sigma_M^2$$

The sum of the weighted averages of all covariances of all securities in the market is the variance of the market portfolio, which is consistent with Equations 5-3 and 5-4. Since

$$\sum_{j=1}^{n} W_j = 1,$$

Then

$$\frac{\sum_{j=1}^{n} COV_{jM}}{\sigma_M^2} = \frac{COV_{MM}}{\sigma_M^2} = \frac{\sigma_M^2}{\sigma_M^2} = \beta_{MM} = 1.0$$

The market portfolio is a portfolio whose beta is one. The beta of each stock times its weight

$$W_j \frac{COV_{jM}}{\sigma_M^2}$$

measures the proportional contribution to the systematic risk of the market portfolio: its proportional contribution to 1.0.

CAPITAL ASSET PRICING MODEL   The beta coefficient can be used to answer the question: What should the expected return be on each stock in the market portfolio of stocks? More precisely, perhaps: What should the return be on a stock over and above the risk-free rate? The answer comes from the works of Sharpe, Lintner, Treynor, and Mossin, and has come to be known as the **Capital Asset Pricing Model** (CAPM).[16]

Under the following assumptions consistent with efficient markets[17]:

1. All investors are risk-averse and maximize their terminal wealth on the basis of expected utility over a single period, choosing among alternative portfolios on the basis of means and standard deviations of returns. Each investor holds a diversified portfolio: the market portfolio.

2. All investors can borrow or lend at the risk-free rate.[18] All investors have identical subjective estimates of the means, variances, and covariances in returns among all assets.

3. All assets are marketable and can be marketed without transactions costs.

4. There are no taxes.

5. All investors are price-takers: they take the price of any or all securities as given—an assumption consistent with perfectly competitive capital markets.

6. The quantities of all assets are given.

7. The rate of inflation is fully anticipated in the expected return.

Hence the market price of the asset is the best estimate of its intrinsic value. Moreover, *the premium a security earns over and above the risk-free rate varies in proportion to its beta coefficient.* For the time being, we shall accept the assumptions underlying the CAPM without further comment and focus our attention on the conclusion.

Consider Figure 5-8. The risk-free rate is *i*. Since there is no covariance with the market, the beta coefficient for the risk-free rate is zero. The beta coefficient for

---

[16] William F. Sharpe. "Capital Asset Prices: A Theory of Market Equilibrium under Risk," *Journal of Finance*, Vol. 19 (September 1964, pp. 425–42). John Lintner. "The Valuation of Risky Assets and the Selection of Risky Investments in Stock Portfolios and Capital Budgets," *Review of Economics and Statistics*, Vol. 47 (February 1965, pp. 13–37). _____. "Security Prices, Risk, and Maximum Gains from Diversification," *Journal of Finance*, Vol. 20 (December 1965, pp. 587–615). Jack L. Treynor. "Towards a Market Value of Risky Assets" (unpublished manuscript, 1961). Jan Mossin. "Equilibrium in a Capital Asset Market," *Econometrica*, Vol. 34 (October 1966, pp. 768–83). For further background into the intellectual development leading to CAPM, see also William F. Sharpe, "A Simplified Model for Portfolio Analysis," *Management Science*, Vol. 9 (January 1963, pp. 277–93).

[17] They follow, with some changes, M. C. Jensen, "Capital Markets: Theory and Evidence," *Bell Journal of Economics and Management Science*, Vol. 3 (Autumn 1972, pp. 358–59).

[18] Also, there are no restrictions on selling securities short: borrowing stock and selling it with the hope of buying it back at a lower price and then returning it to the lender.

Figure 5-8   **The Security Market Line**

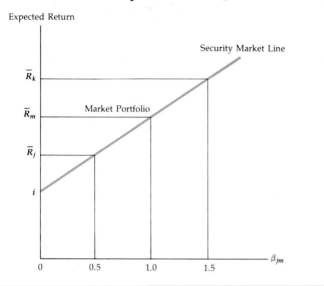

the market portfolio, as we have seen, is 1.0. The expected return is $\bar{R}_m$. The value $(\bar{R}_m - i)$ is the risk premium for holding the market portfolio. According to the CAPM, the expected return on security j is $(\bar{R}_j - i) = \beta_{jm}(\bar{R}_m - i)$.

For securities R_j and R_k, whose beta coefficients are .5 and 1.5 respectively (see Figure 5-8), we obtain

$$(\bar{R}_j - i) = .5(\bar{R}_m - i)$$
$$(\bar{R}_k - i) = 1.5(\bar{R}_m - i)$$

If

$$i = 8\%$$
$$\bar{R}_m = 14\%$$

then for j and k respectively, the returns are

$$(\bar{R}_j - 8\%) = .5(14\% - 8\%)$$
$$\bar{R}_j = 11\%$$
$$(\bar{R}_k - 8\%) = 1.5(14\% - 8\%)$$
$$\bar{R}_k = 17\%$$

The line upon which all investments plot is the **Security Market Line** (SML). Because the market portfolio includes all types of investment opportunities, one could call it the **Investment Market Line**. Since we are confining our discussion to the stock component of the market portfolio, we shall follow convention and use the common term and abbreviation SML.

To state the proposition that the premium on a security is directly related to its beta coefficient can be useful to studying the principles of Modern Portfolio Theory for the first time; to understand why this is the case is another matter. Fortunately, there is a comparatively easy way to explain (under the assumptions made) why the proposition is valid.

Consider security j as an additional investment. To the investor $\bar{R}_j$ must be 14%. Why? Because the investor could create a portfolio from the market and the risk-free rate such that $\beta_p = w(\beta_M) + (1-w)(\beta_i)$, where w is the proportion invested in the market and $1-w$ is the proportion invested at the risk-free rate. Security j has a beta coefficient of .5. As we noted earlier, the beta coefficient of the market portfolio is 1 and the beta coefficient of the risk-free security is zero. To create a portfolio whose beta coefficient is .5, the appropriate weights are

$$.5 = w(1) + (1-w)(0)$$
$$w = .5$$
$$1 - w = .5$$

The expected return $\bar{R}_p$ on this combination is

$$\bar{R}_p = .5(\bar{R}_m) + .5(i)$$
$$\bar{R}_p = .5(14\%) + .5(8\%)$$
$$\bar{R}_p = 11\%$$

Alternatively, 100 percent of the funds could be invested in security j for an expected return of 11 percent.

Consider security k. To earn a 17-percent return, one must borrow at the risk-free rate and invest in the market portfolio so that the beta coefficient for that portfolio is 1.5. Thus

$$1.5 = w(1) + (1-w)(0)$$
$$1.5 = w$$
$$1 - w = -.5$$

In this case, one invests 100 percent of his or her money in the market portfolio and also borrows 50 percent to invest in the market portfolio, so that

$$\bar{R}_p = 1.5(14\%) - .5(8\%)$$
$$\bar{R}_p = 21\% - 4\%$$
$$\bar{R}_p = 17\%$$

Alternatively, one could invest 100 percent of his or her funds in security k.[19]

---

[19] Bear in mind that in the artificial world for which the model holds, there is no stigma to borrowing. The expected return is the same whether one puts 100 percent of the funds in the riskier security k or borrows 50 percent of the funds at the risk-free rate and invests the entire amount in the comparatively less-risky market portfolio.

Consequently, if security k sold at a premium compared to its beta coefficient—its expected return was more than 17 percent—investors would rush to buy it, thereby raising the price and lowering its expected return to 17 percent. Similarly, if the expected return on security k was less than 17 percent, investors would rush to sell it, thereby lowering the price and raising its expected return. A similar argument can be made for security j, ensuring that its expected return will be 14 percent. Since $(\bar{R}_j - i) = \beta_{jm}(\bar{R}_m - i)$, then

$$\beta_{jm} = \frac{(\bar{R}_j - i)}{(\bar{R}_m - i)} \qquad (5\text{-}7)$$

Because the following comments are so important, take an aspirin, prop up your chin with your wrist and elbow, and continue reading.

Equations 5-6 and 5-7 are each expressions for the beta coefficient. In equation 5-6, the rationale was based upon the contribution of a specific security to the market portfolio; it was part of the rationale underlying the SML. Accordingly, Equation 5-7 depends upon the validity of the SML and the assumptions underlying it. Nevertheless, it is Equation 5-7 that provides the basis for calculating systematic risk. The beta coefficients that spew forth from computers of research staffs of brokerage and investment houses are linked to the SML. Recognizing there are variations in practice, let us see how the basic calculations are made.

THE CAPM IN PRACTICE

In Figure 5-9 we suggest the nature of the relationship expressed by SML for securities j, k, and the market portfolio we employed in the previous section. Each of the lines takes the form $y = a + bx$. The equations are shown on the graph. The value for y is the excess return on the security: the risk premiums $(\bar{R}_j - i)$ and $(\bar{R}_k - i)$. The value for x is the excess return (or risk premium) on the market portfolio $(\bar{R}_m - i)$. The slope b is the β coefficient. Because under the SML excess returns on all securities are systematically related to beta, the excess return on any one security—j, k, and so forth—is a function of the excess return on the market portfolio. Consequently, the value for a is zero.

Known as the **characteristic line**, there is such a line for every security and for every portfolio of securities except the market portfolio. For the market portfolio, values of y and x are both $(\bar{R}_m - i)$ and β is one. Characteristic lines of a security whose β is greater than one lie to the left of the characteristic line for the market portfolio; those of a security whose β is less than one lie to the right.

One does not need a Ph.D. in financial economics to take the next step. Raw data necessary to calculate actual (not expected) holding period returns—specifically, market prices and dividends—are readily available. So, too, are yields on treasury bills. What is missing are data on the market portfolio. As a proxy, at least for stocks, the approach is to use changes in a popular index and the dividends on those

Figure 5-9   The Characteristic Line

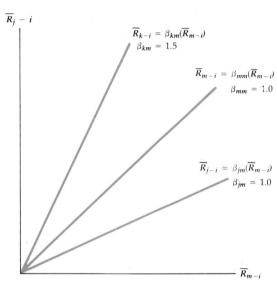

securities in the index. Often the Standard & Poor's 500 (S & P 500) is employed as representative of the market. From such data come historical betas.

The actual procedure for calculating β requires some rudiments of a standard regression model basic to the study of econometrics. Before suggesting what is involved in such a procedure, let us use a hypothetical example based upon equation 5-7:

$$\beta_{jm} = \frac{\bar{R}_j - i}{\bar{R}_m - i}$$

To illustrate, the data in Table 5-1 are the annual holding period returns on security j for ten years. The risk-free rate i we have assumed is the holding period return on a 52-week treasury bill. The holding period return on the market portfolio has been approximated by the holding period return on one of the market indexes. R_j, R_m, and i are then averaged so that

$$\sum_1^{10} R_m = .137 = \bar{R}_m \qquad \sum_1^{10} i = .053 = \bar{i} \qquad \sum_1^{10} R_j = .126 = \bar{R}_j$$

The symbol we have been using for expected return (such as $\bar{R}_j$) is now the symbol for an average historical return.

At the bottom of Table 5-1, we note that $\bar{R}_m - \bar{i} = (\bar{R}_m - \bar{i})$; that is, the average for column 1 minus the average for column 2 equals the average for column 3. The

Table 5-1 Estimating β on Security j

					Column			
1	*2*	*3*	*4*	*5*	*6*	*7*	*8*	*9*
R_m	i	$R_m - i$	R_j	$R_j - i$	$[(R_m - i) -$ $(\bar{R}_m - \bar{i})]$	$[(R_j - i) -$ $(\bar{R}_j - \bar{i})]$	*(column 6)^2*	*(column 6 ×* *column 7)*
Year								
1 .20	.06	.14	.16	.10	.056	.027	.003136	.001512
2 .15	.06	.09	.13	.07	.006	(.003)	.000036	(.000018)
3 .10	.05	.05	.08	.03	(.034)	(.043)	.001156	.001462
4 (.04)	.03	(.07)	(.01)	(.04)	(.154)	(.113)	.023716	.017402
5 .05	.04	.01	.04	.00	(.074)	(.073)	.005476	.005402
6 .10	.05	.05	.11	.06	(.034)	(.013)	.001156	.000442
7 .18	.06	.12	.17	.11	.036	.037	.001296	.001332
8 .21	.06	.15	.19	.13	.066	.057	.004356	.003762
9 .20	.06	.14	.21	.15	.056	.077	.003136	.004312
10 .22	.06	.16	.18	.12	.076	.047	.005776	.003572
Total 1.37	.53	.84	1.26	.73			.049240	.039180

Average $\bar{R}_m - \bar{i} = (\bar{R}_m - \bar{i}); \bar{R}_j - \bar{i} = (\bar{R}_j - \bar{i})$

Return $.137 - .053 = .084; .126 - .053 = .073$

$$\sigma_m^2 = \frac{.049240}{10} = .004924$$

$$COV_{jm} = \frac{.039180}{10} = .003918$$

$$\beta = \frac{.003918}{004924} = .795695$$

same is true for $\bar{R}_j - \bar{i} = (\bar{R}_j - \bar{i})$. Thus, in columns 6 and 7 we subtract $(R_m - i)$ from $(R_m - i)$ and $(\bar{R}_j - \bar{i})$ from $(\bar{R}_j - \bar{i})$ for each of the ten years; that is, we subtract individual observations from their respective average. The results in column 6 are squared in column 8 to obtain the figures necessary to calculate the variance in the market return. Column 6 is multiplied by column 7 in column 9 to obtain the figures necessary to compute the covariance between the return on security j and the return on the market.

Using the total at the base of columns 8 and 9, we have

$$\sigma^2 = \frac{.049240}{10} = .004924$$

$$COV_{jm} = \frac{.039180}{10} = .003918$$

Beta becomes

$$\beta = \frac{.003918}{.004924} = .795695 \approx .796$$

For our hypothetical security, the value of β (.796) suggests that, for every 1-percent change in the excess return on the market portfolio, there will be a .796-percent change in the excess return on the stock. The excess return on a security whose beta is less than one will fall less rapidly than the return on the market portfolio. However, the excess return also will rise less rapidly than the return on the market portfolio. For stocks whose beta is greater than one, the reverse is true. By implication, therefore, we would expect diversified portfolios weighted toward low beta stocks to outperform the market portfolio during periods of falling stock prices. Alternatively, during periods of rising stock prices we would expect the market portfolio to outperform the diversified portfolio weighted toward low beta stocks. The reverse is true for diversified portfolios weighted toward high beta stocks. Portfolios indexed to the market portfolio will perform as the market performs.

Anyone who has sat through (in some cases slept through) presentations by portfolio managers knows that betas for individual securities are part of the quantitative output analyzing the performance of that portfolio. Although in practice the procedure for calculating beta is akin to the arithmetic employed in Table 5-1, the technique is based upon an equation of the form $y = a + bx$, so that using the symbols employed for Table 5-1, $\bar{R}_j = \bar{i} + b(\bar{R}_m - \bar{i}) + e_j$ or $\bar{R}_j - \bar{i} = a + b(\bar{R}_m - \bar{i}) + e_j$. The second form is consistent with the characteristic lines as we have drawn them. In theory, of course, a should be zero: there is no excess return. The term e_j is a random variable whose expected value is zero. In the parlance of econometrics, if $(\bar{R}_j - \bar{i})$ is indeed a function of $(\bar{R}_m - \bar{i})$, then deviations between predicted and actual observations for $R_j - i$ should be random: they should be the result of chance.

Figure 5-10 suggests qualitatively what is involved in the procedure. The points representing observations on $\bar{R}_j - \bar{i}$ and $\bar{R}_m - \bar{i}$ represent successive holding periods. The equation estimated by a line of best fit is calculated from a standard technique known as the *method of least squares* (the procedure is outlined in Appendix 5-A). The line represents an average relationship between the values for $(\bar{R}_j - \bar{i})$ and $(\bar{R}_m - \bar{i})$. Values for a and b can be calculated using this procedure. In keeping with the space age, the slope is called *beta* (β) and the value for a is called *alpha* (α).

If the CAPM holds, the difference between the observed value of alpha and zero is not statistically significant: it is due to chance. On the other hand, the difference between the actual value of beta and zero should be positive. Otherwise, $(\bar{R}_j - \bar{i})$ is not a function of $(\bar{R}_m - \bar{i})$ and the CAPM is not confirmed. Finally, the actual values for $(\bar{R}_j - \bar{i})$ and $(\bar{R}_m - \bar{i})$ will depart from the line of average relationship but should not do so in a systematic way.

Figure 5-10   The Characteristic Line—An Empirical Representation

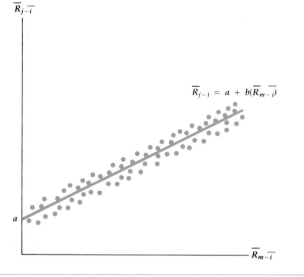

Texts in econometrics describe in detail the techniques and the pitfalls of regression analysis.[20] Suffice it to say that beta calculations are routine outputs of many financial firms. Selected betas and standard deviations of holding period returns from one reporting source for fourth-quarter 1981 are shown in Table 5-2, together with the beta and standard deviation of the Standard & Poor's *500 Composite Index*. As the footnotes to Table 5-2 indicate, the statistical relationships are based upon monthly holding period returns over the preceding 60-month period, a common practice among securities firms. In this instance, the stock of each firm is widely known; each is also included in the S & P 500.

Let us examine the beta for IBM. If the market is generally declining, according to the historical relationship, the return on IBM should be higher than the return on the S & P 500. If the market is generally rising, the return on the market portfolio should be greater than the return on IBM. For first-quarter 1982, the holding period return on IBM was 8.93 percent. The return on the S & P 500 was −2.43 percent. The YTM on a 3-month treasury bill issued December 31, 1981, was 2.98 percent.[21]

---

[20] See, for example, Paul Wonnacott and Thomas A. Wonnacott, *Econometrics*, 2nd ed. (New York: John Wiley & Sons, 1979).

[21] Calculations based on data from the *Wall Street Journal*, Standard & Poor's *Outlook*, and the *U. S. Treasury Bulletin*. The YTM on the treasury bill was calculated using the procedure developed in Chapter 3, but left as a quarterly rate.

Table 5-2   **Selected Betas and Standard Deviations (fourth-quarter 1981)**

Company	Beta[a]	σ[b]
Boeing	1.40	51%
Gillette	0.74	24%
International Business Machines	0.76	19%
J. C. Penney	0.68	30%
Ramada Inns	1.78	56%
Texaco	1.19	28%
(*S & P Composite Index* average	1.0	16%)

[a] Computed by a regression of monthly historical holding period returns for a stock against the monthly historical returns for the Standard & Poor's *500 Composite Index* over the same period (historical returns generally based on most recent 60 months).
[b] Calculated as a deviation on the annual return of a stock computed from monthly total return data for the past 60 months.
SOURCE: Suresh L. Bhivud. *Quantitative Perspective* (New York: First Boston Corporation, December 1981).

On December 31, 1981, one knew the risk-free rate anticipated for a 91-day holding period. One did not, however, know the return on the S & P 500. Assume the forecast was −2.43 percent, the actual outcome. The predicted return on IBM would be

$$R_{IBM} - i = b(R_m - i)$$
$$R_{IBM} - 2.98 = .76(-2.43 - 2.98)$$
$$R_{IBM} = 2.98 - 4.11$$
$$= -1.13\%$$

The predicted return on IBM fell short of the actual return. Although in this instance the actual return was understated, in other cases it could be overstated. Even if we had used a more refined technique, a substantial difference between prediction and actual outcome would come as no surprise to many.[22] In the first place, because the model is based upon expected and not actual returns, the historical relationships need not hold in the future. Secondly, the actual relationships between individual observations of $(R_m - i)$ and $(R_j - i)$ can be very unstable, similar to what is depicted in Figure 5-11(a) and (b). As one moves through time, new observations are replacing old observations and altering the values of both alpha and beta for a

---

[22] If IBM had experienced a positive alpha, for example, one must add this to −1.13 percent. The particular report cited in Table 5-2 did not report alphas. Rather, it relied upon a variation of the fundamental model developed in Chapter 3 to predict the return for 1982. The prediction was 19 percent. The holding period return for 1982, based upon year-end closing prices, was $\dfrac{96.25 - 56.375 + 3.44}{56.375} = 76.83\%$ (See Table 3-4).

The report greatly underestimated the performance of IBM for the year.

Figure 5-11   Comparative Stability of Portfolio and Security Betas

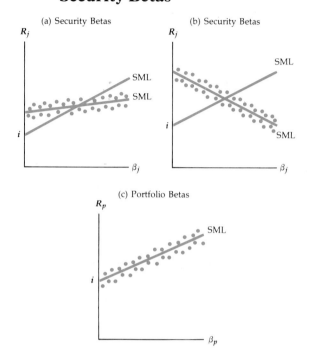

(a) Security Betas

(b) Security Betas

(c) Portfolio Betas

60-month period. Each can change rapidly and be subject to a high degree of statistical error. For individual securities, beta and alpha are often highly unstable. At the same time, for reasons not fully understood, portfolio betas exhibit greater stability than betas of individual securities. As a rule, portfolio betas tend to arrange themselves as the SML suggests [see Figure 5-11(c)].[23]

Not only do betas of individual securities fluctuate wildly—particularly over short periods of time—but the statistical line of average relationship has a flatter slope than is suggested by theory [see SML in Figure 5-11(b)]. As a result, securities with relatively low betas may have positive alphas $(\bar{R}_j - \bar{i})$ statistically significant while securities with relatively high betas may have alphas closer to zero or even negative. Low beta securities are overcompensated and high beta securities

[23] See Marshall Blume, "On Assessment of Risk," *Journal of Finance*, Vol. 26 (March 1972, pp. 1–10); M. C. Jensen, ed., *Studies in the Theory of Capital Markets* (New York: Frederick A. Praeger, 1972); E. F. Fama and J. D. MacBeth, "Risk, Return and Equilibrium: Empirical Tests," *Journal of Political Economy*, Vol. 81 (May 1973, pp. 607–36); Burton G. Malkiel, "Risk and Return: A New Look," in Benjamin M. Friedman, ed., *The Changing Rates of Debt and Equity in U.S. Capital Formation* (Chicago: University of Chicago Press, 1982, pp. 27–45).

undercompensated for risk. Indeed, in some short-run periods, the risk premium decreases with increases in beta [see Figure 5-11(b)]. The evidence, as it pertains to individual securities, is not consistent with the theory. Indeed, it is at times the reverse of what theory predicts![24]

RELAXING THE ASSUMPTIONS

By design, models are unrealistic; they must be to capture the essence of the phenomena one seeks to explain. Scientists often use models based on the assumption the process under study takes place in a vacuum. The real world is not a vacuum. We know the time necessary for an object to fall from the top of the Sears Tower in Chicago to the street below will be affected by air resistance. In the case of a shot put, the effect is negligible; in the case of a feather, it is not.

Natural scientists can often modify a model to take account of factors that have been assumed away; similar efforts by social scientists are often less successful. Nevertheless, by relaxing some assumptions, we may better understand not only why empirical evidence is not as robust as one would hope but also where fruitful areas of further research might lie.

THE BORROWING AND THE LENDING RATE

What happens when we allow the borrowing rate to exceed the lending rate? From Figure 5-12(a), it is apparent the CML drawn from the risk-free rate i to the frontier is now tangent to portfolio P, while the CML drawn from the lending rate L to the frontier is tangent at P'. Under these conditions, the CML includes a curved segment whose end points are P and P'. Those holding lending portfolios would invest in portfolio P; those holding borrowing portfolios would invest in portfolio P'.

If the market portfolio lies between P and P', it is possible for both borrowers and lenders to hold it.[25] To do so, investors would create from risky securities a portfolio whose beta is zero. A line drawn from Z in Figure 5-12(a) and tangent to the market portfolio can be interpreted in the same way as the Capital Market Line was

---

[24] *A Bonus Footnote!*   Before you rush to ask your broker for a list of all stocks with positive alphas, remember that others play the same game. The stock with a low beta and a high alpha today may be the stock with a high beta and a low alpha next month. In efficient markets, this is what one should expect. Investors would rush to buy securities whose risk premiums are not compensatory, thereby bidding up the price and the *actual* holding period return. If the excess return rises relative to the excess return on the market portfolio, the computed beta also will rise. The best approach is to find out what has happened to stocks with positive alphas. Did they subsequently outperform the market? Or was there no discernable trend in evidence?

[25] If there were no restrictions on short sales (selling stock one does not own in the expectation of buying it back at a lower price), the market portfolio would plot between P and P'. For further analysis, see Fischer Black, "Capital Market Equilibrium with Restricted Borrowing," *Journal of Business*, Vol. 45 (July 1972, pp. 444–54). See also Richard Roll, "Orthogonal Portfolio," *Journal of Financial and Quantitative Analysis*, Vol. 15 (December 1980, pp. 1005–11).

Figure 5-12   The CML and SML for a Zero Beta Portfolio

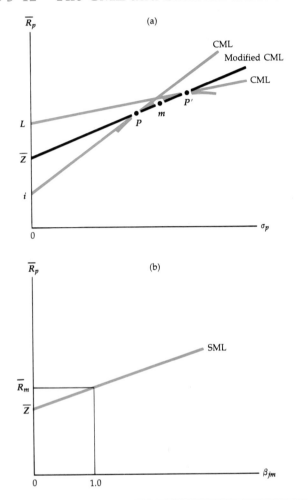

originally drawn. The difference is that the y intercept is above the risk-free rate. In the usual manner, one can plot the SML [Figure 5-12(b)]. The slope of the SML line, however, is based upon $(\bar{R}_j - \bar{Z})$ and $(\bar{R}_m - \bar{Z})$, where $\bar{Z} > \bar{\imath}$. The slope of this SML is, therefore, flatter than the SML pictured in Figure 5-8.

Known as the **zero beta portfolio**, it has one pleasing result of substituting $\bar{Z}$ for $\bar{\imath}$ so that the flatter SML is often more consistent with the actual holding period returns, thereby eliminating many of the positive alphas suggested by Figure 5-11(a). Unlike the yield on a treasury bill, however, the zero beta portfolio cannot be found in the newspapers; it must be inferred from the information on stock returns. If one is not careful, the empirical results can be self-serving. What we know is that the borrowing rate differs from the lending rate. The zero beta portfolio makes it possible to reconcile these differences in rates and, therefore, to maintain the SML and the characteristic lines of each security. Empirically, however, the zero beta portfolio can be elusive.

TAXES

Income taxes, unfortunately, are a fact of life. What is fortunate, at least, is that in this area income taxes are less complex in 1988 than prior to 1987, when federal law made a major distinction between income in the form of dividends or interest and income from selling an investment at a profit. In Chapter 11, when we discuss dividend policy, we develop this distinction. For now, we need only note that the imposition of income taxes will lower the actual return. Although taxes are paid in the year income is received, if the market price of the stock has risen over what the investor paid for the shares, no taxes are due unless the security is sold. To illustrate, suppose during a holding period the stock of XYZ corporation rises from $50 to $60 per share and a $2.00 dividend is paid. If the investor who paid $50 per share for the stock does not sell it and has a marginal tax rate of 28 percent, the holding period return after taxes is

$$HPR = \frac{\$60 - \$50 + \$2.00(1 - .28)}{\$50}$$

$$HPR = \frac{\$10 + \$1.44}{\$50}$$

$$HPR = .2288 \times 100 = 22.88\%$$

If the investor sells the stock at the end of the holding period, the return after taxes is

$$HPR = \frac{(\$60 - \$50 + \$2.00)(1 - .28)}{\$50}$$

$$HPR = .1728 \times 100 = 17.28\%$$

Each result compares with an *HPR* before considering taxes of

$$HPR = \frac{\$60 - \$50 + \$2.00}{\$50}$$

$$HPR = .24 \times 100 = 24\%$$

It is, of course, after-tax returns that guide individual investment decisions. Much empirical work, however, is based upon before-tax returns.

OTHER ASSUMPTIONS

One can relax the other assumptions and modify the CAPM to some extent. For example, the expected holding period return is based upon a nominal risk-free rate and hence upon the real return plus an inflation premium. If there is unanticipated inflation, it may not have a systematic impact upon all securities. Investors may not be risk-averse nor maximize their satisfaction as the models suggest. They may not hold diversified portfolios. In addition, investors may not have identical expectations about the future. Transaction costs do exist and some investments do not have a well-developed market. Capital markets may not be perfectly competitive. The quantity of assets available may not be fixed.

Space does not permit a detailed evaluation of these assumptions; a few comments, however, are in order. In some cases, one can modify the assumptions fairly easily. Transaction costs, for instance, do affect holding period returns. The price paid is net of brokerage commissions and one pays an additional commission to realize any capital gains. In other cases, the assumptions are palpably unrealistic. Investors do not have identical subjective estimates of the means, variances, and covariances in returns among all assets. If, however, there is an expected estimate (the deviations from which are normally distributed), models will hold within the framework of errors due to chance.

THE MARKET PORTFOLIO

In the summer of 1980, a major practitioner's journal ran a cover story entitled "Is Beta Dead?"[26] The story was followed by a commentary on the article in the financial press.[27] In 1977, Richard Roll published a major critique of the CAPM tests that had helped stimulate the interest of practitioners.[28] A major criticism concerned the proxies to measure the market index. For example, the S & P 500, the most popular measure, was not necessarily the most efficient index—it was not on the frontier. Positive or negative alphas for individual securities could, therefore, be partly the result of a poor benchmark.

From the practitioner's point of view, the criticism could be damaging. At the time, perhaps one-third of U.S. pension fund managers used the CAPM as the

---

[26] Artise Wallace. "Is Beta Dead?" *Institutional Investor*, Vol. 14 (July 1980, pp. 23–30).

[27] Paul Blustein. "Money Managers' Bedrock Theory of Investing Comes under Attack," *Wall Street Journal* (September 8, 1980, p. 32).

[28] Richard Roll. "A Critique of the Asset Theory Tests," *Journal of Financial Economics*, Vol. 4 (March 1977, pp. 124–76). See also Richard Roll, "Performance Evaluation and Benchmark Errors," *Journal of Portfolio Management*, Vol. 6 (Summer 1980, pp. 5–12).

central framework for selecting and maintaining securities in their portfolios. In addition, index funds were sold on the assumption that if one could not beat the market, then one could buy it. Index funds were weighted in proportion to the S & P 500. These unmanaged portfolios would move with the market: they would have a beta of 1.0. Because there was little trading, profits would not be nibbled away by brokerage commissions. Yet, if the S & P 500 was not fully reflective of the market, it could underperform more diversified portfolios.

Although people knowledgeable both of security management in theory and practice understood the pitfalls of employing an unrepresentative market index, many in the investment community had always been skeptical of relying on MPT as the basis for professional management of securities.[29] In human terms, the skepticism is understandable. No one—whether fund manager, production-line worker, or diagnostic physician—wants to believe such skills can be programmed and the decisions routinely made by computer. At a philosophical level lies the issue of the purpose of MPT: Is it designed to explain how efficient markets work or is it applicable to real-world markets? We return to this latter point in the chapter summary.

In the meantime, bear in mind, the foundations upon which MPT was built rose from insight by Markowitz: he observed that portfolios were diversified and showed how diversification led one to optimize between risk and return. Subsequent developments in theory have served to underscore the importance of developing a market portfolio. Although a portfolio that includes all investable wealth may be difficult to assemble, one that goes beyond the domestic stocks of the S & P 500 and the bonds of established corporations to include real estate, international securities, small domestic companies, and other types of instruments is certainly comprehensive. Moreover, it is a portfolio that may lead to greater diversification and hence to an upward shift in the efficient frontier. Students of the subject—such as Brinson and Diermier, as well as Ibbotson, Siegel, and Schlarbaum—have worked on this challenge.[30] The result is a composite index, in this instance tailored to the needs of pension funds. Because the index depends on international diversification, we shall reserve further comment until Chapter 22, where we discuss the principles of finance in an international context. Such an index, however, does represent the interplay of theory and practice leading ultimately to a better understanding of what constitutes a feasible market portfolio.

---

[29] See, for example, Stanford Calderwood, "The Truth about Funds," *Financial Analysts Journal*, Vol. 32 (July–August 1977, pp. 36–47). Rex Sinquefield, who introduced the index fund to the financial community, was well aware of the limitations of the S & P 500. See *Wall Street Journal* (September 18, 1979, p. 6).

[30] Gary P. Brinson, Jeffrey J. Diermier, and Gary A. Schlarbaum. "A Composite Portfolio Benchmark for Pension Plans," *Financial Analysts Journal*, Vol. 42. (March–April 1986, pp. 15–24). Roger C. Ibbotson and L. B. Siegel. "The World Market Portfolio," *Journal of Portfolio Management*, Vol. 9 (Winter 1983, pp. 5–17).

ARBITRAGE PRICING THEORY

The fact that the market index or indexes employed in practice may be less than satisfactory is not necessarily a reason for rejecting the CAPM. The fault lies not with the theory but with the practice. The market portfolio should contain all investments—real as well as financial, national as well as international. As suggested earlier, the SML is truly an Investment Market Line in a global context. One can object to the realism of the approach but not to the concept.

From a different perspective, however, the CAPM can be seen as a self-contained system. A single investment is related to the market portfolio; yet this single investment helps determine the total risk of the portfolio. To be sure, its contribution may be so small it can be ignored. Nevertheless, the expected return on any security is related to the expected return on a portfolio of which it is a part.

One might, therefore, do as Ross has done and approach the issue from a different perspective.[31] Briefly, suppose we postulate that the total risk all investments face can be broken into several components—such as expectations about future inflation, level of interest rates, level of national income, and the like. The returns on all securities are related to these several but limited number of components. Other factors, such as changes in the defense budget, may affect specific securities but not all. These and similar risk components may be mitigated through diversification.

To continue with the logic of the approach, assume there are three identifiable factors to which the expected return of each security can be related. If we call these factors 1, 2, and 3, the expected $\bar{R}_j$ is

$$E(R_j) = \bar{R}_j = a + b\beta_{j1} + c\beta_{j2} + d\beta_{j3} \qquad (5\text{-}9)$$

where β_{j1}, β_{j2}, and β_{j3} measure the sensitivity of the return of security j to the common factors 1, 2, and 3; and a, b, c, and d are constants.

Suppose there are n securities that have identical sensitivities with respect to factors 1 and 3; they differ only as to their sensitivity with respect to factor 2. Let us examine five of these securities: j, k, l, m, and q. Can they plot as suggested in Figure 5-13? Given the assumptions made, the answer is "no." Although security m has a higher return than security k, security m appears to show the same sensitivity to factor β_2 as does security k. Similarly, the expected return on security q is below the return for security j even though security q appears to have the same sensitivity to factor β_2 as security k. If so, then in perfect capital markets one could

[31] Stephen A. Ross. "The Arbitrage Theory of Capital Asset Pricing," *Journal of Economic Theory*, Vol. 13 (December 1976, pp. 341–60). See also Richard Roll and Stephen A. Ross, "An Empirical Investigation of the Arbitrage Pricing Theory," *Journal of Finance*, Vol. 35 (December 1980, pp. 1073–1103); Burton G. Malkiel, "Risk and Return: A New Look," in Friedman, pp. 37–45.

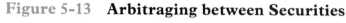

Figure 5-13   **Arbitraging between Securities**

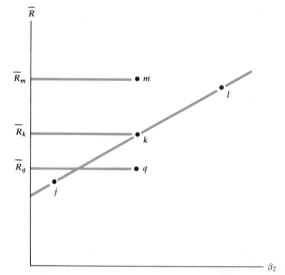

arbitrage the two stocks, simultaneously buying stock m and selling stock q short. The residual $\bar{R}_m - \bar{R}_q$ represents arbitrage profits that result from these transactions.

How can this be? Consider the classic definition of arbitrage—simultaneously buying and selling the same commodity in two different markets. Thus, if gold was selling at the equivalent of $300 an ounce in Zurich and $305 an ounce in London (ignoring transaction costs), one could simultaneously buy 100 ounces in Zurich and sell 100 ounces in London at a profit of $5 per ounce. Similarly, if AT&T was selling at $55 per share on the New York Stock Exchange and $56 per share on the Midwest Stock Exchange, one could sell 100 shares short on the Midwest Stock Exchange, covering the sale with 100 shares purchased on the New York Stock Exchange.

Arbitrage Pricing Theory (APT) makes use of the concept in a subtle way. In terms of Figure 5-13, the price today P_0 of stock q is too high relative to stock k, which is properly priced in terms of its sensitivity to β_2. Similarly, the P_0 for stock m is too low. Nevertheless, arbitrage profits can be earned. One sells stock q short and buys stock m. As others engage in similar transactions, the price of stock q falls and the price of stock m rises. The expected holding period return on stock m falls to the expected holding period return for stock k, while the expected holding period return for stock q rises to the expected holding period return for stock k.[32]

---

[32] Since for stock q the P_0 before arbitrage is greater than the P_0 after arbitrage, the denominator in the equation for expected holding period return falls, thereby raising the expected return. Since the P_0 before arbitrage is less than the P_0 after arbitrage for stock m, the denominator is larger and the expected holding period return falls. The expected holding

As constructed, the one who arbitrages earns a profit in terms of expected return represented by $(\bar{R}_m - \bar{R}_q)$. The profit is first based upon the gains made from selling stock m after its price has risen and its expected holding period return has fallen to $\bar{R}_m - \bar{R}_k$. The remainder comes from covering the short sale on stock q whose price has fallen, which creates profit $\bar{R}_k - \bar{R}_q$ from buying and from returning to the lender stock purchased for less than it is sold.[33]

Through the Arbitrage process, investors in competitive markets ensure that the returns on each security are systematically related to each factor. The expected return on each security would equal the return on the risk-free rate, plus the risk premiums the market attaches to each factor. For our purposes, in Figure 5-13 security l is more sensitive to factor β_2 than either security k or j; each, however, is properly priced with respect to that factor. Nevertheless, a higher proportion of security l's expected return is due more to factor β_2 than is the case for either security k or j. In our simplified presentation, $c\beta_{l2} > c\beta_{k2} > c\beta_{j2}$. Suppose factor β_2 is expected inflation. Then security j is less sensitive than security l to inflationary expectations.

Since what is knowable at any point in time is incorporated in the expected return, the actual return will differ from expected return because of unexpected changes in the factors affecting those returns. To again illustrate using inflationary expectations, because the return on stock l is sensitive to anticipated inflation, presumably its return would be sensitive to unanticipated changes in inflation. Prices of shares of public utilities are notoriously sensitive to changes in the price level. During the 1970s, as actual rates of inflation were exceeding anticipated rates of inflation, total returns on public utility shares fell. Even though betas on such shares are generally less than one, total returns are often lower than total returns on an index of stocks.[34] When the inflationary pattern reversed itself in the early 1980s, returns on utilities tended to lead returns on the market.

Arbitrage Pricing Theory functions on the proposition that the difference between actual and expected returns is due to unexpected changes in factors to which securities are particularly sensitive. But what are the factors and why are they

---

period return on stock k is the terminal point for the arbitrage process. At this point, the expected return on stocks m and q are in direct proportion to their sensitivity to β_2. Because all stocks along the line differ only with respect to their sensitivity to this factor, each is properly priced in relation to the others.

[33] Suppose only a single stock, q, was improperly priced. One could still arbitrage either against k or a combination of securities j and l, for example, weighted so their combined sensitivities were equal to the sensitivity of stock k to β_2. One sells stock q short and buys stock k or some combination of j and l. Since there are n properly priced securities along the lines, one does not expect prices to rise as purchases are spread among them. The arbitrage profits come from buying back stock q at a lower price. The purpose of simultaneously selling short and buying k or some combination is to lock in the profits: to create the perfect hedge. From the proceeds of the short sale, one earns the expected return on k. The arbitrage profits are $\bar{R}_k - \bar{R}_q$.

[34] The scenario is straightforward. Utilities borrow heavily and their prices can only be increased by regulatory commissions. Nominal rates of interest rise with inflation. New or renewed borrowings must be financed at higher rates. Commissions are reluctant to pass on increases to consumers. The resulting *regulatory lag* also works in the opposite direction as nominal rates of interest fall during periods of declining inflationary expectations.

important? To date, Roll and Ross have identified what appear to be four factors that over a long period of time explain the difference between actual and expected returns. Whether they will continue to do so is a moot point. The four factors affecting stocks are *unanticipated changes* in:[35]

1. inflation
2. industrial production
3. risk premiums between high-quality and low-quality debt instruments
4. yields on short- and longer-term debt securities

Factors 1 and 2 require no elaboration. Factor 3 is also known as the structure of risk premiums at any point in time, with risk interpreted to mean the chance for default. Thus, debtholders of IBM are virtually assured of payment of principal and interest when due; those of the Four Star Sand and Gravel Corporation may face greater risk. Such risk is reflected in the relatively lower yield on debt instruments of comparable maturity issued by IBM. Factor 4 holds the risk level constant but varies the term structure of debt. Consequently, there can be an unanticipated change in the yield differential between U.S. Treasury bills and longer-term federal debt.

To date, the jury is still out on whether APT will replace CAPM. The former may require additional theoretical justification for the factors identified. Moreover, no one is certain the factors will hold up over time: others may replace them. APT, however, does strike a chord. CAPM may well mask what is a far more complex explanation of what underlies the expected return on a security. APT, which suggests a multiple rather than a single variable analysis, appears to be the direction of future research. Nevertheless, our primary concern is with the principles of finance, and for all of its weaknesses, CAPM can provide insights into the subject worth pursuing. Hence, we shall continue to rely upon CAPM as we extend our analysis.

SUMMARY

Lyndon Johnson was fond of saying that in politics one must often settle for half a loaf. As a set of propositions that attempts to explain how an investor can maximize return consistent with his or her willingness to bear risk, Modern Portfolio Theory represents at least half a loaf and possibly more.

Perhaps the least controversial of the propositions discussed in this chapter is the concept of diversification. It is worth reiterating that Markowitz and Tobin gave substance to a practice widely employed in the investment community but only

---

[35] Richard Roll and Stephen A. Ross. "The Arbitrage Pricing Theory Approach to Strategic Portfolio Planning," *Financial Analysts Journal*, Vol. 40 (May–June 1984, pp. 14–16).

intuitively understood. From our discussion of the variance–covariance matrix, we know it is possible (when the coefficient of correlation between pairs of securities is less than one) to reduce the standard deviation of the portfolio by increasing the number of securities in it. In principle, one should be able to extend that matrix to include all possible investment opportunities—real as well as financial. In practice, of course, this is impractical. Nevertheless, one can diversify among securities, commodities (gold, silver, and the like), and real estate.

A fully diversified portfolio may lie on or near the frontier of the opportunity set. There is, however, the issue of how to resolve the trade-off between risk and return inherent in all portfolios that lie along the frontier. As demonstrated in this chapter, the Capital Market Line (CML) connecting the risk-free rate to a point of tangency along the frontier offers the opportunity to maximize individual investor satisfaction, by allocating funds between investments earning the risk-free rate and the market portfolio.

Since the market portfolio is fully diversified, its unsystematic risk is minimal; what remains is systematic risk. To measure systematic risk, one calculates the degree to which the return on an individual investment covaries with the return on the market portfolio. The result is known as the beta coefficient. The expected return on any security is a function of the beta coefficient. The graphical representation of this function is called the Security Market Line (SML). The beta for the market portfolio is one. The betas of those securities whose returns rise or fall more than the return on the market are greater than one. The betas of those securities whose returns rise or fall less than the return on the market are less than one.

A convenient way of measuring the beta coefficient is to correlate the expected excess return on an investment $(\bar{R}_j - \bar{\imath})$ with the expected excess return on the market portfolio $(\bar{R}_M - \bar{\imath})$. Known as the characteristic line, it is found when one correlates actual excess returns on a security with actual excess returns on the market portfolio. Beta coefficients, therefore, are part of the quantitative output of many security firms.

The SML and characteristic lines comprise the basis of the Capital Asset Pricing Model (CAPM). The relationship between the excess return on a security and the market portfolio maintains itself under a rigorous set of assumptions that include the absence of taxes, no differences between the borrowing and lending rates, risk-averse investors holding the market portfolio, and efficient capital markets. Empirical results, however, are not always consistent with the theory. The y intercept (or alpha), which should be zero, can be positive or negative. In short-run periods, the SML is sometimes negatively sloped. Portfolio betas, however, tend to conform (broadly) with the anticipated relationship between expected return and systematic risk. When some of the assumptions are relaxed—when one allows for differences in the lending and borrowing rates and in the tax treatment of dividends and capital gains—some of the anomalies in the empirical results are at least partially resolved.

Yet many practitioners are uncomfortable with the model. Although progress has been made toward a more complete measure of the market portfolio, indices employed as proxies for the market may not even lie on the investment frontier. The assumption of risk-aversion places a behavioral constraint on the model that might be eliminated. One alternative to CAPM is Arbitrage Pricing Theory. In diversified portfolios, returns on securities are a function of a few macroeconomic variables. With APT, securities are related to these variables and hence to one another in a systematic way. Investors arbitrage any security whose return is too low or too high relative to the return on other securities. Whether the factors thus far identified provide a better explanation of the return on a security than the simple CAPM awaits further empirical work.

Consequently, whether Arbitrage Pricing Theory succeeds or supplements the CAPM remains to be seen. Each, however, depends on a concept of efficient capital markets, the criteria for which are adumbrated at the beginning of the chapter. In efficient markets, the current market price of an investment is the best estimate of the present value of its future income stream. If all relevant information pertaining to such an investment is not uniformly available to all investors, the current market price is not the best estimate of its present value. The investment is inefficiently priced and expected holding period returns are inaccurate, not representative of the security in relation to others or to the market portfolio.

In the real world of investments, it is likely that information affecting returns on widely held securities (shares of IBM, for example) is quickly disseminated. In an absolute sense, the current market price of IBM may be an efficient price for that security. There may, however, be other investments for which information is not widely distributed; indeed, there may not be a well-developed market at all.

Because some of the tenets of Modern Portfolio Theory hold only under the assumption of efficient capital markets, a portfolio manager might conclude that this and other restrictive assumptions circumscribing the CAPM render the concepts ineffective as operational models. To take this position, however, is to miss a major point. Modern Portfolio Theory offers a long-term investment philosophy, not a short-run decision-making model. As theory and empirical evidence suggest, return is ultimately related to risk. Consequently, as a broad explanation of how prices and (ultimately) returns on investments are determined, Modern Portfolio Theory offers a great deal to practitioners of the art of investing. Short-term strategies, if successful, may still depend upon innate ability, experience, and luck. The nexus between theory and practice may never be so complete as to substitute a model for informed judgment at any given time.

THE STANDARD DEVIATION OF A PORTFOLIO

$$\text{Let } w_j \equiv \text{portfolio weight for security } j$$
$$w_k \equiv \text{portfolio weight for security } k$$
$$w_j = w_k$$
$$\text{Let } R_p \equiv \text{actual return on portfolio}$$
$$\bar{R}_p \equiv \text{expected value of portfolio}$$
$$\sigma_p^2 \equiv \text{variance in portfolio}$$

Then $\sigma_p^2 = E(R_p - \bar{R}_p)^2$, where $E(R_p - \bar{R}_p)^2$ designates the expected value of $R_p - \bar{R}_p$ squared.

Suppose we have two stocks, j and k. The stocks are combined in pairs and summed over all possible pairs of returns. Then, beginning with stock j

$$\sigma_p^2 = E\left(\sum_{j=1}^{N} w_j R_j - \sum_{j=1}^{N} w_j \bar{R}_j \right)^2$$
$$= E\left[\left(\sum_{j=1}^{N} w_j R_j \right)^2 - 2\left(\sum_{j=1}^{N} w_j R_j \right)\left(\sum_{j=1}^{N} w_j \bar{R}_j \right) + \left(\sum_{j=1}^{N} w_j \bar{R}_j \right)^2 \right]$$
$$= E\left[\sum_{j=1}^{N} w_j^2 R_j^2 - 2 \sum_{j=1}^{N} w_j^2 R_j \bar{R}_j + \sum_{j=1}^{N} w_j^2 \bar{R}_j^2 \right]$$

Introducing stock k and carrying out the summation over the pairs of returns, we have (ignoring for simplification $j = 1$ and N)

$$\sigma_p^2 = E[\sum w_j^2 R_j^2 + \sum w_j R_j \sum w_k R_k - 2 \sum w_j^2 R_j \bar{R}_j - \sum w_j R_j \sum w_k \bar{R}_k$$
$$- \sum w_j \bar{R}_j \sum w_k R_k + \sum w_j^2 \bar{R}_j^2 + \sum w_j \bar{R}_j \sum w_k \bar{R}_k]$$

Rearranging the terms

$$\sigma_p^2 = E[(\sum w_j^2 R_j^2 - 2 \sum w_j^2 R_j \bar{R}_j + \sum w_j^2 \bar{R}_j^2) + (\sum \sum w_j w_k R_j R_k$$
$$- \sum w_j R_j \sum w_k \bar{R}_k - \sum w_j \bar{R}_j \sum w_k R_k + \sum \sum w_j w_k \bar{R}_j \bar{R}_k)]$$

As the weights are constant, we can again rearrange so that

$$\sigma_p^2 = \sum w_j^2 [E(R_j - \bar{R}_j)^2] + \sum w_j w_k E[(R_j - \bar{R}_j)(R_k - \bar{R}_k)]$$

Since $E[(R_j - \bar{R}_j)^2]$ equals σ_j^2 and $E[(R_j - \bar{R}_j)(R_k - \bar{R}_k)]$ equals COV_{jk}, then (reintroducing $j = 1$ and N)

$$\sigma_p^2 = \sum_{j=1}^{N} w_j^2 \sigma_j^2 + \sum_{j=1}^{N} \sum_{k=1}^{N} w_j w_k \text{COV}_{jk}$$

Because the variance in the rate of return on any stock j is essentially the covariance between the return and itself, we can replace σ_j^2 with COV_{jj} and condense the expression to

$$\sigma_p^2 = \sum_{j=1}^{N} \sum_{k=1}^{N} w_j w_k \text{COV}_{jk}$$

As COV_{jk} also equals $r_{jk}\sigma_j\sigma_k$, we also have

$$\sigma_p^2 = \sum_{j=1}^{N} \sum_{k=1}^{N} w_j w_k r_{jk} \sigma_j \sigma_k$$

$$\sigma_p = \sqrt{\sum_{j=1}^{N} \sum_{k=1}^{N} w_j w_k r_{jk} \sigma_j \sigma_k}$$

In the case of a two-stock portfolio, j and k would covary with themselves as well as with one another. Then

$$w_j w_j r_{jj} \sigma_j \sigma_j = w_j^2 \sigma_j^2$$
$$w_k w_k r_{kk} \sigma_k \sigma_k = w_k^2 \sigma_k^2$$

Consequently, $\sigma_j^2 = w_j^2 \sigma_j^2 + 2 w_j w_k \text{COV}_{jk} + w_k^2 \sigma_k^2$.

FUNDAMENTALS OF REGRESSION ANALYSIS

The essence of regression analysis is to establish an empirical relationship between a dependent variable, such as the return on stock Y, and one or more independent variables, such as the return on a portfolio representative of the market. Since one can establish an empirical relationship among any set of variables, it is important to derive an analytical framework that suggests why the relationship should exist. We developed such a framework in the text of this chapter for the relationship between residual return on a stock and residual return on the market portfolio: the respective returns on each after subtracting the risk-free rate. In this appendix, we develop the most widely used technique for estimating such a relationship, *least squares regression*.

In the first two columns of Table 5-3, we show excess returns for ten periods for stock Y and the market portfolio. This relationship is portrayed graphically in

Table 5-3   Excess Return on the Market Portfolio and on Stock *Y*

Period	*Excess Return on the Market Portfolio* R_p	*Excess Return on Stock Y* R_y	$R_p R_y$	R_p^2
1	.14	.13	.0182	.0196
2	.10	.09	.0090	.0100
3	.01	.04	.0004	.0001
4	.13	.12	.0156	.0169
5	.09	.10	.0090	.0081
6	.10	.10	.0100	.0100
7	.04	.06	.0024	.0016
8	.12	.14	.0168	.0144
9	.05	.06	.0030	.0025
10	.02	.03	.0006	.0004
Total	*.80*	*.87*	*.0850*	*.0836*

Figure 5-14. As the analytical treatment in the text of this chapter suggests, there appears to be a linear relationship between the observed return on stock *Y* and on the market portfolio. Moreover, as shown in Figure 5-14, this relationship is expressed by the equation $R_y = .024 + .786 R_p$. To derive this equation from the data, we chose the line that minimizes

$$\sum_{i=1}^{N} (R_{yi} - \hat{R}_{yi})^2$$

The term $\hat{R}_{yi}$ is read "*R* hat sub *yi*" and stands for the value of R_y estimated by using the regression line suggested in Figure 5-14. The term *least squares regression analysis* is employed to describe the foregoing expression. The reason for using this formulation is part of statistical theory and beyond the scope of this discussion.[37] Nevertheless, an intuitive reason for employing it lies, first, in the fact that the more remote $\hat{R}_{yi}$ is from R_{yi}, the poorer the *fit* and hence the poorer the equation as an explanation of the relationship between R_y and R_p. This is true whether the difference between R_y and R_p is positive or negative. As there are deviations both above and below the line, the sum of the differences would be small. By squaring each term, we avoid the canceling effect of positive and negative values. Second, squaring the term gives greater weight to greater distances between $\hat{R}_{yi}$ and R_{yi}.

---

[37] For a more complete explanation, see, for example, John E. Freund, *Mathematical Statistics* (Englewood Cliffs, NJ: Prentice-Hall, 1962, pp. 314–25) and later editions. See also Robert Pindyck and Daniel L. Rubenfeld, *Econometric Models and Economic Forecasts* (New York: McGraw-Hill, 1976, pp. 6–9).

Figure 5-14   Excess Return on Stock *Y* and on the Market Portfolio

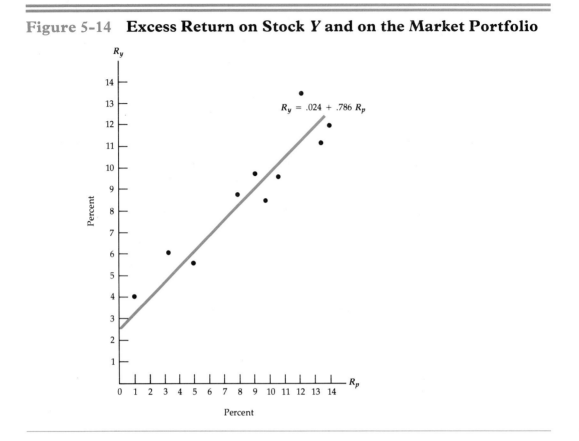

Thus, a distance of 4 percent squared is 16 percent. A distance of 2 percent squared is 4 percent. Squaring, therefore, is a means of weighting the distances.

The linear relationship between R_y and R_p becomes $\hat{R}_y = \hat{a} + \hat{b}R_p$. Substituting, we have

$$\sum_{i=1}^{N} (R_y - \hat{a} - \hat{b}R_p)^2$$

To find the values of $\hat{a}$ and $\hat{b}$ that minimize the sum of the squared error (SE), we must take the partial derivative of SE with respect to a and b. We then set the resulting derivatives equal to zero. Thus

$$\frac{\partial SE}{\partial a} = (-2)\sum(R_y - \hat{a} - \hat{b}R_p) = 0$$

$$\frac{\partial SE}{\partial b} = (-2)\sum[(R_p)(R_y - \hat{a} - \hat{b}R_p)] = 0$$

Dividing by -2 and rearranging, we have

$$\sum R_y = \sum \hat{a} + \hat{b} \sum R_p$$
$$\sum R_y = N\hat{a} + \hat{b} \sum R_p \qquad (5\text{-}9)$$

and

$$\sum R_p R_y = \hat{a} \sum R_p + \hat{b} \sum R_p^2 \qquad (5\text{-}10)$$

Equations 5-9 and 5-10 are *normal equations* and the basis upon which to estimate the regression line. Although simplifications for calculating a and b exist, we proceed by solving the foregoing equations simultaneously.[38] Thus, in columns 1, 2, 3, and 4 of Table 5-3 we have values for $\sum R_p$, $\sum R_y$, $\sum R_p R_y$, and $\sum R_p^2$. Substituting for Equations 5-9 and 5-10, we have $.87 = 10\hat{a} + .80\hat{b}$, and

$$.085 = .80\hat{a} + .0836\hat{b}$$
$$\hat{a} = .106250 - .10450\hat{b}$$

Consequently

$$.87 = 10(.106250 - .10450\hat{b}) + .80\hat{b}$$
$$\hat{b} = .785714 = .786$$

Substituting in Equation 5-10, we have

$$.87 = 10\hat{a} + .80(.785714)$$
$$\hat{a} = .024143 = .024$$
$$R_y = .024 + .786R_p$$

The foregoing regression equation represents the line of best fit. Assuming the future is similar to the past, if the return on the portfolio is expected to be 10 percent for the next year, the return on stock Y is expected to be

$$R_y = .024 + .786(.1)$$
$$R_y = .024 + .0786$$
$$R_y = .1026$$

Several questions pertaining to the significance of the regression equation as a forecasting model remain. For example, our analysis underlying the beta coefficient suggests that a should be zero. Is the value of .024 simply due to chance? Does b represent the beta coefficient for this stock? The statistical procedures for answering

---

[38] See, for example, Taro Yamana, *Statistics: An Introductory Analysis*, 3rd ed. (New York: Harper and Row, 1973, pp. 400–408).

these and similar questions carry us beyond the scope of the book.[39] Suffice it to say: as with the example developed in the text of this chapter, the relationship between R_y and R_p depends upon historical relationships being indicative of the future. To the extent this is not the case, the results will be less useful than they might otherwise have been.

PROBLEMS AND QUESTIONS

1. The stocks of companies X and Y have the following characteristics:

	X	Y
Expected return for next year	10%	8%
Standard deviation in expected return	5%	4%
Coefficient of correlation between X and Y	−.6	−.6

   a. What is the expected portfolio return of the two securities, assuming an investor gives equal weight to each security in his or her portfolio? What is the standard deviation of the portfolio?

   b. Assume the investor chooses to put 60 percent of his or her funds in stock X and 40 percent in stock Y. What is the expected portfolio return? What is the standard deviation?

   c. Would one combination of X and Y be preferred over the other? Explain.

2. The return on a portfolio of securities on the frontier of the Markowitz opportunity set is 14 percent, the standard deviation is 8 percent, and the risk-free rate is 5 percent. An investor desires a portfolio with a standard deviation of 4 percent. What return must the investor be willing to accept to achieve a standard deviation of 4 percent?

3. The stock of company X and the market portfolio have the following characteristics:

Expected return on the market portfolio	= .12
Standard deviation of security X	= .20
Standard deviation of the market portfolio	= .10
Correlation between the returns on security X and the market portfolio	= .70
Risk-free rate	= .06

   In the context of the capital asset pricing model (CAPM), what is the expected return on security X?

---

[39] See [38], pp. 408–98.

4. You are given the following data:

Year	Return on the Market Portfolio	Return on Security j	Risk-free Rate
1	10%	9%	.05
2	9%	11%	.05
3	11%	12%	.05
4	14%	10%	.06
5	18%	21%	.06
6	13%	11%	.05
7	10%	10%	.05

From these data, calculate the beta coefficient for security j. Suppose the market portfolio return for the next period is expected to be 10 percent and the risk-free rate 5 percent. Assuming the past is indicative of the future, what is the expected return on security j for the next period?

5. You are given the following set of portfolios:

Portfolio	A	B	C	D
Expected return	10%	11%	15%	8%
Standard deviation	8%	7%	10%	8%

a. Which portfolios are superior? Why?
b. Is one portfolio clearly preferred over any other? Explain in detail.

6. What primary assumptions underlie the Capital Asset Pricing Model? Suppose these assumptions were relaxed; what are the implications? Explain.

7. You are given the following data:

	Risk-free Rate	Security j	Security k	Market Portfolio
Standard deviation	0	—	—	9%
Covariance with the market portfolio	0	.0081	.010125	—

a. The expected return on the market portfolio is 12 percent and the risk-free rate is 4 percent. What are the beta coefficients for securities j and k? What are the expected returns on securities j and k?
b. What is the beta coefficient for the risk-free rate? Explain why.

8. Assuming the securities are equally weighted in the following portfolio, calculate the expected return and standard deviation:

	Variances and Covariances			
Portfolio	1	2	3	4
1 $\bar{R}_1 = .12$	.02	−.01	−.04	−.01
2 $\bar{R}_2 = .16$	−.01	.06	−.02	−.02
3 $\bar{R}_3 = .18$	−.04	−.02	.08	.04
4 $\bar{R}_4 = .22$	−.01	−.02	.04	.12

9. Three securities are related to one another in the following ways:

	1	2	3
1	.036	0	0
2	0	.045	0
3	0	0	.072

a. Assume all securities are combined in an equally weighted portfolio. What is the standard deviation of such a portfolio?

b. Assume a fourth security is added whose variance is .04 and whose covariances with securities 1, 2, and 3 are

$$COV_{1,4} = -.01$$
$$COV_{2,4} = -.02$$
$$COV_{3,4} = .04$$

Assuming equal weights, what happens to the standard deviation of the portfolio when the fourth security is added? If the expected return on the portfolio remained unchanged, would you add security 4 to the portfolio? Explain.

10. A security whose beta is one has a positive alpha of 4 percent. Do you conclude that the security is underpriced? Explain in detail.

11. Assume the lending rate equals the borrowing rate and that both rates are 6 percent. The return on the market portfolio is 16 percent and the standard deviation is 8 percent. For an individual who borrows 25 percent of his wealth and invests it in the market, what is the return on the portfolio? What is the standard deviation of the portfolio?

SELECTED ADDITIONAL REFERENCES

Baesel, Jerome B. "On the Assessment of Risk: Some Further Considerations," *Journal of Finance*, Vol. 29 (December 1974, pp. 1491–94).

Ben-Zion, Uri and Sol S. Shalit. "Size, Leverage, and Dividend Record as Determinants of Equity Risk," *Journal of Finance*, Vol. 30 (September 1975, pp. 1015–26).

Black, Fischer. "Capital Market Equilibrium with Restricted Borrowing," *Journal of Business*, Vol. 45 (July 1972, pp. 444–54).

Blume, Marshall E. "Betas and Their Regression Tendencies," *Journal of Finance*, Vol. 30 (June 1975, pp. 785–96).

———. "On Assessment of Risk," *Journal of Finance*, Vol. 26 (March 1971, pp. 1–10).

Blume, Marshall and Irwin Friend. "A New Look at the Capital-Asset Pricing Model," *Journal of Finance*, Vol. 28 (March 1973, pp. 19–34).

Brealey, Richard A. *An Introduction to Risk and Return from Common Stocks*, 2nd rev. ed. (Cambridge, MA: MIT Press, 1983).

Brennan, M. J. "Capital Market Equilibrium with Divergent Borrowing and Lending Rates," *Journal of Financial and Quantitative Analysis*, Vol. 6 (December 1971, pp. 1197–1205).

———. "The Optimal Number of Securities in a Risky Asset Portfolio when There Are Fixed Costs of Transacting: Theory and Some Empirical Results," *Journal of Financial and Quantitative Analysis*, Vol. 10 (September 1975, pp. 483–96).

Brenner, Menachem. "The Effect of Misspecification on Tests of the Efficient Market Hypothesis," *Journal of Finance*, Vol. 32 (March 1977, pp. 57–66).

Brinson, Gary P., Jeffrey J. Diermier, and Gary A. Schlarbaum. "A Composite Portfolio Benchmark for Pension Plans," *Financial Analysts Journal*, Vol. 42 (March–April 1986, pp. 13–24).

Carlson, Robert S. "Aggregate Performance of Mutual Funds: 1948–1967," *Journal of Financial and Quantitative Analysis*, Vol. 5 (March 1970, pp. 1–32).

Cass, D. and J. E. Stiglitz. "The Structures of Investor Preference and Asset Returns and Separability in Portfolio Allocation: A Contribution to the Pure Theory of Mutual Funds," *Journal of Economic Theory*, Vol. 2 (June 1970, pp. 122–60).

Clark, John J., Margaret T. Clark, and Peter T. Elgers. *Financial Management: A Capital Market Approach* (Boston: Holbrook Press, 1976, pp. 28–53).

Cootner, Paul H. *The Random Character of Stock Market Prices* (Cambridge, MA: MIT Press, 1964).

Elton, Edwin and Martin J. Gruber. "Estimating the Dependence Structure of Share Prices—Implications for Portfolio Selection," *Journal of Finance*, Vol. 28 (December 1973, pp. 1203–32).

Evans, Jack and Stephen H. Archer. "Diversification and the Reduction of Dispersion: An Empirical Analysis," *Journal of Finance*, Vol. 23 (December 1968, pp. 761–7).

Fama, Eugene F. "Components of Investment Performance," *Journal of Finance*, Vol. 27 (June 1972, pp. 551–67).

———. "Efficient Capital Markets: A Review of the Theory and Empirical Work," *Journal of Finance*, Vol. 25 (May 1970, pp. 383–417).

———. "Efficient Capital Markets: Restatement of the Theory," *Journal of Finance*, Vol. 27 (June 1972, pp. 551–67).

———. "Risk, Return and Equilibrium," *Journal of Political Economy*, Vol. 79 (January–February 1971, pp. 30–55).

———. "Risk, Return and Equilibrium: Some Clarifying Comments," *Journal of Finance*, Vol. 23 (March 1968, pp. 29–40).

Fama, Eugene F. and Marshall Blume. "Filter Rules and Stock Market Trading Profits," *Journal of Business*, Vol. 39 (Special Supplement, January 1966, pp. 226–41).

Fama, Eugene F. and James D. MacBeth. "Risk, Return and Equilibrium: Empirical Tests," *Journal of Political Economy*, Vol. 81 (May–June 1973, pp. 607–36).

Fama, Eugene F. and Merton H. Miller. *The Theory of Finance* (New York: Holt, Rinehart and Winston, 1972).

Francis, Jack Clark. "Intertemporal Difference in Systematic Stock Price Movements," *Journal of Financial and Quantitative Analysis*, Vol. 10 (June 1975, pp. 205–20).

Friend, Irwin, Marshall Blume, and Jean Crockett. *Mutual Funds and Other Institutional Investors* (New York: McGraw-Hill, 1970).

Hakansson, Nils H. "Capital Growth and the Mean-Variance Approach to Portfolio Selection," *Journal of Financial and Quantitative Analysis*, Vol. 6 (January 1971, pp. 517–58).

Hamanda, Robert S. "Portfolio Analysis, Market Equilibrium and Corporation Finance," *Journal of Finance*, Vol. 24 (March 1969, pp. 13–32).

Haugen, Robert A. *Modern Investment Theory* (Englewood Cliffs, NJ: Prentice-Hall, 1986).

Hirshleifer, Jack. "Investment Decisions Under Uncertainty: Application of the State-Preference Approach," *Quarterly Journal of Economics*, Vol. 80 (May 1966, pp. 252–77).

Ibbotson, Roger C. and L. B. Siegel. "The World Market Wealth Portfolio," *Journal of Portfolio Management*, Vol. 9 (Winter 1983, pp. 5–17).

Jacob, Nancy. "The Measurement of Systematic Risk for Securities and Portfolios: Some Empirical Results," *Journal of Financial and Quantitative Analysis*, Vol. 6 (March 1971, pp. 815–34).

Jensen, Michael C. "Capital Markets: Theory and Evidence," *Bell Journal of Economics and Management Science*, Vol. 3 (Autumn 1972, pp. 357–98).

———. "Risk, The Pricing of Assets, and the Evaluation of Investment Portfolios," *Journal of Business*, Vol. 42 (April 1969, pp. 167–247).

———. *Studies in the Theory of Capital Markets* (New York: Praeger, 1972).

Johnson, K. H. and D. S. Shannon. "A Note of Diversification and Reduction of Dispersion," *Journal of Financial Economics*, Vol. 1 (December 1974, pp. 365–72).

Klemkosky, Robert C. and John D. Martin. "The Adjustment of Beta Forecasts," *Journal of Finance*, Vol. 30 (September 1975, pp. 1123–8).

Levy, Robert A. "On the Short Term Stationarity of Beta Coefficients," *Financial Analysts Journal*, Vol. 27 (November–December 1971, pp. 55–62).

Lintner, John. "Security Prices, Risk and Maximal Gains From Diversification," *Journal of Finance*, Vol. 20 (December 1965, pp. 587–616).

———. "The Aggregation of Investors: Judgments and Preferences in Purely Competitive Securities Markets," *Journal of Financial and Quantitative Analysis*, Vol. 4 (December 1969, pp. 347–400).

———. "The Market Price of Risk, Size of Market and Investor's Risk-Aversion," *Review of Economics and Statistics*, Vol. 52 (February 1970, pp. 87–99).

———. "The Valuation of Risky Assets and the Selection of Risky Investments in Stock Portfolios and Capital Budgets," *Review of Economics and Statistics*, Vol. 47 (February 1965, pp. 13–27).

Litzenberger, Robert H. and Alan P. Budd. "Corporate Investment Criteria and the Valuation of Risky Assets," *Journal of Financial and Quantitative Analysis*, Vol. 5 (December 1970, pp. 395–420).

Litzenberger, Robert H. and Krishna Ramaswamy. "The Effect of Personal Taxes and Dividends on Capital Asset Prices," *Journal of Financial Economics*, Vol. 7 (June 1979, pp. 163–95).

Lorie, James and Richard Brealey, eds. *Modern Developments in Investment Management* (New York: Praeger, 1972).

Lorie, James, Peter Dodd, and Mary Hamilton Kimpton. *The Stock Market: Theories and Evidence*, 2nd ed. (Homewood, IL: Richard D. Irwin, 1985).

Malkiel, Burton. "Risk and Return: A New Look," in Benjamin M. Friedman, ed., *The Changing Roles of Debt and Equity in U.S. Capital Formation* (Chicago: University of Chicago Press, 1982, pp. 27–45).

———. *A Random Walk Down Wall Street*, 4th ed. (New York: W. W. Norton, 1985).

Malkiel, Burton and John Cragg. *Expectations and the Valuation of Shares* (National Bureau of Economic Research Working Paper, No. 471, April 1980).

Mao, James C. T. "Security Pricing in an Imperfect Capital Market," *Journal of Financial and Quantitative Analysis*, Vol. 6 (September 1971, pp. 1105–16).

Markowitz, Harry M. "Portfolio Selection," *Journal of Finance*, Vol. 12 (March 1952, pp. 77–91).

———. *Portfolio Selection, Efficient Diversification of Investments* (New York: John Wiley and Sons, 1959).

Mayers, David. "Nonmarketable Assets and the Determination of Capital Asset Prices in the Absence of a Riskless Asset," *Journal of Business*, Vol. 46 (April 1973, pp. 258–67).

McDonald, John C. "Investment Objectives, Diversification, Risk and Exposure to Surprise," *Financial Analysts Journal*, Vol. 32 (March–April 1975, pp. 42–49).

Merton, Robert C. "Theory of Finance from the Perspective of Continuous Time," *Journal of Financial and Quantitative Analysis*, Vol. 10 (November 1975, pp. 659–74).

Modigliani, Franco and Gerald A. Pogue. "An Introduction to Risk and Return," *Financial Analysts Journal*, Vol. 30 (March–April 1974, pp. 68–80 and May–June 1974, pp. 69–86).

Mossin, Jan. "Equilibrium in a Capital Asset Market," *Econometrica*, Vol. 34 (October 1966, pp. 768–83).

———. *Theory of Financial Markets* (Englewood Cliffs, NJ: Prentice-Hall, 1973).

Myers, Stewart C. "A Time-State Preference Model of Security Valuation," *Journal of Financial and Quantitative Analysis*, Vol. 3 (March 1968, pp. 1–34).

Pettit, R. Richardson and Randolph Westerfield. "Using the Capital Asset Pricing Model and the Market Model to Predict Security Returns," *Journal of Financial and Quantitative Analysis*, Vol. 9 (September 1974, pp. 579–606).

Pogue, Gerald A. "An Extension of the Markowitz Portfolio Selection Model to Include Variable Transactions Costs, Short Sales, Leverage Policies, and Taxes," *Journal of Finance*, Vol. 25 (December 1970, pp. 1005–27).

Roll, Richard. "A Critique of the Asset Theory Tests," *Journal of Financial Economics*, Vol. 4 (March 1977, pp. 124–76).

———. "The Arbitrage Pricing Theory Approach to Strategic Portfolio Planning," *Financial Analysts Journal*, Vol. 40 (May–June 1984, pp. 14–26).

———. "Orthogonal Portfolios," *Journal of Financial and Quantitative Analysis*, Vol. 15 (December 1980, pp. 1005–11).

Roll, Richard and Stephen A. Ross. "An Empirical Investigation of the Arbitrage Pricing Theory," *Journal of Finance*, Vol. 35 (December 1980, pp. 1073–1103).

Ross, Stephen A. "The Arbitrage Theory of Capital Asset Pricing," *Journal of Economic Theory*, Vol. 13 (December 1976, pp. 341–60).

———. "The Capital Asset Pricing Model (CAPM), Short Sale Restrictions and Related Issues," *Journal of Finance*, Vol. 32 (March 1977, pp. 177–83).

Rubinstein, Mark. "Securities Market Efficiency in an Arrow–Debreu Economy," *American Economic Review*, Vol. 65 (December 1975, pp. 812–24).

Schwendiman, Carl J. and George E. Pinches. "An Analysis of Alternative

Measures of Investment Risk," *Journal of Finance*, Vol. 30 (March 1975, pp. 193–200).

Seelenfreund, Alan, George G. C. Parker, and James C. VanHorne. "Stock Price Behavior and Trading," *Journal of Financial and Quantitative Analysis*, Vol. 3 (September 1968, pp. 263–82).

Sharpe, William F. "A Simplified Model for Portfolio Analysis," *Management Science*, Vol. 9 (January 1963, pp. 277–93).

———. "Capital Asset Prices: A Theory of Market Equilibrium under Conditions of Risk," *Journal of Finance*, Vol. 19 (September 1964, pp. 425–42).

———. *Portfolio Analysis and Capital Markets* (New York: McGraw-Hill, 1970).

Sharpe, William F. and Guy M. Cooper. "Risk-Return Classes of New York Stock Exchange Common Stocks," *Financial Analysts Journal*, Vol. 28 (March–April 1972, pp. 46–54).

Tobin, James. "Liquidity Preferences as Behavior Towards Risk," *Review of Economic Studies*, Vol. 25 (February 1958, pp. 65–86).

Treynor, Jack L. "Towards a Market Value of Risky Assets" (unpublished manuscript, 1961).

Whitbeck, Volkert S. and Manown Kisor, Jr. "A New Tool in Investment Decision-Making," *Financial Analysts Journal*, Vol. XIX (May–June 1963, pp. 55–62).

Wolfe, Philip. "The Simplex Method for Quadratic Programming," *Econometrica*, Vol. 27 (July 1959, pp. 382–98).

MEASURING THE
COST OF CAPITAL

In developing the principles of Modern Portfolio Theory, we concentrated on the return from a single investment in relation to the return from a portfolio of investments. In principle, an investment portfolio includes all investable wealth; in practice many real assets are excluded. Thus, although you may own shares of stock in an aluminum company, you probably have no direct ownership of its facilities. Presumably, a nonfinancial corporation with appropriate expertise can raise the large sums of money required to build and operate facilities more efficiently than could you or a group of investors who lack the expertise, if not the funds. Hence, as part of your portfolio, you settle for shares of stock in the company rather than in the plant. Even if you want to invest in Professor Hairbrain's latest mutation—vegetables that grow at temperatures below freezing—you probably will do so by purchasing stock or a partnership interest in the project. Hairbrain needs your money; you need his expertise.

Nonfinancial business firms, therefore, construct portfolios of financial claims (primarily debt and ownership interests) and use the proceeds to develop a portfolio consisting primarily of real assets designed to produce goods and services—aluminum, aluminum products, and vegetables that grow at sub-freezing temperatures.

For the next several chapters, we shall view finance from the perspective of the nonfinancial business firm (generally a corporation) or from the nonfinancial subsidiary of a conglomerate that may include a financial subsidiary. We shall assume corporate management is attempting to maximize the market value of its shareholders' wealth. Institutionally, the assumption suggests the corporation is primarily interested in maximizing the market value of the common stock of the company or, in the case of the subsidiary, its market value as an entity. In accepting this assumption, however, we also recognize that investment and financing decisions of management will be viewed by investors in the context of a portfolio of investment alternatives. What real assets management chooses to buy and how it finances them affects the risk and ultimately the return on the stock. Remember that

$$\beta jm = \frac{r_{jm}\sigma j\sigma_m}{\sigma_m{}^2} = \frac{\text{COV}_{jm}}{\sigma_m{}^2}$$

The standard deviation σ_j, and hence beta β_{jm}, is affected by the investment and financing decisions of the management of firm j.

A simple example serves to illustrate the point. Suppose a manufacturer of computers decides to market an innovative product, one that combines software, printer, data storage, and the like in one system (as did Coleco Industries in the fall of 1983). Although, from the press releases of the time it was apparent such an innovation could lead to increased revenues and profits at least over a short-run period, it was also apparent it could lead to lower prices, losses for the firm, and new products to challenge the innovator.[1] In an effort to enhance profits, the company, in this case Coleco, assumed the **business risk** inherent in innovation.

The assets necessary to produce the product—plant, equipment, inventories, and so forth—all required funds. These funds could have come exclusively from the issuance of new stock or the retention of earnings at the expense of dividends. Alternatively, the funds could have come from bank loans, bond issues, or from other types of indebtedness. They also could have come in part from borrowing and in part from the owners.

The decision to borrow, however, is a decision to incur **financial risk**. Debtholders generally have prior claim over owners to the earnings and assets of the company. If the innovation is unprofitable, the company is still liable for the interest and principal on any debt used to finance the assets purchased. Moreover, the claim is general and may apply to the total earnings and assets of the company, not just to assets related to the project the debt financed. In the extreme case, where a company cannot meet interest or principal payments on debt, bankruptcy ensues. The company may be liquidated and the assets sold to satisfy the claims of debtholders. On the other hand, interest and principal payments are fixed by contract. The earnings from a venture whose profitability equals or exceeds expectations accrues, after payment to debtholders, to the company and hence to the owners. Consequently, if it assumes financial risk, management can enhance the earnings available to owners. The tantalizing question is whether the use of debt to enhance profitability will increase the market value of the owners' equity. If it does, there is an optimal portfolio of financial claims divided between debt and equity that management should maintain to maximize the value of the owners' wealth.

Before pursuing this question, we must develop the costs of using each individual source of funds and a weighted (or average) cost of all such sources. Fortunately, most tools for accomplishing this task are already in place, having been developed in the preceding chapters. We need only extend and apply them to the individual firm.

---

[1] Andrew Pollack. "The Coming Crisis in Home Computers," *New York Times* (June 19, 1983, Sec. 3, pp. 1 and 29). See also Richard A. Shaffer, "Small Changes Net Gains in Coleco's Adam Computer," *Wall Street Journal* (June 10, 1983, p. 35) and Laura Landro, "'Adam' Jolting Pricing Tactics in Computers," *Wall Street Journal* (June 19, 1983, p. 35). In this instance, Coleco's product experienced difficulties. As a result, the firm lost money on the computer, subsequently abandoning it and selling off the inventories. *Wall Street Journal* (January 3, 1985, p. 3).

THE EXPLICIT COST OF DEBT CAPITAL

When a firm borrows funds, the explicit cost of debt capital is the interest paid on the funds borrowed. As noted in Chapter 3, one widely used measure of the return on borrowed funds is the **yield to maturity**. Yield to maturity equals the stated rate of interest when the amount raised is equal to the amount to be repaid by the borrower. To illustrate, suppose a firm issued $100 million in debt instruments that mature in twelve years and carry a coupon rate of 12 percent, and issued them in $1,000 denominations. When it marketed the securities, the firm received $100,000,000 in cash from the sale, so that

$$\$100,000,000 = \$12,000,000 \frac{\left[1 - \left(1 + \frac{r}{2}\right)^{-24}\right]}{r} + \frac{\$100,000,000}{\left(1 + \frac{r}{2}\right)^{24}}$$

$$r = 12 \text{ percent}$$

If the individual investor purchased one of these instruments for $1,000, the yield to maturity to the investor is

$$\$1,000 = 120 \frac{\left[1 - \left(1 + \frac{r}{2}\right)^{-24}\right]}{r} + \frac{\$1,000}{\left(1 + \frac{r}{2}\right)^{24}}$$

$$r = 12 \text{ percent}$$

In this case, the yield to maturity to the investor equals what we shall call the **cost to maturity** to the issuing company: both equal the stated, or coupon, rate on the debt instrument.

However, if the company had received only $99,200,000 for the debt instruments, the cost to maturity would be

$$\$99,200,000 = \$12,000,000 \frac{\left[1 - \left(1 + \frac{r}{2}\right)^{-24}\right]}{r} + \frac{\$100,000,000}{\left(1 + \frac{r}{2}\right)^{24}}$$

$$r = 12.128 \text{ percent}$$

If the investor paid $992 per bond, the yield to maturity to the investor is also

$$\$992 = \$120 \frac{\left[1 - \left(1 + \frac{r}{2}\right)^{-24}\right]}{r} + \frac{\$1,000}{\left(1 + \frac{r}{2}\right)^{24}}$$

$r = 12.128$ percent

What yield to maturity is to the investor, cost to maturity is to the issuer.

Suppose, however, the $800,000 difference ($8 per bond) represents the flotation costs of the issue: the costs incurred in engaging the services of an investment banking firm or team of firms to underwrite (guarantee) the proceeds to the issuing company. In so doing, underwriters receive a **spread** equal to the difference between the offering price of the bonds to the public and the proceeds to the company. If, in this instance, the investment bankers offered the bonds to the public at par ($1,000 per bond), the yield to maturity on the bond is 12 percent and the cost to maturity is 12.128 percent. The difference—.128 percent or 12.8 **basis points**—is part of the flotation costs of the issue.[2] For analytical purposes, flotation costs may be ignored; for empirical purposes, they may not. One may either recognize flotation costs as the difference between yield and cost to maturity or add the dollar amount, in this instance $800,000, to the outlay on the projects to be funded by the proceeds from the sale of the securities.[3] Because it is more convenient to follow the practice of theoreticians and ignore *institutional details*, we shall treat cost to maturity as though it were yield to maturity. However, forewarned is forearmed. Taking such details into consideration is an essential part of a practitioner's job, particularly if one expects one's salary to be commensurate with one's age rather than with one's shoe size.

Once issued, the cost to maturity represents what is sometimes called the *imbedded* cost of debt. For the life of the issue in the example employed, the company will pay $6,000,000 semiannually. At the end of the twelve-year period, it will owe the bondholders $100,000,000. The cost, whether 12 percent or 12.128 percent, does not vary; it is impervious to changes in the market rate of interest.

If the company wanted to issue $100,000,000 in twelve-year debt instruments next year, the company might discover it could issue these securities only at a cost to maturity of 14 percent. If so, the *current cost* of debt capital is 14 percent, even though the imbedded cost of last year's debt issue is 12 percent. It is the current cost

---

[2] In Chapter 17 on investment banking, we consider the issue of flotation costs in greater detail.

[3] Adding flotation costs to the projects to be funded lowers the rate of return, or net present value, of each project. The logic of this argument rests upon the principles developed in Chapter 3 and applied in Chapter 8 where we take up the subject of capital budgeting.

of debt, as well as the current cost of other debt instruments, that is important in judging whether new investments will be undertaken.[4]

The current cost of debt is the explicit cost of debt, or cost of using debt, at the time the debt instruments are issued. We emphasize *explicit* because no allowance has been made for the impact the increased financial risk might have on the market price of the stock and hence on the wealth of owners. The full cost of debt, however, takes this effect into account. We shall examine the full cost of debt when we consider the optimal portfolio of financial claims, or optimal capital structure, in Chapter 7.

THE EXPLICIT COST OF PREFERRED STOCK

The explicit cost of preferred stock is the yield on preferred stock at the time of issue. A straight preferred stock, one not convertible into common stock, is effectively a perpetuity.[5] Suppose the firm were raising $20,000,000 through an issue of preferred stock. The current yield on preferred stock of similar quality is 10 percent. The company could issue 1,000,000 shares paying a $2 annual dividend, so that

$$\frac{\$2.00}{.10} = \$20$$

The explicit cost of preferred stock is 10 percent. Since failure to pay dividends on preferred stock can never precipitate bankruptcy, the risk to common stockholders consists only of a single restriction usually found in the preferred-stock contract. Specifically, if the dividend is not paid, it cumulates. Common stockholders generally cannot receive dividends until preferred dividends, both current and cumulated, have been paid. Consequently, management treats preferred dividends as though they were interest payments to be met when due, which is usually every quarter. In the preceding illustration, the dividend is $.50 per quarter.

---

[4] The imbedded cost of debt as well as the principal itself could be a source of value to owners during a period of accelerating inflation. For example, a company with a substantial amount of debt at an imbedded cost well below the current cost of debt may produce a windfall for a company able to price its products so they keep pace with inflation. Because the interest costs are fixed, the debt is repaid in dollars with lower purchasing power: a dollar borrowed ten years ago may be worth 50 cents today. Presumably this potential windfall in efficient markets is fully capitalized in the price of the stock. However, one study suggested it was not. See Franco Modigliani and Richard A. Cohn, "Inflation, Rational Valuation and the Market," *Financial Analysts Journal*, Vol. 35 (March–April 1979, pp. 24–44). The opposite is true if the current cost of debt capital were falling relative to the imbedded cost, causing a windfall loss to the firm. This is often the outcome of a rapid deceleration in the rate of inflation, resulting in declining nominal rate of interest.

[5] Any preferred stock or debt instrument can have a call price. This allows the company to repurchase the instrument at a specific price. Thus, in the preceding illustration, the company may have issued the preferred stock callable at any time at $23 per share. If yields on preferred stock fell to 8 percent, the firm could get $25 per share on new preferred stock with the same dividend ($2.00 ÷ .08 = $25). Depending on costs of calling in the old stock and issuing new shares, it may be worthwhile for the company to pay $23 and issue new shares at $25. (See Chapter 16 for further details.)

Table 6-1   **How the Explicit Cost of Debt and Preferred Stock Affects Corporate Income Taxes**

Assumptions   The corporation has a marginal corporate income-tax rate of 34 percent, can issue $10,000,000 of debt or preferred stock at a cost of 11 percent, and can issue debt at a face value of $1,000 and preferred at $100 per share. Annual earnings before interest and taxes (EBIT) expected from such an investment are $3,000,000.

	If Preferred Is Issued	*If Debt Is Issued*
EBIT	$3,000,000	$3,000,000
Interest		1,100,000
EBT	3,000,000	1,900,000
Taxes at 34%	1,020,000	646,000
EAT	1,980,000	1,254,000
Pfd dividends	1,100,000	
Earnings available to stockholders	$ 880,000	$1,254,000

If interest had not been tax deductible, additional taxes of .34 × $1,100,000 = $374,000 would have been paid on earnings. Thus, the true explicit cost of interest is $1,100,000 − $374,000 = $726,000 ÷ $10,000,000 × 100 = 7.26%. Alternatively .11 (1 − tax rate) = .11(1 − .34) = .0726 × 100 = 7.26%.

TAXES VERSUS THE EXPLICIT COST OF DEBT AND PREFERRED

The complexities of Federal income-tax laws serve to enrich lawyers and accountants and lengthen textbooks in finance. One feature of the tax code involves the differential treatment accorded the issuer in taxing interest and preferred dividends. By law, preferred stock is equity, not debt. To be sure, it is a peculiar form of ownership interest. The stock is generally nonvoting and receives only a fixed dividend payment. Nevertheless, equity it is. This is why preferred stockholders have no recourse in bankruptcy if management fails to pay dividends when due.

The revenue code allows a corporation to deduct interest payments from earnings before taxes: such interest is a tax-deductible expense. Preferred-stock dividends are paid from earnings after taxes. To illustrate the impact of taxes, consider a company with a marginal corporate income-tax rate of 34 percent: 34 cents of every additional dollar of earnings is paid in corporate income taxes. To keep the illustration simple, suppose the company could raise funds from issuing preferred or debt whose cost or cost to maturity in 30 years is 11 percent. The amount issued would be $10,000,000. The investment is expected to produce $3,000,000 per year in earnings before interest and taxes (EBIT). (See calculations in Table 6-1, page 152.) Comparing the two types of financing and ignoring the maturity date on the debt, common stockholders would experience greater earnings from the use of debt rather than from the use of preferred stock. More generally, as the calculations in Table 6-1 suggest, the explicit cost of debt after taxes now becomes cost to maturity $(1 - \text{marginal tax rate}) = \text{after-tax cost of debt}: .11(1 - .34) = .0726 \times 100 = 7.26\%$. The tax laws encourage the corporation to use debt rather than preferred.[6]

THE COST OF EQUITY CAPITAL

The owners have residual claim on company earnings whether they are proprietors, general partners, or, in the case of a corporation, common stockholders. Because corporations dominate American business and because the shares of corporations can be readily bought and sold, we shall view the cost of equity capital from the perspective of common stockholders.

The earnings of a corporation can either be reinvested within the company or distributed as cash dividends. What effect, if any, the decision to raise or lower the proportion of earnings paid as dividends may have on the value of owners' equity is an issue of sufficient importance to devote Chapter 11 to its consideration. Consequently, we shall finesse the question and assume the proportion of earnings paid as cash dividends remains fixed. In the jargon of finance, the *payout ratio* (D/E), where D is dividends and E is earnings, will remain constant.

At the basic level of analysis, therefore, given expected earnings and payout ratio, we may use models already developed to measure the cost of equity capital. Specifically, if annual company earnings are $3 per share and payout ratio is 2/3, then dividends are $2 per year (2/3 × $3 = $2). Suppose earnings are expected to remain at $3 per share indefinitely and that current market price of the stock is

---

[6] *A Bonus Footnote!* Under the current tax laws, an individual should probably not purchase straight preferred stock. Corporate owners of stock receive a substantial tax break from purchasing preferred (or common for that matter): 80 percent of dividends received by one corporation from another are excluded from taxable income; the remaining 20 percent are taxed at regular rates. Corporate owners of corporate bonds, however, must pay income tax on 100 percent of the interest. In the preceding example, if a corporate purchaser with a marginal tax rate of 34 percent bought the bonds, the after-tax yield would be 7.26 percent. However, if the company bought preferred, the after-tax yield on preferred would be $.11 [1 - (.34 \times .20)] = .10252 = 10.252$ percent. Individuals are taxed at the same rate whether they receive bond interest or preferred dividends. The result is that purchasers of preferred stock (most of which is issued by public utilities) are corporations, such as property and casualty insurance companies. See Thomas R. Fausel, "The Supply and Demand Effect on Preferred Stock Yield Behavior" (unpublished paper submitted in partial fulfillment of requirements for M.A. degree, Trinity College, 1982). Even those contemplating preferred stock for pension funds, Investment Retirement Accounts, and the like, would generally be better off with high-quality debt instruments. So strong has the tax effect been that yields on high-quality debt instruments are sometimes 100 to 150 basis points—1 to 1.5 percent above yields on high-quality preferreds. (See, for example, *Moody's Bond Survey*, June 15, 1987, p. 6248.) When funds are tax-exempt or, at least, when taxes are deferred, one is better off reinvesting the higher return.

$12.50. From the analysis in Chapter 3

$$\$12.50 = \$2.00 \frac{[1 - (1 + r)^{-n}]}{r}$$

as $n \to \infty$

$$\$12.50 = \frac{\$2.00}{r}$$

$$r = \frac{\$2.00}{\$12.50}$$

$$r = 16\%$$

To complicate matters slightly, suppose earnings are expected to grow at 6 percent a year indefinitely and that market price of the stock is $20 per share. Since the payout ratio is assumed to be constant, dividends will grow with earnings at 6 percent a year indefinitely. Again, from the analysis in Chapter 3

$$\$20.00 = \$2.00 \frac{\left[1 - \left(\frac{1 + r}{1 + g}\right)^n\right]}{r - g}$$

$$\$20.00 = \$2.00 \frac{\left[1 - \left(\frac{1 + r}{1.06}\right)^n\right]}{r - .06}$$

with $r > g$ as $n \to \infty$

$$\$20.00 = \frac{\$2.00}{r - .06}$$

$$r - .06 = \frac{\$2.00}{\$20.00}$$

$$r - .06 = .10$$

$$r = .16$$

$$r = 16\%$$

There are several points to bear in mind. Preliminarily, what were intrinsic value models used to determine present value of a stock have now been turned into measures of the cost of equity capital. To do this, one uses market price of a stock as a current estimate of its present intrinsic value. When doing so, one implicitly assumes current market price of a stock is the best estimate of its present intrinsic value. In our first case, where no growth is expected, r is 16 percent. In our second case, where g is assumed to be 6 percent, r is also 16 percent. The difference in price—$20 rather than $12.50—is due to anticipated growth in dividends.

From the analysis of risk in Chapter 4, we can envision expected earnings of $3 per share as the mean of a probability distribution. Given a payout ratio of 2/3, the dividend of $2 per share is the mean of a probability distribution, as is the expected growth rate g of 6 percent. Moreover, as we have seen, there could be a short-run as well as a long-run growth rate. Indeed, growth rates could vary from period to period. By analogy, so could values for r.[7]

Such values, of course, can be affected by the forces that shape the revenues and expenses and (ultimately) earnings of the company. Yet, aren't these forces in part at least peculiar to that company? A new discovery of bauxite ore may lower the cost of raw materials to an aluminum manufacturer, adversely impact close substitutes such as steel, but cause only a ripple effect on the revenues and expenses of a national grocery chain. Are we not, therefore, dealing with unsystematic risk? We are indeed. And as Chapter 5 suggested: investors diversify away unsystematic risk, leaving only systematic risk. Nevertheless, as noted earlier: through its investment and financing decisions, management will affect the unsystematic risk of the firm and hence the beta coefficient. Thus

$$E(R_j) = i + \beta_{jm}[E(R_m) - i]$$

and the greater σ_j (other things being the same), the greater the beta coefficient.

If β_{jm} is 1.0, the cost of capital, $E(R_j)$, is simply the expected return on the market portfolio $E(R_m)$. Recall, however, that the measure of expected return is the expected holding period return. For the market portfolio

$$E(R_m) = \frac{E(P_{m1}) - P_{m0} + E(D_{m1})}{P_{m0}}$$

where $E(P_{m1})$ equals the expected value of the market portfolio (or market index) at the end of period 1. $E(D_{m1})$ equals the expected dividends on the market portfolio at the end of period 1. P_{m0} equals the market value (or the index of market value) of the portfolio at the beginning of the period. Thus, suppose the value of a popular market index at the beginning of the year was 160, that at the end of the year it was expected to be 180, and that the dividend on the index is expected to be $5.50. Thus

$$E(R_{m1}) = \frac{180 - 160 + \$5.50}{160} = \frac{25.50}{160} = .159375$$

If the beta coefficient for stock j is 1.25 and the risk-free rate for the annual holding period is 12 percent, expected return and hence expected cost of equity capital for company j is

$$E(R_j) = .12 + 1.25(.159375 - .12)$$
$$ER_j = .169219$$

Based on the CAPM, cost of equity capital for the next annual holding period is 16.92 percent.

---

[7] The growth rate, g equals 6 percent, could be the long-term growth rate at the beginning of year 4. It may result from the following growth rates for years 1, 2, and 3: $(1.055)(1.065)(1.06) = (1.19099)^{1/3} = 1.05992 = 1.06 - 1 = .06$. Similarly, the long-term value for r may result from $(1.14)(1.18)(1.16) = (1.560432)^{1/3} = 1.159885 = 1.16 - 1 = .16$. Other combinations are, of course, possible. By using a single value for g or r at a point in time, we are implicitly using the geometric mean of values for g and r that preceded either.

PRESENT INTRINSIC VALUE AND THE CAPM—A COMPARISON

As techniques for measuring cost of equity capital, present intrinsic value and CAPM offer conceptually different approaches. If one uses present intrinsic value to estimate cost of equity capital, one suggests the return or cost is related only to current dividends and expected growth in those dividends. If however, one uses CAPM to estimate cost of equity capital, the return or cost is the expected holding period return on the security as a function of the holding period return on a diversified portfolio of securities. Nevertheless, the CAPM implicitly uses present intrinsic value. Because

$$r = E(R_j) = i + \beta_{jm}[(E(R_m) - i)]$$

where

$$E(R_j) = \frac{E(P_{j1}) - P_{j0} + E(D_{j1})}{P_{j0}}$$

and, as noted earlier

$$E(R_m) = \frac{E(P_{m1}) - P_{m0} + E(D_{m1})}{P_{m0}}$$

then, assuming an infinite holding period, what CAPM suggests is

$$E(P_{j1}) = \frac{E(D_{j1})}{r_{j1} - g_{j1}}$$

and

$$E(P_{m1}) = \frac{E(D_{m1})}{r_{m1} - g_{m1}}$$

Thus, under CAPM the expected return r, or $E(R_j)$, is

$$\frac{\dfrac{E(D_{j1})}{r_{g1} - g_{j1}} - P_{j0} + E(D_{j1})}{P_{j0}} = i + \beta_{jm}\left[\frac{\dfrac{E(D_{m1})}{r_{m1} - g_{m1}} - P_{m0} + E(D_{m1})}{P_{m0}} - i\right]$$

The preceding algebraic abomination suggests present intrinsic value (in CAPM) is simply one holding period removed: it is viewed in terms of P_1 rather than P_0. Nevertheless, the substantive difference between the two approaches remains. Present intrinsic value depends upon expected growth in dividends. For example, the investment and financing decisions of management will affect expectations and hence the standard deviation of the return on security j. Any change in the standard deviation will be reflected in the beta coefficient and hence in the holding return as viewed in the context of the CAPM.

THE RETURN ON BOOK VALUE

Although modern financial theory offers market-determined measures of the cost of equity capital, there are still practitioners who believe that, in using either present intrinsic value or CAPM or both, one is pursuing a will-o'-the-wisp. Why not base cost of equity capital on what the firm has actually earned on the funds stockholders have invested in the company? In other words, the cost of equity capital may be based upon the return on the **book value** of the common stock.

To illustrate, consider the summary balance sheet of corporation X at the end of 1988 (see Table 6-2). The company has $150,000,000 in assets, $10,000,000 in current liabilities, and $40,000,000 in long-term debt. The preferred stock is carried at its par value ($10,000,000 in total), which we assume was the price at which the stock was sold when first marketed. The sum of the remaining accounts constitute simple book value per share. If the stock carries a par (or stated) value of $20 per share as assumed in this instance, the $20,000,000 par value is the product of $20 times 1,000,000 shares. The capital surplus constitutes value received, possibly at the time of original issue, in excess of $20 per share. Thus, if 1,000,000 shares were sold at $30 per share, $20 per share would be charged to par value and $10 per share to capital surplus. Earned surplus generally reflects the difference between earnings per share and dividends paid over the years; it may also reflect gains or losses on the sale of assets. From this simplified illustration, we conclude that book value is $90,000,000, or $90 per share. If earnings per share after taxes were $15.30, the return on book value per share is

$$\frac{\$15.30}{\$90.00} = .17 = 17\%$$

One might conclude that common stockholders expect to earn 17 percent on current and future capital invested in the company. Such a conclusion would be premature. Whatever the elusive qualities of market-determined cost of equity capital, calculating it from book value is not necessarily based upon better data. A well-known litany of problems stem from the use of original cost as the basis for valuation. Company X, for example, carries its land at an original cost of $10,000,000. It may be worth more in the market. Plant and equipment are carried at historical cost less accumulated depreciation. Book value is probably at variance with current market value and likely to be lower than replacement cost. Inventories may be carried at cost or market, whichever is lower.

Table 6-2   Balance Sheet Summary for Corporation X (end of year 1988)

Assets		Liabilities	
Current		Current debt	$ 10,000,000
Cash	$ 5,000,000	Long-term debt	40,000,000
Marketable securities	3,000,000	Total current liabilities	50,000,000
Receivables	7,000,000	*Equity*	
Inventories	10,000,000		
Total current assets	25,000,000	Preferred stock at par of $10 (1,000,000 shares outstanding)	10,000,000
Fixed			
Land at cost	10,000,000	Common stock at stated value of $20 (1,000,000 shares outstanding)	20,000,000
Plant and equipment cost less accumulated depreciation	115,000,000	Capital surplus	10,000,000
Total fixed assets	125,000,000	Earned surplus	60,000,000
Total assets	$150,000,000	Total equity	100,000,000
		Total liabilities and equity	$150,000,000

Such practices affect book value as well as reported earnings. Although one may adjust each to take into account the weaknesses inherent in original cost accounting, these efforts call for informed judgment (as do attempts to utilize present intrinsic value and CAPM). What return on book value per share offers is another measure with which to compare others. More importantly, return on book value per share may be used as a crude measure of opportunity cost by firms in the same industry employing the same accounting techniques. If other companies in the same industries experienced 17-percent returns on book value, barring unusual accounting entries—such as an extraordinary gain or loss from the sale of an asset recognized in the current year—one might have confidence the company was earning what others were earning on invested capital.

AVERAGE COST OF CAPITAL

Once management has determined the cost of individual sources of funds, there remains the task of determining the **weighted average cost of capital**: the product of the current cost of individual sources of capital weighted by the proportion of total funds accounted for by each source. Average cost of capital suggests what it costs the firm to raise money for investment in real assets. But what proportions: the book value weights as shown on the balance sheet or the proportions accounted for by the current market values of outstanding instruments? If we use book value, employing the numbers in Table 6-2 leads to the conclusion that in company X: debt is 33.33 percent of total liabilities and equity (short- and long-term), preferred stock represents 6.67 percent, and common stock is 60.0 percent. If we follow usual practice and subtract current liabilities from current assets, we have $140,000,000 in total funds: long-term debt is 28.57 percent, preferred is 7.14 percent, and owners' equity represents 64.29 percent.

Although book value weights are often employed in practice, in principle the market values of debt, preferred, and common stock determine the weights to use. Total market value at any point in time represents the value of the concern as an entity. To determine the cost of new money, the company would use the current cost of each individual source of funds multiplied by the proportion of total market value accounted for by that source. Suppose the total market value of a firm is $100,000,000, the market value of its debt is $30,000,000, the market value of its preferred stock is $15,000,000, and the market value of its common stock is $55,000,000. Thus, at this point in time, 30 percent of the capital structure is debt, 15 percent is preferred, and 55 percent is common. If the after-tax cost of new debt is 10 percent, the cost of new preferred is 12 percent, and the cost of new common stock is 18 percent, the weighted average cost of capital is

$$(.10 \times .3) + (.12 \times .15) + (.18 \times .55) =$$
$$3.0\% \quad + \quad 1.8\% \quad + \quad 9.9\% \quad = 14.7\%$$

Thus management, raising funds in proportion to the current market value of outstanding sources and at their respective current costs, has calculated correctly the combined or average cost of new capital. The figure tells management what investors currently expect to earn on the funds raised, and the proportions in which the funds should be raised. Therefore, the firm should (in turn) expect to employ new monies to earn at least the average cost of capital. To the extent management invests funds whose returns exceed the weighted average cost of capital, the market price of the stock may rise. Whether the stock rises or not depends upon the nature of the investments made and, in particular, on the impact such investments have on the overall risk or standard deviation in earnings and (ultimately) dividends. This, in turn, affects the beta coefficient and the expected return for holders of diversified portfolios. At this juncture, the author can only anticipate the results, the details require further clarification later in the book.

Practitioners who might otherwise agree that current average cost of capital as outlined is the appropriate measure of what investors expect to receive for the funds they tender may still demur on pragmatic grounds.

Many companies do not have publicly held debt: they borrow privately through commercial banks, insurance companies, or both. Such companies, however, have access to the current cost of borrowing from these institutions and, accordingly, can impute a current market value to their outstanding debt. For example, suppose a firm

Table 6-3   Cash Flows from $7,000,000 Loan Balance and Their Present Value at 13-percent Interest

End of Year	Principal Outstanding	Interest at 11%	Principal Payment	Interest Plus Principal	Present Value of Interest Plus Principal at $(1.13)^n$
1	$7,000,000	$770,000	$700,000	$1,470,000	$1,300,884.96
2	6,300,000	693,000	700,000	1,393,000	1,090,923.33
3	5,600,000	616,000	700,000	1,316,000	912,054.01
4	4,900,000	539,000	700,000	1,239,000	759,901.90
5	4,200,000	462,000	700,000	1,162,000	630,687.05
6	3,500,000	385,000	700,000	1,085,000	521,145.60
7	2,800,000	308,000	700,000	1,008,000	428,461.13
8	2,100,000	231,000	700,000	931,000	350,204.83
9	1,400,000	154,000	700,000	854,000	284,283.65
10	700,000	77,000	700,000	777,000	228,895.15
					$6,507,441.61

borrowed $10,500,000 from a life insurance company at 11 percent interest five years ago, that $7,000,000 is outstanding, and that the loan has ten years to maturity. The firm could borrow a similar amount today for 13 percent, also maturing in ten years. The terms of the 11-percent loan call for $700,000 to be paid at the end of each year for the next ten years and for 11 percent to be paid annually on the remaining balance. The cash flows from this loan and their present value at 13 percent interest are shown in Table 6-3; they currently total $6,507,441.61. Given a 13-percent yield to maturity on current loans of ten years, investors would pay $6,507,441.61 for the outstanding loan. Similar calculations can be made for other currently outstanding debt. The result is an imputed market value of debt capital. If the company had issued preferred stock that was also in the hands of private investors with no organized market, the company could also impute market value of debt capital based upon what it would cost to issue preferred stock at current rates. Suppose management had a $9 preferred stock outstanding that had been marketed at par or at $100 per share with a 9-percent yield. Currently management could issue new preferred at 11.5 percent. The imputed market value of the $9 preferred is

$$\frac{\$9.00}{.115} = \$78.26087$$

If 100,000 shares had been issued, current imputed value is $7,826,087 (100,000 × 78.26087 = $7,826,087).

This leaves the common stock, which has a current market value. Using the CAPM and the intrinsic value model, management finds it has an estimated cost of

Table 6-4 Firm's Current Cost of Capital Using Imputed Market Values for Debt and Preferred Stock

	Current Cost		Proportion of Current Capital Structure		
After-tax cost of debt	.091	×	.3	=	.02730
Preferred stock	.115	×	.15	=	.01725
Common stock					
Intrinsic value	.16	×	.55	=	.08800
CAPM	.175	×	.55	=	.09625
Return on book value	.17	×	.55	=	.09350

Average Cost of Capital (I)		*Average Cost of Capital (II)*	
Debt	= .02730	Debt	= .02730
Preferred	= .01725	Preferred	= .01725
Common (intrinsic value)	= .08800	Common (CAPM)	= .09625
Average cost	= .13255	Average cost	= .14080
	= 13.3%		= 14.1%

Average Cost of Capital (III)	
Debt	= .02730
Preferred	= .01725
Common (book value)	= .09350
Average cost	= .13805
	= .13.8%

equity capital of 17.5 percent under CAPM and 16.0 percent under the intrinsic value model. Management also finds its return on book value is 17 percent, a figure in accord with what other firms in similar industries earn. Using imputed market values for debt and preferred stock, the firm finds the proportion of total market value of debt, preferred, and common stock is .30, .15, and .55, respectively. The marginal tax rate of the firm is 30 percent. The after-tax cost of debt capital is $.13(1 - .3) = .091 = 9.1\%$. Using all three measures of return on equity capital, management finds its current average cost of capital is between 13.3 and 14.1 percent (see Table 6-4).

Of course, market values can change rapidly, and this may alter drastically the proportion accounted for by each source. As interest rates fall, stock prices tend to rise, raising market values of outstanding instruments. Because bonds and preferred stocks have fixed payments, both upward and downward price movements are usually smaller than those of stocks. A bull market could raise the relative proportion of total value of the firm accounted for by common stock. Management, sensing a receptive market for new issues, may want to raise more funds from the sale of stock. By using the current market values as weights, management may thus be encouraged to do what intuition suggests: raise a larger proportion of current funds from the sale of common stock. If one applied book value weights based on accounting for the sources of the relative contributions of all past fund sources, the resulting financing decisions may not be warranted by current market conditions.

THE COMPOSITION OF FINANCING AS A PORTFOLIO DECISION

It is always important to distinguish between the composition of outstanding funds and the addition of new securities. Assume management does not expect to invest in new projects. The firm will, however, continue to earn a return on existing assets, which will be used to repay those who supplied the funds—debtholders and owners. A major question management should address is whether the composition of financing—the current proportions of debt and equity, again using market value weights—maximizes the return, therefore the market value, and presumably the wealth of the owners. Before going further, *reread the preceding sentence*. Note the transition. In preceding sections you were introduced to the concept of weighted average cost of capital as if management were raising *new* monies. We are now discussing the proportions of debt and equity as if the company were in equilibrium and did not need additional funds. At the basic level of analysis, this distinction is very important. If the composition of outstanding obligations maximizes the wealth of owners, the capital structure is optimal. The cost of new funds raised in the manner described is also optimal. However, if the wealth of stockholders can be increased by altering the composition of debt and equity, this should be done prior to determining the weighted average cost of new capital.

We can view the problem in the context of the opportunity set shown in Figure 6-1. Suppose management has financed a portfolio of real assets by issuing a portfolio of financial claims consisting of debt and equity. The portfolio could include preferred stock. For purposes of analysis, however, management would treat preferred dividends as bond interest; failure to pay them would block the dividends to common stockholders, thereby affecting their return and wealth. Let us further assume the coefficient of correlation between all pairs of debt instruments is one. Consequently, we cannot lower the standard deviation of a portfolio of debt instruments by shifting among them.[8]

What remains is the return on common stock. A firm may finance 30 percent of its total outstanding assets from debt and 70 percent from equity. Alternatively, a

---

[8] In practice, the coefficients are not one. Institutional differences in debt contracts, even in the absence of market imperfections (primarily the tax laws), can result in comparatively greater risk to some debtholders than to others. The result of using these more risky instruments is a higher cost of debt capital and a greater standard deviation in the cost to maturity of the debt portion of the portfolio.

Figure 6-1   Changes in the Expected Average Cost of Capital and the Standard Deviation of a Portfolio of Financial Claims from Altering the Capital Structure

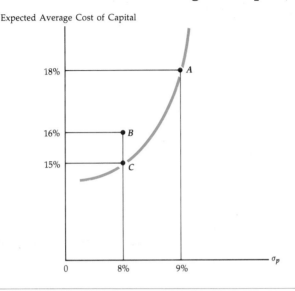

firm may use 40 percent and 60 percent, 60 percent and 40 percent, or some other combination. Because returns on stock historically show greater variability than returns on debt instruments, one would intuitively expect the standard deviation of a portfolio of claims more heavily weighted in stock to have a greater standard deviation. How much greater, as the relative weights change, depends upon the coefficient of correlation and therefore the covariance of the returns on debt and equity.[9] Using Figure 6-1, assume the current composition of financing results in portfolio C, which has an expected average cost of 15 percent and a standard deviation of 8 percent. Management finds that by selling debt and using the proceeds to purchase some of its outstanding stock, it will raise the cost of debt capital and also raise the cost—the return to stockholders—even higher. The result (portfolio A) is a higher average cost of 18 percent and an altered standard deviation of the portfolio (in this instance, it has risen). Why this might happen, even when there is proportionately more debt (with historically lower variability) than equity, will become clearer in Chapter 7. To start you thinking about the problem, contemplate what would happen to expected return and variability of return on equity when more

---

[9] To save you the trouble of returning to Chapter 4, the formula for the standard deviation of the portfolio follows:

$$\sigma_p = \sqrt{w_1^2 \sigma_2^2 + 2w_1 w_2 r_{12} \sigma_1 \sigma_2 + w_2^2 \sigma_2^2}$$

where w_1 and w_2 are the respective portfolio weights for debt and equity, r_{12} is the coefficient of correlation between the returns on debt and equity, and σ_1 and σ_2 are the standard deviations of the returns on debt and equity.

of the expected total earnings on investments in real assets must be used to pay a fixed and now (in absolute terms) larger interest charge.

As Figure 6-1 is drawn, the optimal portfolio of financing obligations is the mirror image of the Markowitz opportunity set. On the frontier, one can only trade off risk against cost (investors' return). In the context, portfolio B is suboptimal relative to C. By altering the proportions of debt and equity, the firm achieves a lower weighted average cost of capital without increasing the standard deviation of cost on that portfolio. Can management construct an efficient (least-cost) portfolio of financial claims? It is this question we next seek to answer.

SUMMARY

Just as long-distance runners must pace themselves at various times during a race, so too must those who undertake the study of financial theory pace themselves at various times along the road to understanding. Runners often pace themselves to conserve strength for a particularly grueling part of the race—Heartbreak Hill in the Boston Marathon, for example. Students must do so to sort out what they have learned in preparation for broadening and deepening that knowledge.

Chapter 6 may be viewed as designed to pace the reader. We began by using the measures of return developed earlier and turning them into the costs of specific sources of funds. For every basic debt instrument except common stock, the procedure is straightforward: yield to maturity on debt becomes cost to maturity; by analogy, yield on preferred stock becomes cost of financing with preferred. Expenses associated with issuing new instruments—flotation costs—cause the latter to be greater than the former. These expenses can be added to outlays for projects funded from monies raised and, for analytical purposes, can be ignored. Other institutional details, particularly the impact of income-tax laws on the cost of funds, can affect the choice of instruments employed. Interest on debt, for example, is a tax-deductible expense; interest on preferred stock is not. The after-tax cost of debt and the cost of preferred represent the explicit costs of using these instruments. Explicit costs do not take into account the effect new issues may have on market price, return, and (ultimately) wealth of the stockholders.

How does one measure the return and, therefore, the cost of common stock? Drawing again upon a previous discussion, we examined more closely the intrinsic value and CAPM models as measures of return and (ultimately) cost of equity capital. Using the intrinsic value model for an infinite holding period, we found the cost of equity capital to be

$$r = \frac{D}{P} + g$$

Using the CAPM, the cost of equity capital is

$$E(R_j) = i + \beta_{jm}(R_m - i)$$

We then briefly explored differences and (ultimately) similarities between the two models, noting that the CAPM—while depending on the relationship between expected return on a security and the market portfolio—implicitly uses present intrinsic value in calculating P_{j1} and P_{m1}. Moreover, although the present intrinsic value model depends on dividends and expected growth in dividends, the investment and financing decisions of management will affect the standard deviation of expected dividends and hence the expected returns. By altering the standard deviation or unsystematic risk of the firm, management also will affect the beta coefficient upon which CAPM depends.

Both the intrinsic value and CAPM models are market-based. By contrast, another measure of the cost of equity—return on book value—depends on accounting conventions. If dividends are a function of earnings, the latter depends on accounting treatment of revenues and expenses. At this point, however, the similarity between return on book value and the other two measure ends. Return on book value offers small comfort to those who believe intrinsic value and CAPM models are sophisticated versions of tea leaves. Nevertheless, the vagaries of accounting practice give one a measure that could be at variance with the way in which the market perceives the cost of new funds to the firm. At best, return on book value is a crude measure of opportunity cost for firms in similar industries with similar accounting practices.

Using all three measures of cost of equity capital as well as the cost of debt and preferred, we then calculated the weighted average cost of new capital. We concluded the weights should be based on the proportion of market value of each source of funds outstanding to the total market value of all fund sources. In this way, we have a market-based and not an accounting-based value of the firm as an entity.

The weighted average cost of new capital, however, presupposes that management cannot raise the market value of outstanding stock and lower the cost of new equity capital by issuing debt and retiring some of those shares. In other words, the capital structure as it currently exists is optimal. We ended Chapter 6 by setting the stage for a subsequent evaluation of this issue.

PROBLEMS AND QUESTIONS

1. The Stalled Computer Corporation is considering issuing either debt or preferred stock. Management can sell preferred stock so that its cost is 10.2 percent. The cost to maturity on a 15-year debt issue is 11.8 percent. If the firm has a marginal tax bracket of 10 percent, which security would have the lower after-tax cost of capital? Why? Would your answer change if the firm's marginal tax bracket was 20 percent? Explain.

2. Distinguish in detail between business risk and financial risk.

3. The Strong Box Corporation maintains a payout ratio of 40 percent. After-tax earnings are currently $7.35 per share and are expected to grow indefinitely at 5 percent per annum. The current market price of the stock is $24.50. Using the intrinsic value model, what is the cost of new equity capital?

4. Assume the beta coefficient for the Strong Box Corporation is .95. The risk-free rate is .08. The expected return on the market portfolio is .20. Using the CAPM, what is the expected return on the Strong Box Corporation?

5. The Strong Box Corporation also has the following values on the company books:

Common stock par value/$5	
1,150,000 shares outstanding	$ 5,750,000
Capital surplus	1,375,000
Earned surplus	21,485,000

Calculate book value per share for the common stockholders and return on book value per share. Contrast the results with your answers to problems 3 and 4. What might account for the differences among your answers?

6. The Burlington Brass Button Corporation has the following capital structure:

	Market Value
Debt	$13,500,000
Preferred stock	4,275,000
Common stock	42,225,000

a. Calculate the respective proportions of total capital accounted for by each source.

b. The current costs of issuing new sources of each type are:

Debt	13.50% YTM
Preferred stock	12.75% yield
Common stock	16.00% return on book value
	17.50% CAPM
	18.00% intrinsic value

Calculate the weighted average cost of new capital using each measure of the cost of common stock. Contrast the results.

7. Long-run growth in value of the market portfolio is expected to be 6 percent. Long-run return from holding the market portfolio is expected to be 15 percent.

Expected dividends from holding 1 percent of the market portfolio for one year are $575,000. Current value of 1 percent of the market portfolio is $6,000,000.

a. What is the expected return from holding the market portfolio for one year based upon 1 percent of the total market value?

b. If the risk-free rate for the expected holding period is 10.5 percent and the beta coefficient for the stock of XYZ Corporation is .85, what is the expected return from holding the stock of XYZ Corporation for one year?

8. Contrast the present intrinsic value model with the CAPM as tools for determining cost of equity capital. Should each give the same measure of cost of equity capital? Explain in detail.

SELECTED ADDITIONAL REFERENCES

Alvazian, Varouj and Jeffrey L. Callen. "Investment, Market Structure, and the Cost of Capital," *Journal of Finance*, Vol. 34 (March 1979, pp. 85–92).

Arditti, Fred D. and Haim Levy. "The Weighted Average Cost of Capital as a Cutoff Rate: A Critical Analysis of the Classical Textbook Weighted Average," *Financial Management*, Vol. 6 (Fall 1977, pp. 24–34).

Beranek, William. "The Weighted Average Cost of Capital and Shareholder Wealth Maximization," *Journal of Financial and Quantitative Analysis*, Vol. 12 (March 1977, pp. 17–32).

Brennan, Michael J. "A New Look at the Weighted Average Cost of Capital," *Journal of Business Finance*, Vol. 5 (Spring 1973, pp. 24–30).

Brigham, Eugene F. and Keith V. Smith. "The Cost of Capital to the Small Firm," *Engineering Economist*, Vol. 13 (Fall 1967, pp. 1–26).

Elliot, J. Walter. "The Cost of Capital and U.S. Investment," *Journal of Finance*, Vol. 35 (September 1980, pp. 981–1000).

Ezzell, John R. and R. Burr Parket. "Flotation Costs and the Weighted Average Cost of Capital," *Journal of Financial and Quantitative Analysis*, Vol. 11 (September 1976, pp. 403–13).

Fama, Eugene and Merton H. Miller. *The Theory of Finance* (New York: Holt, Rinehart and Winston, 1972, Chapter 7).

Gordon, M. J. and L. I. Gould. "The Cost of Equity Capital: A Reconsideration," *Journal of Finance*, Vol. 33 (June 1978, pp. 849–61).

Haley, Charles W. and Lawrence D. Schall. "Problems with the Concept of the Cost of Capital," *Journal of Financial and Quantitative Analysis*, Vol. 13 (December 1978, pp. 847–70).

Hamada, Robert S. "Portfolio Analysis, Market Equilibrium and Corporation Finance," *Journal of Finance*, Vol. 24 (March 1969, pp. 13–31).

McDonald, John G. "Market Measures of Capital Cost," *Journal of Business Finance*, Vol. 2 (Autumn 1970, pp. 27–36).

Mullins, David W. "Does the Capital Asset Pricing Model Work?" *Harvard Business Review*, Vol. 60 (January–February 1982, pp. 105–14).

Myers, Stewart C. "The Application of Finance Theory to Public Utility Rate Cases," *Bell Journal of Economics and Management Science*, Vol. 3 (Spring 1972, pp. 58–97).

Nantell, Timothy J. and Robert Carlson. "The Cost of Capital as a Weighted Average," *Journal of Finance*, Vol. 30 (December 1975, pp. 1343–55).

Ofer, Aharon R. "Investor Expectations of Earning Growth, Their Accuracy and Effects on the Structure of Realized Rates of Return," *Journal of Finance*, Vol. 30 (May 1975, pp. 509–23).

Reilly, Raymond R. and William E. Wecker. "On the Weighted Average Cost of Capital," *Journal of Financial and Quantitative Analysis*, Vol. 8 (January 1973, pp. 123–6).

Scott, David F., Jr. "Determining the Cost of Common Equity Capital: The Direct Method," *Journal of Business Research*, Vol. 8 (March 1980, pp. 89–103).

Solomon, Ezra. "Measuring a Company's Cost of Capital," *Journal of Business*, Vol. 28 (October 1955, pp. 240–52).

7

LEVERAGE, COST OF CAPITAL, AND OPTIMAL CAPITAL STRUCTURE

As we suggested in Chapter 6, one of the most important issues in the theory and practice of finance is whether the average cost of capital is affected by the proportion of assets financed through debt (including, for our purposes, preferred stock). If it is, financial managers seeking to augment the owners' wealth should maintain a proportion of debt in the capital structure that maximizes market value of the owners' equity: management should maintain an optimal capital structure.

To clear the air and minimize confusion, we note at the outset that under a specific set of assumptions (to be adumbrated shortly) there is no optimal capital structure. In practice, there are some reasons for using some debt to finance assets; the optimal proportion, however, remains elusive. To reach this rather unexciting conclusion, we will be trekking through arduous and sometimes tedious intellectual terrain. For some, the experience may be tantamount to scaling the Jungfrau—only to find the view enveloped in clouds. Others, however, will recognize that theoretical analysis sheds light on institutional factors that lend substance to the decision to finance at least some assets through debt. From this perspective, the view from the summit—although not as satisfying as one might have expected—is worth the effort. It is in this spirit that we embark upon our climb.

LEVERAGE

One of the more important phenomena in the field of finance is the effect on the earnings of stockholders called **leverage**. Leverage is divided conceptually into two components: **operating leverage** and **financial leverage**. The former pertains to the effect fixed costs of operations have on earnings before interest and taxes (EBIT); the latter pertains to the effect fixed costs of debt (interest) have on per-share earnings of common stockholders. Financial leverage is of direct concern to us in this chapter, but both financial and operating leverage are interconnected. However, their relationship is sufficiently involved to warrant a separate discussion. Accordingly, we present the discussion in Appendix 7-A for future chief executive officers to read and for future clerks to ignore.

FINANCIAL LEVERAGE Suppose an airline has financed its assets so that 75 percent of its market value is in common stock and 25 percent is in debt. The current market value of the common stock is $150,000,000: 3,000,000 shares at a current market price of $50 per share. The current market value of the debt is $50,000,000. Three widely used ratios measuring the proportions accounted for by debt and equity are

$$\frac{\text{debt}}{\text{debt} + \text{equity}} = \frac{\text{debt}}{\text{total capital}} = \frac{\$50,000,000}{\$50,000,000 + \$150,000,000} = \frac{1}{4} = 25\%$$

$$\frac{\text{equity}}{\text{debt} + \text{equity}} = \frac{\text{equity}}{\text{total capital}} = \frac{\$150,000,000}{\$50,000,000 + \$150,000,000} = \frac{3}{4} = 75\%$$

$$\frac{\text{debt}}{\text{equity}} = \frac{\$50,000,000}{\$150,000,000} = \frac{1}{3} = 33\tfrac{1}{3}\%$$

In terms of market value of the securities, the debt-to-total-capital ratio of the firm is $\frac{1}{4}$ (25 percent), the equity-to-total-capital ratio is $\frac{3}{4}$ (75 percent), and the debt-to-equity ratio is $\frac{1}{3}$ (33$\frac{1}{3}$ percent).[1]

---

[1] Practitioners often use book value weights to calculate these ratios. For reasons developed earlier, we shall use market values. Similarly, if preferred stock is used, it will be included in the market value of debt.

Table 7-1   Effect of Financial Leverage on Earnings per Share[a] for Three Forecasts of EBIT

Total Capital: 75 percent equity / 25 percent debt			
	Pessimistic	Most Likely	Optimistic
EBIT	$10,000,000	$20,000,000	$30,000,000
Interest	3,250,000	3,250,000	3,250,000
EBT	6,750,000	16,750,000	26,750,000
Taxes at .40	2,700,000	6,700,000	10,700,000
EAT	4,050,000	10,050,000	16,050,000
3,000,000 shares outstanding			
EPS	$1.35	$3.35	$5.35

Assets: financed with 100 percent equity			
	Pessimistic	Most Likely	Optimistic
EBIT	$10,000,000	$20,000,000	$30,000,000
Interest	—	—	—
Taxes at .40	4,000,000	8,000,000	12,000,000
EAT	6,000,000	12,000,000	18,000,000
4,000,000 shares outstanding[b]	$1.50	$3.00	$4.50

[a] Current market value of debt is $50,000,000; current market value of equity is $150,000,000. Debt to equity ratio is 1 : 3. There are 3,000,000 shares outstanding at a market value of $50 per share.
[b] 1,000,000 new shares of stock issued at $50 per share and proceeds used to retire $50,000,000 of debt.

In Table 7-1 we present three forecasts of EBIT. The interest payments are imbedded costs of debt whose market value is now $50,000,000; the average tax rate is 40 percent of earnings after interest. From the calculations, we find that forecasted earnings per share are $1.35, $3.35, and $5.35, respectively.

Suppose management were to issue 1,000,000 new shares of stock to existing stockholders at $50 per share and use the proceeds to repurchase the outstanding debt of $50,000,000. Again from Table 7-1 it is apparent that if the pessimistic forecast for EBIT occurred, EPS would be higher for the stockholders than if the debt had not been retired ($1.50 > $1.35). However, if either the most likely or most optimistic forecasts had materialized, the leverage effect of fixed interest charges would have caused EPS with debt in the capital structure to have been greater than EPS without such debt ($3.35 > $3.00 and $5.35 > $4.50).

Indeed, given a specific level of interest payments and a debt ratio, one can readily calculate the EBIT necessary for EPS to be the same whether one leaves the current capital structure undisturbed or retires the debt with a new issue of stock.

The relationship between the two capital structures is

$$\frac{(EBIT' - \text{interest})(1 - \text{tax rate})}{S_1} = \frac{(EBIT')(1 - \text{tax rate})}{S_2} \tag{7-1}$$

where $EBIT'$ results in the same EPS when a given leveraged capital structure is replaced with 100 percent equity:

$$S_1 = \text{number of shares currently outstanding}$$
$$S_2 = \text{number of shares after all debt is retired}$$

In the example, interest is \$3,250,000, the marginal tax rate is .40, S_1 is 3,000,000 shares, and S_2 is 4,000,000 shares. Substituting, we have

$$\frac{(EBIT' - \$3,250,000)(1 - .4)}{3,000,000} = \frac{(EBIT')(1 - .4)}{4,000,000}$$
$$EBIT' = \$13,000,000$$

With an EBIT of \$13,000,000, the calculations shown in the footnote to Figure 7-1 indicate the two modes of financing both yield an EPS of \$1.95 per share.

Figure 7-1 also suggests why the use of debt *leverages* EPS. Fixed-interest charges raise the slope of the line graphing the relationship between EBIT and EPS over what it would otherwise be if all assets were financed from equity. As the arithmetic suggests: for a given proportion of debt in the capital structure, in terms of EPS, stockholders are better off with that amount of debt in the capital structure as long as EBIT exceeds \$13,000,000. They are worse off if EBIT falls below \$13,000,000. If EBIT falls below \$3,250,000, earnings become insufficient to cover interest payments. If the company lacks the cash to meet such payments, bankruptcy can ensue.

Thus, financial leverage increases the variability of EPS for common stockholders. What, if anything, does it do to the market value of the stock and ultimately to the average cost of capital? It is to this question we now turn.

THE THEORY OF THE CAPITAL STRUCTURE— EARLY BASIS FOR CONTROVERSY

Just as Harry Markowitz fomented an intellectual revolution that culminated in Modern Portfolio Theory, so, too, did Franco Modigliani and Merton H. Miller (M & M) generate what, in light of hindsight, might be considered a second but related intellectual revolution concerning the effect of leverage on the cost of capital.[2]

---

[2] The classic article is Franco Modigliani and Merton H. Miller, "The Cost of Capital, Corporation Finance, and the Theory of Investment," *The American Economic Review*, Vol. 58 (June 1958, pp. 261–97). See also Franco Modigliani and Mertin H. Miller, "Corporate Income Taxes and the Cost of Capital: A Correction," *American Economic Review*, Vol. 58 (June 1963, pp. 433–43).

Figure 7-1   The Effect of Leverage on EPS (a graphical representation of the data in Table 7-2)

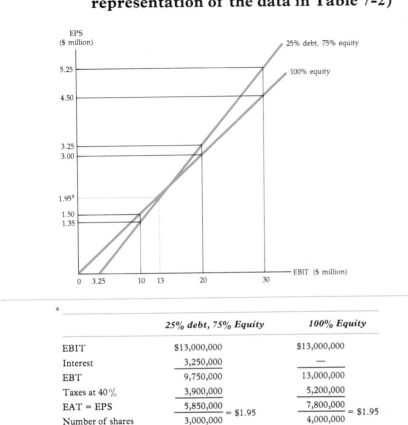

	25% debt, 75% Equity	100% Equity
EBIT	$13,000,000	$13,000,000
Interest	3,250,000	—
EBT	9,750,000	13,000,000
Taxes at 40%	3,900,000	5,200,000
EAT = EPS	5,850,000 = $1.95	7,800,000 = $1.95
Number of shares	3,000,000	4,000,000

Markowitz, observing that investors hold diversified portfolios, proceeded to quantitatively develop the role of diversification in optimizing between risk and return. Modigliani and Miller observed that corporations employed *cheaper* debt in the financing of their assets. Up to some point, it was presumed—so conventional wisdom ran—management could minimize the average cost of capital by using leverage and it was in the interests of the stockholders to do so. According to M & M, this view was incorrect. Their central and, at the time, revolutionary proposition was that the average cost of capital to any firm is independent of its capital structure and equal to the capitalization rate for the earnings of an unleveraged firm with some business risk.[3]

Unlike Markowitz, who was lending substance to what investors intuitively understood, M & M were challenging the conventional view that the average cost of

---

[3] Modigliani and Miller, pp. 276–77.

capital would be lower if the firm used some debt rather than no debt to finance assets. The revolution M & M generated had the effect of forcing both academics and practitioners to rethink the composition of the portfolio of securities employed by corporations to finance the company's assets. The passport to knowledge in this instance begins with a systematic study of the basic M & M proposition

THE THEORY OF THE CAPITAL STRUCTURE—SOME DEFINI- TIONS AND ASSUMPTIONS   Continuing with our simple classification of securities as debt, equity, or common stock, we employ the following assumptions:[4]

1. All markets are frictionless, so capital and other resources are perfectly mobile. As a result, there are no bankruptcy costs.

2. Dividends equal earnings. Because the company pays 100 percent of its earnings as dividends, dividend policy is not a factor in determining the cost of equity capital.

3. Operating earnings of the company are not expected to grow.

4. Individuals borrow and lend at the same interest rate as businesses.

5. There are no income taxes.

6. All investors hold the same view as to the probability distributions of expected future earnings.

7. All investors behave rationally: they maximize the market value of their equity.

8. For purposes of determining the costs of debt and equity, we assume a perpetual time horizon.

9. A corporation alters its capital structure by substituting debt for equity.

10. There are no transactions costs when buying or selling securities.

11. The firm's cost of equity depends upon its business-risk class.

Although these assumptions are restrictive, they offer a basis for building an analytical model with which to verify the M & M proposition that the cost of capital is independent of the capital structure of the firm. In this and subsequent chapters, we relax the most important assumptions in order to develop a more useful model to guide financial decision-makers in constructing a portfolio of financial instruments that minimizes the average cost of capital and thereby maximizes the wealth of owners. In addition to the foregoing assumptions, we denote interest (cost of debt) as k_d where

$$k_d = \frac{\text{interest payments}}{\text{market value of debt}}$$

---

[4] These assumptions differ somewhat from those in the original article: they reflect the development of thought in this area and facilitate the exposition. M & M, for example, would have been better served if they had explicitly stated that in perfect markets there are no bankruptcy costs. Since they did not, they were forced into an elaborate rationalization as to why the cost of debt would rise and the cost of equity correspondingly fall at high indexes of leverage. Modigliani and Miller, pp. 273–76.

Similarly, we denote the cost of leveraged equity capital as k'_e where

$$k'_e = \frac{\text{earnings}}{\text{market value of equity}}$$

Furthermore, using market values we label debt D and equity E, so that the same relationship denoted by k_e is the cost of unleveraged equity.

$$\frac{\text{debt}}{\text{capital}} = \frac{D}{D + E}$$

$$\frac{\text{equity}}{\text{capital}} = \frac{E}{D + E}$$

$$\frac{\text{debt}}{\text{equity}} = \frac{D}{E}$$

If k_o equals overall return to the company, in the absence of taxes, net operating income NOI = interest + earnings. Dividing by the total market value of the firm, D + E, we have

$$\frac{NOI}{D + E} = \frac{\text{interest} + \text{earnings}}{D + E}$$

We shall define

$$k_o = \frac{NOI}{D + E} = \frac{\text{interest} + \text{earnings}}{D + E}$$

But k_o also can be viewed as a weighted average return or cost of capital, so that

$$k_o = k_d\left(\frac{D}{D + E}\right) + k'_e\left(\frac{E}{D + E}\right) \tag{7-2}$$

To facilitate the use of these definitions, we present an arithmetic illustration in Table 7-2. Note that k_o, the return to all investors as well as the average cost of capital, is the same (.145161) whether one uses NOI or the weighted average cost of capital. Before going further, make certain you understand the definitions and are comfortable with the illustration.

THE OPTIMAL CAPITAL STRUCTURE— THE TRADITIONAL VIEW

Until the publication of M & M's seminal article, it was widely assumed, although never proven, that there was indeed an optimal combination of debt and equity in the capital structure of a company that minimized the average cost of capital. Graphically,

Table 7-2   Arithmetic Illustration: Weighted Average Cost of Capital Using M & M Definitions

Interest payments   = $ 1,500,000
Market value of debt   = 12,000,000

Cost of debt (k_d) $= \dfrac{1,500,000}{12,000,000} = .125$

Earnings   = $ 7,500,000
Market value of equity = 50,000,000

Cost of equity (k'_e) $= \dfrac{7,500,000}{50,000,000} = .15$

Net operating income $(NOI) = \$1,500,000 + \$7,500,000 = \$9,000,000$
Market value of firm $(D + E) = \$12,000,000 + \$50,000,000 = \$62,000,000$

$$\frac{\text{Debt}}{\text{Debt} + \text{Equity}} \frac{D}{D + E} = \frac{\$12,000,000}{\$62,000,000} = .193548$$

$$\frac{\text{Equity}}{\text{Debt} + \text{Equity}} \frac{E}{D + E} = \frac{\$50,000,000}{\$62,000,000} = .806452$$

$$\text{Return to investors } (k_0) = \frac{\$9,000,000}{\$62,000,000} = .145161$$

Average cost of cost of capital $(k_o) = (.125)(.193548) + (.15)(.806452) = .145161.$

the traditional approach may be illustrated as suggested in Figure 7-2. As the company increases its leverage, k'_e rises gradually while k_d remains unchanged. Consequently, k_o falls. The rationale for the gradual rise of k'_e, at least initially, is: (1) the relatively low probability small amounts of leverage will cause a fall in EPS and (2) the relatively high probability EPS will rise with the initial leverage.

Continuing, k_d remains constant initially, as the risk that debtholders will not receive their interest and principal payments when due is minimal. At some point, however, the risk to stockholders and ultimately debtholders rises with leverage, so that k'_e increases rapidly. As the debt–equity ratio rises, k_d also increases. As a result, the weighted average cost of capital is minimized at a value for k_o, where the debt–equity ratio (in this instance) is assumed to be .4.

To illustrate arithmetically how k_o falls and then rises, suppose k_e for an all-equity capital structure is 20 percent. The total expected earnings are $200,000 and the stock's market value is, therefore, $1,000,000. As there are 100,000 shares outstanding, the price per share is $10. Assume management issues $200,000 in debt

Figure 7-2   The Optimal Capital Structure (traditional approach)

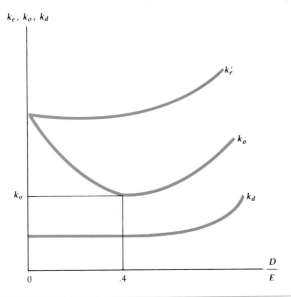

instruments at 8 percent interest and uses the proceeds to retire $200,000 in stock: 20,000 shares at $10 per share. In the absence of income taxes, the effect of leverage on earnings per share is

	All-equity Capital Structure	Capital Structure with Leverage
Earnings before interest (NOI)	$200,000	$200,000
Interest on $200,000 debt at 8%		−16,000
Earnings after interest	$200,000	$184,000
Earnings per share on 100,000 shares	$ 2.00	
Earnings per share on 80,000 shares		$ 2.30

To compensate for financial risk, suppose the market now capitalizes earnings at 21 percent rather than 20 percent. Thus the market price of the stock rises from $10 to

$$\frac{\$2.30}{.21} = \$10.95$$

Furthermore

$$k_o = k_d \left(\frac{\text{debt}}{\text{total capital}} \right) + k_e' \left(\frac{\text{equity}}{\text{total capital}} \right)$$

$$k_o = .08 \left(\frac{\$200,000}{80,000 \times \$10.95 + \$200,000} \right) + .21 \left(\frac{80,000 \times \$10.95}{80,000 \times \$10.95 + \$200,000} \right)$$

$$k_o = .08 \times .186 + .21 \times .814$$

$$k_o = \quad .015 \quad + \quad .171$$

$$k_o = .186 = 18.6\%$$

The average cost of capital has fallen with leverage.

On the other hand, suppose the firm had issued $800,000 instead of $200,000 in debt. At this level, assume the cost of debt capital is 18 percent. Management uses the proceeds from the debt to retire 80,000 shares of stock at $10 per share. Thus

	All-equity Capital Structure	Capital Structure with Leverage
Earnings before interest (NOI)	$200,000	$200,000
Interest on $800,000 debt at 18%		−144,000
Earnings after interest	$200,000	$ 56,000
Earnings per share on 100,000 shares	$ 2.00	
Earnings per share on 20,000 shares		$ 2.80

At these extreme indexes of leverage, assume the market now capitalizes earnings at 38 percent. The market price of the stock falls, so that

$$\frac{\$2.80}{.38} = \$7.37$$

Consequently

$$k_o = .18 \left(\frac{\$800,000}{\$7.37 \times 20,000 + \$800,000} \right) + .38 \left(\frac{20,000 \times \$7.37}{\$7.37 \times 20,000 + \$800,000} \right)$$

$$k_o = .152 + .059$$

$$k_o = .211 = 21.1\%$$

The average cost of capital has risen with leverage.

In the traditional approach to the capital structure, therefore, a corporation through trial and error attempts to find the level at which the average cost of capital is at a minimum. Management will continue to employ debt as long as the rise in the capitalization rate on equity is more than offset by the increase in earnings per share, thereby resulting in a further increase in the market price of the stock. At some point, however, the capitalization rate will begin to accelerate and the market price of the stock will decline. Moreover, as the debt–equity ratio rises, lenders will eventually demand a higher interest rate to compensate them for the increased risk they assume.

Although the traditional approach has intuitive appeal, it suffers from a lack of analytical rigor. The hypothesis fails to specify the functional relationship between k'_e and the debt–equity ratio and k_d and the debt–equity ratio, leaving one with the notion there is an optimal capital structure but no analytical means of determining it.

In short, the traditional view suggested the path that the cost of capital in the real world might follow, but without carefully specifying institutional factors (save perhaps bankruptcy costs) that would bring about an optimal capital structure. By using assumptions similar to those employed by M & M, one can develop a model to show under what conditions the average cost of capital is independent of the capital structure, while shedding light on the forces that give some credence to the traditional view as a representation of reality.

THE CAPITAL STRUCTURE— THE M & M HYPOTHESIS

As noted earlier, M & M postulated that the average cost of capital was independent of the firm's capital structure and equal to the capitalization rate of an unleveraged stream of earnings. The earnings are capitalized (discounted) at a rate appropriate for the business risk faced by that firm and other firms in the same risk class. As a result, the total market value of the firm is independent of the capital structure.

Stated briefly, M & M argued that firms in different industries faced different business risks. A utility, for example, may be subject to less earning variability than an oil company. Hence, in efficient capital markets, earnings of the former would be capitalized at a lower rate than earnings of the latter. If k_o were 10 percent for a utility and 12 percent for a manufacturing firm, these differences would compensate for differences in risks faced by the two companies.

Although we demonstrate later in the chapter that the risk-class assumption M & M made was not necessary to develop their hypothesis, we continue to employ it in order to illustrate their model. The essence of the M & M argument is that income from operations—NOI, or earnings before interest—will always be capitalized at the k_o appropriate to a firm's risk class. For example, if k_o equals 20 percent and NOI equals \$1,000,000, the total market value of the firm would be

$$\text{Market value of the firm} = \frac{\$1,000,000}{.20}$$

$$\$5,000,000 = \frac{\$1,000,000}{.20}$$

This simple calculation follows from our earlier assumptions that earnings do not grow and that all earnings are paid out as dividends. Thus, for this firm we view NOI as an infinite income stream and from our earlier valuation models capitalize it accordingly.

Now suppose this company has an all-equity capital structure with 100,000 shares outstanding. The market price of the stock is

$$\text{Price per share} = \frac{\$5,000,000}{100,000}$$

$$\text{Price per share} = \$50$$

Earnings, hence dividends per share, are

$$EPS = \frac{\$1,000,000}{100,000}$$

$$EPS = \$10$$

Suppose further that management could issue debt securities at 8-percent interest and retire stock with the proceeds. Using an arithmetic illustration, assume management borrows $1,000,000 at 8 percent and uses the proceeds to retire $1,000,000 in stock:

$$\frac{\$1,000,000}{\$50} = 20,000 \text{ shares}$$

Earnings per share for the remaining 80,000 shares are now

$$\text{NOI} = \$1,000,000$$
$$\text{Interest on debt} = \quad -80,000$$
$$\text{Net earnings} = \$ \ \ 920,000$$

$$EPS = \frac{\$920,000}{\$80,000}$$

$$EPS = \$11.50$$

According to M & M, because the cost of equity k_e will rise to k'_e, k_o will remain 20 percent. In short

$$k_o = k_d \frac{D}{D + E} + k'_e \frac{E}{D + E}$$

Because under the M & M Hypothesis total market value of the firm is unchanged, in our illustration

$$\frac{D}{D + E} = \frac{\$1,000,000}{\$5,000,000} = .2$$

$$\frac{E}{D + E} = \frac{\$4,000,000}{\$5,000,000} = .8$$

Substituting, we have

$$.2 = .08(.2) + k'_e(.8)$$
$$.8k'_e = .184$$
$$k'_e = .230, \text{ or } 23\%$$

More formally, if k_e represents only the cost of equity capital for an unleveraged capital structure and k'_e the cost of equity capital for a firm with debt in its capital structure, it can be shown that[5]

$$k'_e = k_e + \frac{D}{E}(k_e - k_d) \qquad (7\text{-}3)$$

---

[5] A simple proof is: for M & M, $k_o = k_e$. But

$$k_o = k_d \frac{D}{D+E} + k'_e \frac{E}{D+E}$$

Therefore

$$k_e = k_d \frac{D}{D+E} + k'_e \frac{E}{D+E}$$

$$k'_e \frac{E}{D+E} = k_e - k_d \frac{D}{D+E}$$

Adding and subtracting the term $k_e \frac{D}{D+E}$ from the equation, we have

$$k'_e \frac{E}{D+E} = k_e - k_d \frac{D}{D+E} + k_e \frac{D}{D+E} - k_e \frac{D}{D+E}$$

Rearranging and simplifying

$$k'_e \frac{E}{D+E} = k_e - k_e \frac{D}{D+E} + k_e \frac{D}{D+E} - k_d \frac{D}{D+E}$$

$$k'_e \frac{E}{D+E} = k_e \left(1 - \frac{D}{D+E}\right) + \frac{D}{D+E}(k_e - k_d)$$

Since

$$\frac{D}{D+E} + \frac{E}{D+E} = 1$$

$$\frac{E}{D+E} = \left(1 - \frac{D}{D+E}\right)$$

Therefore

$$k'_e \frac{E}{D+E} = k_e \frac{E}{D+E} + \frac{D}{D+E}(k_e - k_d)$$

(continued at bottom of page 182)

Figure 7-3   The Modigliani and Miller Hypothesis

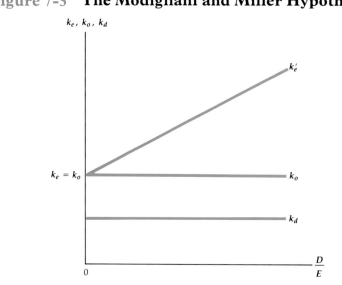

Because the cost of an unleveraged capital structure under the M & M Hypothesis is the average cost of capital, k_o

$$k'_e = .2 + \frac{.2}{.8}(.2 - .08)$$

$$k'_e = 23\%$$

Again

$$k_o = .08(.2) + .23(.8)$$
$$k_o = .016 + .184$$
$$k_o = 20\%$$

Graphically, the relationship between k_e, k_o, and k_d is illustrated in Figure 7-3. Since the average cost of capital equals the cost of an unleveraged capital structure, the capital structure is a mere detail that should not occupy management's time.

In summary, under the M & M Hypothesis, k_o is independent of the capital structure and the cost of equity rises with leverage in a manner specified by Equa-

---

(continued from bottom of page 181)

Multiplying by $\dfrac{D + E}{E}$, we have

$$k'_e = k_e + \frac{D}{E}(k_e - k_d)$$

tion 7-3. In other words, the risk premium to stockholders is simply a linear function of the debt–equity ratio times the difference between the cost of an unleveraged capital structure and the cost of debt capital. This premium is added to the cost of an unleveraged capital structure to obtain the cost of equity capital for a given debt–equity ratio.

THE M & M HYPOTHESIS—THE ROLE OF ARBITRAGE

In M & M's frictionless world of rational investors with homogeneous expectations, the mechanism for ensuring that $k_e = k_o$ is arbitrage. As there are no transaction costs and because individuals can borrow at the same rate as corporations, there is no advantage to stockholders when corporations borrow in order to raise earnings per share. Stockholders, by using *homemade* leverage, can duplicate the leveraged positions of corporations. To illustrate, consider the following two corporations in the same risk class: both face identical business risk. However, corporation A is a *low-roller* firm whose management is unwilling to issue debt in order to leverage EPS. In contrast, the management of corporation B consists of *high rollers* willing to use debt in order to increase earnings. Assume both companies have identical net operating income (NOI), so that

Corporation A low roller		Corporation B high roller	
NOI	$100,000	NOI	$100,000
Interest at 8 percent	—	Interest at 8 percent	32,000
Earnings after interest	$100,000	Earnings after interest	$ 68,000
Number of shares	50,000	Number of shares	30,000
Earnings per share	$2.00	Earnings per share	$2.267
Equity capitalization rate	.125	Equity capitalization rate	.136
Market price per share	$16.00	Market price per share	$16.67
Market value of stock	$800,000	Market value of stock	$500,000
Market value of company debt	—	Market value of company debt	400,000
Total market value	$800,000	Total market value	$900,000

Corporation A has an all-equity capitalization rate of .125 with 50,000 shares outstanding, a net income of $100,000, and a total market value of $800,000 ($100,000 ÷ .125). Earnings per share are $2.00 ($100,000 ÷ 50,000) and market price per share is $16 ($2.00 ÷ .125).

On the other hand, the high rollers managing corporation B have issued $400,000 in debt at 8 percent interest, leaving $68,000 in net income and only 30,000 shares. Capitalization rate on equity is .136—somewhat higher than the capitalization rate for corporation A, but not high enough to offset per-share growth in earnings resulting from use of leverage. As a result, market price per share is $16.67 (2.267 ÷ .136), total market value of the stock is $500,000 ($68,000 ÷ .136), and total value of the firm is $900,000.

Under M & M, this situation cannot continue. A shareholder in corporation B would find it profitable to sell, to borrow at the same rate as the management of corporation B, and to buy shares in corporation A. For instance, suppose an individual held shares representing 1 percent of the market value of corporation B. He or she sells the shares for $5,000 (.01 × $500,000). The stockholder now borrows in proportion to the debt ratio of corporation B and purchases 1 percent of the stock in corporation A. The debt-to-total-capital ratio of corporation B is $\frac{4}{9}\left(\frac{\$400,000}{\$900,000}\right)$.

The cost of shares representing 1 percent of the market value of corporation A is $8,000 (.01 × $800,000). Using the leverage ratio of corporation B, our stockholder can now create his or her leverage so that

Purchase 1 percent of the market value of corporation A	= $8,000.00
Borrow $\frac{4}{9}$ of $8,000	= 3,555.55
Portion of proceeds from sale of 1 percent of corporation B invested	= 4,444.45
1 percent of NOI of corporation A	= 1,000.00
Interest on $3,555.55 at 8 percent	= 284.44
Net income	715.56
Return on shareholder's investment in corporation A	$715.56 ÷ $4,444.45 = 16.1 percent

Clearly, the 16.1 percent return on the stockholder's funds invested in corporation A is superior to the 13.6 percent he or she would have earned by remaining in the leveraged corporation. Moreover, a smaller dollar investment in corporation A exposes the investor to less risk—the same risk exposure as owning shares representing 1 percent of the market value of corporation B.

At their current market price, therefore, shares of corporation B are overvalued. Stockholders of corporation B will sell their shares and purchase shares in corporation A, as well as shares in other unleveraged companies in the same risk class. Consequently, the market price of shares in corporation B will fall. If we further assume several unleveraged companies are in the same risk class, shares of corporation A need not rise as stockholders of corporation B disperse their purchases among the several companies.

The market price of the stock of corporation B will continue to decline until there is no additional profit from arbitraging. As the M & M Hypothesis suggests, the market value of shares in corporation B will fall to $400,000, or $13.33 per share ($400,000 ÷ 30,000). At this point, the total market value of corporations A and B are the same: $800,000. The cost of equity capital for corporation B is 17 percent ($2.267 ÷ $13.33). The ratio of debt to total capital is now .5. The average cost of capital k_o for corporation B is now

$$k_o = (.08)(.5) + (.17)(.5)$$
$$k_o = .125$$

Thus k_o for corporation B is .125, which is equal to k_e for corporation A. At $13.33 per share, if an investor sold 1 percent of the market value of the stock of corporation B, he or she would receive $4,000 (.01 × $400,000). If the investor purchased 1 percent of the market value of the shares in corporation A, he or she would spend $8,000 (.01 × $800,000). Using personal leverage, the stockholder would

Purchase 1 percent of the market value of corporation A	= $8,000
Borrow $\frac{1}{2}$ of $8,000	= 4,000
Portion of proceeds from sale of 1 percent of corporation B invested	= 4,000
1 percent of NOI of corporation A	= 1,000
Interest on $4,000 at 8 percent	= 320
Net income	= 680
Return on shareholder's investment in corporation A	$680 ÷ $4,000 = 17 percent

Thus a shareholder can do no better with an $8,000 investment in corporation B than with a $4,000 investment in corporation A. In the first case, the company provides the leverage; in the second, the individual investor provides the leverage. Since each investment has an identical risk — a ratio of debt to total capital of .5 — and since each investment has an identical return of 17 percent, arbitrage should cease.

LEVERAGE CAPM AND THE COST OF EQUITY CAPITAL

Since M & M wrote their initial article, financial theory has developed along the lines discussed in Chapter 5. As a result, CAPM has become the basis for an alternative explanation of the cost of equity capital with debt in the capital structure. Let us examine CAPM in this context and then compare it with the arbitrage process M & M initially employed.

Because we have shown CAPM can be used as a measure of the cost of equity capital without reference to the capital structure, then using k'_e as the cost of equity for a leveraged firm, CAPM becomes

$$k'_e = i + \beta_{em}(R_m - i)$$

$$k'_e = i + \frac{R_m - i}{\sigma_m^2}(r_{em}\sigma_e\sigma_m)$$

where k'_e = expected holding period return to stockholder and therefore cost of equity capital to firm

i = risk-free rate

R_m = expected return on market portfolio [$E(R_m)$ or $\bar{R}_m$ in Chapter 5]

r_{em} = coefficient of correlation between k'_e and R_m

σ_e = standard deviation of probability distribution of possible values for k'_e

σ_m = standard deviation of probability distribution of possible values for R_m

The CAPM tells us k'_e is a function of the risk-free rate plus a premium equal to

$$\frac{(R_m - i)\text{COV}_{em}}{\sigma_m^2}$$

We can set up a similar expression for the debt of the corporation, so that

$$k_d = i + \frac{(R_m - i)}{\sigma_m^2}(r_{dm}\sigma_d\sigma_m)$$

In this case, r_{dm} is a correlation coefficient between returns on the company's debt and returns on the market portfolio consisting of both debt and equity instruments. The standard deviation of the probability distribution of possible values for k_d is σ_d.

It can be shown that the covariance between expected return on the stock of a leveraged company and expected return on the market portfolio is[6]

$$r_{em}\sigma_e\sigma_m = \frac{D + E}{E}(r_{em}\sigma_e\sigma_m)^* + \left(1 - \frac{D + E}{E}\right)(r_{dm}\sigma_d\sigma_m)$$

The term $(r_{em}\sigma_e\sigma_m)^*$ is the covariance of the expected return on the stock with the expected return on the market portfolio, assuming the company had an all-equity (unleveraged) capital structure. If we substitute the foregoing in our equation for CAPM, we have

$$k'_e = i + \left[\frac{R_m - i}{\sigma_m^2}\right]\left[\frac{D + E}{E}(r_{em}\sigma_e\sigma_m)^* + \left(1 - \frac{D + E}{E}\right)(r_{dm}\sigma_d\sigma_m)\right]$$

---

[6] Robert A. Haugen and James L. Pappas. "Equilibrium in the Pricing of Capital Assets, Risk-Bearing Instruments and the Question of Optimal Capital Structure," *Journal of Financial and Quantitative Analysis*, Vol. 6 (June 1971, 943–54). See also Yutaki Imai and Mark E. Rubinstein, "Comment," and Robert A. Haugen and James L. Pappas, "Reply," *Journal of Financial and Quantitative Analysis*, Vol. 7 (September 1972, pp. 1995–2004).

Since

$$\frac{E}{D+E} + \frac{D}{D+E} = 1$$

Then, multiplying both sides of the expression by $\dfrac{D+E}{E}$, we obtain

$$\left(\frac{D+E}{E}\right)\left(\frac{E}{D+E}\right) + \left(\frac{D+E}{E}\right)\left(\frac{D}{D+E}\right) = \frac{D+E}{E}$$

$$1 + \frac{D}{E} = \frac{D+E}{E}$$

Substituting and rearranging, we have

$$k'_e = i + \left(\frac{R_m - i}{\sigma_m^2}\right)\left[\left(1 + \frac{D}{E}\right)(r_{em}\sigma_e\sigma_m)^* - \frac{D}{E}(r_{dm}\sigma_d\sigma_m)\right]$$

$$k'_e = i + \left[\frac{R_m - i}{\sigma_m}\right](r_{em}\sigma_e)^* + \frac{D}{E}\left[\frac{R_m - i}{\sigma_m}\right](r_{em}\sigma_e)^* - \frac{D}{E}\left[\frac{R_m - i}{\sigma_m}\right](r_{dm}\sigma_d)$$

Since the term

$$i + \frac{R_m - i}{\sigma_m}(r_{em}\sigma_e)^*$$

is the same as the cost of equity capital for an unleveraged firm, k_e, we have

$$k'_e = k_e + \frac{D}{E}(k_e - k_d)$$

ARBITRAGE AND THE CAPM

Lest we become overburdened by the mathematics, let us pause and compare in straightforward prose the two approaches to the cost of equity capital with leverage in the capital structure. In the arbitrage model, M & M began with a risk-class assumption—a logical device suggesting, independent of financial risk, different levels of business risk for different ventures. In terms of the analysis employed, this assumption amounts to stating that the standard deviation of the expected return for one type of business may be greater than that for another type of business. As we have seen under CAPM, one finesses the problem of independent variability by holding a diversified portfolio. The expected return on the stock then depends on the covariance with the market. Included in the covariance, however, is a measure of independent variability that affects the value of beta. As a result, CAPM relieves us of the risk-class assumption.

For arbitrage to work perfectly, one must be able to borrow at the same rate as a leveraged firm. Yet we know this assumption is unrealistic. A similar problem arose in the development of the rationale underlying CAPM. The Capital Market Line (CML) and hence the market portfolio depended on the borrowing rate equaling the lending rate, again an unrealistic assumption. Because each unrealistic assumption is a market imperfection, each is—however minor empirically—a flaw in application of the analysis to the real world.

M & M originally abstracted from the dividend decision by assuming dividends equaled earnings. Moreover, they assumed no growth. Both assumptions can and are relaxed in Chapters 10 and 11. As they stand, however, in terms of a holding period return with no debt in the capital structure

$$\text{holding period return} = \frac{P_1 - P_0 + D_1}{P_0}$$

If $D_1 = E_1$, then P_1 equals P_0. Recall the rationale in Chapter 6, where we discussed the differences between the intrinsic value model and the CAPM. Because there is no growth and 100-percent payout, there is no reason, given the capital structure, for the market price to change. Introducing financial risk (leverage) into either model causes the market value of the stock to change and the cost of equity capital to rise under either M & M or CAPM. In addition, the no-growth assumption implies no further additions to assets from new issues of debt and equity. A firm could pay out all earnings as dividends, issue new debt and equity in proportion to their current values $\left(\dfrac{D}{E} \text{ remains constant}\right)$, and add to the assets and to total operating earnings. Two scenarios are possible. Under M & M, because the addition to earnings from assets purchased does not affect the standard deviation in earnings per share, the risk class is not altered. Similarly, under CAPM, the beta coefficient is unaffected by a change in the standard deviation $\left(\text{remember, } \beta_{jm} = r_{jm}\dfrac{\sigma_j\sigma_m}{\sigma_m^2}\right)$. Under the second scenario, business risk is altered and both the risk class and the beta coefficient change, causing the return or cost of equity capital to rise or fall accordingly. Inasmuch as the capital investment decision is the subject of the next two chapters, this topic receives fuller consideration there.

Finally, there is a basic philosophical point in both analyses. Under M & M, the firm adds nothing of value to shareholders from manipulating the capital structure; under CAPM, one reaches the same conclusion through a different framework. In each case, cost of equity capital rises with financial risk; by implication, average cost of capital remains unchanged. With reference to a point raised at the end of Chapter 6, management need not concern itself with whether the portfolio of liabilities and equity lie on the efficiency frontier. Under M & M, nothing can be done to rearrange the portfolio so as to alter the average cost of capital; under

CAPM, the expected return lies on the Securities Market Line. Manipulating the capital structure merely alters the position of the company's stock along the SML. In theory, management is helpless and the message is clear: six-figure salaries are paid to executives to assume responsibility for business risk the firm undertakes—not for wasting time with capital structure.

Nevertheless, any executive who assumes that on the basis of the foregoing discussion he or she may ignore capital structure should be, if not dismissed, at least demoted—perhaps to corporate economist. We have already suggested that the market portfolio is difficult to determine. Moreover, it is not a foregone conclusion that all stockholders have diversified portfolios. In addition, if the corporation can borrow at a lower rate than the shareholder, corporate leverage is a better substitute than personal leverage. These points aside, two important assumptions in the original version by M & M must be relaxed: (1) the difference in tax treatment of income versus debt and equity and (2) the costs of bankruptcy or, more generally, what we term the costs of financial distress.

CORPORATE INCOME TAXES AND COST OF CAPITAL

Blessed are the income taxes, for they stimulate creativity—particularly creative schemes to avoid them. Any financial vice president worth a six-figure salary knows interest creates a tax shield.

Consider the data in Table 7-3; they depict two situations. In the first, where the firm's capital structure is entirely equity, there is an expected EBIT from operations of $18,000,000. With a marginal tax rate of 46 percent, the expected EAT is $9,720,000. In the second situation, the same firm, with both debt and equity, has a total market value of $54,600,000. In constructing the table, we assumed management replaced its all-equity capital structure by purchasing 200,000 shares from existing stockholders at $50 per share for $10,000,000, with purchases made in proportion to their initial holdings.[7] The monies used to purchase the shares came from the sale of $10,000,000 worth bonds at par and carrying a 14-percent interest rate. To remain consistent with the M & M format, we shall assume the interest rate continues in perpetuity, thereby setting at least the upper limit on the tax advantage from a given rate of interest.

Note the total value of the firm has risen to $54,600,000. Thus, expected total income to both bondholders and stockholders is now $10,364,000. Under an all-equity capital structure, expected total income was $9,720,000. The increase, $644,000, represents the differential between the actual interest cost of $1,400,000

---

[7] Although the phrase "with purchases made in proportion to their initial holdings" is of no analytical significance, it allows one to abstract from the issues of redistribution of income from old stockholders who sold their shares and from those who did not.

Table 7-3 How Taxes Affect Debtholder and Stockholder Income when Leverage Is Employed

	Situation One (100% equity)	Situation Two (with leverage)
Market value of equity	$50,000,000	$44,600,000
Market value of debt	—	10,000,000
Total market value	$50,000,000	$54,600,000
Total number of shares	1,000,000	800,000
Market price per share	$50	$55.75
EBIT	$18,000,000	$18,000,000
Interest at 14%	—	1,400,000
EBT	$18,000,000	$16,600,000
Taxes at 46%	8,280,000	7,636,000
EAT	$ 9,720,000	$ 8,964,000
Number of shares	1,000,000	800,000
EPS	$9.72	$11.205
k_e or k'_e (under M & M)	$\frac{\$9.72}{\$50.00} = 19.44\%$	$\frac{\$11.205}{\$55.75} = 20.10\%$
Total income to bondholders	—	$ 1,400,000
Total income to stockholders	$ 9,720,000	$ 8,964,000
Total income to bondholders and stockholders	9,720,000	10,364,000
Average cost of capital	19.44%	17.8033%

$$\frac{\$10,000,000}{\$54,600,000} \times 14\%(1-.46) + \frac{\$44,600,000}{\$54,600,000} \times 20.10\% = 17.8033\%$$

Debt–equity ratio

$$\frac{D}{E} = \frac{\$10,000,000}{\$44,600,000} = .2242 = 22.42\%$$

and the after-tax cost of $756,000. Thus

$$.14 \times \$10,000,000 = \$1,400,000$$
$$.14(1-.46)\$10,000,000 = \underline{\quad 756,000}$$
$$\$ \ 644,000$$

For stockholders, the risk they assumed in receiving the tax shield was the interest they paid on the debt. Given the perpetuity assumption, the

$$\text{present value of tax shield} = \frac{\$644,000}{.14} = \$4,600,000$$

We obtain the same results in the following way. Let

$$D = \text{market value of debt}$$
$$T_c = \text{corporate tax rate}$$
$$k_d = \text{yield (or cost) in perpetuity on debt}$$

Then

$$\text{present value of tax shield} = \frac{T_c k_d D}{k_d}$$
$$= T_c D$$

In the foregoing illustration, present value of the shield equals $.46 \times \$10,000,000 = \$4,600,000$. In the absence of taxes, under M & M the total market value of the firm equals expected EBIT from operations divided by the average cost of capital that in turn equals the cost of an unleveraged capital structure. Thus, if

$$V_u = \text{value of unleveraged firm}$$
$$k_e = k_o = \text{cost of unleveraged capital structure}$$

Then

$$V_u = \frac{EBIT}{k_e} \tag{7-4}$$

Although introduction of income taxes does not alter the business risk, it does lower the level of earnings, so that

$$EAT = EBIT\,(1 - T_c)$$
$$V_u = \frac{EAT}{k_e} \tag{7-4a}$$

However, given that earnings are tax deductible, then

$$V_L = \frac{EAT}{k_e} + T_c D \tag{7-5}$$

In their analysis of the impact of corporate taxes on the cost of equity capital, M & M demonstrate that[8]

$$k'_e = k_e + \frac{D}{E}\,(k_e - k_i)(1 - T_c) \tag{7-6}$$

---

[8] Franco Modigliani and Merton H. Miller. *Corporate Income Taxes and the Cost of Capital: A Correction*, pp. 437–39. The perceptive student—the one who reads footnotes—is probably wondering whether interest is deductible for individuals who might use the arbitrage model. It is. The presumption (not always correct) is that corporations can borrow at lower rates and that they experience higher taxes than individuals. As we shall see, the personal income tax rate can affect the gains owners enjoy from leverage.

The cost of equity capital for a leveraged firm rises more slowly than in the absence of corporate income taxes: the higher the tax, the flatter the slope of k'_e. As shown in Table 7-3, $\dfrac{D}{E}$ equals .2242 or 22.42 percent. Using the appropriate figures

$$k'_e = .1944 + .2242(.1944 - .14)(1 - .46)$$
$$k'_e = .1944 + .0066$$
$$k'_e = .2010 = 20.10\%$$

This is the same result suggested by the arithmetic in Table 7-3. Furthermore, it has been demonstrated using the CAPM that[9]

$$R_j = k'_e = i + (R_m - i)\beta_{ju}\left[1 + \frac{D}{E}(1 - T_c)\right] \tag{7-7}$$

where R_j is the same as $E(R_j)$ or $\bar{R}_j$ in Chapter 5 and where, assuming an unleveraged capital structure, β_{ju} is the beta coefficient for stock j. If β_{ju} is .802807, return on the market portfolio is 21 percent, and the risk-free rate is 12 percent, then

$$R_j = k'_e = .12 + (.2100 - .1200).802807(1 + .2242(.54))$$
$$k'_e = .12 + (.09).9000$$
$$k'_e = .12 + .0810$$
$$k'_e = .2010 = 20.10\%$$

The effect of introducing corporate income taxes is to flatten the slope of k'_e over what it would otherwise be as debt is substituted for equity. Using M & M, k'_e rises, but not rapidly enough to keep k_o constant. Using CAPM, we obtain the same results. Because the standard deviation of return on the stock increases with leverage, so does the beta coefficient—but not enough to keep k_o constant.

Although the corporate tax rate determines the extent to which a firm benefits from leverage, the lower the rate the smaller the subsidy to the stockholders from using debt. As suggested by the foregoing equations and as shown in Figure 7-4, a falling average-cost-of-capital curve (which is consistent with the traditional view of the relationship between cost of capital and leverage) can be explained by the corporate income tax. However, the traditional view also suggests the weighted average-cost-of-capital curve levels off and eventually rises with increases in leverage. The presumption is that in the real world, bankruptcy costs cause k'_e to begin rising with increases in $\dfrac{D}{E}$, thereby resulting in a rising average-cost-of-capital

---

[9] See Robert S. Hamada, "Portfolio Analysis, Market Equilibrium and Corporation Finance," *Journal of Finance,* Vol. 24 (March 1969), pp. 19–30). Hamada's proof uses the nomenclature of the time; Equation 7-5 is couched in the terminology of this text. The arithmetic examples, of course, derive from the models and illustrate the major point that as debt is substituted for equity, the introduction of corporate income taxes lowers the average cost of capital.

Figure 7-4   Corporate Income Taxes, the Cost of Debt, the Cost of Equity Capital, and the Average Cost of Capital

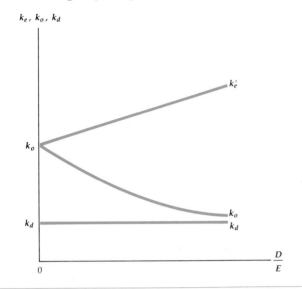

curve. We subsequently examine this proposition more closely. In the meantime we must consider the effect of personal income taxes on the gain firms receive from leverage.

THE EFFECT OF PERSONAL INCOME TAXES ON DEBTHOLDERS AND SHAREHOLDERS

The corporation deducts interest from taxable income of the firm; bondholders—unless the bonds are tax exempt—pay income taxes on the interest they receive. Moreover, individual stockholders pay income taxes on all dividends. Merton H. Miller, among others, has suggested the gain from leverage must be modified to take personal income taxes into account.[10] To understand the effect of personal income

---

[10] Merton H. Miller. "Debt and Taxes," *The Journal of Finance*, Vol. XXXII (May 1977, pp. 261–75, particularly pages 267–69). See also Donald Farrar and Lee L. Selwyn, "Taxes, Corporate Policy and Returns to Investors," *National Tax Journal*, Vol. 20 (December 1967, pp. 444–54); Stewart C. Meyers, "Taxes, Corporate Financial Policy and the Return to Investors: Comment," *National Tax Journal*, Vol. 20 (December 1967, pp. 455–62); R. C. Stapleton, "Taxes, the Cost of Capital and the Theory of Investment," *The Economic Journal*, Vol. 82 (December 1972, pp. 1273–92); Joseph Stiglitz, "Taxation, Corporate Financial Policy, and the Cost of Capital," *Journal of Public Economics*, Vol. 2 (February 1973, pp. 1–34).

taxes, from Equations 7-4a and 7-5 we can write

$$V_L = V_U + T_c D \tag{7-5a}$$

The second term on the right side of the expression, $T_c D$, can be rewritten so that

$$T_c D = D[1 - (1 - T_c)]$$

If we let

$$T_{ps} = \text{personal tax rate of stockholders}$$
$$T_{pd} = \text{personal tax rate of bondholders}$$

then one can reason that when a firm employs leverage, it reduces the number of shares outstanding and hence lowers both corporate income tax and personal taxes paid by shareholders. Retaining our assumption that all earnings are paid out as dividends, *savings* to stockholders from using leverage is

$$k_d D(1 - T_c)(1 - T_{ps})$$

Debtholders, however, must pay taxes on interest received. Consequently, after-tax income to debtholders equals

$$k_d D(1 - T_{pd})$$

Because debtholders are interested in after-tax yields, gain to stockholders from using debt must be compared with loss of income to debtholders from paying income taxes. Assuming a perpetual income stream, the tax advantage to owners of using debt is

$$\frac{T_c D \left[1 - \dfrac{(1 - T_c)(1 - T_{ps})}{(1 - T_{pd})} \right]}{T_c}$$

or tax advantage of debt is

$$D \left[1 - \frac{(1 - T_c)(1 - T_{ps})}{(1 - T_{pd})} \right]$$

or changing Equation 7-4a, we obtain

$$V_L = V_U + D \left[1 - \frac{(1 - T_c)(1 - T_{ps})}{(1 - T_{pd})} \right] \tag{7-8}$$

The bracketed term in Equation 7-8 represents gain from leverage, G_L, so that

$$G_L = D \left[1 - \frac{(1 - T_c)(1 - T_{ps})}{(1 - T_{pd})} \right] \tag{7-9}$$

Thus, gain from leverage depends algebraically on differences in tax rates of the corporation, the shareholders, and the debtholders. For example, if the tax rate on shareholders equaled the tax rate on debtholders or both were zero, then

$$G_L = [1 - (1 - T_c)]D$$
$$G_L = T_c D$$

which is the same as the present value of the tax shield in Equation 7-5. On the other hand, if

$$(1 - T_c)(1 - T_{ps}) = (1 - T_{pd})$$

then the ratio

$$\frac{(1 - T_c)(1 - T_{ps})}{(1 - T_{pd})} = 1$$

and there is no gain from leverage. If the ratio is greater than one, perhaps 1.25, then

$$G_L = [1 - 1.25]D$$
$$G_L = -.25D$$

and there is a loss to the firm from using leverage. Consequently, only if the ratio is less than one is there a gain to the firm from employing leverage.

Some interesting questions emerge from the foregoing analysis. For example, management should know (but rarely does) at least the average tax rate of its stockholders and bondholders. Another issue: for the economy as a whole, do stockholders have a higher or lower tax rate than bondholders? We investigate this and related questions on the debt and dividend decisions in practice in Chapter 11. Our analysis thus far shows, however, that corporate income taxes do cause the average-cost-of-capital curve to fall, with the slope of the curve dependent upon the corporate tax rate. The introduction of personal taxes on dividends to stockholders and of interest payments to bondholders could, depending on comparative rates, retard, reverse, or not affect the advantage corporate income-tax laws bestow on the company from the use of leverage.

FINANCIAL DISTRESS AND AVERAGE COST OF CAPITAL

Like indigestion, the term bankruptcy connotes something unpleasant. Moreover, bankruptcy is associated with a legal procedure that represents the extreme outcome of a situation where a firm is unable to pay principal or interest when due. The term **financial distress**—like caterer, custodian, or sanitary engineer—is not only more delicate and euphonious but also more accurate. Continuing the analogy to indigestion, the pain of financial distress ranges from mild to acute. Although cash needed to meet interest payments may be tight, certain assets can be liquidated. Similarly, wealth is reduced—even though the reduction is marginal—when one invests in an antacid for the relief of gastronomic distress. Acute indigestion may require medical treatment or hospitalization; acute financial distress may require protracted litigation.

From an analytical perspective, there are costs to financial distress. The liquidation of assets decreases the wealth of owners; the use of the courts involves legal and other expenses. When acute indigestion is symptomatic of terminal illness, the patient dies. When financial distress is symptomatic of a condition where the market value of a company's liabilities exceeds the market value of its assets, the legal remedy is generally liquidation of the company, sale of its assets, and distribution of the proceeds to settle a portion (if not all) of the financial claims against the company.

In the real world, therefore, there can be losses to owners and to the debtholders.[11] Although a complete description of bankruptcy procedures is more suited to the study of law than finance, basic analytical issues can be handled with ease if not complete precision. (In Chapter 13, we touch upon some of the more salient institutional features of bankruptcy.)

Firms with publicly held debt are well aware of their bond rating; those with privately held debt can usually obtain a rating that reflects the quality of their credit. The major rating services, Moody's and Standard & Poor's, use a classification system that summarizes their judgment of a company's ability to meet the obligations of the debt contract: payment of principal and interest as they come due. Ratings can change over time. For example, when AT&T was forced to divest itself of Bell System companies, the debt rating for some of those companies was downgraded, reflecting the increased risk associated with holding securities of those firms.[12]

Both rating services employ Aaa (Moody's) and AAA (Standard & Poor's) to rank those issues of highest possible quality with respect to risk of default—ability to pay principal and interest is very strong. Issues rated Aa, A, and Baa (Moody's) and AA, A, BBB (Standard & Poor's) are all considered adequately protected with respect to principal and interest—Aa slightly less so that Aaa, A less so than AA, and Baa less so than A. The last two ratings reflect the judgment of the rating services that adverse economic conditions may affect ability to pay principal and interest when due. Ratings below this level (Ba, B, Caa for Moody's, BBB, CCC, and CC

---

[11] There are also social costs. Former employees must find new jobs. In some instances, where the company was a particulary important factor in the economic health of the community, the entire region can be affected. Because they are outside the scope of our analytical framework, we do not consider these costs.

[12] *Moody's Bond Survey*, Vol. 75 (March 11, 1983).

Table 7-4   Corporate Bond Yield Averages at a Point in Time in 1983 (percent)

	June 2	June 1	May 31	1983 High	1983 Low
Av. Corp	12.53	12.54	12.54	13.12	12.11
Aaa	11.73	11.78	11.79	12.14	11.23
Aa	12.15	12.17	12.18	12.70	11.75
A	12.83	12.80	12.82	13.65	12.51
Baa	13.41	13.41	13.36	14.06	12.90

SOURCE: *Moody's Bond Survey* (June 6, 1983, p. 2566).

for Standard and Poor's) reflect the judgment of the rating services as to various degrees of speculation attached to payment of principal and interest. Ca/CC are highly speculative issues likely to default. Moody's uses C to designate the lowest rated issue with extremely poor prospects. Standard & Poor's employs D to indicate a debt instrument in default. Moody's often uses such codes as A_1, A_2, and A_3 to suggest gradations within the group of A-rated securities. Standard & Poor's employs a($+$) and a($-$) to suggest better- or worse-than-average quality for a particular issue with a specific rating.[13]

At any point in time, there is a differential in yields, such as those shown in Table 7-4 for the first five months of 1983 and specifically for May 31, June 1, and June 2. One, but not the only, factor affecting this differential is the expected risk of default.[14] At the outset, a particular firm may not qualify for an Aaa rating. For example, operations may be affected sufficiently by changes in the general level of economic activity to warrant an A rating—which makes its k_d higher than the k_d for Aa-rated and Aaa-rated corporations and which, in turn, makes the k_d for Aa-rated and Aaa-rated corporations higher than the yield on risk-free U.S. government securities of comparable maturity.

---

[13] The foregoing description is adapted from Moody's *Bond Record* and Standard & Poor's *Bond Guide*. Standard & Poor's uses a C rating to describe an income bond on which management must pay interest only if earned, but which is not being paid because earnings are not available.

[14] Other factors include:

1. Differences in maturities of same-quality instruments.
2. Differences in systematic risk with respect to the market portfolio for debt issues.
3. Differences in coupon rates. Bonds with lower coupons have a lower effective tax rate and therefore sell at lower YTM before taxes.
4. Marketability of different issues can vary. The more marketable an issue is, the lower the required YTM.
5. Differences in call prices. The higher the call premium over the par value of the instrument, the greater the YTM.
6. Random factors, especially as they affect daily yields.

Figure 7-5   The Effect of Leverage on the Cost of Debt Capital and the Cost of Equity Capital

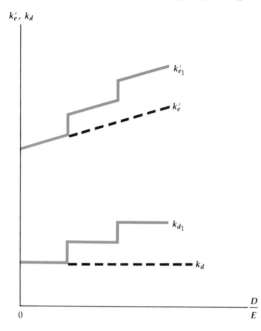

Other things being the same, the key question for the financial manager is, at what $\frac{D}{E}$ ratio does the A rating become a Baa rating, and so on? One can graphically illustrate the problem using Figure 7-5. At some $\frac{D}{E}$ ratio, k_d will rise because of a drop in debt rating. Debtholders, in other words, must be compensated for the increased risk they assume. This rise, however, lowers expected EBT and EAT over what they would otherwise be if k_d had not risen. Given lower expected EAT, the increase in leverage raises the standard deviation of the expected return, which causes risk-averse investors to bid down the market price of the stock, thereby raising k'_e over what it would otherwise be if k_d had not risen.

As depicted in Figure 7-5, k_d and k'_e ratchet upward with each decline in bond rating.[15] If we allow for marginal changes in k_d and k'_e after the first drop in ratings,

---

[15] For a more complete analysis, see Alan Kraus and Robert H. Litzenberger, "A State-Preference Model of Optimal Financial Leverage," *Journal of Finance*, Vol. 28 (September 1973, pp. 911–22).

Figure 7-6   The Optimum Capital Structure Giving Consideration to Taxes and Bankruptcy Costs

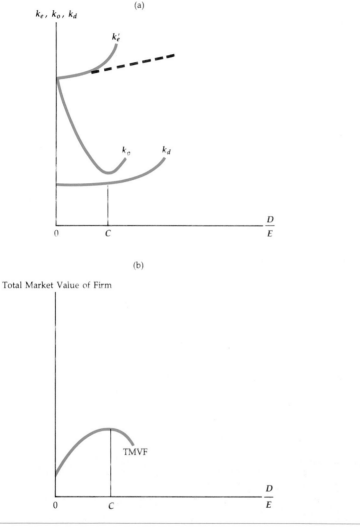

the result is the optimal $\dfrac{D}{E}$ ratio suggested by Figure 7-6(a). The tax advantage from leverage would cause k_0 to fall. However, at some point, increases in k_d will cause k'_e to accelerate and the combination will cause k_0 to rise. At that point the firm has reached the optimal capital structure.

In terms of Figure 7-6(b), the optimal capital structure is consistent with the point at which the total value of the firm is at maximum. Recall Equation 7-8, where

$$V_L = V_u + \left[1 - \frac{(1 - T_c)(1 - T_{ps})}{(1 - T_{pd})} \right] D$$

Assume that $T_{ps} = T_{pd}$, so that

$$V_L = V_u + T_c D$$

Then, if PV_F represents the present value of expected cost due to financial distress

$$V_L = V_u + T_c D - PV_F \tag{7-10}$$

What Equation 7-10 suggests is that the optimal capital structure has been reached when the present value of the tax shield equals the present value of the loss associated with the cost of bankruptcy.

To illustrate the point, we have reproduced in Table 7-5 the second column of Table 7-3, where the firm took advantage of the tax deductibility of interest using a $\frac{D}{E}$ ratio of .2242. At this point the market value of the firm is consistent with $V_L = V_u + T_c D$. We must presume, therefore, that PV_F is zero. Suppose that instead of a $\frac{D}{E}$ ratio of .2242, management changed leverage of the firm from zero to $\frac{D}{E}$ equals 1.36. To do this, however, the firm had to pay 20-percent interest on debt rather than 14 percent. Debtholders, recognizing the increased risk, expect to be compensated accordingly. Since EBIT is independent of the composition of financing, the additional interest not only lowers expected EAT but increases its variability. Because of the reduction from 800,000 to 400,000 shares, expected EPS rises from $11.205 to $16.20. The market price of the stock, however, falls from $55.75 to $55 per share and the total market value of the firm falls from $54,600,000 to $52,000,000. The average cost of capital rises from 17.80 percent to 24 percent.

Considering only the tax advantage of debt, the market value of the firm should be

$$V_L = \$50,000,000 + .46 \times \$30,000,000$$
$$V_L = \$63,800,000$$

Because the total market value of the firm is now $52,000,000, we presume that $PV_F = \$63,800,000 - \$52,000,000 = \$11,800,000$. Apparently the optimal capital structure is greater than a $\frac{D}{E}$ ratio of .2242 but less than a $\frac{D}{E}$ ratio of 1.36.

Table 7-5   How Taxes and Increased Debt Cost Affect Debtholder and Stockholder Income

	$\dfrac{D}{E} = .2242$	$\dfrac{D}{E} = 1.36$
Market value of equity	$44,600,000	$22,000,000
Market value of debt	10,000,000	30,000,000
Total market value	$54,600,000	$52,000,000
Total number of shares	800,000	400,000
Market price per share	$55.75	$55.00
EBIT	$18,000,000	$18,000,000
Interest at 14%	1,400,000	—
Interest at 20%	—	6,000,000
EBT	16,600,000	12,000,000
Taxes at 46%	7,636,000	5,520,000
EAT	8,964,000	6,480,000
Number of shares	800,000	400,000
EPS	$11.205	$16.20
k_e'	$\dfrac{11.205}{55.75} = 20.10\%$	$\dfrac{16.20}{55.00} = 29.45\%$
Total income to bondholders	$1,400,000	$6,000,000
Total income to stockholders	8,964,000	6,480,000
Total income to bondholders and stockholders	$10,364,000	$12,480,000
Average cost of capital	17.8033%	24.00%

$$k_o = .20 \frac{30,000,000}{(52,000,000)} + .2945 \frac{22,000,000}{(52,000,000)} = .23998 = .24 = 24\%$$

If the foregoing scenario seems a bit contrived, you have reason for your skepticism. There is in the literature considerable controversy as to when the average cost of capital begins to rise. Some have even argued that rational investors, creditors, employers, and employees who sense the possibility of bankruptcy avoid the debacle by cooperating to reduce debt with a new issue of stock. It is in their interests to protect the concern.[16] Others argue that if the company is not a viable

---

[16] See Robert A. Haugen and Lemma W. Senbet, "The Irrelevance of Bankruptcy Costs to the Theory of Optimal Capital Structure," *Journal of Finance*, Vol. 33 (June 1978, pp. 383–94).

economic entity it should be liquidated. The process of liquidation, however, may entail losses to both debtholders and owners.

A fundamental feature of common stock is limited liability to owners. If one had purchased a share of W. T. Grant stock in 1972, following its collapse in 1975 and subsequent liquidation, he or she would have lost the price paid for the stock. The common shareholder's home, car, and other property could not be attached to pay off losses banks incurred as a result of the failure.[17] Moreover, recall that rational behavior implies perfect information. In writing off $35 million in bad loans, a spokesman for one of Grant's major lenders noted: "We never knew how bad the internal systems were... The deeper we got in the more bad apples we found."[18]

To monitor the inventories and receivables that are major assets of a retailer necessitates expenditures. Such expenditures are a form of **agency cost** that may be anticipated in higher interest rates on loans made and, consequently, in lower earnings and lower market value for shareholders.[19] In a large modern corporation, management acts as agent for both debtholders and stockholders who are the principals supplying capital to the company. Since common stockholders are the ultimate owners to whom management (in principle) is responsible, it should come as no surprise debtholders want to protect the market value of their loan. Hence, restrictive covenants such as limitations on dividend payments are not uncommon in debt contracts. To protect debtholders completely from loss, however, would involve an incredible number of covenants and would severely limit management in its investment and financing decisions. Monitoring costs incorporated in the interest could become so high as to effectively preclude the use of debt beyond some $\frac{D}{E}$ ratio.

Thus, even if bankruptcy is not an immediate threat, increased interest costs and subsequent limitations on managerial discretion could cause the agent (management) and the principals supplying equity capital from issuing further debt.

In practice, therefore, agency costs may be a significant factor in raising k_d at relatively low levels of $\frac{D}{E}$ and those costs may accelerate as financial risk increases.

The burden of higher interest shifts to the stockholders, who will eventually bid down the price of shares, causing the market value of the firm to decline. Tax advantages from using debt are overwhelmed by agency costs and (ultimately) by expected costs of bankruptcy, eliminating any advantage to additional leverage.

---

[17] See "Investigating the Collapse of W. T. Grant," *Business Week* (July 19, 1976, pp. 60–62).

[18] Business Week, p. 62.

[19] See Michael C. Jensen and William H. Menckling, "Theory of the Firm: Managerial Behavior, Agency Costs and Ownership Structure," *Journal of Financial Economics*, Vol. 3 (October 1976, pp. 305–60). For a somewhat different perspective, see Stewart C. Myers, "Determinants of Corporate Borrowing," *Journal of Financial Economics*, Vol. 5 (November 1977, pp. 147–75). See also Amir Barnea, Robert Haugen, and Lemma W. Senbet, "Market Imperfections, Agency Problems and Capital Structure: A Review," *Financial Management*, Vol. 10 (Summer 1981, pp. 7–22). For a broader analysis of the concept of agency cost, see Eugene F. Fama, "Agency Problems and the Theory of the Firm," *Journal of Political Economy*, Vol. 88 (April 1980, pp. 288–307).

A HAZY VIEW FROM THE SUMMIT

Although we subsequently examine such additional factors as growth and dividend policy that may impact on the cost of capital, we have now reached the point where we can see that k_o and (ultimately) the market value of the firm depend upon $\dfrac{D}{E}$. The work of Modigliani and Miller, among others, sheds light on factors, specifically tax deductability of interest, that encourage the use of debt. Yet, debt was employed long before the corporate income-tax law was enacted and long before taxes were a significant portion of net income.[20] Although earlier financial managers may not have known differential calculus, it is hard to believe they did not have some rationale for using debt. Perhaps the time-honored truth that a corporation is a convenient institution for apportioning risk, income, and control through the issuance of various types of debt and equity instruments carried some substance.[21] One could amass capital and issue securities catering to the specific risk-return trade-offs of individuals or institutions unwilling or unable to diversify portfolios in the modern sense of that word. At the same time, if control of—not an agency relationship with—management is a primary motivation of ownership, then using debt rather than equity to raise funds would help limit stock ownership.

Agency and bankruptcy costs, of course, have always been present and can account for the rising portion of k_o in the traditional notion of an optimal capital structure: such costs may limit the use of debt. On the other hand, even though the tax deductability of interest may explain why management, acting as agent for stockholders, may use some debt in the capital structure, it does not provide a rationale for preferred stock whose dividends are not deductible. However, preferred stock does increase the equity base of the firm and, from that perspective, lowers the agency and bankruptcy costs of additional debt.

As you were cautioned at the outset, the view from the summit leaves something to be desired. Yet, by making the trek, the financial manager now has the tools necessary to examine the firm's existing capital structure to test whether or not some debt is warranted; that is, what is T_c, T_{pd}, and T_{ps}, and at what $\dfrac{D}{E}$ ratio will k_d begin to

---

[20] The corporate income tax took effect March 1, 1913; it was preceded by a corporate excise tax enacted in 1909. In 1914, the corporate income tax averaged less than 1 percent of net income; in 1922, it averaged 10.2 percent of EBT. The excess profits tax that characterized the 1940s and early 1950s raised the tax to a high that averaged, for example, 48.7 percent in 1951. In 1958, the year M & M's seminal article appeared, there was no longer an excess profits tax but corporate income taxes averaged 43.3 percent of EBT. By 1979, the rate averaged 37.3 percent. See U.S. Department of Commerce, *Historical Statistics of the United States*, Bicentennial Edition (Washington, D.C.: U.S. Government Printing Office, 1975, Part 2, pp. 1091 and 1109) and U.S. Department of Commerce, Bureau of the Census, *Statistical Abstract of the United States*, 1982–83, p. 261. The deductability of interest on debt has been a feature of the corporate income-tax law since it took effect in 1913. See 38 U.S.C. § 173 (1913). See also the discussion of current tax law in Chapter 8 and Appendix F of the book.

[21] W. H. Lyon. *Capitalization: A Book on Corporation Finance* (Boston: Houghton Mifflin, 1912, p. 2).

rise? In the context of a specific firm, answers to these questions may not pinpoint the optimum level of $\dfrac{D}{E}$ but will help management determine the threshold level of debt *below* which k_o would be higher and the market price of the stock lower than optimum. Beyond that point, the view is murkier and the financial theorist should not fault management for having second thoughts about whether further increases in $\dfrac{D}{E}$ will increase rather than decrease the market value of the firm.

SUMMARY

At this stage of our discussion we have reached an important juncture on the road toward understanding the principles of modern financial theory. Financial managers raise funds through the issuance of debt and equity instruments. The monies raised are invested in plant equipment and other assets that are, in turn, employed in the production of goods and services. A central management question is whether or not there is an optimal combination of securities, specifically debt and equity, that minimizes the average cost of capital and therefore maximizes the market value of the firm. Using a set of assumptions that abstract from market imperfections, Modigliani and Miller demonstrated that (1) the average cost of capital equals the cost of an unleveraged capital structure for a firm in a given business risk class and (2) the cost of equity capital for a leveraged firm rises as a linear function so that

$$k'_e = k_e + \frac{D}{E}(k_e - k_d)$$

To demonstrate the validity of their propositions, M & M let investors use homemade leverage under the assumption individuals could borrow at the same rate as the firm. Accordingly, an excess premium incorporated in the market price of a leveraged firm's stock would be bid away as investors substituted personal leverage for corporate leverage. We indicated the identical result can be obtained from the CAPM, which, in turn, makes M & M's risk class assumption unnecessary. Since k'_e for the two models is identical, for purposes of corporate policy management can do nothing to increase the wealth of owners through manipulating the capital structure. While management's role is passive, by implication owners adjust portfolios to satisfy their own risk-preference functions.

Once we drop some of the assumptions upon which the M & M model is built, it is possible for k_o to decline and the market value of the firm to rise with increases in leverage. Not only can the firm generally borrow at lower rates than the individual, but interest is tax-deductible. The interest rate may be lower and the tax savings greater from the use of corporate rather than personal leverage. As demonstrated in the text, however, the tax advantage from using debt may be partially offset by the fact that debtholders pay taxes on the interest and stockholders on the dividends. Within these limits, the gain from leverage is

$$G_L = 1 - \left[\frac{(1 - T_c)(1 - T_{ps})}{1 - T_{pd}}\right]D$$

Even if k_o declines because of tax laws, there will come a point where increases in leverage will cause k_d to rise because of agency costs and expected costs of bankruptcy. Although the risk to owners increases with additional leverage, restrictive covenants in the debt contract, if sufficiently broad, can curtail managerial discretion with respect to investment and financing decisions in the future. This, in turn, may impact adversely upon earnings and (ultimately) the market price of the stock, causing k'_e to accelerate. With both k'_e and k_d increasing, k_o begins to rise rapidly and the market value of the firm begins to fall. At the point at which k_o rises—at the minimum point on the average-cost-of-capital curve—the market value of the firm is at a maximum.

In practice, it is difficult for management to know the appropriate $\frac{D}{E}$ ratio for the firm. From its credit rating, at any point in time management knows the rate at which it can borrow and also knows that beyond some $\frac{D}{E}$ ratio the rate will rise. In addition, management may not know the average and marginal tax rates of stockholders and debtholders. Agency and bankruptcy costs for a particular firm are even more difficult to determine, although management can assume that one or the other or both are incorporated in higher interest costs that may accompany increased $\frac{D}{E}$. Consequently, management may only be able to determine an approximate $\frac{D}{E}$ ratio below which k_o is higher and the value of the firm is lower than it otherwise would be. Beyond that point, one would have confidence in recommending additional leverage only if it could be demonstrated that a rise in k_d would not cause k_o to increase.

Finally, the principles developed in this chapter lead toward an equilibrium solution. In a dynamic context, the composition as well as the aggregate supply of new funds may be changing. If other factors remain the same (inflationary expectations, for example), k_d might change because of institutional forces. For instance, life insurance companies are major purchases of corporate debt. If a sudden increase in insurance premiums were collected, these companies might be willing to lend money at lower interest rates. Accordingly, the same credit risk might warrant lower k_d in a different environment. This, in turn, could lead a firm to increase marginally its $\dfrac{D}{E}$ ratio.

More important, however, is the fact that a growing firm will be adding to its assets in the future. Will the income such assets produce affect not only the expected level of EBIT from operations but also the probability distribution? Does this suggest the cost of new capital (abstracting the impact of inflation on returns) is different from the current values of k_d, k'_e, and k_o based upon the existing capital structure? To gain insight into this issue, we now turn to the management of and, particularly, additions to the assets of a company.

OPERATING LEVERAGE, FINANCIAL LEVERAGE, AND THE RELATIONSHIP BETWEEN THEM

Chief executive officers (CEOs) are sometimes referred to as *big-picture* executives; it is their function to understand the business as a whole, leaving details to the lower echelons. Knowing how operating leverage affects total earnings, how financial leverage affects earnings per share, and how the two interrelate is an important element in the big picture.

To illustrate, suppose a manufacturer of calculators determines the total fixed costs of the firm are $1,500,000. Whether the plant is operating or not, these costs—ranging from depreciation to security forces—remain. Average variable costs—costs that are a function of output, such as wages, materials, and the like—are $50 per calculator. Let

$$v = \text{variable costs per unit (average variable costs)}$$
$$x = \text{output}$$
$$F = \text{total fixed costs}$$
$$p = \text{price per unit}$$
$$EBIT = \text{Earnings Before Interest and Taxes from operations}$$

By definition, a firm breaks even—total profits are zero—when

$$\text{total fixed costs} + \text{total variable costs} = \text{total revenues}$$
$$F \qquad + \qquad vx \qquad = \qquad px$$
$$x = \frac{F}{p - v}$$

If management sets a price of $150 for the calculator, the break-even point is

$$x = \frac{\$1,500,000}{\$150 - \$50}$$
$$x = 15,000 \text{ units}$$

At this output, EBIT is zero.

Now let us assume that assets are financed from both debt and equity. The current market value of the debt is $25,000,000 and the current market value of the stock is $100,000,000. There are 2,500,000 shares outstanding at $40 per share. The current interest charges are $3,000,000, 12 percent of the value of outstanding debt. At $40 per share, management could buy all debt outstanding by issuing 625,000 shares. Comparing the current capital structure of the firm with 100-percent equity financing, the EBIT at which EPS would make both equal is

$$\frac{(EBIT' - \$3,000,000)(1 - .4)}{2,500,000} = \frac{(EBIT')(1 - .4)}{3,125,000}$$

$$EBIT' = \$15,000,000$$

Using either capital structure, at this level of EBIT we find that EPS is

	Debt and Equity	*100% Equity*
EBIT	$15,000,000	$15,000,000
Interest	3,000,000	—
EBT	12,000,000	15,000,000
Taxes at .4	4,800,000	6,000,000
EAT	7,200,000	9,000,000
Number of shares	2,500,000	3,125,000
EPS	$2.88	$2.88

Having established the break-even point for operations and the level of EBIT at which EPS is higher using the given capital structure, we can now calculate the output necessary to reach an EBIT of $15,000,000. Simply add the $15,000,000 to the fixed costs, so that

$$x = \frac{\$16,500,000}{\$150 - \$50}$$

$$x = 165,000 \text{ units}$$

The foregoing analysis focuses on the major decisions that determine profitability or lack of it. Consider what information must be available at top levels of management to determine how profitable the firm is. Preliminarily, management needs an estimate from production of unit costs of manufacturing the calculators as well as a realistic estimate of costs independent of output—fixed costs. From marketing must come an estimate of quantities that can be sold at various prices and a justification that the chosen price will maximize total operating profits. Finally, traditionally the province of the financial vice president, comes the rationale for the chosen capital structure. As the discussion in this chapter suggests, there are real-world reasons why a company may use financial leverage for the benefit of owners. Consequently, if (after analyzing the component parts) management concludes in this instance there is virtual certainty that sales at $150 per calculator will exceed 165,000 units a year into the foreseeable future, there is little risk to the stockholders from the current level of debt in the capital structure. On the other hand, if 165,000 units is an optimistic sales forecast, management may want to consider the effect of price changes on the number of units sold, or the reduction of debt in the capital structure, or both.

THE DEGREE OF OPERATING LEVERAGE (DOL)

Given a price, given that more units can be sold at that price (price equals marginal revenue), and given the variable and fixed costs, it is useful to calculate the impact on EBIT of a change in sales. Known as the **degree of operating leverage**

$$DOL = \frac{\% \Delta \text{ in } EBIT}{\% \Delta \text{ in sales}}$$

Since

$$EBIT = \text{total sales} - \text{total variable costs} - \text{total fixed costs}$$
$$= \quad px \quad - \quad\quad vx \quad\quad - \quad\quad F$$
$$= x(p - v) - F$$

Because F is fixed, a change in EBIT results from

$$\Delta EBIT = \Delta x(p - v)$$

Therefore

$$\frac{\Delta EBIT}{EBIT} = \frac{\Delta x(p - v)}{x(p - v) - F}$$

Since

$$DOL = \frac{\% \Delta \text{ in } EBIT}{\% \Delta \text{ in sales}}$$

Then

$$DOL = \frac{\dfrac{\Delta EBIT}{EBIT}}{\dfrac{\Delta px}{px}} = \frac{\dfrac{\Delta x(p - v)}{x(p - v) - F}}{\dfrac{\Delta px}{px}}$$

Since p is constant

$$\frac{\Delta px}{px} = \frac{\Delta x}{x}$$

Then

$$\frac{\frac{\Delta x(p-v)}{x(p-v)-F}}{\frac{\Delta x}{x}} = \frac{\Delta x(p-v)}{x(p-v)-F} \cdot \frac{x}{\Delta x}$$

and

$$DOL = \frac{x(p-v)}{\cdot\; x(p-v)-F} \qquad\qquad \text{(7-A-1)}$$

Because the only difference between the numerator and the denominator is the total fixed costs F, the larger those costs are the greater the profit or loss per unit change in sales. At the break-even point, DOL is zero, below that point, DOL is negative; above that point, it is positive. Using our illustration where x is equal to 10,000 and 20,000 units, respectively, we have

$$DOL = \frac{10,000(\$150 - \$50)}{10,000(\$150 - \$50) - \$1,500,000} = -2.00$$

$$DOL = \frac{20,000(\$150 - \$50)}{20,000(\$150 - \$50) - \$1,500,000} = 4.00$$

At 10,000 units, EBIT from operations is declining twice as fast as sales, whereas at 20,000 units, EBIT is rising four times as fast as sales.

DEGREE OF FINANCIAL LEVERAGE (DFL)

The **degree of financial leverage** is defined as

$$DFL = \frac{\%\,\Delta \text{ in } EPS}{\%\,\Delta \text{ in } EBIT} = \frac{\frac{\Delta EPS}{EPS}}{\frac{\Delta EBIT}{EBIT}}$$

For a given number of shares N, a given level of interest In, and a marginal tax rate equal to the average tax rate t, then

$$EPS = \frac{(EBIT - In)(1 - t)}{N}$$

Since In is fixed, then

$$\Delta EPS = \frac{\Delta(EBIT)(1 - t)}{N}$$

Consequently

$$\frac{\Delta EPS}{EPS} = \frac{\dfrac{(\Delta EBIT)(1-t)}{N}}{\dfrac{(EBIT - In)(1-t)}{N}} = \frac{\Delta EBIT}{EBIT - In}$$

Hence

$$DFL = \frac{\dfrac{\Delta EBIT}{EBIT - In}}{\dfrac{\Delta EBIT}{EBIT}} = \frac{EBIT}{EBIT - In} \qquad (7\text{-}A\text{-}2)$$

In this instance, let In equal \$15,000,000. If EBIT were \$20,000,000, then

$$DFL = \frac{\$20,000,000}{\$20,000,000 - \$15,000,000} = 4.00$$

From this level of EBIT, EPS will increase 4.00 times as rapidly as EBIT.

DEGREE OF OPERATING AND FINANCIAL LEVERAGE (DOFL)

The **degree of operating and financial leverage** is defined as

$$DOFL = DOL \cdot DFL = \frac{x(p-v)}{x(p-v) - F} \cdot \frac{EBIT}{EBIT - In}$$

However

$$\frac{EBIT}{EBIT - In} = \frac{x(p-v) - F}{x(p-v) - F - In}$$

Therefore

$$DOFL = \frac{x(p-v)}{x(p-v) - F} \cdot \frac{x(p-v) - F}{x(p-v) - F - In}$$

$$DOFL = \frac{x(p-v)}{x(p-v) - F - In} \qquad (7\text{-}A\text{-}3)$$

The DOFL tells management what will happen to EPS at x units of output. We know, for example, that at 165,000 units, DOFL is zero. At 200,000 units, however

$$DOFL = \frac{200,000(\$150 - \$50)}{200,000(\$150 - \$50) - \$1,500,000 - \$15,000,000} = 5.71$$

Figure 7-A-1   A Graphical Representation of DOFL

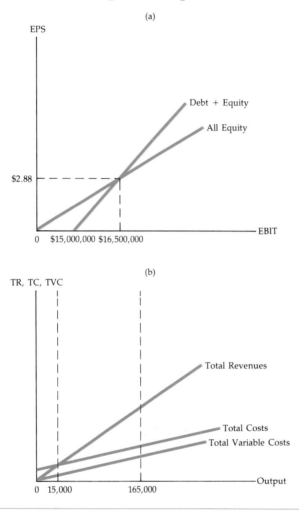

EPS in this instance is rising 5.71 times as rapidly as EBIT. However, if x were 100,000 units

$$DOFL = \frac{100,000(\$150 - \$50)}{100,000(\$150 - \$50) - \$1,500,000 - \$15,000,000} = -1.54$$

EPS would fall 1.54 times as fast as EBIT.

DOFL—SUMMARY   Figure 7-A-1 (a and b) graphically shows the relationship between operating leverage and financial leverage. When the firm breaks even—total costs equal total revenue—EBIT and EPS are zero. Up to an EBIT of $15,000,000, EPS is zero, as interest absorbs all of EBIT. Beyond a $16,500,000 EBIT, EPS rises more rapidly with the current level of interest payments than if all debt were replaced by stock. Simple, is it not?

In fact, judicious application of this analysis can be helpful in understanding how a firm's EBIT and EPS vary. A high degree of operational and financial leverage can cause considerable year-to-year fluctuations in each. One does not, however, become a CEO merely by putting numbers into formulas: the real world is far more complicated. Except in perfectly competitive industries, total revenues do not rise at a linear rate. A jumbo jet, flying from New York to San Francisco on two consecutive days, could be filled to capacity each day yet not generate the same total revenue. The reason lies in the myriad fares from first-class to super-saver to clerical discounts, all designed to take advantage of what are perceived to be differences in elasticities of demand for the service. Depending on the number of tickets sold at each fare, total revenues for the same flight vary. The example, although trivial, when generalized for the entire company may show total revenues rising—as a function of the number of seats sold—at a decreasing rather than at a constant rate.

In addition, it may be difficult to separate fixed from variable costs. Accountants allocate depreciation estimates, which are treated as variable expenses, prior to calculating reported EBIT or EPS. Such estimates, however, may bear slight resemblance to the costs that are truly variable in the event output is zero. Furthermore, firms may produce several products or services; the problem of allocating costs among them is a continuing conundrum, one for which there is no agreed-upon solution.

In summary the foregoing framework suggests reasons for fluctuations in EBIT and EPS. Adapting the analysis to the specifics of a particular company remains an art, not a science.

PROBLEMS AND QUESTIONS

1. Assume company X has an all-equity capital structure. The cost of capital for the company is 17 percent. Management decides to replace some of the equity with debt and issues a series of bonds at 8-percent interest. As a result, the ratio of debt to total capital rises to 20 percent. Under the M & M Hypothesis, what is the new cost of equity capital? What is the average cost of capital? Why?

2. Magna Corp has an all-equity capital structure. Its current cost of capital after taxes is 16 percent. Management is considering adding debt to the capital structure. The current market value of the stock is $1,000,000. There are 100,000 shares of stock outstanding. The corporate income-tax rate is .5. Assume management can replace stock with debt in increments of $200,000. If

it does so, management estimates that

Option	New Issue of Debt	Per-share Market Price of Stock	Before Taxes k_d	After Taxes k'_e
1	$200,000	$12	8%	15.83%
2	$400,000	$10	8%	24.00%
3	$600,000	$ 8	12%	38.75%
4	$800,000	$ 4	30%	50.00%

a. Assuming management selects one of the four options, calculate the average cost of capital. In other words, for each calculation assume management begins with an all-equity capital structure and replaces equity with the debt indicated.

b. Is there an optimal choice among the four? Explain.

3. Suppose the cost of equity capital is 15 percent for a firm with no debt in its capital structure. Management issues a series of bonds. Before tax k_d is 8 percent. The proceeds are used to retire a portion of the stock outstanding. As a result, the ratio of debt to total capital rises from 0 to .30. The cost of equity capital k'_e after taxes is now 18 percent. The corporate income-tax rate is .5.

a. What is the average cost of capital using the after-tax cost of debt capital?

b. Assuming k'_e is 18 percent, k_d is 8 percent, and there are no income taxes, what is the average cost of capital? Is the result consistent with the M & M Hypothesis? Explain.

4. Company X and company Y are both in the same risk class. Company X is a high roller; company Y is a low roller. Company X chooses to finance 50 percent of its capital structure from debt at an interest cost of 10 percent. Company Y retains an all-equity capital structure. The operating results are

	Company X	Company Y
NOI	$1,000,000	$1,000,000
Interest at 10%	—	$ 300,000
Net earnings	$1,000,000	$ 700,000
Number of shares	200,000	100,000
EPS	$5.00	$7.00
k_e or k'_e	16.67%	17.5%
Price per share	$30.00	$40.00
Market value of stock	$6,000,000	$4,000,000
Market value of bonds	—	3,000,000
Total market value	$6,000,000	$7,000,000

Using the M & M assumptions underlying the process of arbitrage, show how an investor is better off selling shares in company Y and purchasing shares in company X, or in other similar companies in the same risk class. At what point should arbitrage cease? Explain.

5. Management of Wallbanger Corporation is concerned about the company's capital structure. Presently it finances all its assets from equity. Although managment is familiar with the current literature in finance, it knows that tax deductibility of interest suggests the company should employ some debt. The corporate tax rate on earnings averages .3; the average personal tax rate for stockholders of the corporation is .2. If Wallbanger issued debt, prospective purchasers would pay income taxes on the interest at a rate of .44. Do you recommend management consider debt financing? Explain.

6. A thorough investigation by Side Car Corporation management of its optimal capital structure revealed the following

After Tax k_e or k'_e	After Tax k_d	Ratio of Debt to Total Capital
16.000%	4%	0
17.000%	4%	.1
19.000%	4%	.2
22.000%	4%	.3
25.000%	5%	.4
29.000%	6%	.5
35.000%	6%	.6
42.000%	8%	.7
50.000%	11%	.8
60.000%	15%	.9

a. Compute the average cost of capital k_o for each ratio of debt to total capital.
b. Plot the results for k_e, k_d, and k_o. Does the Side Car Corporation have an optimal capital structure? Explain.

7. "The M & M Hypothesis was designed to explain behavior in the context of a capital market; it was never meant to be a prescription for financing a capital budget at a given point in time." Do you agree with this statement? Explain in detail.

8. As a project, find the current debt-equity ratios for International Business Machines (IBM) and Commonwealth Edison. How do you account for the substantial differences between the companies regarding the proportion of debt and preferred stock employed.

9. "Although the Capital Asset Pricing Model (CAPM) permits us to eliminate the

arbitrage process upon which the M & M Hypothesis functions, we may well be substituting one unrealistic set of assumptions for another." Do you agree? Explain in detail.

10. The cost of capital for an unleveraged capital structure is 18 percent. EBIT is $4,500,000.

    a. Using the M & M Hypothesis, what is the market value of the firm?

    b. Suppose the marginal corporate tax rate is .4. Under the M & M Hypothesis, modified to take account of corporate income taxes, what is the market value of the firm if management replaced $5,000,000 worth of stock with $5,000,000 worth of debt at 12-percent interest? Would your answer change if interest was 14 percent?

    c. Assume the average personal income-tax rate of stockholders is .30 and the average tax rate of debtholders is .20. Under the M & M Hypothesis, modified for personal taxes, what now is the market value of the firm?

11. Distinguish between bankruptcy and agency costs. Describe their impact on the cost of capital.

12. "In theory, there is no optimal capital structure; in practice, there must be." Evaluate in detail.

SELECTED ADDITIONAL REFERENCES

Arditti, Fred D. and Haim Levy. "The Weighted Average Cost of Capital as a Cutoff Rate: A Critical Analysis of the Classical Textbook Weighted Average," *Financial Management*, Vol. 6 (Fall 1977, pp. 24–34).

Arditti, Fred D. and John M. Pinkerton. "The Valuation and Cost of Capital of the Levered Firm with Growth Opportunities," *Journal of Finance*, Vol. 33 (March 1978, pp. 65–73).

Barnea, Amir, Robert Haugan, and Lemma Senbert. "Market Imperfections, Agency Problems, and Capital Structure: A Review," *Financial Management*, Vol. 10 (Summer 1981, pp. 7–22).

Baron, David P. "Default Risk and the Modigliani-Miller Theorem: A Syntheseis," *American Economic Revue*, Vol. 63 (March 1976, pp. 204–12.)

———. "Default Risk, Homemade Leverage, and the Modigliani and Miller Theorem," *American Economic Review*, Vol. 64 (March 1974, pp. 176–82).

Baxter, Nevins. "Leverage, Risk of Ruin, and the Cost of Capital," *Journal of Finance*, Vol. 22 (September 1967, pp. 395–403).

Bower, Richard S. and Dorothy N. Bower. "Risk and the Valuation of Common Stock," *Journal of Political Economy*, Vol. 77 (May–June 1969, pp. 349–62).

Brennan, M. J. "Taxes, Market Valuation, and Corporate Financial Policy," *National Tax Journal*, Vol. 23 (December 1970, pp. 417–27).

Brennan, M. J. and E. S. Schwartz, "Corporate Income Taxes, Valuation and the Problem of Optimal Capital Structure," *Journal of Business*, Vol. 51 (January 1978, pp. 103–15).

Brigham, Eugene F. and Myron J. Gordon. "Leverage, Dividend Policy, and the Cost of Capital," *Journal of Finance*, Vol. 23 (March 1968, pp. 85–104).

Chen, Andrew H. and E. Han Kim, "Theories of Corporate Debt and Policy: A Synthesis," *Journal of Finance*, Vol. 34 (May 1979, pp. 371–84).

De Angelo, Harry and Ronald Masulis. "Optimal Capital Structure under Corporate and Personal Taxation," *Journal of Financial Economics*, Vol. 8 (March 1980, pp. 3–29).

Donaldson, Gordon. *Corporate Debt Capacity* (Boston: Division of Research, Harvard Business School, 1961).

————. "Strategies for Financial Emergencies," *Harvard Business Review*, Vol. 47 (November–December 1969, pp. 67–79).

Durand, David. "The Cost of Capital, Corporation Finance, and the Theory of Investment: Comment," *American Economic Review*, Vol. 49 (September 1959, pp. 638–69).

Fama, Eugene. "Agency Problems and the Theory of the Firm," *Journal of Political Economy*, Vol. 88 (April 1980, pp. 288–307).

————. "The Effects of a Firm's Investment and Financing Decisions on the Welfare of its Security Holders," *American Economic Review*, Vol. 68 (June 1978, pp. 272–84).

Fama, Eugene F. and Merton H. Miller. *The Theory of Finance*, Ch. 4 (New York: Holt, Rinehart and Winston, 1972).

Flath, David and Charles R. Knober. "Taxes, Failure Costs and the Optimal Industry Capital Structure: An Empirical Test," *Journal of Finance*, Vol. 35 (March 1980, pp. 99–117).

Glenn, David W. "Super Premium Security Prices and Optimal Corporate Financing Decisions," *Journal of Finance*, Vol. 31 (May 1976, pp. 507–24).

Gordon, Myron J. and Clarence C. T. Kwan. "Debt Maturity, Default Risk, and Capital Structure," *Journal of Banking and Finance*, Vol. 3 (December 1979, pp. 313–29).

Gordon, Rodger J. and Burton G. Malkiel. "Taxation and Corporate Finance" (Working Paper, National Bureau of Economic Research, 1980).

Haley, Charles W. and Lawrence D. Schall. "Problems with the Concept of the Cost of Capital," *Journal of Financial and Quantitative Analysis*, Vol. 13 (December 1978, pp. 847–70).

Hamada, Robert S. "Portfolio Analysis, Market Equilibrium, and Corporation Finance," *Journal of Finance*, Vol. 24 (March 1969, pp. 13–31).

————. "The Effect of a Firm's Capital Structure on the Systematic Risk of Common Stocks," *Journal of Finance*, Vol. 27 (May 1972, pp. 435–52).

Haugen, Robert A. "Reply," *Journal of Financial and Quantitative Analysis*, Vol. 7 (September 1972, pp. 2005–09).

Haugan, Robert A. and James L. Pappas. "Equilibrium in the Pricing of Capital Assets, Risk-Bearing Debt Instruments and the Question of Optimal Capital Structure," *Journal of Financial and Quantitative Analysis*, Vol. 6 (June 1971, pp. 943–54).

Haugen, Robert A. and Lemma W. Senbet. "The Irrelevance of Bankruptcy Costs to the Theory of Optimal Capital Structure," *Journal of Finance*, Vol. 24 (June 1978, pp. 383–94).

Heins, A. James and Case M. Sprenkle. "A Comment on the Modigliani and Miller Cost of Capital Thesis," *American Economic Review*, Vol. 59 (September 1969, pp. 590–92).

Hellwig, Martin F. "Bankruptcy, Limited Liability, and the Modigliani-Miller Theorem," *American Economic Review*, Vol. 71 (March 1981, pp. 156–70).

Imai, Yutaki and Mark E. Rubinstein. "Equilibrium in the Pricing of Capital Assets, Risk-Bearing Debt Instruments, and the Question of Optimal Capital Structure: A Comment," *Journal of Financial and Quantitative Analysis*, Vol. 7 (September 1972, pp. 2001–03).

Jensen, Michael C. and William E. Meckling. "The Theory of the Firm: Managerial Behavior, Agency Costs and Ownership Structure," *Journal of Financial Economics*, Vol. 3 (October 1976, pp. 305–60).

Kim, E. Han. "A Mean–Variance Theory of Optimal Structure and Corporate Debt Capacity," *Journal of Finance*, Vol. 33 (March 1978, pp. 45–64).

Kim, E. Han, Wilbur E. Lewellen, and John C. McConnell. "Financial Leverage Clienteles," *Journal of Financial Economics*, Vol. 7 (March 1979, pp. 83–109).

Kraus, Alan and Robert N. Litzenberg. "A State-Preference Model of Optimal Financial Leverage," *Journal of Finance*, Vol. 28 (September 1973, pp. 911–22).

Lee, Wayne Y. and Henry H. Barber. "Bankruptcy Costs and the Firm's Optimal Debt Capacity," *Southern Economic Journal*, Vol. 43 (April 1977, pp. 1453–63).

Lintner, John. "The Cost of Capital and Optimal Financing of Corporate Growth," *Journal of Finance*, Vol. 18 (May 1963, pp. 292–310).

Malkiel, Burton G. *The Debt–Equity Combination of the Firm and the Cost of Capital: An Introductory Analysis* (New York: General Learning Press, 1971).

Miller, Edward M. "Risk, Uncertainty, and Divergence of Opinion," *Journal of Finance*, Vol. 32 (September 1977, pp. 1151–68).

Miller, Merton H. "Debt and Taxes," *Journal of Finance*, Vol. 32 (May 1977, pp. 261–75).

Miller, Merton H. and Franco Modigliani. "Some Estimates of the Cost of Capital to the Electric Utility Industry," *American Economic Review*, Vol. 56 (June 1966, pp. 333–91).

Milne, F. "Choice over Asset Economics: Default, Risk and Corporate Leverage," *Journal of Financial Economics*, Vol. 2 (June 1975, pp. 165–85).

Modigliani, Franco and Merton H. Miller. "Corporate Income Taxes and the Cost of Capital: A Correction," *American Economic Review*, Vol. 53 (June 1963, pp. 433–43).

—— and ——. "The Cost of Capital, Corporate Finance and the Theory of Investment," *American Economic Review*, Vol. 48 (June 1958, pp. 261–97).

Myers, Stewart C. "Determinants of Corporate Borrowing," *Journal of Financial Economics*, Vol. 5 (November 1977, pp. 147–75).

Petry, Glenn H. "Empirical Evidence on Cost of Capital Weights," *Financial Management*, Vol. 4 (November 1977, pp. 58–65).

Rendleman, Richard J. "The Effects of Default Risk on the Firm's Investment and Financing Decision," *Financial Management*, Vol. 7 (Spring 1978, pp. 45–53).

Ross, Stephen A. "The Determination of Financial Structure: The Incentive Signaling Approach," *Bell Journal of Economics*, Vol. 8 (Spring 1977, pp. 23–40).

Rubinstein, Mark E. "A Mean–Variance Synthesis of Corporate Financial Theory," *Journal of Finance*, Vol. 28 (March 1973, pp. 67–82).

Sametz, Arnold W. "Trends in the Volume and Composition of Finance," *Journal of Finance*, Vol. 19 (September 1964, pp. 450–69).

Schall, Lawrence S. "Firm Financial Structure and Investment," *Journal of Financial and Quantitative Analysis*, Vol. 6 (June 1971, pp. 925–42).

Schneller, Meir I. "Taxes and the Optimal.Capital Structure of the Firm," *Journal of Finance*, Vol. 35 (March 1980, pp. 119–27).

Scott, James H., Jr. "A Theory of Optimal Capital Structure," *Bell Journal of Economics*, Vol. 7 (Spring 1976, pp. 33–54).

——. "Bankruptcy, Secured Debt and Optimal Capital Structure," *Journal of Finance*, Vol. 32 (March 1977, pp. 1–20).

Smith, Clifford W., Jr. and Jerold B. Warner. "On Financial Contracting: An Analysis of Bond Covenants," *Journal of Financial Economics*, Vol. 7 (June 1979, pp. 117–61).

Solomon, Ezra. "Leverage and the Cost of Capital," *Journal of Finance*, Vol. 18 (May 1963, pp. 273–74).

Stiglitz, Joseph. "A Re-examination of the Modigliani and Miller Theorem," *American Economic Review*, Vol. 59 (December 1969, pp. 784–93).

——. "On the Irrelevance of Corporate Financial Policy," *American Economic Review*, Vol. 64 (December 1974, pp. 851–66).

——. "Theory of Finance," *Bell Journal of Economics and Management Science*, Vol. 3 (Autumn 1972, pp. 458–82).

Taggart, Robert A., Jr. "Taxes and Corporate Capital Structure in an Incomplete Market," *Journal of Finance*, Vol. 35 (June 1980, pp. 645–60).

VanHorne, James C. "Optimal Initiation of Bankruptcy Proceedings by Debt Holders," *Journal of Finance*, Vol. 32 (June 1976, pp. 897–910).

Warner, Jerald B. "Bankruptcy Costs: Some Evidence," *Journal of Finance*, Vol. 32 (May 1977, pp. 337–47).

Whippern, Ronald F. "Financial Structure and the Value of the Firm," *Journal of Finance*, Vol. 42 (December 1966, pp. 615–34).

White, M. J. "Bankruptcy Costs and the New Bankruptcy Code," *Journal of Finance*, Vol. 37 (May 1983, pp. 477–88).

THE CAPITAL
INVESTMENT
DECISION

Early in the study of finance it is often easier to identify with a portfolio of financial assets than with a portfolio of **real capital assets.** *As individuals, most of us have checking, NOW, or savings accounts, and at various stages of life we may directly own shares in companies. Today, nearly every working person indirectly owns stock or corporate or government debt paid for by contributions to a pension fund. For the majority, however, direct real capital investment is limited to home ownership. Yet, as our discussion of the cost of capital suggested, financial managers of nonfinancial corporations issue financial instruments to purchase plant, equipment, and the like. When we analyze a portfolio of financial assets, we are indirectly analyzing the real assets that underlie these claims.*

The independent trucker who roars past you at 75 miles per hour on the downgrade of a turnpike or freeway may own the truck—a real capital asset. He could, however, consider himself or herself the owner of a concern whose single asset is the truck. Assume the latter is the case. Suppose further that the trucking firm is incorporated, its sole asset is the truck—valued at $50,000 and on which nothing has been borrowed—and the driver owns 100 percent of the stock in the firm. The truck generates annual sales revenue of $80,000 and the driver pays himself or herself $30,000 per year, equal to what he or she could earn working for a large trucking concern. To simplify the example, assume the $80,000 annual sales revenue will continue indefinitely and the owner can invest $15,000 per year in the truck to cover maintenance (thereby keeping the truck going indefinitely). Other expenses of operation—clerical help, storage area for the truck when not in use, and the like—are $25,000. Thus, for an investment with an infinite income stream

$$\$50,000 = \frac{\$80,000 - \$30,000 - \$15,000 - \$25,000}{r}$$

$$\$50,000 = \frac{\$10,000}{r}$$

$$r = 20\%$$

From the viewpoint of the owner, the $10,000 yield or return on investment in the truck is 20 percent before taxes. The owner could also view the $10,000 as a return before taxes on company stock. Suppose the return for truckers in similar positions is 20 percent. Then the market value of the firm's stock is

$$\$50,000 = \frac{\$10,000}{.20}$$

Whether the investor views the asset as the truck or as the stock in the company that owns the truck, the result is the same: in the capital market, both are worth $50,000.

"Before God made profits, he made production, and before production he made capital. So be it."

Drawing by Vietor, ©1976, The New Yorker Magazine, Inc.

Conceptually, therefore, financial assets can just as easily be the real capital assets that underlie them. Reality, of course, is far more complex. Unless they are in business for themselves, individuals generally prefer financial to real assets. Even an independent trucker, who owns stock in a local utility, would consider the stock—not a pro-rata share of the real assets underlying the stock—as his or her investment, even though earnings and (ultimately) dividends on that stock depend on the profitability of plant and equipment.

Management of the modern nonfinancial corporation or nonfinancial subsidiary of a conglomerate—whether a utility, a manufacturing concern, a wholesale or retail trade operation—is preoccupied with the profitability of real capital assets for which it is responsible. Salaries, promotions, bonuses, and so forth are tied to the firm's performance as an entity. The risk–return trade-off is traditionally couched in terms of the expected return or variability of return on the firm itself. Using the language of Modern Portfolio Theory, management focuses on unsystematic risk. The firm may diversify by making various products or supplying various services, the covariance of returns on which are low or negative; the impetus, however, comes from management. Stockholders can and do react to decisions by adjusting their portfolios, and the beta coefficient will change over time as such decisions affect the standard deviation and eventually the covariance of the return on the stock.

All of the foregoing may seem obvious. It is easy, however, to lose perspective—for we are about to embark upon a discussion of the capital investment decision. We shall be developing principles of decision-making that treat stockholders as being concerned with profitability and unsystematic risk of the enterprise itself. Our objective is to maximize market value of the shares and (ultimately) wealth of the shareholders. So for Chapters 8 and 9, put aside what you have learned about MPT and apply the principles of Chapters 3, 4, 6, and 7 to the real assets of the individual firm. Then, in Chapter 10 we discuss in greater detail the implications of MPT and, in particular, CAPM, for a portfolio of real assets, integrating the material into a cohesive framework.

THE NATURE OF THE CAPITAL INVESTMENT DECISION

Real assets of a nonfinancial business consist of land, plant, equipment, and inventories necessary to produce the goods or services the firm markets. Many of these assets have been designed for a specific purpose. Cost overruns and failure to anticipate technical or environmental problems in the operation of a facility may render the business unprofitable. Moreover, the investment may have little value elsewhere: it has little or no opportunity cost. Nuclear generating plants are a vivid illustration of such problems. Other types of investment—such equipment as the rolling stock of railroads, aircraft, and the like—often have opportunity cost in the hands of another user. As a result, a ready secondary market may develop for such assets.

With the exception of inventories, the major categories of real assets are expected to provide returns for several years into the future. Hence such returns, as the trucking example suggests, are amenable to present value calculations. From the perspective of one making the capital investment decision, inventories of finished goods can be viewed as part of the outlay. To illustrate, suppose a computer manufacturer builds a new plant to assemble a product. The manufacturer fully expects to tie up funds between the time the goods are manufactured and the time they are sold. Such outlay is a long-term investment in the additional computers the company will manufacture (new inventories replacing those previously sold) and is conceptually part of the capital outlay for plant and equipment.

The preceding information is important. Beginning students of finance, particularly those with backgrounds in accounting, may wish to categorize assets as *fixed or long-lived* and *current*. The plant is fixed (or long-lived) and inventories (both raw materials and finished goods) are current. It is appropriate to view inventories, as well as all additional investment in such current assets as the extension of credit to new customers (accounts receivable), as part of the capital outlay for the project. Later in the text we treat the subject of **working capital**, more completely examining particular issues pertaining to management of current assets. We also raise questions about the specific treatment accorded short-term liabilities, those that by accounting convention mature in less than a year. For the time being, however, increases in working capital are treated as part of the capital outlay with which they are associated.

As we have seen, financial investments are subject to a degree of risk—risk of default (except for U.S. government securities) and risk that unanticipated inflation will result in zero or negative real returns even in the absence of default. Returns on financial investments are ultimately tied to returns on the real investments that underlie them. We must, therefore, treat expected return in the context of the risk associated with earning that return. We begin our discussion, however, as though returns are certain: there is no risk of default and inflation is fully anticipated in the return. Later in this chapter and in Chapter 9, we gradually relax these assumptions.

CASH FLOWS

In the parlance of the literature on real capital investment, the asset generates a return that (in terms of dollars) is called the **cash flows** of the project. Cash flows consist of profits *after taxes* plus noncash expenses associated with the investment. The most important noncash expense is depreciation of the asset. Profits from an investment arise in one or the other or both of two ways: the investment is either revenue-producing or cost-saving or both. A new production facility can add to existing capacity and the output produced can be sold at a profit. Such additional profit comes from the additional revenue generated. Alternatively, a firm may replace a facility with one that is technologically advanced. The result is it lowers the cost of production and raises profits. The new facility is a cost-saving innovation. Many projects are both cost-saving and revenue-producing. A process that lowers the cost of production allows a company to lower price. If demand is elastic (in the case of perfect competition, demand is infinitely elastic), total revenues and profits rise. The increase in profits results both from additional sales and lower costs; however, the cost-saving component was the impetus for the increase.

To illustrate what is involved in evaluating cash flows, assume a company can invest $500,000 in expanding its facilities, $30,000 of which represents additional working capital. From such an investment, the company will realize $400,000 annually in extra sales. Engineers have estimated the useful life of the expanded facilities is ten years. There are additional annual operating expenses of $200,000 for increased labor, maintenance, and materials. Relying on engineering reports, the accounting staff has concluded there is no scrap value and has chosen to write off the asset using the *straight-line* method of depreciation: an annual depreciation expense of $50,000 ($500,000 ÷ 10) charged against revenues. Assume further the income tax rate applicable to additional profits is 45 percent (reserving to later in the chapter a discussion of current tax law provisions and their impact upon investment).

From Table 8-1 we see that profit after taxes is $82,500 per year—what the company earns on the investment if we assume depreciation is reinvested in the facility to maintain its useful life indefinitely. Such a practice is treated as part of the maintenance expenses to be carried out in perpetuity; in reality, however, its useful life is only ten years. Each year $50,000 is returned to the company for reinvestment elsewhere in the company. Depreciation is a noncash expense that is part of the cash

Table 8-1   Cash Flows from an Expansion in Plant and Equipment

Year	Outlay	Estimated Sales or Revenues		Annual Operating Expenses		Straight-line Depreciation		Taxable Income	Income after Taxes[a]
T_0	$500,000	—		—		—		—	—
T_1		$400,000	—	$200,000	—	$50,000	=	$150,000	$82,500
T_2		400,000	—	200,000	—	50,000	=	150,000	82,500
T_3		400,000	—	200,000	—	50,000	=	150,000	82,500
T_4		400,000	—	200,000	—	50,000	=	150,000	82,500
T_5		400,000	—	200,000	—	50,000	=	150,000	82,500
T_6		400,000	—	200,000	—	50,000	=	150,000	82,500
T_7		400,000	—	200,000	—	50,000	=	150,000	82,500
T_8		400,000	—	200,000	—	50,000	=	150,000	82,500
T_9		400,000	—	200,000	—	50,000	=	150,000	82,500
T_{10}		400,000	—	200,000	—	50,000	=	150,000	82,500
									$825,000

[a] $150,000 − .45($150,000) = (1 − .45)($150,000) = .55($150,000) = $82,500.

flows generated from operations. Future returns, therefore, include both profits and depreciation.[1] In this instance, future returns or after-tax cash flows equal $50,000 + $82,500, or $132,500. More generally, if we let

ΔCF = net cash flow from adopting investment project

ΔR = addition to gross revenues from adopting project

ΔO = addition to total cash operating expenses or total variable costs from adopting project

ΔD = addition to total depreciation expense from adopting project

t = marginal income-tax rate applicable to profits generated from investment

then

$$\Delta CF = \Delta \text{ profits before income taxes} - \text{income taxes}$$
$$\text{profits before income taxes} = \Delta R - \Delta O$$
$$\text{income taxes} = t(\Delta R - \Delta O - \Delta D)$$
$$\Delta CF = (\Delta R - \Delta O) - t(\Delta R - \Delta O - \Delta D) \tag{8-1}$$
$$\Delta CF = \Delta R - \Delta O - t\Delta R + t\Delta O + t\Delta D$$
$$\Delta CF = \Delta R - t\Delta R + t\Delta O - \Delta O + t\Delta D$$
$$\Delta CF = (\Delta R - \Delta O)(1 - t) + t\Delta D$$

Using the appropriate figures from Table 8-1, we have

$$\Delta CF = (\$400{,}000 - \$200{,}000)(1 - .45) + .45 (\$50{,}000)$$
$$\$110{,}000 + \$22{,}500 = \$132{,}500$$

If the project had been designed to lower total operating costs rather than to add to total revenues, the reduction in total operating costs would be designated by ΔO_L. Since costs are less, profits before taxes rise by the amount of the cost savings: by ΔO_L. Equation 8-1 becomes

$$\Delta CF = \Delta O_L(1 - t) + t\Delta D \tag{8-1a}$$

If the project is expected to produce both additional revenues and a savings in cost, Equation 8-1 becomes

$$\Delta CF = [(\Delta R - \Delta O) + \Delta O_L](1 - t) + t\Delta D \tag{8-1b}$$

Finally, although operating expenses associated with the project are deducted from revenues, we have not deducted the costs of financing the project: interest on the

---

[1] By analogy, future returns also include any noncash expenses (such as depletion allowances) that are applicable in some cases to wasting assets.

money borrowed or the dividends stockholders expect to receive from investing funds in the project. The reasons for not including these costs become apparent in the following sections.

THE NET PRESENT VALUE OF THE INVESTMENT

A wag once observed that an economist need only know two words—demand and supply. For the student of finance, three suffice—**net present value**. Just as we can calculate the present value of future interest and the repayment of principal on a bond issue, so can we calculate the present value of the cash flows on a real capital investment. But what is the appropriate discount rate? For a bond, it is the YTM for an issue of comparable quality and maturity with identical interest payments. Do we look for a similar measure of identical facilities elsewhere in the economy? That may be hard to find.

The discussion in Chapters 6 and 7, however, offer the basis for determining the rate. Suppose we accepted the M & M Hypothesis; then the appropriate rate *could be* the cost of new equity capital. Assume management—allowing for institutional imperfections such as the income tax laws—has, to the best of its ability, found an optimal capital structure. Then the appropriate rate *could be* the weighted after-tax average cost of new debt and equity, using the debt and equity ratios of the existing capital structure as weights. Assume further the current debt-to-total-capital ratio is 20 percent and the equity-to-total-capital ratio is 80 percent and the current after-tax cost of debt is 12 percent and the cost of equity 18.25 percent, then the average cost of capital is $.20 \times .12 + .8 \times .1825 = 17.0$ percent.

In each case we emphasize the phrase *could be*. Although funds supplied by investors are used to finance projects, payments made to them—dividends, interest, and so forth—are tied to overall performance of the company, not just to profitability of a specific project. In the real world, overall performance is subject to a degree of risk. Does the addition of such a project alter the probability distribution of cash flows for the entire firm? We have assumed cash flows from such a project are certain. Let us finesse the issue for the time being and assume cash flows from existing assets are also certain.

There remains the premium for anticipated inflation; the cost of capital contains such a premium. For the firm, however, the question is whether or not the cash flows include an allowance for inflation in both revenues and expenses. Table 8-1 suggests that either we have made no allowance for inflation or that *both* revenues and expenses are unaffected by inflation. For the moment we assume the latter.

Bearing the foregoing in mind, in this instance the market-determined cost of individual sources of funds will contain a premium for inflation but no premium for business risk. On the assumption the firm (primarily because of taxes) has approximated an optimal capital structure at 20 percent of its total capital in debt, we employ an average cost of capital of 17 percent as the discount rate.[2] From our discussion of present value, we know that

$$p.v. = \$132,500 \frac{[1 - (1.17)^{-10}]}{.17}$$

$$p.v. = \$617,264.98$$

where $132,500 equals the annual cash flows and .17 is the weighted average cost of capital—assuming interest is compounded annually. This assumption, as we have seen, may be relaxed. To the extent it is, the present value will change.

Net present value is the residual between outlay and present value of future cash flows. Because outlay is an expenditure, it carries a negative sign; present value of the cash flows is positive. In general terms, Net Present Value (NPV) = −outlay + p.v. of cash flows. Using the data in Table 8-1 and the preceding calculations

$$NPV = -\$500,000 + \$617,264.98$$
$$NPV = \$117,264.98$$

One can say in this instance that present value of future cash flows is greater than outlay for the project, so net present value is positive. As long as net present value is greater than zero, there are sufficient cash flows to cover the cost of using the funds (17 percent per annum) and to return the original outlay ($500,000).

INTERNAL RATE OF RETURN

When using financial instruments as illustrations, we often calculated yields on those instruments, such as yield to maturity on a bond. Can we not do the same thing with a capital investment? We can indeed. Recall in Chapter 3 we calculated both internal rate of return and net-percent value on real capital investments. To do so in this case, one structures an equation so that

$$\text{investment (outlay)} = \text{after-tax cash flows} \frac{[1 - (1 + r)^{-n}]}{r}$$

We then solve the equation for r. From the data in Table 8-1

$$\$500,000 = \$132,500 \frac{[1 - (1 + r)^{-10}]}{r}$$

---

[2] In the absence of a risk premium, we expect the cost of debt and equity to be equal. Bankruptcy costs have been ruled out. Depending on the respective tax rates of bondholders, stockholders, and the corporation, the average cost of capital might be lower if the firm further increased the debt-to-total-capital ratio. We ignore this problem, since the assumption of certainty in cash flows is relaxed in Chapter 9.

Using a hand calculator, computer, or the tables in Appendix C, you will find that $r = 23.21423$ percent. This figure is known variously as the **internal rate of return, the marginal efficiency of investment**, or the **yield** on an investment. Because r is greater than the cost of capital—r is greater than 17 percent—the investment is profitable. In other words, the rate of return is greater than the cost of funds employed in financing the project.

DISCOUNTED CASH FLOWS—IMPLICIT REINVESTMENT ASSUMPTIONS

Because both the net present value and internal rate of return include the time value of money in the computations, each (in principle) is considered an acceptable measure of profitability. However, internal rate of return can be misleading; to understand why, we must examine more closely the assumptions implicit in the calculations. Each technique presumes that the return on the project can be deducted annually from cash flows and the residual reinvested at the rate employed in each calculation: 23.21423 percent and 17 percent, respectively. The computations in Table 8-2 show why this is true.

An internal rate of return of 23.21423 percent may be interpreted as follows: Given an investment of $500,000 and cash flows of $132,500 received at the end of each year for ten years, we may subtract from the cash flows $500,000 × .2321423 ($116,071.15) representing annual return on investment. The difference between $132,500 and $116,071.15, $16,428.85, is reinvested at .2321423 percent for each of the remaining nine years. The $16,428.85 received in the final year cannot be reinvested. The sum of the residuals compounded annually recoup the original investment, $500,000, at the end of the tenth year.

The net present value calculation may be interpreted as follows: Given an investment of $500,000 and cash flows of $132,500 received at the end of each year for ten years, we may subtract from the cash flows .17 × $500,000, $85,000, as return on investment. The difference between $132,500 and $85,000, $47,500, is reinvested at the required rate of return, 17 percent, for each of the remaining nine years. The sum of the residuals compounded annually is $1,063,672.72. Subtracting the original outlay, $500,000, leaves $563,672.72. Using a 17-percent cost of capital, the present value of $563,672.72 is (to the nearest dollar) $117,265.

Net present value, therefore, is the value today of an amount of money received (in this instance) ten years in the future that is over and above the funds necessary to cover the required rate of return and outlay for the project. In this context, the internal rate of return can be viewed as a special case of net present value. Because the internal rate of return equates present value of future cash flows with original outlay, it is the rate at which net present value is zero. Only the outlay is recovered at the end of ten years; there is no residual and, therefore, no net present value. Due to

Table 8-2   Arithmetic Illustration of Reinvestment Assumptions Implicit in Discounted Cash-flow Techniques

	Cash Flow	−	$500,000 × .2321423	=	Residual × (1.2321423)ⁿ	=	Compound Value
1	$132,500	−	$116,071.15	=	$16,428.85 $(1.2321423)^9$	=	$107,536.27
2	132,500	−	116,071.15	=	16,428.85 $(1.2321423)^8$	=	87,275.85
3	132,500	−	116,071.15	=	16,428.85 $(1.2321423)^7$	=	70,832.61
4	132,500	−	116,071.15	=	16,428.85 $(1.2321423)^6$	=	57,487.36
5	132,500	−	116,071.15	=	16,428.85 $(1.2321423)^5$	=	46,656.43
6	132,500	−	116,071.15	=	16,428.85 $(1.2321423)^4$	=	37,866.10
7	132,500	−	116,071.15	=	16,428.85 $(1.2321423)^3$	=	30,731.93
8	132,500	−	116,071.15	=	16,428.85 $(1.2321423)^2$	=	24,941.86
9	132,500	−	116,071.15	=	16,428.85 $(1.2321423)^1$	=	20,242.68
10	132,500	−	116,071.15	=	16,428.85	=	16,428.85
							$499,999.94 (or $500,000)

Net Present Value = $117.264.98

	Cash Flow	−	$500,000 × .17	=	Residual × (1.17)ⁿ	=	Compound Value
1	$132,500	−	$85,000	=	$47,500 $(1.17)^9$	=	$ 195,149.02
2	132,500	−	85,000	=	47,500 $(1.17)^8$	=	166,794.03
3	132,500	−	85,000	=	47,500 $(1.17)^7$	=	142,599.00
4	132,500	−	85,000	=	47,500 $(1.17)^6$	=	121,845.30
5	132,500	−	85,000	=	47,500 $(1.17)^5$	=	104,141.28
6	132,500	−	85,000	=	47,500 $(1.17)^4$	=	89,009.64
7	132,500	−	85,000	=	47,500 $(1.17)^3$	=	76,076.69
8	132,500	−	85,000	=	47,500 $(1.17)^2$	=	65,022.76
9	132,500	−	85,000	=	47,500 $(1.17)^1$	=	55,575.00
10	132,500	−	85,000	=		=	47,500.00
							$1,063,672.72
						Outlay	− 500,000.00
						Residual $	563,672.72

$$\text{Present Value of Residual } \frac{\$563,672.72}{(1.17)^{10}} = \$117,264.98 \text{ (or } \$117,265)$$

the implicit reinvestment rate, there is no relationship between profits and depreciation, which comprise the cash-flow estimates and their counterparts in the calculations. The cash flows were based on after-tax profits and depreciation calculated in the conventional accounting format. From Table 8-3, it is apparent that what is *return of* investment and what is *return on* investment differs with the

Table 8-3   Return *on* Investment and Return *of* Investment under Different Conceptual Frameworks

	Cash Flows		
	Conventional Accounting	*Internal Rate of Return (23.21423%)*	*Required Return (17%)*
Return *on* Investment	$ 82,500	$116,071.15	$ 85,000
Return *of* Investment	50,000	16,428.85	47,500
Total	$132,500	$132,500.00	$132,500

technique employed. Under conventional accounting practice, return of the original cost of investment takes place over its useful life; there is no explicit assumption about reinvesting funds, and the implicit assumption is that funds are reinvested at zero rate of interest. We can conceive, therefore, of setting aside $50,000 per year in a noninterest-bearing account that, at the end of ten years, would total $500,000. The $82,500 is after-tax return *on* investment.

As demonstrated, both internal-rate-of-return and net-present-value calculations assume reinvestment. Here the initial investment is returned at the end of ten years from a fund that compounds at an interest rate implied in the calculations. In the real world, depreciation is ordinarily reinvested in the firm. Inasmuch as the reinvestment assumption is implicit in either calculation, which is the more appropriate assumption: reinvestment at the internal rate of return or reinvestment at the cost of capital?

A CONTROVERSY OVER TECHNIQUES

From the perspective of concern for maximizing shareholder wealth, net present value is the appropriate evaluator of capital investment projects. As long as the suppliers of funds receive at least the cost of the monies employed, market value of company shares remains unchanged. To the extent the company invests funds in projects whose net present value is greater than zero, market value of company shares rises. Using the net-present-value approach, management will always rank investment proposals correctly. Employing the internal-rate-of-return approach, however, sometimes causes incorrect decisions.

To illustrate, consider the examples in Table 8-4. Projects 1 and 2 are **mutually exclusive**: the acceptance of project 1 precludes the acceptance of project 2. This is a common occurrence in capital budgeting. For instance, management may have to choose between two different types of machine tools, one with a lower capital outlay but a higher operating expense than the other.

Table 8-4   A Comparison of Three Projects

		Outlay	T_1	T_2	T_3
			Cash Flows		
	Project 1	$ 1,000	$1,500	$1,500	$1,500
	Project 2	8,000	6,000	6,000	6,000
	Project 3	10,000	7,000	7,000	7,000

	Internal Rate of Return	Net Present Value at 10%
Project 1	139.01%	$ 2,730
Project 2	54.77%	6,921
Project 3	48.72%	7,408
Projects 1 + 3	57.49%	$10,138
Projects 2 + 3	51.42%	14,329

Project 3 is independent of either project 1 or 2 and, therefore, can be considered separately. It is apparent from Table 8-4 that management, using internal rate of return, should accept projects 1 and 3. However, if the net-present-value technique is employed, the company should accept projects 2 and 3. From the foregoing discussion of reinvestment assumptions, it is clear net present value is the value today of all future cash flows, assuming a reinvestment rate equal to cost of capital—not an unreasonable assumption when contrasted with reinvestment at the internal rate of return. Therefore, although both techniques signal all three projects are acceptable, projects 2 and 3 add more to total profits and hence to market value of company stock than do projects 1 and 3. Consequently, the net-present-value rather than the internal-rate-of-return technique is consistent with what we assume to be the primary company goal.

The comparatively poor guidance afforded management when it uses the internal-rate-of-return approach can be demonstrated more fully. Assume projects A and B are mutually exclusive. Assume cost of capital is 16 percent.

	Outlay	Cash Flow (end of first year)	Cash Flow (end of second year)
Project A	$10,000	$13,000	—
Project B	$10,000	$ 1,000	$14,000

Project A terminates at the end of the first year; project B carries over to the second year, at the end of which it ceases to be productive. For project A, the rate of return is

$$\$10,000 = \frac{\$13,000}{1 + r}$$
$$r = 30\%$$

To find the yield for project B, we employ a standard computer program or preprogrammed hand calculator, which solves the quadratic that results from

$$\$10,000 = \frac{\$1,000}{1 + r} + \frac{\$14,000}{(1 + r)^2}$$
$$r = 23.43\%$$

Substituting 16 percent (the required rate of return) into each equation and subtracting the outlay from the present value of the cash flows, the net present value of each is

	Net Present Value
Project A	$1,206.90
Project B	$1,266.35

Project A yields a higher rate of return than project B, but the net present value of B is higher than the net present value of A.

Because the rate of return is in excess of 16 percent and the net present value in both instances is positive, either project—if it were not a mutually exclusive investment—would be acceptable. Inasmuch as both are substitutes for the other, however, the problem of ranking arises. The reason for the discrepancy is seen most easily by calling attention to the different terminal dates. Project A has a 30-percent return on the basis of a single year. We may assume, consistent with our discussion of the reinvestment assumption, that if the funds are reinvested, this is the rate applicable during the second year. If so, the *terminal value* of Project A is $13,000(1.30) = $16,900.

For project B, on the other hand, the rate of return is 23.43 percent on cash flows for both the first and second years. Assuming the cash flows for the first year are reinvested at that rate, the terminal value of project B is

$$\$1,000(1.2343) = \$ \ 1,234$$
$$\text{Cash flow (end of second year)} = \$14,000$$
$$\text{Terminal value} = \$15,234$$

Suppose, however, the cash flows for both projects can be reinvested only at the required rate of return, 16 percent. The terminal value of project A is

$13,000(1.16) = \$15,080$, whereas the terminal value of project B is

$$\$1,000(1.16) = \$\ 1,160$$
$$\text{Cash flow (end of second year)} = \$14,000$$
$$\text{Terminal value} = \$15,160$$

Consequently, under the assumption funds are reinvested at their respective yields, project A—with the higher rate of return—also has the higher terminal value than project B. If cost of capital is assumed to be the relevant reinvestment rate, project B—with the higher net present value—also has the higher terminal value than project A.

However, if we use 17 percent as the reinvestment rate, the terminal value of project A is $13,000(1.17) = \$15,210$, whereas the terminal value of project B is

$$\$1,000(1.17) = \$\ 1,170$$
$$\text{Cash flow (end of second year)} = \$14,000$$
$$\text{Terminal value} = \$15,170$$

The different yields of the two techniques are illustrated graphically in Figure 8-1. As the calculations suggest, if the implicit reinvestment rate is less than 17 percent, project B is preferable to project A; however, if we implicitly accept the rate of return as the reinvestment rate, project A is preferable to project B. Therefore, to render mutually exclusive investments strictly comparable, we must make assumptions about the reinvestment rate. From the discussion, it is apparent suppliers

Figure 8-1   Relationship between Reinvestment Rate and Net Present Value for Projects A and B

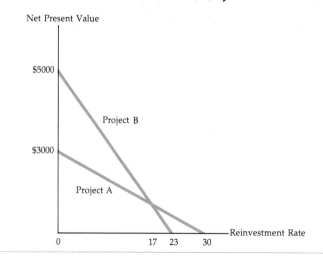

of capital expect all funds to be reinvested at the required rate of return. Thus, for mutually exclusive investments, compute the terminal value on each project and select the project with the higher value. Given a cost of capital of 16 percent (in this instance), project B is preferable to project A.

Another problem that can yield conflicting results stems from differences in the cash outlays. Assume two projects, C and D, are mutually exclusive. The pattern of cash outlays and cash flows are

	Outlay	Cash Flow (end of first year)	Cash Flow (end of second year)
Project C	$ 6,944.40	—	$\dfrac{\$10,000}{(1 + r)^2}$
Project D	$71,818.40	—	$\dfrac{\$100,000}{(1 + r)^2}$

The cost of capital is 15 percent and reinvestment is not a problem because both projects have a common terminal date. For project C, r equals 20 percent; for project D, r equal 18 percent. The net present value of C is $617.04; the net present value of D is $3,795.97.

In this instance, the source of the disparity can be traced to the fact that yield is independent of the absolute size of cash outlay, whereas net present value is not. If we calculate rate of return on the incremental cash flow—on the difference between outlays and cash flows for the two projects—we find that

$$\$64,874 = \frac{\$90,000}{(1 + r)^2}$$
$$r = 17.78\%$$

Since this yield is above the required rate of return, it is in the interests of stockholders to accept the project with the greater capital outlay. Given the reinvestment assumption implicit in this calculation, the decision is confirmed by the fact that net present value and hence total profits are greater if we accept project D than if we accept project C. In this case, therefore, the internal-rate-of-return technique provides the same signal as the net-present-value technique. Nevertheless, the latter technique always tells us which project adds more to the total wealth of owners.

MULTIPLE RATES OF RETURN

A special problem that can arise when using the internal rate of return is the possibility of one or more solutions or (in some instances) no real solution to a problem. Because the internal rate of return is based upon n years, there are n roots to the equation. However, as long as an outlay is followed by one or more positive cash inflows, only one of these roots is a real number. The remaining $n - 1$ roots are imaginary numbers that have no economic significance. Conventional investment proposals of the kind we have been considering follow this pattern. Therefore, we are dealing with only one (unique) solution that has economic meaning.

However, not all capital budgeting proposals are conventional. A classic example is investment in a high-speed oil pump. If the project is accepted, the well will produce more oil in the first year but less in the second and subsequent years. To illustrate, suppose a company has the opportunity to invest $16,000 in high-speed pumping equipment. The effect is to increase production by $100,000 the first year but decrease it by $100,000 the second year. Assume the project has a two-year useful life. Thus

T_0	T_1	T_2
$\$16,000 = \dfrac{\$100,000}{(1 + r)}$		$- \dfrac{\$100,000}{(1 + r)^2}$

$$\$16,000(1 + r)^2 = \$100,000(1 + r) \qquad - \$100,000$$

$$\$16,000(1 + 2r + r^2) = \$100,000 + \$100,000r - \$100,000$$

Rearranging the terms and simplifying, we obtain

$$\$16,000 + \$32,000r + \$16,000r^2 - \$100,000r = 0$$

$$\$16,000r^2 - \$68,000r + \$16,000 = 0$$

$$\$4000(4r^2 - 17r + 4) = 0$$

$$\$4r^2 - 17 + 4 = 0$$

This quadratic equation with two roots can be solved by factoring or by following the quadratic formula:

Quadratic Formula	**Factoring**
$r = x = \dfrac{-b \pm \sqrt{b^2 - 4ac}}{2a}$	$4r^2 - 17 + 4 = 0$
$r = \dfrac{-17 \pm \sqrt{289 - 64}}{8}$	$(4r - 1)(r - 4) = 0$
$r = \dfrac{-17 \pm 15}{8}$	$4r = 1$
$r = .25, 4$	$r = \frac{1}{4} = .25$
	$r - 4 = 0$
	$r = 4$

The rate of return, therefore, is either 25 percent or 400 percent. There are two unique solutions to the equation. Between the two percentages, as illustrated in

Figure 8-2   **Multiple Rates of Return (an illustration)**

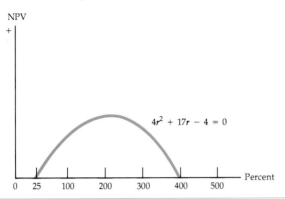

Figure 8-2, the net present value is positive.[3] Fortunately, given our experience to date, in this case we can treat 400 percent as an unrealistic rate of return. We are, however, saying that at 25 percent the company will pay interest of $4,000 each year (25 percent of $16,000) and have $16,000 remaining at the end of year two. Thus

Year	End of T_2
T_1 ($100,000 − $4,000)(1.25) =	$120,000
T_2 (−$100,000 − $4,000) =	−104,000
	$16,000
	−16,000
	0

If the required rate of return had been 15 percent, then

Year	End of T_2
T_1 ($100,000 − $2,400)(1.15) =	$112,240
T_2 (−$100,000 − $2,400) =	−102,400
	$9,840
	−16,000
	−$6,160

$$\text{Present value of } -\$6{,}160 = \frac{-\$6{,}160}{(1.15)^2}$$

$$\text{Present value} \qquad = -\$4{,}657.84$$

---

[3] The first derivative, $4r^2 − 17r + 4 + 0$, is $8r − 17$. Setting the first derivative equal to 0, we have $8r − 17 = 0$. Thus, $r = 2.125$ or 212.50 percent. The second derivative (8) is positive; hence maximum net present value occurs at 212.50 percent.

On the other hand, if the required rate of return had been 30 percent, then

Year	End of T_2
T_1 ($100,000 − $4,800)(1.3) =	$123,760
T_2 (−$100,000 − $4,800) =	−104,800
	$18,960
	− 16,000
	$2,960

Present value of $2,960 $= \dfrac{\$2,960}{(1.3)^2}$

Present value $= \$1,751.48$

In this instance, the higher the required rate of return, the greater the incentive to remove the oil with a high-speed pump. Assuming the funds are reinvested at a return in excess of 25 percent, management can offset the cost of the funds, recoup the investment, and raise the market value of the company stock. However, if the cost of funds (hence the required rate of return) is less than 25 percent, management should not invest in a high-speed pump.

Now consider the following: Management invests $500,000 in an advanced pumping system that will generate an additional $600,000 worth of oil in year T_1 but will cause a $50,000 reduction in oil produced in year T_2. Thus

$$\$500,000 = \frac{\$600,000}{1 + r} - \frac{\$50,000}{(1 + r)^2}$$

$$\$500,000(1 + r)^2 = \$600,000(1 + r) - \$50,000$$

$$10(1 + r)^2 = 12(1 + r) - 1$$

$$10(1 + 2r + r^2) = 12 + 12r - 1$$

$$10 + 20r + 10r^2 = 12 + 12r - 1$$

$$10r^2 + 8r - 1 = 0$$

Because the equation cannot be factored, we employ the quadratic formula, so that

$$r = \frac{-8 \pm \sqrt{64 + 40}}{20}$$

$$r = \frac{-8 \pm 10.198}{20}$$

$$r = \frac{2.198}{20} = 10.99\%$$

$$r = \frac{-18.198}{20} = -90.99\%$$

Figure 8-3   Multiple Rates of Return (another illustration)

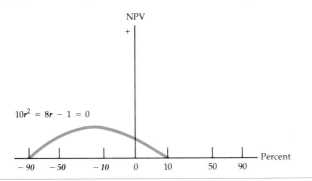

In this instance, we have both a positive and a negative rate of return. The function is pictured in Figure 8-3.[4] As long as the required rate of return is less than 10.99 percent but greater than -90.99 percent, the net present value is positive. In this case, real-world considerations suggest that only positive rates of interest are realistic. Thus, we can ignore values less than zero. If the required rate of return exceeds 10.99 percent, the net present value is negative and the project is unacceptable.

Let us extend our horizons somewhat and consider the following set of cash flows:

$$\$100,000 = \frac{\$150,000}{(1+r)} - \frac{\$75,000}{(1+r)^2} + \frac{\$500,000}{(1+r)^3} - \frac{\$500,000}{(1+r)^4}$$
$$+ \frac{\$100,000}{(1+r)^5} - \frac{\$50,000}{(1+r)^6}$$

Note the sign changes five times. It is possible every time a sign changes there is a new root. Indeed, the maximum number of real solutions is equal to the number of sign changes in the cash flows.[5] Here, using a computer-based solution to the problem, we find there are at least two real solutions.

$$r = -6.009\,\%$$
$$r = 83.178\,\%$$

---

[4] Differentiating $10r^2 + 8r - 1$ and setting the result equal to 0, we have $20r + 8 = 0$. Thus, $r = -.40$ or -40 percent. The second derivative (20) is positive; hence maximum value for r occurs at -40 percent.

[5] See Daniel Teichroew, Alexander A. Robichek, and Michael Montalbano, "An Analysis of Criteria for Investment Financing Decisions under Certainty," *Management Science*, Vol. 12 (November 1965, pp. 159–71). See also Daniel Teichroew, *An Introduction to Management Science: Deterministic Models* (New York: John Wiley and Sons, 1964, pp. 78–82).

Although neither return is realistic, if we assume the required rate of return is 18 percent, then

$$NPV = -\$100,000 + \$127,118.64 - \$53,863.83 + \$304,315.44 - \$257,894.44$$
$$+ \$43,710.92 - \$18,521.58$$
$$NPV = \$44,865.15$$

The preceding examples suggest that, however interesting, the internal rate of return has mathematical properties that can lead to ambiguous results for purposes of capital budgeting. At times, only one root is realistic and using it provides the same *accept* or *reject* results as the net-present-value technique. At other times, as the third example suggests, the real solutions to the equation are unrealistic. With the net-present-value technique, however, the results are always unambiguous.

DIFFERENCE IN THE COST OF CAPITAL

A more subtle problem interpreting internal rate of return lies in the possibility cost of capital can vary through time, so that

$$p.v. = \frac{\text{after-tax cash flow}_1}{1 + r_1} + \frac{\text{after-tax cash flow}_2}{(1 + r_2)^2}$$
$$+ \cdots + \frac{\text{after-tax cash flow}}{(1 + r_n)^n}$$

where $r_1 \neq r_2 \neq r_n$.

Indeed, at the time the project is considered, one might expect the return on all financial instruments to be rising. Such expectations could be observed in the **term structure** of interest rates found in the YTM of various U.S. government debt instruments. Where the return on short-term Treasury bills is lower than the return on longer-term U.S. government notes or bonds, a rising *yield curve* would carry over into the market for corporate debt. A weighted average cost of capital would incorporate these expectations, so that $r_1 < r_2 < r_n$. To illustrate, suppose the term structure of interest rates suggested the weighted average cost of capital for a particular firm considering an investment with a useful life of four years would vary, so that

$$r_1 = 16$$
$$r_2 = 16.5$$
$$r_3 = 17.0$$
$$r_4 = 18.0$$

Projected cash flows are

	After-tax Cash Flow	After-tax Cash Flow	After-tax Cash Flow	After-tax Cash Flow
Outlay	T_1	T_2	T_3	T_4
$100,000	$36,300	$36,300	$36,300	$36,300

Using the net-present-value approach (NPV)

$$\$100,000 \neq \frac{\$36,300}{1.16} + \frac{\$36,300}{(1.16)(1.165)} + \frac{\$36,300}{(1.16)(1.165)(1.17)} + \frac{\$36,300}{(1.16)(1.165)(1.17)(1.18)}$$

$$\$100,000 \neq \$31,293.10 + \$26,861.03 + \$22,958.15 + \$19,456.06$$

$$NPV = -\$100,000 + \$100,568.34$$

$$NPV = \$568.34$$

On the other hand, the internal rate of return on the project is

$$\$100,000 = \$36,300 \frac{[1 - (1 + r)^{-n}]}{r}$$

$$r = 16.79$$

If we calculate the geometric mean of the average cost of capital through time, then

$$\text{geometric mean} = \sqrt[4]{(1.16)(1.165)(1.17)(1.18)} - 1$$

$$\text{geometric mean} = 1.1687 - 1 = 16.87$$

Using the geometric mean to calculate net present value, we obtain

$$\$100,000 = \$36,300 \frac{[1 - (1.1687)^{-4}]}{.1687}$$

$$NPV = -\$164.98$$

Although the internal rate of return remains the same, is it more or less than the cost of capital? If we use the geometric mean of 16.87 percent, the internal rate of return of 16.79 percent is slightly smaller and the net present value is barely negative. If we recognize expectations about the term structure of interest rates in the cost of capital, the present value is slightly positive.

Practitioners may accuse us of academic hairsplitting, but the illustration serves to emphasize the conceptual limitation of the internal rate of return: it remains a percentage that equates the present value of future cash flows with the outlay. Consequently, it has little economic content. In focusing on net present value, however, management is forced to examine the capital markets. It may choose to ignore or perhaps average expectations about the term structure of interest rates as they pertain to the cost of capital. If management employs an average, it will (in this instance) discount earlier cash flows too heavily relative to expected future cash flows. Nevertheless, in either case its decision can be related to investor expectations as perceived in the capital market.

THE AVERAGE RETURN ON INVESTMENT AND THE PAYBACK PERIOD

Those responsible for budgeting capital employ both the internal-rate-of-return and net-present-value techniques.[6] Although we explore actual practice in Chapter 12, it is worth noting that firms also employ two other approaches to the investment decision: *average return on investment* and **payback period**.

THE AVERAGE RETURN ON INVESTMENT   The average return on investment is found by dividing the average annual profit after taxes by the average amount of funds tied up in the project. From the data in Table 8-1, this would be

$$\text{average return on investment} = \frac{\dfrac{\$825,000}{10}}{\dfrac{\$500,000}{2}} = \frac{\$82,500}{\$250,000} = 33\%$$

Those employing the foregoing method assume the company should not treat depreciation as part of cash flows; rather, it should be used to reduce book value of the investment that begins at $500,000 in year T_0 and ends in year T_{10} at $0. The average amount of funds in the project, therefore, is $250,000. After-tax profits are the only source of future benefits. Total profits after taxes for ten years are $825,000, or $82,500 per year. In a variation on this approach, we can calculate the *average annual return on the original investment*.

$$\text{average annual return on original investment} = \frac{\$82,500}{\$500,000} = 16.5\%$$

Neither approach is satisfactory. In the first calculation, management employs conventional accounting techniques to determine the average amount of funds tied

---

[6] See, for example, Lawrence J. Gitman and John R. Forrester, Jr., "A Survey of Capital Budgeting Techniques Used by Major U.S. Firms," *Financial Management*, Vol. 6 (Fall 1977, pp. 66–71). See also James M. Fremgen, "Capital Budgeting Practices: A Survey," *Management Accounting*, Vol. 54 (May 1973, pp. 19–25); Thomas Klammer, "Empirical Evidence on the Adoption of Sophisticated Capital Budgeting Techniques," *Journal of Business*, Vol. 28 (July 1972, pp. 387–97); James C. T. Mao, "Survey of Capital Budgeting: Theory and Practice," *Journal of Finance*, Vol. 25 (May 1970, pp. 349–60); and J. William Petty, David F. Scott, Jr., and Monroe M. Bird, "The Capital Expenditure Decision-Making Process," *The Engineering Economist*, Vol. 20 (Spring 1975, pp. 159–72).

up in the project, $250,000. In the second calculation, management ignores depreciation altogether. Moreover, neither calculation takes into consideration the present value of the benefits to be realized at some point in the future.

THE PAYBACK PERIOD   Rather than using either of the preceding methods, management may employ a simple payback period technique to determine whether or not a project is acceptable. The payback period, as the nomenclature suggests, tells management the length of time required to recoup the original outlay from cash flows. In this instance, given an outlay of $500,000 and an annual cash flow of $132,500, the payback period is

$$\frac{\$500,000}{\$132,500} = 3.77 \text{ years}$$

Suppose the outlay had been the same, $500,000, but there had been irregular cash flows over a useful life of five rather than ten years, so that

	T_1	T_2	T_3	T_4	T_5
Cashflow	$200,000	$250,000	$300,000	$200,000	$100,000

By inspection, we see that all but $50,000 is returned in two years. The $50,000 is one-sixth, or .167, of the cash flows in year T_3. Consequently, the payback period is 2.167 years.

In neither instance does management consider the present value of cash flows nor does it value cash flows that occur after proceeds have been repaid. Nevertheless, the payback period is widely used in practice. In the real world of uncertain cash flows, management often relies upon the payback period as a secondary (if not primary) technique for determining whether or not a project is acceptable.

The combination of either the internal-rate-of-return or net-present-value techniques and a minimum payback period may be used to screen projects.[7] To illustrate, again using the data in Table 8-1, a firm that employs either the internal-rate-of-return or the net-present-value approach would accept the project. However, if management has a three-year payback criterion, the project is unacceptable. And if the required payback period is four years, the project is only marginally acceptable.

If the firm uses a *discounted payback period*, it can calculate how long it takes to return the outlay from the present value of future cash flows. Using 17 percent as the

---

[7] Gitman and Forrester, Jr., p. 68.

cost of capital, then

$$
\begin{array}{ccccccc}
T_1 & T_2 & T_3 & T_4 & T_5 & T_6 & T_7
\end{array}
$$

$$
p.v. = \frac{\$132,500}{1.17} + \frac{\$132,500}{(1.17)^2} + \frac{\$132,500}{(1.17)^3} + \frac{\$132,500}{(1.17)^4} + \frac{\$132,500}{(1.17)^5} + \frac{\$132,500}{(1.17)^6} + \frac{\$132,500}{(1.17)^7}
$$

$$
p.v. = \$113,247.86 + \$96,793.05 + \$82,729.10 + \$70,708.63 + \$60,434.73 + \$51,653.61
$$
$$
+ \$44,148.39
$$

$$
p.v. = \$519,715.37
$$

At the end of seven years, the present value of future cash flows more than covers the original outlay of $500,000. At the end of six years, the present value of future cash flows is $475,566.98 ($519,715.37 − $44,148.39). Thus $24,433.02 ($500,000 − $475,566.98) is the amount that must be recovered in year seven. Because the ratio of $24,433.02 ÷ $44,148.39 is .553, we can say the discounted payback period is approximately 6.553 years. A firm with a six-year payback period or less would not accept the project; one with a seven-year payback period would accept the project.

Although selection of a specific payback period is arbitrary, it may be based on past experience. Nevertheless, adoption of a particular payback period suggests that cash-flow forecasts beyond a specific number of years are widely at variance with reality. In employing the payback-period concept, management implicitly treats all cash flows after the payback period as zero, even though the project may have a positive net present value when they are included. Whether the payback period is an adequate hedge against uncertainty is an issue we explore in Chapter 12.

THE ACCELERATED COST RECOVERY SYSTEM (ACRS) AND THE INVESTMENT TAX CREDIT (ITC)

The decade of the 1980s has been characterized thus far by major changes in Federal Income Tax laws. In less than six years, three acts were passed by Congress and signed into law by President Reagan: Economic Recovery Tax Act of 1981 (ERTA), Tax Equity and Fiscal Responsibility Act of 1982 (TEFRA), and Tax Reform Act of 1986. (Some of the basic features of the Tax Reform Act of 1986— the most sweeping reform in 40 years—are included in Appendix F.) In this chapter, we limit discussion to the effect of the tax laws on capital budgeting. To explain fully what is involved, we offer a comparative analysis—specifically, an analysis of tax law in the early part of the decade and how it has changed under the Tax Reform Act of 1986.

The 1981 legislation (ERTA) established a different concept of depreciation. Known as the Accelerated Cost Recovery System (ACRS), it eliminated any vestige of the notion that for tax purposes, the original cost of the asset must be recovered over its useful life.[8] This concept was not changed by either the 1982 law (TEFRA) or the sweeping overhaul of the tax code in 1986. However, the Tax Reform Act of 1986 lengthens for tax purposes the time required to recover the original cost of many assets.) The 1981 act also reintroduced a notion included in and subsequently eliminated from earlier legislation, the Investment Tax Credit (ITC). In its simplest form, the Investment Tax Credit permits a firm to deduct *from its taxes but not its taxable income* a specific percentage of the purchase price of the asset. Thus, if there is a 10-percent investment tax credit, using our $500,000 outlay taxes are reduced by .10 × $500,000 = $50,000. Depending on legislation in force at the time, the depreciable base ($500,000) may remain unchanged or be reduced by some percentage of the ITC, perhaps 50 percent. If so, then the depreciable base becomes $500,000 − .5 ($50,000) = $475,000.

To take full advantage of the ITC, firms must have taxable income; firms that do not have taxable income cannot make effective use of the provision. As we shall see in Chapter 18, however, firms might have leased the asset from another company that could have taken full advantage of the ITC.

With the Tax Reform Act of 1986, Congress again repealed the Investment Tax Credit. At the same time, however, Congress lowered the maximum tax rate paid by corporations from 46 percent to 34 percent. Because the provisions of the tax laws change periodically, certain text illustrations and end-of-chapter problems/ questions are not consonant with current practice. Nevertheless, using the provisions in effect in 1988, let us see what is the impact of ACRS and what the lower tax rates would be concerning the net present value of the example we have employed.

Since the asset has a useful life of ten years, under current law it falls under what is known as the *7-year 200-percent* class for purposes of the ACRS.[9] This means for tax purposes the original cost of an asset with a useful life of ten years may be recovered over seven years; the *200 percent* refers to the depreciation procedure. This is also known as the *double-declining-balance* technique of depreciation. Thus, if the original cost of the asset can be recovered in seven years, one depreciates the asset so that

$$2\left(\frac{1}{7}\right) = .28571428 = 28.571428\%$$

Consequently, 28.5714 percent of the declining balance can be recovered each

[8] See Commerce Clearing House, Standard Federal Tax Reports, *1983 Depreciation Guide*, No. 26 (May 26, 1983, pp. 15–19). For a discussion of the provisions of the applicable statutes, see Tax Management, Inc., Part 1, "Detailed Analysis," *Economic Recovery Tax Act of 1981* (Washington: The Bureau of National Affairs, Inc., 1981); and Tax Management, Inc., *Tax Equity* and *Fiscal Responsibility Act* (Washington: Bureau of National Affairs, 1983).

[9] United States Joint Committee on Taxation, *Summary of Conference Agreement on H.R. 3838 (Tax Reform Act of 1986)*, (Washington: U.S. Government Printing Office, 1986, p. 7).

year.[10] Moreover, under the code in effect in 1988, a firm may elect to recover the cost over the ACRS life using a straight-line method. In addition, a firm may begin with the double-declining-balance method and shift at any time to the straight-line method to maximize annual depreciation.[11]

In Table 8-5, we summarize the ACRS options available under current law. In so doing, we make use of established practice: assuming the asset purchased is put into place at the midpoint of the year. Known as the *half-year convention*, the asset depreciates for seven years but is allowed only one-half annual depreciation during the first year. The effect is to shift depreciation into eight taxable years.

Employing the double-declining-balance method, annual depreciation allowances taper off rapidly after the fourth year, leaving a large residual in the eighth year. We have shifted to straight-line depreciation in the final year to distribute the remaining depreciation more evenly over the other three years, leaving a smaller residual for the final year.

---

[10] More generally, if n equals the number of years over which the original cost of the asset can be recovered for tax purposes and P equals the percentage of the straight-line method allowable, the general formula for the declining-balance method is

$$P\left(\frac{1}{n}\right) = \text{annual depreciation percentage for the declining balance}$$

Under the current code, P for assets in the 15-year class is 150 percent, so that

$$1.5\left(\frac{1}{15}\right), .10 = 10\%$$

[11] Same as [9], pp. 7 and 8. In a few instances—such as assets used abroad, used by tax-exempt entities, or financed out of proceeds from the sale of tax-exempt bonds—only straight-line depreciation is available. The reintroduction of a standard accelerated-depreciation technique (the declining-balance approach) can be contrasted with the *sum-of-the-years' digits* method. In the case of an asset depreciable for seven years, one sums the number of years, so that $1 + 2 + 3 + 4 + 5 + 6 + 7 = 28$. Then the original cost (not the declining balance) is depreciated, so that

$$\frac{7}{28} \times \text{original cost} = \text{depreciation for first year}$$

$$\frac{6}{28} \times \text{original cost} = \text{depreciation for second year}$$

$$\frac{5}{28} \times \text{original cost} = \text{depreciation for third year}$$

$$\frac{4}{28} \times \text{original cost} = \text{depreciation for fourth year}$$

$$\frac{3}{28} \times \text{original cost} = \text{depreciation for fifth year}$$

$$\frac{2}{28} \times \text{original cost} = \text{depreciation for sixth year}$$

$$\frac{1}{28} \times \text{original cost} = \text{depreciation for the seventh year}$$

Although this option is not available under the current code, it could reappear in the future.

Table 8-5   ACRS Recovery for Asset Classified in Seven-year Category

Depreciation on Straight-line Basis

Year	Amount Recoverable	−	Depreciation[a]	=	Remaining Balance
1	$500,000.00	−	$35,714.29	=	$464,285.71
2	464,285.71	−	71,428.57	=	392,857.14
3	392,857.14	−	71,428.57	=	321,428.57
4	321,428.57	−	71,428.57	=	250,000.00
5	250,000.00	−	71,428.57	=	178,571.43
6	178,571.43	−	71,428.57	=	107,142.86
7	107,142.86	−	71,428.57	=	35,714.29
8	35,714.29	−	35,714.29	=	0
			$500,000.00		

Depreciation Using Double-dealing Balance

Year	Amount Recoverable	−	Depreciation[a,b]	=	Remaining Balance
1	$500,000.00	−	$71,428.57	=	$428,571.43
2	428,571.43	−	122,448.98	=	306,122.45
3	306,122.45	−	87,463.56	=	218,658.89
4	218,658.89	−	62,473.97	=	156,184.92
5	156,184.92	−	44,624.26	=	111,560.66
6	111,560.66	−	31,874.47	=	79,686.19
7	79,686.19	−	22,767.48	=	56,918.71
8	56,918.71	−	56,918.71	=	0
			$500,000.00		

[a] For tax purposes, first-year recovery is one-half the depreciation allowed for that year.

[b] .28571428 of the balance:

$$.28571428 \times \$500,000 = \$142,857.14 \div 2 = \$71,428.57$$
$$\$500,000 - \$71,428.57 = \$428,571.43 \times .28571428 = \$122,448.98$$
$$\$428,571.43 - \$122,448.98 = \$306,122.45 \times .28571428 = \$87,463.56$$

and so on.

[c] (See p. 248.)

$$\$156,184.92 \div 3 = \$52,061.64 \div 2 = \$26,030.82$$
$$\$156,184.92 - \$26,038.82 = \$130,154.10 \div 3 = \$43,384.70$$
$$\$156,184.92 - \$43,384.70 = \$112,800.22$$

and so on.

Table 8-5 (*Continued*)

Depreciation Using Double-declining Balance and Shifting to Straight-line in Fourth Year

Year	Amount Recoverable	−	Depreciation[a,b,c]	=	Remaining Balance
1	$500,000.00	−	$71,428.57	=	$428,571.43
2	428,571.43	−	122,448.98	=	306,122.45
3	306,122.45	−	87,463.56	=	218,658.89
4	218,658.89	−	62,473.97	=	156,184.92
5	156,184.92	−	43,384.70	=	112,800.22
6	112,800.22	−	43,384.70	=	69,415.52
7	69,415.52	−	43,384.70	=	26,030.82
8	26,030.82	−	26,030.82	=	0
			$500,000.00		

To compare results under rates effective in 1988, assume the company is in the 34-percent bracket. Take the data in Table 8-1 and rearrange the cash flows to allow for the different depreciation schedules. Calculating both the internal rate of return and net present value for each option, we present this rearrangement in Table 8-6.

Table 8-6   After-tax Cash Flows Using Depreciation from Table 8-5 (assuming 34-percent tax rate and 17-percent cost of capital)

Depreciation on Straight-line Basis

Year	$(\Delta R - \Delta O)(1 - t)$	+	TcD	=	After-tax Cash Flows
	($400,000 − $200,000)(1 − .34)	+	.34D	=	After-tax Cash Flows
1	($200,000)(.66) = $132,000	+	.34($35,714.29)	=	$144,142.86
2	(200,000)(.66) = 132,000	+	.34(71,428.57)	=	156,285.71
3	(200,000)(.66) = 132,000	+	.34(71,428.57)	=	156,285.71
4	(200,000)(.66) = 132,000	+	.34(71,428.57)	=	156,285.71
5	(200,000)(.66) = 132,000	+	.34(71,428.57)	=	156,285.71
6	(200,000)(.66) = 132,000	+	.34(71,428.57)	=	156,285.71
7	(200,000)(.66) = 132,000	+	.34(71,428.57)	=	156,285.71
8	(200,000)(.66) = 132,000	+	.34(35,714.29)	=	144,142.86
9	(200,000)(.66) = 132,000	+	—	=	132,000.00
10	(200,000)(.66) = 132,000	+	—	=	132,000.00

$IRR = 27.65\%$
$NPV = \$203,273.03$

Table 8-6 (*Continued*)

Depreciation Using Double-declining Balance

Year	$(\Delta R - \Delta O)(1 - .34)$	+	.34D	=	After-tax Cash Flows
1	$132,000	+	.34($71,428.57)	=	$156,285.71
2	132,000	+	.34(122,448.98)	=	173,632.65
3	132,000	+	.34(87,463.56)	=	161,737.61
4	132,000	+	.34(62,473.97)	=	153,241.15
5	132,000	+	.34(44,624.26)	=	147,172.25
6	132,000	+	.34(31,874.47)	=	142,837.32
7	132,000	+	.34(22,767.48)	=	139,740.94
8	132,000	+	.34(56,918.71)	=	151,352.36
9	132,000	+	—	=	132,000.00
10	132,000	+	—	=	132,000.00

$IRR = 28.65\%$
$NPV = \$215,244.03$

Depreciation Using Double-declining Balance and Shifting to Straight-line

Year	$(\Delta R - \Delta O)(1 - .34)$	+	.34D	=	After-tax Cash Flows
1	$132,000	+	.34($71,428.57)	=	$156,285.71
2	132,000	+	.34(122,448.98)	=	173,632.65
3	132,000	+	.34(87,463.56)	=	161,737.61
4	132,000	+	.34(62,473.97)	=	153,241.15
5	132,000	+	.34(43,384.70)	=	146,750.79
6	132,000	+	.34(43,384.70)	=	146,750.79
7	132,000	+	.34(43,384.70)	=	146,750.79
8	132,000	+	.34(26,030.82)	=	140,850.48
9	132,000	+	—	=	132,000.00
10	132,000	+	—	=	132,000.00

$IRR = 28.69\%$
$NPV = \$215,922.32$

The results conform with expectations. Both in terms of IRR and NPV, it is more profitable to use the double-declining-balance method of depreciation than the straight-line method: the former shifts many of the cash flows to the earlier years. By switching from the double-declining-balance method to the straight-line method in the latter part of the recovery period, there is an additional (though nominal) increase in the internal rate of return and the net present value.

INFLATION AND CAPITAL BUDGETING

The original purpose for establishing ACRS was in recognition that "inflation had diminished the value of previous depreciation allowances."[12] In the late 1970s and early 1980s, prices increased in double-digits and at record highs; by the mid-to-late 1980s, prices increased only 3- to 4-percent per year. The volatility of inflation that has characterized our recent experience caused academics and financial practitioners to scrutinize the methods employed in budgeting capital. To examine the impact of inflation, it is convenient to analyze first the cash flows and then the cost of capital. Again employing the data in Table 8-1 and using Equation 8-1, with the illustrative 45-percent tax rate and without ACRS

$$CF = (\Delta R - \Delta O)(1 - t) + tD$$
$$CF = (\$400,000 - \$200,000)(1 - .45) + .45(\$50,000)$$
$$CF = \$110,000 + \$22,500$$
$$CF = \$132,500$$

The $400,000 operating revenues and the $200,000 operating expenses are conceptually distinct from the $50,000 annual depreciation charge. Operating revenues can rise or fall over time with changes in the level of prices; depreciation charges can, as we have seen, only vary with changes in the tax code. Consequently, for purposes of analysis, management should examine the impact of inflation on only operating revenues and expenses. A fundamental question is whether management can pass on expected increases in operating expenses as higher prices. If it can, profits—not depreciation—rise with inflation.

Assume that prices rise at an average rate of 8 percent per year and that the marginal tax rate is unaffected by inflation. Assume further that both revenues and expenses increase by 8 percent compounded annually. For year one

$$CF = [\$400,000(1.08) - \$200,000(1.08)](1 - .45) + .45(\$50,000)$$
$$CF = \$118,800 + \$22,500$$
$$CF = \$141,300$$

For year ten

$$CF = [\$400,000(1.08)^{10} - \$200,000(1.08)^{10}](1 - .45) + .45(\$50,000)$$
$$CF = \$237,481.75 + \$22,500$$
$$CF = \$259,981.75$$

In year one, after-tax revenues less operating expenses (profits after taxes) increase

---

[12] Commerce Clearing House, p. 11.

by 8 percent [$118,800 = $110,000(1.08)$]. The same is true of year ten [$237,481.75 = $110,000(1.08)^{10}$]. However, in year one cash flows increase by

$$\$132,500(1 + r) = \$141,300$$
$$r = 6.6415\%$$

Similarly, in year ten cash flows increase by

$$\$132,500(1 + r)^{10} = \$259,981.75$$
$$r = 6.972636\%$$

Because the depreciation expense is insensitive to inflation, total cash flows do not keep pace with changes in the price level (6.97 percent < 8.0 percent). Thus, one may argue that depreciation expense should rise more rapidly to offset inflation increases. If prices increase at 8 percent per year, the price level will more than double in ten years.[13]

The replacement cost of a $500,000 asset is $500,000(1.08)^{10} = \$1,079,462.50$. Suppose the firm sets aside a sinking fund to replace the asset. Assume such a sinking fund earns 10 percent per year from U.S. Government securities (a real rate of 2 percent and a rate of inflation of 8 percent). From the discussion in Chapter 3, we can establish an annual annuity payment of x dollars, so that

$$\frac{x[(1.10)^{10} - 1]}{.10} = \$1,079,462.50$$
$$15.937425x = \$1,079,462.50$$
$$x = \$67,731.30$$

In principle, this annuity payment is the annual depreciation allowance set aside in a sinking fund to pay for the asset at replacement cost rather than at original cost.

In reality, however, business firms rarely set aside sinking funds to recover the original cost, let alone the replacement cost, of an asset. Rather, the annual depreciation allowances become a source of funds presumably reinvested in the firm, as net present value suggests, at the cost of capital. In promoting accelerated cost recovery, Congress promoted increased net present value for a project, thereby

---

[13] *A Bonus Footnote!* When interviewing for a position requiring some familiarity with the mathematics of compound interest, be ready for the question: *Approximately how long will it take for an investment to double if interest is x percent?* The general answer is: *Assuming interest is compounded annually, divide 72 by the rate in percent.* Thus, 72 divided by 8 percent equals nine years. Lo and behold: $(1.08)^9 = 1.999$ or 2.0 and $1,000 would approximately equal $2,000 at the end of nine years. Knowing that as the *rule of 72*, you also might point out—deftly and without a trace of intellectual arrogance in your manner and voice—that if interest is compounded continuously, one could divide 69.3 by 8 percent, and the investment would double in 8.6625 years ($\$1000e^{.08 \times 8.6625} = \$2000$). The *rule of 69.3* is more precise than the *rule of 72*. Unfortunately, what is true of the investment is also true of the price level. An 8-percent annual rate of inflation will cause the price level to approximately double in nine years if the rate is compounded annually or to exactly double in 8.6625 years if the rate is compounded continuously.

raising the incentive to invest. Whether the policy actually promoted the replacement of existing assets throughout the economy is a moot point: following enactment of ACRS, a major capital boom ensued. Between the fourth quarter of 1982 and the end of 1985, nonresidential fixed investment rose 11.3 percent per year compared with 6.4 percent per year during the average recovery from a recession.[14] Nevertheless, legislation enacted in 1986 brought an end to the investment tax credit—making the ACRS less generous but lowering the corporate tax rate. The jury is still out on the results.

Whatever the tax law provisions, management must consider them in conjunction with inflation in developing a comprehensive approach to capital budgeting. In so doing, a detailed analysis of the cash flows may reveal that only part of the inflation rate is applicable to inflows or outflows. Moreover, revenues may be affected at different rates than expenses. To allow for these modifications, one can establish a general framework for any project, so that[15]

$$\text{inflation-adjusted } NPV = \sum_{n=1}^{t} \frac{[\text{inflow}(1 + aF)^n - \text{expenses}(1 + bF)^n](1 - t) + tD]}{(1 + r)^n} - C_0$$

where

a = proportion of inflation rate applicable to all cash inflows
F = inflation rate
b = proportion of inflation rate applicable to operating expenses
t = marginal tax rate
D = depreciation for tax purposes (D could be zero for some years)
C_0 = cost or outlay for asset in year zero
r = cost of capital

If an abandonment value or scrap value is anticipated at the end of the useful life of the asset, then

$$\text{inflation-adjusted } NPV = \sum_{n=1}^{t} \frac{[\text{inflow}(1 + aF)^n - \text{expenses}(1 + bF)^n](1 - t) + tD}{(1 + r)^n}$$
$$+ \frac{A}{(1 + r)^n} - C_0$$

where A is the projected abandonment value at the end of the useful life of the asset.

---

[14] *1986 Economic Report of the President*, p. 40.

[15] Phillip L. Cooley, Rodney L. Roenfeldt, and It-Keong Chew, "Capital Budgeting Procedures under Inflation," *Financial Management*, Vol. 4 (Winter 1975, pp. 18–26). See also M. Chapman Findlay, III, Alan W. Frankle, Phillip L. Cooley, Rodney L. Roenfeldt, and It-Keong Chew, "Capital Budgeting Procedures under Inflation: Cooley, Roenfeldt, and Chew vs. Findlay and Frankle," *Financial Management*, Vol. 5 (Autumn 1976, pp. 83–90); and Alfred Rappaport and Robert Taggart, Jr., "Evaluation of Capital Expenditure Proposals under Inflation," *Financial Management*, Vol. 11 (Spring 1982, pp. 5–13).

An alternative approach would be to abstract from inflation for both revenues and expenses as well as cost of capital. Suppose the expected rate of inflation is 8 percent compounded annually; then the cost of capital contains a built-in rate of inflation, so that real cost equals 17 percent less the approximately 8-percent premium for inflation.[16] Thus, the real cost of capital is 9 percent. By adjusting the discount rate for inflation, we can return to our original data in Table 8-1, modified only by a depreciation technique consistent with the current tax laws. Consequently, if we had used a cost of capital adjusted for inflation, we would have calculated net present value based upon constant (inflation-adjusted) dollars. But the rate of 9 percent (17 percent − 8 percent) still contains a premium for risk of default. The logic of our analysis suggests that because the cash flows are assumed to be certain, even that premium should be eliminated, bringing the real rate down even farther. We ignore that refinement for the time being.

One substantive criticism of the application of capital budgeting principles is that managers generally do not allow for inflation in the cash flows but continue to discount at a cost of capital that contains a premium for inflation. In doing so, as we suggested at the beginning of the chapter, they implicitly assume after-tax profits will be unaffected by changes in the rate of inflation. The implication is that in real terms profits will decline over time. Although such an assumption is often unwarranted, it may reflect management's desire to hedge against uncertainty in estimating cash flows. Unlike the payback period, however, the bias is more subtle.

PROFITABILITY INDEX (NET-PRESENT-VALUE INDEX)

Throughout this chapter we have emphasized the importance of net present value as the appropriate approach to capital budgeting. However, because practitioners seem to prefer percentages for actual presentations, some may choose to employ the *profitability index* or, as it is sometimes called, the *net-present-value index*.[17] Using our new-found wisdom on the inflation-adjusted cost of capital and employing 9

---

[16] The emphasis is on *approximately*. In Chapter 2, we first encountered the real rate of interest. For risk-free securities—for one year—the nominal rate r is a product of the real rate R and the rate of inflation F, so that $(1 + r) = (1 + R)(1 + F) = 1 + R + F + RF$. The cross product RF is generally small and is ignored in practice, so that $1 + r = 1 + R + F$. Moreover, if interest is compounded continuously, then $e^r = e^R + e^F$.

With business firms, a premium for financial risk is also built into the discount rate. As we have seen, cost of equity capital rises with leverage; in the real world, so does cost of debt. By netting out inflation, real average cost of capital continues to carry a premium for risk-bearing. Because we have assumed certainty in cash flows, the risk premium (as noted in text) also should be netted out, leaving only the risk-free rate. Again, we ignore the refinement at this stage of our analysis.

[17] In the public sector, the phrase *benefit–cost ratio* is employed to measure the present value of future benefits of a project against outlay (cost) of that project.

rather than 17 percent to the data in Table 8-1, we find that

$$\text{present value} = \$132,500 \frac{[1 - (1.09)^{-10}]}{.09}$$

$$= \$850,339.65$$

The profitability index is the ratio of the present value of future cash flows to the original outlay, so that

$$\text{profitability index} = \frac{\$850,339.65}{\$500,000} = 1.70$$

If we had used the original present value discounted at 17 percent, the present value would be $617,264.98 and the profitability index

$$\frac{\$617,264.98}{\$500,000} = 1.23$$

If the net present value of future cash flows had been $500,000, then the profitability index would have been 1.0. Consequently, when the present value of future cash flows equals or exceeds original outlay, the profitability index equals or exceeds 1.0. When the present value of future cash flows is less than outlay, the profitability index is less than 1.0. The decision rule, therefore, is to accept all projects whose profitability index equals or exceeds 1.0 and to reject those whose profitability index is less than 1.0.

Although the profitability index simplifies the presentation of present-value analysis, as with any ratio problems can arise in the case of mutually exclusive investments. Consider the investment opportunities in Table 8–7. According to both internal rate of return and profitability index, project E is preferable to either project F or project G. However, under the net-present-value approach, project G is clearly preferable. Adopting project G adds more to the market

Table 8–7   Comparing Three Mutually Exclusive Investment Opportunities

Project	Outlay	Cash Flow T_1	Internal Rate of Return	Net Present Value at 15%	Profitability Index
E	$ 1,000	$ 1,200	20%	$ 43.48	1.043
F	5,000	5,800	16%	43.48	1.009
G	10,000	11,900	19%	347.82	1.035

value of stockholders' equity than adopting either project E or project F. Therefore, it is advisable—particularly in the case of mutually exclusive investment opportunities—to employ the net-present-value approach. Once the choice is made, however, ranking independent projects on the basis of the profitability index may facilitate presentation of the capital budget for the year in question.

CAPITAL RATIONING

In principle, because management will accept any project where the net present value is positive, the capital budget will consist of all such projects.[18] Our analysis suggests it is the cost of capital that determines the total amount of funds to be invested in any given year. Thus, the size of the capital budget will vary with the number of profitable projects and with the outlay required to implement them.

In practice, however, management often imposes a constraint on the size of the budget—even though this means postponing or not adopting profitable investment opportunities. Sometimes this constraint reflects the belief management can effectively handle only a limited number of projects. A rapidly growing corporation, for example, may find it difficult to organize and train new personnel necessary to implement revenue-producing capital investments. Although such costs should have been taken into consideration when estimating net cash flows, they rarely are. Consequently, personnel constraints manifest themselves as self-imposed capital constraints.

Another reason for limiting the capital budget lies in the mode of financing. Some companies refuse to use such external sources of funds as debt or new issues of stock. Instead, their capital budgets are constrained by internal sources of funds generated from operations: profits and depreciation allowances. Aversion to debt financing is aversion to the consequences of bankruptcy. Refusal to issue new stock may be linked to the desire to maintain control over the corporation: management may pass up profitable investment opportunities rather than let outsiders purchase share in the enterprise.

Although in Chapter 7 we examined the problem of financial risk, constraints arising from personnel adjustments and the issue of control are not treated in this text. We simply recognize these factors as examples of real-world considerations that can lead to limits on the size of the capital budget.

There are several ways of dealing with a constraint on the capital budget. In the simplest scenario, the constraint is for a given year. Suppose, for example, we have a

---

[18] Management will treat mutually exclusive investments separately. Among any set of mutually exclusive investments, the project with the largest net present value will be included in the capital budget.

capital constraint this year of $50,000,000 for the following projects:

	Outlay	Net Present Value
A	$30,000,000	$6,000,000
B	20,000,000	5,000,000
C	15,000,000	4,000,000
D	15,000,000	3,000,000
Total	$80,000,000	

Possible Combination	Outlay	Combined Net Present Value
A and B	$50,000,000	$11,000,000
A and C	45,000,000	10,000,000
A and D	45,000,000	9,000,000
B and C	35,000,000	9,000,000
B and D	35,000,000	8,000,000
B, C, and D	50,000,000	12,000,000
C and D	30,000,000	7,000,000

Of the preceding combinations, only two exhaust the $50,000,000; the other combinations are either less than $50,000,000 or greater than $50,000,000. Combinations such as A, B, and C are not listed because they exceed the budget constraint. Of the projects that use all the budget, projects B, C, and D have higher net present values. Nevertheless, several factors should be considered before recommending B, C, and D. For example, it may be possible to postpone portions of capital outlay until the next budget year to allow the firm to undertake all four projects. In addition, the constraint may be more flexible than initially assumed. Furthermore, some of the projects may have greater cash flows in earlier than in later years. Under a budget constraint, projects with a faster payback may add more to the source of funds for the next year or two than projects with a slower payback. Consequently, it may be useful to employ a multiperiod analysis of a constrained capital budget (the technique for developing this type analysis is in Appendix 7-A).

SUMMARY

We began the chapter discussing the relationship between real assets and their counterparts in financial markets. Behind all securities or financial assets lie real assets. The principles developed in Chapters 3, 4, 6, and 7 can be applied to the capital investment or capital budgeting decision. Such principles abstract from risk and assume future returns are certain.

The dollar return on a real capital investment is its cash flow. Because we are interested in cash flow after taxes, after-tax cash flow equals profits after taxes plus depreciation. A general formula is

$$\text{after-tax cash flow} = (\Delta R - \Delta O)(1 - t) + D$$

The delta may be dropped in practice but serves as a reminder that one is adding to cash flows from existing assets. Since R is the change in revenues, O the change in cash operating expenses from adopting the project, and t the marginal tax rate, the first term in the expression is the annual profits after taxes and D is the depreciation.

To evaluate real capital investments, four techniques have been used in practice: internal rate of return, net present value, payback period, and average return on investment. Based upon principles developed in Chapter 3 both internal-rate-of-return and net-present-value techniques allow for the time value of money. Internal rate of return can be viewed as the percentage that equates present value of future cash flows with outlay on the project. Net present value is the difference between present value of the cash flows discounted at the average cost of capital and outlay on the project. We noted that average cost of capital could be the basis for discounting cash flows; whether it ultimately will be awaits clarification in subsequent chapters.

The payback period is merely the time required to pay back outlay from after-tax cash flows. The average return on the average investment is the ratio of after-tax profits to average amount invested in the project. Although neither takes into account the time value of money, the payback period offers management a simple hedge against uncertainty and is widely used as a secondary technique for budgeting capital.

Of the two primary approaches to budgeting capital, net present value is a more useful measure than internal rate of return. Both internal-rate-of-return and net-present-value techniques contain implicit reinvestment assumptions. In the former, it is assumed that profits equal to the internal rate of return can be subtracted annually from cash flows and the residual can be reinvested at the cost of capital. In the net-present-value technique, funds are reinvested at the cost of capital. The reinvestment assumption is particularly important concerning mutually exclusive investment opportunities. As a result, when using internal rate of return, management sometimes makes incorrect investment decisions. The internal rate of return can also result in multiple solutions to a single problem. Although one can usually determine the appropriate rate, the ambiguity sometimes remains to further detract from the technique.

For accept-or-reject decisions, however, either internal rate of return or net present value gives the same result. In such cases, the project is accepted if internal rate of return exceeds cost of capital or if net present value is positive. Nevertheless, net present value determines the incremental addition to the market value of the company, not internal rate of return. The apparent desire for a percentage rather than a dollar figure can be assuaged by using the profitability index. To calculate the index, divide present value of future cash flows by outlay on the project. As long as the value of the index exceeds 1.0, a project is acceptable.

Current tax laws encourage early recovery of capital. As a result, internal rate of return or net present value of a project can be increased: depreciation is received earlier rather than later. Consequently, the original cost of an asset is fully recovered before its useful life ends. This approach is known as the Accelerated Cost Recovery System (ACRS).

Although accelerated cost recovery may be seen as an offset against an inflationary rise in the replacement cost of an asset, management generally views the depreciation allowance as a source of funds for new projects and not as a sinking fund for replacement existing projects after their useful life ends. Management knows that once the value limit is set, it cannot for tax purposes increase the depreciation allowance to compensate for changes in the price level. Unfortunately, management also appears (in practice) to apply the same approach to revenues and expenses, thereby implicitly assuming after-tax profits do not change with inflation. To offset this bias, one should explicitly recognize the impact of inflation on revenues and expenses or treat them as if they were in constant dollars, reducing the cost of capital by a premium representing expected inflation. However, neither approach is widely used in practice.

Finally, we must recognize that for various reasons constraints will likely be placed on the size of the capital budget. Consequently, it will be necessary to determine from among a series of independent projects the investments that maximize net present value.

MATHEMATICAL PROGRAMMING TECHNIQUES FOR BUDGETING CAPITAL

Some years ago, Lorie and Savage proposed this conundrum: Given a budget constraint, how does one choose among investment opportunities; some of which require outlays in more than one time period? "In such cases, a constraint is imposed not only by the fixed sum available for capital investment in the first period but also by fixed sums available to carry out present commitments in subsequent time periods."[19] The authors illustrated the problem with a budget constraint for two time periods. We reproduce their hypothesis data in Table 8-8. For the current period, the budget constraint is $50; the present value of the budget constraint in the next period is $20.

Using these data as a point of departure, Weingartner has developed a comparative treatment of the problem.[20] We assume cash flows cannot be transferred between time periods and projects are infinitely divisible. Given a cash budget in period 1 of $50 and a cash budget in period 2 of $20, let

$$b_j = \text{net present value of each project}$$
$$X_j = \text{fraction of each project accepted}$$
$$c_{tj} = \text{fraction outlay absorbed by } j^{\text{th}} \text{ project in } j^{\text{th}} \text{ time period}$$

Then, the linear programming problem may be written as

$$\text{maximize} \sum_{j=1}^{n} b_j X_j$$
$$\text{subject to} \sum_{j=1}^{n} c_{tj} X_j \leq C_t$$
$$0 \leq X_j \leq 1$$

---

[19] James H. Lorie and Leonard J. Savage, "Three Problems in Capital Rationing," *Journal of Business*, Vol. XXVIII (October 1955, p. 232).

[20] H. M. Weingartner, *Mathematical Programming and the Analysis of Capital Budgeting Problems* (Englewood Cliffs, NJ: Prentice-Hall, 1963).

Table 8-8   Investment Proposals Available for a Two-period Capital Constraint

Investment Project	Period 1 Outlay	Present Value of Period 2 Outlay	Present Value of Investment
1	$12	$3	$14
2	54	7	17
3	6	6	17
4	6	2	15
5	30	35	40
6	6	6	12
7	48	4	14
8	36	3	10
9	18	3	12

C_t is the total budget constraint. Because we assume the projects are divisible, X_j can have a value anywhere from 0 to 1 or from 0 percent to 100 percent. In linear programming, the foregoing statement is known as the *primal problem*. Since not all the budget may be used in a given time period nor all the projects accepted, we can introduce *slack variables* into the analysis. Therefore, let

S_t = that part of budget not used in time period t

S_j = that portion of project not accepted in time period t

The primal problem can then be rewritten, so that

$$\text{maximize} \sum b_j X_j$$
$$\text{subject to} \sum c_{tj} X_j + S_t = C_t$$
$$X_j + S_j = 1$$

In every linear programming problem, there is a counterpart known as the *dual problem*. The dual problem can be stated

$$\text{minimize} \sum \rho_t c_t + \mu_j \cdot 1$$
$$\text{subject to} \sum \rho_t c_{tj} + \mu_j - \gamma_j = b_j$$
$$\rho_t, \mu_j \geq 0$$

In the dual problem are three new variables designated by the Greek letters ρ, μ, and γ. When $X_j > 0$ in the primal problem, γ_j is zero. Hence, in the dual problem

$$\sum \rho_t c_{tj} + \mu_j - 0 = b_j$$
$$\mu_j = b_j - \sum \rho_t c_{tj}$$

μ_j can be viewed as the difference between net present value of cash flows b_j and imputed value of cash outlays required to undertake the project. When projects are fractionally accepted, the constraint binds the program and $\mu_j = 0$. Thus

$$\sum \rho_t c_{tj} = b_j$$

In other words, net present value of a project we call b_j equals net present value of cash flows. Since the constraint is binding, ρ_t becomes the period 1 discount rate, so that

$$\rho_t = \frac{1}{1 + r_{t+1}}$$

Using the data in Table 8-8, Weingartner established the following as the primal problem.

> maximize
> $14x_1 + 17x_2 + 17x_3 + 15x_4 + 40x_5 + 12x_6 + 14x_7 + 10x_8 + 12x_9$
> subject to
> $12x_1 + 54x_2 + 6x_3 + 6x_4 + 30x_5 + 6x_6 + 48x_7 + 36x_8 + 18x_9 + S_1 = 50$
> $3x_1 + 7x_2 + 6x_3 + 2x_4 + 35x_5 + 6x_6 + 4x_7 + 3x_8 + 3x_9 + S_2 = 20$
> $x_1 + S_1 = 1 \ldots x_9 + S_9 = 1$

Weingartner found the optimal values for x to be

$$
\begin{array}{ll}
x_1 = 1.0 & x_6 = .970 \\
x_2 = 0 & x_7 = .045 \\
x_3 = 1.0 & x_8 = 0 \\
x_4 = 1.0 & x_9 = 1.0 \\
x_5 = 0 &
\end{array}
$$

From the coefficients, we can say projects 1, 3, 4, and 9 are acceptable; projects 2, 5, and 8 are not acceptable. In addition, .97 percent of project 6 is acceptable and 4.5 percent of project 7 is acceptable. Total present value was found to be $70.27. Cash constraints for both periods are binding. Hence, S_1 and $S_2 = 0$ (as pointed out) and become 0 for all projects not adopted or adopted in part.[21]

There are only four positive values for μ.

$$
\begin{array}{ll}
\mu_1 = & 6.77 \\
\mu_3 = & 5.00 \\
\mu_4 = & 10.45 \\
\mu_9 = & 3.95
\end{array}
$$

---

[21] Since $x_1 + S_1 = 1, x_2 + S_2 = 1$, and so on, the slack variables for projects 1, 3, 4, and 9 are each zero and for projects 8 and 2 they are each 1.0. The slack variable for project 6 is .03, or 3 percent. For project 7 it is .955, or 95.5 percent.

At 10.45, μ_4 has the greatest net benefit: it has a smaller net present value than other projects but uses less cash—which is, of course, our constraint. Since γ is a dual slack variable, it has a value only when a project is not accepted in whole or in part—as is the case for projects 2, 5, and 8. The values are

$$\gamma_2 = 3.41$$
$$\gamma_5 = 29.32$$
$$\gamma_8 = .5$$

When compared with μ, we might be tempted to give an opposite interpretation to the values for γ: project 8 does less to reduce net benefits than either projects 2 or 5. More important, however, are the values for ρ. Weingartner found that

$$\rho_1 = 0.136$$
$$\rho_2 = 1.864$$

One interprets the results as follows. For every dollar increase in the budget during period 1, the total net present value increases by 13.6 cents. For every dollar increase in the budget during period 2, the total net present value increases by $1.864. Thus, it is more profitable to relax the constraint during period 2 than during period 1.

We must recognize that although the optimal solution to the problem tells us to undertake fractions of projects 6 and 7, in practice this may be difficult to do. One way to deal with this problem is to assume no projects are divisible. Therefore, x_j must take on an integer value of either 0 or 1. Similarly, where there is a personnel rather than a capital constraint, the program can be modified to take this into account.

Linear programming solutions to capital budgeting are versatile yet not particularly popular. To employ them successfully, one must know all future investment opportunities as well as future budget constraints. Because such knowledge is unlikely, the costs involved in linear programming for more than a few years may not be worth the benefits.

PROBLEMS AND QUESTIONS

Where necessary, use the appropriate tables in the appropriate Appendixes for solving the problems and questions.

1. Find the rate of return on the following project:

Outlay	After-tax Cash Flows		
	First Year	Second Year	Third Year
$10,000	$5,000	$5,000	$5,000

2. Using the data in problem 1, find the net present value under the assumption cost of capital is 10 percent. On the basis of the findings in problems 1 and 2, is the project acceptable? Explain.

3. Find the rate of return on the following project and explain the results. (You may have to use a computer or solve it using the quadratic equation.)

Outlay	After-tax Cash Flows	
	First Year	Second Year
$100,000	−$10,000	$200,000

4. Management is considering the purchase of a computer where original cost is $400,000. It is estimated the computer must be replaced within five years. Management has made a detailed study of the annual savings in total costs that purchasing the computer would generate. It has estimated cost savings at $300,000 per year before taxes. However, management expects to incur an additional $100,000 per year in new expenses associated with operation of the computer. The company has an effective tax rate of 50 percent and its cost of capital is 12 percent. Should the company purchase the computer? Explain.

5. A firm is considering an investment with the following pattern of cash flows:

Outlay	After-tax Cash Flows		
	First Year	Second Year	Third Year
$100,000	$50,000	$100,000	$10,000

The cost of capital is 12 percent and the reinvestment rate is 12 percent. Is the project worth undertaking? Explain in detail.

6. Assume a company with cost of capital and reinvestment rates of 15 percent must choose between the following mutually exclusive investments. Which should it choose? Why?

	Outlay	After-tax Cash Flows	
		First Year	Second Year
Project X	$10,000	$ 5,500	$9,680
Project Y	$20,000	$24,200	—

7. Assume a corporation with a cost of capital rate of 15 percent must choose between the following mutually exclusive investments. Which should it choose? Why?

	Outlay	After-tax Cash Flows	
		First Year	Second Year
Project A	$1,000	$1,300	—
Project B	$1,000	—	$1,562.50

8. XYZ Toolmaking Corporation is considering the purchase of one of two lathes. Outlay on the first is $90,000; outlay on the second is $75,000. The useful life of each is 15 years. Operating expense associated with the $90,000 outlay is $1,000 per year; operating expense associated with the $75,000 outlay is $1,500. The corporate income-tax rate is 40 percent, the required rate of return is 12 percent, and there is no investment tax credit. Assuming no scrap value, straight-line depreciation, and using the net-present-value approach, which project (if either) should you accept? Why?

9.

	Outlay	After-tax Cash Flows		
		T_1	T_2	T_3
A	$110,000	$ 80,000	$ 80,000	$ 80,000
B	$200,000	$150,000	$150,000	$150,000

a. Calculate internal rate of return on each project.
b. Assume average cost of capital is 15 percent. Is one or both projects acceptable? If one, which one? Why?
c. Using net-present-value technique, is either project acceptable? Why? Why not?
d. Suppose you must choose between A and B. Which, if either, should you choose? Why?

10. A company can invest $100,000 in equipment with a useful life of five years and no scrap value. The cost savings would generate an additional $30,000 per year for the next five years. Required rate of return and cost of capital rates are 16 percent. The marginal corporate tax rate is 35 percent. Using straight-line depreciation and net-present-value technique, should the company accept this project? Why?

11. Explain in detail why depreciation is included in cash flows when evaluating a project. Should all noncash expenses be treated in the same way? Explain.

12. "The present-value approach is superior to the yield technique for selecting investments." Evaluate.

13. Using the following data:

Outlay	After-tax Cash Flows				
	T_1	T_2	T_3	T_4	T_5
$75,000	$45,000	$25,000	$20,000	$15,000	$15,000

   a. Compute the payback period.
   b. Assuming there is no scrap value and the asset is depreciated on a straight-line basis, what is the average return on investment given a marginal tax rate of 40 percent?
   c. What is the net present value given a cost of capital of 14 percent?
   d. What is the internal rate of return?

14. Explain why *payback period* and *average return on investments* are poor techniques for evaluating capital projects.

15. "Both net-present-value and internal-rate-of-return approaches to capital budgeting may underestimate true return or net present value on a project." How can this be? Explain.

16. A firm estimates that a $300,000 outlay will generate after-tax profits (exclusive of depreciation) of $50,000 per year for the next ten years. The marginal corporate tax rate is 40 percent. For tax purposes, assume the firm may recover its investment in the asset over the next five years, so that

Year	Percent of Original Cost
1	15
2	22
3	21
4	21
5	21

   a. Calculate after-tax cash flows on the project.
   b. Assuming cost of capital is 15 percent, what is the NPV?
   c. What is the internal rate of return?
   d. Assume the firm had used straight-line depreciation with no scrap value. Would your answers to (b) and (c) change? How?
   e. Suppose tax laws change so the investment can only be depreciated over seven years using a double-declining-balance method with the option to shift to straight-line method. The half-year convention is employed. Compare the results with those in (b), (c), and (d).

17. In problem 16, management estimates inflation to be 9 percent per year. What is the replacement cost of the project in ten years? Should this cost deter management from making the investment? Explain.

SELECTED ADDITIONAL REFERENCES

Bacon, Peter W. "The Evaluation of Mutually Exclusive Investments," *Financial Management*, Vol. 6 (Summer, 1977, pp. 55–58).

Baumol, William J. and Richard E. Quandt. "Investment and Discount Rates under Capital Rationing—A Programming Approach," *Economic Journal*, Vol. 75 (June, 1965, pp. 317–29).

Beedles, William L. "A Note on Evaluating Non-Simple Investments," *Journal of Financial and Quantitative Analysis*, Vol. 13 (March 1978, pp. 173–75).

Bernhard, Richard H. "Mathematical Programming Models for Capital Budgeting—A Survey, Generalization and Critique," *Journal of Financial and Quantitative Analysis*, Vol. 4 (June 1969, pp. 111–58).

Bierman, Harold, Jr. and Seymour Smidt. *The Capital Budgeting Decision*, 6th ed. (New York: Macmillan, 1984).

Bodenhorn, D. "A Cash Flow Concept of Profit," *The Journal of Finance*, Vol. 19 (March 1964, pp. 16–31).

Cooley, Philip L., Rodney L. Roenfeldt, and It-Keong Chew. "Capital Budgeting Procedures under Inflation," *Financial Management*, Vo. 4 (Winter 1975, pp. 18–26).

Dean, Joel. *Capital Budgeting* (New York: Columbia University Press, 1951).

Dorfman, Robert. "The Meaning of the Internal Rate of Return," *Journal of Finance*, Vol. 36, (December 1981, pp. 1010–23).

Fama, Eugene E. and Merton H. Miller. *The Theory of Finance*, Ch. 3 (New York: Holt, Rinehart and Winston, 1972).

Findlay, M. Chapman, III, Alan W. Frankle, Philip L. Cooley, Rodney L. Roenfeldt, and It-Keong Chew. "Capital Budgeting Procedures Under Inflation: Cooley, Roenfeldt and Chew vs. Findlay and Frankle," *Financial Management*, Vol. 5 (Autumn 1976, pp. 83–90).

Fremgen, James M. "Capital Budgeting Practices: A Survey," *Management Accounting*, Vol. 54 (May 1973, pp. 19–25).

Gitman, L. J. "Forecasting and Evaluation Practices and Performances: A survey of Capital Budgeting," *Financial Management*, Vol. 6 (Fall 1977, pp. 66–71).

Gitman, L. J. and G. R. Forrester, Jr. "Capital Budgeting Techniques," *Financial Management*, Vol. 6 (Fall 1977, pp. 66–71).

Hastie, Larry. "One Businessman's View of Capital Budgeting," *Financial Management*, Vol. 3 (Winter 1974, pp. 36–44).

Hunt, Pearson. *Financial Analysis in Capital Budgeting* (Boston: Harvard Graduate School of Business Administration, 1964).

Jean, William H. *Capital Budgeting* (Scranton, PA: International Textbook Company, 1969).

———. "Terminal Value of Present Value in Capital Budgeting Programs," *Journal of Financial and Quantitative Analysis*, Vol. 6 (January 1971, pp. 649–52).

Jeynes, Paul H. "The Significance of Reinvestment Rate," *Engineering Economist*, Vol. 11 (Fall 1965, pp. 1–9).

Johnson, Robert W. *Capital Budgeting* (Belmont, CA: Wadsworth, 1970).

Klammer, Thomas. "Empirical Evidence of the Adoption of Sophisticated Capital Budgeting Techniques," *Journal of Business*, Vol. 28 (July 1972, pp. 387–97).

Lorie, James and Leonard J. Savage. "Three Problems in Capital Rationing," *Journal of Business*, Vol. 28 (October 1955, pp. 229–39).

Lustzig, Peter and Bernhard Schwab. "A Note on the Application of Linear Programming to Capital Budgeting," *Journal of Financial and Quantitative Analysis*, Vol. 3 (December 1968, pp. 427–31).

Lutz, Friedrich and Vern Lutz. *The Theory of Investment of the Firm* (Princeton, NJ: Princeton University Press, 1951).

McCarthy, Daniel E. and William R. McDaniel. "A Note on Expensing versus Depreciating Under the Accelerated Cost Recovery System: Comment," *Financial Management*, Vol. 12 (Summer 1983, pp. 37–39).

Mao, James C. T. "A Survey of Capital Budgeting: Theory and Practice," *Journal of Finance*, Vol. 25 (May 1970, pp. 349–60).

Merrett, A. J. and Allen Sykes. *The Finance and Analysis of Capital Projects* (New York: John Wiley and Sons, 1973).

Nelson, Charles R. "Inflation and Capital Budgeting," *Journal of Finance*, Vol. 45 (July 1972, pp. 387–97).

Oakford, Robert V. *Capital Budgeting* (New York: Ronald Press, 1970).

Petty, J. William and Oswald D. Bowlin. "The Financial Manager and Quantitative Decision Models," *Financial Management*, Vol. V (Winter 1976, pp. 32–41).

Petty, J. William, David F. Scott, Jr., and Monroe M. Bird. "The Capital Expenditure Decision-Making Process," *The Engineering Economist*, Vol. 20 (Spring 1975, pp. 159–72).

Quirin, C. David and John C. Wiginton. *Analyzing Capital Expenditures* (Homewood, IL: Richard D. Irwin, 1981).

Rappaport, Alfred and Robert Taggart, Jr. "Evaluation of Capital Expenditure Proposals Under Inflation," *Financial Management*, Vol. 11 (Spring 1982, pp. 5–13).

Robichek, Alexander A. and James C. Van Horne. "Abandonment Value and Capital Budgeting," *Journal of Finance*, Vol. 22 (December 1967, pp. 557–89).

Schwab, Bernard and Peter Lustzig. "A Comparative Analysis of the Net Present Value and the Benefit–Cost Ratios as Measures of the Economic Desirability of Investments," *Journal of Finance*, Vol. 24 (June 1969, pp. 507–16).

Solomon, Ezra. "The Arithmetic of Capital Budgeting Decisions," *Journal of Business*, Vol. 29 (April 1950, pp. 124–29).

——— (ed.). *The Management of Corporate Capital* (Glencoe, IL: The Free Press, 1959).

———. *The Theory of Financial Management* (New York: Columbia University Press, 1963).

Spies, Richard R. "The Dynamics of Corporate Capital Budgeting," *Journal of Finance*, Vol. 29 (June 1974, pp. 829–46).

Teichroew, Daniel. *An Introduction to Management Science: Deterministic Models* (New York: John Wiley and Sons, 1964, pp. 78–82).

Teichroew, Daniel, Alexander A. Robicheck, and Michael Montalbano. "An Analysis of Criteria for Investment and Finance Decisions Under Certainty," *Management Science*, Vol. 12 (November 1965, pp. 151–79).

Van Horne, J. C. "A Note on Biases in Capital Budgeting Introduced by Inflation," *Journal of Financial and Quantitative Analysis*, Vol. 6 (January 1971, pp. 653–58).

Vandell, Robert and Paul Stonich. "Capital Budgeting: Theory or Results?" *Financial Executive*, Vol. 41 (August 1973, pp. 46–57).

Vickers, Douglas. *The Theory of the Firm: Production, Capital and Finance* (New York: McGraw-Hill, 1968).

Weingartner, H. Martin. "Capital Rationing: Authors in Search of a Plot," *The Journal of Finance*, Vol. 32 (December 1977, pp. 1403–32).

———. *Mathematical Programming and the Analysis of Capital Budgeting Problems* (Englewood Cliffs, NJ: Prentice-Hall, 1963).

———. "Some New Views on the Payback Period and Capital Budgeting Decisions," *Management Science*, Vol. 15 (August 1969, pp. 594–607).

Wilkes, F. M. *Capital Budgeting Techniques* (London: John Wiley and Sons, 1977).

9

RISK
IN CAPITAL
BUDGETING

In Chapter 8 we developed the principles of capital budgeting in a world of certainty: cash flows were predictable over the life of the project. Although unrealistic, the approach allowed us to focus on techniques. In the latter part of the chapter, we took a step toward reality by introducing inflation into the analysis. Because inflation impacts upon all investments—even the risk-free securities of the U.S. government—the subject warranted separate treatment. In this chapter, we take a further step toward reality, drawing upon and extending the analysis developed in Chapter 4.

For a variety of reasons that may be specific to a project, cash flows are not certain. Management may underestimate sales and/or overestimate costs. Consequently, actual cash flows may exceed estimated cash flows. The opposite is also possible. Can one attach probabilities to such an event? If so, how are such probabilities determined? How does taking account of such probabilities affect estimates of net present value or internal rate of return? These are some of the questions we explore in this chapter. The tools employed to answer them are developed in the context of the project itself. Although at this stage we do not consider the impact an investment may have on overall risk to a company, we discuss that issue in some detail in Chapter 10.

INVESTING IN RISKY ASSETS

To help you understand the problems involved in investing in risky assets, consider the following illustration. A prescription drug manufacturer is about to market a new drug for the treatment of a specific disease. Outlay, including research and development, is $6,000,000. We assume the costs are known and recoverable over the useful life or the expected life of the new drug.[1] Because of rapid changes in this field, management assumes therapeutic improvements will be available in four years that will render this particular drug obsolete; in the meantime, management believes it is the most effective treatment available.

To estimate revenues, management must determine—usually from data published on the estimated number of people with the disease—potential demand for the drug and establish a price per unit. Management believes the price can be higher than the price of available alternatives because tests indicate the drug is more effective. Nevertheless, from preliminary tests management has learned of side effects—nausea and vertigo among them—that render the drug contraindicated for a small percentage of sufferers. This limits the potential market. Furthermore, a price that is too high relative to costs of production and distribution encourages substitutes. Although the firm holds a patent on the drug and has received final approval from the Food and Drug Administration (FDA) to market it, other firms may be developing substitutes not covered by the patent.[2] A price well in excess of costs encourages entry and subsequent loss of sales.

Costs, particularly costs of production, also vary. If the drug reaches nearly all the potential market, there are sufficient scale economies to lower the unit costs of

---

[1] The development and marketing of a new drug often requires extensive outlays, not just for the year in which the drug is to be marketed but also in earlier years. Most of these expenses are for research and development. The decision to spend such funds is even riskier than our example suggests. Outlays must be made well in advance of cash inflows, forcing management to estimate cash flows not at t_0 but at t_{0-n}. See Thomas R. Stauffer, "Profitability Measures in the Pharmaceutical Industry," in Robert B. Helms, ed., *Drug Development and Marketing* (Washington: The American Enterprise Institute for Public Policy Research, 1975, pp. 97–129).

[2] For a discussion on the process of testing a new drug, see Henry G. Grabowski and John M. Vernon, *The Regulation of Pharmaceuticals: Balancing the Benefits and Risks* (Washington: American Enterprise Institute for Public Policy Research, 1983, pp. 18–27).

production. On the other hand, the vice president of marketing has learned through experience that additional expenses—including advertising in medical journals and, more importantly, adding sales personnel to call on physicians—will be necessary to bring the drug to the attention of physicians. Because the drug manufacturer has a quality reputation among the medical profession, such additional marketing expenditures are not only necessary to ensure rapid promotion of the product but are viewed by the marketing vice president as essential to effecting maximum penetration of the market.

The foregoing scenario suggests the marketing considerations actually involved; application of the principles of capital budgeting requires an intimate knowledge of the workings of a particular industry or market. Although the specific considerations management of a drug company must address differ from those management of a computer manufacturer must consider, in all instances the bottom line is anticipated future after-tax cash flows from an investment under inevitably different scenarios. The principles developed provide the framework. Management, knowledgeable about the market it serves, gives that framework substance.

Consequently, one way to gain insight into future cash flows is to request that production, marketing, and other appropriate executives develop cost and revenue estimates under identifiable sets of conditions. For a tire manufacturer, introduction of a new longer-life radial must take into consideration the impact of the tire on sales growth. A longer-life tire means fewer replacement sales. Moreover, revenues are greatly affected by the cyclical demand for automobiles and other motor vehicles that provide the greatest source of new-tire sales. Hence, a tire manufacturer may want to estimate sales and costs under various national economic growth forecasts.

However, such considerations may be of scant significance to a drug manufacturer, where demand is relatively inelastic due to desire for effective treatment and because third-party payments (insurance) are available. Recession or growth affects sales only marginally as changing economic conditions impact on employment and on subsequent medical benefits of those who have the disease.[3] More important may be extrapolating to the market as a whole those who suffer from side effects. If test samples underestimate those afflicted by nausea and vertigo, actual sales could be lower than otherwise expected. The opposite would be true if the number of test patients in the sample adversely affected were greater than their actual number in the population as a whole.

Bearing this and other points in mind—such as whether data estimating how many people have the disease understate or overstate their actual numbers, whether additional sales personnel will generate more sales, and whether the price charged will motivate entry into the market—management can identify five possible sales

---

[3] To the extent an illness immobilizes or disables permanently, changing economic conditions may have little or no impact on sales.

Table 9-1 Expected Annual Cash Flows from $6,000,000 New-drug Investment (five individual scenarios)

	Possible Outcomes				
	(1)	(2)	(3)	(4)	(5)
Expected Revenues	$4,000,000	$5,000,000	$6,000,000	$7,000,000	$8,000,000
Expected Operating Expenses	(2,000,000)	(2,250,000)	(2,500,000)	(2,750,000)	(3,000,000)
Depreciation and Amortization	(1,500,000)	(1,500,000)	(1,500,000)	(1,500,000)	(1,500,000)
Profit before taxes	500,000	1,250,000	2,000,000	2,750,000	3,500,000
Taxes at .4	(200,000)	(500,000)	(800,000)	(1,100,000)	(1,400,000)
Profits after taxes	300,000	750,000	1,200,000	1,650,000	2,100,000
Depreciation and Amortization	1,500,000	1,500,000	1,500,000	1,500,000	1,500,000
	1,800,000	2,250,000	2,700,000	3,150,000	3,600,000
Probability	× .1	× .25	× .30	× .25	× .1
Expected Cash Flow =	$180,000 +	$562,500 +	$810,000 +	$787,500 +	$360,000 =
Expected Cash Flow =	$2,700,000				

$$\sigma^2_{cf} = \left[\begin{array}{l} (1,800,000 - 2,700,000)^2(.1) + (2,250,000 - 2,700,000)^2(.25) + (2,700,000 - \\ 2,700,000)^2(.3) + (3,150,000 - 2,700,000)^2(.25) + (3,600,000 - 2,700,000)^2(.1) \end{array} \right]$$

$$\sigma_{cf} = (263,250,000,000)^{\frac{1}{2}}$$

$$\sigma_{cf} = \$513,079$$

figures, each representing a different scenario. Production costs associated with each scenario are estimated and grouped with the other operating expenses. Management chooses to depreciate facilities and amortize research and development expenses on a straight-line basis. The entire $6,000,000 will be recovered in four years: $1,500,000 per year. The marginal tax rate is .4. Relying upon its understanding of the industry, management attached its subjective probabilities to each possible outcome and calculated the expected cash flows and the standard deviation of cash flows. The results are given in Table 9-1.

Drawing upon our earlier analysis, we have subtracted expected operating expenses from expected revenues for each scenario. Depreciation and amortization of research and development expenses also have been subtracted. Cash flows before taxes have been reduced by the amount of the taxes and the noncash expenses have been added back. The result yields expected cash flows after taxes for each outcome identified by management, which are multiplied by the probability management has determined reflects its estimate of chances the result will occur. The weighted average of these outcomes is the expected cash flow of $2,700,000. The standard deviation of the expected cash flow is $513,079.

MONTE CARLO SIMULATION

In the foregoing example, we collated estimates of experts to calculate five possible values for net cash flows. An alternative approach is to program the supersonic moron—the computer—to process the information our experts provide. How would it do so? Would the results be any better than if we relied on what the experts already have given us?

To answer these questions, it is useful to draw upon the gambling analogy we employed in Chapter 4. Suppose a friend suggests you can make money in roulette by employing a particular strategy. He tells you he returned from his last junket to Lake Tahoe with his pockets bulging. Although tempted to tell him not to bother you with the details but to try the strategy three or four more times and then you will listen to him, you choose to hear his story anyway.[4] He believes he can make as much as a 200-percent profit on 100 spins of the roulette wheel, but possibly could lose 50 percent of the money wagered. His strategy is tantamount to a model: the outcomes he anticipates are his most optimistic and pessimistic assumptions. To test the strategy in person can be expensive, but you can do so vicariously through computer simulation. A computer can be programmed to simulate a roulette wheel. The outcome of each simulation can be compared to the bet that would have been placed using the strategy. The process can be repeated 100 times, 1,000 times, or indefinitely. The distribution of *profits* from the simulation and strategy could be plotted. Depending upon your attitude toward risk, you can either disregard the strategy or take the next available plane to Lake Tahoe.

This approach, known as **Monte Carlo Simulation,** has been associated with capital budgeting techniques for several years.[5] The strategy (in this case, the model) employed is the one we have been using. Specifically

after-tax cash flow = (revenues − costs − depreciation − taxes) + depreciation

or

after-tax cash flow = (revenues − costs − depreciation)(1 − tax rate) + depreciation

or

after-tax cash flow = (revenues − cash costs)(1 − tax rate) + tax rate (depreciation)

Although the last expression is in words, it is the same as Equation 8-1a in Chapter 8.

The key components, revenues and costs, were derived from expert opinion; however, each is based on an estimate of physical units sold or produced and on price

---

[4] Your skepticism is warranted. The odds, as we saw, are against you however you choose to play. On the other hand, if your friend had developed a mnemonic device for card counting, it could be useful in Black Jack—where the odds change as each card is turned up and where the dealer could be at a disadvantage. If successful, however, you would be *personna non grata* at the gaming houses.

[5] Among the early advocates were David Hertz and McKinsey and Company. See D. B. Hertz. "Investment Policies That Pay Off," *Harvard Business Review*, Vol. 46 (January–February 1968, pp. 96–108).

or unit cost of production. Our experts developed five individual scenarios. Does this mean they took into consideration changes in price and quantity and changes in unit cost and quantity? Suppose, for example, our marketing expert made no allowance for the effect of inflation on product price. Over a four-year period, the actual price may be much higher than projected. If quantity sold is unaffected by inflation, total revenues will be greater than projected. On the other hand, unit costs of production may be affected differently by inflation.

Another problem is the effect of actual sales in year one on subsequent sales in year two. In other words, are cash flows independent through time? If the drug company finds that first-year sales were higher than forecasted, is it likely second-year sales also will be greater than forecasted? Revenues (and probably expenses) could be dependent over time.

In asking these questions, management is trying to learn how marketing and production experts arrived at their estimates. The quantitative result of this line of inquiry is a series of simultaneous equations relating price to factors affecting it and unit costs to factors affecting it, and ultimately combining revenues and expenses to produce a probability distribution of cash flows. To illustrate, variable costs per unit may rise 1 percent for each 10-percent change in quantity produced, so that

Year 1 variable costs per unit = expected variable costs per unit
$$\times \ (1 + .1 \ \text{change due to error in production forecast})$$

The year-one variable costs per unit is the expected variable costs per unit plus an allowance (positive or negative) representing a proportionate change in variable costs due to forecasting errors. Other factors can be added—such as the impact of inflation on variable costs per unit—which may be more important for estimates of variable costs per unit for years two, three, and four, than for year one. Similar equations would be established for all variables determining cash flows. Otherwise, constants such as the depreciation figure would be entered.

Once the equations are established, specific probabilities are applied. In the case of variable costs per unit, if management is comfortable with the assumption of symmetry, small changes on either side of the forecast of expected variable costs are (notably) more likely to occur than large changes but actual variable costs are just as likely to be 10 percent above expected variable costs as 10 percent below expected variable costs.

A major difference therefore exists between roulette and a capital project. We know the odds for any outcome in a game of roulette. They are *objective*. In applying Monte Carlo Simulation techniques to capital budgeting, the probabilities for errors in the forecast that will cause actual outcome to differ from expected outcome may be based on informed judgment. Nevertheless, the probabilities are *subjective*.

Consequently, in the final analysis, simulation forces decision-makers to specify the equations that led to specific estimates of cash flows. This can be a useful exercise, for it challenges informed people—marketing and production experts—to draw upon their knowledge in a specific way. In the process, they may uncover factors previously overlooked, which in turn may lead to a revision of the five scenarios.

Given the same information, the computer can extend the number of possible outcomes. If management's subjective probability distribution approximates the normal curve, the computer will generate a finite distribution approximating the normal curve with an expected cash flow and standard deviation—instead of five estimates of cash flows. Moreover, depending on the assumptions made about dependency of cash flows through time, the computer will generate an expected value and a standard deviation of cash flows for each of four years. Finally, if we substitute a value for r, the computer will generate a probability distribution of net present values.

Number crunching, however, is easy. How useful are the results? Have we learned more from the exercise or is it garbage in–garbage out (GIGO)? Let us explore the issue further.

CASH FLOWS AND THE NORMAL CURVE

Having employed Monte Carlo Simulation techniques, let us suppose the cash flow estimate based on five finite scenarios (Table 9-1) has been refined to the point where the expected cash flows and standard deviation are presently

$$\text{expected cash flows} = \$2,500,000$$
$$\text{standard deviation} = \$ \ 475,000$$

Further assume, for the time being, the actual cash flows are independent: results in subsequent years are not dependent upon results in earlier years.

From the foregoing information and recalling our discussion in Chapter 4, we can use the normal curve to develop management's expectations of the likelihood cash flows will be more or less than $2,500,000. For example, although asymptotic to the x-axis, the expected return $\pm 3\sigma$s encompasses 99.74 percent of the area under the curve. To phrase it differently, under the assumptions made, management believes there are only 26 chances in 10,000 (.26 percent of 10,000) that cash flows will be less than $1,075,000 or more than $3,925,000 ($2,500,000 $\pm$ 3 × $475,000; see Figure 9-1).

We can carry the analysis one step further. Table 9-2 reproduces columns 1 and 2 of Appendix D and shows the area under the normal curve measured in terms of the standard deviation. Thus

$$Z = \frac{x_1 - E(x)}{\sigma} = \frac{\$1,075,000 - \$2,500,000}{\$475,000} = -3$$

$$Z = \frac{x_2 - E(x)}{\sigma} = \frac{\$3,925,000 - \$2,500,000}{\$475,000} = 3$$

Figure 9-1 Normal Distribution of Expected Cash Flows

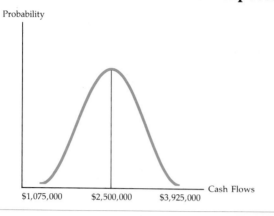

Probability

$1,075,000 $2,500,000 $3,925,000   Cash Flows

Table 9-2 Area under the Normal Curve Measured in Terms of the Standard Deviation

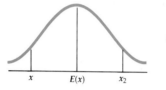

$$\frac{X - E(x)}{\sigma}$$ = distance along abscissa measured in standard deviation units

$\dfrac{X - E(x)}{\sigma}$	Area left or right of $\dfrac{X - E(x)}{\sigma}$	$\dfrac{X - E(x)}{\sigma}$	Area left or right of $\dfrac{X - E(x)}{\sigma}$
0.0	.5000	1.6	.0548
0.1	.4602	1.7	.0446
0.2	.4207	1.8	.0359
0.3	.3821	1.9	.0287
0.4	.3446	2.0	.0228
0.5	.3085	2.1	.0179
0.6	.2743	2.2	.0139
0.7	.2420	2.3	.0107
0.8	.2119	2.4	.0082
0.9	.1841	2.5	.0062
1.0	.1587	2.6	.0047
1.1	.1357	2.7	.0035
1.2	.1151	2.8	.0026
1.3	.0968	2.9	.0019
1.4	.0808	3.0	.0013
1.5	.0668		

As discussed in Chapter 4, the expression $\dfrac{x_1 - E(x)}{\sigma}$ measures the distance left of the expected value of x. In this case, the expected value of the cash flow is $2,500,000. When one subtracts the expected value of the cash flow from x_1 ($1,075,000) and divides it by σ ($475,000), the result is standard deviation units—sometimes referred to (perhaps unfortunately) as *standard deviates*. The area left of x_1 is under the normal curve when x_1 is 3 standard deviations left of the expected value. The value is .0013 or .13 percent of the total area to the left of the expected value. Since the normal curve is symmetrical, 50 percent of the area lies to the left of the expected value and 50 percent to the right. The area beyond x_1, therefore, represents one tail of the distribution.

By analogy, the area beyond x_2 ($3,925,000) is also .13 percent; it is the area in the tail that is the part of the distribution to the right of the expected value. Together (.13% + .13%) the areas under both tails represent .26 percent of the total area under the curve. This is why the odds are 26 in 10,000 the actual cash flow will be less than $1,075,000 or more than $3,925,000.

Based on the simulations, management also believes the likelihood the cash flow will be zero is quite small. Why? If x_1 is 0, then

$$\frac{\$0 - \$2,500,000}{\$475,000} = -5.26$$

The value of x_1 (0) lies 5.26 standard deviations from the expected value. The odds that 0 will be part of a normal distribution of cash flows whose expected value is $2,500,000 and whose standard deviation is $475,000 are so remote as to be virtually nonexistent. Indeed, most people who use the normal curve assume the values that lie more than approximately two standard deviations from the expected value are, for most purposes, statistically insignificant. At this distance, location of the values of x_1 and x_2 are such that chances are fewer than 2.3 (one tail) in 100 there is a value greater than x_2 or smaller than x_1. Similarly, chances that there exist values either greater than x_2 or smaller than x_1 are 4.6 in 100.[6]

EXPECTED NET PRESENT VALUE

Having inferred from the information that management does not expect cash flows to fall below zero, we still have the question of whether or not the project is acceptable on a risk-adjusted basis. Again, outlay is $6,000,000. Based on our earlier analysis,

---

[6] At 1.96 standard deviations from the expected value, the area that lies left of x_1 or right of x_2 represents 2.5 percent of the normal curve. Following convention, we have rounded to 2.0 in the text. Thus, at 1.96 standard deviations, chances are 2.5 in 100 that a value will lie left of x_1 or right of x_2. Chances are 5 in 100 (1 in 20) that there will be values either less than x_1 or more than x_2.

Similarly, at 2.58 standard deviations, the area that lies left of x_1 or right of x_2 is .5 percent. Chances are 1 in 200 that a value will lie left of x_1 or right of x_2. Chances are 1 in 100 that there will be values either less than x_1 or more than x_2.

one could calculate the net present value so that

$$\text{net present value} = -\$6{,}000{,}000 + \frac{\$2{,}500{,}000 \left[1 - (1 + r)^{-4}\right]}{r}$$

All one does is substitute the cost of capital for r and determine whether the net present value is positive, negative, or zero. Right?

Wrong! But the explanation is somewhat involved. We can begin, however, by recalling that the cost of capital includes premiums for risk and for inflation. Because the cash flows have been adjusted for risk, the appropriate value for r is the nominal risk-free rate. If the projected cash flows are in constant dollars, management should employ the real risk-adjusted rate of interest to discount cash flows.

Bear in mind, the purpose of the exercise is to come to grips with the risks involved in accepting the project. Management may conclude the risk is too great. In terms of trading off risk against return or net present value, on a risk-adjusted basis the project may be unacceptable. However, if the project meets this criterion, management may discount expected cash flows in the conventional manner to determine whether the net present value is positive or negative. In other words, we have not discarded the cost of capital but merely set it aside as an inappropriate measure for calculating expected net present value based upon risk-adjusted cash flows.

Assume management chooses not to incorporate estimates of inflation in the cash flows and, therefore, employs the nominal rather than the real risk-free rate in the calculations. Using the yield on U.S. Treasury securities as an appropriate proxy, assume the rate is 9 percent. Then

$$\text{expected net present value} = -\$6{,}000{,}000 + \$2{,}500{,}000 \frac{\left[1 - (1.09)^{-4}\right]}{.09}$$

$$= -\$6{,}000{,}000 + \$8{,}099{,}300$$

$$= \$2{,}099{,}300$$

The expected net present value of $2,099,300 is the mean of a probability distribution of net present values. The standard deviation of this probability distribution depends on the assumptions one makes about the relationship of cash flows in the first year to those in the second and subsequent years. If we continue to assume cash flows are independent of one another, the standard deviation of the probability distribution of net present values can be determined by the equation

$$\sigma \text{ probability distribution of } NVPs = \sqrt{\sum_{n=0}^{\infty} \frac{\sigma_n^2}{(1 + r)^{2n}}} \qquad (9\text{-}1)$$

Using the standard deviation of the cash flows for each of four years, one obtains

$$\sigma = \left[\frac{(\$475,000)^2}{(1.09)^2} + \frac{(\$475,000)^2}{(1.09)^4} + \frac{(\$475,000)^2}{(1.09)^6} + \frac{(\$475,000)^2}{(1.09)^8} \right]^{\frac{1}{2}}$$
$$= [\$597,508,826,100]^{\frac{1}{2}}$$
$$= \$772,987$$

Note the standard deviation of the cash flows is smaller than the standard deviation of the net present value, even though we have explicitly assumed that actual cash flows for any year are independent of actual cash flows for earlier years. We could have assumed the opposite and made cash flows of subsequent years dependent on results of previous years. For example, suppose actual cash flows in year one are one standard deviation right of their expected value. If actual cash flows in years two through n are also one standard deviation right of their expected value, cash flows are said to be perfectly correlated through time. If so, the standard deviation of the probability distribution of net present values is given by the equation

$$\sigma \text{ probability distribution of } NPVs = \sum_{n=0}^{\infty} \frac{\sigma_n}{(1 + r)^n} \qquad (9\text{-}2)$$

Continuing with the same illustration, we obtain

$$\sigma = \frac{\$475,000}{1.09} + \frac{\$475,000}{(1.09)^2} + \frac{\$475,000}{(1.09)^3} + \frac{\$475,000}{(1.09)^4}$$
$$= \$435,780 + \$399,798 + \$366,787 + \$336,502$$
$$= \$1,538,867$$

Although alternative assumptions that do not depend on either perfect correlation or no correlation among cash flows are possible, such extremes suggest what is involved in interpreting a probability distribution of net present values.[7] The standard deviation measures the risk associated with the expected net present value. Again, assuming the probability distribution of net present values is normal, chances the net present value will be zero or less (assuming actual cash flows are interdependent) can be determined first by calculating the normal deviate, so that

$$\frac{X - E(x)}{\sigma} = \frac{0 - \$2,099,300}{\$1,538,867} = 1.36$$

---

[7] Frederick S. Hiller. "The Deviation of Probabilistic Information for the Evaluation of Risky Investments," *Management Science*, Vol. 9 (April 1963, pp. 443–57).

Using Table 9-2 and interpolating linearly between 1.3 and 1.4 and .0968 and .0808 (.0968 − .0808 = .0160) so that

$$\frac{.06}{.10} = \frac{x}{.0160}$$
$$.10x = .000960$$
$$x = .0096$$

Then 1.36 σs from the expected value equals .0968 − .0096 = .0872. This compares with .0869 from Appendix D, which is based on nonlinear interpolation. There are now 8.7 chances in 100 net present value will be zero or less.

The foregoing analysis suggests what is undoubtedly lurking in the minds of management: outlay once made is dependent on a series of cash flows. If the actual results are more or less than the expected value in the first year, this trend is likely to continue into subsequent years. Although the correlation may not be perfect, management intuitively adheres to the principle that both success and failure tend to feed upon themselves.

A DECISION TREE

The possibility that cash flows may be dependent through time adds to the dispersion about the expected net present value. With the risk-aversion assumption on the part of management, the additional variability may cause reconsideration of the commitment. Suppose, however, there is an alternative. For example, the drug manufacturer might invest $3,000,000 rather than $6,000,000, targeting the lower output to specific sections of the country. After a year of experience, management could decide whether to commit additional funds. If sales proved disappointing, it could cap the outlay at $3,000,000.

To help management examine such alternatives, we propose a device known as a **decision tree**. Figure 9-2 illustrates what is involved. Instead of viewing the choice as one of investing, management traces the probable consequences of a $3,000,000 outlay today with the possibility of an additional investment in T_2, contrasted with a $6,000,000 expenditure today and no further investment in the future. Choices are represented by lines (branches) emanating from the square labeled T_0. Management is confident that cash flow estimates for the $6,000,000 outlay (expected return of $2,500,000 and standard deviation of $475,000) are representative of the possible outcomes anticipated for year one. By using techniques described earlier in the chapter, management has determined the expected cash flow for an outlay of $3,000,000 is $1,250,000 and the standard deviation is $237,500.

Reflecting concerns that cash flows may be interdependent through time, management has chosen to concentrate on extreme outcomes: cash flows either two

Figure 9-2   Abbreviated Decision Tree for Marketing a New Prescription Drug

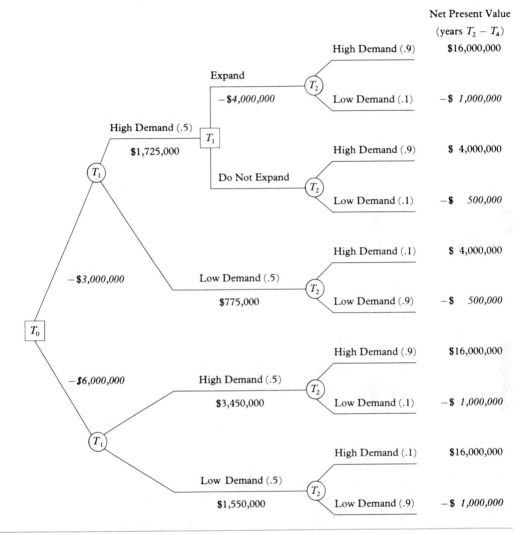

Net Present Value
(years $T_2 - T_4$)

High Demand (.9)	$16,000,000
Low Demand (.1)	− $ 1,000,000
High Demand (.9)	$ 4,000,000
Low Demand (.1)	− $ 500,000
High Demand (.1)	$ 4,000,000
Low Demand (.9)	− $ 500,000
High Demand (.9)	$16,000,000
Low Demand (.1)	− $ 1,000,000
High Demand (.1)	$16,000,000
Low Demand (.9)	− $ 1,000,000

standard deviations above or two standard deviations below the expected cash flow. The former is labeled *high demand,* the latter *low demand.* Because management assumes the probability distribution of cash flows is normally distributed, chances of either outcome occurring are equal. Hence, management attributes a .5 chance to either event—even though it believes the actual outcome lies somewhere between the two extremes. Once the outcome is known, however, the odds surrounding subsequent results change dramatically. Management believes there is a .9 chance a high (low) demand in year T_1 will be followed by a high (low) demand in subsequent years. On the other hand, management believes that there is only a .1 chance a high (low) demand in year T_1 will be followed by a low (high) demand in subsequent years.

Under the assumptions, outcomes will be qualitatively similar whether management chooses to invest $3,000,000 or $6,000,000. Only the magnitudes vary. If management chooses to invest $3,000,000 rather than $6,000,000 at the outset, the outcome will determine whether management invests more money or caps the outlay at $3,000,000. If demand is high, decisions must be made: Should an additional $4,000,000 be invested or should the firm not invest additional funds? Why $4,000,000 rather than $3,000,000? When an investment is broken into two stages, additional costs often (not always) are incurred in order to expand production. Such additional costs can be avoided if the firm makes the necessary investment at T_0. Such is the cost of delay. On the other hand, if demand is low, delay is justified and the firm can adequately serve the existing market with the $3,000,000 outlay. By investing $6,000,000, management avoids further costs if demand is high but exposes the firm to greater losses if demand is low.

From the foregoing discussion, it should be apparent management believes what happens in year T_1 will narrow considerably the uncertainty surrounding years T_2 through T_4. Still, the question remains: Should management invest $3,000,000 or $6,000,000 today? To answer this question, we must begin with the right side of the tree and work left. The numbers $16,000,000, *–$1,000,000*, and so on represent present values of future cash flows for different scenarios for years T_2 through T_4 discounted to the end of T_1. We have abbreviated the tree in order to concentrate on the primary concern: whether to invest in one or two stages.

The appropriate discount rate is moot. One can plausibly argue that because the alternative decisions to commit funds are based on expected cash flows from two positive outcomes (high or low demand), the appropriate rate of discount should be the cost of capital. We accept this argument. Bear in mind, however, that we are finessing an important consideration: To what extent does adoption of the project affect the overall risk or variance of returns to the firm? Does this sound familiar? It should, for the question suggests that variance in total earnings on existing assets will be affected. By using the current cost of capital, we are implicitly assuming the overall risk to the firm is unaffected by the project. Think about this as you take a *sit-up break*.[8]

---

[8] Before dropping to the floor to begin your sit-ups, as a superior student you also will ask yourself whether the owners— all of whom hold diversified portfolios—are concerned at all about the variance in the firm's earnings. Does not Modern Portfolio Theory suggest the owners value the stock because of its systematic, not its unsystematic risk? The answers to these questions are given in Chapter 10. By thinking about the answers now, you stay ahead of students who do not read footnotes.

ROLLING BACK THE DECISION TREE

If demand is high and management selects the $3,000,000 outlay, it must decide at T_1 whether or not to invest $4,000,000. The expected present value of the investment at T_1, if management chooses to invest, is

$$\text{expected net present value} = -\$4,000,000 + (.9)(\$16,000,000) + (.1)(-\$1,000,000)$$
$$= -\$4,000,000 + \$14,400,000 - \$100,000$$
$$= \$10,300,000$$

Thus, if we allow for the additional $4,000,000 outlay and the odds that demand will be low or high for years T_2 through T_4, the expected present value is $10,300,000. Compare this with the alternative of not expanding when demand is high, where the expected net present value is

$$\text{expected net present value} = (.9)(\$4,000,000) - (.1)(\$500,000)$$
$$= \$3,600,000 - \$50,000 = \$3,550,000$$

Clearly, if demand is high, the firm will invest the additional $4,000,000.

We are now in a position to roll back the decision tree for the $3,000,000 investment to T_0. To do this, we first find the present value of the low demand for year T_1 when no further expansion takes place: the expected net present value for years T_2 through T_4.

$$\text{expected net present value} = (.1)(\$4,000,000) - (.9)(\$500,000)$$
$$= \$400,000 - \$450,000 = -\$50,000$$

From T_1 back to T_0, we combine the outcomes for both high and low demand levels and discount the continuation at the cost of capital, which we shall assume is 16 percent.[9] To do so, we employ the following format:

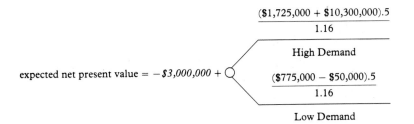

$$\text{expected net present value} = -\$3,000,000 +$$

$$\frac{(\$1,725,000 + \$10,300,000).5}{1.16}$$

High Demand

$$\frac{(\$775,000 - \$50,000).5}{1.16}$$

Low Demand

---

[9] The perceptive student will recognize that a cost of capital of 16 percent also would have been used to arrive at the net present values for the years T_2 through T_4. He or she also will recognize that the percent employed derives from viewing future outcomes in terms of the cost of capital at T_0. At T_1, the cost of capital may change. For this and other reasons discussed in the subsequent section, management will monitor the project to determine whether to continue or abandon it before T_4.

$$\text{expected net present value} = -\$3,000,000 + \frac{(\$6,012,500 + \$362,500)}{1.16}$$

$$= -\$3,000,000 + \$5,495,690$$

$$= \$2,495,690$$

Cash flows for year T_1 (high demand) are added to the present value of cash flows for years T_2 through T_4 and (in this case) multiplied by the same probability of occurrence (.5). Cash flows for year T_1 (low demand) are added to the present value of cash flows for years T_2 through T_4 and (in this case) multiplied by the same probability of occurrence (.5). The combined sum is discounted at the cost of capital for one year (1.16). The $3,000,000 outlay is subtracted, leaving an expected net present value of $2,495,690.

For the $6,000,000 outlay, no further investment is necessary. The price, however, is acceptance of a .9 probability that net present value will be $-\$1,000,000$ for years $T_2 - T_4$ if demand for year T_1 is low. The worst scenario for the $3,000,000 investment is a .9 probability that if demand is low for year T_1, the net present value for years T_2 through T_4 will be $-\$500,000$. In this case, management would not commit the additional $4,000,000. On the other hand, if demand is low for year T_1 but reverses and is high for years T_2 through T_4, by committing $6,000,000 in T_0 there is an outside chance (.1) the present value of future cash flows will be $16,000,000.

To roll back the decision tree, we first calculate the expected net present value for years T_2 through T_4 for high demand at T_1 and for low demand at T_1.

	High Demand (T_1)	Low Demand (T_1)
Expected Net Present Value ($T_2 - T_4$) =	$16,000,000(.9)	$16,000,000(.1)
	+	+
	$-\$1,000,000(.1)$	$-\$1,000,000(.9)$
Expected Net Present Value ($T_2 - T_4$) =	$14,400,000	$1,600,000
	$-100,000$	$-900,000$
	$14,300,000	$ 700,000

Rolling the decision tree back to T_0, we have

$$\text{expected net present value } (T_0) = -\$6,000,000 + \frac{(.5)(\$3,450,000 + \$14,300,000)}{1.16}$$

$$+ \frac{(.5)(\$1,550,000 + \$700,000)}{1.16}$$

$$= -\$6,000,000 + \frac{\$10,000,000}{1.16}$$

$$= \$2,620,690$$

Thus, if management invests $6,000,000 today, the expected net present value is higher. The extra risk incurred is more than offset by the additional $1,000,000 necessary to produce the product in two stages. Unless such costs can be reduced, management will deem it more profitable not to carry out the investment in two stages.

The foregoing example illustrates a genre of investment decisions where two-stage expansion appears to be the safe way to approach uncertainty but which, on subsequent analysis, proves to be less profitable than *taking the plunge* at the start.

Suppose, however, management could invest only $3,000,000 rather than $4,000,000 at the end of T_1 to achieve the same results. In other words, assume there were no additional costs to the firm from expanding in two stages. As a result, the expected net present value at T_1 would have been $1,000,000 higher than originally calculated: $11,300,000 rather than $10,300,000. When multiplied by (.5)—the probability of occurrence for year T_1—and discounted to T_0, the addition to net present value becomes

$$NPV = \frac{(\$1,000,000)(.5)}{1.16}$$
$$NPV = \$431,034$$

Adding the result to our earlier calculation of $2,495,690, we obtain

$$NPV = \$2,495,690 + \$431,034$$
$$NPV = \$2,926,724$$

Under these circumstances, management would prefer to invest in two stages rather than in one. The difference in net present value is $2,926,724 − $2,620,690 = $306,034. If x equals the additional costs incurred at T_1 for a two-stage process, then

$$\$306,034 = \frac{x}{1.16}$$
$$x = \$354,999$$

For additional costs at T_1 of less than $354,999, it is, under the assumptions made, in the best interests of the owners to expand in two stages. Otherwise, management should invest $6,000,000 at the outset.

UTILITY ANALYSIS IN CAPITAL BUDGETING

Although it may appear more profitable to make the entire investment at the outset, there is still the nagging issue presented by the low demand in T_1, where cash flows are $1,550,000. Recall from the discussion of utility analysis involving risk that investors and, by implication, management are assumed to be risk-averse; hence, they do not place the same value on outcomes two standard deviations above the mean as on outcomes two standard deviations below the mean. We have assumed the chances of either happening at T_1 are equal. Thus, at T_1

Investment (T_0)	Expected Net Present Value/ High Demand (T_1)	Expected Net Present Value/ Low Demand (T_1)
$3,000,000	$10,300,000	−$ 50,000
$6,000,000	$14,300,000	$700,000

Suppose we examine each outcome as though it happened, discounting the results from T_1 to T_0 at 16 percent, adding the results from T_0 to T_1 (see Figure 9-2, adding $1,725,000, $775,000, and so on), and subtracting the investment so that

	NPV at T_0 for $3,000,000 Outlay	NPV at T_0 for $6,000,000 Outlay
High Demand	$7,604,310	$9,777,586
Low Demand	−$2,268,103	−$3,846,552

By committing the additional $4,000,000 at T_1, the present value of an actual outcome under conditions of high demand is lower than if the $6,000,000 had been committed ($9,777,586 − $7,604,310 = $2,173,276). If, however, demand is low, the net loss incurred by making the smaller initial investment and capping it is less (−$3,846,552 − −$2,268,103 = −$1,578,449). Risk-averse management would place greater weight on the potential loss than on the potential gain, thereby tipping the scales in favor of the two-stage approach.

ABANDONMENT VALUE IN CAPITAL BUDGETING

We have assumed throughout that once the investment is made, costs are sunk: if the investment is a failure, there is no opportunity to recover the outlay. How realistic is this assumption? If our illustration concerned two levels of investment in transportation equipment (trucks, buses, airplanes, railroad cars, and the like), we would have recognized immediately the existence of a secondary market. Thus, if low demand occurred in T_1, we could sell the equipment. The present value of that sale is subtracted from the outlay to provide a better perspective of costs actually sunken. In short, we reduce the outlay by the present value of abandoning the projects through sale of assets.

Equipment, of course, can usually be readily sold in a secondary market. For the new-prescription drug industry, however, we would expect to write off the entire outlay as sunken costs—would we not? Perhaps, but not necessarily. Abandoning a project does not always mean the facilities are sold in a secondary market or scrapped; another option is to convert them to alternative uses. The critical issue is whether the resources involved have an opportunity cost.

To the extent research and development costs are specific to the drug in question, they may be considered sunken costs, at least with respect to the project. However, the R and D costs may have generated further research into therapeutically superior drugs. Production facilities for the drug in question also may be adapted to producing another drug. To do so, however, may involve conversion costs. If so, such costs reduce expected savings from abandoning the project.

Symmetry demands that if management considers expanding its investment, it also consider the possibility of contracting or abandoning the project when comparing alternative strategies. For example, suppose research and development costs of $2,500,000 are truly sunken but that production facilities can be converted to other uses. For the $3,000,000 outlay, if demand is low in T_1, it will cost $200,000 to convert the facilities to other uses. For the $6,000,000 outlay, it will cost $300,000.

For the time being, we shall ignore costs of converting the additional $4,000,000 outlay should demand be low in subsequent years. Management is initially concerned about results in T_1. Let us examine the two cases of low demand as if they actually occurred. Management, of course, would consider abandoning the project. For the $6,000,000 outlay, $3,200,000 [$6,000,000 − ($2,500,000 + $300,000)] is recoverable. For the $3,000,000 outlay, $300,000 [$3,000,000 − ($2,500,000 + $200,000)] is recoverable. Discounting at 16 percent

	Low Demand				
Outlay	*NPV at T_0*	+	*NPV of Abandonment Value at T_0*	=	*Combined NPV at T_0*
$6,000,000	−$3,846,552	+	$2,758,621	=	−$1,087,931
$3,000,000	−$2,268,103	+	$ 258,621	=	−$2,009,482

Although from this perspective the prospect of abandonment does not necessarily favor investment in a single stage, it certainly reduces the disparity in outcomes if demand is low.

Consider the impact of abandonment on net present value. We recognize the possibility that in the two-stage expansion the additional $4,000,000 may be invested. If so and if demand is low in T_2, assume all facilities can be converted for $300,000, the same conversion costs that would have been incurred if the $6,000,000 outlay had been made. To make the outcomes comparable, conversion costs are incurred at the end of T_2. For the $6,000,000 outlay, the present value of abandonment at the end of T_2 is

$$p.v. \text{ of abandonment} = \frac{\$6,000,000 - \$2,800,000}{(1.16)^2}$$

$$p.v. \text{ of abandonment} = \$2,378,122$$

For the $3,000,000 investment in T_0 and the $4,000,000 investment in T_1 it is somewhat more complicated. Because additional expenditure does not have to be made until T_1, we add the present value of that expenditure (discounted for one year) to $3,000,000 in order to make it comparable with the $6,000,000 outlay in T_0. Thus

$$p.v. \text{ of abandonment} = \frac{\left(\$3,000,000 + \dfrac{\$4,000,000}{1.16} - \$2,800,000\right)}{(1.16)^2}$$

$$p.v. \text{ of abandonment} = \frac{\$3,648,276}{1.3456}$$

$$p.v. \text{ of abandonment} = \$2,711,263$$

Combining the results with the initial calculation of NPV, we have

Outlay	NPV at T_0 +	NPV of Abandonment at T_0 =	Combined NPV at T_0
$3,000,000	$2,495,690 +	$2,711,263 =	$5,206,953
$6,000,000	$2,620,690 +	$2,378,122 =	$4,998,812

By considering abandonment value, we have finally reached a result consistent with intuition and fewer sleepless nights for risk-averse management: accept the project that calls for two-stage investment; the additional outlay does not have to be made for a year. If demand is low, facilities can be converted to other uses. Although research and development costs may be sunk, we are safe in the knowledge there is no justification for expending the larger rather than the smaller sum on production facilities in the hope of spreading sunken costs over a larger volume of sales.

SUMMARY

Or are we? At the beginning of the chapter, it was noted that probabilities attached to outcomes are subjective. Although Monte Carlo Simulation techniques may appear objective, appearances can be deceiving. The models employed, while based on informed judgment, are nevertheless subjective. The value of simulation is to force the decision-maker to specify the equation and in turn to get those responsible for the estimates employed to ask the relevant questions. Has inflation been taken into account? Are the cash flows correlated through time? Is there reason to believe estimates of cash flows are normally distributed or is there reason to assume other than a normal or approximately normal distribution?

To the extent a normal distribution approximates the pattern of cash flows, the expected cash flows (plus or minus three standard deviations) will encompass the entire area below the normal curve. In terms of standard deviation, it is possible to measure the interval $0 - E(x)$ and to determine the likelihood cash flows will be zero or less.

It is net present value, however, that determines whether or not the project is acceptable. When one can calculate expected net present value using expected cash flows, the appropriate measure of discount is the risk-free rate, adjusted or unadjusted for inflation. If cash flows are in constant dollars, the discount rate should be the real rate of interest after subtracting inflation. If an estimate of inflation has been included in the cash flows, the discount rate is the nominal risk-free rate.

The standard deviation of the expected net present value depends on what one assumes about the dependency of cash flows through time. The possibilities range from no correlation to perfect correlation. If there is no correlation, the outcome for one year has no impact upon the next. Perfect correlation, however, implies that if actual cash flows in year one are one standard deviation above the expected cash flows, the actual cash flows for years two through n also will be one standard deviation above the expected cash flows. Management often assumes—indeed may fear—that cash flows are more apt to be correlated (although not perfectly) rather than independent through time. As a result, there may be a chance (in the illustration employed, 8.7 chances in 100) net present value will be zero or less even though chances were negligible that expected cash flows for year one would be zero or less.

To analyze the impact of extreme outcomes on net present value, we used a decision tree. The choices were to invest all funds initially or in two stages, the latter requiring an additional $1,000,000 outlay. We calculated net present value assuming an equal chance of either outcome—*high demand* or *low demand*—occurring in year T_1. However, once the outcome for T_1 is known, chances of the pattern reversing itself would (in management's view) be highly unlikely. High demand in T_1 most likely would be followed by high demand in subsequent years; a low demand in T_1 most likely would be followed by low demand in subsequent years. By rolling back the decision tree, examining the impact of extreme outcomes on the assumption of risk-aversion, and including an estimate of abandonment value, we were able to make a choice: expand in two stages.

As with Monte Carlo Simulation techniques, the decision tree is only as good as the information that goes into it. The probabilities attached to outcomes remain subjective. Again, management should ask more questions. Is management overly optimistic about converting facilities to other uses? Should management employ what it believes to be extreme outcomes as the basis for reaching a decision? Up to some point, not easily defined, asking questions is productive—but diminishing returns eventually set in. For in the final analysis, the decision must be made on the basis of imperfect information. Managers, unlike college professors, are paid for assuming risk.

Nevertheless, academics must remind the decision-maker that whatever form the analysis takes, the risk being measured is specific to that project. Is this not similar to measuring the risk attached to purchasing shares of stock in one company? It is. Did we not learn from Modern Portfolio Theory that diversification can reduce risk? We did indeed. Our task in Chapter 10 is to bring those principles to bear on capital budgeting.

PROBLEMS AND QUESTIONS

1. Shreveport Louisiana Trucking Company moves freight across the Southeastern United States. A proposal is under consideration that will lead to a major expansion of its operations. The outlay required is $20,000,000. The book value of the assets of the firm is $90,000,000. Consequently, the expenditure represents a significant increase in the size of the company. Accordingly, the president of Shreveport has been reviewing the principles of capital budgeting under risk. A management team has concluded from an analysis of revenue and expense projections that for each of the next four years the firm faces the following set of possible outcomes.

Expected Cash Flows Probability of Occurrence				
1	2	3	4	5
$4,000,000	$9,000,000	$14,000,000	$19,000,000	$24,000,000
.1	.25	.3	.25	.1

a. Calculate the expected cash flows and the standard deviation.
b. Using the calculations in (a) and assuming cash flows are normally distributed, what are the chances cash flows will be zero or less?
c. In calculating cash flows, management has taken inflation into account. With a risk-free interest rate of 10 percent, what is the net present value of expected cash flows?
d. What is the standard deviation of the probability distribution of net present values assuming
   i. cash flows are uncorrelated through time?
   ii. cash flows are perfectly correlated through time?
e. If the probability distribution of expected net present values is normal, what is the probability net present value will be zero or less if cash flows are

uncorrelated through time? What is the probability net present value will be zero or less if cash flows are perfectly correlated through time?

  f. Does correlation through time affect the outcome substantially? Explain.

2. In problem 1, assume Shreveport—concerned about the outside chance cash flows could be as low as $4,000,000—decides to compare outcomes under two different scenarios: high demand and low demand. High demand in T_1 for a $20,000,000 outlay would yield cash flows two standard deviations above the expected cash flows calculated in 1(a). Low demand in T_1 would yield cash flows two standard deviations below the expected cash flows calculated in 1(a). The probability of either occurring is .5. As an alternative, management is considering an expenditure of $10,000,000 today. If demand is high in T_1, it can invest an additional $11,000,000 to achieve the same expected net present value in years T_2 through T_4 it would have achieved by investing $20,000,000 in T_0. The expected cash flows and the standard deviation about the expected cash flows are each one-half the values calculated in 1(a). Again, management expects the probability of either occurring to be .5. The cost of capital is 15 percent. The following table summarizes the outcomes from T_1 through T_4 for each possible investment outcome.

Outlay	High Demand (T_1)	High Demand (NPV T_2-T_4)	Probability of Occurrence	Low Demand (NPV T_2-T_4)	Probability of Occurrence
$10,000,000	invest $11,000,000	$72,000,000	.8	−$15,000,000	.2
$10,000,000	do not invest $11,000,000	$18,000,000	.8	−$ 1,000,000	.2
$20,000,000	no additional investment	$72,000,000	.8	−$ 5,000,000	.2

Outlay	High Demand (T_1)	High Demand (NPV T_2-T_4)	Probability of Occurrence	Low Demand (NPV T_2-T_4)	Probability of Occurrence
$10,000,000	no additional investment	$18,000,000	.2	−$ 1,000,000	.8
$20,000,000	no additional investment	$72,000,000	.8	−$ 5,000,000	.2

Using the above information:

  a. Construct an abbreviated decision tree.

  b. *Roll back* the tree to determine which investment has the higher net present value.

3. In problems 1 and 2, assume Shreveport can abandon the project in T_1 by selling off the equipment. Assume further Shreveport can recoup $8,000,000 in T_1 if it makes the $20,000,000 investment and $5,500,000 if it makes the $10,000,000 investment. Would this affect the result in problem 2(b)?

4. Management of Green Mountain Steel Company is considering the addition of a minimill to process scrap iron. The expected net present value of the discounted cash flows is $14,000,000. The standard deviation of the net present value, assuming cash flows are uncorrelated through time, is $2,000,000. If perfectly correlated, the standard deviation is $6,000,000.
   a. What is the probability net present value is zero or less if cash flows are uncorrelated?
   b. What is the probability net present value is zero or less if cash flows are perfectly correlated?
   c. Should management be concerned whether cash flows are perfectly correlated or uncorrelated? Explain.

5. "Even though the probability distribution of net present values for a project may be normal, it does not follow that an outcome x standard deviations below the expected net present value should be given the same weight as an outcome x standard deviations above the mean in determining whether or not to accept or reject the project." Evaluate in detail.

6. Explain why cash flows should be discounted at the risk-free rate when determining the net present value of future cash flows.

7. After reading this chapter, a corporate executive suggested it was illogical to subtract a specific outlay at T_0 from the expected value of future cash flows to determine expected net present value. Rather, it made more sense to subtract the outlay from the present value of each possible set of cash flows to determine the range of net present values and then to examine the effect on profitability, assuming each outcome materialized. Is there substance to this criticism? Explain.

SELECTED ADDITIONAL REFERENCES

Bey, Roger P. and J. Clayton Singleton. "Autocorrelated Cash Flows and the Selection of a Portfolio of Capital Assets," *Decision Sciences*, Vol. 8 (October 1978, pp. 640–57).

Bogue, Marcus C. and Richard Roll. "Capital Budgeting of Risky Projects with Imperfect Markets for Physical Capital," *Journal of Finance*, Vol. 29 (May 1974, pp. 601–13).

Bonini, Charles P. "Capital Investment under Uncertainty with Abandonment

Options," *Journal of Financial and Quantitative Analysis*, Vol. 12 (March 1977, pp. 39–54).

Bussey, Lynn E. and C. T. Stevens, Jr. "Formulating Correlated Cash Flow Streams," *Engineering Economist*, Vol. 18 (Fall 1972, pp. 1–30).

Harney, R. K. and A. V. Cabot. "A Decision Theory Approach to Capital Budgeting under Risk," *Engineering Economist*, Vol. 20 (Fall 1974, pp. 37–49).

Hayes, Robert H. "Incorporating Risk Aversion into Risk Analysis," *Engineering Economist*, Vol. 20 (Winter 1975, pp. 99–121).

Hertz, David R. "Investment Policies That Pay Off," *Harvard Business Review*, Vol. 45 (January–February 1968, pp. 96–108).

———. "Risk Analysis in Capital Investment," *Harvard Business Review*, Vol. 42 (January–February 1964, pp. 95–106).

Hillier, Frederick S. "The Derivation of Probabilistic Information for the Evaluation of Risky Investments," *Management Science*, Vol. 9 (April 1963, pp. 443–57).

Joy, O. Maurice. "Abandonment Values and Abandonment Decisions: A Clarification," *Journal of Finance*, Vol. 31 (December 1976, pp. 425–28).

Keeley, Robert and Rundolf Westerfield. "A Problem for Probability Distribution Techniques on Capital Budgeting," *Journal of Finance*, Vol. 27 (June 1972, pp. 703–9).

Kryzanowski, Lawrence, Peter Lusztig, and Bernhard Schwab. "Monte Carlo Simulation and Capital Expenditure Decisions—A Case Study," *Engineering Economist*, Vol. 18 (Fall 1972, pp. 31–48).

Lewellen, W. G. and M. S. Long. "Simulation vs. Single-Value Estimates in Capital Expenditure Analysis," *Decision Sciences*, Vol. 3 (1973, pp. 19–33).

Magee, J. F. "How to Use Decision Trees in Capital Investment," *Harvard Business Review*, Vol. 42 (September–October 1964, pp. 79–96).

Raiffa, Howard. *Decision Analysis: Introductory Lectures on Choices under Uncertainty* (Reading, MA: Addison-Wesley, 1968).

Robichek, Alexander A. "Interpreting the Results of Risk Analysis," *Journal of Finance*, Vol. 30 (December 1975, pp. 1384–86).

Schall, Lawrence D. and Gary L. Sundem. "Capital Budgeting Methods and Risk: A Further Analysis," *Financial Management*, Vol. 15 (Spring 1980, pp. 7–11).

10

THE COST OF CAPITAL, CAPITAL BUDGETING, AND THE CAPITAL-ASSET PRICING MODEL

Chapters 8 and 9 we treated capital budgeting first in a risk-free world and then under conditions of risk. Attention, however, focused on the independent variability associated with the cash flows, not with the covariance of the return on the project and the return on existing assets. Furthermore, we did not consider, in the light of diversified portfolios, whether systematic or unsystematic risk is the appropriate measure of risk. The purpose of Chapter 10 is to apply what we have learned about Modern Portfolio Theory to the investment and financing decisions of the firm. Chapter 10, therefore, is a synthesis of what we developed earlier.

THE FIRM AND ITS OWNERS

The primary function of management is to maximize market value of stockholders' equity. As we have seen, market value is a function of both profitability and risk. Moreover, as suggested by the Securities Market Line (SML) for diversified portfolios, expected return is a function of systematic risk. But whose diversified portfolio—the firm's or the stockholders'? This is not a frivolous question. Consider the Capital Asset Pricing Model (CAPM) as we left it in Chapter 7.

$$R_j = k'_e = i + (R_m - i)\beta_{ju}\left[1 + \frac{D}{E}(1 - T_c)\right] \qquad \text{(10-1; also 7-7)}$$

β_{ju} represents the beta coefficient for the unleveraged capital structure. The expression $\left[1 + \dfrac{D}{E}(1 - T_c)\right]$ measures the impact on beta and (ultimately) on expected return from employing leverage while taking into account the tax subsidy from doing so. Recognizing the components of beta, then

$$R_j = k'_e = i + (R_m - i)\frac{r_{jm}\sigma_j\sigma_m}{\sigma^2 m}\left[1 + \frac{D}{E}(1 - T_c)\right] \qquad \text{(10-1a)}$$

Management can affect R_j through both its investment and its financial policies. If it chooses to diversify the company's portfolio of real assets, then σ_j will be smaller than if management chooses not to diversify. In any event, the choice of policy will affect the beta coefficient and (ultimately) the expected return on the stock.

Similarly, management's use of debt also will affect the beta coefficient. As the discussion in Chapter 7 suggested, by taking corporate income taxes into consideration (in the more complete model, personal income taxes paid by bondholders and stockholders), it is possible for management to enjoy a lower average cost of capital than if all assets are financed from equity. Although the cost of equity capital (therefore the expected return to the stockholder) rises, the rise is not rapid enough, at least for initial debt increases, to offset the lower cost of debt capital. However, the introduction of bankruptcy costs suggests management must exercise care in adding to its debt. The primary incentives for not expanding beyond a certain point are decline in bond ratings and the subsequent increase in cost of new debt capital that accompany what the market perceives as excessive leverage.

For management then, determining the optimal amount of debt is a useful exercise: it appears to result in a weighted average cost of capital that seems to maximize market value of the company stock. By using the weighted average cost of capital as a cutoff point for new projects, management appears to be adding to plant and equipment in amounts that continue to be in the best interests of the owners.

THE STOCKHOLDER AND MODERN PORTFOLIO THEORY

There is, however, another approach to determining the optimal amount of debt—it comes from Modern Portfolio Theory. Suppose there are only three financial assets: short-term U.S. Treasury bills, which in terms of default are risk-free; corporate debt, which can carry a degree of default risk; and more risky common stock. Suppose further that you and every other investor hold fully diversified portfolios: unsystematic risk has been minimized, leaving only systematic risk. The expected holding period return on your portfolio is the weighted average of the expected return on the stocks and the debt. The return on each is a function of its respective beta coefficients. Ignoring for the time being the impact of taxes on returns and substituting in the CAPM, we obtain

$$\frac{r_{em}\sigma_{em}}{\sigma^2 m} = \beta_{em} = \text{beta for unleveraged equity investment}$$

and

$$\frac{r_{dm}\sigma_d\sigma_m}{\sigma^2 m} = \beta_{dm} = \text{beta coefficient for debt}$$

Thus, the expected holding return on any debt security of firm j is

$$R_{jd} = i + \frac{[R_m - i]r_{jdm}\sigma_{jd}\sigma_m}{\sigma^2 m} \tag{10-2}$$

Similarly, the expected holding period return on any equity security of firm j is

$$R_{je} = i + \frac{[R_m - i]r_{jem}\sigma_{je}\sigma_m}{\sigma^2 m}\left[1 + \frac{D}{E}\right] \tag{10-3}$$

R_m is the expected holding period return on the market portfolio, consisting of all outstanding debt and equity; $\sigma^2 m$ is the variance in that portfolio. Consistent with practice in this book, i is the risk-free rate.

In Equation 10-3, the expression $1 + \dfrac{D}{E}$ (in the absence of a corporate income tax) measures the impact of leverage on beta and hence on the expected return to the stockholders of j, as residual claimants to income.

If we include bankruptcy and agency costs in our discussion, leverage would affect the expected return on debt. In addition, if the holding period return does not coincide with the maturity date of the debt, the market price of the debt at the end of the holding period is technically the expected market price and is, therefore, the mean of a probability distribution of possible market prices. Standard deviations and probability distributions, like cream cheese and bagels, go together. Consequently, there will be some variability in the return on corporate debt. As a result

$$\beta_{jd} = \frac{r_{jm}\sigma_{jd}\sigma_m}{\sigma^2 m} > 0$$

The value of beta for the debt of firm j, while probably not as high as the value of beta for the equity of firm j, is, nevertheless, greater than zero. This nasty complication renders Equations 10-1 and 10-3 inapplicable for calculating the expected return on stock j. Let us see why. Suppose we let

$$R_m = 18\% = \text{expected return on market portfolio}$$
$$k_e = \text{expected return on unleveraged equity}$$
$$R_j = k'_e = \text{expected return on leveraged equity}$$
$$i = 12\% = \text{risk-free rate}$$
$$\beta_{jd} = .25 = \text{beta coefficient of debt of firm } j$$
$$k_d = i + (R_m - i)\beta_{jd} = \text{cost of debt capital before taxes}$$
$$\beta_{ju} = 1.1 \text{ for unleveraged capital structure}$$
$$\frac{D}{E} = .5 = \text{debt–equity ratio}$$

Recall[1] from Chapter 7 the key equation employed in reconciling CAPM with the M & M Hypothesis:

$$R_j = k'_e = i + \left[\frac{R_m - i}{\sigma_m}\right](r_{em}\sigma_m)^* + \frac{D}{E}\left[\frac{R_m - i}{\sigma_m}\right](r_{em}\sigma_e^*) - \frac{D}{E}\left[\frac{R_m - i}{\sigma_m}\right](r_{dm}\sigma_d) \quad (10\text{-}4)$$

In less formidable symbols

$$R_j = k'_e = i + (R_m - i)\beta_{ju} + \frac{D}{E}[(R_m - i)\beta_{ju} - (R_m - i)\beta_{jd}] \quad (10\text{-}5)$$

---

[1] No one expects you to recall the equation. We are being polite.

Substituting, we obtain

$$R_j = k'_e = 12\% + (18\% - 12\%)(1.1) + .5[(18\% - 12\%)(1.1) - (18\% - 12\%).25]$$
$$= 12\% + 6.6\% + .5(6.6\% - 1.5\%)$$
$$= 18.6\% + 2.55\%$$
$$= 21.15\%$$

Because

$$k_d = i + (R_m - i)(\beta_{jd})$$
$$= 12\% + (18\% - 12\%)(.25)$$
$$= 13.5\%$$

18.6 percent is the cost of an unleveraged capital structure. Then under M & M

$$R_j = k'_e = 18.6\% + .5(18.6\% - 13.5\%)$$
$$= 18.6\% + 2.55\%$$
$$= 21.15\%$$

If β_{jd} equaled zero, the corporate debt would have a beta coefficient of zero. In the first calculation of the substitution, 1.5 percent would disappear; in the second calculation of the substitution, k_d would equal i, which equals 12 percent. In both cases

$$R_j = k'_e = 18.6\% + .5(6.6\%)$$
$$= 21.9\%$$

This latter result could have been obtained by using Equation 10-3 and substituting, so that

$$R_{je} = 12\% + (18\% - 12\%)(1.1)(1.5)$$
$$= 12\% + 9.9\%$$
$$= 21.9\%$$

Thus, given the assumption investors hold diversified portfolios, the expected return on a corporation's debt as well as on its equity is a function of systematic risk. Consequently, firms that issue debt do so at a cost that reflects that risk. Otherwise, their debt is risk-free and earns the risk-free return.

Taxes, of course, can be reintroduced into the modified CAPM. Confining ourselves to the corporate income tax rate, then

$$R_j = k'_e = i + (R_m - i)\beta_{ju} + \frac{D}{E}[(R_m - i)\beta_{ju} - (R_m - i)\beta_{jd}](1 - T_c) \qquad (10\text{-}6)$$

Suppose T_c is .4. Then

$$R_j = k'_e = 12\% + 6.6\% + .5(6.6\% - 1.5\%)(1 - .4)$$
$$= 18.6\% + 1.53\%$$
$$= 20.13\%$$

Under M & M, as we discussed in Chapter 7

$$k'_e = k_e + \frac{D}{E}(k_e - k_d)(1 - T_c)$$
$$k'_e = 18.6\% + .5(18.6\% - 13.5\%)(.6)$$
$$= 18.6\% + 1.53\%$$
$$= 20.13\%$$

For financial managers who use CAPM as the basis for determining the cost of equity capital with leverage, it is necessary to use Equations 10-5 and 10-6 rather than 10-1 and 10-3. The former and not the latter are consistent with the M & M Hypothesis in which a firm employs debt that contains a risk premium and is valued by debtholders on the basis of its systematic risk.

Now reread the preceding section until you are comfortable with the analysis. Next take a pizza break and then continue.

COMPANY BETA

Because the company debt has a positive beta, its beta coefficient is the weighted average of the beta coefficients for the firm. Specifically

$$\frac{D}{E} = \frac{debt}{equity}$$
$$\frac{D}{D + E} = \frac{debt}{total\ capital}$$
$$\frac{E}{D + E} = \frac{equity}{total\ capital}$$

Let

$$\beta^*_{je} = \beta_{j\,leveraged} \text{ and } \beta_{firm\,j} = \text{beta for the firm}$$

Then

$$\beta_{firm\,j} = \frac{D}{D + E}\beta_{jd} + \frac{E}{D + E}\beta^*_{je} \tag{10-7}$$

Continuing with the assumption that

$$\frac{D}{E} = .5 = \frac{1}{2}$$

Therefore, $E = 2D$: for every dollar of debt outstanding, there are two dollars of stock or equity also outstanding. Consequently

$$\frac{D}{D + E} = \frac{D}{3D} = \frac{1}{3}$$

Since

$$\frac{D}{D + E} + \frac{E}{D + E} = 1$$

then

$$\frac{D}{D + E} = \frac{2}{3}$$

Retaining the value of β debt as .25, to find β_{je}^* we rearrange Equation 10-5. Thus

$$R_j = i + (R_m - i)\beta_{ju} + \frac{D}{E}(\beta_{ju} - \beta_{jd})(R_m - i)$$

$$R_j = i + (R_m - i)[\beta_{ju} + \frac{D}{E}(\beta_{ju} - \beta_{jd})]$$

(10-8)

The expression

$$\beta_{ju} + \frac{D}{E}(\beta_{ju} - \beta_{jd})$$

in Equation 10-8 is the leveraged beta coefficient for R_j.[2] Substituting, we obtain

$$\beta_{je}^* = 1.1 + .5(1.1 - .25) = 1.1 + .425 = 1.525$$

Using Equation 10-7, the beta for firm j is

$$\beta_{firm\,j} = \frac{1}{3}(.25) + \frac{2}{3}(1.525)$$

$$= .083 + 1.017$$

$$= 1.1$$

The beta for the firm is 1.1, which is the beta for the stock of the unleveraged corporation. The two are logically equivalent. For financial managers, the lesson of the Capital Asset Pricing Model is the same as the lesson of the Modigliani and

---

[2] For footnote aficionados or aficionadas, consider what happens if β_{jd} is 0: the expression becomes

$$\beta_{ju}\left(1 + \frac{D}{E}\right)$$

which is consistent with Equation 10-3, where

$$\beta_{ju} = \frac{r_{jcm}\sigma_j\sigma_m}{\sigma^2 m}$$

and $\beta_j^* = (1.1)(1.5) = 1.65$. When examined on what happens to the beta coefficient of the stock of a leveraged firm when β_{jd} is zero, you will have the answer.

Miller Hypothesis: the firm's risk characteristics ultimately depend on the nature of the portfolio of assets. What are the implications of this finding for the capital budgeting techniques we have developed?

ASSET BETA

Because the nonfinancial firm primarily is a collection of its real assets, its beta coefficient can be viewed as the weighted average of the betas of individual projects. As noted earlier, the firm's unleveraged beta coefficient can be altered as a result of a change in covariance among the returns on assets comprising the portfolio of the firm. Specifically, management can diversify its portfolio of real assets, thereby lowering the standard deviation of the firm and its beta coefficient.

Companies have been doing this with some frequency. For example, beginning in 1972, then Board Chairman Harry J. Gray of United Technologies Corporation (UTC) initiated a program of diversification "in order to reduce its dependency on aerospace activities, which at the time accounted for between 75 to 80 percent of annual revenues."[3] In other words, UTC set out to reduce its unsystematic risk. As a result, it now owns such diverse firms as Otis, the leading manufacturer of elevators, and Carrier, the leading manufacturer of air conditioners.[4]

Another less-frequently used method of diversification concerns building new facilities to manufacture items not currently included in the product mix. There are several reasons why a firm such as UTC prefers to buy established concerns rather than enter the field *de novo*. We examine such reasons in Chapter 21 when we attempt to shed light on the deeper question: does a firm such as UTC offer stockholders something of value through diversification that they cannot achieve on their own? More bluntly, if Otis and Carrier stock (implicitly their assets) were not owned by UTC, the shares would be available to stockholders of a company dependent on the vagaries of the aerospace industries but who could have (or perhaps at the time had) diversified their portfolios.

PROJECT BETAS

Whether or not management consciously seeks to alter the unsystematic risk of its portfolio of real assets, adoption of new projects can have such an impact. To illustrate, suppose the unleveraged beta coefficient of firm j is

$$\beta_{ju} = \frac{r_{jm}\sigma_j\sigma_m}{\sigma^2 m} = \frac{(0.9)(.18)(.14)}{(.14)^2} = 1.157$$

[3] Richard B. Curtiss. "Implementation of the Mergers and Acquisition Program at United Technologies Corporation," in Michael Keenan and Lawrence J. White, eds., *Mergers and Acquisitions* (Lexington, MA: Heath and Co., 1982, p. 349).

[4] Curtiss, p. 352.

Although the return on the firm's portfolio of real assets is closely correlated with the return on the market portfolio (.9), the independent variability of return is higher: .18 rather than .14.

Now suppose management is considering a new investment opportunity: it plans to build a soft-drink bottling plant. Suppose further this is a new line of business not currently included in the firm's portfolio. Following the capital budgeting procedures adumbrated earlier, management finds the net present value is positive. The procedures, however, relate expected cash flows to the firm's average cost of new capital. The implicit assumption in this approach is that the new investment will not alter the unleveraged beta coefficient of the company. If it does, as our analysis in the preceding section suggests, the expected return on the firm's stock will change even though the debt-to-total-capital ratio does not.

In other words, management is considering a project that under conventional capital budgeting procedures is expected to increase the firm's market value and hence the stock's market price. In efficient markets, the expected value of that increase would be anticipated in the market price of the stock at T_1 and, therefore, in the holding period return on that stock.

However, if adoption of the project affects the firm's unleveraged beta coefficient, it also will affect the holding period return on the stock. To phrase it differently: under conventional capital budgeting techniques, the holding period return would rise because of an increase in the firm's net present value reflected in a rise in P_1 (and perhaps even D_1) over what would have occurred if the project had not been adopted. Consequently

$$\text{holding period return} = R_j = \overset{\text{with project}}{\frac{D_1 + P_1 - P_0}{P_0}} > \overset{\text{without project}}{\frac{D_1 + P_1 - P_0}{P_0}}$$

The CAPM, however, suggests that the holding period return also could change because β_{jm} will differ if the project is adopted.

To continue with the illustration, suppose management uses the unleveraged beta coefficients for other bottling companies as a proxy for the beta of the new investment. Suppose further that management finds the beta coefficients of these other bottling companies have averaged .938 while the beta coefficient of the firm has averaged 1.157. The expected net present value of the new investment, added to the market value of the outstanding stock, would represent 10 percent of the total. The new unleveraged beta coefficient then would be

$$\beta_{ju} = .10 \times .938 + .9(1.157)$$
$$\beta_{ju} = 1.1351$$

By adopting the project, management finds the unleveraged beta coefficient of the firm has fallen. Does this mean, other things remaining constant, the stockholders will earn less? The answer is misleading. Because the project adds to the net present value of the firm, it raises the total market value of its stock; however, the project also reduces the systematic risk of the firm's portfolio. Under the assumption stockholders invest in diversified portfolios, they will demand a lower expected return—a lower R_{ju}.

Now recall our earlier question: Whose portfolio should we consider, the firm's or the stockholders'? Presumably stockholders could buy shares in other bottling companies. Unless management can earn a higher return on this type of investment—unless it possesses unusual skills not accounted for in the CAPM analysis of alternatives—adoption of this project, while it does not lower stockholder wealth, apparently does not enhance it.

However, management ordinarily does not see the choice in this light. Consider Figure 10-1. In this instance, the SML includes not only securities but all real capital projects. As we suggested in Chapter 5, the SML is the Investment Market Line. According to the SML, a project with a beta coefficient of .938 should have a return of OD percent. Nevertheless, management has estimated the project has an expected internal rate of return of OH percent, which is greater than OF percent (the firm's weighted average cost of capital). The net present value is, therefore, positive. The difference in results could be due, of course, to the fact the holding period return is shorter than the internal rate of return. Suppose, however, management has used a holding period return based perhaps on a decision tree that permits it to compare the

Figure 10-1   Systematic Risk and the Average Cost of Capital

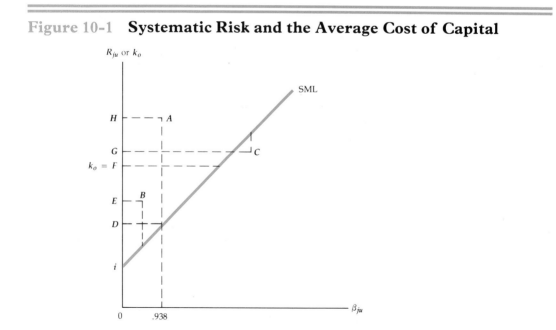

values at T_1 and T_0 as comparable percentages.[5] If so, then it appears management will add to the wealth of stockholders by adopting the project. An expected return higher than market return could be the result of superior managerial skills in organizing production and marketing and/or superior technology. In competitive markets, either could lead to higher returns—at least over the short run. Over the long run—as others adopted similar techniques—returns would fall toward those predicted by the SML.

One way of looking at the conventional capital budgeting procedures and the SML, therefore, is to recognize that a firm could adopt projects that over time merely alter its unleveraged beta coefficient but in the short run generate excess returns that add to the stock's market value.

What about projects B and C in Figure 10-1? From the perspective of the firm, C is acceptable because it compensates for financial risk: the NPV is positive. B, however, is not attractive. If the firm adopts project C, over the long run as returns settle closer to the SML, it will have taken on a project whose systematic risk demands a higher return. On the other hand, project B warrants adoption, at least from the perspective of the market; however, this firm will not be the one that adopts it. Consequently, although employing the SML may be helpful in determining whether a project such as C should be undertaken, the firm will clearly not undertake projects left of the SML and below k_o. The unleveraged systematic risks of such projects are inadequate to compensate for the financial leverage built into the firm and currently incorporated in its leveraged beta coefficient and hence in its expected return on the stock.

For those who rally behind CAPM, however, to ignore projects similar to B is to ignore what the market values. Abandon what you have learned about discounted cash flows, they may cry! For there is no cost-of-capital criteria for capital budgeting: each project has its own cost of capital, which is a function of its systematic risk.

Be of good cheer, however, a revolution is not at hand. You did not pay an inflated price for this text only to learn several chapters are useless. Rather, you mastered the preceding material because you plan to be an executive who is aware of the nuances embodied in conventional rules for making capital investment decisions. CAPM has taught you that investment decisions can slowly (mergers can rapidly) alter the unleveraged beta coefficient of the firm. That is not unimportant. As it exists, however, the firm is a collection of assets financed with a particular combination of leverage. Given that leverage, it is possible to value the firm, as it invests in new assets, at a rate of return that equals the weighted average cost of new capital—in other words, at the marginal cost of new capital.

---

[5] In Chapter 6, when reconciling CAPM with the present intrinsic value model, we noted that P_1 in the latter is the market's determination of the present intrinsic value of dividends, growth, and expected return from P_1 to P_n (or indefinitely). Similarly, the present value of a project at T_1 is the present value of its future cash flows, which management could also label P_1.

THE WEIGHTED AVERAGE COST OF CAPITAL REVISITED

In the discussion of capital budgeting in Chapter 8, we noted the appropriate discount rate *could be* the after-tax weighted average cost of new capital. In light of the foregoing discussion, you can see why we were hesitant. We now take a firmer stand on the issue: management should use the weighted average cost of new capital as its cutoff rate or, more properly, as the basis for determining the net present value of a project. However, in so doing management should recognize the impact, if any, adoption of a project (more likely, the capital budget for the year) will have on the firm's unleveraged beta coefficient.

In Modigliani and Miller terminology, the weighted after-tax cost of capital (as shown earlier) is

$$k_o = k'_e \frac{E}{D+E} + k_d(1 - T_c) \frac{D}{D+E} \qquad (10\text{-}9)$$

where

$$k_o = \text{average cost of capital}$$
$$k'_e = \text{cost of leveraged equity}$$
$$\frac{E}{D+E} = \text{equity-to-total-capital ratio}$$
$$k_d(1 - T_c) = \text{after-tax cost of debt capital to firm}$$
$$\frac{D}{D+E} = \text{debt-to-total-capital ratio}$$

With k_e equal to the cost of unleveraged capital structure, we already have seen that

$$k'_e = k_e + (k_e - k_d) \frac{D}{E} (1 - T_c)$$

It follows that

$$k_o = \left[k_e + (k_e - k_d)(1 - T_c) \frac{D}{E} \right] \frac{E}{D+E} + k_d(1 - T_c) \frac{D}{D+E}$$

Mercifully, the preceding abomination can be simplified

$$k_o = k_e \frac{E}{D+E} + k_e(1 - T_c) \frac{D}{D+E} - k_d(1 - T_c) \frac{D}{D+E} + k_d(1 - T_c) \frac{D}{D+E}$$

$$k_o = k_e \left[\frac{E}{D+E} + \frac{D}{D+E} - T_c \frac{D}{D+E} \right]$$

$$k_o = k_e \left(1 - T_c \frac{D}{D+E} \right) \qquad (10\text{-}10)$$

Equation 10-10 is both simple and easy to apply. For the firm, k_e represents the cost of equity capital in the absence of leverage; it can be interchanged with R_{ju}. If the capital budget alters the unsystematic risk and hence the unleveraged beta coefficient for the firm, k_e can be modified accordingly. On a year-to-year basis, one would not expect k_e to change significantly. However, if management embarked upon an acquisition program such as the one carried out by United Technologies, we would expect k_e to change perceptibly.

The terms within the brackets summarize the impact of financial risk mitigated by the tax subsidy. Therefore, to calculate the current average cost of new capital, one must know the unleveraged cost of equity, the debt-to-total-capital ratio, and the corporate income-tax rate for the year in question. As we have seen, k_e can be approximated by adjusting the leveraged beta coefficient to find β_{ju}. The bottling plant illustration is an example of such an adjustment: the corporate tax rate is readily available and the debt-to-total-capital ratio is easily calculated. Further adjustments can be made where warranted.

CAPITAL BUDGETING AND THE MARKET VALUE OF THE FIRM

As noted in Chapter 7, in the absence of personal income taxes but in the presence of corporate income taxes, a leveraged firm has the value

$$V_L = \frac{EAT}{k_e} + T_c D$$

where EAT equals operating earnings after corporate income taxes. The model, however, does not allow for growth. To do so, we may assume that a percentage K of after-tax earnings would be invested at a positive net present value. In so doing, on average the internal rate of return r would exceed the average cost of capital k_o for N years into the future. Miller and Modigliani have demonstrated that value of growth can be estimated by the term[6]

$$K(EAT)\left[\frac{r - k_o}{k_o(1 + k_o)}\right]N$$

where N is a multiplier, not an exponent, so that the value of a leveraged firm investing at an average rate of $r > k_o$ for N years is

$$V_{\text{firm}} = \frac{EAT}{k_e} + T_c D + K(EAT)\left[\frac{(r - k_o)}{k_o(1 + k_o)}\right]N \qquad (10\text{-}11)$$

---

[6] See Merton H. Miller and Franco Modigliani, "Dividend Policy, Growth and the Valuation of Shares," *The Journal of Business*, Vol. 34 (October 1961, pp. 420–22). See also Thomas C. Copeland and J. Fred Weston, *Financial Theory and Corporate Policy*, 2nd ed. (Reading, MA: Addison-Wesley, 1983, pp. 480–89).

To gain some insight into how the model functions and to review what we have learned, assume there are no taxes and that a firm earns $10,000,000 a year in perpetuity, all of which is paid as dividends. The opportunity cost of capital k_e is 20 percent. The second and third terms in Equation 10-11, therefore, disappear. Consequently

$$V = \frac{\$10,000,000}{.2}$$
$$V = \$50,000,000$$

Because we have shown that under M & M there is no reason to employ debt in the absence of taxes, 20 percent equals the average cost of capital, the cost of equity capital, and the opportunity cost of capital.

Now suppose the government imposes a 40-percent corporate income tax. EAT is now $10,000,000(1 − .4) = $6,000,000. Moreover, the value of the firm falls to

$$V = \frac{\$6,000,000}{.2}$$
$$V = \$30,000,000$$

Interest, however, is tax deductible. Suppose the firm can replace 25 percent of the stock's current market value with a debt issue carrying a 14-percent interest rate in perpetuity. Taking advantage of this opportunity, the firm markets $7,500,000 in bonds (.25 × $30,000,000) and uses the proceeds to repurchase shares from stockholders. Each stockholder retains his or her proportional share in the company: if a person had 1 percent of the stock before the debt was issued, he or she would have 1 percent of the stock after the debt was issued. Using the second factor in the model, we show the value of the firm increases by $T_cD = .4(\$7,500,000) = \$3,000,000$. The total value of the firm is now

$$V = \frac{\$6,000,000}{.2} + .4(\$7,500,000)$$
$$V = \$30,000,000 + \$3,000,000$$
$$V = \$33,000,000$$

Note the first term is still based on capitalization of EAT for an unleveraged capital structure. Subtracting the market value of debt, we obtain the value of the stockholders' equity:

$$V_s = \$33,000,000 - \$7,500,000$$
$$V_s = \$25,500,000$$

If interest had not been deductible, the value of the firm would have remained $30,000,000, the value of the stock $22,500,000, and the value of the debt $7,500,000. Interest payments would have been .14 × $7,500,000 = $1,050,000.

Profits after interest and taxes would have been $6,000,000 − $1,050,000 = $4,950,000. The cost of equity capital with leverage in the capital structure, k'_e, would have been

$$k'_e = \frac{\$4,950,000}{\$22,500,000} = .22$$

The average cost of capital, k_o, would have been

$$k_o = (.22)\frac{\$22,500,000}{\$30,000,000} + (.14)\frac{\$7,500,000}{\$30,000,000}$$

$$k_o = .22(.75) + .14(.25)$$

$$k_o = .165 + .035$$

$$k_o = .20$$

The same result is obtained using the M & M formula for the cost of leveraged equity, so that

$$k'_e = .20 + \frac{\$7,500,000}{\$22,500,000}(.20 - .14)$$

$$k'_e = .22$$

$$k_o = .22(.75) + .14(.25)$$

$$k_o = .20$$

Because interest *is tax deductible*, then

$10,000,000	(earnings before interest and taxes)
−1,050,000	(interest)
8,950,000	(profits before taxes)
−3,580,000	(taxes at 40 percent)
$ 5,370,000	(*EAT*)

With the market value of the firm $33,000,000 and the market value of the debt $7,500,000, then

$33,000,000	
−7,500,000	
$25,500,000	(market value of stock)

Moreover

$$\frac{\text{debt}}{\text{debt} + \text{equity}} = \frac{\$7,500,000}{\$33,000,000} = .227273$$

$$\frac{\text{equity}}{\text{debt} + \text{equity}} = \frac{\$25,500,000}{\$33,000,000} = .772727$$

$$\frac{\text{debt}}{\text{equity}} = \frac{.227273}{.772727} = .294118$$

Again

$$k'_e = \frac{\$5,370,000}{\$25,500,000} = .210588$$

$$k_o = .210588(.772727) + .14(1 - .4)(.227273)$$

$$= .162727 + .019091$$

$$k_o = .181818$$

One can use the M & M formula for cost of leveraged equity, so that

$$k'_e = k_e + \frac{D}{E}(k_e - k_d)(1 - T_c)$$

$$k'_e = .20 + .294118(.20 - .14)(.6)$$

$$k'_e = .20 + .010588$$

$$k'_e = .210588$$

The value for k_o, using Equation 10-10, is

$$k_o = .2[1 - .4(.227273)]$$

$$= .20 - .08(.227273)$$

$$= .181818$$

The third term in the formula may be considered the value added from retaining the earnings and reinvesting them at a rate in excess of the cost of capital. Using EAT for an unleveraged capital structure ($6,000,000), suppose stockholders believe the firm can invest 50 percent of $6,000,000 at a 5-percent differential between $r - k_o$ for five years. Then

$$\text{value of growth} = .5(\$6,000,000)\left[\frac{.05}{.181818(1.181818)}\right]5$$

$$\text{value of growth} = \$3,000,000 \times 1.163463$$

$$\text{value of growth} = \$3,490,389$$

Hence

$$V = \$30,000,000 + \$3,000,000 + \$3,490,389$$

$$V = \$36,490,389$$

For the stockholders

$$\begin{array}{l} \$36,490,389 \\ -7,500,000 \\ \hline \$28,990,389 \quad \text{(value of stockholders' shares)} \end{array}$$

Thus, it is possible to arrive at a valuation of the firm as perceived by the market. The critical variables at this juncture are the unleveraged cost of equity capital, the corporate income-tax rate, the weighted average cost of new capital, and the average return on new investments. CAPM offers management useful insights into how investors value a portfolio of real assets and, therefore, insights into the cost of an unleveraged capital structure. The result, similar to M & M's risk-class assumption, is more robust because it suggests the risk class can be systematically changed through adoption of new projects or acquisition of existing concerns. In that sense, CAPM is a positive guide to determining the value of the firm's assets. Beyond that, however, positive analysis can give way to normative judgments about decisions based only on discounted cash flows. Projects that may be acceptable depend on their returns, the firm's weighted average cost of new capital, and in general only marginally on changes in k_e resulting from changes in the composition of the firm's portfolio of real assets.

SUMMARY

The investment decision can be viewed either in terms of the firm's cost of capital or in terms of the CAPM, specifically the SML for an unleveraged beta coefficient. Each perspective helps shed light on the actual investment decision. Management that seeks to maximize market value of shares in the company recognizes the market can view its stock as a portfolio decision and therefore value it on the basis of its systematic risk. However, systematic risk is a function of both the firm's portfolio of real assets and its composition of financing. Consequently

$$R_j = i + (R_m - i)\left[\beta_{ju} + \frac{D}{E}(\beta_{ju} - \beta_{jd}) \right]$$

where

$$\beta_{ju} + \frac{D}{E}(\beta_{ju} - \beta_{jd})$$

becomes the beta for the leveraged stock. The beta for the firm is

$$\beta_{\text{firm }j} = \frac{D}{D+E}\beta_{jd} + \frac{E}{D+E}\beta_{je}^*$$

and

$$\beta_{\text{firm }j} = \beta_{ju}$$

Thus, CAPM tells us the beta coefficient for the firm equals the beta coefficient for an unleveraged capital structure. It does more than that, however. In calculating the unleveraged beta coefficient, management can also calculate R_{ju} for the firm in the absence of leverage. In turn, this tells management what stockholders expect to earn on a portfolio of real assets. Moreover, the portfolio of real assets can be altered by adopting projects whose systematic risk differs from β_{ju}, thereby altering the unleveraged return on stock j.

The CAPM also appears to suggest each project has its own cost of capital that varies with its systematic risk in a portfolio of diversified assets. However, this perspective, fails to consider that the value of the firm, given its capital structure, depends in part on investing funds at a rate of return in excess of the average cost of new capital. Since

$$k_o = k_e\left(1 - T_c \frac{D}{D + E}\right)$$

where k_e equals R_{ju} and k_o equals the average cost of capital, adoption of new projects that meet the cost of capital standard for the firm but change its unleveraged beta coefficient change k_o by changing k_e. Nevertheless, it is the difference between $r - k_o$ (or a positive net present value) that augments stockholders' wealth. If management accepts projects that lie left of the SML but where $R_{ju} < r - k_o$, the market value of the firm will fall. It is not necessarily true that what is an appropriate investment in the context of MPT is also an appropriate investment for a particular firm with a given capital structure.

PROBLEMS AND QUESTIONS

1. Ms. Ling, treasurer of the Sweet and Sour Sauce Company, a manufacturer of Chinese delicacies, is anxious to determine both the leveraged and the unleveraged cost of equity capital. Her research shows the beta coefficient for the firm has averaged 1.05 for the last 60 quarters. For that same period, the expected return on the market portfolio has averaged 16 percent and the risk-free rate 9.5 percent. The debt-to-total-capital ratio is .2. What are the leveraged and unleveraged costs of equity capital, assuming the beta coefficient for the debt is zero and the company pays no income taxes?

2. In problem 1, suppose the beta coefficient of the debt has averaged .3. What is the unleveraged cost of equity capital? What is the leveraged cost of equity capital?

3. Assume the company in problem 1 has an average tax rate of .25. What is the cost of equity capital for an unleveraged capital structure? What is the cost for a leveraged capital structure, assuming the beta coefficient of the debt is zero and then .3?

4. The financial manager of the Pure Salt Company, which pays no taxes and whose debt-to-equity ratio is .15, knows the company's beta coefficient using the conventional CAPM is 1.2. Is this really the beta coefficient for the firm? Why or

why not? Suppose the beta coefficient of the debt is .1. Would your answer change? Explain in detail.

5. The unleveraged beta coefficient of the Open Pit Sand and Gravel Company is .96. Management is considering the possibility of diversifying its business. The Squigley Company (a manufacturer of chewing gum), whose unleveraged beta coefficient is .80, is for sale. If Open Pit decides to buy Squigley, it estimates its assets will constitute 20 percent of the value of the assets of the combined firms. What is the new unleveraged beta coefficient of the two firms?

6. For problem 5, calculate the cost of unleveraged equity for Open Pit prior to acquisition if R_m is .18 and i is .12. Calculate the same cost for the Squigley Company. What is the unleveraged cost of the combined company?

7. For problems 5 and 6, suppose the corporate income-tax rate of Open Pit is .25. Suppose further that in acquiring Squigley, management of Open Pit maintains the same debt-to-equity ratio as it had before the acquisition: .2.

   a. Calculate the average cost of capital before the acquisition of Squigley. HINT: Use Equation 10-10.)

   b. Calculate the average cost of capital after the acquisition.

   c. If the debt-to-equity ratio following acquisition is .4, how does this affect the average cost of capital (assuming k_d is unchanged)?

8. You are given the following information about The Paradise Creek Mining Corporation:

   a. net operating profits after taxes: $20,000,000

   b. market value of bonds: $40,000,000

   c. corporate income-tax rate: 30 percent

   d. scheduled investment outlays: $10,000,000

   e. average internal rate of return on investments: 24 percent

   f. average cost of capital: 14 percent

   g. number of years for which internal rate of return expected to exceed average cost of capital: five

   h. cost of an unleveraged capital structure: 20 percent

Calculate the firm's market value and the stock's market value.

9. The Pacific Breadnut Company (a leading firm in the development and distribution of macadamia nuts) is located on the sun-drenched island of Paradisea. The company has financed all its assets from equity. Current earnings per share before taxes are $8; current market price of the stock is $24 per share. There are 10,000,000 shares outstanding. The company pays out all earnings as dividends. There is no growth and the corporate income-tax rate is 40 percent.

   a. What is the current cost of equity capital and the total market value of the company?

   b. The company president has just completed an accelerated course in financial management at a local business school. Because interest is tax deductible, the president believes she can raise the market value of stock if she sells debt to stockholders at 12 percent interest in perpetuity and then buys back and retires stock equal to the amount of debt issued. Suppose she retires 25 percent of the stock's market value. Will this repurchase increase the value of the remaining shares?

10. Using the following diagram, the ABC Tool Corporation has plotted its average cost of capital k_o, unleveraged cost of capital k_e (R_{ju}), risk-free rate i, unleveraged beta β_{ju}, and leveraged beta. The firm has also estimated project returns on investments 1 through 4. Should ABC adopt any or all of these investments? Explain in detail.

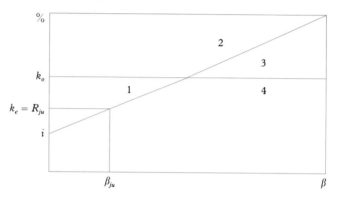

SELECTED ADDITIONAL REFERENCES

Beranek, William. "The WACC Criterion and Shareholder Wealth Maximization," *Journal of Financial and Quantitative Analysis*, Vol. 12 (March 1977, pp. 17–32).

Brennan, M. J. and E. S. Schwartz. "Corporate Income Taxes, Valuation, and the Problem of Optimal Capital Structure," *Journal of Business*, Vol. 50 (January 1978, pp. 103–14).

Chambers, D. R., Robert S. Harris, and John J. Pringle. "Treatment of Financing Mix in Analyzing Investment Opportunities," *Financial Management*, Vol. 11 (September 1982, pp. 27–41).

Chen, Andrew H. and E. Han Kim. "Theories of Corporate Debt Policy: A Synthesis," *Journal of Finance*, Vol. 34 (May 1979, pp. 371–84).

DeAngelo, Harry and Ronald Masulis. "Optimal Capital Structure under Corporate and Personal Taxation," *Journal of Financial Economics*, Vol. 8 (March 1980, pp. 3–30).

Fama, Eugene F. and Merton H. Miller. *The Theory of Finance* (New York: Holt, Rinehart and Winston, 1972).

Farrar, Donald E. and L. Selwyn. "Taxes, Corporate Financial Policies and Returns to Investors," *National Tax Journal*, Vol. 20 (December 1967, pp. 444–54).

Findlay, M. C. and E. E. Williams. "A Positivist Evaluation of the New Finance," *Financial Management*, Vol. 9 (Summer 1980, pp. 7–17).

Hamada, Robert S. "The Effect of the Firm's Capital Structure on the Systematic Risk of Common Stocks," *Journal of Finance*, Vol. 29 (May 1972, pp. 435–52).

Miller, M. and F. Modigliani. "Dividend Policy, Growth and the Valuation of Shares," *Journal of Business*, Vol. 34 (October 1961, pp. 411–33).

Myers, Stewart C. and S. M. Turnbull. "Capital Budgeting and the Capital Asset Pricing Model: Good News and Bad News," *Journal of Finance*, Vol. 32 (May 1977, pp. 321–32).

Pinches, George. "Myopia, Capital Budgeting and Decision Making," *Financial Management*, Vol. 11 (Autumn 1982, pp. 6–19).

Rubinstein, Mark E. "A Mean-Variance Synthesis of Corporate Financial Theory," *Journal of Finance*, Vol. 28 (March 1973, pp. 167–82).

Seitz, Neil. "Shareholder Goals, Firm Goals and Firm Financing Decisions," *Financial Management*, Vol. 11 (Autumn 1982, pp. 20–26).

Stiglitz, Joseph E. "A Re-examination of the Modigliani-Miller Theorem," *American Economic Review*, Vol. 59 (December 1969, pp. 851–66).

———. "On the Irrelevance of Corporate Financial Policy," *American Economic Review*, Vol. 64 (December 1974, pp. 851–66).

THE DIVIDEND
DECISION

To this point in our analysis we have considered in some detail the factors that influence both capital-structure and capital-investment decisions. In one sense, the analysis has come full circle. We began by valuing financial assets based on their future income streams; we now return to and analyze that issue from the perspective of financial management.

Except for common stock, all long-term financial instruments carry a contractual obligation to pay the holders a specified amount at periodic intervals as compensation for the use of their funds. As noted, bondholders receive semiannual interest payments at a specified annual rate until the instruments mature. Preferred stockholders generally receive constant quarterly dividends that continue indefinitely.

No similar provisions exist for common stockholders, however. One can own a share of stock and never receive a dividend. On the other hand, a company may pay a periodic dividend similar to a preferred stock. In-between cases abound. Dividends may fluctuate; extra dividends may be paid at the end of the year. Dividends also may grow with earnings, so that a company maintains a steady payout ratio:

$$payout\ ratio = \frac{dividends}{earnings} = k = constant\ percent$$

The contractual position of common stockholders is that of residual claimant: everyone first receives what is due them, including the Internal Revenue Service. Earnings after taxes can be reinvested within the firm, paid out as dividends, or a combination of both. For financial managers, the critical issue is whether or not there should be a stated dividend policy—perhaps 35 percent of earnings—or whether dividends should fluctuate. Our earlier valuation models—present intrinsic value model and CAPM—both contain an expected dividend component. Indeed, in the former the value of stock is based on future dividends and expected growth; in the latter, at the end of the holding period the stock's market price reflects the present value of future dividends.

However, we have just concluded a chapter in which the firm's value (and, therefore, the stock's value) depends in part on reinvestment of earnings at a rate in excess *of the cost of capital. By implication, if all earnings could be reinvested at an average rate $r > k_0$, management should pay no dividends. If the opposite were true, $k_o > r$, all current earnings should be distributed as dividends; between the two extremes, dividends will fluctuate with investment opportunities. However, do stockholders want dividends to fluctuate? If stockholders are risk-averse, would they value a relatively stable dividend stream more highly than a relatively less stable dividend stream whose present value would otherwise be the same? Let us first consider the issue analytically and then in the context of the real world.*

M & M AND THE IRRELEVANCE OF DIVIDENDS

In their path-breaking article on the dividend decision, Merton H. Miller and Franco Modigliani demonstrated, as they did with the debt decision, that under certain assumptions the dividend decision is irrelevant in determining the stock's market price.[1] Briefly, the basic assumptions are:

1. efficient capital markets
2. no flotation costs
3. no taxes
4. fixed investment outlays (or size of capital budget)
5. fixed capital structure (or debt decision) not subject to change

Under these assumptions, market price of the stock P_o, expected future price P_1, expected dividend D_1, and cost of leveraged equity k'_e (k_e if no debt) are related, so that

$$P_o = \frac{D_1 + P_1}{1 + k'_e} \tag{11-1}$$

Recognizing a given investment decision will be made by issuing stock sufficient to

[1] Merton H. Miller and Franco Modigliani. "Dividend Policy, Growth, and the Valuation of Shares," *Journal of Business*, Vol. 34 (October 1961, pp. 411–33).

maintain the debt ratio, we let

$$n = \text{number of shares currently outstanding}$$
$$m = \text{number of new shares sold at } P_1$$

Then, Equation 11-1 can be rewritten so that

$$nP_o = \frac{1}{1 + k'_e} [nD_1 + (n + m)P_1 - mP_1] \tag{11-2}$$

Consequently, total market value of the stock is the present value of total dividends currently paid plus the total value of all stock outstanding less the value of new stock issued. Because $(n + m)P_1 - mP_1 = nP_1 + mP_1 - mP_1$, we are merely adding and subtracting mP_1 from the numerator. If we let

$$I = \text{total new investment during period 1}$$
$$E = \text{total expected profits for period } T_o \text{ to } T_1,$$

the total amount of new stock issued is

$$mP_1 = I - (E - nD_1) \tag{11-3}$$

Substituting Equation 11-3 for mP_1 in Equation 11-2, we obtain

$$nP_o = \frac{nD_1 + (n + m)P_1 - [I - (E - nD_1)]}{1 + k'_e}$$

$$nP_o = \frac{nD_1 + (n + m)P_1 - I + E - nD_1}{1 + k'_e}$$

$$nP_o = \frac{(n + m)P_1 - I + E}{1 + k'_e} \tag{11-4}$$

Because D_1 does not appear in Equation 11-4 and is replaced by profits less investment outlays for the period, market value of the stock is independent of the dividend decision.

Within the context of the model, new shares are issued because the firm pays dividends. However, suppose I equals E and the firm pays no dividends. From Equation 11-3

$$mP_1 = I - (E - 0)$$
$$mP_1 = I - E = 0$$

No new shares are issued and Equation 11-4 reduces to

$$nP_o = \frac{(n + 0)P_1 - I + E}{1 + k'_e}$$

$$nP_o = \frac{nP_1}{1 + k'_e}$$

Similarly, if the firm pays 100 percent of its profits as dividends so that $E = nD_1$, then

$$mP_1 = I - (E - nD_1)$$
$$mP_1 = I$$

Consequently

$$nP_o = \frac{(n + m)P_1 - I + E}{1 + k'_e}$$
$$nP_o = \frac{nP_1 + mP_1 - I + E}{1 + k'_e}$$
$$nP_o = \frac{nP_1 + E}{1 + k'_e}$$

In essence, the M & M model merely rearranges the income stream to stockholders. If stockholders receive fewer dividends, fewer new shares will be issued. Accordingly, market price per share will be higher. An arithmetic illustration helps shed light on this conclusion. Table 11-1 shows three dividend policies for a firm whose stock has a market price of $100 per share. There are 250,000 shares

---

Table 11-1   Three Arithmetic Illustrations of the Miller-Modigliani Model of Dividend Irrelevancy*

Case I

$$\frac{D}{E} = 100\%$$

$$D_1 = \$4,000,000 \div 250,000$$

$$D_1 = \$16 \text{ per share}$$

$$mP_1 = I - (E - nD_1)$$

$$mP_1 = \$2,000,000$$

$$nP_o = \frac{nP_1 + mP_1 - I + E}{1 + k'_e}$$

$$\$25,000,000 = \frac{250,000P_1 + \$2,000,000 - \$2,000,000 + \$4,000,000}{1.16}$$

$$P_1 = \$100$$

$$D_1 = \$16$$

$$P_1 + D_1 = \$116$$

$$m = \frac{\$2,000,000}{\$100}$$

$$m = 20,000 \text{ share (issued)}$$

Table 11-1 (*Continued*)

Case II

$$\frac{D}{E} = 50\%$$

$$D_1 = \$2,000,000 \div 250,000$$

$$D_1 = \$8 \text{ per share}$$

$$mP_1 = I - (E - nD_1)$$

$$mP_1 = \$2,000,000 - (\$4,000,000 - \$2,000,000)$$

$$mP_1 = 0$$

$$nP_0 = \frac{nP_1 + mP_1 - I + E}{1 + k'_e}$$

$$\$25,000,000 = \frac{250,000P_1 + 0 - \$2,000,000 + \$4,000,000}{1.16}$$

$$P_1 = \$108$$

$$D_1 = \$8$$

$$P_1 + D_1 = \$116$$

$$m = 0 \text{ shares (issued)}$$

Case III

$$\frac{D}{E} = 0\%$$

$$D_1 = \$0 \div 250,000$$

$$D_1 = \$0 \text{ per share}$$

$$mP_1 = I - (E - nD_1)$$

$$mP_1 = \$2,000,000 - (\$4,000,000 - 0)$$

$$mP_1 = -\$2,000,000$$

$$nP_o = \frac{nP_1 + mP - I + E}{1 + k'_e}$$

$$\$25,000,000 = \frac{250,000P_1 - \$2,000,000 - \$2,000,000 + \$4,000,000}{1.16}$$

$$P_1 = \$116$$

$$D_1 = \$0$$

$$P_1 + D_1 = \$116$$

$$m = \frac{-\$2,000,000}{\$116}$$

$$m = 17,241.38 \text{ shares (retired)}$$

*n = number of shares outstanding: 250,000

E = total profits: \$4,000,000

P_o = current market price of stock: \$100

k'_e = cost of equity capital for given leverage: 16%

I = level of investment at T_1: \$2,000,000

P_1 = expected market price at T_1

m = number of new shares

currently outstanding. Total profits are $4,000,000. The level of investment is $2,000,000. Given its debt ratio, cost of equity k'_e is 16 percent.

If management chooses to pay out 100 percent of earnings as dividends (Case I), market price of the stock at P_1 will be $100, the same as P_o. Dividends, however, will be $16 per share. 20,000 new shares will be issued to finance the investment. Total wealth for each stockholder will be $116 ($P_1 + D_1 = \$116$) multiplied by number of shares owned.

Management could choose to finance all investment from earnings (Case II). If it does so, it will pay out 50 percent ($2,000,000) of earnings as dividends. No new shares will have to be issued to finance the investment. Market price of the stock at P_1 will be $108 per share and the dividend will be $8 per share. The shareholder will be just as well off as in Case I: $P_1 + D_1 = \$116$.

Case III is a situation where earnings exceed investment outlay. If the firm chooses not to pay a dividend, it can use the additional funds to repurchase shares. The market price will rise to $116 per share and approximately 17,241.38 shares will be retired. If a stockholder owns 1 percent of the shares at T_0, the value will be $.01 \times 250,000 \times \$100 = \$250,000$. If the company retires 17,241.38 shares, the number of shares outstanding at T_1 will be $250,000 - 17,241.38 = 232,758.62$. If a stockholder retains a proportional interest in the company, holdings at T_1 will be $.01 \times 232,758.62 = 2,327.5862$ shares. Based on the price at P_1, the present value of shares owned at T_1 will be

$$\frac{2,327.5862(\$116)}{1.16} = \$232,758.62$$

However, at T_1 the firm will have purchased 2,327.5862 shares from the stockholder. Consequently, the present value of shares purchased at T_1 will be

$$\frac{(2,500 - 2,327.5862)(\$116)}{1.16} = \$17,241.38$$

The present value of the shares owned and purchased will be

$$\begin{array}{r} \$\ 17,241.38 \\ 232,758.62 \\ \hline \$250,000.00 \end{array}$$

Thus, shareholder wealth will remain unchanged.

The message embodied in the M & M formula, given the underlying assumptions, is that the dividend decision does not affect stockholder wealth. If dividends are distributed as in Case I, new shares will be issued to finance a 100-percent payout. In Case II, no new shares will be issued because sufficient earnings will be retained to finance investment. In Case III, the company will actually retire shares.

Before we relax the assumptions, however, we must clear away one possible source of confusion: it is no riskier for a stockholder to receive the higher dividend

(Case I), the capital gain (Case III), or the combination of both (Case II).[2] He or she will be indifferent to any of the three. The reason is that both investment policy and capital structure decisions are treated as given. If investment policy alters the unleveraged beta coefficient, in efficient capital markets it will be included in β_{ju}. The capital structure decision is already reflected in k'_e. To be sure, D_1, P_1, and E at T_1 could be different than anticipated at T_0; however, the cash flows are the same at T_1. If D, P, and E are lower than anticipated at T_0, total wealth will be lower at T_1. If D, P, and E are higher than anticipated at T_0, total wealth will be higher at T_1. In either case, at T_1 the stockholder has a choice: if D_1 is low, sell shares to acquire cash; if D_1 is high, buy shares. Each stockholder should make the trade-off according to his or her utility function; each should do so, however, at T_1. Meanwhile, between T_0 and T_1 the stockholder with a diversified portfolio earns k'_e—which in efficient markets reflects the appropriate return, given the firm's investment and capital structure decisions.

RELAXING THE ASSUMPTIONS—THE IMPACT OF FEDERAL INCOME-TAX LAWS

Prior to the 1986 major overhaul of federal tax laws, the major effects of which were realized in 1988, cash dividends could be taxed at rates as high as 50 percent. However, if earnings were reinvested profitably and the stock's value rose above its purchase price, the gain (when realized) generally would be taxed at a lower rate. Thus, if a person received $500 in dividends and the marginal tax rate was 50 percent, income after taxes would be $250. Suppose, however, no dividends were paid and total market value of the shares rose by $500. Suppose further the investor held the stock for a year so as to qualify for the long-term capital gains rate and sold the shares at a $500 profit. Under previous tax law, the investor would pay only 50 percent on 40 percent of the gain: $.5 \times .4 \times \$500 = \$100$.

For individuals in high tax brackets there was an incentive to reduce taxes by owning shares in companies with relatively low payout ratios and that profitably reinvested earnings within the firm, thereby increasing the stock's price and effecting a lower tax rate when the shares were sold. By repealing the special treatment accorded capital gains, the 1986 tax reforms eliminated this incentive. However, personal income tax rates were reduced (see Appendix F), so that an individual in the 50-percent bracket in 1985 might be in the 28-percent bracket in 1988. Cash dividends are just as good as capital gains, and from the perspective of current law both are treated equally. Prior to these tax law changes, it was widely believed a policy of paying out a relatively high percentage of earnings as dividends attracted investors from lower income-tax brackets. Similarly, a policy of paying out a

---

[2] See, for example, Myron J. Gordon, "Dividends, Earnings, and Stock Prices," *Review of Economics and Statistics*, Vol. 41 (May 1959, pp. 99–105), and Michael J. Brennan, "A Note on Dividend Irrelevance and the Gordon Valuation Model," *Journal of Finance*, Vol. 26 (December 1971, pp. 1115–22).

relatively low percentage of earnings as dividends was believed to attract investors from comparatively high income-tax brackets.

This *clientele effect*, first recognized by Miller and Modigliani, could have led to management establishing a dividend policy and not altering it radically.[3] Such a policy could have contained comparatively high or low payout ratios; stockholders would have acted accordingly. Once established, however, any sudden policy shift would have at least a short-run impact on the market price of shares as stockholders reassessed after-tax yields relative to alternative investments. Management, concerned with all factors that could have affected the market price of shares, might have sought to neutralize the impact of dividends by maintaining a relatively constant payout ratio.

It has been long recognized that corporations tend to target payout ratios, raising dividends only after management is reasonably sure the new level can be maintained.[4] The actual payout ratio may fluctuate—even fall for awhile—until management is confident the increased earnings that caused the decline in the payout ratio are sufficiently high to raise dividends to a maintenance level. The result may be steady growth in both actual as well as real dividends: dividends adjusted for changes in the price level while payout ratios fluctuate around some target level.

Although policies of firms vary, recent aggregate data on corporate dividends presented in Table 11-2 suggest dividends have grown in both nominal and real terms. The period covered includes two recessions and several years of inflation, some of which reached double-digit proportions. For the 15 years in the table, payout ratios vary from year to year but average 49 percent of adjusted profits: profits after adjustments are made for inventory replacement costs and for plant and equipment worn out from producing goods and services.

Unfortunately, aggregate data not only mask variability in the policies of individual firms but tell us only what they did, not why they did it. Whether the firms tended to target payout ratios, allowing dividends to grow only if they could be maintained to satisfy a particular clientele, is an empirical issue. To date the evidence suggests there may have been a clientele effect. Relatively low-yielding stocks have been held by investors in higher tax brackets; relatively high-yielding stocks have been held by investors in lower tax brackets. Although in some studies the clientele effect was weak, whether strong or weak, the tax incentive upon which the studies were based no longer exists.[5]

---

[3] Same as [1], p. 431.

[4] See, for example, John Lintner, "Distribution of Incomes of Corporations Among Dividends, Retained Earnings, and Taxes," *American Economic Review*, Vol. 56 (May 1956, pp. 97–113). See, also, Eugene Fama and Harvey Babiak, "Dividend Policy and Empirical Analysis," *Journal of the American Statistical Association*, Vol. 63 (December 1968, pp. 1132–61).

[5] Wilbur G. Lewellen, Kenneth R. Stanley, Ronald C. Lease, and Gary G. Schlarbaum. "Some Direct Evidence on the Dividend Clientele Phenomenon," *Journal of Finance*, Vol. 35 (December 1978, pp. 1385–99). See, also, R. Richardson Pettit, "Taxes, Transactions Costs, and Clientele Effects on Dividends," *Journal of Financial Economics*, Vol. 5 (December 1977, pp. 419–36), and Edwin J. Elton and Martin J. Gruber, "Marginal Stockholders' Tax Rates and the Clientele Effect," *Review of Economics and Statistics*, Vol. 52 (February 1970, pp. 68–74).

Table 11-2   American Corporate Dividends and After-tax Real Profits ($ billions)

Year	Adjusted After-tax Profits[a]	Dividends	Dividends on Adjusted After-tax Profits	Real Dividends[b]
1972	$ 58.8	$24.4	41.4%	$52.2
1973	64.1	27.0	42.1	54.4
1974	49.9	29.7	59.5	54.2
1975	66.7	29.6	44.4	50.0
1976	81.0	34.6	42.7	55.3
1977	101.8	39.5	38.8	59.2
1978	113.7	44.7	39.3	62.4
1979	112.1	50.1	44.7	64.1
1980	92.4	54.7	59.2	63.2
1981	106.8	63.6	59.6	67.2
1982	86.9	66.9	77.0	66.9
1983	136.5	71.5	52.4	68.7
1984	169.3	78.3	46.2	72.4
1985	188.9	81.6	43.2	72.9
1986	196.9	87.8	44.6	76.9

[a] After-tax profits plus or minus inventory valuation and capital consumption adjustments that allow primarily for the effect of inflation on replacement costs.
[b] Dividends adjusted for inflation using the personal consumption component of the Implicit Price Deflator for the Gross National Product 1982 = 100.

SOURCE: *1987 Economic Report of the President*, pp. 248 and 343.

RELAXING THE ASSUMPTIONS—ARE CAPITAL MARKETS EFFICIENT?

In Chapter 5 we suggested the bulk of the evidence favors the conclusion that capital markets—at least the market for actively traded stocks—are reasonably efficient in the sense that at any point in time the market price of a firm's shares, given the information available, is the best estimate of the present intrinsic value of those shares. Further, any type of dividend policy is consistent with market efficiency; indeed, it could be part of the information flow that contributes to efficiency.

A characteristic of the modern corporation whose shares are widely held is that ownership is divorced from control. Management selects a payout ratio raising dividends, as suggested earlier, only if it believes the new level can be maintained. Establishing a payout ratio with modest fluctuations about the target is useful to stockholders concerned with tax implications of the dividend policy.

A rise in dividends also adds to the information set. However, financial statements employing conventional accounting techniques may not be as helpful as an established dividend policy in assessing the level and growth of real income.[6] Of course, astute investors and analysts—pouring over reported financial statements in search of a firm's real-income measure—will, in efficient markets, anticipate any dividend increase. Once announced, the new dividend will be fully incorporated in the stock's market price.

The empirical issue, therefore, is not whether a dividend increase raises market price of the shares but whether it is a better source of information about future prospects than available alternatives. If so, the announcement will cause the market price of the stock to rise. Although mixed, recent empirical evidence tends to support the notion that changes in dividends convey information not fully anticipated in the market price of the shares.[7] Such findings are intuitively appealing: institutionally they suggest management is in a better position than outsiders both to interpret the nuances of public information and to access a larger set of more pertinent information about the prospects of the firm. Nevertheless, it is worth reemphasizing that dividends are at best a superior *source* of information: they are not the reason for the stock's increased value. It is anticipated growth in real earnings that offers management an opportunity to signal the market—suggesting the new level of dividends can be comfortably maintained from a higher level of earnings. The anticipated dividend then can be used as a variable in CAPM or present intrinsic value models.

RELAXING THE ASSUMPTIONS—ALTERING THE LEVEL OF INVESTMENT

As noted earlier, the M & M model merely rearranges the income stream for shareholders. However, if management raises or lowers the level of investment, market price of the stock can be affected. In Chapter 10 we pointed out that valuation

---

[6] See, for example, Sudipto Bhattacharya, "Imperfect Information, Dividend Policy, and 'The Bird in Hand Fallacy'," *Bell Journal of Economics*, Vol. 10 (Spring 1974, pp. 259–70); Roger Gordon and Burton G. Malkiel, "Corporate Financial Structure," a paper presented at the Brookings Conference on Economic Effect of Federal Taxes (October 18–19, 1979); and Stephen A. Ross, "The Determination of Financial Structure: The Incentive Signalling Approach," *Bell Journal of Economics*, Vol. 8 (Spring 1977, pp. 23–40).

[7] One can trace the development of empirical evidence from the following sample: Eugene F. Fama, L. Fisher, Michael Jensen, and Richard Roll. "The Adjustment of Stock Prices to New Information," *International Economic Review*, Vol. 10 (February 1969, pp. 1–21). R. Richardson Pettit. "Dividend Announcements, Security Performance, and Capital Market Efficiency," *Journal of Finance*, Vol. 27 (December 1972, pp. 993–1007). Ross Watts. "The Information Content of Dividends," *Journal of Business*, Vol. 46 (April 1973), pp. 191–211). Joseph Aharony and Itzhak Swary. "Quarterly Dividend and Earnings Announcements and Stockholders' Returns: An Empirical Analysis," *Journal of Finance*, Vol. 35 (March 1980, pp. 1–12). Clarence C. Y. Kwan. "Efficient Market Tests of the Informational Content of Dividend Announcements: Critiques and Extension," *Journal of Financial and Quantitative Analysis*, Vol. 16 (June 1981, pp. 193–206).

of company shares depends in part on the proportion of net operating income that can be invested at $r > k_o$. If that proportion changes so that the level of investment changes, market value of company shares varies accordingly.

Suppose, for example, management raises its investment outlay above what was originally anticipated but maintains the firm's current level of dividends. To the extent net operating income after dividends is insufficient to cover the augmented capital budget, new securities are issued in proportion to the current debt ratio and at the current average cost of capital k_o. Because the additional funds can be invested at $r > k_o$, total market value of all shares rises—although addition of new stock mitigates the increase on a per-share basis. A decision to increase investment outlay can, therefore, have a positive impact on the stock's market value. Similarly, a decision to decrease investment over what was originally anticipated can—given the level of dividends—cause the firm to retire both debt and equity, thereby lowering total market value of its shares. By retiring stock, however, the price per share will not decline as rapidly as when the total number of shares remains unchanged. The decrease in anticipated investment outlay would be perceived as a decrease in opportunities to invest at $r > k_o$, and the market would react accordingly.

Note in either case it is the change in investment level that affects market value of the firm, not dividend level. Although management could alter the latter—as we have seen there may be good reasons for not doing so—it chooses to increase external financing. Transaction costs of increasing external financing must be weighed against the clientele effect and the confusing signals a volatile dividend policy may portend for the market value of company shares. Of course, confusing signals could be mitigated by a clear statement that dividends will fluctuate with investment opportunities. Such volatility, however, may not be appreciated by the market, where varying tax consequences of a widely fluctuating payout ratio are unsatisfactory to stockholders in all tax brackets.

In the real world, investment expenditures almost always fluctuate. Data in Table 11-3 cover the same period as the dividend data in Table 11-2 and suggest greater year-to-year volatility in the level of investment outlays compared with the level of dividends. In real terms, gross as well as net outlays for both structures and equipment generally ebb and flow with the level of economic activity.[8] In the aggregate and in real terms, American corporations are more likely to maintain the level of dividends while allowing the level of investment outlays to fluctuate. That management allows investment to fluctuate should come as no surprise: expenditures on plant and equipment take place only if $r > k_o$ or the net present value is positive. For the economy as a whole, an increase in investment expenditures

---

[8] The third component of investment expenditures, changes in business inventories, is also highly volatile. We have not focused on this component because plant and equipment are the primary components of the capital budget. A permanent investment in inventories is included in capital outlays. If a firm's annual capital budget contained no capital outlays, the level of inventories associated with existing productive capacity would change with changes in demand for the goods produced.

Table 11-3   **American Corporate Investment Expenditures[a]—1972–1986 ($ billions)**

	Structures				Equipment			
	Gross[a]		Net[b]		Gross[a]		Net[b]	
Year	Current $	Real[c] $	Current $	Real[c] $	Current $	Real[c] $	Current $	Real[c] $
1972	44.5	109.5	17.4	39.8	78.5	167.5	23.1	45.5
1973	51.4	117.7	21.7	46.8	94.5	199.6	34.4	69.8
1974	57.0	115.2	22.0	42.5	103.6	202.7	33.7	64.4
1975	56.3	102.8	15.6	27.9	106.6	178.4	21.9	32.9
1976	60.1	104.4	16.0	27.3	119.9	186.2	24.8	34.6
1977	66.7	108.3	17.6	28.7	147.4	215.7	41.0	56.5
1978	81.0	119.3	25.0	37.2	178.0	242.8	57.2	74.3
1979	99.5	130.6	34.5	44.8	203.3	258.8	64.5	79.5
1980	113.9	136.2	39.4	47.2	208.9	243.0	49.5	54.1
1981	138.5	148.8	51.7	56.0	230.7	246.4	46.9	49.4
1982	143.3	143.3	45.9	45.9	223.4	223.4	19.6	19.6
1983	124.0	127.2	25.9	26.2	232.8	233.9	19.9	24.1
1984	141.1	143.8	39.3	39.8	274.9	281.4	51.8	63.5
1985	152.5	149.4	45.5	41.8	290.1	304.8	55.9	75.3
1986	137.4	130.3	26.6	20.2	299.5	320.3	54.4	72.2

[a] Gross investment in structures or equipment: includes structures and equipment designed to replace capital used for production.
[b] Net investment after allowances for capital used for production.
[c] 1982 dollars.

SOURCE: *1987 Economic Report of the President*, pp. 244, 246, 262, 263. *U.S. Department of Commerce Survey of Current Business*, Vol. 67 (July 1987, p. 52).

is consistent with a rise or anticipated rise in the level of economic activity; a decrease in investment expenditures is consistent with a decline or an anticipated decline in the level of economic activity.

RELAXING THE ASSUMPTIONS—THE DEBT–EQUITY RATIO

As we concluded in Chapter 7, management is likely to maintain a relatively stable debt-to-total-capital ratio to preserve credit status. Raising the ratio significantly raises the cost of debt capital by lowering the company's credit rating. A higher cost of debt capital raises the probability that the current dividend level cannot be maintained without issuing additional shares. Hence, market price of the stock falls; cost of equity capital rises; and average cost of new capital, k_o, increases.

On the other hand, lowering the debt–equity ratio does not necessarily raise the credit rating and lower the cost of debt capital. In the real world, a firm's credit rating is not only a function of its debt–equity ratio but also its absolute size. For example, the Dexter Corporation of Windsor Locks, Connecticut—ranked 396th in sales and 371st in assets among the 1986 Fortune 500 largest industrial corporations— carries an "A" credit rating.[9] If it were a larger concern, it would have an "AA" rating and therefore a lower cost of debt capital. Only through growth can Dexter earn a higher credit rating; thus its management maintains a debt–equity ratio that preserves the highest possible credit rating and the lowest current cost of debt capital. To the extent all firms follow similar practices, the assumption that the debt–equity ratio is held constant may be consistent with both theory and practice.[10]

An interesting aspect of debt policy concerns those who hold the securities. Consider the second term in the M & M valuation model, which employs both personal tax rates of debtholders as well as stockholders: the portion of the total value of the leveraged firm that depends on

$$\left[1 - \frac{(1 - T_c)(1 - T_{ps})}{(1 - T_{pd})} \right] D$$

where

D = market value of debt

T_c = corporate tax rate

T_{ps} = average personal tax rate of stockholders

T_{pd} = average personal tax rate of debtholders

Because there exist both high quality tax-exempt municipal obligations as well as fully taxed corporate debt of similar quality, holders of debt instruments tend to gravitate toward the highest after-tax yield. At the end of 1982, there were $553.4 billion in corporate bonds outstanding; life insurance companies held $202.3 billion; state and local government retirement funds held $112.1 billion; and private pension funds held $65.1 billion. Together these debtholders accounted for nearly 69 percent of all corporate bonds outstanding; on the other hand, they are not purchasers of state and local government obligations.[11] Because pension funds pay no taxes,

---

[9] *Fortune*, Vol. 115 (April 27, 1987, pp. 378–79).

[10] Even large corporations have difficulty maintaining their credit rating when their debt–equity ratio exceeds a particular level. In 1984, Chevron lost its *aaa* credit rating when it issued $13.3 billion in debt to purchase Gulf Oil. To maintain its lower *aa* rating, Chevron projected its debt-to-total-capital ratio at between 25 and 30 percent by 1989. *Economist* (June 7, 1986, p. 27).

[11] Board of Governors of the Federal Reserve System. *Flow of Funds Accounts, Assets and Liabilities Outstanding, 1959–1982* (August 1983, p. 36). Of the $553.4 billion, $59.9 billion were foreign bonds. Although state and local retirement funds hold small amounts of municipal obligations, of the $424.3 billion of municipals outstanding in 1983, $129 billion and $158.7 billion were held by households and commercial banks, respectively.

debtholders have no incentive to hold municipal bonds; on the other hand, highly taxed households and commercial banks, the largest purchasers of state and local obligations, have an incentive to buy them. Life insurance companies pay taxes but hold bonds that cover the fixed payments inherent in many of their contracts. Consequently, a corporation can usually assume the average tax rate paid by holders of its debt may be lower than the average tax rate paid by its stockholders. Actually, in many cases it may be zero.

With a personal tax rate for debtholders of zero, the tax value of leverage to a firm becomes $[1 - (1 - T_c)(1 - T_{ps})]D$. Of course, the larger the values of both T_c and T_{ps}, the smaller the product of the terms and the greater the value of the firm given the level of debt. Suppose a corporation and its shareholders were both in the highest tax brackets. Under current tax laws, the maximum benefit per dollar of debt would be based on a corporate income tax rate of 34 percent and a personal income tax rate of 28 percent (33 percent at certain income levels; see Appendix F), so that

$$V_L = [1 - (1 - .34)(1 - .28)]D$$
$$V_L = (1 - .4752)D$$
$$V_L = .5248D$$

For every additional dollar of debt in its capital structure, the value of the leveraged firm V_L will rise .5248 cents. Although this increase may sound impressive, recall the arithmetic example in Chapter 10: of a total value of $36,490,389, $30,000,000 resulted from capitalizing net operating profits after taxes at the cost of unleveraged capital k_e, not leveraged. Indeed, leverage often may have a smaller impact on total value than growth.

REPURCHASE OF SHARES

When management chooses to repurchase a portion of its shares outstanding, is there a compelling reason for doing so? One interpretation is that management has exhausted profitable investment opportunities and is signaling the market that future prospects are not robust. Of course, the same signal could be sent through payment of an extra dividend at the end of the year—a dividend that does not represent a permanent increase.

There are, however, other reasons. Share repurchase may take place in order to fund the firm's executive compensation plans. Stock thus purchased, offered to executives at a specified price, is an incentive to management to increase profitability of the firm. If the company prospers and the market price rises, executives can exercise their option to sell the stock, realizing perfectly legal capital gains.

Although purchasing shares for employee compensation programs is the reason management most often cites for share repurchase, other motives—including prevention of unwanted (hostile) takeovers by other companies and desire to increase the debt–equity ratio—are often cited.[12] Publicly held stock is always subject to takeover bids, which management generally resists. In some cases, such as the 1984 attempt by Saul Steinberg to purchase Disney, management pays a premium to repurchase the shares.[13] Whether resistance to a takeover bid is in the best interests of stockholders is a moot point.[14] Reacting to takeover probability, the management of some companies repurchases shares in such large numbers that the companies become private corporations whose shares are no longer traded on the open market.[15]

Of greater concern to our narrative is the possibility share repurchase may be used to raise the debt–equity ratio. Suppose a firm has been successfully reinvesting earnings in the company so the debt-to-total-capital ratio is lower than necessary to maintain its current credit rating. Without increasing k_d, the firm may repurchase shares from the proceeds of a debt issue, thereby taking advantage of the tax deductability of interest in the manner already described.

Whatever the motivation, share repurchases are popular. In 1981, for example, 312 companies listed on the New York Stock Exchange repurchased shares, 113 acquiring more than 100,000 shares and 32 acquiring 1,000,000 shares or more. A total of 148.4 million shares were repurchased, of which 26.4 million were repurchased by Exxon.[16]

Shares can be repurchased in small quantities through the open market or in large quantities through a tender offer. The latter recently has become a topic of increasing interest to scholars.[17] Open-market purchases are often, though not

---

[12] Francis A. Lee. *Repurchasing Common Stock*, Research Bulletin No. 147 (New York: The Conference Board, 1983).

[13] Steinberg paid an average of $63.75 per share for 11.1 percent of Disney's stock; he received $77.50 per share when management repurchased it, for a reported profit of at least $32 million. Following the buyback, Disney's stock plunged nearly $11 per share. *Wall Street Journal* (July 5, 1984, p. 2; July 6, 1984, p. 11). When an investor purchases stock expressly for the purpose of forcing management to repurchase it at a premium, the practice is known as **greenmail**. It is difficult to distinguish a genuine bid to control a company from greenmail.

[14] For example, suppose the company has been poorly managed so that the market value of its assets exceeds the market value of its securities. Unless stockholders can organize to vote out the management—a difficult task in a large publicly held company—they may be better off accepting the premium than acquiesing in the current management.

[15] A technique for accomplishing this objective is **leveraged buyout**. A small group of investors, who may be the management of the company, borrow from banks and repurchase stock from shareholders at a premium over the market price. Presumably the debt is repaid from operations or from sale of company assets, or both. See Anne B. Fisher, "Oops! My Company Is for Sale," *Fortune*, Vol. 110 (July 23, 1984, pp. 16–21). From our analysis, leveraged buyout makes sense for stockholders who sell to the group only if the stock is inefficiently priced or if the debt–equity ratio is less than optimum. The latter is important if the company subsequently goes bankrupt, for those who sold their stock may have to return the cash received in order to satisfy the principal and interest claims on the debt outstanding.

If management forms the buyout group, it may be doing so to protect its position in the firm. Initially, management may have no interest in going private. However, someone else may form a syndicate to purchase the company. Suspecting greenmail or fearful of losing their jobs, or both, management may find another company willing to purchase the firm via a friendly takeover bid.

[16] Same as [12], p. 4.

[17] See, for example, Ronald Masulis, "Stock Repurchase by Tender Offer: An Analysis of the Causes of Common Stock Price Changes," *Journal of Finance*, Vol. 35 (May 1980, pp. 305–15); Larry Dann, "Common Stock Repurchases: An Analysis of Returns to Bondholders and Stockholders," *Journal of Financial Economics*, Vol. 9 (June 1981, pp. 113–38); and Theo Vermaelen, "Common Stock Repurchases and Market Signalling: An Empirical Study," *Journal of Financial Economics*, Vol. 1 (June 1981, pp. 139–83).

always, small. However, when a company makes a tender offer, it is usually for a substantial portion of the stock outstanding. Moreover, the company offers to repurchase the shares at a price substantially above (often in excess) 20 percent of their market price prior to announcement of the tender offer.

As suggested in Figure 11-1, once the tender offer is made, market price of the stock rises. The average price P_A generally remains below the tender price P_T, though perhaps 15 percent above market price before the tender offer was announced. After the tender offer's expiration date, market price of the stock may fall approximately 3 percent (P_E) yet remain above pre-tender price (P_o).

That tender price P_T is greater than average price P_A after tender announcement is largely because the offers on which these studies are based are generally oversubscribed. Firms usually handle oversubscriptions on a pro-rata basis. Thus, if management tenders an offer for 1,000,000 shares and 2,000,000 are tendered, 50 percent would be purchased; a stockholder who tendered 200 shares would receive the tender price for 100. Since the extent of oversubscription is not fully known until expiration date, P_A is based on expected number of shares tendered. A

Figure 11-1   The Effect of a Tender Offer to Repurchase on the Market Price of the Stock*

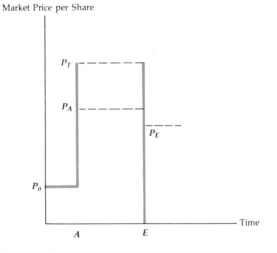

*P_o = market price when tender offer made
 A = announcement date
 P_T = tender price
 E = expiration date
 P_A = average price after announcement date
 P_E = average price after expiration date

3-percent drop in price after expiration date could be within the bounds of statistical error.

The substantive issue involves the effect on wealth caused by the fact P_E (in most cases) is greater than P_o. Assuming the stock is efficiently priced, a tender offer at a premium over market price should lower the price per share compared to what it was prior to the tender offer. To illustrate, suppose a company has 35,000,000 shares of stock outstanding, the current market price of which is $50 per share. If the firm offers to purchase 1,000,000 shares at $62 per share, the effect should be

$$
\begin{array}{r}
35{,}000{,}000 \times \$50 = \$1{,}750{,}000{,}000 \\
-1{,}000{,}000 \times \$62 = -\ \ \ 62{,}000{,}000 \\
\hline
\$1{,}688{,}000{,}000
\end{array}
$$

Because total wealth of the firm drops by $62,000,000, the price per share should fall to

$$
\frac{\$1{,}688{,}000{,}000}{34{,}000{,}000} = \$49.65
$$

Instead, consistent with the thrust of the empirical evidence, market price after expiration date is $57. As suggested by the hypothetical illustration in Table 11-4, the tender offer creates a wealth effect—$250,000,000—which is a 14.3-percent return on the original shares outstanding. The bulk of the return is due to the proportion of shares not tendered, since they represent more than 97 percent of the total. For individuals, of course, the wealth effect varies with the number of shares owned and the percentage tendered.

Possible reasons why market price after expiration of the tender offer is greater on average than market price prior to the announcement include:

1. favorable capital gains rate at the time studies were made
2. leverage effect from repurchasing shares through debt issue
3. favorable signal that earnings are greater than initially predicted from information available prior to repurchase announcement[18]

Of the three reasons, empirical evidence to date suggests the signaling effect plays the greatest role in explaining the increased market price of stock following announcement of a tender offer.[19] As with increased cash dividends, a tender offer to repurchase shares appears to signal the market that the company repurchasing the shares is doing so because its earnings are greater than anticipated: per-share

---

[18] It is possible repurchase may sufficiently reduce the asset base of a firm so as to lower the market price of outstanding debt. However, this would result in a higher cost of debt capital. Moreover, the increased leverage would lower the market price of the stock. Dann, pp. 113–38, found no evidence fixed-income securities decreased in value following repurchase.

[19] Same as [17], Vermaelen, pp. 139–83.

Table 11-4   Hypothetical Illustration of Wealth Effect on Share Repurchase after Tender Offer

Market price before tender announcement	= $50 per share
Tender price	= $62 per share
Price per share after expiration of tender	= $57 per share
Number of shares before tender offer	= 35,000,000
Number of shares tendered	= 1,000,000

Total value of shares before announcement of tender offer (35,000,000 × $50)	= $1,750,000,000
Less total paid for tenders (1,000,000 × $62)	= 62,000,000
	$1,688,000,000
Total value of shares after expiration of tender (34,000,000 × $57)	= $1,938,000,000
Less	1,688,000,000
Total wealth created by tender offer	= $ 250,000,000

$$\frac{\$250,000,000}{\$1,750,000,000} = 14.3\% = \text{total return to stock from tender offer}$$

$$\frac{1,000,000}{35,000,000} \frac{(\$62 - \$50)}{\$50} = 00.7\% = \text{proportion of total return to shares tendered}$$

$$\frac{34,000,000}{35,000,000} \frac{(\$57 - \$50)}{\$50} = 13.6\% = \text{proportion of total wealth to shares not tendered}$$

earnings are greater than initially predicted from information available prior to announcement of repurchase. The market reacts accordingly.

Note the results discussed are for tender offers only: share repurchases in the open market may be made for a greater variety of reasons. The fact tender offers may, on average, signal an increase in earnings is not inconsistent with the possibility some companies repurchase shares from time to time because they cannot otherwise reinvest earnings profitably.

STOCK DIVIDENDS AND SPLITS

A stock dividend, unlike a cash dividend or a repurchase of shares, simply adds to the number of shares outstanding. The same is true of a stock split, except it generally adds a greater number of shares to the total shares outstanding. For example, in June 1984, Chock Full O'Nuts announced a 3-percent stock dividend payable July 31, 1984. At the same time, the Bank of Virginia announced a 100-percent stock dividend to effect a two-for-one split payable July 19, 1984.[20] In the former case, a shareholder

---

[20] Moody's *Dividend Record* (June 29, 1984, p. 4).

received 3 shares for every 100 shares owned; in the latter case, a shareholder received 1 additional share for each share owned—hence the term *two-for-one split*.

Because either a stock dividend or a stock split increases the number of shares outstanding, either lowers market price per share but not the firm's total value. Suppose a company whose stock is selling at $50 per share splits the stock two for one. The market price per share becomes $25. Those owning 100 shares prior to the split now own 200 shares. In both cases total shares owned are worth $500.

Stock splits, in particular, are often accompanied by increased cash dividends. The split usually follows a price run-up that anticipates earnings growth and a subsequent increase in dividends. Consistent with the semi-strong form of the efficient market hypothesis, dividend increase is generally anticipated and the stock's market price does not change significantly following a split.[21] Of course, stock dividends (unlike cash dividends) are taxed only when sold.

SUMMARY

We have explored the dividend decision at some length. What we found was that policy is not consistent with theory. As with their path-breaking analysis of the debt decision, Miller and Modigliani demonstrate that in efficient financial markets—given capital structure, level of investment, no flotation costs, and no taxes—the dividend decision is irrelevant. This is true even in a world of uncertainty. In the case of a leveraged corporation, the market capitalizes its cash flows at k_e or k'_e. Because factors over which management has control—level of investment and debt–equity ratio—are fixed at T_o, there are no surprises from these factors at T_1. Actual values for P_1, E_1, and D_1 may differ from what was initially anticipated at T_o; however, in efficient markets this has been fully accounted for in k_e or k'_e. Thus, for M & M the issue is whether management uses earnings to pay dividends and finances such payments through additional stock, whether it issues no new shares, or whether it repurchases outstanding shares when $E_1 > I_1$, letting market price of the stock rise accordingly. Given the operant assumptions, the stockholder is indifferent to receiving dividends or increased per-share price of the stock.

Once assumptions are relaxed, however, a case can be made for a dividend policy; that case, however, is weaker today than in the past. With elimination of differences in tax treatment between ordinary income and capital gains, there is little incentive to create clientele based on low- or high-payout ratios. Even when that incentive existed, American corporations tended to distribute a relatively high percentage of their after-tax profits. Perhaps more significant is the fact that whatever the ratio, management tends to keep it stable, increasing dividends only when it is reasonably certain the increased level can be maintained.

---

[21] Same as [7], Fama, Fisher, Jensen, and Roll, pp. 1–21.

If markets are not completely efficient, a dividend policy may actually add to the available information: a dividend increase would signal that the firm's prospects appear more robust than could be gleaned initially from information available prior to the increase. Empirical evidence on the signaling hypothesis is encouraging and appears to be a fruitful area for future research. Share repurchase through tender offer also appears to signal that the firm's prospects are better than originally anticipated: on average, the stock's market price is generally greater after expiration of the tender offer than before it was made.

Finally, dividends are sometimes paid in stock rather than cash. Stock dividends and stock splits do not add value to the stock; they merely increase the number of shares outstanding. Only increases in cash payments are valued by the stockholders. Cash payments are justified only when earnings have increased and, under the signaling hypothesis, are expected to have increased permanently.

PROBLEMS AND QUESTIONS

1. Applejack Corporation has targeted its payout ratio at 25 percent of earnings. Last year's earnings were $6 per share. This year, earnings are expected to increase to $8 per share but decrease to $7 per share next year.

   a. If Applejack maintains its dividend policy, what was the dividend last year and what will it be this year and next year?

   b. Should management maintain a constant payout ratio? Explain.

2. Suppose Magnolia Corporation has an opportunity to invest the equivalent of $3 per share within the firm for one year at $r - k_o$ of 8 percent, where k_o is 14 percent. Alternatively, Magnolia could declare an extra dividend of $3 per share. Assume a stockholder is in the 30-percent tax bracket and a capital gains tax of 15 percent exists.

   a. What is the potential difference in wealth for 100 shares of stock, excluding transaction costs, if the firm pays an extra dividend rather than reinvesting the funds within the company?

   b. Would your answer be different if the shareholder was tax exempt? Explain.

3. Using the M & M model for the irrelevance of dividends, suppose

$$n = 3,000,000 \text{ shares}$$
$$E = \$9,000,000$$
$$P_o = \$20$$
$$k'_e = 15 \text{ percent}$$
$$I = \$1,500,000$$
$$P_1 = \text{expected market price at } T_1$$
$$D_1 = \text{expected dividends at } T_1$$
$$m = \text{number of new shares}$$

a. What are the values for P_1, D_1, and m if the payout ratio is 25 percent of earnings?

b. What are the values for P_1, D_1, and m if the payout ratio is 150 percent of earnings?

c. Given the assumptions underlying the M & M model, is it riskier for stockholders if the firm pays out 25 percent or 150 percent of earnings? Explain.

4. Rubric Corporation expects to earn $8 per share next year. There are 5,500,000 shares outstanding. Suppose management decides to pay 50 percent of earnings as dividends, the remainder to be reinvested within the company for one year at $r - k_o$ of 10 percent. Current market price of Rubric stock is $64 and k'_e is 12.5 percent.

a. Under this policy, by how much should the stock's price increase? What will be the firm's total value?

b. Suppose that in addition to paying 50 percent of earnings as dividends, Rubric declares a 3-percent stock dividend. Will the stock price rise or fall over what it is projected to be in (a)? Will the firm's total value change? Explain.

c. Suppose that instead of a 3-percent stock dividend, the same cash dividend was paid but the stock was split two for one. What should happen to the market price per share? To the firm's total value?

5. On January 13, Open Pit Sand and Gravel Company declares a dividend of 75 cents per share payable to stockholders of record on February 15. The stock closes at $38 per share on February 15. Other factors remaining constant, what should happen to the stock price on February 16? Why?

6. Two corporations have the following characteristics:

Corporation A

$$\text{marginal tax rate of bondholders} = .10$$
$$\text{marginal tax rate of company} = .46$$
$$\text{average marginal tax rate of stockholders} = .40$$

Corporation B

$$\text{marginal tax rate of bondholders} = .10$$
$$\text{marginal tax rate of company} = .22$$
$$\text{average marginal tax rate of stockholders} = .20$$

a. What can you infer about the dividend policies of each company?

b. If each company has the same cost of unleveraged equity k_e, should one company be more apt to fund a greater proportion of its assets through debt than the other? Explain.

7. Explain in detail why a stock split or stock dividend adds nothing to the firm's value but why an increase in the cash dividend or a tender offer to repurchase shares could add to the firm's value.

SELECTED ADDITIONAL REFERENCES

Aharony, Joseph and Itzhak Swary. "Quarterly Dividend and Earnings Announcements and Stockholders' Returns: An Empirical Analysis," *Journal of Finance*, Vol. 35 (March 1980, pp. 1–12).

Ang, James S. "Do Dividends Matter? A Review of Corporate Dividend Theories and Evidence," *Monograph Series in Finance and Economics*, 1987–2 (New York: New York University Graduate School of Business Administration).

Asquith, Paul and David W. Mullins, Jr. "Signalling with Dividends, Stock Repurchases and Equity Issues," *Financial Management*, Vol. 15 (Autumn 1986, pp. 27–44).

Bhattacharya, Sudipto. "Imperfect Information, Dividend Policy and 'The Bird in Hand Fallacy,'" *Bell Journal of Economics*, Vol. 10 (Spring 1979, pp. 259–70).

Black, Fischer and Myron Scholes. "The Effects of Dividend Policy on Common Stock Prices and Returns," *Journal of Financial Economics*, Vol. 1 (May 1974, pp. 1–22).

Brennan, Michael. "A Note on Dividend Irrelevance and the Gordon Valuation Model," *Journal of Finance*, Vol. 26 (December 1971, pp. 1115–22).

Brickley, James A. "Shareholder Wealth, Information Signaling and the Specially Designated Dividend," *Journal of Financial Economics*, Vol. 12 (August 1983, pp. 187–209).

Dann, Larry. "Common Stock Repurchases: An Analysis of Returns to Bondholders and Stockholders," *Journal of Financial Economics*, Vol. 9 (June 1981, pp. 113–38.

Divecha, Arjun and Dale Morse. "Market Response to Dividend Increases and Payout Ratios," *Journal of Financial and Quantitative Analysis*, Vol. 18 (June 1983, pp. 163–73.

Elton, Edward J. and Martin J. Gruber. "Marginal Stockholders' Tax Rates and the Clientele Effect," *Review of Economics and Statistics*, Vol. 52 (February 1970, pp. 68–74).

Fama, Eugene F. and Harvey Babiak. "Dividend Policy: An Empirical Analysis," *Journal of the American Statistical Association*, Vol. 63 (December 1968, pp. 1132–61).

Fama, Eugene F., Lawrence Fisher, Michael Jensen, and Richard Roll. "The Adjustment of Stock Prices to New Information," *International Economic Review*, Vol. 10 (February, 1969, pp. 1–21).

Feenberg, Daniel. "Does the Investment Interest Limitation Explain the Existence of Dividends?" *Journal of Financial Economics*, Vol. 9 (September 1981, pp. 265–69).

Feldstein, Martin and Jerry Green. "Why Do Companies Pay Dividends?" *American Economic Review*, Vol. 73 (March 1983, pp. 17–30).

Ferris, Kenneth R., Arie Melnik, and Alfred Rappaport. "Factors Influencing the Pricing of Stock Repurchase Tenders," *Quarterly Review of Economics and Business*, Vol. 18 (Spring 1978, pp. 31–39).

Fung, William K. and Michael Theobold. "Dividends and Debt Under Alternative Tax Systems," *Journal of Financial and Quantitative Analysis*, Vol. 19 (March 1984, pp. 59–72).

Gordon, Myron J. "Dividends, Earnings and Stock Prices," *Review of Economics and Statistics*, Vol. 41 (May 1959, pp. 99–105).

Gordon, Roger and Burton G. Malkiel. "Corporate Financial Structure," a paper presented at the Brookings Conference on the Economic Effect of Federal Taxes (October 18, 1979).

Handjinicolaou, George and Avner Kalay. "Wealth Redistribution or Changes in Firm Value: An Analysis of Returns to Bondholders and Stockholders Around Dividend Announcements," *Journal of Financial Economics*, Vol. 13 (March 1984, pp. 35–64).

Haugen, Robert and Lemma W. Senbet. "Corporate Finance and Taxes: A Review," *Financial Management*, Vol. 15 (Autumn 1986, pp. 5–26).

Kwan, Clarence C. Y. "Efficient Market Tests of the Informational Content of Dividend Announcements: Critique and Extension," *Journal of Financial and Quantitative Analysis*, Vol. 16 (June 1981, pp. 193–206).

Lee, Francis A. *Repurchasing Common Stock*, Research Bulletin No. 147 (New York: The Conference Board, 1983).

Lewellen, William K., Stanley R. Lease, and Gary Schlarbaum. "Some Direct Evidence on the Dividend Clientele Phenomenon," *Journal of Finance*, Vol. 33 (December 1978, pp. 1385–99).

Lintner, John. "Distribution of Incomes of Corporations Among Dividends, Retained Earnings and Taxes," *American Economic Review*, Vol. 46 (May 1956, pp. 97–113).

Litzenberg, Robert and Krishna Ramiswamy. "The Effect of Personal Taxes and Dividends on Capital Asset Prices," *Journal of Financial Economics*, Vol. 7 (June 1979, pp. 163–96).

Long, John, Jr. "The Market Valuation of Cash Dividends: A Case to Consider," *Journal of Financial Economics*, Vol. 6 (June/September 1978, pp. 235–64).

Marsh, Terry and Robert C. Merton. "Dividend Variability and Variance Bounds Tests for the Rationality of Stock Market Prices," *American Economic Review*, Vol. 76 (June 1986, pp. 483–98).

Masulis, Ronald. "Stock Repurchase by Tender Offer: An Analysis of the Causes of Common Stock Price Changes," *Journal of Finance*, Vol. 35 (May 1980, pp. 305–18).

Miller, Merton H. "Dividends and Taxes: Some Empirical Evidence," *Journal of Political Economy*, Vol. 90 (December 1982, pp. 1118–41).

Miller, Merton H. and Franco Modigliani. "Dividend Policy, Growth and the Valuation of Shares," *Journal of Business*, Vol. 34 (October 1961, pp. 411–33).

Miller, Merton H. and Myron Scholes. "Dividends and Taxes," *Journal of Financial Economics*, Vol. 6 (December 1978, pp. 333–64).

Petit, R. Richardson. "Dividend Announcements, Security Performance and Capital Market Efficiency," *Journal of Finance*, Vol. 27 (December 1972, pp. 993–1007).

———. "Taxes, Transactions Costs and Clientele Effects of Dividends," *Journal of Financial Economics*, Vol. 5 (December 1977, pp. 419–36).

Ross, Stephen A. "The Determination of Financial Structures: The Incentive Signalling Approach," *Bell Journal of Economics*, Vol. 8 (Spring 1977, pp. 23–40).

Rozeff, M. "Growth, Beta and Agency Costs as Determinants of Dividend Payout Ratios," University of Iowa Working Paper Series, No. 81–11 (June 1981).

Schiller, Robert. "The Marsh-Merton Model of Managers' Smoothing of Dividends," *American Economic Review*, Vol. 76 (June 1986, pp. 499–503).

Vermaelen, Theo. "Common Stock Purchases and Market Signalling: An Empirical Study," *Journal of Financial Economics*, Vol. 1 (June 1981, pp. 139–83).

Watts, Ross. "The Information Content of Dividends," *Journal of Business*, Vol. 48 (April 1973, pp. 191–211).

FINANCIAL THEORY
IN PRACTICE

Whether standing near the cabin high above Zermatt that marks the final ascent to the top of the Matterhorn or resting at the Lake of the Clouds hut before trekking to the top of Mount Washington, climbers and hikers have an opportunity both to survey the landscape and to gain a perspective on where they have been and where they are going. Those who stop at these points along the way know their journey is not completed, yet they enjoy the respite. On a clear day, what one has seen along the way can only be enhanced by the view from the summit.

Likewise, our trek through financial theory is not complete: we have yet to develop several topics. Nevertheless, we have come far enough to take stock of what we have learned and, in particular, to learn whether it is employed by management. We have strongly suggested, along the way, that financial theory is employed. However, if you have become increasingly skeptical of this claim following our discussion of the dividend decision, it is understandable. Because scholars have been curious about whether or not the principles of financial theory have been widely adopted, numerous surveys have been conducted, most surveys focusing on the largest nonfinancial U.S. corporations. Through such firms enormous quantities of real investment dollars flow. These companies often have specialists in capital budgeting and, in addition, they employ consulting firms adept at distilling academic literature to a form readily applied by busy executives.

Of course, surveys all carry with them the risk that those interviewed may tell the researcher, often an academic, what he or she wants to hear. More crucial, a sample based on a population that includes perhaps only the 1,000 largest U.S. corporations may not be representative of American business in general. In addition, corporate management in one industry may be more receptive to some component of the principles of financial theory than corporate management in another industry. For example, the techniques of capital budgeting may be of greater interest to a manufacturer or a public utility than to a retail trade concern, the bulk of whose assets are in inventories and finished goods. These and related problems are usually addressed in the studies conducted. For our purposes, we simply require evidence that theory does in fact influence practice—not that it dominates all decision-making.

THE GOALS OF THE FIRM

Financial theory focuses on the owner. Management presumably strives to maximize wealth of the owners by maximizing market value of company shares. However, is wealth maximization the prime objective toward which management strives? In the surveys conducted, sometimes other objectives seem to be of greater importance. Among them are the following:[1]

1. maximizing return on assets
2. maximizing growth of per-share earnings
3. maximizing return on equity
4. maximizing aggregate dollar earnings
5. maximizing market share

Although these objectives can be measured crudely, whether any one is maximized is a moot point. Yet, management can argue with some credence that by minimizing costs while maximizing sales revenue, it is maximizing total dollar earnings—the classic concept of profit. Given the total assets and the number of shares outstanding, pursuing the preceding objective will maximize the percentage return on assets and earnings per share.

Growth, however, ultimately requires increased assets, which in turn require additional financing. The essence of capital budgeting is to maximize net present value of additional investments and hence the stock's market value. Growth in earnings per share can, of course, be achieved through increased leverage, which may or may not cause market price of the stock to rise. Growth in earnings also can be

---

[1] See, for example, A. Stonehill and I. Nathanson, "Capital Budgeting and the Multinational Corporation," *California Management Review*, Vol. 10 (Summer 1968, pp. 39–54); A. Stonehill et al., "Financial Goals and Debt Ratio Determinants: A Survey of Practice in Five Countries," *Financial Management*, Vol. 2 (Autumn 1973, pp. 27–41); and William Petty II, David F. Scott, Jr., and Monroe M. Bird, "The Capital Expenditure Decision-Making Process of the the Large Corporations," *The Engineering Economist* Vol. 20 (Spring 1975, pp. 159–72). See also David F. Scott, Jr. and J. William Petty II, "Capital Budgeting Practices in Large American Firms: A Retrospective Analysis," *The Financial Review*, Vol. 19 (March 1984, pp. 111–23).

achieved through reinvestment of earnings in projects that raise the unleveraged beta coefficient of the firm, causing market price of the stock to fall rather than rise. Thus, financial theory suggests that management may be focusing on the wrong goal.

Nevertheless, one must keep two points in mind. First, financial managers may use such objectives as operational targets yet still act as though they are pursuing (through capital budgeting procedures) strategies that maximize the stock's market value. Second, the goals cited are from surveys conducted in the late 1960s and mid-1970s. Although the comparison may be crude, in at least one more-recent survey of large multinational corporations there seems to be evidence financial managers are focusing greater attention on policies that maximize market value of the firm's securities, specifically the stock. If true, this objective should become more prominent in future surveys.[2]

CAPITAL BUDGETING IN PRACTICE

In Chapter 8, we developed five possible methods of capital budgeting:

1. internal rate of return
2. net present value
3. profitability index
4. payback period
5. average return on investment

Of the five, only the first three are theoretically correct: they make allowance for the time value of money. All, however, are discounted cash flow (DCF) models. We have consistently argued that the net present value is the preferred technique because it leads to maximization of the market value of shareholder equity. For those who want a convenient way to view present value relative to outlay, profitability index is second, and internal rate of return third.

Profitability index, although using present value of cash flows as the numerator, suffers from the fact ratios are divorced from absolute magnitudes. It is the difference between outlay and present value that adds to stockholder wealth. Internal rate of return suffers from the same problem and, in addition, the implicit assumption that cash flows are reinvested at the internal rate of return is usually incorrect. Finally, the possibility of multiple solutions to the quadratic equation can be a source of confusion. Nevertheless, on an accept-or-reject basis, all DCF techniques yield the

---

[2] Marjorie T. Stanley and Stanley B. Block. "A Survey of Multinational Capital Budgeting," *The Financial Review*, Vol. 19 (March 1984, pp. 36–54).

same result (the problems generally surface when management considers mutually exclusive investment opportunities). Hence, financial economists favor any DCF technique over either payback period or average return on investment.

What about the practice? A recent survey of the literature reveals some interesting results.[3] First, early investigations (circa 1960 and 1961) indicated that as many as 30 percent of firms surveyed used DCF models. Within a decade, the percentage of firms employing DCF models had risen to 57 percent. More recent studies suggest even higher percentages. One set of authors, reporting results of a survey conducted in 1981, found that more than 81 percent of the firms surveyed used either internal rate of return or net present value as the primary technique for budgeting capital.[4] Second, in spite of widespread misgivings in the academic community, internal rate of return is more popular than either net present value or profitability index. Even payback period (average return on investment) is preferred to either. The typical firm surveyed combines internal rate of return with payback period, using each as a criterion for budgeting capital.[5] Indeed, a project may have to satisfy both criteria before funds are committed. However, if two models are to be employed, why not use net present value and payback period? Part—but only part—of the explanation may lie in the fact that only in recent years has net present value received widespread approval over internal rate of return for capital budgeting decisions, even though the former model carries greater weight in the development of economic thought in this area.[6] Perhaps more important is the fact that net present value, when properly implemented, requires a measure of the cost of capital.

---

[3] Same as [1], Scott and Petty, pp. 114–16. Their conclusions are based on these articles in the following sequence: James H. Miller. "A Glimpse at Practice in Calculating and Using Return on Investment," *N.A.A. Bulletin*, now *Management Accounting* (June 1960, pp. 65–76). Donald F. Istvan. *Capital Expenditure Decisions: How They Are Made in Large Corporations* (Bloomington, IN: Bureau of Business Research, Indiana University, 1961). James C. T. Mao. "Survey of Capital Budgeting: Theory and Practice," *Journal of Finance*, Vol. 25 (May 1970, pp. 349–60). Ronald B. Williams, Jr. "Industry Practice in Allocating Capital Resources," *Managerial Planning*, Vol. 18 (May–June 1970, pp. 15–22). Thomas Klammer. "Empirical Evidence of the Adoption of Sophisticated Capital Budgeting Techniques," *Journal of Business*, Vol. 45 (July 1972, pp. 387–97). James Fremgen. "Capital Budgeting Practices: A Survey," *Management Accounting*, Vol. 54 (May 1973, pp. 19–25). Eugene F. Brigham. "Hurdle Rates for Screening Capital Expenditure Proposals," *Financial Management*, Vol. 4 (Autumn 1975, pp. 17–26). Glenn H. Petry. "Effective Use of Capital Budgeting Tools," *Business Horizons*, Vol. 19 (October 1975, pp. 57–65).

Same as [1], Petty, Scott, and Bird, pp. 159–72). Lawrence J. Gitman and John R. Forrester, Jr. "A Survey of Capital Budgeting Techniques Used by Major U.S. Firms," *Financial Management*, Vol. 6 (Fall 1977, pp. 66–71). Lawrence G. Scholl, Gary L. Sundem, and William R. Geijsbeck, Jr. "Survey and Analysis of Capital Budgeting Methods," *Journal of Finance*, Vol. 33 (March 1978, pp. 281–87).

[4] Same as [2], p. 46.

[5] Same as [1], Scott and Petty, p. 115.

[6] One can contrast the strong preference for internal rate of return in A. J. Merrett and Allen Sykes, *The Finance and Analysis of Capital Projects*, 2nd ed. (New York: Wiley and Sons, 1973, pp. 120–42) with the rationale for the net present value approach in Harold Bierman, Jr. and Seymour Smidt, *The Capital Budgeting Decision Economic Analysis of Investment Projects* (New York: Macmillan, 1984, pp. 52–79). In the modern era, the topic of capital budgeting was first popularized by Joel Dean, *Capital Budgeting* (New York: Columbia University Press, 1951) but treated more extensively and by the standards of the time more formidably in Friedrich and Vera Luiz, *The Theory of Investment of the Firm* (Princeton, NJ: Princeton University Press, 1951). See also, Ward S. Curran, *Principles of Financial Management* (New York: McGraw-Hill, 1970, pp. 89–116).

NET PRESENT VALUE AND THE COST OF CAPITAL

Although the internal rate of return should be compared with the cost of capital before a project is accepted or rejected, the calculations can be effected independently as a staff function. At higher levels, management can accept or reject a project using whatever cutoff rate it chooses. The cutoff rate, often called the **hurdle rate**, may or may not be the cost of capital; moreover, it may vary with the investment—riskier projects held to higher internal rates of return. If net present value is employed, the cutoff rate or rates must be applied at staff levels. Top-level management, however, may choose to make that judgment and would therefore favor the internal rate of return.

Should management use different hurdle rates? We have analyzed the controversy and concluded that each firm should use the weighted average cost of new capital for all projects, even though each individual project may have its own holding period return or its own *cost of capital* in a diversified portfolio.[7] Without belaboring the point and at the risk of oversimplification, we conclude the weighted average cost of new capital is the appropriate rate of return because a project that meets this criteria has a positive net present value. In turn, positive net present value increases market value of the firm's shares—which, we have argued, should be management's objective. The portfolio decision remains in the hands of the individual stockholder. Although there is no obligation to act as though shareholders own diversified portfolios, management may consider the impact of a project on the unleveraged beta coefficient and hence on the cost of equity capital if adopted.

Again, what is the practice? Surveys focusing on capital budgeting techniques have lacked, somewhat curiously, detailed analysis of cost of capital. Although many surveys have found that weighted average cost of capital is popular, they are not always clear as to the weighting schemes employed. Moreover, many firms appear to use costs of specific funding sources, past experience, and management-determined target rates of return.[8] To date, studies that focus on determining the cost of capital in practice are relatively rare; hence, generalizations based on such results must be carefully qualified.[9] A survey of Fortune 1000 firms offered some interesting

---

[7] Some controversy exists as to whether one uses k_d or $k_d (1 - t_c)$ as the cost of the debt component, the argument against the latter being that all tax savings are incorporated in k'_c. See, for example, Fred D. Arditti and Haim Levy, "The Weighted Average Cost of Capital Cutoff Rate: A Critical Analysis of the Classical Textbook Weighted Average," *Financial Management*, Vol. 6 (Fall 1977, pp. 24–34). In defense of our approach, see Glenn V. Henderson, Jr., "In Defense of the Weighted Average Cost of Capital," *Financial Management*, Vol. 8 (Autumn 1979, pp. 57–61).

[8] Same as [1], Scott and Petty, pp. 44–46).

[9] See, for example, Lawrence J. Gitman and Vincent A. Mercurio, "Cost of Capital Techniques Used by Major U.S. Firms: Survey and Analysis of Fortune's 1000," *Financial Management*, Vol. 11 (Winter 1982, pp. 21–29). See, also, Eugene F. Brigham, "Hurdle Rates for Screening Capital Expenditure Proposals," *Financial Management*, Vol. 4 (Autumn 1975, pp. 17–26).

results.[10] Although responses leaned toward the top 300 firms and were heavily weighted with manufacturing concerns, respondents tended to use either some target ratio of debt to total capital or market value weights for each capital structure component. A few employed value weights and some used the cost of specific fund sources to finance a particular project as the cost of capital. With respect to specific funding sources two-thirds of respondents used current market-value based costs of debt and preferred shares; the remainder used historical costs.

More than 33 percent of respondents recognized that cost of equity was the return required by investors. Approximately 26 percent of respondents estimated equity return by employing the $\frac{D}{P} + g$ model developed earlier. Others attempted to employ a risk-adjusted market return and a few used the current cost of debt plus a premium for equity. Formal use of the Capital Asset Pricing Model for determining cost of capital and for capital budgeting was reported by approximately 22 percent of respondents. Unfortunately, nearly 17 percent of respondents based cost of equity capital solely on $\frac{D}{P}$ or $\frac{E}{P}$. Once estimated, however, the cost of capital was used by nearly all respondents in the evaluation of new projects.

It appears, therefore, the theoretical techniques with which we are concerned have made some inroads into financial practice. Acceptance, however, is far from universal. Any reliance by firms on such misconstrued measures of equity costs as $\frac{D}{P}$ or $\frac{E}{P}$ without considering growth or their failure to use DCF models is unfortunate. Is the lack of universal acceptance due to the failure of academics to communicate financial theory to practitioners or are there other reasons?

RISK IN FINANCIAL THEORY AND PRACTICE

Although financial theory has made several contributions to the problem of risk—for example, the concept of covariance—to date our analysis suggests that at the project level, making forecasts of expected cash flows and variability about them is fraught with difficulty. The impact of inflation on both revenues and expenses is difficult to estimate. Moreover, changes in inflationary expectations can alter the nominal returns that security holders expect, which alters the cost of capital over the life of the project. Most important perhaps is the question: To what extent are expected cash flows correlated through time?

Techniques for dealing with such problems continue to occupy the minds of academicians; nevertheless, to be adopted they must be shown to add significantly to

---

[10] Gitman and Mercurio, pp. 21–29).

the ability of management to make decisions where actual outcomes are more consonant with forecasts. To the extent refinements of the measurement process are unproductive, they are not adopted.[11] Consequently, even though the concept of discounted cash flows is now widely employed by practitioners, sophisticated techniques for risk-adjusting are apparently less popular. Employing a required rate of return in excess of cost of capital and using a payback criteria are far more popular approaches to risk than simulation, probabilistic analysis of possible cash flows, and even crude sensitivity analysis where one changes a key assumption (such as a shift in demand or net cash flows) and calculates the new result. No probabilities are attached to the outcome, but a wide range of possible outcomes may affect the decision to invest or not to invest.[12]

INSTITUTIONAL CONSTRAINTS

A broad array of institutional constraints within a company also may affect adoption of several principles of modern finance.[13] To the extent capital budgeting is a staff function, those performing the task may not fully comprehend the techniques involved. Training, of course, can overcome this deficiency. More difficult is the case when capital is rationed, as it often is: lower level managers may scramble to get their projects adopted, tend to emphasize project strengths, and fail to raise important questions concerning key factors and assumptions. In effect, top management diffuses its decision-making role by allowing the investment process to oversimplify the information it reviews.[14] Consequently, even when top management is well-schooled in techniques, it must force lower levels to employ them and to spell out the assumptions on which the information is based. Clearly, top management has the clout to do this.

But will it? Top corporate executives tend to be compensated for increasing total earnings, improving earnings per share, and raising returns on existing investment (ROI). Such incentives often lead to short-run profit maximization and occasionally to the neglect of new technology and of the investment that accompanies it. Moreover, short payback periods (two to three years) may constrain investments with potentially higher net present values but that fail to meet such criteria. Meanwhile, if profits rise for a period, executive bonuses also increase. Should the company begin to falter, the chief executive officer (CEO) can bail out in

[11] See, for example, James S. Ang and Wilbur C. Lewellen, "Risk Adjustment in Capital Investment Project Evaluations," *Financial Management*, Vol. 11 (Summmer 1982, pp. 5–14).

[12] Same as [1], Scott and Petty, pp. 117–19. Same as [9], Gitman and Mercurio, p. 27. Same as [2], p. 46.

[13] See, for example, K. Larry Hastie, "One Businessman's View of Capital Budgeting," *Financial Management*, Vol. 3 (Winter 1974, pp. 36–44).

[14] Hastie, p. 44. See, also, Stephen W. Pruitt and Lawrence J. Gitman, "Capital Budgeting Forecast Biases: Evidence from the Fortune 500," *Financial Management*, Vol. 16 (Spring, 1987, pp. 46–51).

his golden parachute of severance compensation to early retirement or to seek out another concern and repeat the process.

To some, this preoccupation with the short run has helped, over time, to erode America's technological leadership in favor of countries where executives appear to have a longer-term perspective.[15] There may be some validity to this argument: rewards for short-term performance may not necessarily be in the long-term interests of either the stockholders or the nation. However, one can be wrong about the source of the difficulties. Some argue that as discounted cash-flow techniques

> have gained ever wider use in decision making, the growth of capital investment and R & D spending in this country has slowed.... We submit that the discounting approach has contributed to a decreased willingness to invest for two reasons: (1) it is often based on misperceptions of the past and present economic environment, and (2) it is biased against investment because of critical errors in the way the theory is applied. Bluntly stated, the willingness of management to view the future through the reversed telescope of discounted cash flow is seriously shortchanging the futures of their companies.[16]

Although the authors emphasize misuse rather than use of discounted cash flows, it is difficult enough for scholars to measure the contribution of investment to productivity and ultimately to economic growth without attempting to link changes to adoption or nonadoption of specific techniques of capital budgeting.[17]

In addition, if correctly applied, DCF techniques are designed to take into account expected cash flows over the useful life of the project. However, misapplication is always possible. Payback periods may prevail over DCF and management may not take the risks that some believe they should. Nevertheless, one should not blame the techniques; rather, one should look more deeply into the nature of the modern corporation and its system of incentives.

From our perspective, the limited information available suggests that top management is aware of the principles of modern financial theory as they apply to company investment and financing. Actually, in many cases these principles are applied to a degree unknown two decades ago. As knowledge of this area grows, particularly as it is packaged in a readily applicable form, new generations of managers (most of them schooled in these techniques) will make even better use of the principles of modern financial theory. Of course, adapting theory to practice is

---

[15] Robert H. Hayes and William J. Abernathy. "Managing Our Way to Economic Decline," *Harvard Business Review*, Vol. 58 (July–August 1980, pp. 67–77).

[16] Robert H. Hayes and David A. Garvin. "Managing as if Tomorrow Mattered: Investment Decisions that Discount the Future May Result in High Present Values but Bleak Tomorrows," *Harvard Business Review*, Vol. 60 (May–June 1982, pp. 71–72).

[17] See, for example, John W. Kendrick, "Productivity and Economic Growth," The *AEI Economist* (November 1980, pp. 1–12). See, also, Edward F. Denison, *Accounting for United States Economic Growth 1948–1969* (Washington, D.C.: Brookings Institution, 1974) and *Accounting for Slower Economic Growth* (Washington, D.C.: Brookings Institution, 1979).

an art, not a science. Just as two people viewing the same painting may react differently to it, so two people reading the same body of literature on the application of modern financial theory may reach different conclusions about its success to date.

APPLYING FINANCIAL THEORY—THE CASE OF THE DEXTER CORPORATION

One can gain insight both as to the progress made in applying financial theory to practice and in the difficulties involved in doing so by examining how a company familiar with the principles of modern finance actually employs them. Such a company is Dexter Corporation of Windsor Locks, Connecticut. Dexter operates 40 plants in more than eight countries and is the oldest company listed on the New York Stock Exchange. As noted in Chapter 11, in 1986 Dexter was among the 500 largest industrial corporations. Sales in excess of $650 million placed it 396th and book value of nearly $566 million made it 391st in assets. In terms of total return to investors, however, in 1986 Dexter ranked 126th. For the ten-year period 1976–1986, its geometric average of total returns to investors was 17.18 percent, ranking it 175th of 500.[18]

Although classified by the Commerce Department as a manufacturer of chemicals and allied products [Standard Industrial Classification (SIC) 28], its four business groups are:

1. *Coatings and Encapsulants*   Range from food and beverage container coatings to encapsulants for semiconductors.

2. *Life Science Group*   Produces tissue cultures, microbiological media, and other biological products and laboratory materials widely used in virus and cancer research.

3. *Nonwoven Group*   Employs a modified paper-making process for the production of high-strength, porous, and absorbent nonwoven materials for use as filters. Also produces paper for such diverse items as tea bags and surgical masks.

4. *Water Treatment Group*   Production centers on chemical compounds used to prevent corrosion and microbiological fouling of water-supply systems, steam-generating plants, and air-conditioning equipment. Also produces line of sanitizing, cleaning, and building-maintenance chemicals.

Dexter's management is acutely aware of the principles of modern financial theory and has attempted to apply them to the company. For example, discounted cash

---

[18] *Fortune*, Vol. 115 (April 27, 1987, pp. 378–79. Total return includes both price appreciation and dividend yield to an investor in the company's stock, assuming a calendar-year holding period and assuming reinvestment of cash dividends at the end of the year.

flows are an integral part of Dexter's capital budgeting procedures. Both internal rate of return and net present value have been used (the former preferred in actual practice). Although book-value rather than market-value weights are used to estimate the average cost of capital, they are applied to the current costs of both new debt and equity. However, Dexter's management has yet to apply simulation techniques to capital budgeting. Instead, it holds projects to a six-year payback period and to a hurdle rate equal to the measured average cost of capital plus 2 percent.

Nevertheless, Dexter's top management attempts to apply a modified version of the Modigliani and Miller valuation model to its operations by separating the firm's market value into its component parts and giving particular emphasis to the growth component.[19] In doing so, it targets the capital budget with a view toward maintaining a relatively constant debt ratio of 25 to 30 percent of book value and a payout ratio of about 30 to 35 percent of earnings.[20] What management appears to have established is a capital expenditures pattern that includes acquisitions designed to maximize $r - k_o$[21] but that appears to be circumscribed by a target debt ratio, the desire to maintain the dividend (once established), and a reluctance to issue new common stock.[22]

CAPITAL BUDGETING IN THE DEXTER CORPORATION—A CASE ILLUSTRATION

Early in 1979, Dexter Corporation management was considering an outlay to return to service a 1,000-kilowatt turbogenerator that had been idle for some time. Electricity costs had reached a point where it appeared feasible to buy a back-pressure turbine to operate the generator. The expected outlay, including repair work on the generator, was $252,876. In calculating electricity savings, they assumed the generator would operate at 97.5 percent of its 24-hour-a-day capacity for 337 days. Each kilowatt hour of electricity generated would result in a savings of .0307 cents. Annually, total savings were expected to be 1,000kw × .975 × 337 × 24 × $.0307 = $242,094. However, generating the electricity required an additional 4,328 BTUs (British Thermal Units) at an estimated cost of $3.51 per 1,000 BTU

---

[19] Worth Loomis. "Strategic Planning in Uncertain Times," *Chief Executive*, Vol. 14 (Winter 1980–81, pp. 7–12).

[20] *1984 Annual Report of the Dexter Corporation*, p. 17. Subsequent annual reports suggest adherence to these objectives.

[21] Same as [19], pp. 7–12.

[22] At the end of 1984, Dexter had 400,000 shares of preferred stock authorized, none of which were outstanding. Of the 30,000,000 shares of common stock authorized, approximately 15,449,000 shares were outstanding. Adjusted for stock splits, there were 14,980,000 shares outstanding at the end of 1984. See *1984 Annual Report of the Dexter Corporation*, pp. 18, 19, and 32–33. Bear in mind that because of the costs of flotation, the cost of new equity, however measured, is more expensive than retained earnings.

($.00351 per BTU). Annually, the additional expenses were expected to be

$$4,328 \times 337 \times 24 \times \frac{\$3.51}{1,000} = \$122,867$$

Consequently, Dexter anticipated a net savings before taxes of

gross savings	= \$242,094
additional costs	= −122,867
net savings before taxes	= \$119,227

With straight-line depreciation and an estimated useful life of 16 years, the annual depreciation allowance would be $252,876 \div 16 = \$15,804.75$. When we employ a marginal tax rate of 50 percent, which approximated Dexter's tax status at the time, the expected increase in operating profits from this cost-saving innovation would be $(\$119,227 − \$15,805)(1 − .5) = \$51,711$. However, Dexter began the project in 1979, claiming only one-half the first year's depreciation and deferring the remainder until the last year of the project. Thus, estimated operating profits for those two years (the first and last) would be $(\$119,227 − \$7902) \times (1 − .5) = \$55,662$.

With an estimated current cost of capital of 16 percent plus 2 percent (or 18 percent as the hurdle), the net present value of the expected cash flows as shown in Table 12-1 is $158,949,78. The internal rate of return is 35.38 percent. The payback period of 3.8 years is calculated as follows:

Year	Cash Flow	
		$252,876 outlay
1979	$ 63,564	− 198,596 cashflow
1980	67,516	$ 54,280
1981	67,516	
	$198,596	$\dfrac{\$54,280}{\$67,516} = 0.8$ year

Because $198,596 has been received from 1979 through 1981 and because it will require 0.8 of 1982 to return the remainder of the outlay from cash flows for 1982, the payback period is $3 + 0.8 = 3.8$ years.

Although several technical questions can be raised, we have chosen to include them in the problems and questions at the end of the chapter. At this juncture, we need only note that the project met the criteria and was accepted.

Dexter monitors performance of its capital expenditures to determine whether a project meets expectations and (in some cases) to decide whether to continue or to abandon it. In addition, monitoring performance is a learning experience: when mistakes are made, perhaps steps can be taken to avoid similar pitfalls in the future.

Table 12-1   Retrofitting a Turbogenerator—A Capital Budget

Year	Outlay	Net Operating Profit (after taxes)	Depreciation	Net Cash Flows
1979	−$252,876 +	$55,662 +	$ 7902	−$189.312
1980		51,711	15,805	67,516
1981		51,711	15,805	67,516
1982		51,711	15,805	67,516
1983		51,711	15,805	67,516
1984		51,711	15,805	67,516
1985		51,711	15,805	67,516
1986		51,711	15,805	67,516
1987		51,711	15,805	67,516
1988		51,711	15,805	67,516
1989		51,711	15,805	67,516
1990		51,711	15,805	67,516
1991		51,711	15,805	67,516
1992		51,711	15,805	67,516
1993		51,711	15,805	67,516
1994		51,711	15,805	67,516
1995		55,662	7902	63,564

$$NPV = -\$189,312 + \$67,516 \frac{[1 - (1.18)^{-15}]}{.18} + \frac{\$63,564}{(1.18)^{16}} = \$158,949.78$$

$$\$189,312 = \$67,516 \frac{[1 - (1 + r)^{-15}]}{r} + \frac{\$63,564}{(1 + r)^{16}} = 35.38\%$$

Payback period $= 3.8$ years

In this particular instance, results were far from expectations. Due to unforeseen problems in refurbishing the existing generator, actual outlay soared to $426,000, a 68.5 percent increase over estimates. Since textbook examples of capital expenditure decisions tend to focus on the uncertainty associated with future cash flows, the novice is sometimes left with the feeling that estimated outlay is virtually certain. Experience suggests otherwise. The obvious question for management is: Could the estimate have been more accurate without actually initiating the project? To phrase it differently: What would the costs (real and opportunity) be to ensure that the initial estimate was virtually certain? In hindsight, a more detailed analysis of costs associated with bringing idled equipment on line would have been justified.

Perhaps less surprising was the fact actual cash flows in the project's early years differed markedly from expectations. Once operational, demand for the plant's output (paper) declined. Given the cyclical nature of the paper business, this decline might have been anticipated. However, by mid-1983 it appeared as though even under improved economic conditions the assumption the generator would function 24 hours a day for 337 days was overly optimistic and additional work was required to improve performance. Moreover, between 1979 and 1983, fuel and power costs rose rapidly, although the latter had declined somewhat from 1982 peaks. For example

	Electricity (per 1,000 kw)	*Fuel (per 1,000 BTUs)*
1st Quarter 1982	$70.0	$5.85
2nd Quarter 1982	64.4	6.23
January–June 1983	52.4	6.25
Budget Assumptions	$30.7 = .037 \times 1,000$	3.51

In light of the firm's experience, management decided to redo the computations under the assumption that the outlay was made in 1983. Expected after-tax cash flows were recalculated using current costs of fuel and electricity and under the assumption the generator would operate at 90-percent capacity, or 21.6 kwh per day ($.9 \times 24$). Moreover, taking advantage of the investment tax credit and the accelerated cost-recovery scheme enacted in 1981 but no longer available (see Chapter 8 for greater detail), management assumed a useful life of approximately ten years. The results yielded operating profits of $54,150 after taxes, assuming a 50-percent tax rate. The cash flows actually employed in the calculations are shown in Table 12-2.

The cost of new capital in 1983 was 13.5 percent. Adding 2 percent to this figure yields a hurdle rate of 15.5 percent. Under these assumptions, net present value was $72,085.87 and internal rate of return 21.97 percent.[23] Although still profitable under assumptions made at the time, the project is closer to being a marginal investment than initial projections indicated.

Again, the reader is invited to undertake the problems and questions at the end of the chapter so as to probe more deeply into certain of the technical issues the example raises. A case study serves to illustrate problems involved in applying discounted cash-flow techniques to capital budgeting and also points to the need for developing accurate information. In this instance, management must ask: Could the

---

[23] In practice, the company uses continuous discounting to calculate internal rate of return. Moreover, it was assumed the project would have been operational July 1, 1983. The company discounted on the basis of 10.5 years. Continuous discounting and an additional half year yielded an internal rate of return of 19.9 percent. To simplify the exposition, we use annual discounting and assume 10 rather than 10.5 years.

Table 12-2   Retrofitting a Turbogenerator—Reexamination of a Capital Budget

Year	Outlay	Net Operating Profit (after taxes)	Accelerated Capital Cost Recovery	Investment Tax Credit	Net Cash Flows
1983	− $426,000 +	$54,150 +	$18,637 +	$42,600	− $310,613
1984		54,150	35,499		89,649
1985		54,150	31,950		86,100
1986		54,150	28,401		82,551
1987		54,150	24,849		78,999
1988		54,150	21,300		75,450
1989		54,150	17,751		71,901
1990		54,150	14,199		68,349
1991		54,150	10,650		64,800
1992		54,150	7,101		61,251
1993		54,150	2,662		56,812

Internal rate of return = 21.97%

Net present value = $72,085.86

Payback period = 4.66 years

cost overrun have been anticipated in advance? Moreover, were there sufficient reasons at the time for management to question whether the generator would actually operate at 97.5 percent of its 1,000 kw capacity 24 hours a day for 337 days of the year? Finally, could management have anticipated the changes in the costs of electricity and fuel? The answer to the last question is no. However, at the time prudent management might have made assumptions about changes in such costs so as to understand more fully their potential impact on net cash flows (see problem 3).

The answer to the second question depends in part on whether assumptions about plant use were consistent with historical experience and whether or not something was overlooked in the technical design that underlay the project.

Finally, the answer to the first question depends on whether the technical staff could have probed more deeply into the feasibility of refurbishing the generator without actually initiating the project.

Whatever the answers, management learns from the experience. Although this particular project was small relative to the nearly $29.5 million in capital expenditures for 1979, Dexter's management, seeking to improve its performance in this area, continues to learn from postaudits of this and other investments.

DEXTER'S WEIGHTED AVERAGE COST OF NEW CAPITAL

In its annual report, Dexter publishes the estimated average cost of capital targeted for the year and the actual results. Thus, in its 1983 annual report Dexter reported[24]

	Annual Target **($ millions)**				**Result** **($ millions)**		
Estimated Cost	1984	1983	1982	1981	1983	1982	1981
of New Capital	14%	13+%	15+%	15+%	14%	14%	15%

To understand how the target is computed, one must first know the proportion of capital budget financed from debt. As a continuing target, Dexter maintains a debt-to-equity ratio of between 25 and 30 percent based on book value. In 1983, book value of long-term debt was $66,702,000 and total book value of equity was $186,118,000.[25] Hence

$$\text{debt-to-equity ratio} = \frac{\$66,702,000}{\$66,702,000 + \$186,118,000} + 26.4\%$$

The preceding year, the debt-to-equity ratio was 25 percent. Since recent results placed the debt ratio near the lower end of its target, in 1983 management chose to finance 35 percent of its capital budget from debt and 65 percent from equity.[26]

Using outside consultants who employed a variation of CAPM, management learned Dexter's beta coefficient was .92. For 1983, the cost of new equity was estimated to be

$$k'_e = i + .92\,(R_m - i)$$
$$k'_e = .1145 + .92\,(.059)$$
$$k'_e = .1688 \times 100 = 16.88\%$$

---

[24] *1983 Annual Report of the Dexter Corporation*, p. 17. The annual target for 1981 is from the *1980 Annual Report of the Dexter Corporation*, p. 19.

[25] Book value of equity equals

common stock (par value $1) = $	15,439,000
additional paid-in capital =	14,275,000
retained earnings =	175,098,000
currency exchange effects =	− 18,694,000
	$ 186,118,000

Because Dexter operates plants in several countries, the effects of changes in financial statements of those subsidiaries plus gains or losses on currency and related tax effects are charged directly to stockholders' equity. See *1983 Annual Report of the Dexter Corporation*, pp. 21 and 32.

[26] Use of financial targets are widespread. See David F. Scott, Jr. and Dana J. Johnson, "Financing Policies and Practices of Large Corporations," *Financial Management*, Vol. 11 (Summer 1982, pp. 51–59).

With CAPM, the primary difference between k'_e calculated for Dexter and k'_e outlined in this text is the figure for risk-free rate. We employ the yield on short-term Treasury bills. As calculated for Dexter, risk-free rate is the yield on long-term U.S. Government bond issues (2008–2013). R_m, however, is the holding period return on the S & P 500. Given its "A" credit rating at the time, Dexter's long-term borrowing rate was estimated at 12.27 percent.

In 1980, Dexter Corporation had an average tax rate of 49 percent. Subsequent changes in tax law decreased the rate to 44.5 percent in 1982 and 42.3 percent in 1983. Nevertheless, in estimating the marginal tax rate in 1983, outside consultants employed a figure of 48 percent. Hence[27]

$$k_d = .1227 (1 - .48)$$
$$= .0638 = 6.38\%$$
$$k_o = .35 (.0638) + .65 (.1688)$$
$$= .0223 + .1097$$
$$= .1320$$
$$= 13.20 (13.2\%)$$

Subsequent revisions and actual borrowing brought the weighted average cost of capital to 14 percent for the year. Thus, while one might dicker over such details as the proxy for the risk-free rate and the use of 48 percent rather than 44 or 46 percent as the marginal tax rate, it is clear that companywide the cost of new capital is based on methodology consistent with the principles of modern financial theory.

Although Dexter's management targets its debt ratios in terms of book value, we shall see it also uses an estimated market value of its debt, all of which has been placed privately with institutional investors. Of course, more important is the fact the book value of new debt equals the market value at the time the debt is placed. In perfect markets, institutional investors desire returns similar to what they could earn in the market on debt of comparable quality.[28] It is worth emphasizing again that the average cost of new capital is the current (marginal) cost of capital. Costs of individual sources are market determined; management's primary input is the weight it uses for each source.[29] At Dexter, such weights are determined with a view toward maintaining a continuing target, which in turn is related to its credit status and ultimately to the cost of new debt capital.[30]

---

[27] Based on a memorandum to Mr. Worth Loomis, President, dated September 27, 1983. The cost of capital, therefore, reflects an estimate to that date. Average tax rates paid are given in the *1983 Annual Report of the Dexter Corporation*, pp. 18 and 19.

[28] Certain savings on flotation costs may accrue to the company from placing debt privately rather than through a public offering. We discuss this issue in Chapter 17.

[29] Management has some control over its marginal tax rate: investment and acquisition policies can have an impact on taxes paid. Even so, management is reacting to policy determined elsewhere—specifically, in Congress.

[30] Based on external evaluation, Dexter's debt-to-total-capital ratio warranted an "AA" rating. As noted earlier, it is the total size of the company that decreases its overall rating to "A." "Dexter Corporation Bond Rating Summary" (S & P, September 26, 1983).

APPLYING THE M & M VALUATION MODEL TO THE DEXTER CORPORATION

Dexter's top management is also concerned about how the market perceives its investment and financing decisions. Consequently, Dexter has used the M & M valuation model to shed some light on the components of its market value. Recall that

$$V_f = \frac{EAT}{k_e} + T_c D + K(EAT)\left[\frac{r - k_o}{k_o(1 + k_o)}\right] N$$

To implement the model, management needed a value for k_e. To calculate k_e using the analysis developed in Chapter 10, we use Equation 10-10, so that

$$k_o = k_e\left(1 - T_c \frac{D}{D + E}\right)$$

Hence

$$k_e = \frac{k_o}{\left(1 - T_c \frac{D}{D + E}\right)}$$

Employing the appropriate figures for Dexter, we obtain

$$k_e = \frac{.132}{1 - .48(.35)}$$
$$k_e = 15.87\% (16.0\%)$$

In the absence of growth and with an all-equity capital structure assumption, depreciation and other noncash expenses would be reinvested in the firm at k_e. Thus, EAT becomes after-tax cash flows from operations (exclusive of the tax subsidy because of interest), which is consistent with the M & M model. For 1983, Dexter estimated this figure to be $35.3 million.

The second term in the equation is based on an average tax rate rounded to the nearest tenth: .5 times book value of debt outstanding ($66.7 million in 1983).

The third term in the equation is the proportion of EAT that can be invested for N years at $r - k_o$. If new financing is required, the proportion K would be greater than one. Of course, management thinks in terms of absolute dollars. In 1983, expenditures for plant and equipment (including working capital and new acquisitions) were $40 million, all of which was financed from debt and retained earnings.[31]

---

[31] In 1983, net working capital actually fell as some cash and marketable securities were liquidated to help finance acquisitions. See *1983 Annual Report of the Dexter Corporation*, p. 29.

Thus, the cost of new common-stock capital did not have to be included in k_o. Management estimated its total budget would average a 20-percent return. But, for how long?

At the end of 1983, the market price of Dexter's stock was $22 per share. There were approximately 15.4 million shares outstanding (a total of $339 million). Although book value of Dexter's debt was $66.7 million, imbedded interest cost was below the current cost of debt capital. Thus, market value was less than book value. Using the actual cost of existing debt, management estimated market value to be $47 million. Dexter's estimated total value in 1983 was, therefore, $386 million ($339 million + $47 million). Management could then solve for N, so that

$$\$386 = \frac{\$35.3}{.16} + .5(\$66.7) + \$40\left[\frac{(.20 - .13)}{.13(1.13)}\right]N$$

$$\$386 = \$220 + \$33 + 19N$$

$$19N = \$133$$

$$N = 7 \text{ years}$$

In public presentations, management emphasizes its approach suggests an *apparent* application of the M & M model. Even if numbers were altered, it is doubtful the relative magnitudes would change a great deal. As with most corporations, the bulk of Dexter's market value lies in reinvesting its cash flows from operations at k_e. Although leverage adds to market value, in terms of the foregoing calculations, this term represents only about 9 percent of the firm's total value. Consequently, the key to increasing value is growth coupled with the length of time over which the market believes the firm can continue to invest at $r - k_o > 0$.

With respect to increasing value, Dexter's capital expenditure program (including acquisitions) is designed to discover opportunities where growth is most promising—that is, to continue widening $r - k_o$. Just as important, Dexter seeks to terminate existing investments where $r < k_o$.[32] Clearly, management must always bear in mind that changing the composition of its assets will affect β_{ju} and k'_e and, therefore, k_o.

With respect to n, management is interested in the market's perception of its ability to sustain expected levels of growth. In the late 1960s, consistent calculations over several years suggested a value for n of approximately ten. By the late 1970s, n had declined to five; by 1983 (as the computations suggest), it was seven—and has stayed at approximately seven throughout the mid-1980s. Management can only react to market forces; however, by employing the M & M valuation model, it can gain some insight into the components of the total value investors place on the firm.

---

[32] Same as [27].

SUMMARY

In this chapter, we have paused to seek answers to the question: Are the principles of financial theory, as they apply to the firm, being employed in practice? In short: Is anyone out there listening? The answer is yes. There is evidence that much of what this text concerns is being heard and implemented by those who must make the decisions: DCF techniques are widely used in capital budgeting. To the extent the experience of Dexter Corporation represents a growing interest in sophisticated measures of cost of capital and firm valuation, it suggests that practitioners listen, learn, and employ such concepts.

To be sure, much remains to be done. The approach to risk measurement is still crude—payback period and hurdle rates in excess of the cost of new capital are commonly employed—and academics are not unified on the appropriate treatment of risk. Simulation, decision trees, and sensitivity analysis all have a place; however, from the practitioner's viewpoint, do they yield better results than the crude but more easily applied measures generally employed? Until the benefits of the more sophisticated techniques exceed their costs, payback period and other rules of thumb will continue to be employed as supplemental measures.

Meanwhile, some in the academic community argue that DCF emphasizes the short run over the long run, ultimately to the detriment of the nation's future. Yet, this places too heavy a burden on the techniques themselves, rather than on their misapplication or, more importantly, on deeper forces that may have affected attitudes toward the future. "Men at some time are masters of their fates. The fault, dear Brutus, is not in our stars, But in ourselves . . ."[33]

PROBLEMS AND QUESTIONS

1. Examine the data in Table 12-1.
   a. Assuming the outlay was made at the beginning of 1979, are net present value and internal rate of return correctly calculated? If so, why? If not, recalculate both. Would the payback period be affected? Why? Why not?
   b. Suppose the turbogenerator was not operational until January 1, 1980. What would the internal rate of return and net present value be? Would the payback period be affected? Why? Why not?

2. In 1979, the investment tax credit for a new asset with a useful life of seven years or more was 10 percent. Why would Dexter Corporation management *not* want to

---

[33] William Shakespeare, *Julius Caesar*, Act I, Scene II, 139–41, *Shakespeare: The Complete Works*, G. B. Harrison, ed. (New York: Harcourt, Brace, 1952, p. 818).

consider the 10-percent investment tax credit when initially calculating the expected return on investment?

3. In 1979, suppose management had anticipated increases in the price of both electricity (budgeted at .0307 per kwh) and fuel (budgeted at $3.57 per 1,000 BTU). Explain what would happen to projected net cash flows before taxes and depreciation allowances if:
   a. both the cost of electricity and fuel doubled
   b. the cost of electricity doubled but the cost of fuel rose 2.5 times
   c. the cost of electricity increased 1.5 times but the cost of fuel rose 2.5 times
   d. the cost of electricity increased 1.5 times and the cost of fuel doubled

4. In 1989, suppose the leveraged beta coefficient for Dexter Corporation decreased to .75 and the risk-free rate rose to 12 percent. $R_m - i$, however, remained at .059. The cost of new debt capital rose to 13 percent and the corporate tax rate fell to 34 percent.
   a. Calculate k'_e.
   b. Calculate the weighted average cost of capital if debt is 30 percent and equity 70 percent of new funding.
   c. Calculate k_e.
   d. Compare these results with those estimated for 1983.

5. Suppose that in financing past acquisitions, Dexter Corporation could have employed $100 million instead of $66.7 million worth of debt without disturbing its credit rating and hence its current cost of debt or equity. Suppose further that in doing so, no new shares would have been issued.
   a. Should market price of the stock have been higher than $22 at the end of 1983? Explain.
   b. Given the relative importance investors appear to attach to the components of total value, does the debt decision materially impact that value? Explain.

6. From using the M & M valuation model, in 1983 Dexter Corporation learned that investors do not expect sustained growth rates of $r - k_o$ for more than seven years. Indeed, calculations for some earlier years showed n to be lower. Assuming a five-to-seven-year time frame continued throughout the 1980s, is this consistent with Dexter's approach to capital expenditure decisions as outlined in the chapter? Do you recommend revisions in their procedures? Explain.

7. In 1986, the president of Dexter Corporation was given the following information:

risk-free rate	= 9.25%
beta coefficient	= .92
return on market portfolio	= 15.15%
corporate tax rate	= 48%
current cost of debt capital	= 10.14%

a. Using CAPM, calculate the cost of leveraged equity.

b. Calculate the after-tax cost of debt capital.

c. Assuming the ratio of debt-to-total capital is 0.3, calculate the weighted average cost of capital.

d. Calculate the cost of unleveraged equity.

SELECTED ADDITIONAL REFERENCES

Ang, James S. and Wilbur G. Lewellen. "Risk Adjustment in Capital Investment Project Evaluation," *Financial Management*, Vol. 11 (Summer 1982, pp. 5–14).

Arditti, Fred D. and Haim Levy. "The Weighted Average Cost of Capital as a Cutoff Rate: A Critical Analysis of the Classical Textbook Weighted Average," *Financial Management*, Vol. 6 (Fall 1977, pp. 24–34).

Brerman, Harold, Jr. and Seymour Smidt. *The Capital Budgeting Decision Economic Analysis of Investment Projects*, 6th ed. (New York: Macmillan, 1984).

Brigham, Eugene F. "Hurdle Rates for Screening Capital Expenditure Proposals," *Financial Management*, Vol. 4 (Autumn 1975, pp. 17–26).

Curran, Ward S. *Principles of Financial Management* (New York: McGraw-Hill, 1970, pp. 89–116).

Dean, Joel. *Capital Budgeting* (New York: Columbia University Press, 1951).

Fremgen, James. "Capital Budgeting Practices: A Survey," *Management Accounting*, Vol. 54 (May 1973, pp. 19–25).

Gitman, Lawrence J. and John R. Forrester, Jr. "A Survey of Capital Budgeting Techniques Used by Major U.S. Firms," *Financial Management*, Vol. 6 (Fall 1977, pp. 66–71).

Gitman, Lawrence J. and Vincent A. Mercurio. "Cost of Capital Techniques Used by Major U.S. Firms: Survey and Analysis of Fortune's 1000," *Financial Management*, Vol. 11 (Winter 1982, pp. 21–29).

Hayes, Robert and William J. Abernathy. "Managing Our Way to Economic Decline," *Harvard Business Review*, Vol. 58 (July–August 1980, pp. 67–77).

Hayes, Robert and David A. Garvin. "Managing as if Tomorrow Mattered: Investment Decisions that Distort the Future May Result in High Present Values but Bleak Tomorrows," *Harvard Business Review*, Vol. 60 (May–June 1982, pp. 70–79).

Henderson, Glenn V., Jr. "In Defense of the Weighted Average Cost of Capital," Vol. 8 (Autumn 1979, pp. 57–61).

Istvan, Donald F. *Capital Expenditure Decisions: How They Are Made in Large Corporations* (Bloomington, IN: Bureau of Business Research, Indiana University, 1961).

Klammer, Thomas. "Empirical Evidence of the Adoption of Sophisticated Capital Budgeting Techniques," *Journal of Business*, Vol. 45 (July 1972, pp. 387–97).

Loomis, Worth. "Strategic Planning in Uncertain Times," *Chief Executive*, Vol. 14 (Winter 1980–1981, pp. 7–12).

Lutz, Friedrich and Vera Lutz. *The Theory of Investment of the Firm* (Princeton, NJ: Princeton University Press, 1951).

Mao, James C. T. "Survey of Capital Budgeting: Theory and Practice," *Journal of Finance*, Vol. 25 (May 1970, pp. 349–60).

Merrett, A. J. and Allen Sykes. *The Finance and Analysis of Capital Projects*, 2nd ed. (New York: John Wiley & Sons, 1973).

Miller, James H. "A Glimpse of Practice in Calculating and Using Return on Investment," *NAA Bulletin* (now *Management Accounting*), (June 1960, pp. 65–76).

Petry, Glenn H. "Effective Use of Capital Budgeting Tools," *Business Horizons*, Vol. 19 (October 1975, pp. 57–65).

Petty, J. William II, David F. Scott, Jr., and Monroe M. Bird. "The Capital Expenditure Decision-Making Process of the Large Corporation," *The Engineering Economist*, Vol. 20 (Spring 1959, pp. 159–72).

Pruitt, Stephen and Lawrence J. Gitman. "Capital Budgeting Forecast Biases: Evidence from the Fortune 500," *Financial Management*, Vol. 16 (Spring 1987, pp. 46–51).

Schall, Lawrence G., Gary L. Sundem, and William Geijsbeck. "Survey and Analysis of Capital Budgeting Methods," *Journal of Finance*, Vol. 33 (March 1978, pp. 281–87).

Scott, David F. and Dana J. Johnson. "Financing Policies and Practices in Large Corporations," *Financial Management*, Vol. 11 (Summer 1982, pp. 51–59).

Scott, David F. and J. William Petty II. "Capital Budgeting Practices in Large American Firms: A Retrospective Analysis," *The Financial Review*, Vol. 19 (March 1984, pp. 111–23).

Stanley, Majorie and Stanley R. Block. "A Survey of Multinational Capital Budgeting," *The Financial Review*, Vol. 19 (March 1984, pp. 35–54).

Stonehill, Arthur and I. Nathanson. "Capital Budgeting and the Multinational Corporation," *California Management Review*, Vol. 10 (Summer 1968, pp. 39–54).

Stonehill, Arthur, et al. "Financial Goals and Debt Ratio Determinants: A Survey of Practice in Five Countries," *Financial Management*, Vol. 4 (Autumn 1975, pp. 27–41).

13

WHY WORKING CAPITAL?

To this point in our analysis, we have centered the discussion on the capital investment decision and cost of capital of the firm. In doing so, we have set aside what to an earlier generation of financial economists and practitioners was a focus of considerable attention—working-capital analysis. The neglect, although deliberate, was not because the subject lacked importance. Lexicographer Samuel Johnson once observed, "When a man knows he is to be hanged in a fortnight it concentrates his mind wonderfully." Similarly, when a chief financial officer discovers the firm is not generating sufficient cash to meet obligations as they come due, the liquidity crisis that ensues "concentrates his mind wonderfully"—assuming, of course, he still retains his position. We have neglected working-capital analysis because conceptually the primary assets that comprise it (for example, cash, marketable securities, inventories, receivables) are augmented as management adds to plant and equipment. In other words, working capital is part of the investment outlay.

Similarly, current liabilities (short-term bank loans, commercial paper, credit extended by trade credit suppliers, and the like) can be viewed as funding sources. By convention, current liabilities mature in less than a year. Each liability, however, has a cost and can be included in the weighted average cost of capital. To date, we have followed the practice of using only long-term funding sources in determining the weighted average cost of capital. Those who adopt this position usually think of increases in working capital as the difference between current assets and current liabilities: as increases in net working capital. As a firm expands, it requires additional short-term funds to finance increases in inventories and receivables. Because those who supply short-term funds rarely finance 100 percent of the increases in current assets, a permanent investment in net working capital is required. This is financed from long-term funding sources, debt or equity, or a combination of both.

Consequently, either explicitly or implicitly, we have ignored working capital because there has been no reason to consider it. We now learn why it is important to give the subject individual attention.

THE OPERATING CYCLE

The primary reason why working capital warrants specific consideration is because production/sale of a product and collection of receivables/payment of bills do not occur uniformly and instantaneously (see Figure 13-1). If they did, this book would be a few chapters shorter. Reality, however, is more complicated for some companies than for others. Management of a manufacturing concern typically faces a production cycle. Raw materials must be employed to produce the goods sold. Between input of supplies and output of product lies a hiatus the length of which is dictated by the current state of technology. Breakthroughs may shorten this

Figure 13-1   The Operating Cycle

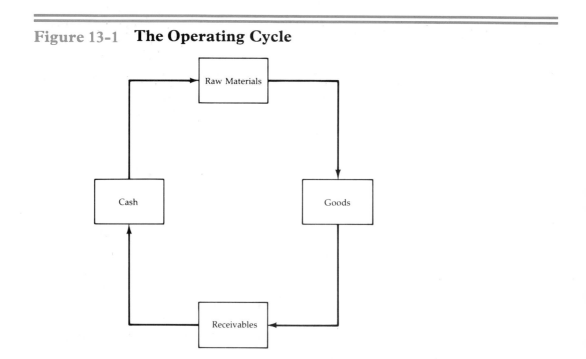

period—the introduction of continuous casting in steel manufacturing, for example—but the process is rarely instantaneous. Moreover, at either end of the manufacturing process lie other factors that lengthen the process: the time required to obtain raw materials and the time necessary to bring the finished goods to market. Although plant location may help ameliorate both factors, if markets are some distance from their source of materials, there is a trade-off that can be resolved only by a comparison of costs. To complicate matters further, demand for many products—toys, fertilizers, canned soups, to name a few—is distinctly seasonal and production, therefore, is not uniform over the course of a year.

Once products are marketed, the buyer is generally given time to pay: credit is extended from manufacturer to wholesaler, wholesaler to retailer, and retailer to consumer. Convention rather than technology dictates the length of time involved in collecting receivables. To shorten the process in some industries, middlemen or wholesalers are bypassed and some retailers offer lower prices for cash payment—the sale of gasoline being a prime example in the United States.

Consequently, not all firms experience the same operating cycle. The supplier of services such as a physician has limited investment in inventories but often a lengthy waiting period before collecting from a patient or more likely from the patient's health insurance provider. A large national retailer such as J. C. Penney invests heavily in inventories of finished goods while maintaining an extensive investment in enormous numbers of accounts receivable. The nature of Penney's operating cycle may, therefore, differ from that of an aluminum manufacturer, whose production cycle is dictated by technology and whose customers buy in large quantities. In contrast, the local utility has a huge investment in depreciable plant and equipment but comparatively little in working capital. As a result, management is concerned more with the former than with the latter. Thus the details and even the relative importance of working capital differ from industry to industry. Nevertheless, this inability to obtain uniform and instantaneous transformation of cash into goods and services and back into cash gives rise to an operating cycle and hence the need to manage it so as to meet production schedules and financial obligations.

CURRENT LIABILITIES

Although current assets can be rationalized in terms of an operating cycle, can the same be said for current liabilities? Or is the conventional distinction between short- and long-term liabilities largely an accounting artifact? In the process of manufacturing and marketing a product, raw materials are used up, sales are made, and receivables are collected. The period of time required to go from cash back to cash is generally a few weeks or a few months. In the case of seasonal industries, the cycle may extend for an entire year. A toy manufacturer, for example, depends heavily on the Christmas season. Retailers usually build inventories to accommodate the bulk of their sales in the fourth quarter of the year. Because the operating cycle is most often confined to a period no greater than a year or less, symmetry suggests that current assets be financed largely from liabilities discharged from cash generated at the end of the cycle. The venerable if sometimes ignored rule of commercial banking is to make short-term, self-liquidating loans: loans to finance inventories and receivables. If management views the operating cycle as a necessary cost of doing business, it is important to minimize such costs by (1) shortening the cycle, (2) minimizing the level of current assets relative to sales, and (3) employing the lowest-cost financing available—usually short-term credit. The shorter the maturity, the lower the risk of loss to creditors due to default on the principal or to changes in the purchasing power of money. Firms with high credit ratings often can borrow, at a point in time, at a short-term rate lower than the long-term rate on that date.[1] Hence, management relates current assets to short-term sources of funding: to current liabilities.

CAPM AND WORKING CAPITAL

While it is sometimes convenient to examine working capital in isolation, we must not lose sight of the lessons of Modern Portfolio Theory and particularly of CAPM. As we know, the composition of assets affects the firm's unleveraged beta coefficient. If, relative to other assets, management invests heavily in short-term government securities, the company's unleveraged beta coefficient likely will be relatively low. However, if government securities are simply a temporary depository for seasonally idle cash that will be reinvested in inventories and ultimately in receivables, it is the systematic risk of the latter that affects the beta coefficient of the firm.

The point is simple but not trivial. Consider two firms: A and B. Both firms are in the same business and the book value of the assets of each is identical. During the slack season, marketable securities comprise as much as 40 percent of each firm's total assets. During the peak season, when marketable securities are liquidated and the proceeds invested in inventories and receivables, the account balance of firm A is zero whereas that in the account of firm B is 10 percent of total assets. Clearly, there is a difference in the composition of the assets of the two firms: management of firm B is investing a larger proportion of its funds in marketable securities than is management of firm A. Moreover, the unleveraged beta coefficient of the two firms differs. Assuming the beta coefficient for marketable securities approximates zero, we find the unleveraged beta coefficient of firm B is lower than the unleveraged beta coefficient of firm A.

---

[1] At times, particularly during periods of so-called *tight money*, long-term rates may be lower than short-term rates. The result is overall curtailment of borrowing.

What about liabilities? Again, assume that on the basis of book value each firm maintains the same debt-to-total-capital ratio when short-term liabilities are included in the calculations. However, management of firm A chooses to finance more of its total assets from short-term debt whereas management of firm B chooses to rely more heavily on long-term debt. As a result, the only difference between firms A and B is the ratio of current assets to current liabilities: the so-called **current ratio** is smaller for firm A than for firm B. Similarly, the net working capital of firm A is also smaller than the net working capital of firm B. Does this mean not only because of its lower permanent investment in marketable securities and hence its higher unleveraged beta coefficient, but also because of differences in the maturity or term structure of its debt, that the leveraged beta coefficient is higher for firm A than for firm B? As leveraged beta depends only on the debt ratio, the quick answer is no.

The question, however, is intriguing. Firm A has chosen to substitute short-term debt for long-term debt. Of course, it could duplicate firm B's liability structure by marketing long-term bonds and using the proceeds to retire short-term debt. Whether firm A would experience the same cost of servicing the debt is moot. Because firm A made its choice on a different date, its overall cost of outstanding debt capital could be higher or lower depending on interest rates at the time.

Thus, the relevant question is whether firm A enjoys a more flexible position than firm B: enjoys a better position to lower its overall cost of debt capital than firm B by taking advantage of a decline in interest rates to shift funding from short-term to long-term debt. If so, the market price of firm A's stock will be marginally higher and its debt ratio, on a market-value basis, will be marginally lower than firm B's. Again, in perfect markets investors will have capitalized any perceived advantage into the stock's market price.

Suppose, however, interest rates had risen. Long-term debt would have been funded from short-term debt at higher rates or renewed (re-funded) also at higher rates. In such circumstances, the term structure of firm B's debt, whose long-term rate was locked in at a lower level, appears more advantageous to owners.

The difficulty evaluating term structure is similar to the problem portfolio managers face in timing investment shifts from short-term to long-term maturities: they do so when they anticipate a fall in interest rates, thereby locking up high-yielding bonds. Corporate financial officers, on the other hand, shift short-term to long-term debt when interest rates *have* fallen and they anticipate rates may be ready to rise again. This was the case in mid-1983 when many chief financial officers, perceiving that interest rates had temporarily bottomed out, began to shift short-term to long-term liabilities.[2]

Timing, however, is an art. In our discussion of the efficient market hypothesis, we raised questions about the ability of security analysts consistently to select stocks

---

[2] Richard Karp and Gregory Miller. "Sadder but Wiser about Debt," *Institutional Investor*, Vol. 17 (July 1983, pp. 214–18).

that outperform the market. Whether an issuer or purchaser, their timing the term structure of a portfolio of fixed income securities falls in the same category. What does he or she know that is not already incorporated in the market price and hence the yield on such securities? Economists, portfolio managers, and chief financial officers are often caught at the wrong end of a prediction about interest rates. There is no systematic evidence that any are consistently correct.[3] Indeed, the volatility that has characterized interest rates in recent years has led (as we shall see in later chapters) to the issuance of more variable-rate and less fixed-rate long-term debt securities and to the more recent use of financial futures as a hedge against fluctuations in interest rates.

Nevertheless, chief financial officers alter the term structure of debt when they anticipate changes in interest rates. Borrowing short in the expectation of shifting short-term debt to long-term securities is a common practice. Firms are always looking for a *window* in the market through which a drop in rates can facilitate extending the maturity of its liabilities. At any given moment, however, not all current liabilities are used to finance short-term, self-liquidating loans.[4]

In addition, over the years there has been a general drift toward shortening the term structure of debt. According to one estimate, in 1960 the ratio of long-term to short-term debt was 2.39; by 1983 it had fallen to 1.19.[5] For nonfinancial corporations as a group, the current ratio also appears to have declined and, in real terms at least, so has net working capital. As shown in Table 13-1, although net working capital in current dollars has risen since 1974, the current ratio has declined. In real terms, however, net working capital actually fell from 1977 through 1982 but has been fluctuating since that time.

SHORT-TERM DEBT AND THE DEBT RATIO

Whatever the aggregate trends, our primary concern is with the firm. From our analysis of companies *A* and *B*, it is quite possible the only substantive difference lies in the unleveraged beta coefficients of the two firms. We would expect leveraged beta coefficients to differ, but only because the unleveraged beta coefficients differ. However, if the debt-to-total-capital ratio of firm *A* is larger than the debt-to-total-capital ratio of firm *B* when short-term debt is included in the capital structure, the leveraged beta coefficient of firm *A* would be greater than the leveraged beta coefficient of firm *B* because (1) the unleveraged beta coefficient of firm *A* is larger

---

[3] Lynn Brenner. "How CFO's Make Interest Rate Calls," *Institutional Investor*, Vol. XVIII (January 1984, pp. 83–85).

[4] Some of the funds borrowed may not, in conventional accounting terminology, be short-term loans: their maturities may extend from two to five years. The major consideration is whether or not management expects to shift these loans to long-term maturities extending 20 years or more into the future.

[5] Same as [2], p. 294.

Table 13-1   Net Working Capital and Current Ratios of Nonfinancial Corporations—1974–1986 ($ billions)

Year	Net Working Capital	Real Net Working Capital[a]	Current Ratio[b]
1974	$282.0	$522.2	1.662
1975	307.4	518.4	1.681
1976	332.4	526.8	2.671
1977	355.5	528.2	1.638
1978	374.3	518.4	1.559
1979	407.5	518.4	1.505
1980	437.8	510.9	1.492
1981	448.3	473.9	1.462
1982	451.1	451.1	1.458
1983	516.3	496.9	1.487
1984	539.5	500.0	1.464
1985	551.0	494.2	1.447
1986[c]	573.4	507.9	1.469

[a] Net working capital divided by the Implicit Price Deflator for each year, where 1982 = 100.
[b] Ratio of current assets to current liabilities.
[c] First quarter of 1986 only.

SOURCE: Board of Governors of the Federal Reserve, Department of Commerce, Bureau of Census, Federal Trade Commission, Securities and Exchange Commission. Summarized in U.S. Joint Economic Committee, *Economic Indicators* (July 1984, pp. 29; May 1986, p. 29; July 1987, pp. 29).

than the unleveraged beta coefficient of firm B and (2) the debt-to-total-capital ratio is greater for firm A than for firm B.

Management of firm A may still shift short-term debt to long-term debt, but may do so only at a higher cost of debt capital. A higher k_d may have been taken into consideration when k_o was initially calculated for purposes of capital budgeting. If not, k_o has been underestimated. At a minimum, management should include short-term debt that is expected to be shifted to long-term debt as part of its permanent debt-to-total-capital ratio.

We summarize the foregoing analysis in Figure 13-2. Again, firms A and B are in the same industry, face identical business risks, grow over time at the same rate, and have the same level of fixed assets. Both face identical seasonal needs and must carry additional inventories and receivables to meet them. Management of firm B has chosen to finance more of its seasonal needs from permanent working capital by carrying a larger permanent balance of marketable securities and relying less heavily on short-term credit from suppliers and commercial banks. Management of firm A has chosen to finance all its seasonal needs from short-term funding sources. Given the greater permanent level of marketable securities in the asset structure of firm B, it is reasonable to conclude—assuming a beta coefficient for marketable securities of

Figure 13-2   A Comparison of Asset Structures for Firms _A_ and _B_

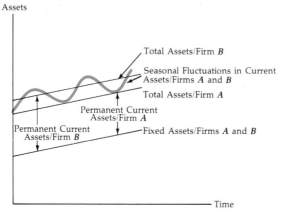

zero—that the unleveraged beta coefficient of firm _B_ is lower than the unleveraged beta coefficient of firm _A_.

How the permanent assets of both firms _A_ and _B_ are financed also can affect their respective betas. To the extent total debt ratios (including short-term debt) are the same but term structures differ, there may be no difference in their beta coefficients because of leverage. If, however, total debt ratio of firm _A_ is higher than total debt ratio of firm _B_, the leveraged beta coefficient of firm _A_ will rise accordingly.

FLEXIBILITY AND WORKING CAPITAL

The fascinating question is why management of firm _B_ would choose to employ a permanently higher level of current assets—specifically, marketable securities—to finance seasonal needs. One answer is flexibility. Suppose firms _A_ and _B_ were manufacturing ski equipment. In anticipation of the usual seasonal increase in demand, during the summer the firms manufacture the equipment and begin shipping to retailers. As the skiing season approaches, sales usually start to rise. The snow, however, does not fall. More importantly, an unusually mild winter precludes successful snowmaking in the markets served. As a result, ski slopes close down early and demand for equipments falls. Both firms have stockpiled their unsold inventory. Because management of firm _B_ has relied less heavily on short-term financing of inventory than has management of firm _A_, the latter firm may have to cut prices and incur losses to induce retailers and ultimate buyers to purchase now and to wait for the next season. Management of firm _B_ may be able to retain a larger stock of equipment, thereby temporarily rearranging composition of its current assets: fewer marketable securities and larger inventories. Firm B may then curtail production for next season yet receive full price for what it produced and stored for the year.

Which strategy is more profitable depends on a comparison of the costs of dumping or retaining inventories. Management of firm B, however, is in a better position to make that choice.

LIQUIDITY AND WORKING CAPITAL

Another answer to the question of why management of firm B would choose to employ a permanently higher level of current assets to finance seasonal needs is liquidity. The greater the difference between current assets and current liabilities—the larger the net working capital—the less likely it is a firm will be unable to meet its financial obligations. Inability to pay bills as they come due suggests a firm lacks liquidity. In the preceding illustration, because management of firm A had to sell inventories (perhaps at a loss) to meet current liabilities and management of firm B did not have to sell inventories, neither firm lacked liquidity: assets could be sold to pay bills. Management of firm B, however, had a choice; management of firm A did not.

When management cannot meet financial obligations as they come due either through selling assets or through shifting short-term debt to long-term debt, the result is bankruptcy. Although bankruptcy is an extreme form of **financial distress**, a firm can experience financial distress and not experience bankruptcy. To be forced to sell assets at a loss to meet current liabilities is a manifestation of financial distress: the total wealth of stockholders declines. Similarly, to shift short-term temporary borrowing to long-term debt raises the permanent debt-to-total-capital ratio and can reduce the market value of the stock, which also can be viewed as a sign of financial distress. However, the crisis may pass: the snows may fall in abundance next year and the demand for ski equipment be greater than anticipated. On the other hand, a second successive mild winter may deepen the distress, particularly for firm A.

Through the working capital decision, as through the leverage decision, management expresses its attitude toward risk. In this instance, management of firm A appears less risk-averse than management of firm B. However, firm B may rationalize its philosophy as follows: a permanent working capital position designed to ensure flexibility, minimize financial distress, and in the extreme avoid bankruptcy is in the interest of stockholders because it safeguards, insofar as possible, the firm's long-run viability.

Management of firm A might argue with equal vigor that it is a waste of long-term financing to tie up funds in marketable securities whose return is probably lower than the cost of capital. Consequently, it is in the long-run interests of stockholders to minimize permanent investment in working capital by using fewer total assets to finance the same volume of business.

Neither, of course, is wrong. It is true that total investment in permanent assets employed by firm A is less than employed by firm B to generate the same expected sales. Assuming both use the same proportion of short-term and long-term debt to finance such assets, firm A would have proportionately fewer shares outstanding. Therefore, firm A's earnings and dividends per share could be greater. The trade-off, however, is a relatively greater variability in per-share earnings. To compensate, firm A may have a lower payout ratio than firm B. Also, there is the difference in the beta coefficients of the two firms, suggesting that stockholders are willing to accept a lower expected return on the shares with the lower systematic risk: the shares of firm B.

Thus, management understandably identifies with the firm. A relatively risk-averse management will follow the working capital philosophy suggested by firm B; a less risk-averse management will follow the working capital philosophy suggested by firm A. Assuming investors hold diversified portfolios and securities are traded in efficient markets, their expected returns will be affected by how these respective philosophies impact on the expected dividends, the market price at the end of the holding period, and the beta coefficients of each firm.

WORKING CAPITAL AND AGENCY COSTS

Even if information about different levels of working capital is effectively incorporated in the stock's market price, it does not follow that the subject is of no further significance. For those who loan funds to the company, monitoring working capital is a means of gauging the ability of firms to meet payments when due. Yet, monitoring working capital on a day-to-day basis is costly, even for those who act as their own agents: banks and insurance companies, among others.

To make such tasks less expensive, agents have come to rely on a set of implicit or explicit covenants they expect management to follow. In the case of many debt instruments, the monitored factors have been memorialized in the contract or indenture underlying the loan. Because debt holders have agreed to loan a specific amount at a fixed rate of interest for a certain period of time, covenants are often placed in such contracts to ensure that management will make no decisions that will jeopardize payment of interest and repayment of principal. One such covenant may be a restriction on working capital: perhaps that the level of working capital should remain above a specific amount or, more likely, that the current ratio should not fall below 2:1.

The purpose of this and such covenants as restrictions on dividends, limits on the debt-to-total-capital ratio, and the like is to lower debtholder **agency costs**.[6]

---

[6] An excellent source for specific provisions on debt contracts is found in *Commentaries on Model Debenture/Indenture Provisions* (Chicago: American Bar Association, 1971).

Specifically, the trustee for the bondholders or for the institution that has made the loan monitors the financial statements as they pertain to specific covenants. If adhered to, presumably such covenants help ensure payment of interest and repayment of principal, and thus help maintain debt quality. Management (which generally has nothing to hide) in turn cooperates, thereby ensuring access to capital markets at a k_d lower than it might otherwise enjoy.

In the context of firms A and B, each may be adhering to the working capital standards prescribed or implied in the various contracts that underlie their respective debt issues. Management of firm B, however, may have a standard higher than that required in the indenture or implicitly expected by the lending agent. Whether this enhances the debt quality of firm B over firm A and thereby marginally lowers the cost of new debt capital is a moot point. It may depend, as we have suggested, on whether the aggregate ratio of long-term and short-term debt is higher for firm A than for firm B.

Nevertheless, as with dividend policy, management attends to working capital; it may even state an objective and attempt to maintain it. Returning to the Dexter Corporation: the company publicly states that it attempts to maintain a continuing 2:1 target as a current ratio.[7] Generally, Dexter has stayed within and usually slightly above the target.

BANKRUPTCY—THE INSTITUTIONAL SETTING

The ultimate or extreme experience for any firm is the involuntary liquidation of its assets to satisfy the financial claims against it. The event that usually triggers bankruptcy is failure to meet interest payments on a loan when due. Before bankruptcy occurs, however, management generally exhausts every conceivable opportunity to raise the necessary funds: assets may be sold or other sources of funds sought. Bankruptcy itself is the last resort.

Yet businesses do fail. Table 13-2 shows the rate and number of industrial and commercial failures in recent years. Many of these firms were comparatively small. Although the failure rate of the mid-1980s can be contrasted with the 154 per 10,000 (a total of 31,822) firms that collapsed in 1932 during the depths of the Great Depression, in real terms the GNP of the mid-1980s was about seven times larger.[8] Hence, recent data do not suggest the same degree of distress. Nevertheless, recent data include such spectacular failures as W. T. Grant and Braniff International. Johns-Manville Corporation (an otherwise solvent company) applied for protection

---

[7] *1983 Annual Report of the Dexter Corporation*, p. 17.

[8] U.S. Department of Commerce, Bureau of the Census. *Historical Statistics of the United States, Colonial Times to 1970* (Washington: U.S. Government Printing Office, 1975, Part 2, p. 912).

Table 13-2   **Business Failures—1974–1986**[a]

Year	Failure Rate per 10,000	Total Number of Failures
1974	38.4	9,915
1975	42.6	11,432
1976	34.8	9,628
1977	28.4	7,919
1978	23.9	6,619
1979	27.8	7,564
1980	42.1	11,742
1981	61.3	16,794
1982	89.0	24,908
1983	110.0	31,334
1984	107.0	52,078
1985	114.0	57,068
1986	122.2[b]	61,183

[a] Commercial and industrial failures only. Excludes failures of banks and railroads; real-estate, insurance, holding, and financial companies; steamship lines, travel agencies, and so forth.
[b] Estimated.

SOURCE: *1987 Economic Report of the President*, p. 351; 1986 data on number of failures are from U.S. Department of Commerce, *Survey of Current Business*, Vol. 67 (July 1987, p. S-5).

under the bankruptcy laws, claiming that pending damages arising out of litigation over the use of asbestos it once manufactured would bankrupt the firm.[9]

The Manville action was novel.[10] Generally, a debtor—either an individual or a firm—initiates voluntary proceedings under state or federal bankruptcy laws to prevent seizure of assets by creditors attempting to satisfy unpaid claims. For instance, most debt contracts specify that if interest is not paid when due, the amount borrowed (principal plus accrued interest) is payable immediately even though the loan or bond may have several years to maturity. To satisfy their claims, creditors may obtain a court order to seize the debtor's property that can be liquidated. Some loans are even secured by such property as plant, land, and equipment. In principle, such collateral can be seized and sold to meet unpaid obligations. For example, in the case of an individual, a home secured by a mortgage may be seized. The bank or creditor simply forecloses on the mortgage because the debtor has not met the monthly payments. Initiating voluntary pro-

---

[9] Richard A. Epstein. "Manville: The Bankruptcy of Product Liability Law," *Regulation*, Vol. 6 (September–October 1982, pp. 14–19 and 43–46).

[10] But not that novel. The federal bankruptcy law had been used by several firms—for example, Continental Airlines—to abrogate, in whole or in part, labor contracts. See "Good Law Abused," *Economist*, Vol. 289 (October 18, 1983, p. 16). More recently, Texaco filed for bankruptcy to protect itself from Pennzoil's multibillion dollar jury award for damages sustained by Pennzoil when Texaco intentionally interfered with merger plans between Pennzoil and Getty Oil. See Stratford P. Sherman, "The Gambler Who Refused $2 billion," *Fortune*, Vol. 115 (May 11, 1987, pp. 50–54 and 58).

ceedings under the bankruptcy laws prevents foreclosure or property seizure. Subsequently, property may be sold and the firm liquidated to satisfy unpaid claims.

Creditors may also institute involuntary bankruptcy proceedings against a debtor. Suppose a firm cannot pay interest on debt secured by a plant lien: it is in arrears on credit extended by suppliers to carry the firm's inventories. The suppliers may be unsecured creditors of the firm. Fearing that secured creditors may seize the plant, the suppliers institute involuntary bankruptcy proceedings.

Thus, either debtor or creditor may employ the bankruptcy laws. For the debtor, if incorporated, creditors may eventually satisfy a portion of their claims out of the debtor's assets. However, if creditors are not repaid in full, they have no further claim against the owners or stockholders of that corporation. Stockholders have limited liability: they may lose all they have invested, but no more. If you own shares in the bankrupt XYZ Corporation, the creditors of that company have no claim on your earnings, bank account, or home. Your shares may have zero but not negative value. Later we suggest that corporation owners treat creditors as though they had given creditors an option on corporate assets in exchange for funds. Should the venture fail, creditors would have a claim on such assets. Nevertheless, there is no guarantee creditors will recover what is due them.

Unincorporated firms and individuals have unlimited liability.[11] Although while this might bring to mind such horrors as seizure of the homestead, the family car, and anything else that is marketable, reality is more sanguine. The debtors prisons we associate with Dickens have long since disappeared. Maine, which offers this option to the creditor, forces the creditor to pay the debtor's room and board. Better to garnish the wages of the debtor than to let him or her languish in jail. In many cases, state laws also protect certain property from seizure by creditors. If one chooses to file for bankruptcy under federal rather than state laws, there are lists of federal exemptions.[12]

Even though the purpose of bankruptcy laws is to give individual debtors a chance to start anew, certain debts cannot be discharged by declaring bankruptcy. The old adage that only death and taxes are certain remains intact under the bankruptcy laws. Taxes must be paid, even if the bankrupt is relieved of other debts.

---

[11] *A Bonus Footnote!* You may have seen the letters *P. C.* in the United States after the names of physicians and other professionals and *Ltd.* after the names of British corporations. P. C. means professional corporation; Ltd. means limited liability. Although they cannot use the corporate veil to protect themselves from malpractice suits, physicians and other professionals may prefer the limited liability feature of corporations to the unlimited liability that accompanies proprietorship or partnership organizations. In the context of British law, the joint stock company employed to amass large amounts of funds has unlimited liability unless Ltd. is specifically included in its charter.

Because the Tax Reform Act of 1986 lowered personal income-tax rates relative to corporate rates (see Appendix F), a business form (structure) known as the Master Limited Partnership has become popular. Although its owners have limited liability and its shares trade as shares of a corporation, the owners avoid the corporate income tax. See *Wall Street Journal*, June 30, 1987, pp. 1 and 14.

[12] The Constitution specifically permits the federal government to enact bankruptcy laws. Our modern system dates from the Federal Bankruptcy Act of 1898. States, however, have the right to prevent individuals from using federal exemptions. A few, Florida for example, have exercised this right.

CORPORATIONS AND THE BANKRUPTCY LAWS

Although a corporation or its creditors may resort to bankruptcy, the procedure is not costless. Legal and administrative fees may run as high as 5 percent of the market value of the securities immediately prior to bankruptcy, but are more likely to range from 2 to 3 percent of market value.[13] However, perhaps more significant is the redistribution of wealth and income that may accompany bankruptcy proceedings. For example, stockholders may be compelled to forfeit all assets to creditors. On the one hand, creditors may not realize all the claims due them; on the other hand, creditors may choose to own the firm rather than liquidate it. In subsequent years, profits may exceed expectations and the firm's value may exceed what was anticipated at the time of bankruptcy. Both the costs of such proceedings and the unanticipated losses or gains often cause the debtor or creditors to compromise claims rather than institute proceedings. Thus, creditors may agree to an *extension* that postpones maturity of their claims. If, for example, creditors conclude the firm is fundamentally sound and its insolvency the result of temporary or unusual conditions (perhaps three mild winters in a row), they may prefer an extension. As a condition of the extension, creditors may insist, however, on greater equity investment in permanent working capital so as to reduce the threat of future insolvency.

A more drastic step involves a *composition* in which creditors agree on a pro-rata settlement of their claims. If the creditors are suppliers, they may value the outlet and be willing to incur a partial loss so as to avoid bankruptcy costs, perceiving they may do no better or even worse in legal proceedings.

Whether an extension or a composition is employed, it must be acceptable to all creditors. Dissenters must be paid in full or they can initiate involuntary bankruptcy proceedings against the company. Thus, for an extension or a composition to be successful, the number of creditors involved must be small.

BANKRUPTCY—LIQUIDATION OF CORPORATIONS

Although the details of bankruptcy law must be left to specialized courses, there are specific points germane to the study of finance that bear upon the risk security holders assume. In other words, what can one expect if the worst indeed happens? Corporations, like individuals, may use either state or federal laws to accomplish an orderly liquidation of assets under bankruptcy proceedings. While the individual

---

[13] J. B. Warner. "Bankruptcy Costs: Some Evidence," *Journal of Finance*, Vol. 32 (May 1977, pp. 337–48). Warner's estimates were based on eleven particularly complex railroad bankruptcies with proceedings averaging 13 years.

may lose certain assets to satisfy claims, he or she remains intact. The corporation, on the other hand, is liquidated. At the funeral are the creditors. From proceeds of the sale of company assets, creditors receive compensation in accordance with established pecking order. Because the federal bankruptcy system is designed to be self-supporting, at the head of the pecking order are the United States Treasury, the federal court officers, the trustees appointed to preside over the assets until sold, and, of course, the lawyers. Unpaid taxes also have a high priority, as do debts of certain federal agencies. Employees with unpaid wages of up to $2,000 are next in line; their earned pension benefits also rank ahead of the claims of other creditors.

If any flesh remains on the carcass, creditors are next. Creditors with loans secured by property have prior claim over unsecured creditors, at least to the extent the property has value. Thus, if the sale of equipment used as collateral for a loan brought 80 percent of the principal and accrued interest, 80 percent of such claims would be satisfied. The remaining 20 percent is treated as an unsecured obligation. After secured loans are satisfied, unsecured creditors are next to feed. Assuming the remaining proceeds cover only 50 percent of such claims, the secured creditors discussed earlier would receive one-half the remaining 20 percent, or 90 percent of the total amount owed.

What about preferred and common stockholders? They are, to put it bluntly, wiped out. The firm's assets have been sold and the proceeds are not adequate to satisfy all prior claims. The technical reason for bankruptcy—inability to pay debts when due—has, ex post facto, resulted in insolvency. Because the claims against the firm (including bankruptcy costs) exceed the value of the firm's assets, no equity remains.

There are, as we learn in Chapter 16 on individual securities, ways to move forward or backward in the pecking order. Contracts can be written so as to enhance or retard a security holder's status in bankruptcy. The redistribution of risk is compensated for by the difference in required return for such security holders.

REORGANIZATION

Although bankruptcy often means liquidation, it is possible the company may be reorganized. What factors dictate the approach? Rolling stock, trucks, and airplanes, for example, are easily sold: they have an opportunity cost. If they are the primary assets of the firm, creditors may satisfy almost all their claims through liquidation. On the other hand, if the company markets a service that depends heavily on the use of highly skilled labor and sophisticated equipment—the Silicon Valley or Boston's Route 128, for example—creditors may gain more from reorganization than liquidation. If, under the circumstances, the firm has greater value as a going concern—better to be alive than dead.

Reorganization, therefore, is a distinct possibility. Corporations such as Toys "R" Us, Miller-Wahl, Dynamics Corporation of America, Continental Steel (formerly Penn-Dixie Steel Corporation), and the Penn Central Corporation have successfully reorganized.[14] Although the procedures currently followed result from the Bankruptcy Reform Act of 1978 and subsequent legislation enacted in 1984, much of the substantive treatment of creditor claims dates from legislation and Supreme Court decisions of the late 1930s.[15]

Under modern procedures, either a debtor corporation or a group of creditors may file a petition under Chapter 11 of the Act. Once the petition has been accepted, an independent trustee can be appointed to operate the company. However, it is more likely that present management will be left in charge. If management continues to operate the company, it has 120 days to file a petition to reorganize; otherwise, the plan of reorganization is the responsibility of the trustee. In any event, the debtor, creditors, or committee for creditors may file an alternative plan of reorganization. The court reviews the plan or plans to ensure the final outcome is "fair and equitable and feasible." To be "fair and equitable," security holders must be treated in accordance with the provisions of their contracts. "Feasible" suggests that once the company is reorganized it is unlikely to find itself in bankruptcy again. The fair and equitable standard is constitutional; the feasibility standard is economic and financial. To implement either necessarily involves participants in classic conflict resolution. Let us see why.

CRITERIA FOR FEASIBILITY   Assume Deep in Debt corporation has the following simplified capital structure:

	Book Value
Short-term Debt	
Bank loans (secured by inventory)	$10,000,000
Trade credit	25,000,000
Long-term debt	
75,000 mortgage bonds (secured by plant lien)	75,000,000
100,000 unsecured debentures	100,000,000
Equity	
400,000 shares of preferred stock at par or at original selling price	40,000,000
500,000 shares of common stock (book value)	50,000,000
Total Book Value of Capital Structure	**$300,000,000**

---

[14] Harvey R. Miller. "Often It Pays to Go Bankrupt," *New York Times* (April 18, 1982, Sec. 3, p. 2).

[15] See, for example, Case v. Los Angeles Lumber Products Company, 308 U.S. 116 (1939) and Consolidated Rock Products Company et al. v. DuBois, 312 U.S. 526 (1940).

From a legal perspective, $210,000,000 in unpaid debt is on the company books, exclusive of any interest due but not yet paid. Assume further that Deep in Debt was unable to meet interest payments on both the bank loans and the mortgage bonds due to "inadequate" working capital. Assume also that interest charges amounted to $500,000 on the bank loans and $6,500,000 on the mortgage bonds. Management filed a Chapter 11 petition to avoid seizure of its property by these secured creditors. In addition, assume that market value of the inventory securing the bank loans is in excess of $10,500,000 (more than the principal and interest due on the bank loans) and that market value of the property securing the mortgage bonds is in excess of $81,500,000 (more than the principal and interest due the bondholders). Finally, prior to bankruptcy the company reported annual earnings before interest and taxes of $20,000,000. Interest and related charges, however, had reduced taxable income to zero. Hence, the company paid no dividends on either preferred or common stock. Dividends, which under the preferred-stock contract cumulate if not paid, are $1,000,000 in arrears. Even though Deep in Debt generates income, in order to reorganize so the company will not fail again—to make the reorganization feasible—there must be less debt in the capital structure. But how much less?

VALUING A BANKRUPT CORPORATION

Before the foregoing question can be answered the value of Deep in Debt as a going concern must be determined. Theory suggests that we look at market value of the securities. Both bank loans and trade credit are held by institutions; at best, their market value can be imputed. Assume, however, the remaining securities are publicly traded and their current market values are:

	Market Value
Long-term Debt	
75,000 mortgage bonds	$50,000,000
100,000 unsecured debentures	25,000,000
Equity	
400,000 shares of preferred stock	2,000,000
500,000 shares of common stock	1,000,000
	$78,000,000

The mortgage bonds are worth two-thirds their original value exclusive of unpaid interest and the unsecured debentures are worth one-quarter their original value exclusive of unpaid interest. Because the bank loans are secured and the trade credit is not, the imputed market value of each is two-thirds and one-quarter their respective book values:

	Imputed Market Value
Short-term Debt	
Bank loans	$ 6,667,000
Trade credit	6,250,000
	$12,917,000

Preferred stock, which originally sold at $100 per share ($40,000,000 ÷ 400,000), is now trading at $5 per share; common stock is trading at $2 per share. The total actual and imputed market values exceed $90,000,000 ($78,000,000 + $12,917,000 = $90,917,000).

Assume there is general agreement that as a going concern the company would continue to earn $20,000,000 indefinitely before interest and taxes. Research suggests companies producing similar products have expected returns based on unleveraged beta coefficients of 16 percent. Ignoring income taxes and assuming the reorganized company had an all-equity capital structure, we find its total value as a going concern earning $20,000,000 a year indefinitely is

$$\$125,000,000 = \frac{\$20,000,000}{.16}$$

Under these assumptions, market value of the company as a going concern appears to exceed market value of its outstanding claims. Based primarily on the assets used as collateral for the bank loans and mortgage bonds, the estimate is the assets of Deep in Debt would generate approximately $100,000,000 if sold. Thus, company value as a going concern appears somewhat higher than current liquidation value. In light of the foregoing analysis one might ask, why are the market values of the securities — particularly the secured debt — so low? Alternatively, should the stockholders assume — given their place in the pecking order — their claims have any value at all?

THE CROSSCURRENTS IN REORGANIZATION

Although somewhat artificial, the circumstances in which the security holders of Deep in Debt find themselves are not atypical. Secured creditors, in particular, often have collateral whose market value approximates or exceeds their claims. And in terms of pecking order, their claims rank high. However, if the company is reorganized using the $125,000,000 valuation figure, it is clear that to meet the criteria of feasibility Deep in Debt must become Less in Debt in the future. Otherwise, interest charges will severely compromise the working capital and hence the liquidity position of Deep in Debt, placing it in the same position as before. Consequently, the company could again find itself in bankruptcy. At the same time, interest charges are tax deductible. Assuming the company can generate $20,000,000 in pretax profits, interest will lower any tax liability. If the tax liability is not lowered thereby, the value of the company must be reduced. Thus, if its average tax rate was 30 percent and there was no debt in the capital structure, the valuation figure for an unleveraged cost of equity of 16 percent is

$$V = \frac{\$20,000,000(1 - .3)}{.16} = \$87,500,000$$

The claims of security holders with collateral now appear less secure in reorganization than initially. Yet, the valuation figure could be wrong. Indeed, earnings could be higher or lower than projected. Hence, by nature reorganization contains an element of uncertainty that can be eliminated only by the auctioneer's hammer. Liquidation, of course, resolves these dilemmas.

Resolution, however, may be based on broader considerations. For instance, if a company is a major local employer and is liquidated, such action may have a deleterious impact on the area's economy. Such externalities are not lost on the court, which may make every effort to keep a company alive even when the valuation figure suggests liquidation.[16] Because delays, externalities, and the need to make a reorganization feasible are all issues that may ultimately work against the claims of secured creditors, they may prefer (and in some cases manage) to have the company liquidated and their claims satisfied.[17]

ABSOLUTE VERSUS RELATIVE PRIORITY

In legal theory, if secured creditors have claims equal to the value of their collateral, their priority in reorganization should be the same as their priority in liquidation: they should receive, dollar for dollar, claims equal to the value of the claims they would forfeit in reorganization. Known as the **absolute priority** theory of reorganization, it was sanctioned by the U.S. Supreme Court years ago.[18]

To illustrate the principle, continue to assume the valuation figure of $125,000,000. Suppose in this instance an independent trustee was appointed and developed a reorganization plan. To keep the company in business during bankruptcy, the court authorized it to borrow up to $10,000,000. Under the law, this claim takes priority. An additional $5,000,000 went for court costs, legal fees, and the

---

[16] For an interesting illustration of this problem, see Jacob J. Kaplan, Daniel J. Lyne, and C. Keefe Hurley, "The Reorganization of the Waltham Watch Company: A Clinical Study," *Harvard Law Review*, Vol. 64 (June 1951, pp. 1262–86).

[17] See, for example, "Investigating the Collapse of W. T. Grant," *Business Week* (July 19, 1976, pp. 60–62).

[18] Case v. Los Angeles Lumber Products Company, 308 U.S. 106 (1939). For an ancient but nevertheless enlightening commentary on creditors' rights in bankruptcy that formed part of the intellectual basis for that decision, see James C. Bonbright and Milton C. Bergerman, "Two Rival Theories of Priority Rights of Security Holders in a Corporate Reorganization," *Columbia Law Review*, Vol. 28 (February 1928, pp. 127–65).

like. Thus, there remain $110,000,000 to be distributed in new securities to old security holders on the basis of their pecking order. Since book value of secured claims totals $92,000,000 in principal and interest ($10,500,000 + $81,500,000), security holders will be honored in full. This leaves $18,000,000 in new securities to be distributed to unsecured creditors. Since their claims cannot be fully satisfied, under absolute priority theory stockholders are wiped out.

The reorganization, however, must be feasible. Consequently, the trustee decides that bondholders with plant and equipment liens will become the majority stockholders in the company. In other words, bondholders will exchange their bonds for stock. The bank loans will remain intact, partly because bank ownership of stock in any company is restricted and also because the company will need future short-term loans to operate the business. Hence, the banking connection should be maintained. The unsecured creditors—trade creditors and debenture holders—will receive (in stock) $\dfrac{\$18,000,000}{\$100,000,000 + \$25,000,000} = 14.4$ percent of their claims.

Focusing our attention on the claims of creditors only, a simplified capital structure for a reorganized Deep in Debt would reflect

Short-term Bank Loans and Accrued Interest	$ 10,500,000
Common Stock	
Bondholders' share (book value)	81,500,000
Unsecured creditors' share (book value) at 14.4% × $125,000,000	18,000,000
	$110,000,000

In principle, the value of the total claims is satisfied by the issuance of new securities. If the court and the participating security holders approve the reorganization, the company will be released from bankruptcy and allowed to continue in business.

In this instance, however, approval may not be forthcoming. One-half of each class of creditors (representing two-thirds of the value of claims outstanding) must approve. It is highly unlikely bondholders, in particular, would accept this plan. Even if they did, the court might question whether it could approve a plan where bondholders may be better off under liquidation. Furthermore, one should not assume stockholders will contemplate their fate philosophically. On the contrary, they are likely to protest vigorously.

The slender thread from which this distribution hangs is the valuation figure. The company could, of course, be more or less successful than forecasted.[19] The difficulty with absolute priority theory in reorganization is its implicit assumption that the valuation figure is certain. But only liquidation offers certainty. Hence, an alternative concept, the *relative priority* theory of reorganization, is often advocated.

---

[19] In Case v. Los Angeles Lumber Products, where absolute priority was established as the law of the land, the stockholders were eliminated from the reorganization. The valuation estimate, however, proved to be too low. Indeed, the firm prospered. In light of hindsight, one might argue that stockholders were treated unfairly. See Arthur Stone Dewing, *The Financial Policy of Corporations*, 5th ed. (New York: The Ronald Press, 1953, Vol. II, p. 1306, footnote i).

Relative priority implies that each security holder should make some sacrifice, but that the sacrifice be in proportion to the pecking order. Secured creditors accept modifications in their contracts to help make reorganization feasible. Bondholders, for example, agree to interest being paid only if earned. Known as *mortgage income bonds*, they are secured by collateral but failure to pay future interest if unearned does not precipitate bankruptcy. Further down the pecking order, stockholders may lose a considerable portion of their investment but are not wiped out. The relative sacrifices of unsecured creditors lie somewhere in between.

How are these relative sacrifices determined? One approach is to use the present market value of claims. Recall in the case of Deep in Debt that claims of secured creditors were presently valued at two-thirds their face value, claims of unsecured creditors at one-fourth, and claims of stockholders were nominal. Moreover, the aggregate present market value of these claims was only $90,917,000. Given the value of the collateral, however, it is unlikely either the bank or the bondholders would accept a one-third loss of the face value of their claims. On the other hand, stockholders would welcome any chance to participate.

The actual plan thus becomes an exercise in conflict resolution and compromise is inevitable. From the court's perspective, the major concerns are feasibility and (in this case) fairness to secured creditors who, in the absence of bankruptcy laws, could have seized the pledged property and satisfied their entire claims. The plan that is finally hammered out will take such legitimate concerns into consideration. For secured creditors, whose collateral has value equal to or exceeding their claims, reorganization may often affect somewhat adversely the value of such claims. Unsecured creditors generally can expect severe losses from either reorganization or liquidation.

THE COSTS OF BANKRUPTCY

Although our narrative suggests that bankruptcy costs are real, their measurement remains elusive. The 2- to 5-percent figure suggested earlier was based on reported legal and administrative expenses: the direct costs of bankruptcy. More specifically, the percentages pertained to railroads. Indirect costs or losses to security holders can be substantially higher. However, early warnings of distress manifest themselves in company financial statements—deteriorating working capital being one of a number of signals.[20] If heeded, bankruptcy may be avoided. Thus, some have suggested that

---

[20] See, for example, William H. Beaver, "Financial Ratios as Predictors of Failure," *Empirical Research in Accounting: Selected Studies*, supplement to the *Journal of Accounting Research* (1966, pp. 71–111). Edward J. Altman. "Financial Ratios, Discriminant Analysis and the Prediction of Corporate Bankruptcy," *Journal of Finance*, Vol. 23 (September 1968, pp. 589–609). Ismael G. Dambolena and Sarkis J. Khoury. "Ratio Stability and Corporate Failure," *Journal of Finance*, Vol. 35 (September 1980, pp. 1017–26). R. Charles Moyer. "Forecasting Financial Failure: A Re-examination," *Financial Management*, Vol. 6 (Spring 1977, pp. 11–17). Edward I. Altman, Robert G. Haldeman, and P. Narayanan. "Zeta Analysis: A New Model to Identify Bankruptcy Risks of Corporations," *Journal of Banking and Finance*, Vol. 1 (June 1977, pp. 29–54). Robert A. Collins. "An Empirical Comparison of Bankruptcy Prediction Models," *Financial Management*, Vol. 9 (Summer 1980, pp. 52–57).

rational investors would be more apt to conduct an informal reorganization—the bondholders, for example, buying out the stockholders—and reversing company policies rather than incurring the expenses of bankruptcy. Accordingly, transaction costs of the buyout could place an upward limit on bankruptcy costs.[21] This approach is consistent with the view that bankruptcy costs are small or can be easily finessed.[22] Others, however, suggest they can be very large.[23] The issue is far from resolved. As noted in the discussion of optimal capital structure, neither financial managers nor credit rating agencies act as though k_d is independent of leverage. The costs are real; their magnitude is at issue.

SUMMARY

The chapter title asks the question: "Why Working Capital?" On the surface, the answer seems obvious. However, the working capital decision is linked to the operating cycle: production, marketing, and collection of receivables do not occur simultaneously. Consequently, a firm must maintain a cash balance, a level of inventories, and an investment in receivables consistent with its credit policy. Technology will dictate the production aspect of the operating cycle. But management, through its credit policies, may be able to lengthen or shorten the time involved in collecting receivables; its actions, however, will be influenced by what its competitors do.

Though its ability to determine the length of the operating cycle may be limited, management enjoys greater latitude in establishing the proportion of total assets that will comprise working capital, as well as the composition of its financing. Of course, what management does will affect the firm's beta coefficient. However, the beta coefficient is inevitably linked with the cost of capital. Hence, decisions as to the level and the financing of working capital will affect how investors view the firm's systematic risk.

Because inadequate working capital is both a sign of financial distress and often the proximate cause of bankruptcy, the two conditions are bound together. Institutional practices for dealing with a bankrupt firm are such that creditors as well as stockholders may lose all or part of their investment. Although their magnitude remains in dispute, the direct and indirect costs of bankruptcy are real.

In perfect markets, direct bankruptcy costs are incorporated in the expected returns on securities used to finance the enterprise; however, other costs are not.

---

[21] Robert A. Haugen and Lemma W. Senbet. "The Insignificance of Bankruptcy Costs to the Theory of Optimal Capital Structure," *Journal of Finance*, Vol. 33 (May 1978, pp. 383–93). Of course, it is possible stockholders might buy out bondholders.

[22] See Merton Miller, "Debt and Taxes," *Journal of Finance*, Vol. 32 (May 1977, pp. 261–75).

[23] Robert E. Kalaba, Terence C. Longetieg, Nima Rasakhoo, and Mark Weinstein. "Estimation of Implicit Bankruptcy Costs," *Journal of Finance*, Vol. 39 (July 1984, pp. 629–42).

Liquidation always means loss of jobs and in some cases economic hardship for the entire community. But if resources are mobile, these negative factors can be minimized. Nevertheless, management and employees identify with the firm and not with MPT: working capital decisions look to the viability of the firm and not their impact on expected returns. A decision to reduce the amount of working capital financed from debt may have a marginal effect on the firm's beta coefficient, yet have a remarkable impact on management's ability to sleep well at night.

PROBLEMS AND QUESTIONS

1. Firms X and Y both have an unleveraged beta coefficient of 1.1 and both have a debt-to-equity ratio of .5 and a tax rate of .25. If R_m is 15 percent and i is 11 percent, what should their expected returns be?

2. Suppose in problem 1 firm X decides to finance more of its working capital and less of its long-term assets from debt than does firm Y. Hence, the term structure of its debt is shorter than that of firm Y. Would you expect the leveraged beta coefficients and thus expected returns of the two firms to differ even though the debt-to-equity ratio of both is the same? Explain.

3. "By increasing investment in current assets relative to total assets, management will lower the unleveraged beta coefficient of the firm." Comment.

4. It requires 10 days to convert inventory to finished goods, 3 days to acquire new inventory, 2 days to transport goods to customers, and 30 days for payment. How long is the firm's operating cycle? How long is the production portion of the operating cycle?

5. What is the difference between the absolute and relative priority theories of reorganization?

6. The One-Too-Many Corporation has gone into bankruptcy. It has the following capital structure:

	Principal or Book Value Plus Accrued Interest
Short-term Debt	
Secured bank loans	$ 11,400,000
Trade credit	20,000,000
Long-term Debt	
Secured equipment loans	32,600,000
Debentures	50,000,000
Equity	
Preferred stock	20,000,000
Common stock	40,000,000
	$174,000,000

In addition, there are court costs of $5,300,000 and unpaid salaries of $500,000 (no single individual owed more than $2,000). Also, $200,000 is owed for local property taxes. The company assets were sold at auction and brought $60,000,000; the equipment underlying the equipment loans and collateral securing the bank loans were sold and brought $25,000,000 and $9,000,000 respectively. How much will each security holder receive?

7. In problem 6 it was estimated that as a going concern One-Too-Many had a market value of $100,000,000. If the court reorganized the firm under absolute priority but consonant with the legal requirement of feasibility, develop a reorganization plan using the valuation figure. In establishing the reorganization plan, assume the court knows the equipment market value and collateral underlying the loans are $25,000,000 and $9,000,000, respectively. Before reorganization is completed, however, the court had to authorize an additional $4,000,000 in loans with priority over other securities but not over unpaid salaries, taxes, and court costs.

8. "Bankruptcy costs are not fully reflected in market price of the securities, even in perfect capital markets." Comment.

SELECTED ADDITIONAL REFERENCES

Altman, Edward. "A Further Empirical Investigation of the Bankruptcy Cost Question," *Journal of Finance*, Vol. 39 (September 1984, pp. 1067–89).

———. "Bankruptcy and Reorganization," in Edward I. Altman, ed., *Financial Handbook*, 5th ed. (New York: Wiley & Sons, 1982).

———. *Corporate Bankruptcy in America* (Lexington, MA: Lexington Books, 1971).

———. *Corporate Financial Distress* (New York: Wiley & Sons, 1983).

———. "Financial Ratios, Discriminant Analysis and the Prediction of Corporate Bankruptcy," *Journal of Finance*, Vol. 23 (September 1968, pp. 589–609).

Altman, Edward, Robert G. Haldeman, and P. Narayanan. "Zeta Analysis: A New Model to Identify Bankruptcy Risks of Corporations," *Journal of Banking and Finance*, Vol. 1 (June 1977, pp. 29–54).

Beaver, William H. "Financial Ratios as Prediction of Failure," *Empirical Research in Accounting: Selected Studies*, supplement to the *Journal of Accounting Research* (1966, pp. 71–111).

Bulow, J. I. and J. B. Shoven. "The Bankruptcy Decision," *Bell Journal of Economics and Management Science*, Vol. 9 (Autumn 1978, pp. 437–57).

Collins, Robert A. "An Empirical Comparison of Bankruptcy Prediction Models," *Financial Management*, Vol. 9 (Summer 1980, pp. 52–57).

Dambolena, Ismael G. and Sarkis J. Khoury. "Ratio Stability and Corporate Failure," *Journal of Finance*, Vol. 35 (September 1980, pp. 1017–26).

Epstein, David. *Debtor-Creditor Law*, 3rd ed. (St. Paul, MN: West Publishing Company, 1985).

Haugen, Robert A. and Lemma A. Senbet. "The Insignificance of Bankruptcy Costs to the Theory of Optimal Capital Structure," *Journal of Finance*, Vol. 33 (May 1978, pp. 383–93).

Kalaba, Robert E., Terence C. Langetieg, Nima Rasakhoo, and Mark Weinstein. "Estimation of Implicit Bankruptcy Costs," *Journal of Finance*, Vol. 39 (July 1984, pp. 629–42).

Knight, W. D. "Working Capital Management—Satisfaction vs. Optimization," *Financial Management*, Vol. 1 (Spring 1972, pp. 33–40).

Mehta, D. R. *Working Capital Management* (Englewood Cliffs, NJ: Prentice-Hall, 1974).

Miller, Merton. "Debt and Taxes," *Journal of Finance*, Vol. 32 (May 1977, pp. 261–75).

Moyer, R. Charles. "Forecasting Financial Failure: A Re-examination," *Financial Management*, Vol. 6 (Spring 1977, pp. 11–17).

Petty, J. William and David F. Scott. "The Analysis of Corporate Liquidity," *Journal of Economics and Business*, Vol. 32 (Spring/Summer 1980, pp. 206–18).

Silvers, J. B. "Liquidity, Risk and Duration Patterns in Corporate Financing," *Financial Management*, Vol. 5 (Autumn 1976, pp. 54–64).

Smith, K. V. *Guide to Working Capital Management* (New York: McGraw-Hill, 1974).

Tinsley, P. A. "Capital Structure, Precautionary Balances and Valuation of the Firm: The Problem of Financial Risk," *Journal of Financial and Quantitative Analysis*, Vol. 5 (March 1970, pp. 33–62).

Warner, J. B. "Bankruptcy, Absolute Priority, and the Pricing of Risky Debt Claims," *Journal of Financial Economics*, Vol. 4 (May 1977, pp. 239–76).

———. "Bankruptcy Costs: Some Evidence," *Journal of Finance*, Vol. 32 (May 1977, pp. 337–48).

White, Michelle J. "Bankruptcy Costs and the New Bankruptcy Code," *Journal of Finance*, Vol. 38 (May 1983, pp. 477–88).

———. "Public Policy Toward Bankruptcy: Me-First and Other Priority Rules," *Bell Journal of Economics*, Vol. 11 (Autumn 1980, pp. 550–64).

14

COMPONENTS OF
CURRENT ASSETS

As suggested in Chapter 13, components of current assets depend heavily on the nature of the operating cycle. Generally, a manufacturer has a comparatively high level of investment in inventories, both raw materials and finished goods. A personal-service firm has no investment in either; a retail-trade firm depends on turning inventories of finished goods into sales to earn a profit. All firms usually extend credit to customers and therefore use funds to carry accounts receivable. Cash balances, of course, are universally required to meet obligations as they are due. Idle funds, however, have an opportunity cost. Consequently, management attempts to minimize these balances. The alternative to cash is marketable securities. Thus cash, marketable securities, inventories, and receivables comprise the primary components of a firm's current assets. Each has unique characteristics that we examine in this chapter.

INVENTORIES

Of the major components of current assets, inventories have perhaps received the most extensive analytical treatment.[1] The reason for this is straightforward: in manufacturing, attention is focused on the efficient operation of the plant. Both the level of raw-material stocks held and their effective use figure prominently in efficiency of operations. Assuming the plant manager was told what to produce over a given period, perhaps a year, it is her responsibility to operate the plant so as to produce the output at the lowest possible cost given the available technology.

To illustrate, suppose the production manager was told she was to produce a specific amount of product over the year. Production will continue at a constant rate for the entire period. The output, metal tubes, will require specific amounts of raw materials in fixed proportions to produce each unit with uniform quality. A major task is to determine the optimal amount of inventory she must carry to run the plant efficiently. The amount necessary is shown in Figure 14-1(a); how that amount is determined is suggested in Figure 14-1(b).

Figure 14-1(a) indicates that inventory Q—what we shall call metal, the raw material employed in the manufacture of the tube—will be used over time as suggested by the line segment QT_n. In other words, in manufacturing metal tubes under the technological conditions obtained in the plant, the firm will exhaust its supply of metal in T_n days. Because it requires x days to deliver a new order of raw material, the production manager will ensure that the order is placed at $T_n - x$ days. If T_n is 30 days and x is four days, a new order for Q units is placed on the 26th day, arrives on the 30th day, and its production continues uninterrupted (or so the graph suggests).

---

[1] The literature is abundant. For an overview, sample E. S. Buffa and William H. Taubert, *Production-Inventory Systems: Planning and Control*, rev. ed. (Homewood, IL: Irwin, 1972); G. W. Plossi and O. W. Wright, *Production and Inventory Control: Principles and Techniques* (Englewood Cliffs, NJ: Prentice-Hall, 1967); John F. Magee and Harlan C. Meal, "Inventory Management and Standards," in J. Fred Weston and Maurice B. Goudzwaard, ed., *The Treasurer's Handbook* (Homewood, IL: Dow Jones-Irwin, 1976, pp. 496–542); Shizuo Senju and Seii Chi Fujita, "An Applied Procedure for Determining the Economic Lot Sizes of Multiple Products," *Decision Sciences*, Vol. 11 (July 1980, pp. 503–13).

Figure 14-1   Determining the Economic Order Quantity (EOQ)

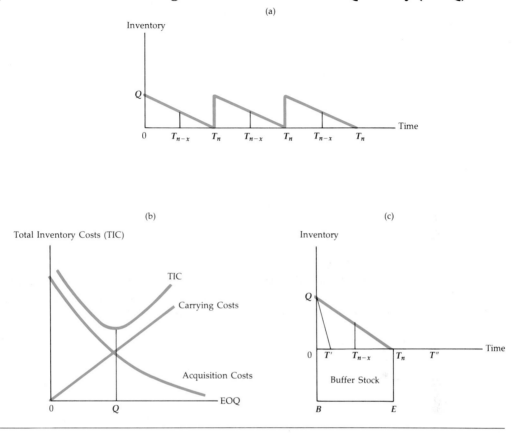

Determining Q is somewhat more complicated. Known as the **Economic Order Quantity** (EOQ), it represents the most efficient (lowest cost) level of inventory. Conceptually, there are two broad categories of costs associated with inventories. The first category is the cost of acquiring (ordering) them. The paperwork involved in placing orders and the opportunity cost of the personnel time are all about the same regardless of the order size. Thus, the larger the order, the lower the costs per unit of inventory purchased. Total acquisition costs are approximately constant. When graphed so that the two axes represent the quantity ordered and ordering cost per unit, the product of the two is a constant and the curve depicted an equilateral hyperbole of the form $xy = k$.

The second broad category is the cost of carrying the inventory. The larger the quantity stored the greater the amount of funds tied up in raw materials. Carrying costs rise at approximately a constant rate as more inventory is ordered. Although volume discounts for large orders may cause the slope to change, we shall ignore that refinement. As a result, carrying costs per unit of inventory are constant and total inventory cost increases linearly with the number of units ordered. Algebraically, let

Q = Economic Order Quantity (EOQ)

A = acquisition (ordering) costs

D = total demand for raw materials

C = carrying costs

$\dfrac{D}{Q}$ = number of inventory purchases per period

Then

Total Inventory Costs = Total Acquisition Costs + Total Carrying Costs

$$TIC \quad = \quad A\left(\frac{D}{Q}\right) \quad + \quad C\left(\frac{Q}{2}\right) \qquad \text{(14-1)}$$

Acquisition costs for the entire year are the product of the derived demand D for raw materials divided by the Economic Order Quantity Q. Each time the firm orders, it costs A dollars; the number of items it orders is $\dfrac{D}{Q}$. To carry Q units does not cost C dollars because the inventory is being used up over T_n days. The amount Q is in stock only on the first day. On day T_n, the firm runs out of inventory. Consequently, $\dfrac{Q}{2}$ represents the average amount of inventory held for T_n days. When we multiply by C, the cost of carrying the average amount of inventory, we obtain the total carrying costs.

Since acquisition costs decline and carrying costs rise with increases in inventory purchased, the EOQ is the minimum point on the curve that represents the total inventory costs (TIC). While the graph is easy to follow, determining EOQ (Q) in Figure 14-1(b) requires a little calculus. Differentiating the function, we obtain

$$\frac{d(TIC)}{dQ} = \frac{C}{2} - \frac{DA}{Q^2}$$

Setting the derivative equal to zero so as to calculate the minimum point Q, we obtain

$$CQ^2 - 2DA = 0$$

$$Q^2 = \frac{2DA}{C}$$

$$Q = \sqrt{\frac{2DA}{C}} \qquad \text{(14-2)}$$

Consequently, if D is 1,000,000 units, A is \$100, and C is \$5,000, then

$$Q^2 = \frac{2(1,000,000)(\$100)}{\$5,000}$$

$$Q^2 = \frac{\$20,000,000}{\$5,000}$$

$$Q = \sqrt{\$40,000}$$

$$Q = 200 \text{ units of raw material}$$

Although our production manager—who is probably an engineer—can no doubt perform the computations, this type analysis is usually performed by an employee with a calculator or preprogrammed computer. She is a production manager in part because she knows that models assist the decision-making process— they are not substitutes for it. No efficient production manager operates to the point at which a key raw material is depleted just as the next trainload or truckload arrives. The order point at $T_n - x$ must allow for transportation delays.

Suppose top management, responding to an unforeseen increase in demand, raises its production objectives. The sales manager wants product, not excuses. Top management responds by telling the production manager to use overtime or a second shift. Because the production manager is expected to deliver, she will always maintain a buffer stock of raw materials. Buffer stock ensures she can supply the product at an increased rate in the short run while allowing her staff to recompute the Economic Order Quantity. The change is suggested in Figure 14-1(c), where the time for using Q falls from T_n to T'. More orders must now be placed over the year to accommodate the increased demand. Thus, $\frac{D}{Q}$ becomes $\frac{D'}{Q}$ where $D' > D$. Hence, Q will change. While adjusting to the new EOQ, the production manager will make use of the buffer stock OT_nBE. If she is fortunate, the transition will be smooth and a bonus will await her at the end of a prosperous year.

However, buffer stocks tie up funds. Although buffer stocks assist in meeting unexpected increases in demand, there is a bleak side to the outlay for them. Suppose demand was overestimated and the EOQ required T''' days (longer than T_n days) to deplete. Again, the production manager must recalculate the EOQ. In the meantime, the financial manager is pressing for a reduction in buffer stock and curtailment of new orders of raw materials.

Because the actual rate of use depends on an accurate demand forecast, the EOQ estimate is only as good as the information on which it is based. The key variable is demand. Acquisition costs are comparatively easy to determine and reasonably stable. However, inventory carrying costs can change, sometimes rapidly. If interest rates—and therefore the cost of capital—rise, so do carrying costs. As a result, EOQ shifts left and levels of inventory decline. In the aggregate economy, rising interest rates can be associated with an overall decline and even a liquidation of inventories by business in general. Thus, demand and carrying costs will cause management to reassess inventory stocks.

Whether we are discussing raw materials or finished goods, the basic analysis is the same: each has a carrying cost but each is less expensive to acquire if purchased in large quantities. Although the balancing act can be performed using comparatively simple calculations, the EOQ is subject to change as the value of the variables, particularly demand, changes. Again, buffer stocks of raw materials and finished goods help management adjust to unexpected increases in demand. However, buffer stocks may appear excessive if demand is less than originally anticipated. Too little reserve causes the sales and production managers to reach for the Alka-Seltzer; too much sends the financial manager to the same remedy. In any event, the tolerance for large buffer stocks may be greater for the sales and production managers than for the financial manager. Clearly we have another example of conflict within the firm. To resolve the conflict, however, would take us beyond the scope of this volume.[2] Consequently, we draw the curtain on the scene, leaving the protagonists to their own devices.[3]

CASH MANAGEMENT

Although one can make long-range forecasts of cash needs consistent with long-range planning, the primary concern of management is with day-to-day cash inflows and outflows. Realistically, a planning horizon of one year is sufficient to allow for seasonal changes in the cash account. When developing the capital budget, management can include increases in net working capital in the outlay necessary for the projects being considered. Since growth implies an upward trend in all assets including cash, that trend would be factored into the cash needs for the year. Thus, if a company anticipates a 10-percent growth in sales next year, the additional working capital necessary to finance such sales would be included in the forecast. If the 10-percent increase meant the firm would have to expand production facilities, the working capital outlay would be part of the capital budget.

---

[2] To determine the appropriate buffer stock, one must know (in technical jargon) *the stockout acceptance factor.* Production specialists have retreated to formulas for the answer. See, for example, Arthur Snyder, "Principles of Inventory Management," *Financial Executive,* Vol. 32 (April 1964, pp. 13–21). Although the formulas are helpful in specifying the problem, the solution remains one of resolving the conflict between managers charged with different responsibilities. The problems associated with excessive inventories are of greater concern to the financial manager than are stockouts due to unexpected increases in demand. For the sales and production managers, the reverse is true.

[3] *A Bonus Footnote!*   As a rising young star in the company, you notice the managers appear polarized over the issue. Discretely, you suggest that departures from the EOQ may not be as inefficient as Figure 14-1(b) suggests. By your computations, a 10-percent increase or decrease in EOQ raises TIC by only 1 percent. The curve, in other words, slopes gently near the EOQ. Perhaps there is greater flexibility in ordering and hence less need for as large a buffer stock as the sales and production managers originally desired. Assuming you are right, a bonus and promotion await you following the next merit evaluation.

For our purposes, we shall assume management already has taken the trend into account and that its current concern is a cash forecast that allows for seasonal fluctuations in the cash account over the course of a year. The problem is illustrated in Figure 14-2. The label O represents cash outlays; the label I represents cash inflows. Management anticipates a cash outlay of $10 million per month throughout

Figure 14-2 **Seasonal Pattern of Cash Balances for a Hypothetical Firm**

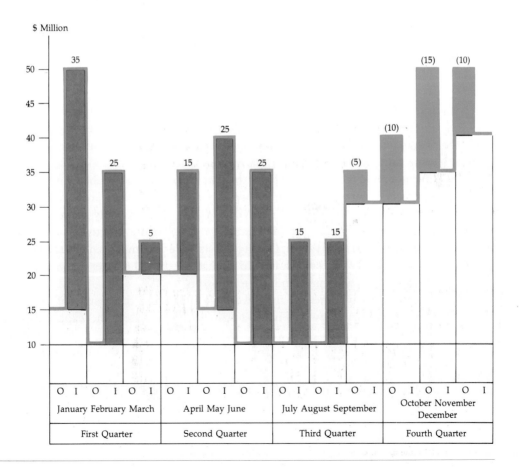

its various facilities. Given the projections, this amount represents wages, salaries, and other necessary expenses, in the absence of any seasonal pattern. For a growing firm, this figure will rise over time.

Management also anticipates a distinct seasonal pattern in cash inflows and outflows. For example, a large retail concern with national outlets could experience a first-quarter inflow of cash as receivables representing Christmas buying are liquidated and January sales bring in a flow of cash. During the second quarter there may be a rise, first in cash outflows and then in cash inflows, as firms prepare for the spring and Easter seasons and subsequently as they liquidate their stock. Inventories require investment. Once sold, inventories are replaced with receivables and receivables ultimately turned into cash. Much of the third quarter represents summer sales as stock is reduced. The fourth quarter, which in some instances represents 50 percent of annual sales, suggests a major buildup of inventories and receivables and an outflow of cash. Although part of these inventories and receivables will be financed from short-term loans, banks usually finance only 70 to 80 percent of the cost of inventories and the face value of receivables. The balance must come from permanent financing: long-term debt or equity. As a result, some of the cash generated in surplus months may be placed in short-term marketable securities for reinvestment in inventories and receivables during the seasonal peak. This is the story suggested by the cash pattern shown in Figure 14-3.

There are, however, two important elements missing. The first missing element is the category of outlays that may not be periodic expenses, as are wages or salaries. For instance, management may wish to use some of the cash generated earlier in the year to repay a portion of the principal on long-term debt not due periodically. At the same time, management will plan to liquidate short-term loans secured to carry inventory and receivables. The latter plan we have placed in the months of January, February, March, April, and May, where cash outflows are greater than those represented by the black line. Management will probably want its short-term borrowing at or near zero immediately prior to the fourth-quarter buildup of inventories and receivables. During the slack period, management also may wish to use some of the excess cash to help finance the capital budget for the year, thereby reinvesting cash earnings in long-term assets.[4]

For our hypothetical firm, we have illustrated the results of the foregoing planned cash outlays in Figure 14-3. The bars reflect the expected difference between cash inflows and outflows for the twelve months shown in Figure 14-2. In this instance the black line represents planned use of cash for other than monthly expenses and repayment of short-term loans. The numbers at the top of each bar suggest the level of cash balances after taking these planned expenditures into account.

---

[4] Assuming management has determined its *optimal* combination of debt and equity financing, retained earnings over and above planned dividends may be employed (in lieu of a new issue of stock) to finance the equity portion of the capital budget.

Figure 14-3   **Seasonal Pattern of Cash Balances for a Hypothetical Firm**

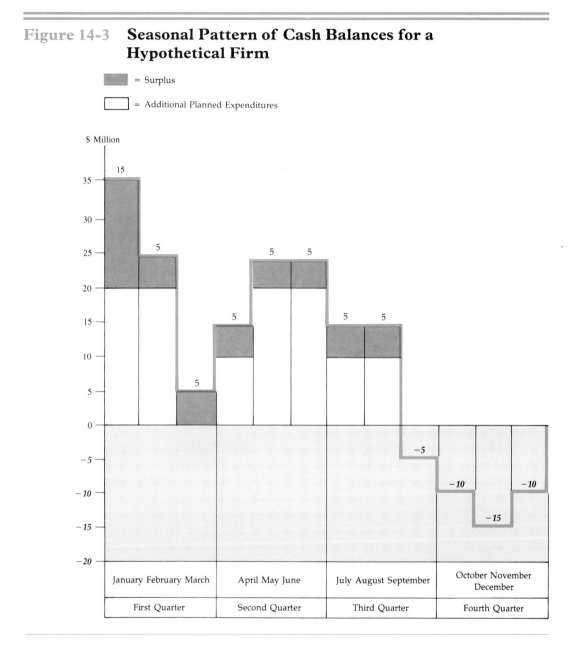

The second missing element in our analysis is the random (or stochastic) nature of cash flows. It is in the cash account that the firm experiences the nature of the business and financial risks it is undertaking. Sales may rise, yet receivables may not be paid as rapidly as projected. Alternatively, sales may not be as robust as initially anticipated. Moreover, unexpected expenses may materialize, such as unplanned repairs of plant and equipment. The pitfalls are numerous and the cash-flow forecast may have to be revised throughout the year.

Nevertheless, it is useful to start with a plan and revise it when necessary. Accordingly, we have summarized the planned cash outflows, including periodic expenses, in Figure 14-4. The dark shaded areas suggest that for the first eight

Figure 14-4   Total Projected Cash Inflow and Outflow for a Hypothetical Firm

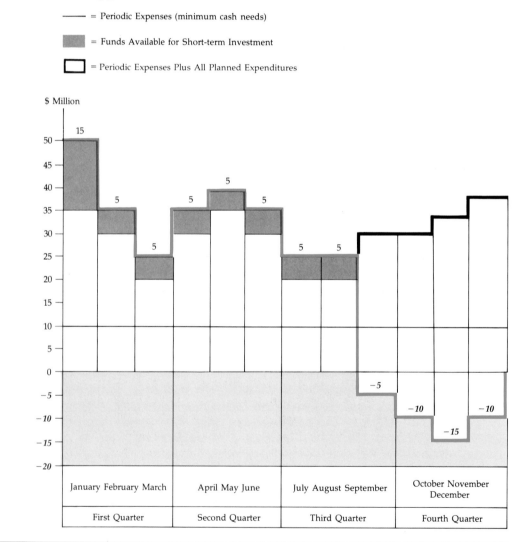

months of the year management expected to set aside funds in short-term investments and to liquidate those securities during the seasonal peak, thereby providing the additional funds necessary to cover the cash deficits expected in the last four months. Consequently, the additional $15 million cash generated in January could be invested for as long as eight months, and longer, since only $5 million would be needed in September and an additional $10 million in October. Furthermore, an additional $5 million cash is expected to be generated from February through August. Of this $35 million total, $25 million would be needed for November and December. Thus, $10 million could be left indefinitely in marketable securities, as it would not be needed to finance seasonal needs. Has management overestimated its cash needs? Should some of these funds be added to the capital budget or used to declare an extra dividend? Let us examine these issues.

MODELING CASH FLOWS

John Maynard Keynes, the famous British economist, noted that individuals have three reasons for holding cash: (1) the transaction motive, (2) the precautionary motive, and (3) the speculative motive. If we adapt these motives to the firm, we can assume management invests cash within the firm in long-term assets based on the capital budgeting principles adumbrated earlier. For our purposes this is the speculative motive, and the cash plan calls for expenditures on plant and equipment. Hence, we shall concentrate on the transaction and precautionary motives.

If demand for cash were similar to demand for raw materials, we could apply the inventory model developed earlier (see Equation 14-2). Carrying costs would represent the opportunity costs of cash: interest lost by not investing the funds in marketable securities. In this instance, carrying costs C would be expressed as a percentage rather than as dollars (as is the case with inventory). Acquisition costs would represent the ordering costs in buying or selling securities. As in the case of inventories, ordering costs are largely invariant with the order size.

In principle, therefore, one could determine the EOQ or, in this instance, the optimal cash balance. But what time period should we use? If a year is employed, we would sum the unshaded areas in Figure 14-4: $355 million. There would, however, be considerable variation in outlays over the course of the year. Because there are expenses that must be incurred each month, it is more plausible to estimate the EOQ on a monthly basis. The periodic expenses (the transactions demand for cash) are $10,000,000 per month. If the costs of buying or selling securities were $100 per order and the interest rate were .01 (1 percent per month), the optimal cash balance would be

$$EOQ = \sqrt{\frac{2(\$10,000,000)(\$100)}{.01}}$$
$$= \$447,213.60$$

To meet the periodic expenses of the firm, management should have available a $447,213.60 cash balance. This means the firm would make

$$\frac{\$10,000,000}{\$447,213.60} = 22.36$$

transactions of marketable securities into cash per month. However, the cash balance does not take into account planned outlays during the slack season and additional cash outlays during seasonal peaks. Furthermore, there is no guarantee cash will be consumed at a constant rate. For example, the payroll may be met weekly, biweekly, or at the end of the month. In fact, there may be sufficient random aspects in cash outlays to warrant a buffer stock or a precautionary balance to meet unforeseen contingencies. In this instance, it is the financial manager—not the production or marketing managers—who is primarily concerned with the lack of inventory: cash inventory. Finally, one must consider the inflows of cash. Even good credit risks may pay bills randomly during the payment period or there may be some bunching near the end of the month.

Thus, when applied to cash balances, the inventory model may not be particularly useful. An alternative approach would provide for uncertainty in cash flows. One such model was developed by Merton H. Miller and Daniel Orr.[5] As in the case of inventories, the model depends on both the fixed costs associated with securities transactions and with the opportunity costs of cash. In addition, the model depends on the variance in daily cash flows.

As shown in Figure 14-5, the key element in the model is the return point Z, which represents the optimal daily cash balance. Balances are allowed to fluctuate between the upper control limit h (which equals $3Z$) and the lower control point, which is either zero or some positive cash level representing management's precautionary motive or buffer stock. When the cash balance reaches h, securities are purchased and the balance is returned to Z. When the balance reaches the lower control limit, securities are sold and the cash balance is returned to Z. Since developing the model further takes us beyond the scope of the text, we simply show the final result:

$$Z = \sqrt[3]{\frac{3b\sigma^2}{4i}} \tag{14-3}$$

where

$$b = \text{fixed costs associated with securities}$$
$$i = \text{daily interest rate on marketable securities}$$
$$\sigma^2 = \text{variance in daily cash flows}$$

---

[5] See Merton H. Miller and Daniel Orr, "A Model of the Demand for Money by Firms," *Quarterly Journal of Economics*, Vol. 80 (August 1966, pp. 413–35). For an application of the technique, see ————, "The Demand for Money by Firms: Extension of Analytic Results," *Journal of Finance*, Vol. 23 (December 1968, pp. 735–59).

Figure 14-5   **Graphical Representation of the Miller-Orr Model for Cash Management**

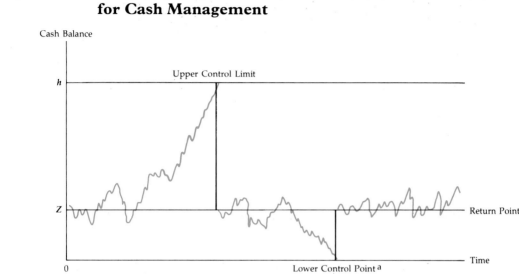

ᵃ Lower control point shown is zero. If management had chosen a positive balance to satisfy its precautionary motive, the lower control point would be greater than zero.

The measure of variance may be historical. Again, the model could be applied on a monthly basis, with a new value for Z calculated each month. For example, suppose the historical pattern of cash balances were to suggest that during January daily cash balances averaged $1,500,000, with a variance of $400,000. The fixed costs of securities purchased or sold is $100. The annual rate of interest on marketable securities is 12 percent, so the daily rate is

$$\frac{.12}{365} = .000329$$

Therefore,

$$Z = \sqrt[3]{\frac{3(\$100)(\$400,000)}{4(.000329)}}$$
$$Z = \$4,500.99 = \$4,500$$

Because $h = 3Z$, the upper control limit would be $4,500 \times 3 = \$13,500$. These figures assume the lower control point is zero. If, however, management expects (for precautionary reasons) to maintain a minimum cash balance of $10,000, Z would be $14,500 and h would be $23,500. The values, of course, could change as variance changed month by month.

CONTROLLING THE TRANSACTIONS DEMAND FOR CASH

Management is likely to find that the transactions demand for cash is neither totally stochastic nor always predictable. Consequently, determining the optimal cash balance requires considerable judgment. Moreover, modern techniques for collecting funds and controlling disbursements can help reduce some of the stochastic elements in cash flows. Let us see how this is accomplished.

If management can concentrate payment of bills so that the firm can anticipate receiving the funds on a specific date, it will reduce the randomness of daily cash flows. To do this, the firm might employ **preauthorized checks** for customers making periodic payments on installment contracts. The customer simply signs an agreement that permits the firm or the firm's bank to write a check on the customer's account on a specified date and for a fixed amount. This is programmed through the firm's computer and the bank automatically transfers the funds to the firm's account on the specified date. A **preauthorized debit** has the same effect as a preauthorized check: the funds are charged against the customer's account and automatically transferred by wire to the firm's account. If such funds are deposited in several banks throughout the country, management may nominate banks in specific regions—one in Chicago, Boston, New York, Atlanta, San Francisco, and so forth—as regional centers, where **concentration accounts** are maintained and funds are wired from local banks. Even if management does not employ preauthorized checks or debits, it may reduce the time necessary to process a check by having the customer mail payment to a centrally located post office box or **lock box**, from which the firm's bank obtains the mail, deposits the check, and periodically transfers the funds to the concentration account.

Similarly, firms attempt to slow cash payments through controlled disbursements. While centralizing receipts, firms may decentralize payments. Thus, a firm may write checks on an account that receives only one shipment of checks from the Federal Reserve each day. The receiving bank can debit the firm's account and immediately inform management of the remaining funds available for investment that day. Alternatively, instead of maintaining funds at banks on which checks are written, the firm may utilize a **zero balance account**. When the checks drawn against that account are tabulated, the firm transfers funds from the central account.[6]

Modern computer services allow companies to fine-tune both receipts and disbursements to a degree unknown prior to 1970. Although there are costs to the

---

[6] Michael Dotsey. "An Investigation of Cash Management Practices and Their Effects on the Demand for Money," *Economic Review*, Vol. 70 (September–October 1984, pp. 3–12).

process, they have fallen over time. Moreover, a complementary development in financial instruments even accommodates daily cash balances. In principle, a corporation should be able to reduce its noninterest-bearing transaction accounts virtually to zero. This is a major goal of modern cash management.

CASH AND MARKETABLE SECURITIES

In Table 14-1 we list and briefly describe some of the more conventional instruments available for investing temporarily idle funds. For the financial manager, the choice involves certain essential considerations, the first of which is safety: investments are substitutes for cash. Most managers, whether their concern is variance or systematic risk, view this portfolio as virtually risk-free. This is true for U.S. Treasury bills and federal agency securities, although the latter are only indirectly backed by the U.S. Treasury and hence yield slightly more than Treasury bills with the same maturity. The remainder are at risk. In 1970, for example, Penn Central defaulted on $82 million in outstanding commercial paper.[7] In 1984, if the Federal Deposit Insurance Corporation had not agreed to guarantee all deposits of Continental Illinois (the statutory limit was $100,000), holders of large certificates of deposit (CDs) would have suffered considerable losses.[8] In 1979, when First Pennsylvania failed, the FDIC did not guarantee deposits in excess of $100,000. Although both were bank holding companies, the former was intimately involved with the movement of funds from all over the world, whereas the latter was a regional banking company. To prevent what might have created a major panic, the FDIC took an unprecedented step. Once it is taken, financial managers may assume that deposits, regardless of size, are guaranteed; however, as of this writing, regulations do not require any such guarantee.

A related consideration is liquidity: some instruments have poor secondary markets. The market for Treasury bills is excellent and easily accessed; the market for directly placed commercial paper depends on the willingness of the issuer to buy it back before maturity. For instance, a financial manager may develop a relationship with General Motors Acceptance Corporation whereby GMAC will repurchase its commercial paper prior to maturity. Such private arrangements are widespread and can be tailored to suit the needs of both issuer and buyer.

A third consideration is interest-rate risk. Even if a financial manager can commit funds for six months and chooses U.S. Treasury bills as the vehicle, it is

---

[7] Peter Abken. "Commercial Paper," *Economic Review*, Vol. 67 (March–April 1981, pp. 11–22).

[8] Gary Hector. "The Nationalization of Continental Illinois," *Fortune*, Vol. 110 (August 20, 1984, pp. 135, 136, and 140).

Table 14-1   A Potpourri of Marketable Securities

Security	Description	Maturity (new issues)	Standard Denomination	Interest Payment	Secondary Market
U.S. Treasury Bills	Direct obligation of U.S. government	91, 182, 364 days	$10,000 (minimum)	Discount only	Excellent at all maturities
Federal Agency Issues	Notes of agencies and corporations enacted by but not directly backed by U.S. government	Short-term to several years—much of it less than one year	$5,000 (minimum)	Discount and interest-bearing	Good to excellent
Short-term Tax-exempt Notes	Issued by states, municipalities, and related agencies; interest exempt from federal income tax.	Two months to one year	$1,000 (minimum)	Either discount or interest-bearing with payment at maturity	Good
Commercial Paper (dealer placed)	Unsecured notes issued by industrial firms, non-U.S.–based companies, and small finance companies	30 to 270 days	$100,000	Discount only	None, but dealer may arrange buyout
Commercial Paper (finance company)	Unsecured notes issued by large finance companies and some bank holding companies	3 to 270 days	$100,000	Discount only	None, but company will usually redeem before maturity if asked
Negotiable Certificates of Deposit (CDs)	Receipts for large time-deposits at commercial banks	30 to 91 days or longer	$1,000,000	Interest-bearing with payment at maturity	Good
Eurodollars	Dollar-denominated time-deposits at foreign banks	1 to 365 days	$1,000,000	Interest-bearing with payment at maturity	None
Banker's Acceptances	A time-draft issued by a firm and accepted (hence guaranteed) by a bank	30 to 180 days	$100,000	Discount only	Good
Repurchase Agreements (repos)	Sale of government securities by bank or dealer with agreement to repurchase	One day to three months	$500,000	Repurchase price set higher than selling price	Limited
Money-Market Mutual Funds	Pool of short-term money market instruments	Shares may be sold anytime	$500	Interest credited to account monthly	Fund provides liquidity by buying back shares

possible for yields to rise or fall during the period. When the funds are actually invested until maturity, the rate is *locked up*. Suppose, however, an unforeseen demand for cash arises three months after the investment is made. If interest rates have risen, the yield on the outstanding six-month issue now three months from maturity approximates the yield on a newly issued 91-day Treasury bill. To illustrate (recalling the discussion in Appendix 3-A), suppose on a bank discount basis that the yield on a 180-day Treasury bill when issued is 8 percent, so that the price paid is

$$.08 = \frac{360}{182}\left(\frac{100 - p}{100}\right)$$
$$8.00 = 197.802198 - 1.97802198p$$
$$p = 95.9556$$

Now suppose at the end of three months, when the company needs the funds, that the yield on a 91-day Treasury bill is 12 percent on a bank discount basis, so that

$$.12 = \frac{360}{91}\left(\frac{100 - p}{100}\right)$$
$$12 = 395.6043956 - 3.95604956p$$
$$p = 96.9667$$

In the secondary market, the outstanding 6-month issue with 91 days remaining will be priced so as to yield approximately 12 percent on a bank discount basis. In terms of simple interest, the financial manager has realized

$$i = \frac{365}{91}\left(\frac{96.9667 - 95.9556}{95.9556}\right)$$
$$i = 4.223\%$$

If held to maturity, the original investment would have yielded

$$i = \frac{365}{182}\left(\frac{100 - 95.9556}{95.9556}\right)$$
$$i = 8.45\%$$

Thus, by selling the securities prior to maturity, the financial manager has realized an economic (if not an accounting) loss. Of course, if interest rates had declined, he or she would have experienced a gain. For example, if the bank discount on a 91-day Treasury bill is 6 percent rather than 12 percent, then

$$.06 = \frac{360}{91}\left(\frac{100 - p}{100}\right)$$
$$p = 98.4833$$

The simple interest yield on a six-month bill, if sold after three months, would be

$$i = \frac{365}{91}\left(\frac{98.4833 - 95.9556}{95.9556}\right)$$
$$i = 10.57\%$$

To hedge against interest-rate risks, financial managers may use the financial futures market. How this market functions is discussed in Chapter 20.

A fourth consideration is minimum maturities. It is one thing to anticipate seasonal needs and invest a portion of surplus cash in longer maturities. As suggested earlier, a major goal of modern cash management is to keep noninterest-bearing demand deposits as close to zero as possible. Because random factors affect cash balances, it is difficult to keep all idle funds invested unless instruments of short maturities are available and their transaction costs do not absorb all the returns that might be earned.

To accomplish this end, firms may purchase outstanding Treasury bills or newly issued commercial paper maturing in a few days. Transaction costs for short-term bills may be fairly high. Directly placed issues of commercial paper maturing in a few days may represent only a fraction of the commercial paper issued. Consequently, what many firms find useful are repurchase agreements or RPs (repos) negotiated with commercial banks in which concentration accounts are maintained. Under a repurchase agreement, the buyer, a commercial bank, acquires funds through the sale of securities to the depositing firm and simultaneously agrees to repurchase the securities at a later date.[9] Maturities can be as short as one day. Moreover, the financial manager may have a continuing contract with the bank by which excess funds are supplied daily and the contract is treated as though the account were reestablished daily. As long as the instruments used as collateral for the RPs are securities of the federal government or a federal agency, the bank is not required to maintain reserves against the funds borrowed from depositors. From the financial manager's viewpoint, RPs are collateralized with risk-free securities. On balance, the net yield after taxes and transaction costs may be higher than on Treasury securities of comparable maturities. Because the firm is a major depositor in the bank and because the bank has direct access to federal funds — the market for Federal Reserve funds of other banks — it is comparatively easy for the bank to make cash available to the firm through wire transfers of funds on a day-to-day basis.

Thus, financial managers of nonfinancial business firms — indeed, managers of any firm with a seasonal pattern of cash flows punctuated by daily random fluctuations — are in a position to develop a portfolio of marketable securities that allows them to maintain cash balances sufficient to meet anticipated daily cash needs.

---

[9] Norman N. Bowsher. "Repurchase Agreements," *Monthly Review*, Federal Reserve Bank of St. Louis (September 1979, pp. 17–22). Charles M. Lucas, Marcos T. Jones, and Thom Thurston. "Federal Funds and Repurchase Agreements," *Quarterly Review*, Federal Reserve Bank of New York, Vol. 2 (Summer 1977, pp. 33–48).

Some small firms may be shut out of certain markets because they lack the funds necessary for minimum purchases. However, with commercial banking facing an increasingly competitive environment, it is likely that the RP or some variation of it will soon be available to smaller companies.[10]

ACCOUNTS RECEIVABLE

The decision to extend credit is a decision to invest funds in accounts receivable. The investment entails some risk, since the customer may not be able to pay the bill when due. Cash on delivery (COD) would eliminate the risk, yet credit is an integral part of doing business. In 1986, credit among nonfinancial corporations, **trade credit**, accounted for 41 percent of the financial assets of nonfinancial corporations and more than 15 percent of total assets.[11] For most business firms, the decision is not whether credit will be extended but to whom it will be extended and in what amount.

To determine whether or not to grant credit, management sometimes examines the financial statements of customers but more often consults Dun & Bradstreet, its reference book, or the computer-based retrieval system of the National Association of Credit Management. The firm also may use banks or trade associations for the same purpose. In some cases, past experience with other customers may provide the information required to determine the creditworthiness of a specific customer. Although there are sophisticated methods for separating good and bad credit risks, in extending credit most firms try to rely on the track records of prospective customers charted by banks and rating services.[12] For this, of course, a price must be paid. Once the information is obtained, its price is a sunken cost. However, whether the cost is $50 or $500, without the information management will be unable to evaluate the profitability of extending credit. Let us examine the issue more closely.

THE DECISION TO EXTEND CREDIT— THE BASIC MODEL

Credit extension can be viewed in the same framework as investment in plant and equipment. The details, however, will differ. Presumably one extends credit because the present value of the increased sales is greater than the costs associated with

---

[10] See, for example, George G. Kaufman, "Banking as a Line of Commerce: The Changing Competitive Environment," in Thomas M. Havrilesky and Robert Schweitzer, *Contemporary Developments in Financial Institutions and Markets* (Arlington Heights, IL: Harlan Davidson, 1983, pp. 156–83).

[11] Calculated from data in Board of Governors of the Federal Reserve System. *Balance Sheets for the U.S. Economy 1945–86* (Washington: U.S. Government Printing Office, May 1987, p. 21).

[12] See, for example, Robert A. Eisenbeis and Robert B. Avery, *Discriminant Analysis and Classification Procedures* (Lexington, MA: D. C. Heath, 1972); Robert A. Eisenbeis, "Pitfalls in the Application of Discriminant Analysis in Business, Finance and Economics," *Journal of Finance*, Vol. 32 (June 1977, pp. 875–900); O. Maurice Joy and John O. Tollefson, "On Financial Applications of Discriminant Analysis," *Journal of Financial and Quantitative Analysis*, Vol. 10 (December 1975, pp. 723–40).

carrying the customer. Thus, the key question is: What will net increased sales and ultimate profit be from extending credit? When entering a particular business *de novo*, a firm may find that its competitors extend credit as a matter of policy: customers appear to demand both the goods and the credit. Hence, the firm must also extend credit as a matter of policy.[13] In practical terms, the firm determines whether to extend credit to a new customer on the basis of the net present value of the sales less the cost associated with them.

Suppose, for example, a potential customer is willing to buy $100,000 worth of merchandise each year. Variable costs of supplying the merchandise are $80,000.[14] Credit check indicates the customer pays bills when due. Normal credit terms are 30 days. In this instance, therefore, the firm carrying this potential customer will have an average investment or outlay in accounts receivable of

$$\$80,000 \times \frac{30}{365} = \$6,575$$

More generally, the initial investment in accounts receivable for a new customer typical of the firm's clientele is

$$O = \frac{V}{S} \times \frac{R}{\dfrac{S}{365}} \times \frac{S}{365} \tag{14-4}$$

where

$$O = \text{outlay}$$
$$V = \text{variable costs}$$
$$R = \text{accounts receivable balance for period}$$
$$S = \text{total sales for period made on credit}$$

The expression $\dfrac{R}{\dfrac{S}{365}}$ equals the average collection period, which we have assumed is 30 days. If that period is typical, the average collection period is also 30 days. Similarly, variable costs are 80 percent of sales. If that is typical both for this potential customer and more generally for the firm, then

$$O = \frac{\$80,000}{\$100,000} \times 30 \times \frac{\$100,000}{365} = \$6,575$$

---

[13] It is, of course, not unusual for firms to offer discounts for prompt (if not immediate) cash payment. A 2-percent discount for payment made within ten days is common. This discount, however, is an option open to the customer. It is rare—particularly for sales from one business firm to another—to conduct business exclusively on a COD basis, even when prices are lower than those charged by competitors.

[14] It is generally assumed that capacity to produce is available: the marginal customer does not force management to add to plant and equipment.

Cash flows equal profits on sales less cash expenses for credit and collection costs plus bad-debt allowance. The residual is reduced by taxes paid, resulting in the familiar after-tax cash flow. In general terms: $ATCF = [S - V - S(BD) - C](1 - T)$, where

$$ATCF = \text{after-tax cash flow}$$
$$S = \text{sales}$$
$$V = \text{variable costs}$$
$$BD = \text{percent of sales that are bad debts}$$
$$C = \text{credit and collection costs}$$
$$T = \text{marginal corporate tax rate}$$

Assume BD for the firm is typically 1 percent. This potential customer's credit rating suggests it fits into the group that on average experiences a 1-percent loss due to bad debts. Assume further that credit and collection costs involved in servicing this type of account are $1,000 and the marginal tax rate for the firm is 40 percent. Thus

$$ATCF = [\$100,000 - \$80,000 - \$100,000(.01) - \$1,000](1 - .4)$$
$$= [\$20,000 - \$1,000 - \$1,000](1 - .4)$$
$$= \$10,800$$

Assuming a k_o of 18 percent, we find the net present value of an investment in an account receivable is

$$NPV = -O + ATCF \frac{[1 - (1 + r)^{-n}]}{r}$$

To simplify the mathematics, assume the firm anticipates sales of $100,000 per year indefinitely. Therefore

$$NPV = -\$6,575 + \frac{\$10,800}{.18}$$
$$NPV = -\$6,575 + \$60,000$$
$$NPV = \$53,425$$

In this instance, the computations indicate the firm should accept the new account. Although the model is consistent with present value calculations for capital budgeting, some qualifications prevail. Specifically, it may be necessary to raise or lower the probability of bad-debt losses for a particular customer. The purpose of the credit check is to forecast the risk involved in extending credit. When multiplying that risk by the percentage of sales, we attribute average experience to the customer. However, in this instance, the customer may not in fact default. If there are 100 customers in the same risk class, each with $100,000 in purchases, the total sales are $10,000,000 and tax deductible bad-debt loss is $100,000

($10,000,000 × .01). The technique employed in the calculations is a pro-rata allocation of bad-debt losses under the assumption that marginal risk and average risk are the same. Likewise, the figure for credit and collection costs is based on typical experience with similar customers. The marginal cost of credit and collection is presumably equal to the average cost. If this is not true, adjustments must be made in the calculations.

Using average cost of capital k_o as the discount rate necessarily brings us back to our earlier quandary: Is it the systematic risk of the marginal investment or is it the average cost of capital that should determine the investment decision? Since we have discussed this issue at suitable length, we shall not repeat the controversy here.

In addition, there is the outlay or information cost of determining creditworthiness of the customer. Such costs, as noted, must be incurred or one runs the risk of granting credit to those who cannot or will not pay. To minimize these costs, management may want to conduct a worst-case scenario to determine whether a thorough analysis is warranted. Suppose, for example, that policy limits credit extension to customers whose accounts are outstanding for an average of 60 days, who are likely to average credit and collection costs of $2,000 per year, and for whom the bad-debt allowance is 4 percent. Then

$$O = \frac{\$80,000}{\$100,000} \times 60 \times \frac{\$100,000}{365} = \$13,151$$

$$ATCF = [(\$100,000 - \$80,000) - 4\%(\$100,000) - \$2,000](1 - .4)$$
$$= [(\$20,000 - \$4,000 - \$2,000].6$$
$$= \$8,400$$

Assuming an indefinite annual sales volume at this level, then

$$NPV = -\$13,151 + \frac{\$8,400}{.18}$$
$$= -\$13,151 + \$46,667$$
$$= \$33,516$$

The calculations suggest it is in the interests of the company to run the credit check. Suppose, however, it was questionable whether the account would extend beyond a year. Assuming $100,000 in sales during the year and a $13,151 investment in receivables, then[15]

$$NPV = -\$13,151 + \frac{\$8,400 + \$13,151}{1.18}$$
$$= -\$13,151 + \$18,264$$
$$= \$5,113$$

---

[15] In this instance, profits would occur periodically. The $13,151 would be liquidated after approximately 14 months, not at the end of the year. We ignore these refinements, however, in order to develop the central point.

Because the expected *NPV* is positive, management will make the necessary credit check. In most cases, however, the customer wants a quick response or will seek a competitor that offers similar terms. Thus, management must often commit to information costs rapidly. However, with experience, managers quickly learn to discern whether to incur the costs of a credit check. In this instance, preliminary tests suggest the firm should do so. Generally, the cost of a credit check is small relative to potential profits from large orders.[16]

TERMS AND CONDITIONS OF SALES

Once credit is extended, the terms and conditions will vary with the customer. In addition, often there are terms and conditions common to the industry. For marginal credit risks, COD may be the only term offered; more generally, however, customs of the industry prevail.

Such industries as chemicals, plastics, and industrial machinery employ a net-30 basis: bills must be paid in 30 days. Retail customers—those of us who are consumers—understand such conditions. If we pay within the billing cycle of approximately 30 days, there is no service charge.[17] If we meet the minimum payment requirements, credit continues to be granted up to a predefined limit; however, there is a service charge of from 1 to 1.5 percent each month on the balance outstanding.

In granting trade credit, however, firms generally do not impose service charges on one another. They may carry a customer beyond the due date, valuing the outlet. Although sporadically late payments present no undue difficulties, consistently late payments lower a customer's credit status.

It is not uncommon for industries to grant the following terms:

1/10 net 30

2/10 net 30

2/10 net 60

In all cases, the customer is given a choice: pay the bill within 10 days and receive a 1- or 2-percent discount. If that discount is not taken, the full amount is due in 30 days

---

[16] *Large* is a relative term. A $100,000 order for hosiery by a retail chain could be significant compared with an ordinary sale. On the other hand, it may be small if it represents tires purchased by an automobile manufacturer. In either case, however, the credit check may be routine, costing only a few dollars.

[17] *A Bonus Footnote!*   Watch the billing date on your credit statement. If, for example, the statement date is the 5th of the month and all bills must be paid by the last day of the month to avoid a service charge, you have approximately 25 or 26 days to pay the bill. If you purchase on the 6th of the month, however, you will not be billed until the next cycle—giving you an entire month plus 25 or 26 days. Of course, if you make it a habit to buy and pay in this manner, it becomes known to services that run credit checks. Consequently, as a consumer, your credit rating becomes marginally lower than one who pays bills promptly upon receipt.

or, in such industries as stationery, paints, and wire goods, 60 days. Many sellers find the discount profitable. Using our earlier illustration, suppose the customer is given 1/10 net-30 terms. If accepted, the supplier's outlay is

$$O = \frac{\$80,000}{\$99,000} \times 10 \times \frac{\$99,000}{365} = \$2,192$$

After-tax cash flow is

$$
\begin{aligned}
ATCF &= [(\$99,000 - \$80,000) - \$1,000 - \$1,000](1 - .4) \\
&= [\$19,000 - \$2,000].6 \\
&= \$10,200
\end{aligned}
$$

$$
\begin{aligned}
NPV &= -\$2,192 + \frac{\$10,200}{.18} \\
&= -\$2,192 + \$56,667 \\
&= \$54,475
\end{aligned}
$$

Granting a 1-percent discount suggests that net present value is greater (\$54,475 > \$53,425). From the customer's perspective, he or she receives a 20-day loan with an interest payment of \$1,000. In terms of simple interest, the customer pays

$$i = \frac{\$1,000}{\$99,000} \times \frac{365}{20} = 18.43\% \text{ per year}$$

The customer may be able to acquire a lower rate of simple interest from a commercial bank. If so, because both parties would appear to benefit from early payment, the discount is likely to be offered and taken.

Whatever terms are granted, and even conventional terms may change during periods of tight money, most trade credit is granted on *open account*.[18] Occasionally, **sight drafts** or **time drafts** are employed; each is an order to pay a specified amount at a point in time to a given person or to the bearer. The sight draft is similar to COD: the customer does not take title to the goods until the draft is paid. A time draft, however, allows the customer to pay within a certain number of days. If the customer's bank accepts the draft, it becomes a **banker's acceptance** and hence a marketable short-term security, one of the several available for cash management portfolios.

Although sight and time drafts may be used by firms when they have insufficient information about the credit status of the customer or when the goods delivered are

---

[18] Other common terms are 2/10 net 60 with seasonal dating. This is used for agricultural equipment, where seasonal patterns are distinct. Equipment is delivered early but the invoice is postdated so the customer can take advantage of the discount 10 days thereafter. Net 10 EOM is common for knitted garments and outerwear. EOM (end of month) is assumed to mean 25th of the month, with payment due the 10th of the following month. 2/10 EOM means 2-percent discount if paid by the 10th of the following month. Sometimes the word *proximo* is substituted, so that 2/10 proximo is the same as 2/10 EOM. Peculiarities abound in particular industries. Gas stations often purchase load-to-load, paying for the previous load when the next load arrives.

large (transportation equipment, for instance), the primary use of a draft, particularly a time draft, is in international trade. It is routine for the seller, an exporter, to receive a letter of credit from the foreign customer's (importer's) bank (in another country) guaranteeing payment or honoring a draft drawn on the foreign bank in the name of the importer. When the letter of credit is received by the exporter, the goods are shipped together with a draft and a **bill of lading**. The bill of lading serves as a contract between buyer and seller, and provides title to the goods on acceptance of the draft. (See Chapter 22 for discussion on the financing of international trade.)

MONITORING RECEIVABLES

As noted, the average collection period is the receivables balance at the end of a year divided by the ratio of the credit sales for the year to 365. Thus, if a firm has a receivables balance of $35,000,000 and its credit sales for the year were $219,000,000, its average collection period is

$$\frac{\$35,000,000}{\dfrac{\$292,000,000}{365}} = 43.75 \text{ days}$$

On the average, it takes the firm 43.75 days to collect a bill.

Averages, however, can mask seasonal collection patterns. For example, credit sales in December may exhibit the following pattern:

December Sales	Percent Collected
December	5
January	40
February	40
March	15

Credit sales in June, however, may exhibit the following pattern:

June Sales	Percent Collected
June	30
July	20
August	10

Accordingly, firms may have to vary their investment in receivables. This pattern, as we have seen, will affect cash amounts available for investment in short-term securities.

Individual accounts also will be monitored to determine whether they continue to be profitable. For example, if payments are late—so that what was assumed to be 30 days now averages 90 days, the outlay increases considerably. Again turning to our earlier example

$$O = \frac{\$80,000}{\$100,000} \times 90 \times \frac{\$100,000}{365} = \$19,726$$

If credit and collection costs rise to $3,000 and bad-debt probability increases to 15 percent, then

$$ATCF = [(\$100,000 - \$80,000) - .15(\$100,000) - \$3,000](1 - .4)$$
$$= \$1,200$$

$$NPV = -\$19,726 + \frac{\$1,200}{.18}$$
$$= -\$19,726 + \$6,666.67$$
$$= -\$13,059$$

Thus, delays in payment, increases in credit and collection costs, and a rise in bad-debt probability can turn a before-the-fact profitable credit sale into an after-the-fact loss.

SUMMARY

In this chapter, we have briefly surveyed the principles underlying management of the four major working capital components—inventory, cash, marketable securities, and receivables—the order dictated in part by the level of analytical sophistication attached to the management of each. Within the manufacturing process, once the production has been made, the EOQ model provides management with some insight into efficient levels and use of raw materials. Even if production schedules change, it is possible to adapt the inventory model to the new levels.

By contrast, sophisticated management of cash and marketable securities is of relatively recent vintage. Attempts to apply the inventory model to cash management have given way to stochastic models designed to deal with the short-term variability that accompanies cash flows. In addition, the rapidly changing institutional environment has affected both cash receipts and disbursements—management trying to speed up the former while slowing down the latter. The means has also developed whereby firms can invest virtually their entire cash balance at approximately risk-free rates for periods as short as one day. Consequently, the marketable securities component of the portfolio can be accommodated not only to traditional/seasonal cash needs but also to random fluctuations in cash balances.

The principles underlying extension of credit have not been affected quite so much by the changing institutional environment. A firm must still determine whether to extend credit to a new customer. Although access to modern computers offers the firm better information concerning the payment patterns of a potential customer than existed several years ago, management must still incur the cost to make an informed decision. It must then set the terms and conditions on which credit is granted and subsequently monitor the collection process.

Trade credit extended is in part offset by trade credit received. Thus, accounts receivable have a counterpart, accounts payable—a major component of short-term financing—a topic to which we now turn.

PROBLEMS AND QUESTIONS

1. Windy Widget Corporation requires 200,000 units of raw materials to meet expected demand for the coming quarter. Acquisition costs are $200 and carrying costs are $2,000.

   a. What is the Economic Order Quantity (EOQ)? The Total Inventory Cost (TIC)?

   b. Suppose management expects demand to be either 10-percent higher or 10-percent lower than anticipated. How would the EOQ and TIC be affected?

   c. Would your answers to (b) play a role in determining the buffer stock? Explain in detail.

2. Suppose Bangor Bobsled, a manufacturer of winter sports equipment, has monthly cash expenses of $75,000. Because of the seasonal nature of its business, cash inflows and outflows over and above basic expenses are as follows:

	Inflows	Outflows		Inflows	Outflows
Jan	$200,000	$20,000	Jul	$ 10,000	$ 60,000
Feb	175,000	15,000	Aug	10,000	90,000
Mar	150,000	10,000	Sep	40,000	100,000
Apr	150,000	0	Oct	80,000	200,000
May	90,000	0	Nov	250,000	50,000
Jun	10,000	0	Dec	300,000	20,000

   a. What is the net of cash inflows and outflows for each month of the year?

   b. Assume the firm begins each year with no short-term loans outstanding. It pays all its bills and receives all its revenues at the end of the month. Develop a schedule of maturities for short-term investments and loans that will carry Bangor Bobsled through the year.

3. Niantic Educational Research and Development (NERD), a postgraduate think tank, depends solely on seminar fees for revenue. Fees are paid quarterly. The treasurer estimates he must pay $1,000,000 in salaries and other expenses every three months. Fees, payable in advance, are expected to equal $1,050,000 per quarter.

   a. Using the inventory model, develop an optimal cash balance on the assumption that interest rates are 4 percent per quarter and transaction costs are $100.

   b. What would happen to the optimal cash balance if interest rates fell to 2 percent per quarter?

   c. Is the inventory model useful to a business such as NERD? Explain in detail.

4. The treasurer of Reno, Las Vegas, and Winnemucca Trucking finds a variance in daily net cash flows of approximately $10,000. The opportunity cost of funds is 16 percent per year. It costs $100 to process an order for securities. Using the stochastic model, estimate the optimal cash balance toward which the treasurer should strive.

5. Suppose in problem 4 the treasurer estimates the variance could be as high as $12,000 or as low as $8,000. What might he do with the firm's cash balance to ensure sufficient cash at all times?

6. What are the four major factors management must consider before investing temporarily idle funds in short-term securities?

7. Between May 1982 and April 1985, five major U.S. Government Securities dealers failed. All were involved in the *repo* market. What is that market? How can managers of nonfinancial corporations who invest short-term funds in the repo market ensure the safety of their funds?

8. Suppose a potential customer with an expected annual sales volume of $175,000 applies for credit at ABC Corporation. The variable costs of the merchandise to be purchased are 75 percent of sales and the average collection period is expected to be 45 days.

   a. What is the average investment in accounts receivable?

   b. Assuming bad-debt losses of 2 percent of sales, collection costs of $500, and a marginal tax rate of .35, what is the expected after-tax cash flow?

   c. The firm's average cost of capital is 16.5 percent. It expects the potential customer to account for $175,000 in sales for the next five years. What is the net present value of accepting the credit risk?

9. In problem 8, suppose the average collection period was 60 days and the bad-debt probability was .10. All else remains unchanged.

a. What is the net present value of the potential account?

b. Would you expect bad-debt loss to be independent of credit and collection costs? Explain in detail.

SELECTED ADDITIONAL REFERENCES

Abken, Peter. "Commercial Paper," *Economic Review*, Federal Reserve Bank of Richmond, Vol. 67 (March–April 1981, pp. 11–22).

Bowsher, Norman. "Repurchase Agreements," *Monthly Review*, Federal Reserve Bank of St. Louis (September 1979, pp. 17–22).

Brick, Ivan E. and William K. H. Fury. "The Effect of Taxes on the Trade Credit Decision," *Financial Management*, Vol. 13 (Summer 1984, pp. 24–30).

Buffa, Elwood S. *Modern Production-Operations Management*, 7th ed. (New York: Wiley & Sons, 1980).

Buffa, Elwood S. and William H. Taubert. *Production-Inventory Systems: Planning and Control*, rev. ed. (Homewood, IL: Irwin, 1972).

Christie, George N. and Albert E. Bracuti. *Credit Management* (Lake Success, NY: Credit Research Foundation, 1981).

Dotsey, Michael. "An Investigation of Cash Management Practices and Their Effect on the Demand for Money," *Economic Review*, Federal Reserve Bank of Richmond, Vol. 70 (September–October 1984, pp. 3–12).

Eisenbeis, Robert A. "Pitfalls in the Application of Discriminant Analysis in Business Finance and Economics," *Journal of Finance*, Vol. 32 (June 1977, pp. 875–900).

Eisenbeis, Robert A. and Robert B. Avery. *Discriminant Analysis and Classification Procedures* (Lexington, MA: D. C. Heath, 1972).

Joy, O. Maurice and John O. Tollefson. "On Financial Applications of Discriminant Analysis," *Journal of Financial and Quantitative Analysis*, Vol. 10 (December 1975, pp. 723–40).

Kaufman, George G. "Banking as a Line of Commerce: The Changing Competitive Environment," in Thomas M. Havrilesky and Robert Schweitzer, *Contemporary Developments in Financial Institutions and Markets* (Arlington Heights, IL: Harlan Davidson, 1983, pp. 156–63).

Lucas, Charles M., Marcos T. Jones, and Thom Thurston. "Federal Funds and Repurchase Agreements," *Quarterly Review*, Federal Reserve Bank of New York, Vol. 2 (Summer 1977, pp. 33–48).

Magee, John F. and Hurlan C. Meal. "Inventory Management and Standards," in J. Fred Weston and Maurice B. Goudzewaard, ed., *The Treasurer's Handbook* (Homewood, IL: Dow Jones-Irwin, 1976, pp. 476–542).

Miller, Merton H. and Daniel Orr. "A Model of the Demand for Money by Firms," *Quarterly Journal of Economics*, Vol. 80 (August 1966, pp. 413–35).

————. "The Demand for Money by Firms: Extension of Analytic Results," *Journal of Finance*, Vol. 23 (December 1968, pp. 735–59).

Plossi, George and O. Wright. *Production and Inventory Control: Principles and Techniques* (Englewood Cliffs, NJ: Prentice-Hall, 1967).

Sachdeva, Kanwal S. and Lawrence J. Gitman. "Accounts Receivable Decisions in a Capital Budgeting Framework," *Financial Management*, Vol. 10 (Winter 1981, pp. 45–49).

Senju, Shizuo and Seii Chi Fujita. "An Applied Procedure for Determining the Economic Lot Sizes of Multiple Products," *Decision Sciences*, Vol. 11 (July 1980, pp. 503–13).

Vander Weide, James and Steven F. Maier. *Managing Corporate Liquidity* (New York: Wiley & Sons, 1985).

15

SHORT- AND INTERMEDIATE-TERM FINANCING

As noted in Chapter 13, the term structure of debt can affect the average cost of capital k_o. A firm with a preponderance of assets financed primarily with relatively short-term loans could be faced with the need to refinance these assets with longer-term loans at higher rates of interest. Alternatively, if interest rates decline and a firm has considerable short-term debt outstanding, management could choose to lengthen the maturity of such debt. Modern financial theory, of course, suggests that predicting changes in the level and term structure of interest rates is difficult. Few (if any) analysts are consistently successful in spotting underlying trends.

The problem can be finessed if the term structure of a firm's assets are matched by the term structure of the firm's financing. Thus, inventories and receivables are current assets: by convention they are presumed liquidated in less than a year. Hence, they could be matched: financed from current liabilities such as short-term bank loans or trade credit extended by inventory suppliers. Similarly, longer-term assets (transportation equipment, for example) could be financed with loans designed to be repaid over the useful life of the asset—perhaps a term loan to be repaid in five years. Carried to its logical conclusion, investment in certain long-term assets (new plant, for example) would be financed with long-term funding sources, such as bonds that mature in 20 or 30 years or some interim period that represents the useful life of the asset.

If the matching principle is taken literally, the nature of the business determines the term structure of the liabilities. To a degree, this is what actually happens. Public utilities, for example, have a comparatively high proportion of investment in long-term assets. As a result, the capital structure of many utilities consists of a comparatively high proportion of long-term liabilities. Many manufacturing industries rely heavily on long-term assets and finance them accordingly. Because of their greater variability in operating earnings, manufacturers rely more heavily than utilities on equity rather than long-term debt. Where inventories and receivables constitute a major proportion of total assets, as in wholesale and retail trades and in some areas of manufacturing, heavy reliance is placed on short-term funding sources.

Notwithstanding, there is never complete symmetry in matching assets with liabilities. Convention dictates that short-term lenders expect some long-term investment in working capital. Otherwise, current assets would equal current liabilities and not working capital: current assets less current liabilities would be zero. Since the firm maintains a long-term equity investment in all its assets, net working capital is positive, not zero. Of course, accounting practice can result in anomalies explicable only by scrutinizing the details. For example, current liabilities may exceed current assets, giving the appearance of negative working capital. The bulk of current liabilities, however, may be a construction loan to provide interim financing for a new plant. This loan will be **funded** (shifted) into long-term debt as the plant nears completion. When that happens, short-term financing disappears and current assets again exceed current liabilities.

None of the foregoing precludes management from deliberately creating greater asymmetry between the term structure of assets and the term structure of debt, which might not otherwise occur in the normal course of financing. As we have seen, management might choose to fund a relatively high proportion of current assets from long-term sources, thereby maintaining a comparatively high level of net working capital. Alternatively, to the extent it can do so, management may choose to borrow heavily using short-term maturities to finance long-term assets (rolling over or renegotiating construction loans, for example) in the hope of funding such assets at lower interest rates than those currently in force.

Whatever the strategy, in this and in Chapter 16 we examine in some detail the basic sources open to management. The emphasis in this chapter, however, is on current sources: those maturing within a year or less. Although we do consider certain types of term loans that mature within a few years, we reserve the discussion of long-term financing for Chapter 16.

Our primary purpose here is to introduce the major types of instruments employed. Because variations abound and innovations can be rapid, do not assume that what follows encompasses the full range of alternatives. Rather, view the exercise in much the same way as you would view the sight-seeing tour of a large city. Your guide covers the major points of interest, and you return to explore those that seem most intriguing. Chapter 15 covers the major points of interest only; the Selected Additional References offer an opportunity to explore particular topics more deeply.

PRIMARY SHORT-TERM SOURCES

If we accept the conventional definition of a short-term funding source as one that matures within a year, we can identify three primary types: trade credit, commercial bank loans, and commercial paper. The first and second types are standard sources employed by nearly every business firm. The third type is employed by a growing number of firms with access to national credit markets: large well-known corporations.

Because they mature within a year, one can compare the costs of each funding source using the standard equation for calculating a simple or nominal rate of interest initially employed in Appendix 3-A for calculating the yield on a Treasury bill. Thus

$$k_i = \text{cost of funds} = \frac{\$ \text{ of interest}}{\text{amount borrowed}} \times \frac{365}{\text{number of days funds borrowed}}$$

We employ this basic approach to calculate the cost of each type of short-term funding source discussed in this chapter. Because we are comparing alternatives for which all expenses are tax deductible, we limit our computations to the pretax cost of capital.

TRADE CREDIT

As noted in Chapter 14, in 1986 trade credit accounted for 41 percent of the financial assets of nonfinancial corporations and more than 15 percent of their total assets. In Chapter 14, we were concerned with the terms and conditions under which credit is granted. An asset to the firm granting credit is, of course, a liability to the firm accepting credit. To the recipient, trade credit has a cost and the terms under which it is granted may be a considerable incentive to repay the loan or fund it from another source. Thus, as we suggested in Chapter 14, a customer who obtains 1/10 net-30 terms on $100,000 worth of merchandise is effectively paying $1,000 (0.1 ×

$100,000) for a 20-day loan, so that

$$k_i = \frac{\$1,000}{\$99,000} \times \frac{365}{20} \times 100 = 18.43 \text{ percent}$$

Similarly, if the discount had been 2 percent, then

$$k_i = \frac{\$2,000}{\$98,000} \times \frac{365}{20} \times 100 = 37.24 \text{ percent}$$

For many customers, the opportunity cost of cash or the cost of an alternative funding source is often less than the implicit cost of the loan; hence, they will take advantage of the discount. On the other hand, net 30 terms offer the customer an interest-free loan for thirty days; hence, there is no cost incentive to repay before the due date.

When trade credit is granted, the supplier becomes an unsecured creditor of the company to which credit has been extended. If the supplier, because of insufficient credit information or poor past experience, refuses to supply the goods except for cash on or before delivery, there is in effect no credit granted and the funds must come from some other source.

COMMERCIAL BANK LOANS

After trade credit, perhaps the most pervasive short-term funding source is the commercial bank loan. Because of rapid institutional change (which cannot be discussed in detail in this volume), terms under which commercial banks lend money are in a state of flux. Suffice it to say that commercial banks, once the exclusive suppliers of short-term funds to most businesses, are now being challenged by other financial institutions—including life insurance companies and foreign banks—as well as by freer access to the commercial paper market.[1]

---

[1] In 1987, for example, the state of Connecticut completely eliminated the legal distinctions between state-chartered thrift institutions and commercial banks. For a further discussion of changes in intermediaries, see Thomas F. Brady, "Changes in Loan Pricing and Business Lending at Commercial Banks," *Federal Reserve Bulletin*, Vol. 71 (January 1985, pp. 1–13); Evelyn M. Hurley, "The Commercial Paper Market Since the Mid-Seventies," *Federal Reserve Bulletin*, Vol. 68 (June 1982, pp. 326–34); Peter Abken, "Commercial Paper," *Economic Review*, Federal Reserve Bank of Richmond, Vol. 67 (March–April 1981, pp. 11–22); Alfred Broaddus, "Financial Innovation in the United States—Background, Current Status and Prospects," *Economic Review*, Federal Reserve Bank of Richmond, Vol. 71 (January–February 1985, pp. 2–22); Peter S. Rose and Donald R. Fraser, *Financial Institutions*, 2nd ed. (Plano, TX: Business Publications, 1985, pp. 535–55). Legislative changes are summarized in "Research Staff of the Federal Reserve Bank of Chicago: The Depository Institutions Deregulation and Monetary Control Act of 1980," *Economic Perspectives*, Vol. 4 (September/October 1980, pp. 3–23) and Gillian Garcia et al., "The Garn-St. Germain Depository Institutions Act of 1982," *Economic Perspectives*, Vol. 7 (March/April 1983, pp. 3–31). See also, Andrew S. Carron, *Reforming the Bank Regulatory Structure* (Washington, DC: The Brookings Institution, 1984); Thomas F. Cargill and Gillian G. Garcia, *Financial Reform in the 1980's* (Palo Alto, CA: Hoover Institution Press, 1985); Arnold Sametz, ed., *The Emerging Financial Industry* (Lexington, MA: Heath and Company, 1984); Kerry Cooper and Donald Fraser, *Bank Deregulation and the New Competition in Financial Services* (Cambridge, MA: Bellinger Publishing Company, 1986).

Nevertheless, one can distinguish among basic loan types. For example, a loan may be made to cover a single transaction. The borrower signs a promissory note that specifies (1) interest rate; (2) amount borrowed; (3) collateral, if any; and (4) maturity date as well as any other terms to which the parties agree. Such a loan usually has a specific purpose: it may be to fund the purchase of inventory or to finance accounts receivable. In such cases, either may be pledged as collateral.

More generally, a firm with an excellent credit rating may seek an unsecured **line of credit** to meet seasonal needs; under such an agreement, a firm can borrow up to a specified amount. A firm with a $100,000 line of credit may borrow up to that amount at any time during the life of the agreement. When the agreement expires, the balance outstanding must be repaid and a new line of credit established. At one time firms anticipated the availability of lines of credit; however, the periodic credit shortages of recent years caused many banks to reduce their lines of credit, leaving firms to scramble for funds or curtail their purchases of inventories even in the face of rising demand.

As a result, banks began to make greater use of **revolving loan commitments** that guaranteed corporations a specific amount of credit over an extended period of time, often two to three and possibly up to ten years.[2] Although guaranteed, the firm had to pay a commitment fee on any unused portion of the commitment. Thus, if a firm had a $1,000,000 revolving loan commitment and was using $600,000 only, the firm would pay a fee of perhaps three-fourths of 1-percent interest per year on the unused $400,000. Assuming the firm did not commit itself to borrowing the $400,000 for a year, the cost of having it available would be $3,000. Revolving loan commitments are becoming the dominant type of commercial and industrial loans. One sample indicated that such loans rose from 24.7 percent of all commercial and industrial loans in the fourth quarter of 1977 to 44.2 percent in the fourth quarter of 1983.[3] Another sample at about the same time estimated that more than half the outstanding commercial and industrial loans were revolving loan commitments.[4]

THE PRICE OF BANK LOANS

At one time, the price (interest) charged on nearly all commercial bank loans was based on the **prime rate**: the rate a bank charged its best customers. Other customers often paid the prime rate plus 2 percent. Although the prime still plays a major role in determining the price of smaller loans, commitments in excess of $1,000,000 are—because of competition from other sources—more closely tied to

---

[2] Karlyn Mitchell. "Trends in Corporation Finance," *The Economic Review*, The Federal Reserve Bank of Kansas City, Vol. 68 (March 1983, pp. 14–15).

[3] Same as [1], Brady, p. 2.

[4] Same as [2], p. 15.

money-market rates. Thus, a bank may make a short-term loan of perhaps 90 days using a markup over the rate it offers depositors on a 90-day certificate of deposit (CD). If the 90-day CD rate were 9 percent, a 2 percent markup to 11 percent still might be below the prime rate existing at the time, yet competitive with commercial paper. Similarly, multimillion-dollar loan commitments may be tied to a CD with a fixed maturity selected by the borrower, or to the **London Interbank Offered Rate (LIBOR)**. The latter is the rate at which banks in different countries trade. A potential customer may have access to loans in dollars deposited in U.S. branches abroad or in foreign banks. Such deposits are known as **Eurodollars**. A domestic bank competing for this loan may have to offer a rate that represents a markup based on the LIBOR, particularly if the LIBOR is lower than the prevailing rates on domestic CDs. For customers with access to alternative funding sources, competition is sufficient to bring actual rates in line with the cost of funds to the lender, plus a competitive markup for servicing the loan.

THE COST OF BANK LOANS

The rate, of course, only represents the loan cost if paid at maturity. Thus, the cost of a twelve-month loan for $1,000,000 at 11 percent is

$$k_i = \frac{\$110,000}{\$1,000,000} \times 100 = 11\%$$

Similarly, if the loan matured in 90 days with interest paid at maturity, interest equals

$$.11 \times \$1,000,000 \times \frac{90}{365} = \$27,123.29$$

and

$$k_i = \frac{\$27,123.29}{\$1,000,000} \times \frac{365}{90} \times 100 = 11.00\%$$

Although loans may be tailored so that the stated rate of interest is the cost of the funds, in practice the cost is likely to be higher. The least expensive increment would come from using a 360- rather than a 365-day year, a practice virtually universal among banks. If so, in the above illustration interest equals

$$.11 \times \$1,000,000 \times \frac{90}{360} = \$27,500$$

and

$$k_i = \frac{\$27,500}{\$1,000,000} \times \frac{365}{90} \times 100 = 11.153\%$$

Interest will more likely be based on a 360-day year and taken out in advance: the loan is *discounted*, so that net proceeds = $1,000,000 − $27,500 = $972,500.

$$k_i = \frac{\$27,500}{\$972,500} \times \frac{365}{90} \times 100 = 11.468\%$$

In addition, the bank could demand **compensating balances** on the loan: the borrower must maintain a percentage of the loan (on balance) in the account at all times. Reflecting on our discussion of cash management in Chapter 14, compensating balances can impose a burden on management expecting to invest all excess dollars at interest. Thus, if the compensating balance was 20 percent of the principal, the firm would have only the use of $800,000 ($1,000,000 − .2 × $1,000,000). Consequently

$$k_i = \frac{\$27,500}{\$1,000,000 - \$200,000 - \$27,500} \times \frac{365}{90} \times 100 = 14.437\%$$

Because such an increase in the effective rate often turns borrowers to alternative sources, competition has forced a decline in the use of compensating balances. Moreover, because competition has forced banks to relate fees more closely to costs—at least for loans where competition is effective—commitment fees rather than compensating balances are more closely associated with the costs of making loans. When a borrower exercises rights under a commitment, a bank must be in a position to honor it. Hence, a portion of the bank's portfolio must be invested in instruments that are easily liquidated but whose yield is comparatively low. Alternatively, the bank may have to borrow, employing repos (as discussed in Chapter 14) in order to honor its commitments. Because the bank adjusts its portfolio to make commitments, a fee is justified when the entire amount committed is not used.

Continuing with our 11-percent 90-day loan, suppose the borrower uses 50 percent of the loan commitment for 45 days and 90 percent for the additional 45 days, and repays the loan at the end of 90 days. The commitment fee is .75 percent and interest is deducted in advance (there are no compensating balances). With the banker's 360-day year, the commitment fee is (unused portion) × (annual commitment fee) × (portion of year):

$$\text{first 45 days} = (\$1,000,000 - \$500,000)(.0075)\frac{45}{360} = \$468.75$$

$$\text{next 45 days} = (\$1,000,000 - \$900,000)(.0075)\frac{45}{360} = \frac{\$\ 93.75}{\$562.50}$$

The discount payments are:

$$90 \text{ days} = \$500,000 \times .11 \times \frac{90}{360} = \$13,750$$

$$45 \text{ days} = \$400,000 \times .11 \times \frac{45}{360} = \frac{\$ 5,500}{\$19,250}$$

For our purposes, we can view the interest payments as broken into two 45-day periods, so that

$$\text{first 45 days} = \$500,000 \times .11 \times \frac{45}{360} = \$ 6,875$$

$$\text{next 45 days} = \$900,000 \times .11 \times \frac{45}{360} = \frac{\$12,375}{\$19,250}$$

k_i on the loan is now additive, so that

$$k_i = \left[\frac{\$6,875 + \$468.75}{\$500,000 - \$13,750} + \frac{\$12,375 + \$93.75}{\$900,000 - \$5,500} \right] \left[\frac{365}{45 + 45} \right] \times 100$$

$$k_i = (.015103 + .013939)4.05\overline{5} \times 100$$

$$k_i = (.029042)4.05\overline{5} \times 100$$

$$k_i = 11.778\%$$

Note that interest is calculated subtracting discounts as they occur. Interest, however, is based on a $500,000 loan for 45 days and a $900,000 loan for 90 days. If the commitment fee is due at the end of 90 days, we can rearrange the arithmetic:

$$k_i = \left[\frac{\$6,875}{\$500,000 - \$13,750} + \frac{\$12,375 + \$562.50}{\$900,000 - \$5,500} \right] \left[\frac{365}{45 + 45} \right] \times 100$$

$$k_i = (.014139 + .014463)4.05\overline{5} \times 100$$

$$k_i = (.028602)4.05\overline{5} \times 100$$

$$k_i = 11.60\%$$

Let us now assume the loan commitment is for 180 days. However, for the second 90 days it is tied to the 180-day CD rate prevailing at the time the commitment is made. Assume further this rate is 10 percent and the premium remains 2 percent. This is known as a *variable-rate loan commitment*, with the rate specified at 2 percent above the 90- and 180-day CD rates prevailing at the time of commitment.[5] Assume also that the borrower follows the foregoing pattern; for the second 90 days, however, the borrower uses the entire $1,000,000 line of credit, with

---

[5] Alternatively, the second rate may be the prevailing rate 90 days from the date of commitment.

interest discounted in advance, and commitment fee paid at maturity. The discount payments are now:

$$90 \text{ days} = \$500,000 \times .11 \times \frac{90}{360} = \$13,750$$

$$\$28,750$$

$$90 \text{ days} = \$500,000 \times .12 \times \frac{90}{360} = \$15,000$$

$$45 \text{ days} = \$400,000 \times .11 \times \frac{45}{360} = \$\ 5,500$$

$$\$17,500$$

$$90 \text{ days} = \$400,000 \times .12 \times \frac{90}{360} = \$12,000$$

$$90 \text{ days} = \$100,000 \times .12 \times \frac{90}{360} = \$\ 3,000$$

$$\$49,250$$

The interest payments (the sum of which equal the bank discounts) are now:

$$45 \text{ days} = \$500,000 \quad \times .11 \times \frac{45}{360} = \$\ 6,875$$

$$45 \text{ days} = \$900,000 \quad \times .11 \times \frac{45}{360} = \$12,375$$

$$90 \text{ days} = \$1,000,000 \times .12 \times \frac{90}{360} = \$30,000$$

$$\$49,250$$

The loan configuration is now:

$$k_i = \left[\frac{\$6,875}{\$500,000 - \$28,750} + \frac{\$12,375}{\$900,000 - \$17,500} + \frac{\$30,562.50}{\$1,000,000 - \$3,000} \right]$$

$$\times \left[\frac{365}{45 + 45 + 90} \right] \times 100$$

$$k_i = (.014589 + .014023 + .030654)2.02\overline{7}$$

$$k_i = 12.018\%$$

The preceding calculations illustrate the complexities involved in attempting to measure the cost of a loan with variable rates of interest and a commitment fee when interest is discounted in advance. The approach is arithmetic, which permits discounts to be subtracted as they occur. However, interest payments are based on balances outstanding: interest on $500,000 for 45 days, $900,000 for 45 days, and $1,000,000 for 180 days. As long as the face amount of the loan is due at maturity and the commitment is a year or less, this approach to calculating simple interest is adequate.

Suppose, however, the contract is set up as an **installment loan** and the firm borrows $1,000,000 at 11 percent for one calendar year. A monthly payment based on principal and total interest of $110,000 is:

$$\frac{\$1,000,000 + \$110,000}{12} = \$92,500$$

Interest is paid on the entire principal even though approximately one-half the principal is returned within six months. The approximate annual percentage rate on such a loan is:

$$k_i = \frac{\$110,000}{\dfrac{\$1,000,000}{2}} \times 100 = 22.00\%$$

Viewed somewhat differently, a geometric average of monthly interest rates on a declining principal (see Table 15-1) reveals that the purchaser pays (on average) 2.8085 percent per month in interest for the year.

Needless to say, installment loans are not employed by banks seeking to attract commercial customers with access to alternative funding sources. Installment loans are, however, popular when banks extend credit to consumers purchasing automobiles, refrigerators, and the like. Although the dollar amount financed is relatively low and the dollar interest payment comparatively low, the percentage paid on installment loans is relatively high.

SECURED LOANS

In general, commitments of the foregoing type are unsecured. Firms and even individuals may obtain unsecured loans: if the credit rating is excellent and the banking relationship successful—payments in the past made on schedule—it is possible to obtain unsecured credit. Those who cannot meet prescribed standards may have to use collateral.[6] Since much of short-term financing is for the purpose of carrying receivables or inventories, these assets become standard sources of collateral for such loans. Under the Uniform Commercial Code (operational in nearly every state), a standardized document (security agreement) is used to list the

---

[6] *A Bonus Footnote!*   As an individual seeking a loan for a single purpose, not a line of credit, you may have established a credit rating sufficient to warrant an unsecured loan. However, you may still want to use collateral (U.S. government securities, for example) because the bank charges a lower rate when collateral is employed.

Table 15-1 Effect of Installment Payments on Interest[a]

Month		Interest	Month		Interest
(1)	$\dfrac{\$9,166.67}{\$1,000,000}$	= .009167	(7)	$\dfrac{\$9,166.67}{\$1,000,000 - 6(\$83,333.33)}$	= .018333
(2)	$\dfrac{\$9,166.67}{\$1,000,000 - \$83,333.33}$	= .010000	(8)	$\dfrac{\$9,166.67}{\$1,000,000 - 7(\$83,333.33)}$	= .022000
(3)	$\dfrac{\$9,166.67}{\$1,000,000 - 2(\$83,333.33)}$	= .011000	(9)	$\dfrac{\$9,166.67}{\$1,000,000 - 8(\$83,333.33)}$	= .027500
(4)	$\dfrac{\$9,166.67}{\$1,000,000 - 3(\$83,333.33)}$	= .012222	(10)	$\dfrac{\$9,166.67}{\$1,000,000 - 9(\$83,333.33)}$	= .036666
(5)	$\dfrac{\$9,166.67}{\$1,000,000 - 4(\$83,333.33)}$	= .013750	(11)	$\dfrac{\$9,166.67}{\$1,000,000 - 10(\$83,333.33)}$	= .055000
(6)	$\dfrac{\$9,166.67}{\$1,000,000 - 5(\$83,333.33)}$	= .015714	(12)	$\dfrac{\$9,166.67}{\$1,000,000 - 11(\$83,333.33)}$	= .110000

$$k_i = [(1.009167)(1.01)(1.011)(1.01\overline{2})(1.0375)(1.015714)(1.018\overline{3})(1.022)(1.0275)(1.03\overline{6})(1.055)(1.11)]^{1/12} - 1$$

$$k_i = [(1.394293)]^{1/12} - 1 = .028085 \times 100 = 2.8085\% \text{ per month}$$

[a] Assumptions

Amount borrowed: $1,000,000 for one year
Terms: 11% nominal annual rate of interest (interest and principal paid in 12 monthly installments)
Monthly payment: $1,000,000 × .11 ÷ 12 = $ 9,166.67
$1,000,000 ÷ 12   = 83,333.33
Total monthly payment   = $92,500.00

assets pledged as collateral. Hence, details of loan agreements are similar throughout the country.

ACCOUNTS RECEIVABLE FINANCING

If a bank elects to loan funds on pledged accounts receivable, it must do so on the basis of all receivables or only on those it carefully screens. In the former case, the bank will often lend from 60 to 70 percent of the receivables. However, if the bank screens the receivables, it may lend as much as 85 to 90 percent of the face value of those it accepts. In either case, the bank usually charges a processing fee to cover the cost of screening. On the one hand, the processing fee may be standard or vary with the intensity of the screening process; on the other hand, the interest charge may vary from two to four percent above either the prime or some other money-market rate, the premium depending on the quality of the receivables. A more intensive screening process could mean a higher processing fee but a lower interest rate on the loan. For receivables, financing at the base rate is apt to mean the prime rate plus two to four percent. Those who pledge receivables are often small, less creditworthy companies whose access to broader capital markets is limited. Although management may shop among banks for better terms, it is unlikely management will obtain rates based on current money-market yields, which are generally below the prime.

For purposes of illustration, suppose a bank charges a 1-percent processing fee to ABC Novelty Corporation and agrees to finance 70 percent of its accounts receivable. ABC has a policy of $n/30$ with no discount for early payment. The firm averages \$15,000 per day in credit sales, but takes nearly 45 days from the time the merchandise is sold to receipt and clearance of the customer checks. Thus, the average receivables balance is \$675,000 (\$15,000 × 45). Assume the processing fee is 1 percent of the average balance, the interest rate is 3 percent above the current prime rate of 12 percent (15 percent), and the loan is not discounted. For the average collection period:

$$\text{processing fee} = (.01)(\$675,000) \qquad\qquad\; = \$\;6,750.00$$
$$\text{interest} = (.15)(.70)(\$675,000)\left(\frac{45}{360}\right) = \frac{\$\;8,859.38}{\$15,609.38}$$
$$\text{loan} = .70 \times \$675,000 = \$472,500$$
$$k_i = \frac{\$15,609.38}{\$472,500} \times \frac{365}{45} \times 100 = 26.80\%$$

The effective rate can, of course, change with changes in the prime rate and changes in the average collection period. However, the example suggests how expensive receivable financing can be.

FACTORING ACCOUNTS RECEIVABLE

There is an alternative to pledging accounts receivable as collateral for a bank loan: *factoring* (selling) accounts receivable to a commercial factor or a factor subsidiary of a commercial bank. Factoring accounts receivable has a long history in certain industries, such as textiles, and is widely employed in carpeting, furniture, electronics, and several other industries.[7]

In deciding whether to factor accounts receivable, the firm should consider that it may be more costly to incur the bookkeeping and collection expenses than to factor them. For a fee that ranges between .75 percent and 2 percent of the receivables purchased, the factor will incur such costs as well as the risk of bad debts. In other words, there is no recourse to the firm: the factor assumes responsibility. Moreover,

---

[7] See, for example, Clyde W. Phelps, "*The Rule of Factoring in Modern Business Finance*" (Baltimore: Commercial Credit Company, 1956). Commercial finance companies also loan on and factor accounts receivable.

at the end of each month the factor pays the firm on the basis of the average due date of the receivables. In the case of ABC Novelty, we noted that its average daily sales were $15,000 but that its average collection period was 45 days. By factoring the receivables, at the end of each month ABC will find its account credited with the amount collected less the commission. Assuming the fee is 1.75 percent, for an average month ABC would receive $30 \times \$15,000 \times (1 - .0175) = \$442,125$.

Of course, variations on this arrangement are possible and the factor may refuse to accept certain accounts; however, the firm usually reaches an accommodation whereby credit and collection costs are eliminated and cash is credited monthly to its account. This process is known as **maturity factoring**. Because credit and collection costs are eliminated, the gross fee of 1.75 percent overstates the cost of factoring receivables. For example, if experience suggests that credit and collection costs are also 1.75 percent of the receivables balance, then factoring is actually as efficient as incurring the credit and collection costs; indeed it may be more efficient, since the factor guarantees payments on a nonrecourse basis.

Factors also advance funds at a rate typically 2 to 4 percent above the prime rate, inasmuch as they base the rate on the face value of the accounts and not on their discounted value. Suppose ABC Novelty seeks an advance on $450,000 worth of accounts receivable with an average due date of 30 days. The factor will base the loan on $360,000, 80 percent of the receivables ($.80 \times \$450,000$), at 3 percent above the prime rate of 12 percent (15 percent). Because the factor's fee offsets the credit and collection costs ABC would otherwise incur, the effective cost of the loan includes only the interest on it:

$$.15 \times \$360,000 \times \frac{30}{360} = \$4,500$$

Therefore

$$k_i = \frac{\$4,500}{\$360,000} \times \frac{365}{30} \times 100 = 15.21\%$$

Although factoring is often treated as an expensive source of credit, its true cost must reflect any savings in credit and collection costs; it becomes expensive when the firm's credit and collection costs are less than the factor's fee. Suppose, for example, that credit and collection costs are 1.0 percent of accounts receivable. The factor's charge of 1.75 percent suggests the firm is paying a net fee of .75 percent to factor its receivables. The costs of both factoring and borrowing $360,000 for 30 days would include the net fee of .0075 ($360,000), or $2,700, so that

$$k_i = \frac{\$4,500 + \$2,700}{\$360,000} \times \frac{365}{30} \times 100 = 24.333\%$$

For many firms, the full cost of factoring and advances exceeds the cost of a bank loan secured by accounts receivable. For other firms, however, savings from the elimination of credit and collection costs coupled with the certainty of monthly cash payments may tilt the balance in favor of factoring.[8]

INVENTORY LOANS

Both inventory of raw materials and finished goods are commonly used as collateral for bank loans. The automobile dealer may finance his or her stock with bank loans secured by that very inventory. In turn, the bank may finance the loan required by the person purchasing the car. The cereal manufacturer may use wheat, oats, and other grains as collateral for short-term loans during the manufacturing and marketing phases of operation. As in the case of accounts receivable, the bank determines the percentage of the market value it will loan. For inventories with a ready market price, the bank may loan from 75 to 80 percent of their current value. Such commodities as grains, metals, and other raw materials for which there is a readily available current price fall into this category. Because inventories of specialized finished goods, such as specific-purpose machine tools, do not fall into this category, the loan may be for a smaller percentage of their estimated value.

There are several methods by which inventories can be secured, the most universal of which (under the Uniform Commercial Code) is a *blanket (floating) lien* on all inventories. However, the bank has no control over the sale of inventories under a blanket lien, where the collateral might be sold and the proceeds not used to repay the loan. To preclude this event, the bank may require a *trust receipt*. With a trust receipt, the lender can specify that the goods are held in trust for the bank. Such a procedure might be used to finance the operations of an automobile, truck, farm equipment, or yard equipment dealer. The goods are held in trust. When they are sold, the dealer obtains a release from the bank and the sale proceeds are used to reduce the loan.

Another approach is to use a warehouse. Under this technique, goods are stored either in a public warehouse or on the borrower's property but in an area or building where the inventory securing the loan can be physically separated from other inventory. When goods are stored in a public warehouse, *warehouse receipts* are issued that do not permit removal of the goods without express approval of the

---

[8] Although some resent being billed by a third party, in many cases customers do not even know their account has been factored. In fact, the bill may be sent on company letterhead and payment is made to the company but sent to a post-office box. The factor, which may be a commercial-bank subsidiary, processes and collects the checks. The company has authorized the bank to endorse them to the factor.

At one time—except in such industries as textiles, where factoring was a tradition—selling accounts receivable was a sign of financial weakness. Today, it is more apt to be viewed as a cost-effective means of finance and used as such or viewed as a cost-ineffective means of finance and therefore avoided.

lender. When goods are stored on the borrower's property, **field warehouse** receipts are issued that do not permit removal of the goods without express approval of the lender. In either case, the lender controls the inventory. Assuming the public warehouser or field warehouser discharges his or her responsibilities for supervising disbursement of inventory as approved by the lender, the loan is adequately secured. Although warehousers generally discharge such responsibilities in accord with lenders' directions, it is not uncommon that inventory is used without permission. Sometimes the collateral thought to be in the warehouse is in fact not there.[9] When the collateral is not in the bank's *vault*, the loan is marginally more risky.

COST OF INVENTORY LOANS

The loan is also more expensive. Warehouses are not eleemosynary institutions. Whether the borrower uses a public or field warehouse, there is a cost. Hence, warehouse fees must be added to the interest on the loan. To illustrate, suppose a local brewer must draw frequently on a stock of grain to produce beer and the bank has approved a loan secured by the grain. For convenience, the grain is kept on the brewer's property under the supervision of a field warehouser. The brewery has an average loan of $1,000,000 outstanding that represents 70 percent of the inventory's current market value. Interest and warehouse costs are paid every 90 days. The interest rate is currently 3 percent more than the prime rate of 11 percent (14 percent) and the field warehouser charges $75 per day. Thus

$$\text{field warehouse} = 90 \times \$75 = \$6,750$$

$$\text{interest on loan} = \$1,000,000 \times .14 \times \frac{90}{360} = \$35,000$$

$$k_i = \frac{\$35,000 + \$6,750}{\$1,000,000} \times \frac{365}{90} = 16.93\%$$

Because loans based on inventories as well as receivables are reduced as the collateral is converted to cash, k_i is merely an average rate. To the extent a firm can speed up the operating cycle, it can lower the loan balance and hence reduce its dollar outlay for interest.

Financing secured by inventories and receivables is often more expensive than an unsecured line of credit. There are several reasons for this. First, those who can obtain lines of credit are prime-quality customers who can tap alternative funding

---

[9] The great salad-oil scandal was one such event: the storage facilities presumably containing the oil were filled with water. See "Lessons from the Haupt Affair," an editorial in *Fortune*, Vol. 69 (January 1964), pp. 74–78). See, also, Monroe R. Lazere, "Swinging Swindles and Creepy Frauds," *Journal of Commercial Bank Lending*, Vol. 60 (September 1977, pp. 44–52).

sources. Consequently, the interest rate on a line of credit is likely tied to money-market rates. Loans secured by receivables or inventories are likely tied to the current prime lending rate, which is higher than current money-market rates. Those who use the latter financing mode either lack access to alternative funding sources or their lines of credit are insufficient to meet borrowing requirements.

Second, using receivables and inventory as collateral is expensive due to costs of processing the former and monitoring the latter. A firm could, of course, substitute such other collateral as marketable securities and lower the cost of borrowing. However, since marketable securities are repositories for temporarily idle cash, they will be liquidated during periods of maximum borrowing need.

Third, although our calculations do not reflect it, loans secured by receivables or inventories may be discounted. Moreover, if the bank has a policy of requiring compensating balances, the requirement may also apply to loans secured by collateral. Consequently, the bottom line is that although loans secured by receivables and/or inventories are more expensive than unsecured lines of credit, they may be less expensive than deliberately slowing payment of bills and thereby compromising the valuable customer-supplier relationship.

COMMERCIAL PAPER

One of the options available to those with sufficiently high credit ratings is **commercial paper**. Unlike the foregoing funding sources, commercial paper is an unsecured note of the issuing corporation sold directly through dealers to investors. As noted in Table 14-1, although commercial paper does not enjoy an active secondary market, dealers will repurchase the paper prior to maturity and companies that place their paper directly with investors will repurchase it as a customer service.

Even though it is offered directly to the public, most commercial paper is purchased by such institutional investors as bank trust departments, pension funds, colleges and universities, life insurance companies, and nonfinancial corporations. Because most sales are in $50,000 to $100,000 blocks, individual investors do not generally participate directly. However, mutual funds that sell shares to the public and invest the proceeds in money-market instruments (including commercial paper) have grown rapidly since the early 1970s. Most shareholders in such *money-market mutual funds* are individuals.[10]

Commercial paper is a uniquely American institution, sparked in part by the fragmented banking system that has characterized the United States for much

---

[10] Evelyn M. Hurley. "The Commercial Paper Market Since the Mid-Seventies," *Federal Reserve Bulletin*, Vol. 68 (June 1982, pp. 327–34).

of its history.[11] Because of loan limits, major corporations that could not obtain sufficiently large lines of credit would use commercial paper as a means of supplementing their bank loans. When federal regulation of new security issues was enacted in 1933, commercial paper (with maturities of 270 days or less) was exempt from registration requirements under the law. Consequently, the commercial paper market is limited to maturities of 270 days or less. Otherwise, the cost of frequent registration with the Securities and Exchange Commission (SEC) under the Securities Act of 1933 would render commercial paper of longer maturities a costly and hence inefficient funding source.

As both nominal and real interest rates rose in the 1970s, the commercial paper market expanded. For example, at the end of 1974, $50.5 billion worth of commercial paper had been issued by approximately 700 firms. By the first quarter of 1982, 1,205 financial *and* nonfinancial business firms had $171.4 billion worth of commercial paper outstanding.[12] At the end of 1982, nonfinancial corporations alone had $37.6 billion worth of commercial paper on their balance sheets. By 1986, the figure had risen to $62.9 billion.[13]

Although commercial paper is unsecured, smaller companies that might not otherwise have a sufficient credit rating to access the market may do so through a **letter of credit** from a commercial bank. A letter of credit guarantees payment at maturity to the purchaser of commercial paper in the event the issurer defaults. Hence, the credit rating of the commercial paper is based on the credit rating of the financial institution issuing the letter of credit.

Finally, industrial firms are the most frequent issuers of commercial paper; however, public utilities also tap the market. Among financial institutions, finance companies, savings and loan associations, and bank holding companies are the major issuers. Finance companies and bank holding companies are more apt to place paper directly with investors; other institutions are more likely to use the nine major commercial paper dealers (located primarily in New York) to place commercial paper.[14]

---

[11] From the demise of the Second Bank of the United States in 1836 until the passage of the Garn-St. Germain Act in 1982 and the 1985 Supreme Court decision affirming mergers through holding companies of banks in different states when state laws permit, American banks (unlike those of other countries) were confined to operating branches in a single state and, sometimes, depending on state law, to operating a single bank with no branches. Same as [1], Garcia et al. and *Northeast Bancorp, Inc., et al. v. Board of Governors of Federal Reserve*, No. 84-363, United States Supreme Court, 1985.

[12] Same as [10], p. 329.

[13] Federal Reserve System. *Balance Sheets for the U.S. Economy* (May 1987, p. 25). At the end of 1986, there was $393 billion worth open market paper, much of it commercial paper, outstanding. *Federal Reserve Statistical Release* (June 5, 1987, Table 1).

[14] Same as [10], p. 330. Again, the rapidly changing institutional environment suggests that others, specifically commercial banks, may act as dealers in commercial paper. See Theresa A. Einhorn, "National Banks' Discount Brokerage Services Are Permissable under Glass-Steagall Act, but an Office at which such Services Are Offered Constitutes a Branch," *Banking Law Journal*, Vol. 101, (May–June 1984, pp. 349–61). See, also, Edwin B. Cox, *Bankers Desk Reference* (New York: Warren, Gorham & Lamont, 1983, p. 35).

THE COST OF COMMERCIAL PAPER

As in the case of Treasury bills, commercial paper is sold at a discount from par. Unlike the U.S. Treasury, however, the issuer faces additional costs:

1. A fee of between $5,000 and $25,000 to obtain a rating from a rating agency such as Standard & Poor's, Moody's, or Fitch Investors Services.

2. Fees paid to a commercial bank or others acting as agents for the issuers. If the bank issues a letter of credit, it also will charge a fee for the service.

3. If the paper is placed through a dealer, there is a commission of 1/8 of 1 percent for the services rendered.

4. Issuers of commercial paper are usually expected to back the notes with a standby loan commitment for which there is a fee of up to .75 of 1 percent of the amount issued.

Given these additional costs, it is understandable why issuers of commercial paper, although growing in number, represent a small proportion of corporate borrowing. Corporations that issue substantial amounts of commercial paper can, of course, minimize these costs. The rating fee is a small percentage of a large issue and the paper may be placed directly. Although a firm may internalize the cost of this service, it may still be lower than if the paper is sold through dealers. Moreover, a corporation with a high credit rating does not need a letter of credit from a bank. Such a firm may incur a commitment fee, but the rate paid may be closer to .25 of 1 percent than .75 of 1 percent of the amount issued. As a result, the net cost may be lower than the prime rate. As suggested earlier, a commercial bank competing for the business will tie the interest rate to a premium over money-market rates in order to entice the firm to borrow directly rather than to issue commercial paper. On the other hand, if the Federal Reserve tightens credit, the commercial bank may not *compete* for the loan. In these circumstances, the company can still obtain the funds it seeks in the commercial paper market, albeit at rates that reflect temporarily tight credit market conditions.

Bearing these factors in mind, if a firm finds its total flotation costs are .5 of 1 percent of the face value of the commercial paper and it markets the paper at a bank discount rate of 8.5 percent for 60 days, the total effective cost of a $20,000,000 issue is

$$\text{costs of flotation} = \$20,000,000 \times .005 = \$100,000$$

$$\text{discount} = \$20,000,000 \times \frac{60}{360} \times .085 = \frac{\$283,333}{\$383,333}$$

$$k_i = \frac{\$383,333}{\$20,000,000 - \$383,333} \times \frac{365}{60} \times 100 = 11.89\%$$

For firms that anticipate a decline in long-term rates, commercial paper is one means of temporarily financing long-term assets. Commercial paper can be used as a *bridge loan* issued prior to marketing long-term debt instruments. Commercial bank loans, of course, can serve the same purpose.

EURODOLLARS

A firm, particularly a multinational corporation, will often borrow in the **Eurodollar** market to meet the working capital needs of its international subsidiaries. Eurodollars are dollar deposits in banks outside of the United States. Although they began in Europe and the bulk of such deposits remain there, Eurodollars are found in other countries. When a firm borrows Eurodollars, it does so in a manner similar to borrowing dollars domestically. However, the major difference is that the borrowing rate is tied neither to the prime rate nor to a money-market domestic CD, but to the London Interbank Offered Rate (LIBOR). Because this is the rate "at which major international banks are willing to offer term Eurodollar deposits to each other,"[15] it becomes the basis on which the interest on Eurodollar loans is determined. Such loans are commonly made at 2 percent to 4 percent above the LIBOR rate and discounted in the usual manner.

BANKER'S ACCEPTANCES

A **banker's acceptance** is a written order to pay: a check or draft drawn on a specific bank by a seller. The purpose of the draft is to obtain payment for goods sold to a specific customer. By accepting the draft, the bank guarantees payment on the due date.

Used almost exclusively in international commerce, a banker's acceptance is a source of funds for an importer. For example, suppose an American grocery chain orders a $100,000 supply of mustard from Dijon, France. The French manufacturer agrees to ship the mustard using a 90-day banker's acceptance. To implement the transaction, the grocery company negotiates a letter of credit whereby its American bank agrees to honor drafts drawn on that account through a French bank. Once the paperwork is complete, the French company ships the goods and draws a draft on the American company's account through its French bank that is, in turn, honored by the American bank. The American bank accepts the draft, agreeing to make payment in 90 days. Once the draft is accepted by the American bank, it can be held to

---

[15] Marvin Goodfriend. "Eurodollars," in John R. Brick et al., eds. *Financial Markets Instruments and Concepts*, 2nd ed. (Richmond, VA: Robert F. Dame, 1986, p. 123).

maturity or marketed at a discount by the French company. In either case, the holder of the banker's acceptance will present it for collection at the American bank upon maturity. The bank will honor its acceptance and charge the grocery company $100,000 plus fees for services rendered, including those involved in preparing the original letter of credit.

The American company has effectively borrowed funds for 90 days. The true cost of that loan depends on the alternatives available to the American importer. Presumably, the French exporter would have charged a lower price for the mustard if the American company had paid cash in francs. The grocery chain might have borrowed the necessary funds using a conventional line of credit, converted the dollars to francs, and paid for the mustard prior to its shipment. However, since the mustard cannot be sold until it arrives in the United States, using a banker's acceptance may be the least expensive way to finance the purchase: no cash is actually paid until the acceptance matures. Meanwhile, the French exporter assumed any exchange-rate risk by specifying the dollar equivalent in francs at the time the transaction was consummated.[16] Depending on demand for mustard at the time, the French manufacturer—recognizing that it may be discounting the banker's acceptance—may have already taken into account any such risk when determining the price. If demand is weak, the exporter may have to absorb the discount.

The banker's acceptance plays a major role in international trade primarily because it offers both parties, importer and exporter, the opportunity to substitute the credit of internationally known banks for their own, thereby facilitating the flow of commerce between countries. We return to this instrument when we discuss international finance in greater detail (see Chapter 22).

TERM LOANS

By convention, a **term loan** or *intermediate term credit* matures somewhere between one and ten years. The time frame is somewhat arbitrary and term loans may extend beyond ten years. What tends to distinguish a term loan from long-term borrowing (discussed in Chapter 16) is that the former will be liquidated or paid off in the life of the loan, whereas long-term borrowing is often viewed as a permanent funding source to be renewed or refunded at maturity. Generally, a term loan is sufficiently small that it can be repaid from cash flows of the firm.

The bulk of term loans are made by banks and insurance companies, the former concentrating at the lower end of maturities and the latter at the upper end. Such

---

[16] Even that risk can be hedged by making appropriate use of exchange rates or forward contracts. Some aspects of the futures market are discussed in Chapter 20. The reader may wish to consult Robert W. Kolb, *Understanding Futures Markets* (Glenview, IL: Scott Foresman, 1985, pp. 185–221).

other institutions as pension funds and certain federal government agencies (for example, the Small Business Administration and government-licensed Small Business Investment companies) also make term loans. Specific types of equipment—particularly transportation equipment—are often financed by banks, insurance companies, and sales finance companies through term loans, the equipment used as collateral for the loans.

THE COST OF TERM LOANS

Term loans carry a fixed or variable rate of interest. Some are allowed to float with the prime or, for Eurodollar loans, with the LIBOR. All, of course, carry a rate above the base. For example, a bank may charge .5 to 2.5 percent above the prime rate for a term loan, using the higher figure for a fixed- rather than a variable-rate loan.

Whatever the base, the rate charged equals the stated rate of interest on the loan. Suppose, for example, a firm negotiated a five-year term loan at a fixed rate of 12 percent. Table 15-2 displays three widely used schedules for paying principal and interest. The first is the **amortization** schedule. The terms state that at the end of each year the firm will make an annuity payment equal to a specific amount of money. This payment is determined in the usual manner:

$$\$100,000 = \frac{a[1 - (1.12)^{-5}]}{.12}$$

$$a = \$27,740.97$$

At the end of year 1, interest is 12 percent of $100,000 ($12,000). Subtracting $12,000 from the year-end payment of $27,740.97, we obtain $15,740.97. Subtracting $15,740.97 from $100,000 yields $84,259.03. At the end of the second year, interest calculated on $84,259.03 at 12 percent is $10,111.08. We subtract $10,111.08 from $27,740.97, the payment made at the end of the second year, and the difference ($17,629.89) reduces the principal to $66,629.14. The important point to note is that interest declines as the principal is repaid: the rate applies only to the remaining principal and the loan is not discounted. If a commercial bank is the lender, it may require collateral and, sometimes, compensating balances. The latter could raise the true cost of the loan, particularly if the balances exceed what is customarily held on deposit. If the borrower has access to lenders that do not require compensating balances, one of those lenders will obtain the business.

The second schedule of principal and interest repayment is the **balloon payment**. Under this approach, the borrower repays a portion of the loan each year but the bulk of the principal is paid at maturity. In the example shown in Table 15-2, payments are $10,000 per year for four years followed by a $60,000 payment for the fifth year and interest is on the remaining principal.

Table 15-2   Three Principal and Interest Repayment Schedules[a]

Amortization

Year	Annuity	−	Interest (12%)	=	Principal Repayment	Remaining Principal
0						**$100,000.00**
1	$ 27,740.97	−	$12,000.00	=	$ 15,740.97	84,259.03
2	27,740.97	−	10,111.08	=	17,629.89	66,629.14
3	27,740.97	−	7,995.50	=	19,745.47	46,883.67
4	27,740.97	−	5,626.03	=	22,114.94	24,768.73
5	27,740.97	−	2,972.24	=	24,768.73	0
	$138,704.85	−	$38,704.85	=	$100,000.00	

Balloon Loan

Year	Interest (12%)	Principal Repayment	Remaining Principal
0			**$100,000**
1	$12,000	$ 10,000	90,000
2	10,800	10,000	80,000
3	9,600	10,000	70,000
4	8,400	10,000	60,000
5	7,200	60,000	0
	$48,000	$100,000	

Bullet Loan

Year	Interest (12%)	Principal Repayment	Remaining Principal
0			**$100,000**
1	$12,000	0	100,000
2	12,000	0	100,000
3	12,000	0	100,000
4	12,000	0	100,000
5	12,000	$100,000	0
	$60,000	$100,000	

[a] $100,000 term loan maturing in five years at 12 percent interest payable annually.

The third schedule of principal and interest repayment calls for repayment of the entire principal at the end of the loan; in the interim, interest is paid on the entire $100,000. This type of term loan is called a **bullet loan**, the sobriquet suggesting that the amount borrowed *hits* the borrower all at once.

As shown in Table 15-2, not only is the interest rate fixed for the period of the loan but interest is paid annually. Of course, other arrangements can be made: quarterly principal and interest payments are common. If amortized, quarterly payments would be

$$\$100,000 = \frac{\dfrac{a}{4}\left[1 - \left(1 + \dfrac{.12}{4}\right)^{-5 \times 4}\right]}{\dfrac{.12}{4}}$$

$$a = \$26,886.28$$

$$\frac{a}{4} = \$6,721.57$$

In the case of the balloon loan, quarterly principal payments would be $2,500 for four years and $15,000 for the fifth year. Quarterly interest payments would be .03 × $97,500 = $2,925 for the second quarter of the first year and .03 × $45,000 = $1,350 for the second quarter of the fifth year. For the bullet loan, quarterly interest payments would be .03 × $100,000 = $3,000 for the five years.

Terms and conditions actually negotiated depend on the prevailing economic conditions at the time, the degree of competition among lenders, and the borrower's credit rating. If the term loan is used to finance such readily marketable equipment as trucks, airplanes, railroad cars, automobiles, and the like, the borrower usually must make a 20- to 30-percent down payment; the actual loan is for the remaining principal. Moreover, the length of the loan is closely tied to the economic life of the asset. If the equipment purchaser receives the money from a bank, an insurance company, or other financial intermediary, the lending institution retains a lien on the property known as a **chattel mortgage**, a legal term applied to liens on all property other than real estate. If the borrower defaults on the payments, the lender can usually repossess the equipment.[17]

If the equipment is financed directly by the manufacturer, the purchaser signs a **conditional sales contract** or **purchase money mortgage** whereby the seller retains title until the buyer has performed in accordance with the contract

---

[17] It is possible for the bankruptcy court to delay repossession until it is determined whether or not the company will be reorganized or liquidated. In either case, because the value of the collateral generally exceeds the balance of the loan, the lender is in a strong position.

provisions. The conditional sales contract is similar to the purchase of an asset on the installment plan: one does not own the asset until all payments are made. Although a financial institution may not participate directly, it may be financing the manufacturer rather than the equipment buyer.

PRIVATELY PLACED AND PUBLICLY OFFERED SECURITIES

A common thread running through the narrative thus far is that the funds have come directly from other institutions. All loans were made by financial intermediaries; all commercial paper and (perhaps) banker's acceptances were purchased in the open market by nonfinancial corporations, financial intermediaries, and endowment funds of eleemosynary and educational institutions. Individuals or households, however, were never involved and rarely, if ever, are.[18]

The point is significant. With the exception of commercial paper and banker's acceptances, we can say that the notes or agreements underlying the loans were privately negotiated. In subsequent chapters, we shall use the expression **privately placed (directly placed)** to describe notes directly purchased by investors with the express intent of holding them until maturity. The alternative is a **public offering** of securities, where the holders of such instruments may or may not keep them to maturity. Equipment, for example, may be financed through a marketable debt instrument sold to the general public rather than financed with a term loan.

Public offerings, as we shall see, are more commonly associated with long-term funding sources. To conduct a public offering, however, the corporation must conform to certain requirements specified by the Securities Act of 1933. The additional costs involved in complying with the law are not part of the funding sources discussed in this chapter.

SUMMARY

In Chapter 15 we have examined certain of the major sources of short-term funds. For the bulk of American companies, trade credit and bank loans—the latter made on a secured or unsecured basis—are the primary sources of such funds. Although short-term costs vary, they are always higher than the stated interest rate. Banks base their charges on a 360-day year and generally discount the loan by collecting interest in advance. Banks may also require compensating balances. The cost of trade credit

---

[18] Accurate information on the amount of commercial paper held by individuals is unavailable. Although probably not sizeable, individual participation is believed to have increased in the recent years. Same as [10], p. 334.

depends on the credit and collection policy. A 2/10 net-30 term offers a powerful incentive to take the 2-percent discount in 10 days rather than borrowing the net amount for 30 days.

The general formula for determining the cost of short-term credit is

$$k_i = \text{cost of funds} = \frac{\$ \text{ of interest}}{\text{amount borrowed}} \times \frac{365}{\text{number of days funds are borrowed}}$$

As developed in the chapter, certain additional factors account for specific features of the loan: commitment fee on a line of credit, processing fee for accounts receivable, and warehouse costs for loans secured by inventory. These costs are added to the dollar interest payments. If interest is deducted in advance, the amount borrowed is less than the loan's face amount. Both the additional factors and the discount cause k_i to rise.

The costs of such other types of short-term credit as commercial paper, Eurodollar loans, and banker's acceptances are amenable to the same calculations; they are, however, less likely to be employed by companies. Commercial paper, although an expanding funding source, is still confined to several hundred corporations. Eurodollar loans are important to multinational companies and banker's acceptances to importers/exporters.

In contrast to short-term credit, the stated rate of interest on a term loan is the true cost of the loan. Although the stated rate on the term loan may be higher than on the short-term loan and may vary in the life of the commitment, the entire principal is borrowed. As principal is repaid, the interest rate is applied to the declining balance.

Finally, all funding sources discussed involved institutions: individuals are rarely involved. Commercial paper is a partial exception to the generalization because a variety of investors, including some individuals, do participate. As long as the instrument matures in 270 days or less, it does not qualify as a public offering; the funds received, therefore, are based on privately negotiated agreements. As we shall learn in Chapter 16, long-term funding sources can be both privately placed and publicly offered.

PROBLEMS AND QUESTIONS

1. Last National Bank has a policy of discounting loans and requiring compensating balances of 10 percent. However, the rate charged top-rated customers is 2 percent above prevailing CD rates. Meanwhile, Next-to-last National Bank does not require compensating balances, discounts loans, and charges its top-rated customers the prime rate. Currently, the six-month CD rate is 10.5 percent and the prime rate is 13.25 percent. What is the cost at each bank of a $1,000,000

loan for six months to customers with the highest credit rating? Assume customers have a cash management policy that reduces cash balances to zero.

2. The Tex-Mex national chain of restaurants has an annual unsecured loan commitment of $500,000. A commitment fee of .75 of 1 percent on the unused portion is deducted at the end of every quarter. Interest is charged quarterly at the prime rate prevailing at the beginning of the quarter and deducted in advance. The balance of the loan is liquidated at the end of the year. Tex-Mex borrowed the following amounts at the beginning of each quarter:

	Amount	Prime Rate
1st Q	$400,000	11%
2nd Q	500,000	12%
3rd Q	500,000	13%
4th Q	300,000	10%

What are the geometrical and arithmetical average annual rates of interest at which Tex-Mex borrowed?

3. XYZ Corporation has a 180-day loan commitment from its bank for $2,000,000 with a .5 of 1 percent commitment fee on the unused balance. Interest is 2 percent above 90- and 180-day CD rates of 10.25 percent and 11.75 percent, respectively. The interest is discounted in advance but the commitment fee is paid at the loan termination. XYZ borrows the following amounts at four different intervals:

180 days	$1,500,000
150 days	1,700,000
120 days	1,900,000
90 days	2,000,000

What is the cost of the loan?

4. Acutemp Corporation, a leading manufacturer of thermometers, obtains the following credit terms from its suppliers:

Supplier A	1/15 net, 30
Supplier B	2/10 net, 45
Supplier C	2/10 and 1/30 net, 60

What is the cost of trade credit for each funding source per $100,000 worth of credit extended?

5. Grand National Wholesale Corporation, a distributor of electrical appliances, averages $25,000 per day in credit sales. Approximately 60 days elapse from the time the firm sells its products until the accounts are paid. Using an accounts-receivable loan from its bank, Grand National can borrow 75 percent of its outstanding balance at 2 percent above the prime rate. The bank always charges a .5 of 1 percent processing fee on the value of the receivables. If the prime rate is currently 11.5 percent, what is the cost of the loan for an average collection period assuming interest is not discounted?

6. In problem 5, suppose Grand National chose to factor accounts receivable. The factor agrees to purchase all accounts and to pay Grand National the net proceeds less a factoring fee of 1.5 percent. Grand National estimates that by eliminating its credit and collection department, it will save .75 of 1 percent of the face value of the receivables.

   a. What is the net cost of factoring?
   b. Suppose Grand National can obtain an advance at 3 percent above the prime rate (currently 11.5 percent) on accounts due within 30 days (approximately one-half the average receivables balance). What is the cost of the loan assuming no discount?

7. ABC Corporation has a heavy commitment to inventory. Using its inventory as collateral, a bank loans ABC an average of $4,000,000 every 90 days at 2 percent above the prime rate, which is currently 10.75 percent. The inventory is supervised by a field warehouser who charges $65 per day. Assuming the bank discounts the loan, and the warehouse fee is paid at the end of 90 days, what is the current cost of borrowing for ABC?

8. Comfort First, a leading manufacturer of lingerie, is negotiating the sale of commercial paper. For a $50,000,000 issue, the rating fee is $7,500. The fee for a standby loan commitment is .25 of 1 percent of the face value of the issue multiplied by the portion of the 360-day year during which the loan is outstanding. Although Comfort First does not have to use a commercial bank's credit rating, it does have to use a dealer. The dealer charges .125 of 1 percent of the face value of the commercial paper marketed. The paper is sold at a bank discount of 9.35 percent and matures in 210 days. What is the cost of this funding source?

9. Redeye Trucking Company purchases much of its equipment using six-year term loans with a 20-percent down payment. It has contracted with a bank to purchase $1,000,000 in equipment. After making the down payment, it amortizes the loan annually by paying 14-percent interest. Determine the loan's principal and interest amortization schedule.

10. Suppose in problem 9 that a balloon loan was used, with 10 percent of the initial balance paid each year and the residual paid in the sixth year. Interest remains 14 percent and is paid annually. Determine the amortization schedule for both principal and interest.

SELECTED ADDITIONAL REFERENCES

Abken, Peter. "Commercial Paper," *Economic Review*, Federal Reserve Bank of Richmond, Vol. 67 (March–April 1981, pp. 11–22).

Arnold, Jasper H., III. "How to Negotiate a Term Loan," *Harvard Business Review*, Vol. 60 (March–April 1982, 131–38).

Banaitis, Sy J. *International Letters of Credit* (Chicago: First National City Bank of Chicago, 1977).

Berger, Paul D. and William K. Harper. "Determination of an Optimal Revolving Credit," *Journal of Finance and Quantitative Analysis*, Vol. 8 (June 1973, pp. 491–98).

Bogen, Jules, ed. *Financial Handbook*, 4th ed. (New York: Ronald Press, 1964).

Brady, Thomas F. "Changes in Loan Pricing and Business Lending at Commercial Banks," *Federal Reserve Bulletin*, Vol. 71 (January 1985, pp. 1–13).

Brick, John R. et al., eds. *Financial Markets Instruments and Concepts*, 2nd ed. (Richmond, VA: Robert F. Dame, 1986).

Broaddus, Alfred. "Financial Innovation in the United States—Background, Current Status and Prospects," *Economic Review*, Federal Reserve Bank of Richmond, Vol. 71 (January–February 1985, pp. 2–22).

Brosky, John J. *The Implicit Cost of Trade Credit and Theory of Optimal Terms of Sale* (New York: Credit Research Foundation, 1969).

Campbell, Tim S. "A Model of the Market for Lines of Credit," *Journal of Finance*, Vol. 33 (March 1978, pp. 231–43).

Carron, Andrew S. *Reforming the Bank Regulatory Structure* (Washington, DC: The Brookings Institution, 1984).

Cook, Timothy Q. and Bruce J. Summers. *Instruments of the Money Market*, 5th ed. (Richmond, VA: Federal Reserve Bank of Richmond, 1981).

Cox, Edwin B. *Bankers' Desk Reference* (New York: Warren, Gorham & Lamont, 1983).

Davis, Lance. "The Evolution of the American Capital Market, 1860–1940: A Case Study in Institutional Change," in William Silber, *Financial Innovation* (Lexington, MA: D.C. Heath, 1975).

Dennon, Lester E. "The Security Agreement," *Journal of Commercial Bank Lending*, Vol. 50 (February 1968, pp. 32–40).

Einhorn, Theresa A. "National Banks' Discount Brokerage Services Are Permissable under Glass-Stengall Act, but an Office at which such Services Are Offered Constitutes a Branch," *Banking Law Journal*, Vol. 101 (May–June 1984, pp. 349–61).

First National Bank of Chicago. *Collections, Letters of Credit, and Banker's Acceptances* (Chicago: First National City Bank of Chicago, 1981).

Garcia, Gillian et. al. "The Garn-St. Germain Depository Institutions Act of 1982," *Economic Perspectives*, Vol. 7 (March–April 1983, pp. 3–31).

Gill, Richard C. "Term Loan Agreements," *Journal of Commercial Bank Lending*, Vol. 62 (February 1980, pp. 22–27).

Greef, Albert O. *The Commercial Paper House in the United States* (Cambridge, MA: Harvard University Press, 1938).

Hayes, Douglas A. *Bank Lending Policies: Domestic and International* (Ann Arbor, MI: University of Michigan, 1977).

Hervey, Jack L. "Banker's Acceptances," *Business Conditions* (Federal Reserve Bank of Chicago, May 1976, pp. 3–11).

———. "Banker's Acceptances Revisited," *Economic Perspectives* (Federal Reserve Bank of Chicago, May–June 1983, pp. 21–31).

Hurley, Evelyn M. "The Commercial Paper Market Since the Mid-Seventies," *Federal Reserve Bulletin*, Vol. 68 (June 1982, pp. 326–34).

James, Christopher. "Self-Selection and the Pricing of Bank Services: An Analysis of the Market for Loan Commitments and the Role of Compensating Balance Requirements," *Journal of Financial and Quantitative Analysis*, Vol. 16 (December 1981, pp. 725–46).

James, John A. *Money and Capital Markets in Postbellum America* (Princeton, NJ: Princeton University Press, 1978).

Judd, John P. "Competition Between the Commercial Paper Market and Commercial Banks," *Economic Review* (Federal Reserve Bank of San Francisco, Winter 1979, pp. 39–53).

Lazere, Monroe R. "Swinging Swindles and Creepy Frauds," *Journal of Commercial Bank Lending*, Vol. 60 (September 1977, pp. 44–52).

Melton, William C. and Jean M. Mahr. "Banker's Acceptances," *Quarterly Review* (Federal Reserve Bank of New York, Vol. 6, Summer 1981, pp. 39–55).

Merris, Randall C. "Loan Commitments and Facility Fees," *Economic Perspectives* (Federal Reserve Bank of Chicago, Vol. 2, March–April 1978, pp. 14–21).

Mitchell, Karlyn. "Trends in Corporation Finance," *The Economic Review* (Federal Reserve Bank of Kansas City, Vol. 68, pp. 2–15).

Phelps, Clyde W. *The Role of Factoring in Modern Business Finance* (Baltimore: Commercial Credit Company, 1956).

Quarles, J. Carson, "The Floating Lien," *Journal of Commercial Bank Lending*, Vol. 53 (November 1970, pp. 44–52).

Quill, Gerald D., John C. Cresci, and Bruce D. Shuter. "Some Considerations about

Secured Lending," *Journal of Commercial Bank Lending*, Vol. 59 (April 1977, pp. 41–56).

Rodgers, Robert W. "Warehouse Receipts and Their Use in Financing," *Bulletin of the Robert Morris Associates*, Vol. 46 (April 1964, pp. 41–56).

Rose, Peter S. and Donald R. Fraser. *Financial Institutions*, 2nd ed. (Plano, TX: Business Publications, 1985).

Schwartz, Gilbert T. and Robert G. Ballen. "Banker's Acceptance Financing: The Expanding Opportunities," *Banking Law Journal*, Vol. 101 (May–June 1984, pp. 331–47).

Schwartz, Robert A. "An Economic Analysis of Trade Credit," *Journal of Financial and Quantitative Analysis*, Vol. 9 (September 1974, pp. 643–58).

Selden, Richard T. *Trends and Cycles in Commercial Paper* (Cambridge, MA: National Bureau of Economic Research, 1963, occasional paper 85.

Stigum, Marcia. *The Money Market*, rev. ed. (Homewood, IL: Dow Jones-Irwin, 1983).

Stone, Bernell K. "The Cost of Bank Loans," *Journal of Financial and Quantitative Analysis*, Vol. 7 (December 1972, pp. 2077–86.

Taggart, Robert. "A Model of Corporate Financing Decisions," *Journal of Finance*, Vol. 31 (December 1977, pp. 1467–84).

Uniform Commercial Code, 3 vols. (St. Paul, MN: West Publishing, 1968).

White, William. "Debt Management and Form of Business Financing," *Journal of Finance*, Vol. 29 (May 1974, pp. 565–77).

16

LONG-TERM
FUNDING SOURCES

Long-term funding sources consist of two major classes: debt and equity. Debt represents loans to corporations; equity represents ownership interests. Because the distinction, although legal, is analytically substantive, we have employed the classification throughout the text in our discussion of the cost of capital.

*Traditionally, long-term debt instruments have carried a fixed rate of interest with maturities of between 10 and 30 years. Many still do. Since the mid-1970s, however, debt issues with floating or variable rates are more common and maturities have shortened.[1] Some even carry no interest rate: **zero coupon** instruments, marketed at a discount in much the same way as Treasury bills or commercial paper, except that maturity is years not months away.*

Equity is subclassified into two broad groups: preferred and common stock. Both are perpetuities; preferred stock, however, has traditionally carried a fixed dividend rate. As in the case of debt, variable rate preferred has been employed.

Common equity represents residual ownership. Although there is no stated rate of payment, as our discussion of dividend policy suggested, there is a distinct bias in favor of a stable or at least a known rate that may grow but does not decline over time under ordinary circumstances.

Unlike the funding sources discussed in Chapter 15, long-term debt and equity may be marketed to the public. Traditionally, long-term debt has been held primarily by financial institutions, particularly life insurance companies and pension funds. Equity, on the other hand, has been owned primarily by households. Although this generalization still holds, it is less true today than in the past. In 1960, for example, 11.1 percent of the book value of financial assets owned by households was long-term corporate debt; by 1980, this figure had risen to 17.2 percent. Common stock represented 87.7 percent of financial assets owned by households in 1960 but had fallen to 74.3 percent by 1980. In 1960, long-term corporate debt of nonbank financial intermediaries constituted

---

[1] Alfred Broaddus. "Financial Innovation in the United States—Background, Current Status and Prospects," *Economic Review* (Federal Reserve Bank of Richmond, Vol. 71, January–February 1985, p. 14).

78.6 percent of financial assets owned by households and stock 4.8 percent; by 1980, the percentages were 66.0 and 16.6, respectively.[2]

Having discussed at some length the costs of major sources of long-term funds, we concentrate here on the salient institutional details that characterize various types of debt and equity instruments.

LONG-TERM DEBT INSTRUMENTS

Debt instruments are of two basic classes: secured and unsecured. A secured instrument offered to the public is known as a **mortgage bond**. The collateral underlying a mortgage bond is either *real property* (generically, that which is not portable, such as plant and land) or *personal property* (that which is portable, such as equipment or marketable securities). An unsecured instrument is generally known as a **debenture** (the term *debenture bond* is occasionally employed). As a result, the term *bond* often denotes any publicly offered instrument whose maturity date at issue usually exceeds 10 or perhaps 15 years.

The term **note** primarily, if not exclusively, denotes—following the practice of the U.S. government—publicly offered securities with a maturity date of less than ten years. Again, notes can be secured or unsecured. The term **note** also denotes privately placed debt instruments. Thus, a company might issue a series of unsecured debentures maturing in 20 years and sell them to the public. Alternatively, it might raise the same amount of funds from an issue of unsecured notes maturing in 20 years but sell them to five insurance companies. The debentures would be publicly offered; the notes would be privately placed with a few investors. Privately placed notes cannot be resold to the general public unless registered with the Securities and Exchange Commission under regulations discussed in Chapter 17. Once debentures, bonds, or notes have been publicly offered under SEC regulations, they may be resold; in other words, a secondary market may develop for such instruments.

---

[2] Karlyn Mitchell. "Trends in Corporation Finance," *Economic Review* (Federal Reserve Bank of Kansas City, Vol. 68, March 1983, p. 13). Annual summaries of holdings by economic sectors are published in *Balance Sheets for the U.S. Economy* (Board of Governors of the Federal Reserve System).

TYPES OF SECURED INSTRUMENTS

Although bonds secured by real property may be issued with varying features, there is a tendency to standardize such instruments. This is particularly true of public utilities, which account for the bulk of publicly offered mortgage bonds. Given a substantial plant investment, it is relatively easy for a utility company to issue a series of bonds under the same contract or **indenture**. For example, in April 1982, Texas Electric Service Company undertook to market $75 million in *first mortgage bonds* due approximately 30 years after issue (2012).[3] The term *first mortgage* implies that in the event of default bondholders have first priority or prior lien on the collateral to meet their claims of unpaid principal and interest. In this case, the collateral is a first lien on all company properties presently owned or *after acquired*. In addition, subject to certain restrictions, Texas Electric could issue an unlimited amount of bonds under the same mortgage or indenture. These two provisions, an *after-acquired clause* and an *open-end mortgage*, are common features in such contracts. In effect, they permit the company, in this case the utility, to issue a new series of bonds to finance approximately 60 percent of the cost of the new plant. Each time an additional plant must be added, a new series of bonds will be issued. Thus, a utility that issues series Y bonds under the original indenture already has marketed series A through X bonds on property already built: series Y is merely the next issue. Series Y bonds will be secured by all company property in existence at issue plus any future additions; all the bonds are **senior securities** with equal claim on all the property. The company may still issue **junior securities** or debentures that represent unsecured company obligations.[4]

Obligations secured by personal property vary with the nature of the collateral. For example, in transportation, particularly among railroads, it is common to market **equipment trust certificates** to finance the rolling stock of the railroad. Unlike the **conditional sales contract** or the **purchase money mortgage** discussed in Chapter 15, equipment trust certificates are obligations marketed to the public. Holders of equipment trust certificates are represented by a trustee, often a commercial bank or trust company, that oversees payment of principal and interest (in this case, the term *dividends* is used).

What distinguishes equipment trust certificates from other bonds is that the issuer does not mortgage its equipment. On the contrary, the issuer does not even have title to the equipment; title is in the hands of the equipment trust-certificate holders. The transportation company merely leases the equipment until principal

---

[3] *Moody's Bond Survey* (April 5, 1982, pp. 2335–36).

[4] It is possible for a company to issue various types of secured debt with different senior statuses. A second-mortgage bond is junior to a first-mortgage bond but senior to an unsecured debenture. In the event of bankruptcy, however, claims of first-mortgage bondholders may exhaust the collateral, leaving second-mortgage bondholders in the position of unsecured creditors—on a par with debenture holders.

and interest are paid, at which time title reverts to the company. Known as the *Philadelphia Plan*, it ensures that in the event of bankruptcy the equipment trust-certificate holders can seize the collateral: the court must honor all the contract provisions, something it may not have to do if the equipment were collateral for a mortgage bond.[5]

Under the Philadelphia Plan, it is standard practice for the issuer to make a 20-percent down payment with the remainder financed through an issue of equipment trust certificates. Some portion of the certificates matures each year; those that remain have a face value less than the equipment market value. To illustrate equipment trust certificates, in November 1984 Seaboard Coast Line Railroad issued $26,025,000 in equipment trust certificates to finance 80 percent of the purchase price of 35 diesel-electric locomotives, which are standard equipment for any railroad.[6] Each year—specifically, March 15, 1985, through March 15, 1999, approximately 15 years—$1,735,000 worth of obligations would be retired. Therefore, investors could choose their maturities.

Equipment trust certificates, unlike some forms of long-term debt, are not designed to be refunded at maturity. As such, they are more like a secured term loan that is publicly offered. By contrast, Texas Electric first mortgage bonds permitted the company to issue (under the same open-end indenture) new securities to replace those it retired, thereby ensuring a relatively permanent form of financing on a portion of its real property.

There are good reasons for these differences: although some plant and equipment eventually may be removed from service, new plant and equipment are added. The open-end indenture and after-acquired clauses attempt to ensure that the collateral will equal some percentage, usually 60 percent, of the cost of the plant and equipment. As long as regulatory commissions continue to ensure that utility rates cover the costs of financing plant and equipment—a contingency that is less certain as nuclear power plants experience large cost overruns—this arrangement is satisfactory to potential bondholders.

Railroads provide a different scenario. The bankruptcy proceedings that have characterized numerous railroads have tied up their assets for years. However, because the equipment trust certificate—through its leasing feature—offers holders an opportunity to seize equipment and sell it, principal and interest is almost always paid, even during bankruptcy.

Another type of collateral sometimes employed involves marketable securities; the obligations issued are called **collateral trust bonds**. They are ideal instruments for a holding company whose primary assets are the stocks of its subsidiaries. Because the holding company is the parent concern, it can loan money to a subsidiary

---

[5] The reader may wish to reexamine our discussion of absolute and relative priority theories of corporate reorganization in Chapter 13.

[6] *Moody's Bond Survey* (November 5, 1984, pp. 2744–45).

as collateral or can use securities of a subsidiary as collateral for bonds, to purchase additional subsidiaries. Alternatively, if the parent company's credit rating is sufficiently high, it may instead raise the funds through issuing debentures. Thus in 1985, the Kmart Corporation issued $250,000,000 in debentures to help finance in part the purchase of Pay Less Drug Stores Northwest, Inc., thereby adding to its subsidiaries.[7]

DEBENTURES

The standard debenture contract often contains one of two basic provisions: no restriction on the issuance of secured (senior) debt as well as additional unsecured instruments, or a restriction on the issuance of one or the other or both. The Kmart debentures issued in 1985 carried no such restrictions. Thus, the company presumably could issue additional debt, perhaps collateral trust obligations, or use the real assets of its subsidiaries for secured loans. In so doing, Kmart would run the risk of lowering what at the time was an A_1 credit rating for the outstanding debentures, which in turn would lower its credit rating for new debentures. The result, of course, would be a higher cost of debt capital.[8]

Restrictions placed on the debentures of Mountain Fuel Resources Inc. provide a case in point. The $60-million issue in March 1985 (due March 15, 2010) carried a **negative pledge clause** that, in part, prohibited the company from issuing secured debt in excess of 5 percent of the firm's total capitalization unless it also secured the debentures. In addition, debt limits and dividend restrictions were placed on the company.[9]

Subordinated debentures, a subset of debentures, are subordinated to all other debt, making them junior to all debt obligations unless specifically exempted by contract. The practical effect of such subordination is to place them last in the pecking order for payment of principal and interest in the event of bankruptcy. Because they participate after all other debt, subordinated debentures are highly speculative instruments. For example, in March 1984, Arrow Electronics Inc. issued $70 million worth of 13-percent subordinated debentures due March 15, 2004. The debenture placed no restriction on issuing additional debt. As a result, the bonds were sold at $900 per $1000 of principal, for a yield to maturity of 15.37 percent.[10]

---

[7] *Moody's Bond Survey* (March 11, 1985, pp. 4459–60).

[8] "If subsidiary or secured borrowings grow to unacceptable levels, . . . we will reexamine the appropriateness of current public ratings of Kmart Corporation." *Moody's Bond Survey* (March 11, 1985, p. 4459).

[9] *Moody's Bond Survey* (March 18, 1985, p. 4406).

[10] *Moody's Bond Survey* (March 19, 1984, p. 4407).

INCOME BONDS

Both bonds and debentures carry the obligation to pay interest at stated intervals; failure to do so can precipitate bankruptcy. The major difference between the two instruments is the strength of the claim: their place in the pecking order of security holders. The **income bond**, in some cases the **income debenture**, is a unique debt instrument. Under its terms, principal must be paid at maturity (which likens it to a debt instrument); interest, however, is paid only if earned. (The definition of *when* interest is earned is set forth in the bond contract or indenture). This anomaly has fared poorly with potential investors. Hence, income bonds are not widely employed. Most income bonds resulted from reorganizations, particularly railroad reorganizations, where reduction of fixed charges seemed necessary. Although industrial corporations rarely issue income bonds, Gamble-Skogmo had some $237 million in income bonds outstanding prior to its acquisition by Wickes Companies in 1980.[11]

THE INDENTURE, THE TRUSTEE, AND THE SINKING FUND

As indicated, the indenture is the contract between the issuer of long-term debt securities and the holders or lenders. The indenture lists in detail the nature of the issue and the terms and conditions under which principal and interest must be paid. Any restrictions or *covenants* are also listed in the indenture. For example, firms may have to adhere to working capital requirements, dividend restrictions, and the like. Although details differ and some indentures become quite complex, all debtholders of publicly issued bonds or debentures are required under the Trust Indenture Act to be represented by a trustee who ensures that any restrictions and/or covenants of the indenture are observed. When they are not, appropriate action is taken, which in extreme cases can lead to bankruptcy. The trustee is usually a commercial bank or trust company whose specialized personnel handle such tasks; the issuing corporation pays the trustee's expenses.

Among the restrictions and/or covenants for which the trustee is responsible (when applicable) is the **sinking fund**. Although the purpose of the sinking fund may be to set aside monies with which to retire an issue at maturity, this is rarely

---

[11] Wickes filed for bankruptcy in 1982. For a recent discussion of income bonds, see J. J. McConnell and G. G. Schlarbaum, "Returns, Risks and Pricing of Income Bonds, 1956–76," *Journal of Business*, Vol. 54 (January 1981, pp. 33–64).

done. The opportunity cost of funds often suggests that such monies set aside each year be used to purchase some of the outstanding securities, thereby reducing annual interest charges. Otherwise, such funds probably would be invested in risk-free and, therefore, lower yielding securities.

Moreover, the sinking fund provision may not become operative immediately. For example, beginning in March 1996—eleven years after the initial issue—K mart is required to set aside $12.5 million each year with which to purchase some of the outstanding debentures. Thus, by 2014, virtually 95 percent of the debentures will be retired. In the case of the subordinated debentures issued by Arrow Electronics, annual sinking fund payments begin in 1994, ten years after the securities were issued. They are designed to retire 75 percent of the issue before it matures in March 2004.

By contrast, when the debt financing is considered more or less permanent, sinking funds are not employed. The 1982 mortgage bond issue of Texas Electric Service Company required no sinking fund. Instead, there was a *replacement fund* under which the company must set aside annually a specific sum with which to improve or replace property included in the mortgage.

As agent for the debtholders, it is the trustee's responsibility to ensure that management adheres to all restrictions and/or covenants in the indenture, including those pertaining to sinking and/or replacement funds. But what if management fails to comply? Then the trustee must exercise prudent judgment. Failure to pay interest when due is sufficient grounds for default on all debt issues except income bonds. Failure to meet sinking-fund payments may also result in a trip to bankruptcy court. And then again, it may not. The trustee may have limited discretion, depending on the contract language. Alternatively, the trustee may have no choice. Although failure to meet working-capital requirements probably would not signal default, such an occurrence could suggest difficulties in meeting interest payments as they come due.

Management, of course, makes every effort to adhere to restrictions and/or covenants, since failure to do so results at a minimum in a lower rating on securities outstanding, an increase in perceived risk, and hence a rise in the cost of new debt capital.

CALL PRICE

Call price on a debt instrument is the price at which the security may be called in by the company prior to maturity. Call price is greater than the face value of an instrument. However, call price usually declines as the bond gets closer to maturity. The $1,000 K mart debentures maturing in 2015 are callable at 112.5 percent or

$1,125 with 30- to 60-day notice. The **call premium** declines March 1 of each year by .625 percent or $6.25 until the call value reaches 100 percent or $1,000 on March 1, 2005. Thus in 1995 the call price will be 106.25 percent or $1,062.50.[12]

THE REFUNDING DECISION

The call feature on a debt instrument allows the issuer to pay a premium over the par or stated value (face value) of the security in order to retire the debt early. The usual reason for calling the issue is to take advantage of lower interest rates.[13] The calculations are a straightforward example of net present value.

To illustrate, suppose that 5 years ago Everready Power and Light Company issued $150,000,000 in first mortgage bonds maturing in 25 years. The coupon rate is 12 percent but the bonds sold at a $2,000,000 discount from par. Flotation costs associated with the issue were $800,000. The bonds are currently callable at 108 percent or $1,080. In the interim, interest rates have fallen. Everready can presently issue a comparable quality bond at par, maturing in 20 years, carrying a 10-percent coupon rate, and with flotation costs of $750,000. The company's marginal tax rate is 45 percent. To ensure adequate capital, Everready expects a 30-day overlap during which both issues will be outstanding. The relevant information is summarized below.

	Outstanding Bonds	*Proposed Issue*
Face Value (principal)	$150,000,000	$150,000,000
Stated rate of interest (coupon)	12%	10%
Original life of issue	25 years	20 years
Unamortized flotation costs	$ 640,000[a]	$ 750,000
Unamortized bond discount	1,600,000[b]	—
Call premium on existing bonds	8%	—
Marginal tax rate	45%	
Interest overlap	30 days	

[a] $800,000/25 = $32,000; $32,000 × 5 = $160,000; $800,000 − $160,000 = $640,000
[b] $2,000,000/25 = $80,000; $80,000 × 5 = $400,000; $2,000,000 − $400,000 = $1,600,000

The first step is to determine the after-tax outlay Everready must incur to refund the bonds. Conceptually, this is similar to the outlay necessary to make a conventional capital budgeting decision that reduces costs: lowers cash outflows (in this case, lowers interest charges). Here the major outlay is the premium over par that

[12] *Moody's Bond Survey* (March 11, 1985, pp. 4459).

[13] As we learn in Chapter 19, when a security is convertible to stock, exercising the call option forces conversion. In this chapter, however, we are concerned only with nonconvertible securities.

must be paid to retire the bonds. However, there are also overlapping interest costs and flotation costs incurred in selling the new bonds. The call premium, the unamortized flotation costs, the discount on the old issue, and the additional interest paid during the 30-day overlap are tax deductible. Consequently, it is helpful in arriving at the outlay to consider first the investment necessary before taxes and then to subtract the tax savings in determining the net outlay. As illustrated, the calculations yield a net outlay of $7,155,698.66.

Before-tax Investment

Call value of old bonds (1.08 × $150,000,000)	$162,000,000.00
Additional interest ($150,000,000 × .12 × 30/365)	1,479,452.06
Less net proceeds from new issue ($150,000,000 − $750,000)	−149,250,000.00
	$ 14,229,452.06

Tax-deductible Expenses

Call premium ($162,000,000 − $150,000,000)	$ 12,000,000.00
Unamortized flotation costs of old bonds	640,000.00
Unamortized bond discount	1,600,000.00
Additional interest during overlap	1,479,452.00
	$ 15,719,452.00
Tax savings ($15,719,452 × .45)	7,073,753.40

Initial Investment

Before-tax outlay	$ 14,229,452.06
Less tax savings	−7,073,753.40
Net outlay	$ 7,155,698.66

The next step is to determine the savings in annual cash flows that result from refunding. If the old bonds remain outstanding, the annual interest payments, the unamortized flotation costs on the bonds, and the unamortized discount are tax deductible. If there is a new issue floated at par, only the interest and flotation costs are tax deductible. The net savings is the difference between the two cash outflows. Thus:

Old Bonds

Interest ($150,000,000 × .12)	$18,000,000
Amortization of remaining flotation costs ($640,000/20)	32,000
Unamortized bond discount ($1,600,000/20)	80,000
	$18,112,000
After-tax cash outflow [$18,112,000(1 − .45)]	$ 9,961,600

New Bonds

Interest ($150,000,000 × .10)	$15,000,000
Amortization of flotation costs ($750,000/20)	37,500
	$15,037,500
After-tax cash outflow [$15,037,500(1 − .45)]	$ 8,270,625

Cash outflow—old bonds	$ 9,961,600
Cash outflow—new bonds	−8,270,625
Annual savings in cash outflows from refunding	$ 1,690,975

We are now able to evaluate the refunding option by determining the net present value if the bonds are refunded. Thus

$$NPV = -\$7,155,698.66 + \frac{\$1,690,975[1 - (1 + r)^{-20}]}{r}$$

Because the purpose of the exercise is to replace one set of bonds with another, r in this example is not the weighted average cost of capital but the after-tax cost of debt capital, which is $.10(1 - .45) = .055$.[14] Thus

$$NPV = -\$7,155,698.66 + \$1,690,975 \frac{[1 - (1.055)^{-20}]}{.055} = -\$7,155,698.66 + \$20,207,798.03$$

$$NPV = \$13,052,099.37$$

Refunding is profitable and should be undertaken.

Consequently, the refunding decision is a relatively straightforward example of the application of net present value and suggests the importance of the call feature in the debt contract.[15] Nevertheless, sometimes that feature can be very restrictive. For example, in the case of the K mart sinking-fund debentures, although the issue can be recalled at any time, the indenture explicitly states that the securities are

---

[14] Viewed differently, the present value of the net savings in cash outflows equals the size of the term loan that could be borrowed under the same configuration—10 percent for 20 years—and have a neutral impact on after-tax cash flows of the firm. As long as the present value of the term loan is greater than the outlay, refunding should take place. See Wilbur A. Lewellen and Douglas R. Emery, "On the Matter of Parity Among Financial Obligations," *Journal of Finance*, Vol. 35 (March 1981, pp. 97–111). The decision is the same regardless of how one views the outlay. The approach emphasizes, however, that the firm (the owner) benefits from the increased after-tax cash flows.

[15] One might argue that because interest is paid semiannually, it is appropriate to express this fact in the computations. Consequently

$$NPV = -\$7,155,698.66 + \$1,690,975 \left[\frac{1 - \left(1 + \frac{.055}{2}\right)^{-40}}{.055} \right] = \$13,202,034.81$$

nonrefundable for purposes of lower interest debt until March 1, 1995.[16] This provision ensures investors that the debentures will remain outstanding ten years from date of issue or, if recalled, that the company will do so in order to retire, not to refund, the debt.

ORIGINAL-ISSUE DISCOUNT BONDS

Securities' features vary with changes in the desires of participants and with market conditions. A major market trend has been the participation of pension funds. Among the fastest growing types of financial intermediation, pension fund reserves were a modest 8.6 percent of the total liabilities of financial institutions in 1953. Thirty years later in 1983, pension fund reserves were 24.1 percent of the total liabilities of financial institutions.[17] Pension funds pay no taxes on income the fund earns. Because many pension funds currently pay out very little in pensions, income can be reinvested. During periods of what are perceived to be high nominal interest rates relative to the long-term trend, pension-fund managers like to *lock in* the tax-free interest at such rates over the years. Thus, if interest rates are 15 percent for "A"-rated corporate bonds at a time when historical trends suggest 10 to 11 percent, pension funds (as well as others) are interested in reinvesting income at 15 percent a year.

Meanwhile, corporations raising funds through debt instruments are neither anxious to pay 15 percent a year nor to be locked into a bond or debenture that limits the refunding option implicit in the call premium. Instead, they prefer to shorten the term structure of debt expecting, correctly or incorrectly, to shift the borrowing to long-term instruments as credit conditions ease.

Enter the **Original Issue Discount** (OID) bond, which was very popular during the period of historically high interest rates that characterized the early 1980s. The bonds or debentures generally carry a low 3- or 4-percent interest or a zero coupon and must be marketed at a deep discount from par to yield to maturity a rate comparable to current yields on high-coupon bonds of similar quality. For example, assume a corporation issues a zero-coupon bond maturing in 15 years and that comparable outstanding issues have a yield to maturity of 16 percent. To market this instrument

$$price = \frac{\$1,000}{\left(1 + \dfrac{.16}{2}\right)^{30}}$$

$$price = \$99.38$$

[16] *Moody's Bond Survey* (March 11, 1985, p. 4459).

[17] "Balance Sheets for the U.S. Economy 1945–83" (Board of Governors of the Federal Reserve System, November 1984, pp. 48–49 and 54–55).

If the firm puts a nominal coupon rate of 3 percent on the instrument

$$\text{price} = \frac{\$30\left[1 - \left(1 + \dfrac{.16}{2}\right)^{-30}\right]}{.16} + \frac{\$1,000}{\left(1 + \dfrac{.16}{2}\right)^{30}}$$

$$\text{price} = \$268.24$$

In the first case, the company receives $99.38 for each $1,000 borrowed, repaying the principal at maturity. In the second case, the company receives $268.24, paying $30 a year in interest and $1,000 at maturity.

The term **original issue discount** reflects the fact that the bonds or debentures were originally issued at a discount, as distinct from an outstanding issue that an investor might subsequently purchase at a discount. Although the Internal Revenue Service requires investors to amortize the discount for tax purposes, corporations may deduct a pro-rata share of the discount from the company's taxable income. In late 1984, Exxon Corporation sold zero-coupon bonds in Europe at a lower rate than paid by the U.S. government. In what was essentially an arbitrage opportunity, Exxon used the proceeds from the sale of the zero-coupon issue to purchase enough Treasury securities to pay off the bonds when they matured, making about a $20 million profit on the transaction.[18] The volatility that has characterized the pattern of nominal interest rates in recent years suggests that corporations and the investment bankers who advise them will develop other strategies to cope with or profit from such volatility as long as it continues.[19]

PREFERRED STOCK

Preferred stock represents ownership in the corporation. From a legal perspective, it is not debt; therefore, preferred stockholders have minimal claim on the corporation in the event obligations are not met. From the corporate perspective, because dividend payments are not tax deductible, preferred is issued primarily to preserve

---

[18] Ann Monroe. "Financial Ploys: How Companies Get Funds Through Array of Arcane Maneuvers," *Wall Street Journal* (January 16, 1985, pp. 1 and 18).

[19] To improve their debt rating and often-reported earnings, corporations have engaged in a variety of techniques including repurchasing debt, exchanging debt for equity, and, most recently, establishing a trust containing U.S. government securities whose cash flows match the cash flows of a specific debt obligation on the company's books. In so doing, the debt is defeased: the obligation is satisfied and may be removed from the balance sheet. In 1982, Exxon Corporation used this trust procedure to remove $515 million of debt from its balance sheet. See Pamela Peterson, David Peterson, and James Ang, "The Extinguishment of Debt Through In-Substance Defeasance," *Financial Management*, Vol. 14 (Spring 1985, pp. 59–67). For further discussion of OIDs, see Andrew J. Kalotay, "An Analysis of Original Issue Discount Bonds," *Financial Management*, Vol. 13 (Autumn 1984, pp. 29–38).

the credit rating of the company. Otherwise, debt would be used. Under current law, however, corporate buyers of preferred (or common) stock may exclude 80 percent of the dividends from their taxable income. Hence, preferred stock tends to be purchased by institutions in relatively high tax brackets (for example, property and casualty insurance companies during a profitable stage of the underwriting cycle).[20] For similar reasons, nonfinancial corporations often trade in preferred stock as a cash management tool for collecting the highly tax-sheltered dividend.[21] As a result, "Preferred stock in recent years has yielded a rate that is comparable to the yield on senior bonds of the same corporation—often preferred yields are even lower."[22]

A preferred-stock contract generally contains the following features. First, dividends are a stated percentage of the par or face value of the instrument or the dividend is a specified rate. For example, a 10-percent preferred may be a stock whose annual dividend is 10 percent of the $100 par value of the instrument: $10 per year. Alternatively, the security may be referred to as a $10 preferred. When speaking of preferred stock: *By your dividends ye shall be known.*

Second, the dividend is generally cumulative. In other words, management does not have to meet the obligation as it comes due and can, therefore,—as long as it meets its debt obligations—escape the consequences of extreme financial distress: a trip to the bankruptcy courts. Once in arrears, however, the dividends accumulate. Dividends cannot be paid to residual owners—common stockholders—until they are paid to preferred owners. Moreover, when preferred-stock dividends are in arrears for several quarters, preferred stockholders are usually permitted to elect several directors to the company's board of directors.[23] Although the voting rights of preferred stockholders are sometimes limited in other matters and in some cases altogether nonvoting, the election feature could allow preferred stockholders to control the company when dividends are in arrears for several quarters. Consequently, corporate management tends to treat preferred dividends the same as bond interest—to be paid when due.

Third, perpetuity and fixed-dividend features are characteristic of preferred stock, but are not attractive to investors during periods of volatile yields. Debt instruments with variable interest rates were issued during the mid-1970s and variable dividend rates were introduced in the early 1980s. In each case, interest or

---

[20] Thomas R. Fausel. "The Supply and Demand Effect on Preferred Stock Yield Behavior," unpublished paper written in partial fulfillment of the requirements for an M. A. in Economics (Hartford, CT: Trinity College, 1982). William R. McDaniel. "Sinking Fund Preferred Stock," *Financial Management*, Vol. 13 (Spring 1984, pp. 45–52).

[21] Michael D. Joehnk, Oswald D. Bowlin, and J. William Petty. "Preferred Dividend Rolls: A Viable Strategy for Corporate Money Managers?" *Financial Management*, Vol. 9 (Summer 1980, pp. 78–87).

[22] Joehnk, Bowlin, and Petty, p. 46. This phenomenon goes back even earlier. See Ward S. Curran, "Preferred Stock for Public Utilities," *Financial Analysts Journal*, Vol. 28 (March–April 1972, pp. 71–76).

[23] John D. Finnerty. "Preferred Stock Refunding Analysis: Synthesis and Extension," *Financial Management*, Vol. 13 (Autumn 1984, p. 22).

dividend rates are indexed to yields on U.S. Treasury securities and, within limits, fluctuate with changes in these yields.[24]

Nevertheless, tying a perpetuity to an index is not a comfortable thought to many executives: yields could rise—but not the profits of the corporation—and larger preferred dividends would have to be met from shrinking after-tax profits. Because fixed-rate perpetuities are not an attractive investment in a period of volatile interest rates, one answer is to issue a preferred stock that can be retired within a reasonable period of time. This fact, plus certain regulatory changes affecting how preferred stock is treated as reserves by property and casualty companies, may have contributed to the recent popularity of *sinking-fund preferred* stock.[25]

Fourth, although in the past preferred stock was sometimes issued with a sinking-fund provision, today virtually all preferred stock is issued with that provision in the contract. The provisions of the sinking fund generally begin five years after the date of issue: 5 percent of the issue is retired each year and the stock is completely retired at the end of 25 years. The redemption price is the par value of the preferred and the requisite amount is often redeemed by lottery. In addition, the firm may call all the preferred at declining premiums (the first call price is usually par plus a year's dividend). Thus, a $100 preferred carrying a $9 dividend is callable at $109. The call premium drops over the years, subsequently terminating at par.[26] Although claims are made that sinking-fund preferred sells at .5–1.5 percent (50 to 150 basis points) below preferred of comparable quality without sinking-fund provisions, there is some evidence that the savings, though real, are exaggerated.[27]

In spite of innovations in the preferred-stock contract, such an issue remains a small proportion of the capital structure of most companies, except public utilities, where it may comprise 10–15 percent of total financing. In the regulated environment of public-utility finance, income taxes are treated as operating expense that may be passed on to consumers. Moreover, as with fixed-interest debt, fixed-rate preferred carries a known rate when issued. A public utility's average cost of capital is the basis for determining the allowable rate of return to all investors; what

---

[24] Claire Makin. "The Boom in Uncommon Stock," *Institutional Investor*, Vol. 19 (June 1985, pp. 101–2). The technical term for the stock is *adjustable-rate preferred* (ARP). With the former 85-percent (now 80-percent) dividend exclusion and protection against fluctuations in interest rates, ARPs were initially very popular. By mid-1983, however, investors discovered that these risk-free instruments were trading as much as 20 percent above or below par, depending on the issuer's perceived financial health. Consequently, a new issue termed *money market preferred* (MMP) has been introduced. The price of an MMP is fixed and the dividend allowed to change every seven weeks. This is accomplished through a **Dutch auction**, in which holders of the preferred and potential buyers bid for the yield they are willing to accept for the next seven weeks. Shares, therefore, can change hands. Although the issuer pays varying rates depending on the outcome of the auction, the price of the instrument is unchanged. Needless to say, the number of holders must be small to conduct such an auction. In one instance, Glen Fed Finance Inc., a subsidiary of a savings and loan association, issued MMPs with a face value of $500,000. Yields were limited to 110–125 percent of the 60-day Aa commercial-paper rate. *Moody's Bond Survey* (March 25, 1985, p. 4377).

[25] Same as [20], McDaniel, pp. 46–48. Qualified sinking-fund preferred may be carried at par for purposes of determining reserves rather than at market, thereby reducing the variability in the value of a property and casualty company's reserves.

[26] McDaniel, pp. 46–47.

[27] McDaniel, pp. 47–52.

remains unmeasured is the cost of common equity. Regulatory commissions must deal (as we have dealt) with this seemingly intractable problem.[28] Anxious to hold down rate increases suggested by higher costs of capital, utility management, rightly or wrongly, could easily conclude that regulatory commissions prefer the lowest possible return to common stockholders—consistent with modern financial theory, in harmony with the company's need to attract capital, but not so low as to violate the Due Process Clause of the U.S. Constitution. Within such constraints, one might assume the return on equity would be minimal. However, because utilities finance nearly 50 percent of their investment from debt, the use of preferred not only enhances the equity base and preserves the bond rating, it offers a known cost that reduces the uncertainty in the commission's final determination of the allowable rate of return.

COMMON STOCK

Because we have discussed at some length the principles underlying the cost of common stock and have treated the dividend decision in some detail, we need only review briefly a few points, confining our attention to certain relevant institutional aspects with which a student of finance should be familiar.

As noted, the common stockholder is the residual claimant to the income of the corporation. As such, he or she can receive dividends, enjoy the capital appreciation of spectacular success in reinvesting earnings, experience the despair that accompanies an unsuccessful attempt to launch a new product or to drill an oil well, or learn firsthand what it means to be last in the pecking order of claimants in bankruptcy proceedings. The stockholder, however, is comforted in the knowledge that his or her loss is limited to the amount invested—a limitation that derives from the fact that a share of common stock has a **par (stated) value**. When stock was initially issued by the corporation, purchasers gave the company cash or assets whose value at least equaled the stock's par or stated value. Consequently, the owner—and all subsequent owners who might purchase these shares in the secondary market—enjoys *limited* liability: no owner can lose more than was paid for such shares. In a rare instance, when payment is less than the stock's par or stated value, the shares are said to be watered and the shareholder is liable for the difference. A not uncommon occurrence in the financing of some companies in the latter part of the nineteenth century, *watered stock* is virtually unknown today.[29] Thus, limited liability is almost

---

[28] See, for example, Philip L. Cooley, "A Review of the Use of Beta in Regulatory Proceedings," *Financial Management*, Vol. 10 (Winter 1981, pp. 75–81).

[29] Devotees of the nonessential fact will appreciate knowing that the term *watered stock* comes from the old-west practice of allowing cattle to lick on blocks of salt and then drink water before being weighed at the stockyards for sale by the pound.

a certainty of common-stock ownership. But there are exceptions. Although the corporation is a separate legal entity, the protective shield can be penetrated if stockholders use the corporation for illegal purposes—not a common practice among companies where shareholders purchase the stock for investment purposes and take no active role in management.

Upon obtaining a charter of incorporation from the state in which it is domiciled, a company becomes *authorized* to issue a specific number of shares. Issued shares are either outstanding or have been repurchased by the issuer. Repurchased shares are called *treasury stock*. When all authorized shares have been issued, authorization can be increased by vote of the shareholders. For example, in 1983, shareholders of MCI Communications Corporation authorized an increase in shares from 200,000,000 to 400,000,000. The stock was subsequently split, the split effected in the form of a 100-percent stock dividend (see Chapter 11 for a discussion of stock splits and stock dividends). The shareholders' equity account of MCI in the company's 1984 annual report reflected the following:

	Fiscal Year Ending March 31, 1984
Preferred stock (20,000,000 shares authorized/ none issued)	
Common stock ($.10 par value/400,000,000 shares authorized/235,746,702 issued)	$ 23,575,000
Capital in excess of par value (capital surplus)	784,108,000
Retained earnings	332,352,000
	$1,140,035,000
Common stock held by subsidiaries at cost (2,720,436 shares)	4,292,000
Total stockholders' equity	$1,135,743,000

Book value per share, $\dfrac{\$1,135,743,000}{235,746,702} = \$4.82$

Market price per share $8.38

The company listed no treasury stock but noted 57,384,000 shares could be issued in connection with various employee stock-compensation plans and securities convertible to common stock. In calculating stockholders' equity, the company excluded shares held by its subsidiaries.

Note that par value of the stock is only ten cents. Such shares are known as *nominal-* or *low-par value stock*. The capital surplus indicates the shares received consideration in excess of par value. Futhermore, in the case of stock dividend, standard accounting practice is to transfer some of the retained earnings to the capital surplus account. In a conventional stock split, only the par value is reduced.

To illustrate, assume XYZ corporation has the following capital structure:

	End of Fiscal Year
Common stock par value = $2 per share (10,000,000 shares authorized/5,000,000 issued and outstanding)	$10,000,000
Capital surplus	5,000,000
Retained earnings	65,000,000
Stockholders' equity	$80,000,000

If the current market price of the stock is $20 per share and the company declares a 100-percent stock dividend, it will issue 5,000,000 shares at $2 per share. Since the market price will fall to $10 per share because of the increase in shares outstanding, the difference between $10 and $2 per share, $8, can be charged to retained earnings and capital surplus increased accordingly. Thus, XYZ now has the following capital structure:

	End of Fiscal Year
Common stock par value = $2 per share (10,000,000 shares authorized and issued)	$20,000,000
Capital surplus	45,000,000
Retained earnings	15,000,000
Stockholders' equity	$80,000,000

Capital surplus is increased by $40,000,000 ($8 × 5,000,000) and retained earnings are decreased by $50,000,000 to cover the capital surplus increase and the additional stock issue.

If the stock had split two for one, only the par value would have changed. The shareholders' equity account would have reflected:

	End of Fiscal Year
Common stock par value = $1 per share (10,000,000 shares authorized and issued)	$10,000,000
Capital surplus	5,000,000
Retained earnings	65,000,000
Stockholders' equity	$80,000,000

Since MCI effected a two-for-one stock split with a 100-percent stock dividend, the capital surplus and retained earnings were rearranged but the par value was unchanged. As noted in Chapter 11, in either instance the stockholder receives nothing of value. In this case, the split did not signal a dividend increase because

MCI did not pay dividends at the time; in its 1984 annual report, management stated it had no plans to declare dividends.

Although no preferred stock was outstanding, the par or stated value and capital surplus, if any, would have been included in shareholders' equity but would have been subtracted to determine common stockholder equity and book value per share of common stock. If some stock had been repurchased and placed in the treasury, it would have been retired at cost and retained earnings charged accordingly. The par value account, however, would not have been reduced. The stock could be used subsequently by the corporation for any number of purposes, including stock options for participating employees. If, for example, the shares were purchased in the open market at an average price of $15 per share, retained earnings would be charged accordingly. If executives had stock options at $20 and the market price subsequently rose to $50, those options could be exercised. The stock would be purchased at $15 per share and reissued. Retained earnings would rise accordingly but the par value would remain unchanged.

The salient features of the stockholders' equity account are summarized in Table 16-1 using the hypothetical ABC Toy Corporation. Preferred shares have been sold at par, so there is no capital surplus. Half the authorized preferred shares are issued and outstanding. The common stock has a par value of $3 per share and 50,000,000 of 200,000,000 authorized shares are issued; 1,000,000 shares, however,

Table 16-1   Stockholders' Equity Account— ABC Toy Corporation

	End of Fiscal Year
Preferred stock par value = $10 per share (10,000,000 shares authorized/5,000,000 issued and outstanding)	$ 50,000,000
Common stock par value = $3 per share (200,000,000 shares authorized/50,000,000 issued, including treasury stock)	150,000,000
Capital surplus	200,000,000
Retained earnings	462,000,000
Less treasury stock (1,000,000 shares at cost)	−27,000,000
Total stockholders' equity	835,000,000
Less preferred stock	−50,000,000
Total equity of common stockholders	**$785,000,000**

Book value per share $\dfrac{\$785,000,000}{50,000,000} = \$15.70$

Market price (end of fiscal year) $= \$30.25$

Ratio of market price to book value $\dfrac{\$30.25}{\$15.70} = 1.93$

have been repurchased at an average price of $27 per share. The retained earnings account has been charged accordingly. Although total stockholders' equity is $835,000,000, that amount has been reduced by book value of the preferred stock to arrive at total equity of common stockholders and ultimately book value per share. As might be expected, market price differs from book value: nearly twice book value. Given our discussion of financial theory, this should come as no surprise. Accounting procedures do not pretend to measure market value unless all assets are liquid securities or inventories with a ready market price. For a toy manufacturer, this is highly unlikely. Presumably, the market capitalizes future dividends of this company, so that market price exceeds book value of the stockholders' equity.[30]

CONTROL

In principle, stockholders control the company. In closely held corporations, this may be true; owners and managers may be the same people. In large publicly held corporations, stock ownership is generally viewed as an investment; control is usually in the hands of management.[31] The legal fiction through which stockholders exercise *control* is the board of directors—generally handpicked by management—the terms of whom are staggered. Prior to the annual ritual known as the stockholders' meeting, management sends proxies to all shareholders touting a slate of candidates and requesting that stockholders vote for them or return the proxy statement authorizing someone to cast their vote in favor of the slate. Shareholders also are asked to approve the firm's auditors, to vote (as in the case of MCI) on increasing the number of authorized shares, to approve merger terms (when applicable), and to cast their vote on other matters that by law must be approved by them. In any event, management carefully orchestrates the results. If successful, the outcome is bathos. The most exciting part of the meeting is when the corporate gadfly who owns a few shares launches a tirade against the president, questioning whether the annual increase in compensation for executive officers is justified in light of the operating results. Although such gadflies are sometimes hooted down by others at the meeting, most managers tend to treat them with deference, often allowing them to exercise rights of privilege that stockholders rarely use: examining, within limits, the books of the company or discussing issues with high-level officers prior to the stockholders' meeting.

---

[30] In the standard accounting format, total stockholders' equity equals book value of assets less book value of liabilities.

[31] Even in the case of venture capital, where a group of investors purchase stock in a young firm, they often do so with the view of selling their shares in a public offering at some later date when the company has established a track record or at least has a concept marketable to the general public. Venture capitalists, however, often actively participate in management, being careful not to undercut the entrepreneur who must take responsibility for day-to-day operations. See George Kozmetsky, Michael D. Gill, Jr., and Raymond W. Smilor, *Financing and Managing Fast-Growth Companies: The Venture Capital Process* (Lexington, MA: Heath and Co., 1985, pp. 4–8).

CUMULATIVE VOTING

The general rule is that each share of stock is entitled to one vote. If management has a slate of directors up for election and there are 1,200,000 shares outstanding, 600,001 shares (assuming all shares are voted) are necessary to elect the slate. However, some states require, as do some corporate charters, **cumulative voting**. Under cumulative voting, shareholders have as many votes as they have shares multiplied by the number of directors up for election. If 11 directors are on the board, a stockholder owning 100 shares has 1,100 votes. Moreover, under cumulative voting all votes may be cast for a limited number of directors.

The purpose of cumulative voting is to provide for minority representation on the board. Under standard voting arrangements, 600,001 shares would elect a majority. Suppose, however, a dissident group controlled 100,001 shares. They could elect one director by casting all their votes for him or her.

The general formula for cumulative voting is

$$\text{number of shares required to elect } Y \text{ number of directors} = \frac{\text{total number of shares outstanding} \times Y \text{ number of directors desired}}{\text{total number of directors to be elected} + 1} + 1$$

If 12 directors are up for election, in order to elect 1 director

$$\text{number of shares required to elect } Y \text{ number of directors} = \frac{(1,200,000)(1)}{11 + 1} + 1 = 100,001$$

If all other directors are the choice of management and this particular director is not, at worst the remaining votes will be cast among the 11 management favorites, each receiving

$$\frac{(1,099,999)(11)}{11} = 1,099,999$$

the director chosen by the dissidents receiving $100,001 \times 11 = 1,100,011$ votes.

Other arrangements are possible. All the dissidents must do is make certain the 100,001 shares are voted only for their candidate.[32]

Cumulative voting can make life troublesome for management. When cumulative voting is not mandatory and is put to the vote at shareholder request,

---

[32] Suppose the minority controlled 100,001 shares; it could determine the number of directors to be elected as follows

$$\text{number of directors that can be elected with shares owned} = \frac{(\text{number of shares owned} - 1)(\text{total number of directors to be elected} + 1)}{\text{total number of shares outstanding}}$$

$$= \frac{(100,001 - 1)(12)}{1,200,000} = 1 \text{ director}$$

management is likely to oppose it. When cumulative voting is mandatory, one strategy management can employ is to reduce the number of directors on the board and to stagger their terms. To elect 1 person to a 7-member board, for example, the minority would require

$$\frac{(1,200,000)(1)}{7 + 1} + 1 = 150,001 \text{ shares}$$

If the board contained 15 members and 3 were elected each year to serve five-year terms, to elect 1 member in any given year the minority would require

$$\frac{(1,200,000)(1)}{3 + 1} + 1 = 300,001 \text{ shares}$$

PREEMPTIVE RIGHT

Some state statutes and some corporate charters mandate what is termed the **preemptive right**: stockholders may purchase new shares in the same proportion as their current ownership. Thus, if a corporation has 10,000,000 shares outstanding and proposes to issue 2,000,000 new shares and the preemptive right applies, a holder of 100 shares has the right to purchase 20 new shares. The reason for the preemptive right is to prevent shareholder dilution. Some companies, such as General Motors, have the preemptive right; others, such as Sears, Roebuck, have no such provision. Often, the preemptive right can be waived by stockholder vote. Given that firms use stock for mergers and other purposes, the preemptive right can be a constraint. Consequently, there is considerable likelihood today (compared with the practice of finance years ago) that the preemptive right can be waived.

Nevertheless, firms still make use of the preemptive right, particularly those with a broad shareholder base. When it is used, the company prices the stock well below the going market price and issues *rights* to its stockholders. Such rights enable shareholders to purchase the new stock during the subscription period at the privileged price. To illustrate, suppose a company has 8,000,000 shares outstanding and the current market price is $50 per share. The company wishes to raise $80,000,000 in new capital through a privileged subscription to its stockholders at $40 per share. Thus, it must issue 2,000,000 new shares ($80,000,000/$40 = 2,000,000). Because 8,000,000 shares are currently outstanding, each shareholder is entitled to purchase one new share for each four shares owned. To accomplish this, the shareholders are given rights: one right per share, four rights necessary to purchase one new share. Consequently, a person owning 100 shares is given 100 rights and is entitled to purchase 25 new shares at the subscription price of $40 per share.

During the subscription period, rights have value; those who own or purchase stock during the subscription period enjoy preemptive rights. Accordingly, during the subscription period, the stock sells or trades **cum rights**; once the subscription period ends, the stock sells **ex rights**. Because the rights themselves can be sold or purchased, there is a going market price for them. Stockholders who do not choose to exercise such rights can sell them. The company ensures, through brokerage firms, that stockholders with a fractional number of rights can sell or purchase them. For example, a stockholder with 150 shares can purchase 37.5 shares; therefore, he or she must sell or purchase fractional rights to sell or purchase a whole number of shares.

What determines the value of a right? During the time the stock sells *cum* rights, the value of the right is

$$\text{value of right } cum \text{ rights} = \frac{\text{market price of outstanding stock} - \text{subscription price}}{\text{number of rights to purchase one share} + 1}$$

Since there is one new share for every 4 old shares, add 1 to the denominator. Because the subscription price is $40 and the market price is $50

$$\text{value of right } cum \text{ rights} = \frac{\$50 - \$40}{4 + 1} = \$2$$

During the subscription period, the stock's market price is the variable that determines the value of a right. The stockholder can gain protection against subsequent dilution in market value by exercising the privilege to purchase the shares at the subscription price. When the stock goes *ex* rights, this is no longer possible. To illustrate, assume the price is still $50 on the day the stock is *ex* rights. There will soon be 10,000,000 rather than 8,000,000 shares. The original 8,000,000 shares had a market value of $400,000,000; the new shares sold for $80,000,000. Dividing the total, $480,000,000, by 10,000,000 shares yields a market price of $48 per share. When the stock goes *ex* rights, the market price adjusts so that the denominator no longer reflects the dilution. Consequently

$$\text{value of a right } ex \text{ rights} = \frac{\$48 - \$40}{4} = \$2$$

If the market price of the stock had been $60 the day before the stock sold *ex* rights

$$\text{value of a right } cum \text{ rights} = \frac{\$60 - \$40}{4 + 1} = \$4$$

When the stock goes *ex* rights, the value of each share is ($60 × 8,000,000 + $40 × 2,000,000)/10,000,000 = $56. Furthermore

$$\text{value of a right } ex \text{ rights} = \frac{\$56 - \$40}{4} = \$4$$

Although the stock's value falls when the subscription period expires, other factors can affect the opening price on the day the stock trades *ex* rights. However, if the closing price on the day the subscription period ends is $60, the likelihood (in this instance) is that the stock will open the following day at $56.

When a firm uses a privileged subscription, it may sell the stock at any price. However, the lower the subscription price relative to the market price, the greater the number of new shares that must be issued. In practice, most privileged subscriptions are offered at 10 to 20 percent below the market price. Since the rights have value, the shareholder must either exercise or sell them. To permit the rights to expire unexercised would cause the shareholder to lose some of his or her wealth; moreover, the company would not realize its $80,000,000 goal. Hence, the company would avail itself of an investment banker (on a standby basis) committed to buying the unsubscribed shares, which may account for 2 to 3 percent of the total offering.

RIGHT OF TRANSFER

Owners of publicly held stock can freely transfer ownership; corporate management provides a registrar and transfer agent, often a commercial bank or trust company, for this purpose. The registrar and transfer agent for MCI, for example, is the First National Bank of Chicago. Although the registrar and transfer agent distributes dividends, disseminates notices of shareholder meetings, and so forth, shareholders rarely come into direct contact with the agent.[33] To facilitate transfer, there may be a securities firm or several firms marketing the shares. Alternatively, the shares may be listed on an exchange. In 1987, the shares of MCI were not listed on an exchange but traded over the counter. A shareholder wishing to sell shares goes through a brokerage firm that in turn sells the shares to a dealer buying and selling for his or her own account. If the shares are listed on an exchange, such as the New York Stock Exchange, the broker may get a price from the dealer who is the specialist in the stock. In either case, the transfer agent merely cancels the stock sold and issues new shares to the buyer: it deals with the back office of the securities firm, not the shareholder.

CLASSES OF COMMON STOCK

Thus far we have distinguished only between preferred and common stock. Some firms, however, issue classes of common stock. One not-well-known company, Citizens Utilities, created two classes, one paying cash and the other paying stock

---

[33] Similar arrangements are used for bondholders. However, since the debt is an obligation of the company, the registrar of the bonds, as we have seen, is also the trustee for the bondholder.

dividends. Other firms create classes for different reasons. Ford Motor Company, for example, has Class-A and Class-B common stock. The latter class is owned by the Ford family and enjoys approximately six times as many votes per share as the Class-A common held by the general public. Adolf Coors Company, the Colorado brewer, also employs Class-A and Class-B common stock. Class-A is owned by the family and enjoys full voting power; Class B is owned by the public and has restricted voting power.

As a result of its acquisition of Electronic Data Systems (EDS) in 1984, General Motors issued a Class-E common stock. Although many of the initial shares went to EDS employees who owned stock in EDS, every GM shareholder received one share of Class-E stock for every 20 shares of GM owned.

What was unique about the security was that while the stock was issued in the name of General Motors, its dividends and (ultimately) capital gains depended on the performance of EDS alone. In 1985, GM was preparing a similar issue (subsequently issued) of Class-H common stock to reflect its acquisition of Hughes, now GM-Hughes Electronics Corporation.[34]

The use of Class-A and Class-B stock to ensure that control remains in the hands of the family (as in the Ford and Coors cases) is a common reason for issuing various types of common stock. The GM innovation, however, is unusual: the rationale, in part, was to provide incentive for Hughes to perform. (GM, of course, has no family per se.)

VARIATIONS ON A THEME

In the history of corporate finance, there are attempts at times to market exotic securities—variations on the basic debt and equity contract.[35] In 1983, for example, Refinement, Inc., a Rhode Island processor of precious metals scrap, issued a gold bond. Although investors paid cash for the instrument, it was redeemable in gold and paid interest in gold: 0.325 ounces yearly on a ten-ounce bond. Bonds backed by silver have, on occasion, been issued.

There is also the less exotic. More conventional debt instruments—issued in such large amounts as to lower the debt rating of the issuer—have been popular, particularly in the takeover of one corporation by another. Known as **junk bonds** to their detractors, such instruments are below the investment grade of most institutional purchasers. Their high yields, however, are attractive to less risk-averse individuals and to institutional investors that are not legally constrained in their

---

[34] Same as [24], p. 102. Arise C. Wallace. "The 'New' GM May Still Be Roadbound," *New York Times* (June 16, 1985, Sec. 3, p. 12).

[35] Same as [24], pp. 101–2. Ann Monroe. "New-Securities Ideas Are Often Hatched, But Most Flop," *Wall Street Journal* (March 25, 1986, pp. 1 and 72).

purchases. Such instruments often represent the first public offering of many small companies that might not otherwise have access to securities markets.[36]

In the equity area, firms have begun to employ *putable stock*. Although we develop the put concept more fully in Chapter 19, we note here that a company issuing such a stock grants to the buyer the right to sell back that issue to the company at a specific price. Thus, Gearhart Industries issued equity units consisting of five shares with five rights to sell back those shares to the company at a guaranteed price of at least $14.68 per share. Payment could be made in cash, debt, or additional shares of common stock.[37] A company employs this technique to get people to buy the security at a premium: to pay for the right to exercise the option.

SUMMARY

In this chapter we have focused on the descriptive rather than the analytical. What we have seen is that the permutations on the basic debt-and-equity contracts are numerous. Our theoretical discussion abstracted from such detail in order to develop a useful analytical framework. Thus, we may pose the question: Are such variations necessary? In a world in which institutional investors' portfolios are constrained by certain legal impediments, where the relative importance of such impediments waxes and wanes with the relative importance of such investors in the market— pension funds relative to other intermediaries, for example—the answer is yes. Moreover, as often demonstrated, provisions of the income tax laws affect the use of particular instruments. Neither can we lose sight of the fact that there are differences in the willingness of people to bear risk. The success of the corporation as a vehicle with which resources are organized can be attributed to the fact that management can finely tune the trade-offs among risk, income, and (sometimes) control inherent in any business venture.

Finally, to some extent, we are all a product or victim of our times. The domination of railroads in the latter part of the nineteenth century impacted on the types of financial instruments issued. The carryover to manufacturing and, to a lesser extent, utilities was imperfect; many early variations on the basic debt-and-equity contracts have since fallen into limbo. Interest rate volatility, the increasing role of foreign capital in domestic capital markets, and the increasing competition

---

[36] There is some question as to whether these high-risk issues are efficiently priced. The relatively high yield over comparable Treasury issues represents a default premium. However, there is evidence that suggests investors earn more than necessary—in terms of the Securities Market Line—compensation for the risk they assume. See Jerome S. Fons, "The Default Premium and Corporate Bond Experience" (Working Paper 8604, Federal Reserve Bank of Cleveland, June 1986). See, also, Marshall E. Blume and Jerome E. Hass, "Risk and Return Characteristics of Lower-Grade Bonds" (Rodney L. White Center for Financial Research, The Wharton School, University of Pennsylvania, December 1984). For further discussion on the increased importance of low-grade bonds (Baa for Moody's, BBB for Standard & Poor's), see Jan Loeys, *Business Review* (Federal Reserve Bank of Philadelphia, November–December 1986, pp. 3–12).

[37] Same as [24], pp. 101–2).

among financial institutions have dominated recent experience. As a result, there has been a proliferation of new instruments, some of which may have a short life cycle and others of which may find their way into standard use. The source of many such innovations is the investment banking industry; the role of that industry in shaping capital markets is an important part of Chapter 17.

PROBLEMS AND QUESTIONS

1. The treasurer of Invent-a-Ride, a manufacturer of amusement-park equipment, is considering a public offering to raise $50,000,000 through debt securities. The company is profitable and has an "A" credit rating. Current yields on 15-year zero-coupon bonds of "A" rated companies are 14 percent. If the treasurer of Invest-a-Ride were to issue 15-year coupon debt at par, the rate would be 15 percent. The zero-coupon bonds are callable any time at par. The 15-percent coupon issue is not callable for five years, after which it is callable at par.

   a. What is the expected market value of each bond at issue? In each case, how many bonds must be issued to raise the $50,000,000? (Assume flotation costs are equal and therefore can be ignored.)

   b. What major factors should the treasurer consider in choosing between the possibilities?

2. The financial vice president of Over-the-Hill Retirement Homes is considering a refunding operation. The appropriate data are:

	Outstanding Bonds	*New Bonds*
Face value	$75,000,000	$75,000,000
Stated rate of interest	11.75%	9.875%
Original life of issue	20 years	16 years
Unamortized flotation costs	$480,000	$520,000
Call premium on existing bonds	7%	—
Marginal tax rate	40%	
Interest overlap	31 days	

Assume the original issue sold at par and the new issue would also sell at par. Explain in detail whether or not refunding is profitable.

3. At the end of its fiscal year, Reliable Home Appliance Corporation has 10,000,000 preferred shares authorized at a par value of $10 per share and 50,000,000 common shares authorized at a par value of $2 per share. 25,000,000 shares have been issued and 15,000,000 are outstanding. The company has repurchased 10,000,000 shares at an average price of $10 per share. The capi-

tal or paid-in surplus account totals $17,500,000. Retained earnings are $525,500,000. Develop Reliable's stockholders' equity account. What is the book value per share? If the market price per share is $25 at the end of its fiscal year, what is Reliable's rate of market value to book value per share?

4. In problem 3, if Reliable effected a two-for-one split of its common stock through a stock dividend, project the changes that would occur in the stockholders' equity account. If the split were handled in the *usual* manner, how would this change the shareholders' equity account?

5. Management of Toasty Bakery Company elects its entire slate of 13 directors at one time. There are 2,800,000 shares outstanding. What is the minimum number of shares necessary to elect a majority of directors if state law requires cumulative voting? Suppose the rule is that one share receives one vote. Would the number of shares required to elect a majority of directors change?

6. In problem 5, suppose a dissident group attempts to elect one director. How many shares must the group control? Suppose the terms of the directors are staggered so that one director is elected each year to serve 13 years. How many shares must the dissidents control?

7. Define a mortgage bond, a collateral trust bond, a debenture, a subordinated debenture, and an income bond.

8. Define a variable- or adjustable-rate preferred stock. If marketed at par, would you expect the stock to trade indefinitely around par?

9. Using the preemptive right, a company plans to raise $60,000,000. There are currently 12,000,000 shares outstanding. The stock's market price is $21 per share. Management will offer the stock to the shareholders at $15 per share.
   a. How many new shares must be issued?
   b. How many preemptive rights are necessary to purchase one share?
   c. What is the value of the preemptive right when the stock sells *cum* rights?

10. In problem 9, if the market price of the stock falls to $18 per share when the stock sells *cum* rights, what is the value of each preemptive right? Does the value of the preemptive right change when the stock goes from *cum* rights to *ex* rights? Explain.

SELECTED ADDITIONAL REFERENCES

Blume, Marshall E. and Jerome E. Hass. "Risk and Return Characteristics of Lower-Grade Bonds" (Rodney L. White Center for Financial Research, The Wharton School, University of Pennsylvania, December, 1984).

Bowlin, Oswald D. "The Refunding Decision: Another Special Case in Capital Budgeting," *Journal of Finance*, Vol. 21 (March 1966, pp. 55–68).

Broaddus, Alfred. "Financial Innovation in the United States: Background, Current Status and Prospects," *Economic Review* (Federal Reserve Bank of Richmond, Vol. 71, January–February 1985, pp. 2–22).

Childs, John F. *Long Term Financing* (New York: Prentice-Hall, 1961, Ch. 5).

Cooley, Philip. "A Review of the Use of Beta in Regulatory Proceedings," *Financial Management*, Vol. 10 (Winter 1981, pp. 75–81).

Curran, Ward S. "Preferred Stock for Public Utilities," *Financial Analysts Journal*, Vol. 28 (March–April 1972, pp. 71–76).

Dewing, Arthur Stone. *Financial Policies of Corporation*, 5th ed. (New York: The Ronald Press, 1953, Vol. 1, Chs. 3–9).

Donaldson, Gordon. "In Defense of Preferred Stock," *Harvard Business Review*, Vol. 40 (July–August 1962, pp. 123–36).

Dyl, Edward and William J. Sawaya. "Sinking Funds and the Cost of Corporate Debt," *Journal of Finance*, Vol. 34 (September 1979, pp. 887–94).

Elton, Edwin J. and Martin J. Gruber. "The Economic Value of the Call Option," *Journal of Finance*, Vol. 27 (September 1972, pp. 891–902).

Fausel, Thomas R. "The Supply and Demand Effect on Preferred Stock Yield Behavior" (Hartford, CT: Trinity College, 1982, pp. 1–42).

Finnerty, John D. "Preferred Stock Refunding Analysis: Synthesis and Extension," *Financial Management*, Vol. 13 (Autumn 1984, pp. 22–28).

Fons, Jerome S. "Default Premium and Corporate Bond Experience" (Working Paper 8604, Federal Reserve Bank of Cleveland, June 1986).

Jansson, Solveig. "The Deep Discount Bond Fad," *Institutional Investor*, Vol. 15 (August 1981, pp. 64–75).

Jochunk, Michael, Oswald D. Bowlin, and J. William Petty. "Preferred Dividend Rolls: A Viable Strategy for Corporate Money Managers?" *Financial Management*, Vol. 9 (Summer 1980, pp. 78–87).

Kalotay, Andrew J. "An Analysis of Original Issue Discount Bonds," *Financial Management*, Vol. 13 (Autumn 1984, pp. 29–38).

Kozmetsky, George, Michael D. Gill, Jr., and Raymond W. Smilor. *Financing and Managing Fast-Growth Companies. The Venture Capital Process* (Lexington, MA: Heath and Company, 1985).

Laber, Gene. "Repurchase of Bonds Through Tender Offers: Implications for Shareholder Wealth," *Financial Management*, Vol. 7 (Summer 1978, pp. 7–13).

Lewellen, Wilbur G. and Douglas R. Emory. "On the Matter of Parity Among Financial Obligations," *Journal of Finance*, Vol. 35 (March 1981, pp. 97–111).

Makin, Claire. "The Boom in Uncommon Stock," *Institutional Investor*, Vol. 19 (June 1985, pp. 101–2).

Marshall, William J. and Jess B. Yawitz. "Optimal Terms of the Call Provision on a Corporate Bond," *Journal of Financial Research*, Vol. 3 (Fall 1980, pp. 203–11).

McConnell, J. J. and G. G. Schlarbaum. "Returns, Risks, and Pricing of Income Bonds 1956–1976," *Journal of Business*, Vol. 54 (January 1981, pp. 33–64).

McDaniel, William R. "Sinking Fund Preferred Stock," *Financial Management*, Vol. 13 (Spring 1984, pp. 45–52).

Mitchell, Karlyn. "Trends in Corporation Finance," *Economic Review* (Federal Reserve Bank of Kansas City, Vol. 68, March 1983, pp. 3–15).

Moody's Bond Survey (selected weekly issues).

Peterson, Pamela, David Peterson, and James Ang. "The Extinguishment of Debt Through In-Substance Defeasance," *Financial Management*, Vol. 14 (Spring 1985, pp. 59–67).

Pinches, George E. "The Role of Subordination and Industrial Bond Ratings," *Journal of Finance*, Vol. 30 (March 1975, pp. 201–6).

Yawitz, Jess B. and James A. Anderson. "The Effect of Bond Refunding on Shareholder Wealth," *Journal of Finance*, Vol. 32 (December 1977, pp. 1738–46).

17

INVESTMENT BANKING AND
THE SECURITIES MARKETS

On average, nonfinancial corporations raise approximately 30 percent of their funds from external sources; approximately 70 percent of their funds come from plowing back profits and depreciation (more precisely, capital consumption allowances). Concerning external sources, the proportions of short-term borrowing—trade credit, long-term securities, and mortgages—can vary substantially. Selected external source data for 1982– 1986 (Table 17-1) reflect the volatility that has characterized recent experience. Although internal funding sources always dominate, various external sources change in importance from year to year. As interest rates fell from 1984 to 1986, corporations shifted from short-term to long-term funding sources. The negative figures for common stock, particularly in the mid-1980s, are due in part to repurchase of shares by corporations—in some cases for the purpose of becoming a private corporation.

*With the exception of commercial paper, we have already suggested that short-term lending occurs between the borrower (the nonfinancial firm) and the lending institution. Generally, there are no intermediaries between the two. However, raising funds in long-term capital markets often entails third parties commonly known as **investment***

Table 17-1 **Funding Sources for Nonfarm/Nonfinancial Corporations—1982–1986 ($ billions)**

Year	Total	Internal[a]	Equity	Bonds	Bank Loans	Commercial Paper
1982	$306.0	$242.3	$ 11.4	$ 18.7	$39.7	$ −6.1
1983	342.2	285.7	28.3	16.0	18.0	−0.8
1984	394.1	326.3	−77.0	46.1	77.0	21.7
1985	396.8	352.5	−81.6	73.9	37.4	14.6
1986	443.3	359.0	−80.8	113.7	60.7	−9.3

[a] After-tax profits, dividends, capital consumption allowances, foreign-branch profits, and subsidiaries' earnings retained abroad.

SOURCE: *Federal Reserve Flow of Funds Summary Statistical Release*, June 3, 1986, Table 4 (for 1981 statistics); *Federal Reserve Flow of Funds Summary Statistical Release*, June 5, 1987, Table 4 (for 1982–1986 statistics).

bankers. *A primary function of an investment banker is to act as intermediary between those who must raise money in long-term capital markets and those who invest in the securities issued to raise these funds. In this chapter, we discuss the investment banking function and its role in the new-issues market. We also contrast the new-issues (primary) market with the outstanding securities market (secondary or trading markets). Finally, we examine briefly the role of public policy as it pertains to the issuance of and trading in corporate securities.*

THE INVESTMENT BANKING FUNCTION

Although investment banking firms still exist, few engage solely in the purchase of new issues for resale. J. P. Morgan survives within the investment banking firm of Morgan Stanley, which remains a leader in the field. Whether father or son would be comfortable with the changes in the industry, particularly during the last decade, is moot.[1] What was once a clubby industry dominated by an old-boy network has rapidly spawned a more competitive environment. Although the hours are long, some salaries and bonuses reach seven figures in a good year. Those earning such sums are usually at the innovative forefront of financial instruments and/or in charge of corporate mergers or acquisitions.

Traditionally, an investment banker was a wholesaler in the new-issues market. For example, J. P. Morgan—together with a few others in an underwriting syndicate—might purchase a new stock issue offered by a company at $50 per share, mark it up to $52, and reissue it to a group of security dealers that in turn would also mark it up and sell it to the general public. Today, intermediation between issuer and buyer is simpler: a syndicate (group of securities firms) both underwrites and distributes (markets) the securities to the ultimate investors. Moreover, for most securities firms today, investment banking is a component of their corporate finance

---

[1] See, for example, A. F. Ehrbar, "Upheaval in Investment Banking," *Fortune*, Vol. 106 (August 23, 1982, pp. 90–95) and Ann Monroe, "Pinstripe Power: Morgan Stanley Banks on a Hybrid Strategy as Its World Changes," *Wall Street Journal* (June 27, 1985, pp. 1–22). See, also, Samuel L. Hayes III, A. Michael Spence, and David Marks, *Competition in the Investment Banking Industry* (Cambridge, MA: Harvard University Press, 1983); Joseph Auerbach and Samuel L. Hayes III, *Investment Banking and Diligence: What Price Deregulation* (Boston: Harvard University Press, 1986. For a comparison with early practice, see Vincent P. Carosso, *The Morgans: Private International Bankers 1854–1913* (Cambridge, MA: Harvard University Press, 1987.)

Figure 17-1   Investment Banking in the New Issues Market

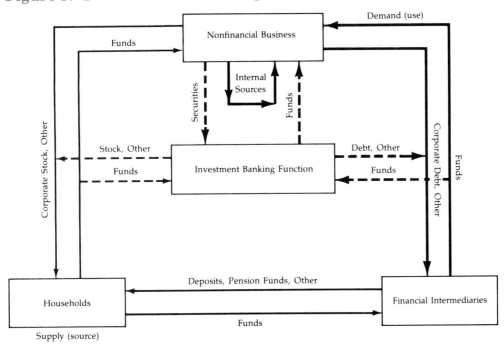

division, which provides an array of financial services.[2] Consequently, it is more appropriate to speak of an **investment banking** *function* performed by corporate finance specialists, whose primary expertise lies in translating the nuances of the new-securities market at any point in time and who advise financial managers of nonfinancial corporations on raising capital and long-run planning and strategy. Because our earlier discussion of financial theory concerned the problems of minimizing cost of capital in perfect capital markets, this function was ignored. At any point in time, however, a firm must make choices based on imperfect information. Should it issue short-term or long-term debt? Are there instruments or particular securities currently popular with investors? Is there a shift in the flow of funds to types of financial institutions not approached before? The financial manager is often aware of but not fully informed on such matters; consequently, the investment banking function is a useful service to management.

To understand more fully the dimensions of investment banking and the new-issues market, examine Figure 17-1. *Déjà vu* it may seem but *déjà vu* it is not.

---

[2] Leslie Wayne. "New Pressure in Investment Banking," *The New York Times* (April 15, 1984, Sec. 3, pp. 1 and 24).

Although a similar figure appears in Chapter 2, at the center of this illustration lies the investment banking function—which is or can be the catalyst in the new-issues market. To reiterate, the corporation seeking funds has several choices. It may go directly to owners, be they households or financial institutions, offering them securities in exchange for cash. Under a preemptive right, as we have seen, a sale of stock might take place. Similarly, a corporation may seek a loan from a bank or insurance company. Or it may avoid capital markets altogether, funding its requirements from internal sources. Finally, the company may issue long-term debt or stock in the public market.

In all but funding from internal sources, those performing investment banking functions may play a role. In the case of the preemptive right, investment banking specialists may be hired to purchase the unexpired rights so as to ensure a successful offering. In the case of the direct (private) placement of notes or securities with a financial institution, the specialists may have acted as intermediary or contact in helping to arrange mutually acceptable terms and conditions. As we shall see, it is in the public offering of securities that investment banking plays the pivotal role.

PRIVATE PLACEMENT OR PUBLIC OFFERING

The distinction between private placement and public offering of corporate securities is significant because the latter requires that the issuer comply with the requirements of the Securities Act of 1933 (the former does not). Under the Act's Rule 506 of Regulation D, the Securities and Exchange Commission can permit an issuer to sell an unlimited number of securities to "accredited investors" (many of them financial institutions) as well as to up to 35 other purchasers. If the SEC permits the issuer to place securities under Regulation D, it is a private placement. When privately placed, securities cannot be resold to the general public without first complying with the Securities Act of 1933. This is less a burden for debt than for common stock: debt is often held to maturity; it is ordinarily not intended to be resold by the investor (generally a life insurance company but sometimes a bank, a thrift institution, or a pension fund).[3] For stock, there is no maturity date; hence, the debt market tends to account for more than 80 percent of privately placed securities.[4] Of equity issues privately placed, only a small portion are conventional preferred and common stock. The bulk of issues privately placed are limited-partnership interests in companies purchased privately, sometimes to avoid takeover by another firm. Other limited-partnership interests and sometimes letter stock are privately placed in venture capital firms. In the case of the former, the

---

[3] Kidder, Peabody & Co. *Private Placements Review* (1984, p. 6).

[4] Kidder, Peabody & Co., p. 5.

firm goes private so management can retain control. In the case of the latter, management generally expects to make a public stock offering at some point in the future.

Aside from such variations, common and preferred stock are generally publicly offered whereas debt may be privately placed or publicly offered. In addition, much publicly offered conventional long-term debt is issued by corporations with credit ratings of A or above—particularly Aa- and Aaa-rated companies. There are five major reasons for this. First, Aa- and Aaa-rated corporations are the largest U.S. corporations. When they enter the long-term debt market, such corporations often borrow in excess of $100 million. Costs of complying with the provisions of the Securities Act of 1933 are largely independent of the size of the issue; hence, the larger the total issue the smaller the compliance costs per dollar of capital raised. Second, the underwriters' compensation (**underwriting spread**) between the price to the issuer and the price to the public) also declines with the size of the issue. The first two reasons combine to bring total flotation costs for small issues, $2,000,000 or less, to about 15 percent of proceeds. However, flotation costs decline rapidly— leveling off at about 4 percent or less of total proceeds—as the issue size exceeds $50 million.[5]

Third, the capacity of a few institutional investors to absorb large privately placed issues is limited. Although placements in excess of $100 million are more common today than a few years ago, it is nevertheless true that a large private placement of securities requires more investors and hence comes closer to being a public offering.[6] As important, perhaps, is the fact that the more investors involved, the less likely the firm can enjoy the advantage of the fourth reason for private placement: a custom-designed or tailor-made contract more finely tuned to the desires of both borrower and lender. As the number of lenders increases, the chances of unanimity decrease. Consequently, the more investors there are the more likely the securities offer will mirror the standard contract types discussed in Chapter 16, contracts suitable for public offerings.

Finally, the spread between A-rated and Baa/BBB-rated credit risks is lower in the private market than in the public market. For example, for the years 1975–1984, the average spread between such ratings was 79 basis points in the public market but only 35 in the private market.[7]

---

[5] Although costs are larger for equity issues than for debt issues of the same size, they level off in the $50-million range. See C. W. Smith, "Alternative Methods for Raising Capital: Rights Versus Underwritten Offerings," *Journal of Financial Economics*, Vol. 15 (December 1977, p. 277); R. Hilstrom and R. King, eds., *1960–69: A Decade of Corporate and International Finance* (New York: Investment Dealers Digest, Inc., 1972, p. 18); Securities and Exchange Commission, "Costs of Flotation of Corporate Securities 1951–55" (Washington: U.S. Government Printing Office, 1957, pp. 18–19 and 21).

[6] Same as [3], p. 5.

[7] Same as [3], p. 18. The public-market low was 37 basis points in 1984 and the high was 129 in 1974. The private-market low was 17 basis points in 1978 and the high was 51 in 1982.

REGISTERING SECURITIES FOR A PUBLIC OFFERING

If a firm elects to market an issue publicly, it must register the securities with the Securities and Exchange Commission. Given the high average-fixed costs associated with small issues, Regulation D permits small companies—those not subject to the Securities Exchange Act of 1934—to sell up to $500,000 in securities during a 12-month period to any investors without furnishing them any information. Some information, but not a complete registration, may be required for issues between $500,000 and $5,000,000. If the issuer can qualify, many first-time offerings make use of these exemptions.

Table 17-2 presents the cash-sales data for publicly offered securities of U.S. business firms from 1982–1986. Unlike the data in Table 17-1, these are gross proceeds and do not account for funds used to retire securities. Although debt instruments ordinarily account for more of the total offerings than stock, in recent years the equity portion has been high because it includes not only conventional common stock but also such noncorporate ownership interests as limited partnerships that qualify as public offerings. Manufacturing, finance, and real-estate firms as well as traditional public utilities account for the bulk of public offerings. The contribution of this group is particularly overweighted relative to Gross National Product (GNP). The reason, as suggested in Chapter 16, is regulated rate of return. By raising the bulk of their funds in public markets, public utilities have an explicit cost of capital for a substantial proportion of the funds they employ.

For a conventional public offering, the registration procedure can be somewhat cumbersome. In the past, registration statements contained hundreds, even thousands, of pages and often contained information that might be duplicated elsewhere. Today, companies whose stock is publicly traded must file annual reports (10-K Report) with the Securities and Exchange Commission. However, much of the information contained in a registration statement can be "incorporated by reference" to the 10-K Report or to other materials filed with the SEC. Companies offering securities to the public for the first time (generally unseasoned stock issues) must file an even lengthier document, unless they qualify for Regulation-D exemptions.

Perusal of the registration statement in Washington can take as long as 20 days. Although the SEC may approve the registration statement in a shorter period, it can request (by "deficiency memorandum") further information or require other changes it deems necessary. As a result, the approval period is extended. Following acceptance of the registration statement by the SEC, the issue can be marketed to the public.

During the waiting period, however, neither can the securities be sold nor orders taken. The purpose of this *waiting* period is to disseminate information that

Table 17-2 Cash-sales Data for Publicly Offered Securities of U.S. Business Firms—1982–1986 ($ millions)

Year	Total[a]	Bonds[b]	Percent of Total	Preferred Stock	Percent of Total	Other Equity[c]	Percent of Total
1982	$ 73,519	$44,771	60.9	$4,952	6.7	$23,796	32.4
1983	102,406	49,485	48.3	7,693	7.5	45,228	44.2
1984	85,853	59,483	69.3	4,219	4.9	22,151	25.8
1985	129,085	86,279	66.8	6,374	4.9	36,432	28.3
1986	224,341	158,128	70.5	11,374	5.1	54,839	24.4

Bonds by Industry

Year	Total	Manufacturing	Electric, Gas, Water	Sales, Finance, Real Estate	Other[d]
1982	$44,771	$10,556	$9,141	$17,372	$ 7,702
1983	49,485	8,922	7,050	22,439	11,074
1984	59,483	10,957	5,910	32,591	10,025
1985	86,279	19,924	8,087	42,902	15,366
1986	158,128	29,048	20,434	82,787	25,859

Preferred Stocks by Industry

Year	Total	Manufacturing	Electric, Gas, Water	Sales, Finance, Real Estate	Other
1982	$4,952	$ 507	$2,105	$1,997	$ 343
1983	7,693	1,243	1,900	3,350	1,200
1984	4,219	826	613	2,017	763
1985	6,374	1,230	430	3,786	928
1986	11,374	3,091	1,530	4,346	2,407

Other Equity by Industry

Year	Total	Manufacturing	Electric, Gas, Water	Sales, Finance, Real Estate	Other
1982	$23,796	$ 2,689	$5,270	$ 4,277	$11,560
1983	45,228	12,793	3,799	9,913	18,723
1984	22,151	2,684	1,000	10,542	7,925
1985	36,432	4,597	1,497	19,144	11,194
1986	54,839	9,295	1,969	28,376	15,199

[a] Data include foreign corporate offerings: $1,323, $2,583, $879, $1,799 and $2,300 million, respectively, in 1982, 1983, 1984, 1985, and 1986.
[b] Data include convertibles: $3,075, $5,871, $3,408, $8,018, and $8,463 million, respectively, in 1982, 1983, 1984, 1985, and 1986.
[c] Data include conventional common stock as well as limited-partnership interests, voting-trust certificates, and condominium securities. Conventional common stock issues were $13,361, $29,794, $8,669, $18,348, and $31,323 million, respectively, in 1982, 1983, 1984, 1985, and 1986.
[d] Data include mining (extractive), transportation, communications, and commercial sectors.

SOURCE: Data for 1985 and 1986 adapted from SEC *Monthly Statistical Review*, Vol. 46 (May 1987, pp. 15–21). Data for 1983 and 1984 adapted from SEC *Monthly Statistical Review*, Vol. 45 (May 1986, pp. 23–28). Data for 1982 from SEC *Monthly Statistical Review*, Vol. 44 (May 1985, pp. 14–19). Data represent cash sales of securities registered with the SEC pursuant to the requirements of the Securities Act of 1933 or exempted under Regulation A of the Act.

aids investors in determining whether or not to purchase the securities. In this way, the company secures evidence of interest in the offering from potential buyers. To assist in securing such evidence, a **preliminary (red-herring) prospectus** is employed. This prospectus summarizes the information contained in the registration statement. The term **red herring** comes from the bold red letters on the left side of the prospectus noting that a registration statement has been filed but is not yet effective and may indeed be amended. Conspicuously absent from the preliminary prospectus is any mention of sale price to the public, proceeds to the company, or investment banker's spread. Nevertheless, at times one can gain some insight as to the price or, in the case of debt or preferred, the yield investors expect in order to sell the issue. In addition, because market conditions can change rather quickly, price and investment banker's spread are determined on the day the issue is marketed.

Figure 17-2 is a red-herring prospectus (you will have to color it yourself) for a $500,000,000 note and sinking-fund debenture issue offered by the R. J. Reynolds Company on July 26, 1985. For contrast, compare Figure 17-2 with Figure 17-3, the latter of which shows the price to the public, the spread, and the proceeds to the company.

In this instance, the price to the public was $998.42 per $1,000 of face value for the note. However, the debentures were sold at par, or $1,000. The rate on the notes was 10.75 percent; the rate on the debentures was 11.75 percent. The syndicate charged $6.50 per note and $8.75 per debenture to cover the risk of underwriting and marketing each instrument. The company was guaranteed $991.92 per note and $991.25 per debenture. The other, largely fixed expenses associated with the registration and distribution of the securities totaled $325,000, or $0.65 per $1,000 of face value for the combined issue.

Note the SEC neither approves nor disapproves of the securities offer; it only accepts the registration statement qualifying them for public offering. Liability for false and misleading statements arguably rests with the underwriters if they fail to exercise due diligence in their examination of the issuer's documents. The underwriters, however, can negotiate the issuer's indemnification from such liability. In this case, R. J. Reynolds agreed to such indemnification. Liability for false and misleading statements can also rest on those who helped prepare the registration statements—such as accountants, lawyers, and others. Ultimate responsibility, of course, lies with the issuer.

THE UNDERWRITING SYNDICATE

In conventional or legal terms, it is in the S-3 offering that investment bankers play the major role. The Reynolds' underwriting is a classic illustration of the investment banking syndicate executing its traditional function. The syndicate consists of a manager (sometimes comanagers) and a group of firms interested in sharing the risks of underwriting the offer. For its effort, the manager receives approximately

Figure 17-2 Preliminary Prospectus of R. J. Reynolds Industries, Inc.—A Note and Debenture Offer

> **A registration statement relating to these securities has been filed with the Securities and Exchange Commission but has not yet become effective. Information contained herein is subject to completion or amendment. These securities may not be sold nor may offers to buy be accepted prior to the time the registration statement becomes effective. This prospectus shall not constitute an offer to sell or the solicitation of an offer to buy nor shall there be any sale of these securities in any State in which such offer, solicitation or sale would be unlawful prior to registration or qualification under the securities laws of any such State.**

PRELIMINARY PROSPECTUS DATED JULY 19, 1985

$500,000,000

R. J. Reynolds Industries, Inc.

$250,000,000 % Notes, Due August 1, 1993

$250,000,000 % Sinking Fund Debentures, Due August 1, 2015

(Interest on the Notes and Debentures payable February 1 and August 1)

The Notes may not be redeemed prior to August 1, 1991. On or after that date, the Notes may be redeemed at the option of Industries on 30 days' notice, in whole or in part, at par. The Debentures may be redeemed at any time at the option of Industries on 30 days' notice, in whole or in part, as set forth herein, except that no such optional redemption may be effected prior to August 1, 1995 directly or indirectly from moneys borrowed at an interest cost of less than % per annum. A mandatory annual sinking fund beginning August 1, 1996 will be sufficient to retire at par 95% of the aggregate principal amount of the Debentures prior to maturity. Industries may increase its sinking fund payment in any year by an additional amount of up to 150% of the mandatory sinking fund payment in that year.

THESE SECURITIES HAVE NOT BEEN APPROVED OR DISAPPROVED BY THE SECURITIES AND EXCHANGE COMMISSION NOR HAS THE COMMISSION PASSED UPON THE ACCURACY OR ADEQUACY OF THIS PROSPECTUS. ANY REPRESENTATION TO THE CONTRARY IS A CRIMINAL OFFENSE.

	Price to Public*	Underwriting Discounts and Commissions†	Proceeds to Company*‡
Per Note	%	%	%
Total	$	$	$
Per Debenture	%	%	%
Total	$	$	$

* Plus accrued interest, if any, from August , 1985.

† Industries has agreed to indemnify the several Underwriters against certain liabilities, including certain liabilities under the Securities Act of 1933.

‡ Before deduction of expenses payable by Industries estimated at $

The Notes and Debentures are being offered by the Underwriters as set forth under "Underwriting" herein. It is expected that delivery of the Notes and the Debentures will be made on or about August , 1985 at the office of Dillon, Read & Co. Inc., New York, N. Y., against payment therefor in New York funds. The Underwriters include:

Dillon, Read & Co. Inc.

The date of this Prospectus is July 1985.

SOURCE: Dillon, Read & Co. Inc.

10 percent of the spread on each bond or stock sold. The manager assists the issuer in preparing the registration statements, in choosing specific features of the proposed instrument, and in forming the syndicate. Hence, the override is compensation for such services. The underwriting risk accounts for 35 to 40 percent of the spread; the remainder is sales commission.

Figure 17-3   Final Prospectus of R. J. Reynolds Industries, Inc.—A Note and Debenture Offer

$500,000,000

R. J. Reynolds Industries, Inc.

$250,000,000 10¾% Notes, Due August 1, 1993
$250,000,000 11¾% Sinking Fund Debentures, Due August 1, 2015

(Interest on the Notes and Debentures payable February 1 and August 1)

The Notes may not be redeemed prior to August 1, 1991. On or after that date, the Notes may be redeemed at the option of Industries on 30 days' notice, in whole or in part, at par. The Debentures may be redeemed at any time at the option of Industries on 30 days' notice, in whole or in part, as set forth herein, except that no such optional redemption may be effected prior to August 1, 1995 directly or indirectly from moneys borrowed at an interest cost of less than 11¾% per annum. A mandatory annual sinking fund beginning August 1, 1996 will be sufficient to retire at par 95% of the aggregate principal amount of the Debentures prior to maturity. Industries may increase its sinking fund payment in any year by an additional amount of up to 150% of the mandatory sinking fund payment in that year.

THESE SECURITIES HAVE NOT BEEN APPROVED OR DISAPPROVED BY THE SECURITIES AND EXCHANGE COMMISSION NOR HAS THE COMMISSION PASSED UPON THE ACCURACY OR ADEQUACY OF THIS PROSPECTUS. ANY REPRESENTATION TO THE CONTRARY IS A CRIMINAL OFFENSE.

	Price to Public*	Underwriting Discounts and Commissions†	Proceeds to Company*‡
Per Note	99.842%	.65%	99.192%
Total	$249,605,000	$1,625,000	$247,980,000
Per Debenture	100%	.875%	99.125%
Total	$250,000,000	$2,187,500	$247,812,500

* Plus accrued interest, if any, from August 1, 1985.

† Industries has agreed to indemnify the several Underwriters against certain liabilities, including certain liabilities under the Securities Act of 1933.

‡ Before deduction of expenses payable by Industries estimated at $325,000.

The Notes and Debentures are being offered by the Underwriters as set forth under "Underwriting" herein. It is expected that delivery of the Notes and the Debentures will be made on or about August 1, 1985 at the office of Dillon, Read & Co. Inc., New York, N. Y., against payment therefor in New York funds. The Underwriters include:

Dillon, Read & Co. Inc.

The date of this Prospectus is July 25, 1985.

SOURCE: Dillon, Read & Co. Inc.

The syndicate manager assumes the greatest underwriting risk; others participate in lesser amounts. Each underwriter is responsible for its proportional share of unsold securities. Thus, if the syndicate sells only 80 percent of the securities at the offering price, the balance (20 percent) is divided among the underwriters in proportion to their participation. For example, a firm with a 5-percent participation in a $200,000,000 offering, 20 percent of which is unsold, must purchase $2,000,000 worth of securities (5 percent × 20 percent × $200,000,000). In this event, the syndicate is terminated and the underwriters cut the price to the public in order to sell the issue. The price to the company, however, is unchanged. Hence, the spread is reduced. Inevitably, in some cases, it is necessary to take a loss in order to sell the issue. Because syndicates exist for only a few days, the sales commissions (available to all participants and on special terms to other dealers) are a considerable incentive to market the issue at the offering price. Most issues are marketed on Tuesday, Wednesday, or perhaps Thursday. In investment banking, happiness is taking the 5:15 PM train to Greenwich on Friday afternoon, knowing that all securities were sold at the offering price and the syndicate terminated. Ecstasy is opening the books on a new issue at 10 AM and closing them before lunch.

Life, however, is rarely that cooperative. In the Reynolds offering, the syndicate manager—the old-line investment banking firm of Dillon, Read—chose, at the company's behest, to market the issue on Friday.[8] The registration statement had been filed one week earlier and accepted by the SEC on July 25, 1985, a short waiting period. Most of the securities, of course, would be purchased by institutional investors. Because the securities could not be advertised legally until the day of the offering, the only legal means of calling attention to the issue—the tombstone advertisement—was published in the *Wall Street Journal* (often other newspapers as well) on July 26, 1985 (see Figure 17-4). Somewhat concerned that yields on debt securities had been rising throughout the week and that the U.S. government would be scheduling sales of securities during the following week, Reynolds wanted to place the issue. The syndicate accommodated Reynolds.[9] With the debentures priced at par to yield 11.75 percent, the offering was approximately two basis points below the average for industrial-bond yields of comparably rated securities.[10]

If the issue were not fully subscribed by day's end, the syndicate would have to stay in existence through the weekend. One of the obligations of a syndicate is to peg the issue price, until it has been fully distributed, to the primary buyers.[11] Thus, if

---

[8] Tim Carrington, "Dillon, Read, Old Line Investment Banker Gets into Takeovers and Other New Lines," *Wall Street Journal* (June 23, 1982, p. 30). See, also, Samuel L. Hayes III, "The Transformation of Investment Banking." *Harvard Business Review*, Vol. 57 (January–February 1979, pp. 153–70).

[9] Based on conversations with Oliver C. Hazard, senior vice president of Dillon, Read & Co. (Boston).

[10] The issue was rated A_1 by Moody's. On July 25, 1985, the composite yield on A-rated industrial bonds was 11.77, having risen from Monday, July 19, when the yield was 11.69. See *Moody's Bond Survey* (July 29, 1985, pp. 3236, 3237, and 3272).

[11] The legality of this policy was upheld in *U.S. v. Morgan*, opinion of Hon. Harold R. Medina (New York: The Record Press, 1953, pp. 111–32).

Figure 17-4   Tombstone Advertisement for R. J. Reynolds Industries, Inc.—A Note and Debenture Offer

This announcement is not an offer of securities for sale or a solicitation of an offer to buy securities.

New Issues

July 26, 1985

$500,000,000

R. J. Reynolds Industries, Inc.

$250,000,000 10¾% Notes, Due August 1, 1993

$250,000,000 11¾% Sinking Fund Debentures, Due August 1, 2015

Prices:

Notes 99.842%

Sinking Fund Debentures 100%
plus accrued interest, if any, from August 1, 1985

Copies of the prospectus may be obtained from such of the undersigned (who are among the underwriters named in the prospectus) as may legally offer these securities under applicable securities laws.

Dillon, Read & Co. Inc.

Morgan Stanley & Co. Incorporated	**Shearson Lehman Brothers Inc.**	**Goldman, Sachs & Co.**
Kidder, Peabody & Co. Incorporated	**Merrill Lynch Capital Markets**	**Salomon Brothers Inc**
Bear, Stearns & Co. Incorporated	**Alex. Brown & Sons** Incorporated	**Deutsche Bank Capital** Corporation
Donaldson, Lufkin & Jenrette Securities Corporation	**Drexel Burnham Lambert** Incorporated	**E. F. Hutton & Company Inc.**
Lazard Frères & Co.	**PaineWebber** Incorporated **Prudential-Bache** Securities	**L. F. Rothschild, Unterberg, Towbin**
Smith Barney, Harris Upham & Co. Incorporated	**Swiss Bank Corporation International Securities Inc.**	
UBS Securities Inc.	**Wertheim & Co., Inc.**	**Dean Witter Reynolds Inc.**
Daiwa Securities America Inc.	**Moseley, Hallgarten, Estabrook & Weeden Inc.**	
The Nikko Securities Co. International, Inc.	**Nomura Securities International, Inc.**	**Oppenheimer & Co., Inc.**
Thomson McKinnon Securities Inc.	**Yamaichi International (America), Inc.**	
Sanford C. Bernstein & Co., Inc.	**Furman Selz Mager Dietz & Birney** Incorporated	**Janney Montgomery Scott Inc.**
Cyrus J. Lawrence Incorporated	**Neuberger & Berman**	**Tucker, Anthony & R. L. Day, Inc.**

SOURCE: Prepared for Dillon, Read–R. J. Reynolds by Doremus & Company, 120 Broadway, NY 10271, July 22, 1985.

events over the weekend caused bond prices to fall and yields to rise, the syndicate would be faced with the obligation of repurchasing some debt it was thought to have placed. Although a slightly higher spread may partially compensate for the additional risk, a reversal is a definite possiblity.

In this instance, placement of nearly 80 percent of both the notes and debentures on Friday necessitated maintaining the syndicate over the weekend. However, the markets held sufficiently, so that by Tuesday the entire $500,000,000 had been placed.[12]

COMPETITIVE BIDDING

The competitive bid is a variation in traditional underwriting. In the corporate arena, competitive bidding is used almost exclusively by public utilities and railroads. Federal and state regulatory agencies often require publicly offered securities, particularly debt issues of utilities, to be sold only by competitive bid. In such instances, the issuer must file the registration statement; if investment banking firms assist in its preparation, they are not eligible to bid on the issue. When the registration statement is accepted, the issuer receives a date for receipt of sealed bids from competing investment banking syndicates. Upon the opening of the sealed bids, the lowest-cost offer to the issuer is the successful bid. For example, on Wednesday, July 24, 1985, a group led by Morgan Stanley submitted a successful bid of $995.39 per $1,000 of face value for a $125,000,000 issue of Public Service Electric Gas Company's first mortgage bonds due July 1, 2015. The bonds carried a 9.5 percent coupon and were priced to the public at $998. The bonds are redeemable at par at the option of either the issuer or the holder each July 1, beginning in 1988; depending on prevailing interest rates at the time, the interest rate can be changed by the issuer, such option available to maturity.[13] In effect, the utility company issued a three-year fixed-interest bond with a variable interest rate thereafter to maturity. In addition, options to liquidate were available to both issuer and holder. Implicitly, future lower interest rates would flow through as lower utility costs to consumers; future higher interest rates would flow through as higher utility costs. No such features existed for either the notes or debentures of R. J. Reynolds' issue.[14]

---

[12] One of the nuances of this offering is that another $175,000,000 in debt was scheduled for shelf registration (discussed later in the chapter). Moreover, Reynolds was completing a $4.9-billion acquisition of Nabisco Brands, Inc. Noting a sizeable increase in company debt, thereby reducing its financial flexibility, one rating service, Moody's, considered the debt issue only upper medium-grade quality. Hence, the A_1 rating. *Moody's Bond Survey* (July 29, 1985, p. 3237).

[13] *Moody's Bond Survey* (July 29, 1985, p. 3232). See, also, *Moody's Bond Survey* (July 22, 1985, pp. 3299–3300).

[14] The notes cannot be redeemed at par until August 1, 1991; the debentures are nonredeemable prior to August 1, 1995, with low-interest-cost debt. (See Figure 17-3.)

SHELF REGISTRATION

Until March 1982, a company whose registration statement had been approved and that had set the date for the public offering or for the competitive bid expected to market all the registered securities. Although it was possible to postpone the issue date, the amounts were not variable: it was all or nothing. On March 5, 1982, the SEC promulgated Rule 415—**shelf registration**, as it is now called. Adopted initially on an experimental basis and made permanent on November 10, 1983, Rule 415 permits eligible corporations (generally, firms with more than $150 million in shares held by outside investors) considerable flexibility in the sale of new securities to the public.[15]

Briefly, Rule 415 permits the issuer, once registered, to sell the securities virtually anytime and in any amounts over a two-year period. Thus, Rule 415 permits the issuer to market some or all securities when management believes the market timing is correct. Moreover, the company can combine a conventional offering with a shelf registration. Consequently, in Reynolds' issue discussed earlier, the company self-registered $175,000,000 in debt securities to be issued from time to time and in varying amounts while simultaneously offering the $500,000,000 in notes and debentures, creating a classically negotiated underwriting.[16] Finally, under Rule 415, a firm is not required to contract with only one investment banker or, as in the case of certain utilities, required to offer the entire issue for competitive bidding at one time.

So appealing was the opportunity to sell securities under Rule 415 that, in the first ten months of its existence, $16 billion in debt and $1.9 billion in preferred and common stock were issued in this manner. This meant that approximately 33 percent of the total debt and 12 percent of the total stock eligible for flotation under Rule 415 were shelf-registered.[17] There is no indication that the popularity of shelf registration, particularly concerning the issuance of corporate debt, has waned.[18]

However, for a shelf registration to differ from a conventionally negotiated underwriting, the issuer must offer the securities to an underwriter or syndicate through an auction that awards them to the highest bidder: to the bidder that offers the lowest cost to maturity by paying the highest price for a given coupon. Nevertheless, not all shelf registrations are auction bids; those that are differ from

---

[15] Robert J. Rogowski and Eric H. Sorensen. "Deregulation in Investment Banking," *Financial Management*, Vol. 14 (Spring 1985, pp. 5–15). Beth McGoldrick. "Life with Rule 415," *Institutional Investor*, Vol. 17 (February 1983, pp. 129–33). Technically, firms eligible to use Forms S-3 or F-3 can utilize shelf registration: generally, large capitalization firms with publicly held securities. See, also, Francis J. Feeney, Jr., "The Saga of Rule 415: Registration for the Shelf," *Corporation Law Review*, Vol. 9 (Winter 1986, pp. 41–69).

[16] *Moody's Bond Survey* (July 29, 1985, pp. 3236 and 3237).

[17] Same as [15], p. 130.

[18] In 1983 and 1984, 52 and 58 percent of conventional debt contracts were shelf registrations.

conventional competitive bids when a portion but not all of the registered securities are offered.

Shelf registration has the potential for altering the entire system of distributing new issues. For example, when firms bid on shelf-registered securities, to what extent are they underwriters, investors, or institutions purchasing securities for investment purposes or with the intent to distribute them at a markup? Might we be returning, albeit through auction bids, to a time reminiscent of J. P. Morgan and others who acted as wholesaler between the issuer and the retail market?

This is not a trivial question. Since the passage of the Banking Act of 1933 (The Glass-Steagall Act), commercial banking and investment banking have been separate functions (at least with respect to corporate issues). Nationally chartered commercial banks and state-chartered banks that are members of the Federal Reserve System cannot underwrite corporate securities. Suppose, however, that commercial banks purchase securities from the issuer. What is the legal distinction between executing a *bought deal* and underwriting securities? Today, the line is a thin one. The SEC defines a statutory underwriter as one who purchases more than 10 percent of a securities offering.[19] Although this limits the participation of commercial banks and institutional investors unwilling to assume the responsibility for exercising due diligence in marketing securities as an underwriter, it does not preclude participation altogether.

From the issuer's perspective, limited evidence to date suggests that shelf registration has lowered (on average) the cost of debt capital by perhaps 20 or more basis points compared to the cost of debt capital under non-shelf offerings. There is some disagreement as to whether shelf registration or the number of potential competitors, including direct participation by other institutions, is responsible for such results.[20] Moreover, there is some evidence that cost savings in shelf registration of equities is offset or more-than-offset by negative performance of stock prices.[21]

Although no panacea for across-the-board lower securities costs in general, shelf registration must be viewed as a potentially far-reaching innovation in the marketing of publicly offered corporate securities, particularly standard types of issues such as those discussed in Chapter 16.

---

[19] J. P. Ketels. "SEC Rule 415 — The New Experimental Procedures for Shelf Registration," *Securities Regulation Law Journal*, Vol. 10 (Winter 1983, pp. 318–38).

[20] Same as [15], Rogowski and Sorensen, pp. 7–11. D. S. Kadwell, M. Wayne Marr, and C. Rodney Thompson. "SEC Rule 415: The Ultimate Competitive Bid," *Journal of Financial and Quantitative Analysis*, Vol. 19 (June 1984, pp. 183–96). Office of Chief Economist, Securities and Exchange Commission. "Explaining the Savings from Rule 415: The Debt Markets" (September 14, 1984, pp. 1–15).

[21] Securities Industry Association Research Department. "SEC Rule 415: Benefits and Costs for Equity Issuers," *Security Industry Trends*, Vol. X (August 22, 1984, pp. 1–17). Office of Chief Economist, Securities and Exchange Commission. "Update — Rule 415 and Equity Markets" (September 4, 1984, pp. 1–29). Sanjai Bhagat, M. Wayne Marr, and C. Rodney Thompson. "The Rule 415 Experiment: Equity Markets," *Journal of Finance*, Vol. 40 (December 1985, pp. 1385–1401), Norman H. Moore, David R. Peterson, and Pamela P. Peterson. "Shelf Registrations and Shareholder Wealth: A Comparison of Shelf and Traditional Equity Offerings," *Journal of Finance*, Vol. 41 (June 1986, pp. 451–63).

Table 17-3   Percentage Breakdown of Primary Corporate Securities Issues—1982–1986[a]

Underwritten

	Total	Debt	Preferred	Common
1982	72.3	84.8	99.7	50.9
1983	78.6	97.0	99.0	65.4
1984	73.2	96.7	94.9	36.9
1985	81.3	97.5	98.9	59.0
1986	79.3	95.4	99.8	68.6

Best Efforts

	Total	Debt	Preferred	Common
1982	19.4	5.2	0.2	41.1
1983	16.6	0.9	0.3	27.5
1984	19.9	1.0	0.2	49.5
1985	14.9	1.5	0.1	33.2
1986	10.5	0.9	0.1	25.0

Issued Directly

	Total	Debt	Preferred	Common
1982	8.3	10.0	0.1	8.0
1983	4.9	2.1	0.7	7.1
1984	6.9	2.3	4.9	13.6
1985	3.9	0.9	0.9	7.8
1986	10.1	3.7	0.1	6.4

[a] By method of distribution and type of security.

SOURCE: *SEC Monthly Statistical Review*, Vol. 45 (May 1986, p. 40). Data for 1982 are from *SEC Monthly Statistical Review*, Vol. 44 (May 1985, p. 30). Percentages calculated from raw data for primary issues registered under The Securities Act of 1933.

BEST-EFFORTS SALES

Firms making public offerings cannot always find investment bankers willing to assume the risk of underwriting the securities at a spread acceptable to the issuer. This is particularly true of the common stocks of unseasoned companies going public for the first time in industries not currently in vogue. Table 17-3 shows the percentage breakdown of primary (new) issues by method of distribution and type of security for 1982–1986. Although the bulk of the debt issues are *underwritten*, a substantial percentage of common stock is sold on a *best-efforts* basis, suggesting that underwriters will market but not guarantee a specific amount to the company for its securities. During 1982, which was perceived to be a year of unusually high nominal interest rates, 5.2 percent of primary debt issues were sold on a best-efforts basis. Needless to say, the commission for selling securities on a best-efforts basis is similar to a brokerage fee and is, therefore, less than the spread for underwriting and marketing the securities.

DIRECT SALES BY ISSUER

As noted in Chapter 16, stock can be sold as a rights offering. Also pointed out was that firms tend to annul rights offerings where possible.[22] Nevertheless, each year small percentages of common stock are *issued directly* by corporations, most of it to existing stockholders. Again in 1982, companies finding credit markets unreceptive turned to direct offerings of debt to customers, stockholders and others. What may be a blip in the data could be repeated, under similar conditions, in the future.

TRADING MARKETS FOR CORPORATE SECURITIES

Once securities are issued, a secondary (trading) market for them may develop. And again, it may not. The nature of the security and those who purchase it have considerable impact on whether or not a secondary market develops. Straight debt issues, such as the offerings of R. J. Reynolds discussed earlier, are purchased primarily by institutional investors. Although some trading may take place, many will hold the debt—particularly the notes—to maturity.

Stock issues are different. Because issues have no maturity date, a secondary market is likely to develop so holders may sell their shares. To be sure, stock of closely held companies is not actively traded whereas stock of small publicly held companies (such as a local utility or a small commercial bank) may be traded only in local or regional markets. Debt issues convertible to stock also may have an active secondary market. The driving force behind the secondary market is demand for liquidity. If such demand is sufficiently strong securities dealers will create an active market in the issue, buying and selling for their own accounts and hoping to profit from the transaction.

---

[22] The reasons remain elusive. See R. S. Hansen and J. M. Pinkerton, "Direct Equity Financing: A Resolution of a Paradox," *Journal of Finance*, Vol. 37 (June 1982, pp. 651–80).

In the United States there are two ways to trade securities: over the counter or on an exchange. **Over-the-counter** securities are traded through a network of brokers and dealers, nearly all of whom are members of the National Association of Securities Dealers (NASD). For years these securities dealers were loosely linked by telephone and teletype. However, beginning in 1971, the NASD introduced an automatic quotation system (NASDAQ) since perfected into a national market list of stocks for which it is possible to determine highest-bid and lowest-asked prices as well as last-sale price on a video terminal. There is also a list of bids and askeds for less actively traded securities and a supplemental list. If there is a NASD member trading in a stock, it is possible to secure a quote on it. Modern technology has linked market participants throughout the country—even throughout the world—in a way not feasible until only recently.

By contrast, an exchange offers a trading floor on which orders to buy and sell are channeled from member firms, who are brokers, usually to a single trader, the specialist, who buys and sells for his or her own account. The exchange views the specialist as providing a close and continuous market in the stock. Thus, if the last-sale price of a stock is 65, the specialist may hold *limited price orders* from brokers for customers. The limited price order can be exercised only at the price specified or better. Suppose, for example, the specialist held a limited price order to buy 100 at 64 and to sell 100 at 66. To decrease volatility from transaction to transaction, the specialist can straddle the last-sale price, buying for his or her own account at $64\frac{7}{8}$ and selling at $65\frac{1}{8}$. One of two things is likely to happen. Two brokers, each with *market orders*—orders that can be executed immediately—meet at the post where the stock is trading. One has a market order to sell 100 shares; the other has a market order to buy 100 shares. Upon asking for the quote from the specialist—$64\frac{7}{8}$ bid, $65\frac{1}{8}$ asked—the two cross orders at 65.

Alternatively, one broker with a market order to buy can come to the post, hear the quote, and accept the asked at $65\frac{1}{8}$. The same broker could, of course, if he or she had a market order to sell, accept the bid at $64\frac{7}{8}$. In either case, the sale would take place within $\frac{1}{8}$ of a point of the preceding transaction. An exchange, such as the New York Stock Exchange that accounts for approximately 86 percent of the dollar volume of exchange-traded stock, prides itself on maintaining price continuity.[23] In 1986, for example, 90.2 percent of all transactions occurred at either no change or at $\frac{1}{8}$ of a point from the previous transaction.[24]

Much has been made of the distinctions between a specialist on the floor of the exchange and a dealer in the over-the-counter market, and whether one or the other

---

[23] Calculated from data in *SEC Monthly Statistical Review*, Vol. 46, U.S. Securities and Exchange Commission, April 1, 1987, p. 4.

[24] *New York Stock Exchange 1987 Fact Book*, p. 15. Specialists purchased at prices below or sold at prices above the last-sale price in 90.2 percent of the transactions in which they participated. For trades of 1,000 shares in 89.2 percent of the trades, the average price of the stock showed either no price change or a movement of only $\frac{1}{8}$ of a point.

provides greater efficiency to buyers and sellers.[25] To understand what is involved, we can think of the dealer-function costs as the size of the bid–asked spread: the smaller the spread the lower the transaction costs, for both buyer and seller.[26] The size of the bid–asked spread is a function of several variables, two of which, on *a priori* grounds, are critical: the flow of orders and the number of traders or dealers in the security.

If the flow of orders is reasonably continuous, so there is a thick trading market with a random sequence of buy-and-sell orders around the current equilibrium price, the risk to the dealer is comparatively low. Continuing with the illustration of the specialist, suppose after buying 100 shares at $64\frac{7}{8}$ that he or she quotes the market at $64\frac{3}{4}$ bid and 65 asked. In a random sequence of events, a market order to buy 100 shares comes to the floor and the specialist sells the stock from his or her own account at 65. In the process, the specialist has earned a $12.50 profit.

As long as trading is active—the market is thick— the specialist will not hold a position in a security for any substantial length of time. To be sure, the equilibrium price can change quickly, as new information causes investors to reasses the present intrinsic value of the security. Depending on the nature of the news, there will be an increase in buy or sell orders. The specialist may incur some losses as he or she buys when others are selling or sells when others are buying. As transaction prices move up or down at $\frac{1}{8}$ of a point intervals, the specialist soon will be able to quote from the book of limited price orders. Thus, if the price declined to $64\frac{1}{8}$ and the specialist quoted the market at 64 bid and $64\frac{1}{4}$ asked, the limited price order of 64 on the book would support the bid whereas the specialist would sell for his own account at $64\frac{1}{4}$. Public orders take precedence over orders of the specialist.

If the market is thin, so that orders flow infrequently, the risk to the trader increases. Although random flows around the equilibrium price are less frequent, the specialist is still subject to the risks inherent in shifts in the equilibrium price. One could widen the bid–asked spread to compensate for such risks, but this would be contrary to exchange policy. One solution the NYSE implements is to give the specialist stocks with comparatively thick as well as stocks with relatively thin markets. The presumption is that profits from trading in the former more than compensate for risks involved: they are quasi-monopoly profits that subsidize risks inherent in maintaining small bid–asked spreads in thinner markets.

In contrast to this *agency-auction market* (as it is called) in which orders are

[25] Thomas S. Y. Ho and Richard G. Macris. "Dealer Market Structure and Performance," in Yakov Amihud, Thomas S. Y. Ho, and Robert A. Schwartz, *Market Making and the Changing Structure of the Securities Industry* (Lexington, MA: Heath andCompany, 1985, pp. 42–66). In the same book, see, also, Hans, T. Stoll, "Alternative Views of Market Making," pp. 69–91; Donald T. Stone, "The View from the Trading Floor," pp. 113–15; and John T. Wall, "The Competitive Environment of the Securities Market," pp. 131–44).

[26] Harold Demsetz. "The Cost of Transacting," *Quarterly Journal of Economics*, Vol. 82 (February 1968, pp. 33–53). Seha M. Tinic. "The Economics of Liquidity Services," *Quarterly Journal of Economics*, Vol. 86 (February 1972, pp. 79–110). Ward S. Curran. *An Economic Approach to Regulation of the Corporate Securities Markets* (Morristown, NJ: General Learning Press, 1976, pp. 11–14).

channeled to a single specialist who is both an agent for a broker with a limited price order as well as a dealer, the over-the-counter (OTC) markets function on the basis of multiple traders. Proponents of the OTC system argue that companies that might otherwise list their stock on an exchange "stay on NASDAQ because they would rather have competitive market makers than a single exchange specialist."[27]

To be sure, competing dealers can affect the bid–asked spread, causing it to decline to levels consistent with risks they are willing to assume. However, this system is more likely to work in thick rather than thin markets. To the extent that profits from trading in minimum intervals are large relative to the capital placed at risk, more people will want to trade in those securities. On the other hand, because of the risks incurred in thin markets, the bid–asked spread is relatively high. Competing dealers may minimize their exposure to such risks by taking smaller positions. Hence, the impact on the spread may be minimal. Nevertheless, the fixed costs of trading are still present and smaller commitments necessitate larger transaction fees to cover those costs. Consequently, markets for thinly traded securities might be more competitive if orders were centralized. This line of reasoning leads to the conclusion that thickly traded stocks are better suited to multiple dealers and thinly traded stocks are better suited to the stock exchange system of auction markets.[28] Unfortunately, many stocks with thin markets are traded over the counter while those with thick markets are more likely to be listed on the New York Stock Exchange.

Taking a different tack, one could raise the following question: Why not eliminate the trader function altogether? Considering the present state of technological sophistication, could not all orders be centralized by computer—each order a limited price order to buy or to sell—all participants have access to the market, and order filled in sequence? Spreads between bids and askeds would hold until a buyer placed (typed in) an order at a higher price and a seller at a lower price. This was the vision of a central securities market adopted by Congress as public policy in 1975. And beginning in 1978, the Cincinnati Stock Exchange attempted such an experiment but response was limited. Apparently there was considerable reluctance abdicating responsibility to the *black box* (to computers rather than to individuals).[29]

In April 1978, the New York and Philadelphia Stock Exchanges inaugurated an electronic communications system linking their markets. The American, Boston, Midwest, and Pacific Stock Exchanges joined later that year. The Cincinnati Exchange followed in 1981. A dealer-trading system operated by the NASD was also linked to the system by order of the SEC. Known as the Intermarket Trading System (ITS), it permits brokers, dealers, and specialists in the various markets to

[27] Same as [25], Wall, p. 132.

[28] Same as [25], Amihud, Ho, and Schwartz, p. 63.

[29] Same as [25], Jeffrey L. Davis, "The Intermarket Trading System and the Cincinnati Experiment," in Amihud, Ho, and Schwartz, pp. 274–76.

interact. The Composite Quotation System (CQS) used by the ITS is designed to permit the broker to fill the customer's order at the best possible price. Stocks traded in multiple markets automatically become part of ITS.

In April 1979, the Securities and Exchange Commission ruled that stocks subsequently listed on any exchange could be traded off the floor of the NYSE.[30] It was the general policy of the New York Stock Exchange to prohibit members from trading securities off the floor. Exceptions had been made for large orders—10,000 or more shares—that could not be accommodated easily by specialists charged with ongoing trading in the stock. So called *upstairs trading* by *block positioners* who are members of securities firms is designed to accommodate the growing institutional participation in the equities market. Otherwise, such transactions would take place on the floor of the exchange. For stocks listed after April 26, 1979, there are no off-board trading rules: ITS was designed to facilitate trading in these stocks as well as in those listed on more than one exchange. Approximately 44 percent of stocks listed on the New York Stock Exchange are traded via the ITS. Because specialists today indeed face competing market makers, the distinctive ways securities are traded over the counter and on an exchange are blurring rapidly.

The increasing importance of institutional investors has a considerable impact on securities trading. As sophisticated traders, institutional investors prefer to control their orders and to shop for the best possible prices. This may be easier in the over-the-counter market than on the exchange floor. Today, the continuous auction market serves largely as a reference point from which to discount prices for large orders rather than as a forum in which to place those orders. Block positioning developed to meet this demand.

There are striking similarities between block trading in stocks and over-the-counter trading in corporate bonds.[31] The New York Stock Exchange lists more bonds than stocks.[32] In 1986, the dollar volume of stock trading was $1.304 trillion as compared to $10.464 billion for bonds.[33] Because there are no specialists in bonds, members wishing to buy or sell small lots (nine or less) for their customers step into the trading ring and wait for a counteroffer, if any, from another member. Meanwhile, the bulk of bond trading takes place over the counter, where institutional investors (when they trade) buy or sell hundreds of thousands of dollars worth in a single transaction. Securities firms with bond traders take positions in bonds to service their clients.

---

[30] Same as [25], Stephen L. Williams, "The Evolving National Market System," in Amihud, Ho, and Schwartz, p. 264.

[31] Virtually all trading in U.S. government and municipal obligations is over the counter.

[32] In 1983, there were 3,600 bonds and 2,307 stocks listed. *New York Stock Exchange 1984 Fact Book*, p. 82. (Some of the bonds are those of foreign governments not corporations.)

[33] *New York Stock Exchange 1987 Fact Book*, pp. 5 and 74. In 1986, market value of the bonds was approximately $1.5 billion, or .07 percent of the $2.199 trillion in stocks listed.

Suppose the stock market becomes as heavily institutionalized as the bond market, would trading shift almost exclusively to over-the-counter? Would the exchanges and the services they offer become less important and perhaps even disappear? The question is intriguing because public policy makers continue to have difficulty coping with the implications of a market place where institutional investors are becoming increasingly important relative to individuals.

PUBLIC REGULATION OF SECURITIES MARKETS

The *raison d'être* for public regulation of securities markets is investor protection. Conceived in the depths of the Great Depression, the Securities Act of 1933 and the Securities Exchange Act of 1934 initiated, for the first time, federal control over the issuance of new securities and the trading thereof in secondary markets.[34] The concerns of the times were rooted in the Crash of 1929. (See Appendix I.) There was widespread belief that fraud, stock-price manipulation, and other unsavory practices were in large measure responsible for both the crash and the subsequent depression.[35] The small investor had been hurt; the belief was that federal legislation would prevent future occurrences. If not, then under pain of criminal and civil penalties, those who violated the law would be punished.

As discussion of the stock-registration process suggests, the Securities Act of 1933 was modeled on the philosophy that disclosure of relevant information would be sufficient to apprise investors of the risks inherent in a new offering: the individual investor could accept or reject a security in light of the full disclosure of pertinent information. Prescribed criminal and civil penalties would apply to those who placed false or misleading information in the registration statement or who failed to exercise due diligence—underwriters, for example, during their investigation of disclosures made in the prospectus prior to marketing a security. Thus, the SEC would not prohibit the sale of stock in an oil drilling company if the registration statement and prospectus contained a geologist's report stating that under the best scientific methods available the chances of finding oil were 100 to 1. If, however, the report had been falsified so as to indicate that chances were 2 to 1, fines and imprisonment

---

[34] For a recent account of the history of the SEC, see Joel Seligman, *The Transformation of Wall Street: A History of the Securities and Exchange Commission and Modern Corporate Finance* (Boston: Houghton Mifflin, 1982). Contrast this account with Susan M. Phillips and J. Richard Zecher, *The SEC and the Public Interest* (Cambridge, MA: The MIT Press, 1981).

[35] There is dispute as to whether fraud and manipulation were so widespread and, more importantly, whether the SEC has been effective in preventing it. See George J. Benston, "Required Disclosure and the Stock Market: An Evaluation of the Securities Exchange Act of 1934," *American Economic Review*, Vol. 63 (March 1973, pp. 133–55). See, also, George J. Benston, "The Costs and Benefits of Government Required Disclosure: SEC and FTC Requirements, an Appraisal," in D. A. DeMott, ed., *Corporations at the Crossroads: Governance and Reform* (New York: McGraw-Hill, 1979, pp. 37 and 54–55).

are possible for those responsible should a subsequent failure to strike oil result in losses to investors who relied reasonably on the information in their decision to purchase the stock. Once the fraud is discovered, criminal proceedings follow. As long as the information disclosed is deemed sufficient, federal law is permissive of risk-taking.[36]

The Securities Exchange Act of 1934 is a more complex statute.[37] The Act continues the philosophy of disclosure and subsequent amendments virtually mandate that any firm whose stock is publicly traded must file annual reports with the SEC. The Act, and subsequent SEC regulations thereunder, contain such restrictions as the prohibition against short selling by company officers, directors, and major stockholders. Insider trading is also prohibited, and the SEC has spent years attempting to define what constitutes both an *insider* and *inside information*. Moreover, the courts have not always agreed with the SEC.[38] (See Appendix 17-A for further discussion of insider trading.)

The act also gives the SEC broad powers concerning registration of broker-dealers, listing securities on an exchange, trading on the exchanges, and (by subsequent amendment) trading over the counter. Relying on the principle of *supervised self-regulation*, enforcement remains in the hands of the exchanges and, for over-the-counter securities, in the hands of the NASD. The Commission can interject itself at any time it believes that provisions of the Act or rules thereunder have been violated. The thrust of such regulations, particularly SEC intervention, is a continuing concern for manipulative trading and purchasing or selling stock on the basis of inside information.

Following enactment of the two statutes and passage of subsequent legislation regulating public-utility holding companies, investment companies, and investment advisors, the SEC has settled into a case-by-case approach to regulation consistent with legal practice. This approach has also characterised SEC special investigations. One such investigation (following on the heels of a stock manipulation scandal on the American Stock Exchange) resulted, in 1964, in extensive amendments to the Securities Exchange Act that presently govern disclosure requirements for all companies as well as the standards of practice for broker-dealers.

The ASE investigation also prompted a trenchant economic analysis of public policy toward securities markets by later-to-be Nobel Laureate George Stigler.[39]

---

[36] States can exact more restrictive measures within their borders prohibiting the sale of what are deemed to be risky securities.

[37] For brief summary, see Richard J. Teweles and Edward S. Bradley, *The Stock Market*, 4th ed. (New York: Wiley & Sons, 1982, Ch. 18).

[38] Dirks v. Securities and Exchange Commission, 463 U.S. 646(1983).

[39] George J. Stigler. "Public Regulation of the Securities Markets," *Journal of Business*, Vol. 37 (April 1964, pp. 117–42). See also Gregg A. Jarrell, "The Economic Effects of Federal Regulation of the Market for New Security Issues," *Journal of Law and Economics*, Vol. 24 (December 1981, pp. 613–75).

Critical of the case-by-case approach to public policy in this area, Stigler launched what became a series of heated exchanges between academics and regulators.[40]

Briefly, conventional microeconomics suggests that regulation might be warranted if the market fails to allocate resources efficiently. Scale economies in production leading to natural monopoly is a textbook example of the fact that price will exceed marginal cost of production. Regulation is one alternative. The market may also fail because all costs are not included in the price of the product. Air and water pollution devices are frequently cited examples of market failures.

Is there market failure in the case of the securities industry? Has regulation corrected it? Consider the new-issues market. Has public regulation not promoted the flow of information and prevented the fraudulent sale of securities? Unfortunately, fraud is still uncovered and whether, in the absence of the SEC, a private market for similar information would develop is a moot point. Of course, wrongdoers may be punished, which in the eyes of many is sufficient justification for the laws.

Regulation may have some impact on the new-issues market. For example, performance of new issues of common stock may not conform to the efficient market hypothesis.[41] It is also possible that the advent of registration, with attendant overhead costs, has reduced variability in returns on new issues.[42] A company may be less likely to go public until the firm is of sufficient size to spread such costs over a larger public offering than might otherwise be the case. Moreover, investors may conceivably but not necessarily have a better idea of the probability distribution of expected returns than if the company began *de novo* with a public offering. However, even if true, it does not necessarily follow that investors benefit. From our earlier discussion of portfolio diversification, we know one can easily reduce variability without the assistance of the SEC.

What about the pricing of brokerage and investment-banking services? In the trading markets, for years brokers operated as a cartel. From the signing of the Buttonwood Tree Agreement in 1792 until 1968, commissions for securities traded

---

[40] In concluding his analysis, Stigler noted that "The SEC has been run by its lawyers on a subprofessional economic basis for thirty years, and the commission will have no difficulty in so continuing for the next few years." *Ibid* Stigler, p. 416. The core of the controversy—equity (fairness) versus efficiency—was spelled out early. See Irwin Friend and Edward S. Herman, "The SEC Through a Glass Darkly," *Journal of Business*, Vol. 37 (October 1964, pp. 382–405); —— and ——, "Professor Stigler on Securities Regulation: A Further Comment," *Journal of Business*, Vol. 38 (January 1965, pp.106–10); George J. Stigler, "Comment," *Journal of Business*, Vol. 37 (October 1964, pp. 414–22); Sidney Robbins and Walter Werner, "Professor Stigler Revisited," *Journal of Business*, Vol. 37 (October 1964, pp. 414–22). See also Jarrell[39], pp. 646–50.

[41] See, for example, Roger C. Ibbotson, "Price Performance of Common Stock New Issue," *Journal of Financial Economics*, Vol. 2 (September 1975, pp. 235–71). Ibbotson found initial excess positive returns on new issues for short-run holding periods. Whether this is the result of a fixed offering price rather than an auction bid—similar perhaps to U.S. Treasury bill auctions—is an open question. But if it is, shelf registration may help alleviate this inefficiency.

[42] Same as [40], Stigler, "Comment," pp. 415–19. The standard deviation of returns on new issues in the 1920s (pre-SEC) was greater than the standard deviation of returns on new issues in the 1950s (post-SEC). One must be careful about reading too much into differences in variances for different time periods.

on the New York Stock Exchange were a function of the value of the stocks traded and independent of the number of shares involved in the transaction: it cost ten times as much to buy or sell 1,000 shares as it did 100 shares.[43] Other exchanges and over-the-counter dealers followed similar practices. More importantly, the number of seats on the NYSE were fixed. To the extent members channeled orders to the floor and limited off-floor trading, these seats had value: as Schwert has shown, they behave in a fashion similar to other capital assets discussed in this book.[44]

One rationale for sanctioning this cartel was because individual investors often received such services as safekeeping of securities, up-to-date securities analysts' reports and the like, at no additional cost. Even if an investor wanted these services, why could they not be priced separately? In competitive markets, there would be those who would supply a full line of services at a composite price and those who would offer discount brokerage services with no frills. In the brokerage industry, where economies of scale are minimal and entry is easy, breakup of the cartel would have little impact on concentration and thus one type of monopoly (the cartel) would not be replaced by another (the single-firm or dominant-firm oligopolist.)

Although this line of reasoning turned out to be essentially correct, the SEC did not actively seek an end to the cartel until market forces helped push the agency in that direction. The increasing importance of institutional trading in the stock market was a primary reason for the change in SEC posture.[45] Institutional investors, led primarily by pension funds, sought the least-expensive way to execute orders. Institutional investors were often accommodated at lower rates by brokers and dealers who, although not members of the New York Stock Exchange, would buy and sell stocks listed on the NYSE yet traded over the counter in the so-called *third market*. Prodded in part by the Justice Department,[46] following several hearings and its own institutional-investor study recommending an end to fixed-commission fees, the SEC sided with the growing number of advocates for competitive brokerage

---

[43] At first, the minimum rate was a percent of the par value of the stock. By the twentieth century, it was in cents per share regardless of the number of shares traded. Same as [34], Phillips and Zecher, p. 54.

[44] G. William Schwert. "Public Regulation of National Securities Exchange: A Test of the Capture Hypothesis," *Bell Journal of Economics*, Vol. 8 (Spring 1977, pp. 128–50). ———. "Stock Exchange Seats as Capital Assets," *Journal of Financial Economics*, Vol. 4 (January 1977, pp. 51–78).

[45] Same as [34], Phillips and Zecher, pp. 54–89; Hans R. Stoll, *Regulation of the Securities Market: An Examination of the Effects of Increased Competition* (New York University: Graduate School of Business Administration/Salomon Brothers Center for Study of Financial Institutions, 1979, pp. 12–40). For background, see Richard R. West and Seha M. Tinic, *The Economics of the Securities Markets* (New York: Praeger Publishers, 1971, pp. 108–42) and ——— and ———, "Minimum Commission Rates on New York Stock Exchange Transactions," *Bell Journal of Economics and Management Science*, Vol. 2 (Autumn 1971, pp. 577–605)? Seha M. Tinic and Richard R. West, "The Securities Industry Under Negotiated Brokerage Commissions: Changes in Structure and Performance of New York Stock Exchange Member Firms," *Bell Journal of Economics*, Vol. 11 (Spring 1980, pp. 29–41).

[46] In *Silver v. the New York Stock Exchange*, 393 U.S. 341 (1963), the SEC testified on behalf of the NYSE and in defense of immunity from the Sherman Act. After the NYSE lost the case, the Justice Department subsequently pressed the SEC to eliminate fixed commissions.

rates.[47] Congressional amendments to the securities laws ended fixed-commission sales on May 1, 1975.[48]

Mounting pressure from issuers led the SEC to adopt Rule 415.[49] However, in this instance, the move toward greater price competition in the new-issues market took place somewhat more quickly. Nevertheless, as in the case of brokerage services, the SEC responded to pressures and failed to lead the movement toward what appears to be greater efficiency in the provision of services. Although the reasons why a regulatory agency follows rather than leads go beyond the scope of this volume,[50] it is certain the issues of equity that prompted the original legislation have been augmented by concerns for efficiency in a rapidly changing financial industry.[51] Commercial banks are offering brokerage services. Brokerage houses are offering deposit accounts. Retail outlets (such as Sears, Roebuck) are offering brokerage services and consumer banking. The boutique approach, wherein firms specialize in specific areas, is fast giving way to institutionalized department stores of finance. The central securities market envisioned in the 1975 amendments to the Securities Act is becoming a reality on a national and even an international basis. Individuals—less directly involved in equity ownership—participate through institutions: pension funds, mutual funds, and the like. To date, there is no sign the pattern will reverse itself. In the final analysis, however, it is possible individual investors may benefit as much if not more from an SEC that encourages price competition than from an SEC that focuses on fraudulent disclosures and insider trading.

---

[47] U.S. Securities and Exchange Commission. *Institutional Investor Study Report*, summary volume (Washington: U.S. Government Printing Office, 1971, pp. 104–5).

[48] Between 1969 and 1975, a series of interim changes resulted in lower rates on larger orders. In real terms, however, rates fell for both institutions and individuals (except for 200 shares or less). See, for example, Richard West and Seha Tinic, "The Securities Industry Under Negotiated Commissions: Changes in Structure and Performance of New York Stock Exchange Member Firms," *Bell Journal of Economics*, Vol. 11 (Spring 1980, pp. 35–37).

[49] Same as [15], Rogowski and Sorensen, p. 6.

[50] Briefly, there are two primary theories of regulatory behavior: the *capture hypothesis* and the *theory of public choice*. The former postulates that regulatory agencies serve the industries they regulate. The latter suggests that regulations subsidize relatively small, well-organized groups with a particularly high stake in the regulations and that can influence resources going to the regulatory agency and perhaps influence the professional advancement of regulators. In each case, the agency responds rather than leads. If those with high stakes are the regulated, as they often are, results are the same regardless of the hypothesis employed. However, in the case of brokerage services and possibly investment-banking firms those demanding the services (large institutions and issuers) have as high a stake in the outcome as those supplying them. Hence, the regulated do not always benefit from the regulatory agency. Same as [34], Phillips and Zecher, pp. 60–87. Same as [15], Rogowski and Sorensen, pp. 7–11. For analytical background on the two regulatory theories, see George J. Stigler, "The Theory of Economic Regulation," *Bell Journal of Economics and Management Science*, Vol. 2 (Spring 1971, pp. 3–21); Sam Peltzman, "Toward a more General Theory of Regulation," *Journal of Law and Economics*, Vol. 19 (August 1976, pp. 212–40). For the public-choice approach, see Barry R. Weingast, "The Congressional-Bureautic System: A Principal-Agent Perspective (with application to the SEC)," *Public Choice*, Vol. 44 (No. 1, pp. 147–94).

[51] Arnold W. Sametz. "The New Financial Environment," in Arnold W. Sametz, ed., *The Emerging Financial Industry* (Lexington, MA: Heath and Company, 1984, pp. 3–19).

SUMMARY

In this chapter we have examined the new-issues market and the role investment banking plays in it, the secondary (trading) markets in securities, and public policy toward securities markets. Corporations may choose to sell securities privately or to market them through a public offering. The former involves a sale to a limited number of purchasers, usually institutional investors. Most private placements are debt issues—although equity is raised from venture-capital firms—and are not easily resold, as a secondary (trading) market is not available. Unless exempted, only securities registered with the SEC under the Securities Act of 1933 can be publicly offered and subsequently traded in the aftermarket. Because debt is often held to maturity, it is more likely than equity to be privately placed.

When offering securities to the public, the issuer almost always engages the services of an investment banking firm, which in turn usually forms a syndicate. In a classic underwritten offering, the securities are registered with the SEC and a red-herring prospectus is distributed to potential buyers. When the securities are marketed, the price to the public, the proceeds to the issuers, and the investment-banking spread are determined. The syndicate maintains the price of the securities until the issue is distributed entirely or until the syndicate is dissolved and the offering price is reduced.

An alternative to a negotiated underwriting is a competitive bid. Competitive bidding was designed to create competition in the issuance of new securities. Since 1982, major corporations have been able to register securities with the SEC under a shelf-registration procedure that permits issuance of securities in installments for a two-year period. Shelf registration not only permits the issuer to market the total shares registered all at once or in installments, but also permits the issuer to negotiate with an investment banking firm or to seek competitive bids for the shares offered.

If a corporation cannot secure underwriters for an issue, it may engage the services of investment bankers on a best-efforts basis. A best-efforts offering most often occurs for common stock of unseasoned companies. Corporations, particularly those with a large number of stockholders, may make (or, if the preemptive right applies, must make) a direct offer to their shareholders. At times, a firm may even sell debt directly.

Securities may be traded in secondary markets. Stocks are traded both over the counter, with competing dealers trading in them, and on the floor of an exchange. In the exchange format, the specialist maintains a close and continuous market by inserting himself or herself as a dealer between the bid and asked. Transactions tend to take place at $\frac{1}{8}$ of a point intervals, lowering what might otherwise be rather wide random fluctuations around the equilibrium price. Bonds are traded almost exclusively over the counter.

The *raison d'être* for public policy toward the securities market is protection of the individual investor. Much of securities law is based on the principle of full disclosure of relevant information necessary to make an informed judgment about a new security. Full disclosure and equal access to all material information is deemed necessary for those who trade in securities. However, only recently have traditional economic issues become important. When the rise of institutional investors helped bring an end to fixed-brokerage rates, this dose of price competition may have proved as beneficial to individual investors as any efforts of the SEC to promote full disclosure and to punish fraud.

APPENDIX 17-A

INSIDER TRADING

Economists are often at odds with regulators over a recurring practice that has recently surfaced in the popular press: *insider trading*. In conjunction with our discussion of the Efficient Market Hypothesis (EMH), we included in the strong form of the hypothesis what many regard as inside information—specifically, what is knowable (Chapter 5). To have inside information is to have knowledge of facts that, if generally available, would materially affect the market price of the security. In other words, inside information is not information that is generally known.

The publicity surrounding insider trading (provided by Ivan Boesky, Dennis Levine, and others) and the widespread popular support for prosecution of insider traders is understandable.[52] Why should someone profit from the purchase or sale of a security because he or she happens to possess information that, if generally known, would alter the price of that security? In the context of a recent phenomenon known as the **takeover**, suppose an individual purchases shares of company A with the knowledge that the management of company B is about to offer the share holders of company A the opportunity to tender (sell) their shares at $50 per share even though the going market price is $38 per share. If the individual is an investment banker or lawyer working on behalf of company B to effect the takeover of company A, securing a position in the shares of company A violates the fiduciary (trust) relationship created when he or she was hired. Although many economists would applaud the prosecution of such individuals, a few would demur on the ground that profits from this type of activity are simply part of the compensation package. In other words, if these insiders could not make such profits in the market, they would charge higher fees for their services.

---

[52] See, for example, Ford S. Worthy, "Wall Street's Spreading Scandal," *Fortune*, Vol. 114 (December 22, 1986, pp. 20–29).

Rather than debate the point, for our purposes it is more instructive to ask a different question: Why would company B pay a premium for the shares of company A? Are markets inefficient? Does the management of company B know something about company A not generally available to the public? Not necessarily. Indeed, it is possible for the market price of the stock to rise in anticipation of an offer and for those buying it to have no inside information that company B is about to make an offer. What sometimes happens is that in ferreting out what is knowable, skilled investors and/or their representatives discover that the market value of company B's assets is greater than the market value of its outstanding securities (debt plus equity). Because of our discussion in Chapter 10, it is apparent that a result of this type is inconsistent with the CAPM. Nevertheless, assets must be managed. Perhaps the market is suggesting the firm is poorly managed. If so, management of company B may believe it can manage the assets more effectively than can management of company A. In making an offer to purchase the shares of company A at a price above the going market price of its stock, management of company B is bidding for the right to manage those assets. Of course, management of company B may fail. In making an offer, however, management of company B is signaling its intention to try. (See Chapter 21 on mergers).

Successful investors who expend the search costs necessary to ferret out the appropriate information should not run afoul of the law if such activities are confined to determining whether or not the market price of a company's securities is undervalued in relation to the market value of its assets. Suppose, however, that an investor hears about the takeover from another person who is close to an officer of company B. That other person is certain that company B is about to offer the shareholders of company A $50 per share for their stock, even though the current price is $38 per share.

Although that information could be wrong, it might be consistent with the investor's analysis that the per-share market value of company A's assets is at least $50. Consequently, the investor purchases some stock. Shortly thereafter, company B publicly announces it is willing to purchase all the shares of company A at $50 per share. The market price of company A's stock rises accordingly. Has our investor traded on inside information?

The Securities Act of 1934 is of little help in this regard. By statute, an insider is a company officer, director, or 10-percent stockholder. Any profit these insiders make from the purchase and subsequent sale of company stock within a six-month period can be recovered by the company.[53] Section 10(b) of the Securities Exchange Act of 1934, however, grants the SEC broad powers to develop rules against the use of manipulative or deceptive devices. One such rule is the SEC's Rule 10b-5 that prohibits, among other things, any person from engaging in any act or practice that

---

[53] David L. Ratner. *Securities Regulation in a Nutshell* (St. Paul, MN: West Publishing Company, 1982, pp. 116–22).

would "operate as a fraud or deceit upon any person."[54] Adopted in 1942, this rule has been the basis for SEC policy on the use of privileged information by anyone. Carried to an extreme, the SEC could attempt to suppress entirely the flow of all material information. Under this scenario and using our illustration of the potential tender offer by company B for the shares of company A, no one could use the information until it was available to all investors. Anyone doing so could be in violation of the law. Thus, an investor who determined independently that the market value of the assets of company A is greater than the market value of its securities might be prosecuted as a *tippee* if he or she purchases stock in company A. The investor (tippee) was told by a person who in turn was told by an officer of company B.

The SEC may have trouble proving in court that the investor relied on the tip rather than on his or her own independent investigation. Moreover, the courts, particularly the United States Supreme Court, may not be sympathetic to an attempt to prosecute an individual under no fiduciary responsibility to either company A or company B. For example, Vincent Chiarella, a mark-up man in the composing room of a financial printer, happened to be a skilled cryptographer. Companies preparing to make offers to take over another company delivered extensive financial information to the printer for preparation of appropriate documents. Although the name of the takeover target was in code, Chiarella broke the code, bought the stock, and later sold it at a higher price following announcement of the tender offer. Although Chiarella was convicted under Rule 10b-5 for engaging in fraudulent trade resulting from unfair informational advantage, the U.S. Supreme Court later reversed the conviction. The majority of the Court reasoned that "Chiarella had no duty to disclose to the people from whom he bought stock because he had no relationship, fiduciary or otherwise, to the sellers."[55]

Despite this setback, the SEC continues to test the limits of what constitutes insider trading. Although he discovered that an insurance company, Equity Funding, was falsifying its accounts and thereby deceiving the public, securities analyst Raymond Dirks was censured by the SEC for violation of Rule 10b-5. Even though he held no stock in the company, he freely advised clients that he was trying to determine whether Equity Funding had indeed falsified its financial statements. Many of his clients sold before the information was generally available. Rather than congratulating Dirks for his efforts, the SEC chose only to censure and not to prosecute him under Rule 10b-5. Dirks appealed that censure. In 1983 he was exonerated by the U.S. Supreme Court.[56]

---

[54] Ratner, p. 132.

[55] Frank H. Easterbrook. "Insider Trading, Secret Agents, Evidentiary Privileges and the Production of Information," in Philip B. Kurland, Gerhard Casper, and Dennis J. Hutchinson, eds., *1981 Supreme Court Review* (Chicago: University of Chicago Press, 1982, p. 315).

[56] *Dirks v. Securities and Exchange Commission*, 463 U.S. 646–79.

Before the end of the decade, the nation may see further Supreme Court decisions clarifying what constitutes misappropriation of inside information. Perhaps there will be additional amendments to the Securities Act of 1934 that extend the scope of what constitutes insider trading. This analysis, however, suggests that care should be exercised in extending such prohibition. There are legitimate search costs involved in obtaining information. For Chiarella, perhaps such costs were minimal. For Dirks, however, such costs consisted of an investigation into the claim made by a disgruntled employee of Equity Funding that the company was engaging in fraud. Investigating these claims, Dirks understandably met with considerable resistance from company officers and less understandably received little help from insurance regulators, the SEC, and the *Wall Street Journal* (who declined to publish an article, at Dirk's request, on the allegations of fraudulent activities).[57] Moreover, Dirks had a fiduciary relationship with his own clients: his reputation and compensation depended on his ability to perform for those clients.

Thus, the continued search for what is knowable is a necessary element in an efficient market. However, the costs of that search must be pitted against what is perceived to be the insider's unfair advantage. The trade-off between efficiency and equity is a pervasive problem in applying economic or financial theory to public policy. As Easterbrook notes: "Scholars are only beginning to understand how information is created, transmitted, and used. Ideas percolate through the bar to the (Supreme) Court slowly. It is not out of line, though, that treatment of information problems will improve in time."[58]

PROBLEMS AND QUESTIONS

1. Oriental Rug Company is considering a public offering of debentures maturing in 20 years. The principal sought is $75,000,000 and each debenture would have a face value of $1,000. Investment bankers believe the coupon on the debentures should be 10.5 percent; at that rate the issue could be marketed at par. Costs of flotation—preparing and filing the registration statements, printing of securities, and so forth—would be $250,000. The investment banker's spread would be .85 percent of gross proceeds.

   a. What are the net proceeds to the company?

   b. Allowing for flotation costs and the investment banker's spread, what is the cost to maturity to the company?

2. Referring to question 1: an insurance company is willing to loan Oriental Rug $75,000,000 at 10.75 percent; interest paid semiannually (as in the sale of a bond)

---

[57] *Dirks v. Securities and Exchange Commission*, pp. 646–65.

[58] Same as [55], p. 365.

and the loan due in 20 years. Should Oriental place the securities privately or offer them publicly? Why? Why not?

3. Sour Mash Bourbon Corporation is a national distillery with a solid "Aa" credit rating. Management is considering a $250,000,000 shelf registration of 20-year debentures. Harvey Dismal, the corporate economist, predicts that interest rates for the next year will remain at about current levels. If so, Sour Mash could acquire long-term debt at par with a 10.25-percent coupon. Fixed costs of flotation are $300,000. If Dismal is correct, the issue could be floated at any time during the year, either in whole or in part. Sour Mash estimates the investment banker's spread would be .5 percent of proceeds on a shelf registration but .84 percent on a conventional underwriting.

   a. What are the net savings from shelf registration?
   b. Assuming interest rates do not change, what is the difference in basis points on cost to maturity between the two approaches to marketing new securities?

4. For corporate securities, contrast shelf registration with conventional competitive bidding. Does the latter usually lead to lower underwriting spread and to lower cost to maturity? Explain.

5. There is limited evidence that shelf registration of common stock negatively impacts the performance of the company's shares. Why do you think this could occur? Is such a result consistent with the efficient market hypothesis? Explain in detail.

6. Distinguish between a dealer in the over-the-counter market and a specialist on the exchange. Which trading approach, if either, will likely minimize the bid–asked spread? Why?

7. There is some evidence that the new-issues market is such that the stock is often underpriced, at least in the short run. Why do you think this could occur? Assuming this is possible, should management consider a rights offering over a conventional public offering? Explain in detail.

8. "Price competition for services in securities markets has done more for individual investors than government efforts to prevent fraud and manipulation of prices." Evaluate.

SELECTED ADDITIONAL REFERENCES

Amihud, Yakov, Thomas S. Y. Ho, and Robert A. Schwartz. *Market Making and the Changing Structure of the Securities Industry* (Lexington, MA: Heath and Company, 1985).

Auerbach, Joseph and Samuel L. Hayes III. *Investment Banking and Diligence: What Price Deregulation?* (Boston: Harvard University Press, 1986).

Baron, D. P. and B. Holstrom. "The Investment Banking Contract for New Issues Under Asymmetric Information Delegation and the Incentive Problem," *Journal of Finance*, Vol. 35 (December 1980, pp. 1115–38).

Benston, George J. "Required Disclosure and the Stock Market: An Evaluation of the Securities Exchange Act of 1934," *American Economic Review*, Vol. 63 (March 1973, pp. 133–55).

Benston, George J. and R. L. Hagerman. "Determinants of Bid–Asked Spreads in the Over the Counter Market," *Journal of Financial Economics*, Vol. 1 (December 1974, pp. 353–64).

Bhagat, Sanjai, M. Wayne Marr, and G. Rodney Thompson. "The Rule 415 Experiment: Equity Markets," *Journal of Finance*, Vol. 50 (December 1985, pp. 1385–1401).

Carosso, Vincent P. *Investment Banking in America: A History* (Cambridge, MA: Harvard University Press, 1970).

Curran, Ward S. *An Economic Approach to Regulation of the Corporate Securities Markets* (Morristown, NJ: General Learning Press, 1976).

DeMott, D. A., ed. *Corporations at the Crossroads: Governance and Reform* (New York: McGraw-Hill Book Company, 1979).

Demsetz, Harold. "The Cost of Transacting," *Quarterly Journal of Economics*, Vol. 82 (February 1968, pp. 33–53).

Easterbrook, Frank H. "Insider Trading, Secret Agents, Evidentiary Privileges, and the Production of Information," in Phillip B. Kurland, Gerhard Casper, and Dennis J. Hutchinson, eds., *Supreme Court Review* (Chicago: University of Chicago Press, 1982, pp. 309–65).

Ehrbar, A. F. "Upheaval in Investment Banking," *Fortune*, Vol. 106 (August 23, 1982, pp. 40–59).

Eisenach, Jeffrey A. and James C. Miller. "Price Competition on the NYSE," *Regulation*, Vol. 5 (January–February 1981, pp. 16–19).

Fabozzi, F. J. and Richard R. West. "Negotiated vs. Competitive Underwritings of Public Utility Bonds: Just One More Time," *Journal of Financial and Quantitative Analysis*, Vol. 16 (September 1981, pp. 323–39).

Farrar, Donald E. "Toward a Central Market System: Wall Street's Slow Retreat into the Future," *Journal of Financial and Quantitative Analysis*, Vol. IX (November 1974, pp. 815–28).

Friend, Irwin, et al. *Investment Banking and the New Issues Market* (New York: World Publishing, 1967).

Friend, Irwin and Edward S. Herman. "Professor Stigler on Securities Regulation: A Further Comment," *Journal of Business*, Vol. 38 (January 1965, pp. 106–10).

——— and ———. "The SEC Through a Glass Darkly," *Journal of Business*, Vol. 37 (October 1964, pp. 382–405).

Hamilton, James C. "Competition, Scale Economies and Transactions Cost in the Stock Market," *Journal of Financial and Quantitative Analysis*, Vol. XI (December 1976, pp. 779–802).

Hansen, R. S. and J. M. Pinkerton. "Direct Equity Financing: A Resolution of a Paradox," *Journal of Finance*, Vol. 37 (June 1982, pp. 651–86).

Hayes, Samuel L. III. "The Transformation of Investment Banking," *Harvard Business Review*, Vol. 57 (January–February 1979, pp. 153–70).

———, A. Michael Spence, and David Marks. *Competition in the Investment Banking Industry* (Cambridge, MA: Harvard University Press, 1983).

Hilstrom, R. and R. King, eds. *1960–69: A Decade of Corporate and International Finance* (New York: Investment Dealers Digest, 1972).

Ibbotson, Roger G. "Price Performance of Common Stock New Issues," *Journal of Financial Economics*, Vol. 2 (September 1978, pp. 235–72).

Jarrell, Gregg A. "The Economic Effects of Federal Regulation of the Market for New Securities Issues," *Journal of Law and Economics*, Vol. 24 (December 1981, pp. 613–75).

Ketels, J. P. "SEC Rule 415—The New Experimental Procedures for Shelf Registration," *Securities Regulation Law Journal*, Vol. 10 (Winter 1983, pp. 318–38).

Kidder, Peabody & Co. *Private Placements Review*, annual issues.

Kripke, Homer. *The SEC and Corporate Disclosure: Regulation in Search of a Purpose* (New York: Harcourt Brace Jovanovich, 1979).

Manne, Henry G., ed. *Economic Policy and Regulation of Corporate Securities— Conference Proceedings.* (Washington, DC: American Enterprise Institute for Public Policy Research, 1969).

Marr, Wayne and C. Rodney Thompson. "SEC Rule 415: The Ultimate Competitive Bid," *Journal of Financial and Quantitative Analysis*, Vol. 19 (June 1984, pp. 183–96).

McGoldrick, Beth. "Life with Rule 415," *Institutional Investor*, Vol. 17 (February 1983, pp. 129–33).

Moore, Norman H., David R. Peterson, and Pamela P. Peterson. "Shelf Registration and Shareholder Wealth: A Comparison of Shelf and Traditional Equity Offerings," *Journal of Finance*, Vol. 41 (June 1986, pp. 451–63).

New York Stock Exchange. *Fact Book*, annual issues.

Ofer, Aharon and Arie Melnick. "Price Deregulation in the Brokerage Industry: An Empirical Analysis," *The Bell Journal of Economics*, Vol. 19 (Autumn 1978, pp. 633–41).

Office of Chief Economist, Securities and Exchange Commission. "Explaining the Savings from Rule 415: The Debt Markets" (September 14, 1984, unpublished paper).

Office of Chief Economist, Securities and Exchange Commission. "Updating Rule 415 and Equity Markets" (September 4, 1984, unpublished paper).

Phillips, Susan M. and J. Richard Zecher. *The SEC and the Public Interest* (Cambridge, MA: The MIT Press, 1981).

Robbins, Sidney and Werner Walker. "Professor Stigler Revisited," *Journal of Business*, Vol. 37 (October 1964, pp. 414–22).

Rogowski, Robert J. and Eric H. Sorensen, "Deregulation in Investment Banking," *Financial Management*, Vol. 14 (Spring 1985, pp. 5–15).

Sametz, Arnold W. *The Emerging Financial Industry* (Lexington, MA: Heath and Company, 1984).

Schwert, G. William. "Public Regulation of National Securities Exchanges: A Test of the Capture Hypothesis," *Bell Journal of Economics*, Vol. 8 (Spring 1977, pp. 128–50).

————. "Stock Exchange Seats as Capital Assets," *Journal of Financial Economics*, Vol. 4 (January 1977, pp. 51–78).

Securities Industry Association Research Department. "SEC Rule 415: Benefits and Costs for Equity Issuers," Security Industry Trends. Vol. X (August 22, 1984. pp. 1–17).

Securities and Exchange Commission. *SEC Monthly Statistical Review.*

Seligman, Joel. *The Transformation of Wall Street: A History of the Securities and Exchange Commission and Modern Corporate Finance* (Boston: Houghton Mifflin, 1982).

Shapiro, Eli and Charles R. Wolf. *The Role of Private Placements in Corporate Finance* (Boston: Harvard University Graduate School of Business Administration, 1972).

Smith, C. W. "Alternative Methods for Raising Capital: Rights Versus Underwritten Offerings," *Journal of Financial Economics*, Vol. 5 (December 1977, pp. 275–307).

Smith, Richard L. "The Choice of Issuance Procedure and the Cost of Competitive and Negotiated Underwriting: an Examination of the Impact of Rule 50," *Journal of Finance*, Vol. 52 (July 1987, pp. 703–20).

Sorensen, Eric H. "The Impact of Underwriting Method Upon Corporate Bond Interest," *Journal of Finance*, Vol. 34 (September 1979, pp. 863–70).

Stigler, George J. "Comment," *Journal of Business*, Vol. 37 (October 1964, pp. 414–42).

————. "Public Regulation of the Securities Markets," *Journal of Business*, Vol. 37 (April 1964, pp. 117–42).

Stoll, Hans R. *Regulation of the Securities Market: An Examination of the Effects of Increased Competition* (New York University: Graduate School of Business Administration, Salomon Brothers Center for the Study of Financial Institutions, 1974).

Teweles, Richard J. and Edward S. Bradley. *The Stock Market*, 4th ed. (New York: Wiley & Sons, 1982).

Tinic, Seha M. "The Economics of Liquidity Services," *Quarterly Journal of Economics*, Vol. 86 (February 1972, pp. 79–110).

Tinic, Seha M. and Richard West. "The Securities Industry under Negotiated Brokerage Commissions: Changes in Structure and Performance of New York Stock Exchange Member Firms," *The Bell Journal of Economics*, Vol. 11 (Spring 1980, pp. 29–41).

U.S. Securities and Exchange Commission. *Institutional Investor Study Report*, summary volume (Washington: U.S. Government Printing Office, 1971).

U.S. v. Morgan, Opinion of Hon. Harold R. Medina (New York: Record Press, 1953).

Weingast, Barry. "The Congressional Bureaucratic System: A Principal-Agent Perspective (with application to the SEC)," *Public Choice*, Vol. 44 (No. 1, pp. 174–91).

West, Richard and Seha M. Tinic. "Minimum Commission Rates on New York Stock Exchange Transactions," *Bell Journal of Economics and Management Science*, Vol. 2 (Autumn 1971, pp. 577–605).

Wolfson, Nicholas. *The Modern Corporation: Free Markets versus Regulation* (New York: The Free Press, 1984, Chs. 13, 14, and 15).

18

LEASE
FINANCING

To this point in our study of finance, we have assumed that a business will purchase its assets, paying for them through the retention of profits or by the issuance of new securities. There is, however, an alternative: the firm may **lease** *the assets. Simply stated, the lessor retains ownership in the property; the lessee uses the property for a specific period of time and then returns it to the owner. Lease payments are made periodically— monthly, quarterly, or annually—through the life of the lease. We are all familiar with leasing. The young professional starting her first job signs a lease to rent an apartment. She may work for a law firm that leases office space from the building's owners. She may have leased rather than purchased her car. We touched briefly on leasing when we discussed equipment trust certificates: Legally, equipment is leased even though the certificates are the obligation of the lessee (usually a railroad or possibly a trucking concern).*

Why do firms lease assets? In some cases, there is no choice: a shipping company can only lease space from a port authority; an airline may only be able to lease airport facilities. In other cases, although there may be choices, the firm may prefer to lease. Several arguments for leasing have been suggested, but only four are substantive:

1. *convenience*
2. *service*
3. *obsolescence*
4. *tax savings*

If a company needs space only seasonally, leasing is convenient. If specialized maintenance is necessary—such as for certain computers, copiers, and sophisticated medical equipment—leasing with full-service maintenance may be more convenient or less costly than outright purchase with a service contract. In addition, the equipment manufacturer may realize scale economies in servicing the product.[1] In competitive

---

[1] Some argue that one preserves capital by leasing, yet nearly all leases require advance payments. Sometimes, however, firms cannot raise the necessary funds. In such instances, there is no choice. A less substantive argument is that leasing increases the firm's debt capacity. Believe that and you probably believe that bankers and other sophisticated lenders are unaware that leasing obligations must be met the same as interest payments must be met. To be sure, in bankruptcy the lessor can walk away with the assets whereas debtholders may have to await liquidation before learning whether their claims will be satisfied. The risks are present in either case; the issue is one of degree. Debt is debt, and lenders and security analysts know it. Markets may not be completely perfect; however, the argument that a firm can increase debt capacity through leasing is not convincing.

markets (alternatives being independent service agencies or in-house maintenance crews), the full-service lease may be the most cost-effective way of using equipment.

In some instance—computers have been a prime example—assets obsolesce rapidly. When state-of-the-art equipment is crucial to maintaining a competitive edge in the product market, management may choose to lease rather than to purchase. Equipment leasing specialists may be able to lease what is technologically obsolete for one user to another whose needs do not depend quite so much on state-of-the-art technology. Although purchase and subsequent sale in a secondhand equipment market is an alternative, the lease may be more cost-effective. The combination of convenience, service, and obsolescence in one asset is a powerful incentive to lease rather than purchase.

TAX SAVINGS

Although convenience, service, and obsolescence offer a substantive rationale for leasing, are they sufficient to explain its widespread use? Equipment leasing alone may amount to $150–200 billion; the leasing of real property would, of course, add significantly to this figure.[2] Nevertheless, how much of this leasing is to effect tax savings? Although lease payments are tax deductible expenses, so, too, are depreciation on owned assets and interest on the loans used to finance the assets. When tax laws permit, owners of assets may deduct an investment tax credit (ITC) directly from taxes owed. However, as noted in Chapter 8, the ITC is a tax advantage that is in and out of force (it was repealed in the 1986 tax reforms).

From the perspective of the federal income-tax laws, therefore, those in relatively high tax brackets gain proportionately more from ownership than do those in lower tax brackets. As we learned in Chapters 7 and 8, if the top tax bracket is 45 percent, a firm in that bracket could lower its taxes by 45 cents for every dollar of depreciation taken and interest paid. Furthermore, if there is an ITC in force of 10 percent, 10 percent of the purchase price could be deducted directly from income taxes. The value of such benefits is less for a firm in the 10-percent bracket and, of course, worthless to a firm in the zero tax bracket.

---

[2] *Leasing: Experiences and Expectations*, Report No. 791 (New York: The Conference Board, 1979, p. 1).

Although lease payments are deductible, they are of little value to firms in low tax brackets. Such firms benefit more when companies in higher tax brackets own their assets and take advantage of ownership tax savings. In a competitive leasing market, most of these savings are passed on through lower lease payments than those in lesser tax brackets might otherwise enjoy.

Clearly, the potential for a competitive leasing market exists. For example, a company may own real property, sell it to another company in a higher tax bracket, and lease it back. Such a technique, known as a **sale leaseback** arrangement, may offer tax advantages to the purchaser not available to the former owner. These additional savings could, in part at least, be passed on to the former owner through lease payments below the sum of the depreciation and interest payments after taxes.

In the preceding example, there are two parties: lessor and lessee. Often, however, there is a third party involved. If the lessor owns the asset but borrows heavily against it, the lessor employs financial leverage through a third party—often a financial intermediary—as the source of funds. The lessee continues to make lease payments to the lessor, who in turn covers the principal and interest on the loan. The lessor, in the higher tax bracket and with a strong credit rating, borrows (often through a subsidiary) the bulk of the purchase price, thereby taking full advantage of the tax deductibility of interest. Such an arrangement is known as a **leveraged lease**. It seems particularly suited to equipment that has an opportunity cost: if the lessee defaults on lease payments, the lessor can remove the equipment and lease it to someone else.

Although the foregoing analysis is consistent with a market fueled by tax differentials, does such a market exist? The answer is *yes*, but that its importance waxes and wanes with changes in the tax laws. Just how difficult does Congress make it for firms to take advantage of tax differentials? Consider, for example, that prior to 1981, Congress placed such severe restrictions on the use of leveraged leasing that the only way to know with reasonable certainty whether or not a lease was acceptable was to obtain an IRS ruling.[3] With the passage of the Economic Tax Recovery Act of 1981, Congress greatly liberalized the rules but tightened them somewhat with the enactment of the Tax Equity and Fiscal Responsibility Act of 1982. The Tax Reform Act of 1986 returned the rules to where they were prior to the passage of the 1981 Act. During that brief period, however, leasing specialists were understandably interested in showing clients what the tax laws could do for them.[4]

For the lessee today that uses leveraged leasing to finance equipment rather than purchase it directly, the useful life of the equipment must be the greater of one year

---

[3] Same as [2], p. 21. See, also, Harold Bierman, Jr., *The Lease Versus Buy Decision* (Englewood Cliffs, NJ: Prentice-Hall, 1982, p. 65).

[4] Peter K. Nevitt. *The Impact of TEFRA on Tax Benefit Transfer "TBT" Equipment Leasing* (San Francisco, CA: Bankamerilease Group, 1982). For the 1986 changes, see U.S. Congress, House of Representatives, *Tax Reform Act of 1986*, Conference Report to Accompany H.R. 3838 (Washington: U.S. Government Printing Office, 1986, Vol. II, pp. 51–52).

or 20 percent of the original estimated useful life at the expiration of the lease. Moreover, when the lease begins, the estimated fair-market value of the equipment must be at least 20 percent of the original cost at the expiration of the lease. Finally, the lessor must have at least a 20-percent equity position, borrowing no more than 80 percent of the cost of the asset from the third party.[5]

The current tax law is less conducive to financing assets through leases than it was just prior to 1981 in two respects. First, there is no investment tax credit now as then. Second, the maximum corporate-tax rate is 34 percent not 46 percent, thereby lowering the dollar benefits from leveraging the asset and leasing it to someone else.

LEASE OR BUY VERSUS LEASING AS A MEANS OF FINANCING

In analyzing a lease, much confusion can arise over whether management is leasing or buying or whether leasing is simply a means of financing. To minimize such confusion, it is helpful to recall the principles of capital budgeting. The project, in this case the equipment, is acceptable if the net present value discounted at the average cost of capital, k_o, is positive. If we assume the firm decides to lease and finds the project acceptable, we can view (with two exceptions) the lease as an alternative to debt financing. The present value of the lease payments would be included in the debt ratio. If the firm uses additional leases to finance its capital budget, it would use less conventional debt financing; the choice would be made on the basis of the after-tax cost of debt capital. In this context, if management chooses leasing, it does so because leasing minimizes the marginal cost of debt capital and ultimately the average cost of capital. The decision to lease or borrow is made, however, only after the equipment passes muster under the conventional capital budgeting analysis.

The two exceptions referred to earlier are the purchase option and the service (maintenance) expense. If the lease contains a purchase option, the present value of that option must be accounted for in the analysis. If the lease contains a service contract, the present value of projected maintenance expense must be taken into account as well. If such services as well as a purchase option are provided, the lessor takes them into account when setting the lease payments. However, ignoring these issues temporarily permits us to treat the lease as an alternative to debt financing in that it puts each on approximately the same risk basis. (In bankruptcy, although the lessor can recover the equipment, debtholders with a lien on the equipment may not be able to do so.)

---

[5] Tax Reform Act of 1986, pp. 6 and 16. See, also, 3, Bierman, Jr., p. 65.

LEASE OR BORROW—THE BASIC CONCEPTUAL FRAMEWORK

Having determined on the basis of net present value that the equipment is profitable, we set about establishing the basic conceptual framework. If the equipment is purchased, the firm makes a cash outlay and recovers the original cost on the basis of a straight-line depreciation schedule or by using the accelerated cost recovery format outlined in Chapter 8. If the equipment is leased, by convention the firm makes the first lease payment when the lease begins, at T_o. Because depreciation is scheduled at the end of the tax year, it will lag the lease payments by one year. Both the lease payments and the depreciation allowances are tax deductible.

Inevitably, we ask the question: Is it more advantageous to lease or to borrow? To answer, we must calculate the **net leasing advantage (NLA)**. Let:

$$C = \text{cost of asset (if purchased) and amount borrowed}$$
$$L = \text{lease payment}$$
$$D = \text{depreciation}$$
$$T_c = \text{corporate income-tax rate}$$
$$k_d' = \text{after-tax cost of debt capital } [k_d(1 - T_c)]$$
$$t = \text{time period 0 to } n \text{ (corresponding to lease term)}$$

Then

$$NLA = C_0 - L_0(1 - T_c) - \left[\sum_{t=1}^{n-1} \frac{L_t(1 - T_c)}{(1 + k_d')^t} + \sum_{t=1}^{n} \frac{T_c D}{(1 + k_d')^t} \right] \tag{18-1}$$

Although another nasty algebraic concept, it is straightforward: borrowing the funds and buying the asset gains the opportunity cost of not making the initial lease payment. Hence, the advantage of leasing must be reduced by $L_0(1 - T_c)$.

Similarly, when leasing, the company makes lease payments and loses the opportunity to capture the tax benefits from depreciation. True to practice, the terms $\sum_{t=1}^{n}$ compared with $\sum_{t=1}^{n-1}$ yield

$$\left[\sum_{t=1}^{n-1} \frac{L_t(1 - T_c)}{(1 + k_d')^t} + \sum_{t=1}^{n} \frac{T_c D}{(1 + k_d')^t} \right]$$

which indicate that future annual depreciation charges lag future annual lease charges by one year.[6] Both are reduced to their present value by the after-tax cost of debt capital, k_d'.

---

[6] *A Bonus Footnote!*   In practice, some equations do not allow for these differences, treating all lease payments as though made in the future. No doubt you will change this when you are in charge of leasing for your company, if not before.

The after-tax cost to maturity of debt is the appropriate discount rate: because it suggests the opportunity cost of borrowing the funds necessary to purchase the asset, it is the appropriate rate for discounting the future real and opportunity costs of leasing rather than borrowing.[7] Since all information necessary to solve Equation 18-1 is available, the calculations can be readily made. If all real and opportunity costs of leasing are less than borrowing the amount necessary to finance the asset, the NLA is positive and the asset should be leased. Although we have not yet considered the positive benefits from exercising the purchase option and receiving service (maintenance) as part of the lease, rest assured the lessor has: the lease payments are accordingly higher. If analysis shows the NLA is positive without these factors being considered, no further investigation is necessary and the company should lease the equipment. If the NLA is negative, management must evaluate the purchase option and the service expense to decide whether to lease or purchase through borrowing.[8]

APPLYING THE BASIC FORMULA

Firm Foundation Construction Company, a regional commercial contractor, is considering whether to purchase ($150,000) or lease ($26,000 per year) construction equipment necessary for its operations. For purposes of cost recovery, the estimated useful life of the equipment is ten years. The company is in the 34-percent tax bracket and the before-tax cost of debt capital is 14.545 percent. Using the cost recovery basis in effect at the time for a ten-year asset (see Table 18-1), management calculates the NLA. Given a before-tax cost of debt capital of 14.545 percent, after-tax cost of debt capital is .096. Hence, $NLA =$ outlay $-$ (initial lease payment) $-$ (present value of nine lease payments + present value of depreciation).

$$NLA = \$150,000 - \$26,000(1 - .34)$$
$$- \left[\frac{\$26,000(1 - .34)[1 - (1.096)^{-9}]}{.096} + \sum_{t=1}^{n} \frac{T_c D}{(1 + 1.096)^t} \right]$$

Where

$$\frac{\$26,000(1 - .34)[1 - (1.096)^{-9}]}{.096} = \sum_{t=1}^{n-1} \frac{\$26,000(1 - .34)}{(1.096)^t}$$

---

[7] The debt-alternative cost to maturity will differ depending on repayment schedules. Being a sophisticated student of present value, you (we assume) have investigated possible alternatives and are using the lowest available cost to maturity consistent with maintaining the company's debt ratio.

[8] If the equipment is purchased, the firm must make a down payment and borrow the rest. Under our assumption—that the equipment already has been screened under conventional capital budgeting procedures—-this is of no consequence. Again, company management has a target debt ratio; distribution of debt and equity among projects has no analytical significance.

Table 18-1   Illustrating NLA for Company in 34-percent Tax Bracket[a]

End of Year	Cost of Asset	Lease Payments	Depreciation[b]	Present Value of Depreciation[c]
0	$150,000	$26,000		
1		26,000	$21,428.57	$ 6,647.55
2		26,000	36,734.69	10,397.63
3		26,000	26,239.07	6,776.35
4		26,000	18,742.19	4,416.28
5		26,000	13,015.41	2,798.23
6		26,000	13,015.41	2,553.13
7		26,000	13,015.41	2,329.50
8		26,000	7,809.25	1,275.25
9		26,000	0	0.00
10			0	0.00
				$37,193.92[d]

[a] After-tax cost of debt capital = .1454(1 − .34) = .096.

[b] See Appendix F.

[c] $\dfrac{T_c D_t}{(1.096)^t}$

[d] $\displaystyle\sum_{t=1}^{n} \dfrac{T_c D}{(1.096)^t} = \$37,193.92$

Using the data in Table 18-1 and solving, we find that $NLA = \$150,000 - \$17,160 - (\$100,415.86 + \$37,193.92) = -\$4769.78$.

In this instance, the NLA is negative; consequently, unless the lease contract includes service and a purchase option, it appears the company should buy rather than lease.

EFFECT OF TAX RATE ON LEASING DECISION

In the preceding illustration, we assume the company is in the 34-percent tax bracket. If the tax bracket were lower, management might find the lease more attractive. Consider the situation of a company in the zero tax bracket—for mnemonic purposes, Zerocorp—but otherwise in the same circumstances. Zerocorp does not expect to pay taxes for the remainder of the life of the lease. Suppose the cost of debt capital is 16 percent. Consequently[9]

$$NLA = \$150,000 - \$26,000 - \frac{\$26,000[1 - (1.16)^{-9}]}{.16} - 0$$

$$= \$150,000 - \$26,000 - \$119,770.14$$

$$= \$4,229.86$$

Loss of the tax shelter and higher cost of debt capital renders leasing more attractive than purchasing. Although lease payments are no longer tax-sheltered, loss of interest deductibility and depreciation tax shelter more than offset tax-savings loss due to lease payments. In general: the lower the user's tax bracket the more likely leasing is preferable to purchasing.

What about the lessor? Because companies that lease equipment to others are (as noted) in higher tax brackets, they can enjoy the tax advantages of ownership and (in a competitive leasing market) pass on some of the benefits to the lessee. Moreover, if the leasing concern is a subsidiary of a major corporation with a top-level credit rating, it may be able to leverage the lease, borrowing heavily against the equipment (as collateral) at rates lower than those available to the lessee. Interest paid is, of course, tax sheltered. The lender is willing to commit the funds because the subsidiary's credit rating is really the parent company's credit rating.

Suppose in the foregoing scenario that the lessor can borrow at 11.75 percent, has a marginal tax rate of 34 percent, and a cost of equity capital of 18 percent. As a subsidiary of the manufacturer, the lessor can borrow 80 percent of the market value of any equipment and hence has a debt-to-total capital ratio of .8.[10] Thus, its weighted-average cost of capital k_o is

$$k_o = .1175(1 - .34)(.8) + .18(.2)$$

$$= .06204 + .036$$

$$= .09804$$

Viewing the equipment investment as a capital budgeting decision and ignoring the service contract and scrap value at the end of ten years, we find the cash flows from investing in the equipment shown in Table 18-2. The net present value from the investment is

$$NPV = -\$150,000 + \$17,160 + \$136,568.86$$

$$= \$3,728.86$$

---

[9] With conventional capital budgeting analysis, loss of the tax advantage will also lower NPV. We shall assume, however, that NPV is still positive.

[10] From our earlier discussion of k_o, one could argue that if the firm is viewed as a whole, the subsidiary's asset structure affects its unleveraged beta coefficient and its 80-percent debt ratio could be weighted in the company's debt ratio, thereby using the company's not the subsidiary's k_o as the rate of discount.

Table 18-2   Cash Flows from Lessor Investment in Equipment

End of Year	Outlay	After-tax Revenues from Lease[a]	Depreciation	T_cD $T_c = .34$	After-tax Cash Flows[b]	Discounted Cash Flows[c]
0	$150,000	$17,160			$17,160.00	
1		17,160	$21,428.57	$ 7,285.71	24,445.71	$ 22,263.04
2		17,160	36,734.69	12,489.79	29,649.79	24,591.52
3		17,160	26,239.07	8,921.28	26,081.28	19,700.37
4		17,160	18,742.19	6,372.34	23,532.34	16,187.97
5		17,160	13,015.41	4,425.24	21,585.24	13,522.78
6		17,160	13,015.41	4,425.24	21,585.24	12,315.38
7		17,160	13,015.41	4,425.24	21,585.24	11,215.79
8		17,160	7,809.25	2,655.15	19,815.15	9,376.74
9		17,160	0	0	17,160.00	7,395.27
10			0	0	0	0.00
						$136,568.86

[a] $26,000(1 - .34) = $17,160
[b] After-tax cash flows $= (1 - T_c)(L_T) + T_cD$
[c] $\sum_{t=1}^{9} \frac{Lt(1 - .34)}{(1.09804)^t} + \sum_{t=1}^{10} \frac{.34D}{(1.09804)^t} = $136,568.86$

Although lease payments are taxable to the lessor, tax advantages from depreciation and interest deductibility make it profitable for the lessor in the higher tax bracket to own and then lease the asset to the lessee in the low or zero tax bracket. The higher-taxed lessors and the low-taxed lessees (*Zerocorps*) often do business with one another.

SERVICE CONTRACTS

Although lessor-lessee tax differences help fuel leasing, one cannot ignore the service contract as a factor. Although when an asset is leased payments usually include service, one can often purchase the equipment and buy a service contract as well. Alternatively, one can often purchase service (maintenance) in the open market or establish a service department. An example with which most consumers are familiar is the extended warranty that can be purchased on many automobiles. Some manufacturers include certain systems, parts, and repairs in the warranty for up to 50,000 miles or five years, whichever comes first. (More recently, certain manufacturers have included 60,000- and 70,000-mile warranties in the car's price.) The consumer is buying a type of insurance, in this instance insurance against major car repairs. Routine service, of course, is not covered. When one leases a car, the ultimate responsibility for repairs lies with the lessor. However, the lease contract may or may not make the lessee responsible for such routine services as oil, lubrication, and the like.

Although details differ, similar arrangements can be made regarding the purchase or lease of other equipment. Moreover, just as a consumer can forego the price of extended warranty, so the company can sometimes forego the service contract when purchasing or when leasing.

The economists' favorite cliche—there is no free lunch—applies to service contracts as it does to every other type of transaction. Consequently, lease payments include a service fee. *A priori*, there are grounds for assuming the lessor can provide the service at a lower cost than if the lessee or buyer provided the service. First, there are economies of scale in repair service, including experience gained by personnel servicing the equipment over time. Second, although all equipment requires service, sometimes major repairs are necessary. Because the lessor services many units, the probabilities of major repairs (particularly for parts or equipment whose technology does not change rapidly) are reasonably well-known—the probability of a major breakdown for a straight six-cylinder engine, for example, after 50,000 miles. Hence, the lessor can price the service accordingly and spread the costs to all users. To be sure, the lessee or buyer can take the risk that he or she will not experience major repairs. Nevertheless, the owner of an automobile whose engine gives out at 20,000 miles is justifiably irked—particularly if it occurs at an inconvenient time (such as 300 miles from home on the second day of a two-week vacation). Such anger, however, is partially assuaged by the knowledge that repairs are covered under extended warranty. Analogous situations arise in business.

In addition, if technology is changing rapidly and equipment is new, the lessor—who may be a subsidiary of the manufacturer—will obtain rapid information through service contracts should something be consistently wrong with the product. This procedure allows the manufacturer to monitor and perhaps alter the assembly operation more quickly, thereby reducing the number of defective products. For the lessee, there is comfort in knowing the defective machinery can easily be returned for new equipment.

THE PRESENT VALUE OF THE SERVICE CONTRACT

When an asset is accepted on a conventional basis, the cash flows include an estimated outlay for repair and maintenance. On a leasing basis, payments include a charge for the service contract. Although the charge may not be explicit, for purposes of our analysis the portion of the lease that covers service and maintenance *should be explicit*. Bear in mind that our analysis compares debt with leasing as a means of financing the asset alone. What our analysis compares now is the portion of lease payments that represents repair and maintenance with the estimate of repair and maintenance expenses.

In this case, we assume management can obtain such information in a straight-forward way: lease payments minus service contract are $26,000 per year. As noted, because the lessor barely covers the cost of capital with these payments, he or she will charge extra for the service contract. If such charges are not explicit, they may be estimated indirectly by the cost of a service contract if the asset were purchased.

To illustrate, suppose that if equipment is leased the lessee must pay an additional service charge of $4,000 per year in the life of the lease. Enter our original lessor, Firm Foundation Construction Company, in the 34-percent tax bracket. Since service charges are deductible, the after-tax outlay would be $2,640: $4,000 $(1 - .34)$. Suppose further that a service contract for the life of the lease (ten years) is available at $27,000.

The potential lessee, of course, is not privy to how the lessor arrives at either figure. Presumably, in light of the foregoing discussion, the lessor can predict from experience what the service problems are for the equipment. The lessor expects to deduct service expenses and earn an after-tax profit that covers the cost of capital. Because some equipment will experience more problems than other equipment, the lessor will average such experience, charging the same rate for all: for our purposes assumed to be $4,000 after taxes. From there, it is but a short step to determining the price of the service contract: the present value of the future lease payments for service discounted at the lessor's average cost of capital. Thus

$$\text{present value} = \$4,000 + \frac{\$4,000[1 - (1.09804)^{-9}]}{.09804}$$

$$= \$27,217 \equiv \$27,000$$

Although the cost of a service contract is tax deductible for the lessee, the cost must be amortized during the life of the contract. In addition, since the cost of the service contract represents service of the asset and not its purchase, the opportunity cost of the funds employed is the average cost of capital for the potential lessee (buyer). To illustrate, suppose Firm Foundation's cost of equity capital is .20 and that it carries a debt-to-total-capital ratio of .5 and an equity-to-total-capital ratio of .5; consequently

$$k_o = .14545(1 - .34)(.5) + .2(.5)$$

$$= .048 + .10$$

$$= .148$$

Because the cost of the service contract is deductible for a ten-year period, the after-tax cost to Firm Foundation equals the outlay less the present value of future tax benefits. Thus

$$\text{after-tax cost of service} = \$27,000 - \frac{(.34)\dfrac{(\$27,000)}{10}[1 - (1.148)^{-10}]}{.148}$$

$$= \$27,000 - 918[5.057264]$$
$$= \$27,000 - 4,642.57$$
$$= \$22,357.43$$

Because lease payments are tax deductible for the year in which they are taken

$$\text{after-tax cost of service through leasing} = \$4,000(1 - .34) + \frac{\$4,000(1 - .34)[1 - (1.148)^{-9}]}{.148}$$

$$= \$2,640 + \$2,640[4.805739]$$
$$= \$15,327.15$$

The cost of service is $7,030.28 greater than the cost of leasing with service included ($22,357.43 − $15,327.15). This changes the NLA from a deficit of $4,769.78 to a positive $2,260.50 ($7,030.28 − $4,769.78). Leasing is now marginally profitable.

What about Firm Foundation incurring its own expenses for service? Suppose when the project was being considered in the capital budget that management estimated repair and maintenance costs at $5,000 per year. The after-tax present value of such costs is[11]

$$\text{present value} = \frac{\$5,000(1 - .34)[1 - (1.148)^{-10}]}{.148}$$

$$\text{estimated expenses} = \$16,688.97$$

It appears from the calculations that leasing with service payments is preferable to Firm Foundation incurring its own expenses. Although actual expenses could be lower or higher, assuming a risk-averse management, the company should lease with service costs built into lease payments.

What about Zerocorp? It already found leasing advantageous, but the NLA was small. Perhaps the service contract would reduce the advantage. Assume Zerocorp has a cost of equity of .2, a debt-to-total capital ratio of .5, and an equity-to-total-capital ratio of .5. Because its cost of debt at .16 cannot be tax-sheltered

$$k_o = .16(.5) + .2(.5)$$
$$= .18$$

As there are no tax savings from either the lease or the service contract, we can compare $27,000 with the present value of the additional lease payments, so that

---

[11] From our earlier discussion of risk-aversion, however, management may choose to lease the asset without service if the amount involved is small relative to total company wealth.

$$\text{cost of service as part of lease} = \$4,000 + \frac{\$4,000[1 - (1.18)^{-9}]}{.18}$$

$$= \$4,000 + \$17,212.09$$

$$= \$21,212.09$$

Clearly, the lease is more advantageous than it was without service included. This advantage could be mitigated somewhat if the expected value of the service costs was lower than the cost of service included in the lease. Again, assuming \$5,000 for maintenance

$$\text{present value of maintenance expenses} = \frac{\$5,000[1 - (1.18)^{-10}]}{.18}$$

$$= \$22,470.43$$

Leasing apparently retains its advantage over purchase—with or without the service contract.

The real world, unfortunately, is far more complicated. For instance, the service provided under the lump-sum contract may not be the same as the service provided under the leasing contract. If the latter service is more extensive, this may tip companies with marginally negative NLAs toward leasing. Moreover, potential lessees may not be able to determine the portion of lease payments that represents service costs. To estimate service costs indirectly, one must know the lessor's average cost of capital, so that

$$\$27,000 = \$x + \frac{\$x[1 - (1 + k_o)^{-n}]}{k_o}$$

Although this is rarely known, by using its own cost of capital a potential lessee can estimate the value of such services. Suppose lease payments are \$29,000 per year *including service*. Management can estimate (from the \$27,000 service contract) that portion of the lease that represents service by substituting .148 for k_o. Thus

$$\$27,000 = \$x + \frac{\$x[1 - (1.148)^{-9}]}{.148}$$

$$= \$x + 4.805739x$$

$$= 5.805739x$$

$$x = \$4,650.57$$

From Firm Foundation's perspective, the lease payments are now \$29,000 − \$4,650.57 = \$24,349.43. Accordingly, figures for the lease-or-borrow decision change, so that

$$NLA = \$150,000 - \$24,349.43(1 - .34) - [\$24,349.43(1 - .34)(5.85174027) + \$37,193.92]$$
$$NLA = \$150,000 - \$16,070.62 - (\$94,041.12 + \$37,193.92)$$
$$NLA = \$2,694.34$$

As management now views the results, there is a slight advantage to leasing once it accounts for service: what management perceived as lower lease payments for use of the asset changed the NLA from slightly negative to slightly positive. However, when calculating after-tax cost of service in the lease payments, management learns that

$$\text{after-tax cost of service through leasing} = \$4,650.57(1-.34) + \$4,650.57(1-.34)[4.805739]$$
$$= \$3,069.38 + \$14,750.62$$
$$= \$17,820.00$$

Because the after-tax cost of the service contract remains unchanged at $22,357.43, it costs $4,537.43 ($22,357.43 − $17,820) less to finance service charges through a lease than through a service contract. This adds to the NLA, continuing to tilt Firm Foundation toward leasing the asset rather than purchasing it and buying a service contract. Admittedly, since the choice is based on a small advantage, management will examine service under leasing and compare it with service under contract to ascertain they are identical.

In conclusion, once we treat leasing as an alternative to debt financing, we must divide the payments into those that represent debt service for leasing the equipment and those that represent the cost of servicing (maintaining) it. In principle, there are three ways to pay for service: service contract, incurred expenses, and lease payments. We have assumed the first and last are fixed amounts that shift the risk to the seller or lessor who in turn spreads the risk to all the equipment, charging each buyer a uniform price and each lessee a uniform rate. The seller or lessor calculates the price or rate using its own average cost of capital. The potential lessee may or may not know how much of the annual lease payment represents service. Lacking such information, a potential lessee can use the price of the service contract and its own average cost of capital to impute the annual service charge and can calculate the NLA by subtracting the imputed service charge from the lease payment. The results should be compared with the advantage or disadvantage of a service contract.

Although conceptually it is easy to separate the three ways to pay for service, in practice it can be difficult to make comparisons. Unless management has had considerable experience with the equipment, estimates for repair and maintenance may be inaccurate. Both the service contract and lease payments that include service are *sums certain*. In assuming the service burden, the potential buyer or lessee accepts the risk—a risk that may be better appraised and more accurately calculated by the manufacturer or the lessor. It is a classic illustration of utility analysis under risk. If the potential loss in wealth from buying or leasing without service is small, management may accept the risk; if the potential loss is large, management will insure itself either through a service contract or through service included in the lease. The trick is to determine whether or not the two are comparable. If they are not, the approach suggested here must be supplemented by detailed analysis of the differences in the service contracts.

THE PURCHASE OPTION

Between 1981 and 1986, it was possible (under leveraged leasing) to offer the lessee the option of purchasing the asset at a price below its estimated market value. When the Tax Reform Act of 1986 essentially returned leasing to the practices prevailing in 1981, the purchase option became less valuable. Presumably, the lessor could offer the option only at a price greater than or equal to the equipment market value at lease expiration.[12] Of course, the market value may turn out to be higher than estimated. For example, in the case of real property, the land may increase in value even if the structure on it does not. It is also possible for an asset to become more useful: its NPV at lease expiration is greater than the going market price. Under such circumstances, an option may have some value.

To illustrate, suppose the lessor anticipates the fair market value of the equipment at the time the lease expires will be $30,000, or 20 percent of the purchase price. However, management of Firm Foundation estimates that at the time the lease expires the equipment will be worth $37,500 to the firm. For Firm Foundation then, the expected net present value of the purchase option at $30,000 is

$$\frac{\$37,500 - \$30,000}{(1.148)^{10}} = \$1,886.44$$

Assuming Zerocorp reached the same conclusion, the expected net present value of the purchase option is

$$\frac{\$37,500 - \$30,000}{(1.18)^{10}} = \$1,432.98$$

For Firm Foundation, the purchase option with service included in lease payments tilts the company toward leasing over purchasing: the purchase option merely adds to the value of leasing. For Zerocorp, further analysis is unnecessary because the NLA without service included in lease payments is positive.

SUMMARY

The lease-or-buy or lease-or-borrow decision continues to be the subject of considerable controversy. We have departed from our custom of examining controversy (see Selected Additional References at the end of the chapter) in order to cut through to the core of the problem. If an asset has a positive net present value when discounted at the average cost of capital, it should be purchased. The legal distinction between ownership and nonownership is important only insofar as it

---

[12] Same as ³, Bierman, Jr., p. 65.

Table 18-3   **Summary of Steps in the Lease-or-Buy or Lease-or-Borrow Decision**

Step 1   Using the average cost of capital, determine whether or not NPV is positive.

Step 2   If NPV is positive, the asset is an acceptable purchase. Treat the lease-or-buy decision as a lease-or-borrow decision, using after-tax cost of debt capital as the discount rate.[a]

Step 3   Using Equation 18-1, determine the net leasing advantage (NLA). Lease payments should include only what is necessary to finance the asset, not to service it.

Step 4   If NLA is positive, no further analysis is required. If NLA is negative, compare the after-tax cost of the service contract available to the purchaser with the after-tax cost of the service included in lease payments. Both should be reduced to present value by using the average cost of capital and each should be compared with the present value of future lease payments for service as estimated by the potential buyer or lessee. If the present value of the future lease payments for service is less than the present value of the service contract, use the difference between the two to raise NLA. If NLA is positive, the firm should lease rather than purchase. If the present value of estimated service expenses is less than either the present value of the service contract or the future lease payments for service, any decision to avoid the outlay should be made on the basis of management's attitude toward risk.

Step 5   If NLA is still negative, determine the present value of the purchase option by using the average cost of capital as the discount rate. If positive, add the purchase option to the NLA to determine whether or not NLA is now positive.

[a] It is possible for NPV to be marginally negative and NLA to be marginally positive.

permits the lessor to repossess the asset if lease payments are not made. If the asset was purchased and financed in part from debt, legal claims of debtholders differ from those of the lessor in the event of default. Otherwise, the decision to lease rather than to borrow is a decision to seek the lowest cost of debt capital. Implicit in our approach is that the debt-to-total capital ratio of the company does not change; the present value of the lease payments is included in the company's debt burden, and the asset leased is part of its capital budget.[13]

The steps involved in our analysis are summarized in Table 18-3 and the results for Firm Foundation and Zerocorp are reported in Table 18-4. In its analysis, management must be able to separate financing the asset from servicing (maintaining) it. Our arithmetic examples are broadly consistent with what one finds in the real world. Specifically, the *Zerocorps* in low- or zero-tax brackets lease from those who

---

[13] In modern accounting practice, they are also included as debt on the corporation's balance sheet, thereby giving recognition to what analysts already knew—that leasing is not "off balance sheet" financing.

Table 18-4 Results of Applying Lease-or-Buy or Lease-or-Borrow Decision Steps to Firm Foundation and Zerocorp

	Firm Foundation		*Zerocorp*
Step 1[a]	Assume *NPV* is positive		Assume *NPV* is positive
Step 2	$k'_d = (1 - .34)(.14545) = .096$		$k'_d = (1 - 0)(.16) = .16$
Step 3	Using Equation 18-1, $NLA = -\$4,769.78$		Using Equation 18-1, $NLA = \$4,229.86$
	(further analysis necessary)		*(project can be leased)*
Step 4[b]	(a)	(b)	
	Assume explicit service payment of \$4,000 in lease:	Estimate using service contract price with implicit service payment of \$4,650.57 in lease:	*p.v.* of explicit service contract = \$27,000
	p.v. of \$27,000 service contract = \$22,357.43	Recalculated NLA = \$ 2,694.34	*p.v.* of explicit lease payments (\$4,000) = \$21,212.09
	p.v. of lease payments = $-15,327.15$	*p.v.* of \$27,000 service contract = 22,357.43	Additional NLA = \$ 5,787.91
	$\overline{}$ \$ 7,030.28	*p.v.* of lease payments = $-17,820.00$	*p.v.* of annual maintenance expenses (\$5,000) = \$22,470.43
	p.v. of maintenance expenses = \$16,688.97	$\overline{}$ \$ 4,537.43	
		p.v. of maintenance expenses = \$16,688.97	
Step 5[b]	*p.v.* of purchase option = \$1,886.44		*p.v.* of purchase option = \$1,432.98
	4(a)	4(b)	
	$NLA = (\$4,769.78)$	$NLA = \$2,694.34$	$NLA = \$ 4,299.86$
	7,030.28	4,537.43	5,787.91
	1,886.44	1,886.44	1,432.98
	$NLA = \$4,146.94$	$NLA = \$9,118.21$	$NLA = \$11,520.75$

[a] It is possible for NPV to be negative for Zerocorp but NLA to be positive.

[b] The average cost of capital is the discount rate: .148 for Firm Foundation and .18 for Zerocorp.

enjoy the tax advantages of ownership that include leverage. On occasion, for corporations in low-tax brackets, equipment that cannot pass the NPV muster may nevertheless have a positive NLA. Other aspects of leasing, including service and purchase option, simply raise the NLA for the *Zerocorps*.

For the *Firm Foundations* in higher tax brackets, even if the lessor is sufficiently large to enjoy a somewhat lower before-tax cost of debt capital, leasing is not usually advantageous. What is involved are rather complex quantitative and qualitative analyses of the value of service and the risk of obsolescence. Although the lessor or manufacturer may enjoy some scale economies from spreading the risk over a large number of assets, the potential lessee or buyer may find the risk so small relative to change in total wealth that he or she is willing to assume it.

In the absence of the ability to pass on tax advantages through purchasing by high-tax bracket firms and subsequent leasing to low-tax bracket firms, leasing would not disappear. However, leasing would be confined primarily to the assets of large-scale ownership, which permits the lessor to enjoy economies by spreading the risk of maintenance and obsolescence over a large number of units.

PROBLEMS AND QUESTIONS

1. Hardy Baked Beans Corporation, a leading manufacturer of canned foods, is considering whether to purchase or lease can-closing machinery for its new plant. The purchase price is $25,000,000. However, the machinery can be leased for $3,200,000 per year exclusive of service contract and purchase option. The lease expires in 15 years. For tax purposes, assume that only straight-line depreciation less salvage value is available and that the machine has an estimated salvage value of $2,500,000. The asset is acceptable on a conventional capital-budgeting basis. Hardy's before-tax cost of debt capital is 13.5 percent, current cost of equity capital is 17 percent, debt-to-total-capital ratio is .3, the marginal tax rate is .25. Determine the NLA for Hardy. Should Hardy lease or buy? Why? Why not?

2. In problem 1, suppose Hardy's marginal tax rate is .45 and that all other conditions remain the same. Determine the new NLA for Hardy. Should Hardy lease or buy? Why? Why not?

3. In problem 1, Hardy management learns that if it purchases the can-closing machinery it can also purchase a service contract for the life of the lease for $2,100,000. Alternatively, Hardy can pay an additional $400,000 a year in lease payments for the same service. How does each alternative affect Hardy's NLA if it is in the 25-percent tax bracket? In the 45-percent tax bracket?

4. Acme Marketing Association is considering leasing a fleet of 20 cars for its sales force. The lease runs for five years at $60,000 per year and includes full service on the cars. Acme estimates it will cost $8,000 per year to service the fleet. Acme's before-tax cost of debt capital is 14 percent, cost of equity is .18, debt-to-total-capital ratio is .35, and marginal tax rate is 38 percent.
   a. Calculate the cost of acquiring the asset through leasing.
   b. Calculate the cost of service for the five-year period.
   c. What is the cost of the lease?

5. In problem 4, Acme has the option of purchasing the fleet for $225,000. For tax purposes, costs can be recovered on the following schedule:

Year 1	15% of $225,000
Year 2	22% of $225,000
Years 3–5	21% of $225,000

Fleet scrap value at the end of five years is $40,000. If leased, the lessor offers to sell the fleet to Acme for $15,000. Calculate the NLA for leasing.

6. "Leasing is advantageous primarily to firms in low tax brackets." Evaluate.

7. "If a company anticipates rapid inflation, it is better to lease than to purchase assets." Evaluate.

8. "The confusion in evaluating leasing as an alternative to debt financing or to purchasing an asset arises from the failure to separate the finance decision from the capital budgeting decision." Evaluate.

9. Dry Hole Oil and Gas Drilling Company is considering purchasing or leasing a new drill. The purchase price is $500,000. For tax purposes, cost recovery can be completed in five years using the following schedule:

Year 1	15% of $500,000
Year 2	22% of $500,000
Year 3–5	21% of $500,000

Dry Hole has a debt-to-total-capital ratio of .2, a marginal tax rate of .35, an equity cost of 17 percent, and a before-tax debt cost of 13 percent.

Alternatively, Dry Hole may lease the equipment for five years at $116,000 per year, pay an additional $20,000 per year for service, and receive a purchase option of $50,000 on expiration of the lease. Secondhand drilling equipment of the same age is currently selling at $80,000.

If Dry Hole purchases the equipment, it can pay $19,000 per year (the first payment in advance) to receive the same service offered for leasing; service costs however, rise 5 percent per year (compounded annually) for the four years remaining.

Should Dry Hole purchase or lease? Discuss in detail.

SELECTED ADDITIONAL REFERENCES

Anderson, Paul F. and John D. Martin. "Lease Versus Purchase Decisions: A Survey of Current Practice," *Financial Management*, Vol. 6 (Spring 1977, pp. 41–47).

Bierman, Harold Jr. *The Lease Versus Buy Decision* (Englewood Cliffs, NJ: Prentice-Hall, 1982).

Bower, Richard S. "Issues in Lease Financing," *Financial Management*, Vol. 12 (Winter 1973, pp. 25–33).

Brealey, R. A. and C. M. Young. "Debt, Taxes and Leasing—A Note," *Journal of Finance*, Vol. 35 (December, 1980, pp. 1245–50).

Capettini, Robert and Howard Toole. "Designing Leveraged Leases: A Mixed Integer Linear Programming Approach," *Financial Management*, Vol. 10 (Autumn 1981, pp. 15–23).

Crawford, Peggy J., Charles P. Harper, and John J. McConnell. "Further Evidence on the Terms of Financial Leases," *Financial Management*, Vol. 10 (Autumn 1981, pp. 7–14).

Dyl, Edward A. and Stanley A. Martin, Jr. "Setting Terms for Leverage Leasing." *Financial Management*, Vol. 6 (Winter 1977, pp. 20–27).

Gordon, Myron J. "A General Solution to the Buy or Lease Decision: A Pedagogical Note," *Journal of Finance*, Vol. 29 (March 1974, pp. 245–50).

Hockman, Shalom and Ramon Rabinovitch. "Financial Leasing Under Inflation," *Financial Management*, Vol. 13 (Spring 1984, pp. 17–26).

Idol, Charles R. "A Note on Specifying Debt Displacement and Tax Shield Borrowing Opportunities in Financial Lease Valuation Models," *Financial Management*, Vol. 9 (Summer 1980, pp. 24–29).

Johnson, Robert W. and Wilbur G. Lewellen. "Analysis of Lease or Buy Decision," *Journal of Finance*, Vol. 27 (September 1972, pp. 815–24).

Kim, E. Han, Wilbur G. Lewellen, and John J. McConnell. "Sale and Leaseback Agreements and Enterprise Valuation," *Journal of Financial and Quantitative Analysis*, Vol. 13 (December 1978, pp. 871–84).

Lewellen, Wilbur G. and Douglas R. Emery. "On the Matter of Parity Among Financial Obligations," *Journal of Finance*, Vol. 36 (March 1981, pp. 97–111).

Lewellen, Wilbur G., Michael S. Long, and John J. McConnell. "Asset Leasing in Competitive Capital Markets," *Journal of Finance*, Vol. 31 (June 1976, pp. 787–98).

Long, Michael S. "Leasing and the Cost of Capital," *Journal of Financial and Quantitative Analysis*, Vol. 12 (November 1977, pp. 579–86).

McConnell, John J. and James S. Schallheim. "Valuation of Asset Leasing Contracts," *Journal of Financial Economics*, Vol. 12 (August 1983, pp. 237–61).

McGugan, Vincent J. and Richard Caves. "Integration and Competition in the Equipment Leasing Industry," *Journal of Business*, Vol. 47 (July 1974, pp. 382–96).

Miller, Merton H. and Charles W. Upton. "Leasing, Buying and the Cost of Capital Services," *Journal of Finance*, Vol. 31 (June 1976, pp. 787–98).

Myers, Stewart C., David A. Dill, and Alberto J. Bautista. "Valuation of Financial Lease Contracts," *Journal of Finance*, Vol. 31 (June 1976, pp. 799–820).

O'Brien, Thomas J. and Bennie H. Nunnally, Jr. "A 1982 Survey of Corporate Leasing Analysis," *Financial Management*, Vol. 12 (Summer 1983, pp. 30–36).

Ofer, Aharon R. "The Evaluation of the Lease versus Purchase Alternatives," *Financial Management*, Vol. 5 (Summer 1976, pp. 67–74).

Roenfeldt, Rodney L. and Jerome S. Osteryoung. "Analysis of Financial Leases," *Financial Management*, Vol. 2 (Spring 1973, pp. 74–87).

Schall, Lawrence D. "The Lease-or-Buy and Asset Acquisition Decisions," *Journal of Finance*, Vol. 24 (September 1974, pp. 1203–14).

Sorensen, Ivar W. and Johnson, Ramon E. "Equipment Financial Leasing Practices and Costs: An Empirical Study," *Financial Management*, Vol. 6 (Spring 1977, pp. 33–40).

Vancil, Richard F. "Lease or Borrow: New Method of Analysis," *Harvard Business Review*, Vol. 39 (September–October 1961, pp. 122–36).

19

*Of late, financial instruments have proliferated. Although many have relatively unimportant antecedents in securities and other markets, two broad groups are of interest to students of finance—***options*** and ***futures***. *Each has been around for a number of years in one form or another, but not until the 1970s was there a satisfactory analytical framework to discuss options. Once that framework was developed, some rather traditional financial arrangements could be viewed, or at least better understood, in the context of an options model.*

*On the other hand, futures contracts have been analyzed in their traditional setting for some time. Notwithstanding, ***financial futures*** *are a relatively recent phenomenon. Although futures were confined largely to such commodities as agricultural goods and raw materials, their extension to the world of finance makes them a proper subject for this text.*

*New concepts continue to unfold: among the latest is the ***interest-rate swap***. *It differs from either an options or a futures contract because it is not traded on an open market. Rather, the swap is an agreement between two firms to exchange interest payments on loans, effectively altering the term structure of their debt obligations.*

A detailed analysis of why these instruments have proliferated would take us beyond the scope of the text. Suffice it to say that part of the explanation lies in the desire to hedge or shift risk—at a price, of course—from those not willing to bear it to those who are. Although this is an incomplete explanation of their rise to prominence, options, futures, and interest-rate swaps can be and undoubtedly are used for this purpose. In that sense, then, they have a common objective.

As we shall see, however, the options model has a broader range—a more general applicability—whereas interest-rate swaps may be substitutes for financial futures. Consequently, we shall treat the former in this chapter and the latter in the next.

WHAT IS AN OPTION?

In financial parlance, an option gives one the right to buy or sell an asset at a specific price, often during or at the end of a particular time period. A lease contract that allows one to purchase the asset at a specified price when the lease expires is an example of a **call option**. A corporation that issues a debt security that allows the buyer to sell the instrument back to that corporation at a specific price has sold not only a security but also a **put option** on that security. In either case, there are four significant aspects of the option. The first is the exercise price: the price at which the asset can be bought or sold. The second is the time period within which the option may be exercised. The third is the underlying market price of the instrument on which the option will be exercised. The fourth is the right of the buyer not to exer-

SOURCE: Reprinted by permission of Tribune Media Services

cise the option. If the buyer does exercise the option, however, the **writer** (maker) must sell (writer of a call option) or buy (writer of a put option). In other words, if the buyer chooses to exercise the option, the writer must honor his or her obligation. For the privilege of exercising the option, the buyer explicitly or implicitly pays the writer a fee.

Given the foregoing information, what determines the value and hence the market price of the option?

VALUE OF AN OPTION—CONCEPTUAL FRAMEWORK

Albert Einstein, whose work revolutionized physics, observed that everything should be made as simple as possible but not simpler. Bearing this admonition in mind, suppose a shareholder of ABC Corporation expected the market price of ABC stock either to rise from its current level of $40 to $50 at the end of six months or to fall to $32. The probability the stock will rise to $50 is .75; the probability it will fall to $32 is .25. No dividends will be paid in the interim and other investors have the same expectations, so that

$$\$50 = uV_s = 1.25(\$40)$$

.75

$$V_s = \$40$$

.25

$$u = (1 + \$10/\$40) = 1.25$$
$$d = (1 - \$8/\$40) = .80$$

$$\$32 = dV_s = .80(\$40)$$

In the jargon of option theory, u equals $1 +$ holding-period return (assuming no dividends) and d equals $1 -$ holding-period return. The letters u and d are mnemonic abbreviations for up and down. At the end of the period, the expected value from holding the stock is

$$\text{expected value} = .75(\$50) + .25(\$32)$$
$$= \$37.50 + \$8$$
$$= \$45.50$$

The holding-period return on the expected value of this investment is

$$HPR = \frac{\$45.50 - \$40}{40} = .1375 = 13.75\%$$

If a six-month call option were available on the stock at an exercise price equal to the current market price of $40, at the end of the period the option would have a value of $10 if the price of the stock rose ($50 − $40 = $10). If, on the other hand, the market price of the stock declined to $32, the value of the option would be $-$8$ ($32 - $40 = -$8$). Because no one (at least no rational individual) would exercise an option at a negative value, one can say that the value of the option is zero when the price at which it can be exercised is greater than the stock's market value at the end of the option period. More formally and if we ignore all transaction costs, the option values at the expiration date are[1]

$$\text{stock rises to } \$50, \max (\$50 - \$40, 0) = \$10$$
$$\text{stock falls to } \$32, \max (\$32 - \$40, 0) = 0$$

The expected value of the option at the expiration date is $.75(\$10) + .25(0) = \$7.50$.

Now suppose our ABC investor wishes to hedge his or her position so that whatever the outcome—the price rises to $50 or falls to $32—the value of his or her wealth remains unchanged. As an owner of the stock, the investor is said to be *long* in ABC. To hedge the investment, he or she will write call options, thus becoming *short* in ABC. Our investor knows that if the stock price rises to $50, the value of the options will be $10 and that he or she will have to buy back the options or allow the stock to be called at the exercise price of $40 per share. On the other hand, if the stock's market price should fall to $32, the option would expire unexercised.

The next logical step involves determining the appropriate number of options one should write relative to the number of shares owned and the value of each in today's market. In short, what is the **hedge ratio**? To determine this ratio, we must consider what happens to the value of the option at the end of the holding period. Given that the option will be either $10 or $0, the difference is $10. Given that the market price of the stock will be either $50 or $32, the difference is $18. The hedge ratio is simply the ratio of these two differences. Thus

$$\text{hedge ratio} = \frac{\$10 - 0}{\$50 - 32} = \frac{5}{9}$$

More formally

$$\text{hedge ratio} = \frac{uV_o - dV_o}{uV_s - dV_s}$$

where uV_o is the value of the option at the end of the period when the stock price is $50 and dV_o is the value of the option when the market price falls to $32.

The numerator of the ratio, in this case 5, suggests that for every 5 shares in which the investor is long he or she should write 9 (the denominator of the ratio) call options. So if the stock's market price should fall to $32, the total value of the 5 shares would be: $32 \times 5 = \$160$. If, however, the stock's market price should

---

[1] Einstein would approve, because what we are doing is analogous to modeling within a frictionless world in physics. The introduction of these costs alters the final value of the option but not the underlying principles.

rise to $50, the options would be convertible into stock at $40 per share and the writer would lose $10 per share: ($50 × 5) − ($10 × 9) = $160.

In either case, the effect of the hedge on wealth is the same: $160. Of course, the writer of the option has no incentive to create the hedge if his or her total wealth is $160 per 5 shares owned and 9 calls written; he or she would be no better off than if the stock had fallen to $32. Moreover, because the expected value per share at the beginning of the option period was $45.50, the expected wealth per 5 shares at the time the hedge is initiated would be $45.50 × 5 = $227.50. As we have seen, the expected holding period return on such an investment is 13.75 percent. Unless the investor can receive sufficient compensation for writing the options, he or she would be better off accepting the rise.

But what is *sufficient*? What price would tempt our investor to write the options? The term *hedge* implies offsetting transactions that reduce risk to zero—in this case, guaranteeing the investor is no worse off if the stock rises to $50 or falls to $32—yet allow the investor to earn something for writing the options. If the investor could receive compensation equal to the risk-free rate, he or she would have an incentive to write the 9 options. Let us see why this is true. Suppose the risk-free rate for six months is 6 percent and the value of the ABC call option at the beginning of the period is V_{OB}.

We know that at the beginning of the holding period the investor has 5 shares of stock valued at $200 (5 shares × $40). We also know that if the investor writes 9 options, he or she could potentially lose money on those options. In addition, we know that the value of the hedge six months from today is $160. Therefore

$$\$200 - 9\,V_{OB} = \frac{\$160}{1 + r_f}$$

$$(\$200 - 9\,V_{OB})(1.06) = \$160$$

$$\$212 - 9.54\,V_{OB} = \$160$$

$$V_{OB} = \frac{\$52}{\$9.54}$$

$$V_{OB} = \$5.451$$

Thus, the ABC investor can write 9 call options per 5 shares owned. If the stock price falls to $32, the options are not exercised and the portfolio's total value is

at T_1, 5 shares × $32	= $160.00
writes at T_0, 9 options × $5.451 =	49.06
total value at T_1	= $209.06

If the stock price rises to $50 per share, the buyer can exercise the option and call the stock. The investor can buy 9 options now worth $10 each, exercise them at $40 per share, and deliver the stock to the option buyer at $40 per share. Alternatively, the investor might buy back the options at $10 each. In either case, the investor must

Table 19-1 Option Model Summary (known outcomes under known probabilities)

1.

$$\$50 = uV_s = 1.25(\$40)$$

with branches $.75$ (up) and $.25$ (down) from $V_s = \$40$

$$\$32 = dV_s = .80(\$40)$$

$$u = \left(1 + \frac{\$10}{\$40}\right) = 1.25$$

$$d = \left(1 - \frac{\$8}{\$40}\right) = .80$$

2. stock rises to $50, max ($50 − $40, 0) = $10 = uV_o
stock falls to $32, max ($32 − $40, 0) = −$8 = dV_o

3. hedge ratio $= \dfrac{uV_o - dV_o}{uV_s - dV_s} = \dfrac{\$10 - \$0}{\$50 - \$32} = \dfrac{\$10}{\$18} = \dfrac{5}{9}$

[buy (long) 5 shares, write (short) 9 options]

4.

stock price end of period	value of long position	value of short position	value of combined hedge
$50	5 × $50 = $250	−9($10) = −$90	$160
$32	5 × $32 = $160	−9($ 0) = $ 0	$160

5. With risk-free rate of .06, value of option V_{OB} is

$$5(\$40) - 9(V_{OB}) = \frac{\$160}{1.06}$$

$$V_{OB} = \$5.451$$

6. With option value of $5.451, hedge is perfect. Thus

Stock Rises to $50		**Stock Falls to $32**	
5 shares × $50	= $250	5 shares × $32	= $160
write 9 options at $5.451	= $ 49.06	write 9 options at $5.451	= $ 49.06
	$299.06		= $209.06
buy 9 options at $10	−$ 90		
	$209.06		

7. Risk-free rate earned on the hedge is

$$\text{gain} = \$209.06 - \$200 = \$\ 9.04$$
$$9 \times \$5.451 \times .06 \quad = \underline{\quad 2.96}$$
$$\$12.00$$

THUS original investment = $40 × 5 shares = $200

$$\frac{\$12.00}{\$200.00} = .06 \times 100 = 6\%$$

$$\text{expected return on unhedged position} = \frac{[.75(\$50) + .25(\$32)] - \$40}{\$40} = .1375 \times 100 = 13.75\%$$

$$\text{expected return for option buyer} = \frac{[.75(\$10) + .25(\$0)] - \$5.451}{\$5.451} = .3759 \times 100 = 37.59\%$$

spend $90. The portfolio value in this instance is

5 shares × $50	= $250.00
writes at T_o, 9 options × $5.451	= 49.06
	$299.06
loss on options at T_1, 9 options × $10	= −90.00
total value at T_1	= $209.06

If our investor can write options at $5.451 each at T_o, he or she has executed the perfect hedge. In either case, the total value of the portfolio is the same. In so doing, our investor forgoes a possible market value of $250 on five shares in exchange for a guarantee against a market value of $160 on 5 shares. From the viewpoint of our investor, current value ($200) is protected and there is an assured gain of $9.06 ($209.06 − $200). Moreover, the funds received for writing the options can be invested at 6 percent, so that $9 \times \$5.451 = 49.059 \times .06 = \$2.94$. Therefore, total gain at expiration of the option is

$ 9.06
2.94
$12.00

and total return is

$$\frac{\$12}{\$200} = 6\%$$

From the foregoing analysis, summarized in the Table 19-1, we see how under the conditions postulated an investor might be willing to hedge his or her investment. As suggested in item seven of Table 19-1, the buyer of the options has the greatest expected return: the buyer assumed greater risk due to a .25 probability that the option value will be zero. Although the investor need not write options nor write them in sufficient numbers to fully hedge the portfolio, the option contract permits doing so. When risk is shifted, the bearer of the risk does so for the higher expected return.

VALUE OF A CALL OPTION—AN INTUITIVE ANALYSIS

The foregoing arithmetic approach hinges on knowledge of outcomes and probabilities of occurrence of such outcomes. We know from our earlier discussion (Chapter 4) of the normal curve that when one tosses n coins, the specific yield of heads or tails is computed by $(p + q)^n$ where p is the probability of heads and

q is the probability of tails. Since $p = q = 1/2$, for two coins

$$(p + q)^2 = p^2 + 2pq + q^2$$

$$= \left(\frac{1}{2}\right)^2 + 2\left(\frac{1}{2}\right)\left(\frac{1}{2}\right) + \left(\frac{1}{2}\right)^2$$

$$= \frac{1}{4} + \frac{1}{2} + \frac{1}{4}$$

The chance of two heads or two tails appearing is 1 in 4 and the chance of one head and one tail appearing is 1 in 2. Using the binomial expansion, we develop additional outcomes as the number of coins tossed increases. As $n \to \infty$, the result is the normal curve.

Although the mathematics are more complex, a similar intuition underlies the value of an option. Continuing with a call option that expires at the end of a given time interval, perhaps a year, we find the price of the underlying instrument (in this case a stock) is available on a transaction-to-transaction basis. Beginning at $40, the price may rise or fall, so that

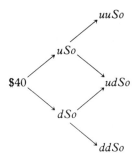

At the end of the first transaction, the stock price either rises to uSo or falls to dSo. If it rises to uSo, after the second transaction, it may rise to $uuSo$ or fall to $udSo$. Alternatively, if the stock price falls to dSo, it may thereafter rise to $udSo$ or fall even farther to $ddSo$. As the number of transactions expands, the possible outcomes increase.[2]

If we think of the stock price as changing continuously, we can generate a continuous stochastic (random) process through time. Does such distribution, however, tend toward normality?

The straightforward answer is no: the probability distribution of stock prices does not tend toward normality. However, because the logarithms of expected prices do approximate normality, formal option models use the logarithms (in the case of continuous functions, natural logarithms) of stock prices.

---

[2] We will not complicate the expansion by considering the possibility that price remains unchanged from one transaction to another.

Unfortunately, there are other complications. First, if the stock price does not exceed the exercise price, the option will not be employed. Consequently, in terms of a normal probability distribution, 50 percent of the outcomes would not be exercised. As in the case of the two-outcome model, when the exercise price is greater than the stock's market price, the option buyer maximizes value at zero: he or she does not exercise the option.

Second, if we consider that a call option is only valuable to the buyer if the stock's market price exceeds the exercise price, it follows that the greater that difference the more valuable the option. In terms of the normal curve, the greater the variance (standard deviation) the greater the potential difference between the exercise price and the stock's market price. Again, the option buyer is interested only in a positive difference, treating a negative difference as zero. Our intuition, therefore, suggests that the greater the variance (standard deviation) in the probability distribution the more valuable the option.

Finally, our intuition suggests that the longer the time period before expiration of the option the greater the chances of a large price change. As discussed in Chapter 5, empirical evidence suggests that stock prices follow a random walk through time; consequently, successive price changes are independent of one another. Suppose one is measuring daily price changes and calculating the variance, σ^2, of those price changes. The longer the time period before the option expires the greater the number of daily price changes. Suppose the stock sells at $40 per share when the contract is made and the price is $50 when the option expires. The price change ($10) is the sum of the daily price changes, all of which are independent random variables. In statistics, the variance of a sum of independent random variables is the sum of the variances of those variables. Thus, if one has a measure of the σ^2 of daily price changes and the option expires in 30 days, the variance of the cumulative price change is 30 σ^2. If the option expires in 60 days, the variance is 60 σ^2. If the option expires in t days, the variance is $t\sigma^2$.

Imagine a stock with a given variance in daily price changes. You are confident that all changes will be random. Although volatility can move the stock up or down from its current level, the greater the variance the greater the chance for a large gain. If the option expires tomorrow, chances of realizing such gain are smaller than if the option expires six months from tomorrow. For the stock purchaser, the value of the option—hence the price the investor is willing to pay—depends both on the amount of variance and the time remaining before the contract expires.

The often repeated Chinese proverb that one picture is worth more than one thousand words is relevant to options. Let us save three thousand words, yet deepen our intuitive understanding of options by examining Figure 19-1 (a, b, and c). All three graphs depict the value of a call option as a function of the stock's market price. E is the exercise price ($40), which we shall continue to assume is the stock's current market price. In the jargon of the trade, the option is "at the

Figure 19-1   Factors to Consider in Determining Call Option Value

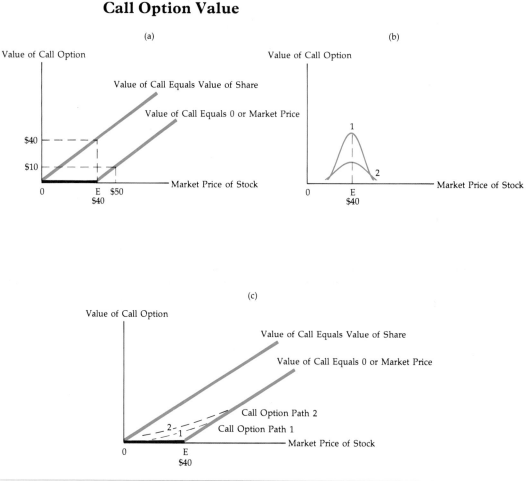

money."[3] The line segment OE, joined at E by the line extending from the x axis, forms the lower boundary of option value. If the current market price of the stock is less than E ($40 in this case), the option is worthless if exercised immediately. No one should exercise a call option at $40 and sell the stock immediately for less than $40, lest they be of greater interest to psychiatrists than to financial economists. If the stock's current market price is $50, a call option to buy a share at $40 is worth $10 if exercised (if the stock is sold immediately). (We later modify the lower boundary.)

_____

[3] When the current market price is less than the exercise price, the option is "out of the money"; when the current market price is greater than the exercise price, the option is "in the money."

The line extending from the origin bisects the x and y axes, and represents the upper boundary of the value of a call option. The line suggests that the current value of the option could never exceed the current market price of the underlying stock. In other words, no one will pay more for the option when the stock itself can be purchased immediately for less.

As one might expect, the value (price) of an option lies between the two extremes. As we suggest, variance and contract length are the major forces that determine option value. Figure 19-1(b) depicts two probability distributions, where probability distribution 2 has greater variance than probability distribution 1. Hence, there is a greater chance the market price will exceed the exercise price ($40). Assuming each has the same maturity date, the call option represented by probability distribution 2 has greater value than the call option represented by probability distribution 1.

Figure 19-1(c) suggests the pattern traced by the value of each call option. As the market price approaches zero, the value of both call options also approaches zero. The higher the stock's market price relative to the exercise price, the closer the value of the option to the difference between the two. However, between those extremes the value of the call option represented by probability distribution 2 is always greater than the value of the call option represented by probability distribution 1. Although it is not shown in Figure 19-1(c), one would expect the dashed lines traced to move closer to the lower boundary (to the abscissa if $E > P$) as the number of days left to exercise the option declines (as t grows smaller).

THE BLACK-SCHOLES OPTION MODEL

Having exhausted what can be accomplished intuitively, we will now examine the basic option model. As is true of the Markowitz contribution to the standard deviation of a portfolio and the Modigliani and Miller Hypothesis on the cost of capital and (ultimately) the firm's value, the first option model was a major intellectual breakthrough that continues to spawn a myriad of applications extending beyond the basic stock option. Although the path-breaking work published in 1973 by Fischer Black and Myron Scholes has since been modified and extended, the basic assumptions underlying their approach are:[4]

1. There is a risk-free rate known and invariant over the life of the option.

2. There are no transaction costs and no taxes.

3. The market functions continuously.

[4] Fischer Black and Myron Scholes. "The Pricing of Options and Corporate Liabilities," *Journal of Political Economy*, Vol. 81 (May–June 1973, pp. 637–59). For further developments, see Menachem Brenner, ed., *Option Pricing Theory and Applications* (Lexington, MA: Heath and Company, 1983). See, also, Robert A. Jarrow and Andrew Rudd, *Option Pricing* (Homewood, IL: Richard D. Irwin, 1983).

4. The stock prices are a lognormal distribution that represents a continuous function of time.[5]

5. The stock pays no cash dividends.

6. The option cannot be exercised until maturity (European option).

7. Short sales of the stock can be transacted without restrictions.

If all of these assumptions hold, the current value of the call option, C, can be determined by the following equation:

$$C = SN(d_1) - Ee^{-rt}N(d_2) \qquad (19\text{-}1)$$

where

S = current market price of the stock
E = exercise price
e = base of the natural logarithms = 2.71828
r = risk-free rate compounded continuously
t = remaining time to expiration of call expressed as fraction of year

$N(d_1)$ and $N(d_2)$ are cumulative normal-probability density functions at specific points—d_1 and d_2—along the curve from which one can measure the area to the left or to the right of the curve. The values for d_1 and d_2, respectively, are given without further proof by the following equations:

$$d_1 = \frac{ln(S/E) + rt}{\sigma\sqrt{t}} + \frac{1}{2}\sigma\sqrt{t} \qquad (19\text{-}2)$$

$$d_2 = d_1 - \sigma\sqrt{t}$$

The letters ln represent the natural logarithm of the ratio of the current stock price to the exercise price. The standard deviation represents the σ of the continuously compounded annual rates of return on the stock.

If we ignore $N(d_1)$ and $N(d_2)$ for a moment, the incomplete expression for the call value is

$$C = S - Ee^{-rt} \qquad (19\text{-}3)$$

When the stock's market price is high relative to the exercise price, $N(d_1)$ approaches $N(d_2)$ and both approach 1. Thus in Figure 19-2, the lower boundary of the call value is determined by Equation 19-3. Although the Black-Scholes model is based on a European option that cannot be exercised until maturity, in Figure 19-1(a) we based the lower boundary on the assumption that the option would be exercised immediately.

---

[5] For a more complete explanation, see Jarrow and Rudd, pp. 89–91.

Figure 19-2   Relationship among Hedge Ratio, Call Value, and Option Maturity Date

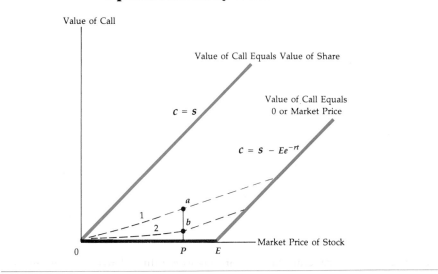

The curves labeled 1 and 2 trace the value of the call option. (The only difference between curve 1 and curve 2 is one expires sooner.) The call value declines as the option approaches maturity, holding other variables constant. Note that at one extreme—at zero or at the lower boundary—curve 1 approaches curve 2.

$N(d_1)$ is the hedge ratio for the current market price of the stock at P, and is depicted in Figure 19-2 as the slope of curve 1 at **a** or curve 2 at **b**. More formally, the hedge ratio is the change in the call value per unit change in the stock price when all other variables hold constant. It is a partial derivative, so that

$$\frac{\partial C}{\partial S} = N(d_1)$$

APPLYING THE BLACK-SCHOLES MODEL

To calculate the theoretical value of a call option, five values must be known. Three of them—current market price of the stock, exercise price, and time until maturity—are known. The continuously compounded risk-free rate can be estimated from prevailing yields on Treasury securities for the option period. However, the standard deviation of the continuously compounded annual rates of return on the stock can be estimated only from the past record of holding period returns. Consequently, variability in past data may not be the same for the future.

We shall, however, assume that it is. Accordingly

$$S = \$45$$
$$E = \$40$$
$$t = .25 \text{ years (three months)}$$
$$r = .11 \text{ compounded continuously}$$
$$\sigma = .54$$

$$d_1 = \frac{ln\left(\dfrac{\$45}{\$40}\right) + (.11)(.25)}{.54\sqrt{.25}} + \frac{.54\sqrt{.25}}{2}$$

$$= \frac{.117783 + .0275}{.27} + \frac{.27}{2}$$

$$= .538085 + .135$$

$$= .673085$$

$$d_2 = .673085 - .54\sqrt{.25}$$

$$= .403085$$

Once d_1 and d_2 are calculated, we can employ the area under the normal curve as we did in Chapter 9, Table 9-2, where we used the formula

$$\frac{x - E(x)}{\sigma}$$

to measure distance along the abscissa in units of standard deviation.[6] Appendix D contains more complete formulations of $\dfrac{x - E(x)}{\sigma}$, which equals d_1 in the Black-Scholes model. The body of Appendix D is accurate to the nearest .01. Hence, $d_1 = .673085$ lies between .67 and .68. Thus

	Area Under Normal Curve
$d_1 = .67$	.2514
$d_1 = .68$	.2483
difference	.0031

Interpolating, we have

$$.2514 - \left(\frac{.673085 - .67}{.01}\right)(.0031) = .250444$$

---

[6] In case you have forgotten your algebra: provided that n is a real number, the natural log (ln) of any expression e^n is n or the exponent of 2.71828. In the foregoing example, $ln\left(\dfrac{P}{E}\right) = ln\left(\dfrac{45}{40}\right) = ln\, 1.125$. In this case, $2.71828^{.117783} = 1.125$.

Although some calculators are programmed to compute natural logarithms, tables are available. In any event, we provide the value of the natural logarithm for $\dfrac{P}{E}$ in the problems.

which represents the portion of the area under the curve that is .250444 greater than the mean. Because the sum of the two areas is one, $N(d_1) = 1 - .250444 = .749556$.
   Similarly, d_2 of .403085 lies between .40 and .41, so that

	Area Under Normal Curve
$d_2 = .40$	.3446
$d_2 = .41$	.3409
difference	.0037

Interpolating, we obtain

$$.3446 - \left(\frac{.403085 - .40}{.01}\right)(.0037) = .343459$$

Therefore, $N(d_2) = 1 - .343459 = .656541$.
   Under the Black-Scholes model, the option value becomes

$$V_o = \$45(.749556) - \$40e^{-(.11)(.25)}(.656541)$$
$$= \$33.73002 - \$25.549285$$
$$= \$8.180735 \approx \$8.18$$

The hedge ratio (.749556) suggests that an investor should own or buy .749556 shares of stock for each option written, or approximately 3 shares for every 4 options.
   Suppose the market price is below the exercise price, perhaps \$35, and all other variables affecting d_1 remain the same. Because the stock's market price is less than the exercise price, the ratio is less than one. The natural logarithm of a number less than 1 is negative. Thus

$$ln\left(\frac{35}{40}\right) = ln(.875) = -.133531$$

Consequently

$$d_1 = \frac{-.133531 + (.11)(.25)}{.54\sqrt{.25}} + \frac{.54\sqrt{.25}}{2}$$
$$d_1 = -.257707$$
$$d_2 = -.257707 - (.27)$$
$$d_2 = -.527707$$

In terms of the normal deviation

$$d = \frac{x - E(x)}{\sigma} = -.257707 \text{ or } -.527707$$

Accordingly, the expected value, $E(x)$, of $x - E(x)$ is greater than x. The exercise price exceeds the market price and in this case is not offset by $\sqrt{t}$ and $\sigma\sqrt{t}$. Therefore, when one calculates d_1 and uses the table for the normal curve, the area found (left of d_1) is $N(d_1)$. The area is not subtracted from 1. The same is true for d_2.

Area Under Normal Curve		Area Under Normal Curve	
$d_1 = .25$	.4013	$d_2 = .52$	.3015
$d_1 = .26$	.3974	$d_2 = .53$	.2981
difference	(.0039)	difference	(.0034)

Interpolation	Interpolation
$d_1 = .4013 - \dfrac{(.257707 - .25)}{.01}(.0039)$	$d_2 = .3015 - \dfrac{(.527707 - .52)}{.01}(.0034)$
$= .398294$	$= .298880$
$N(d_1) = .398294$	$N(d_2) = .298880$

$$V_o = \$35(.398294) - \$40e^{-(.11)(.25)}(.298880)$$
$$= \$13.940290 - \$11.630912$$
$$= \$2.309378 \approx \$2.31$$

Even though the stock price is \$5 below the exercise price, the option time remaining and the risk-free rate combine algebraically with $\sigma\sqrt{t}$ to give the option a positive value. The hedge ratio (.398294) indicates that for every .4 shares owned, 1 option should be written to earn a risk-free rate of return on the portfolio of stock and options.

Finally, we examine an option in which the stock's current market price equals the exercise price (\$40), whereas the other variables remain unchanged. In this case

$$ln\left(\frac{\$40}{\$40}\right) = ln(1) = 0$$

As a result

$$d_1 = \frac{0 + .0275}{.27} + .135$$
$$d_1 = .236852$$
$$d_2 = .236852 - .27$$
$$d_2 = -.033148$$

Therefore

Area Under Normal Curve		Area Under Normal Curve	
$d_1 = .23$	.4090	$d_2 = .03$	.4880
$d_2 = .24$	.4052	$d_2 = .04$	.4840
	.0042		.0040

Interpolation	*Interpolation*
$d_1 = .4090 - \dfrac{(.263852 - .23)}{.01}(.0042)$	$d_2 = .4880 - \dfrac{(.033148 - .03)}{.01}(.0040)$
$= .406122$	$= .486741$
$N(d_1) = 1 - .406122 = .593878$	Because d_2 is negative, $(d_2) = .486741$

$$V_o = \$40(.593878) - \$40e^{-(.11)(.25)}(.486741)$$
$$= \$23.755120 - \$18.941520$$
$$= \$4.813600 \gtrapprox \$4.81$$

hedge ratio $= .593878 =$ approximately .6 shares owned per 1 option written

The results of the preceding calculations are summarized in Figure 19-3. Again, d_1 and d_2 locate points on the abscissa; $N(d_1)$ and $N(d_2)$ are areas left of d_1 and d_2, respectively. The hedge ratio, $N(d_1)$, is the slope at that point on the Black-Scholes option path between market price and value of call. And, of course, $N(d_2)$ is always smaller than $N(d_1)$. Remember: to calculate $N(d_2)$, subtract $\sigma\sqrt{t}$ from $N(d_1)$. Accordingly, the option value is larger than if E is multiplied by $N(d_1)$: $EN(d_1) > EN(d_2)$. Intuitively, we recognize in the subtraction of a smaller number that greater variability and an extended option enhance the option value.

CRITICISMS OF THE BLACK-SCHOLES MODEL

Although a major intellectual breakthrough in understanding option value, the Black-Scholes model must be viewed as a conceptual framework and must be modified in practice. First, the calculus of the hedge ratio justifying the risk-free rate on the combined portfolio implies that the position will be altered continuously because of changes in underlying variables. Real-world transaction costs involved in altering the portfolio daily, if not continuously, would be prohibitive. Transaction costs, of course, are assumed away in the model.[7]

Second, the distribution of stock prices often exhibits discontinuities (jumps). A continuous function, even as an approximation, may be inaccurate.[8] Third, the model does not allow for dividends or taxes. Fourth, the European option differs from the American option: the latter can be exercised anytime before the expiration

---

[7] *A Bonus Footnote!* On the basis of the foregoing information, *never* believe a broker who tells you he or she can design a perfectly hedged portfolio that is risk-free. Even if you do not alter the portfolio daily, the hedge ratio will rise or fall sufficiently to induce you to make changes that will enrich the broker as your account is churned—but not you. Although options can be used to hedge portfolios, they should be used to offset shifts or jumps in the market, not used in the way envisioned by the model.

[8] This difficulty can be overcome in part. See John Cox and Steven Ross, "The Valuation of Options for Alternative Stochastic Processes," *Journal of Financial Economics*, Vol. 3 (January–March, 1976, pp. 145–66).

Figure 19-3   Option Price under Three Value Ratios of Market Price to Exercise Price

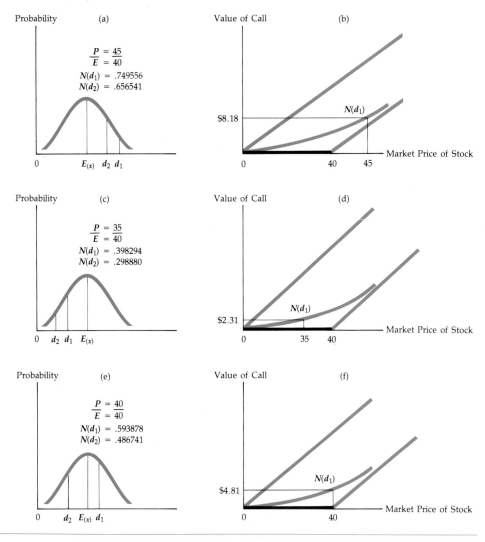

date. Although none of these problems is insurmountable, they weaken the model as an applied tool.

One problem, however, is difficult to overcome: Using past measures of variability as representative of future variability can yield a value for a call option not indicative of the future. When the value is compared with the market price of the option and the two differ, is the model wrong or has the variance changed—past data being no longer relevant? Alternatively, even though past data may be indicative of the future, the options market may be inefficient. Finally, the options market may be efficient and the variance may be correct but the model is an incorrect explanation of how options are priced.[9]

Consequently, empirical tests of the Black-Scholes model are difficult to conduct. Those that have been conducted suggest the model performs relatively well for options near the exercise price: *at-the-money*-options. However, the model is not as useful for stocks whose current market price is much greater or much less than their exercise price. At the same time, variations on or alternative approaches to the Black-Scholes model do not yet offer better predictions than the original model. Where opportunities for profits over and above the risk-free rate appear to exist, transaction costs may well reduce or eliminate them.[10]

THE VALUE OF A PUT

Although most of its emphasis and application relates to the call option, the Black-Scholes model can also be applied to the put option (graphically illustrated in Figure 19-4). Because the put buyer can sell the stock to the put writer at the exercise price, the lower the market price the higher the put option value. If the exercise price is $40 and the market price is $20, the buyer can purchase the stock at $20 and sell it to the writer at $40.

As the opposite of a call, conceptually we expect the put value to move up as the stock's market price goes down and to move down as the stock's market price goes up—indeed, this is what happens. Once call value is determined, the first step in calculating put value is to subtract the stock's market price from the call value. However, when calculating put value, we must add present value of exercise price (that is what the buyer receives when exercised at maturity). Hence, put value is calculated by the equation

$$\text{put value} = C - S + Ex/e^{rt} \tag{19-4}$$

Given the value of each call summarized in Figure 19-3, we obtain

1. put value = $8.18 − $45 + $38.91 = $2.09

2. put value = $2.31 − $35 + $38.91 = $6.22

3. put value = $4.81 − $40 + $38.91 = $3.72

---

[9] See, Robert C. Merton, "Rational Theory of Option Pricing," *Bell Journal of Economics*, Vol. 4; (Spring 1973, pp. 142–145); Eduardo S. Schwartz, "The Valuation of Warrants: Implementing a New Approach," *Journal of Financial Economics*, Vol. 4 (January 1977, pp. 79–93).

[10] For an excellent summary of the empirical evidence, see Dan Galai, "A Survey of Empirical Tests of Option-Pricing Models," in Brenner, pp. 45–80.

Figure 19-4   A Graphic Illustration of the Put Option

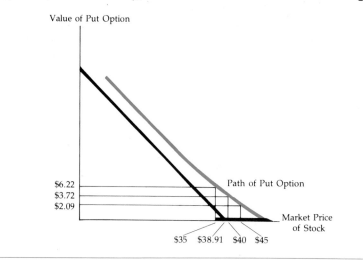

Value of Put Option

$6.22

$3.72

$2.09

Path of Put Option

Market Price
of Stock

$35 $38.91 $40 $45

Note that put value is smaller than call value for a corresponding differential between market price and exercise price. For example, when market price equals call price, put value is $3.72 and call value is $4.81. When market price exceeds exercise price by $5, call value is $8.18; when market price is less than exercise price by $5, put value is $6.22. Only when each option is *out-of-the-money*—market price is less than exercise price in the case of a call or above exercise price in the case of a put—does the value of each approximate one another (the call is $2.31 at a market price of $35 and the put is $2.09 at a market price of $45). If other variables in the model are unchanged, put buyers have a lower limit, the market price of zero, from which to calculate a gain; the upper limit on the stock's market price is infinity. Hence, an *in-the-money* call option has a potentially higher value than an *in-the-money* put option. In each case, *out-of-the-money* options have the same value at maturity—zero.

SUMMARY (OPTION PRICING)

To this point, we have developed the concept of an option in terms of the known probabilities of two possible outcomes and in terms of the Black-Scholes model. Neither is realistic, but then no model is. The Black-Scholes model establishes the hedge ratio given the risk-free rate, the option length, the exercise price, the stock's current market price, and the σ of the continuously compounded annual rate of return on the stock. However, one cannot easily hedge a portfolio of securities by changing the ratio of shares owned to calls written on a continuous or even daily basis without incurring prohibitive transaction costs.

It is still possible to look for undervalued or overvalued puts and calls, taking a position accordingly. For example, if the market price of a call is $3.45 and the Black-Scholes model indicates the price should be $4.50, an investor would buy calls on the stock in anticipation they will rise in value. Similarly, if the Black-Scholes model suggests a put currently selling at $3.24 should be selling at $2.28, one could sell (write) puts on the assumption the put's market value will decline. By using either strategy, however, the investor is no longer hedging: he or she is assuming that the Black-Scholes model adequately reflects what the option value should be and that the market is inefficient. Although this may be true, one cannot assume that it is. Since variance is based on past data, the model makes no allowances for dividends and assumes the option is held to maturity. When stocks go **ex-dividend**, the market price falls by the dividend amount, which in turn affects the value of an option held to maturity.[11]

EXTENDING THE SCOPE OF OPTIONS

Although the Black-Scholes model has been used primarily to value puts and calls and to determine the hedge ratio with specific reference to outstanding shares of common stock, there is no reason why the concept cannot be extended to other securities. In some instances, the analogy is nearly perfect; in others, severe modifications must be made. Nevertheless, the conceptual framework in which options are discussed is useful, for it offers insight into particular financial arrangements, a few of which we now examine more closely.

THE WARRANT

The **warrant** is a straightforward application of the conventional Black-Scholes model with variations. A warrant represents the right to buy shares of stock at a specified price: in short, it is call option. Although the warrant appears similar to rights issued stockholders in a privileged subscription, such stockholder rights are offered to existing stockholders at a price below the stock's current market price and are therefore expected to be sold (exercised) immediately. Even though the rights' period is short, often only a few weeks, privileged subscription rights can be treated in the Black-Scholes context and we do so later in the chapter. Warrants, on the other hand, may be outstanding for several years.

---

[11] To allow for this, one can (as a rough approximation) subtract from the stock price the present value of dividend payments for the life of the stock (as though it were held to maturity) before calculating the present value of the option. Unfortunately, in the case of a put at very low market values, there is little additional gain from holding the put to maturity. The option should be exercised and the money invested elsewhere. See Robert C. Merton, "Theory of the Rational Option Pricing," *Bell Journal of Economics and Management Science*, Vol. 4 (Spring 1973, pp. 156–60).

Warrants are usually issued with debt securities as *sweetners*. The issuer pays a slightly lower interest rate on the debentures but gives the debenture holders the option to buy new shares of stock at a specified price, a price above the stock's current market price. For example, in 1984, International Harvester issued warrants to purchase common stock at $5 per share. The warrants were due to expire December 15, 1993, but could be extended at the option of the company until December 15, 1999. Another series of warrants was issued in 1985, due to expire December 31, 1990, with which the stock could be purchased at $9 per share. The warrants were issued in connection with a debenture offering in the first instance and with a note offering in the second. At the time, International Harvester was reporting losses. The warrants (sweetners) were issued to help market the debt issues.[12]

The theoretical value of a warrant can be given by the equation

$$NS - E = \text{warrant value} \tag{19-5}$$

where

N = number of shares that can be purchased with one warrant

E = option price associated with purchase of N shares

S = market price of the stock

If $N = 1$ (which is often the case) and $E = S$, the theoretical value is zero. However, as we know, options have positive value when their theoretical value is zero or negative. For example, in 1985, the Golden Nugget Casino had warrants outstanding, each warrant entitling the holder to purchase one share of stock at $18. The warrants expired July 1, 1988.[13] As of November 22, 1985 — when the time remaining to maturity was approximately $2\frac{2}{3}$ years[14] — the market price of the stock (which paid no dividends) closed at $11.25; the warrant closed at $2.25.[15] The theoretical value was $-\$6.75$ ($11.25 − $18). In light of our discussion on the Black-Scholes model and considering the long maturity ahead of it, a positive value would be justified.[16]

---

[12] *1985 Moody's Industrial Manual*, Vol. I, p. 2902.

[13] *1985 Moody's Industrial Manual*, p. 2902. There were other warrants outstanding, some of which entitled the holder to purchase more than one share of stock with each warrant. At the time, however, the warrants under discussion represented 13,500,000 of the 14,282,875 shares that could be purchased by exercising the warrants.

[14] November 23, 1985 (the next day) to July 1, 1986, totaled 220 days, or .655 years. (The period includes February 29, 1988.) Allowing for leap year and including November 23, 1985, the option had 951 days remaining and would mature in $951/365 = 2.605$ years.

[15] *Wall Street Journal*, November 22, 1985, p. 62.

[16] But is it $2.25? Because in this instance one does not have (or expect to have) a dividend-paying stock, no allowance need be made for one. The key variables in the model are the risk-free rate and the σ of the annual rate of return compounded continuously. At the time, a 9.5-percent risk-free rate would have reasonably approximated reality. Using the Black-Scholes model and the more precise measure for t calculated in footnote [14], then

$$\$2.25 = 11.25 \, N(d_1) - \frac{\$18}{e^{(.095)(2.605)}} \, N(d_2)$$
$$\$2.25 = 11.25 \, N(d_1) - 14.05 \, N(d_2)$$

CONVERTIBLE SECURITIES

Although there were warrants before the Black-Scholes model, not until after the Black-Scholes model could warrant value be approximated and compared with the going market price. And although there also were **convertibles** before the Black Scholes model, convertibles—even though they can be viewed as call options—are not as easily understood in terms of the model.

A peculiar security, the convertible starts out as one type of instrument—usually a low form of debt, often a debenture, and in many cases a subordinated debenture—and ends its days, generally, as common stock. (Preferred stock is also sometimes convertible to common stock.)

The conventional wisdom has been that management issued convertibles because it believed the stock's market price was below its present intrinsic value. A convertible is a delayed issue of common stock, and the conversion price is set above the common stock's current market price or closer to its intrinsic value. When the stock's market price eventually rose to or above the conversion price, management—which also had set a call price on the securities below its conversion price—would call in the issue. Instead of accepting the lower call price, investors would exchange convertibles for common stock at the conversion price.

Another strand of conventional wisdom has been that certain institutional investors, such as life insurance companies, were limited in the amount of stock they could hold. A debenture convertible to common stock would rise in price as the underlying stock rose in price. Although this would give the issue the flavor of common stock, as long as the underlying debt instrument was investment grade it would meet legal requirements for constrained portfolios.

The expressions for d_1 and d_2 can be rewritten so that

$$d_1 = \frac{\ln S/E + (r + .5\sigma^2)t}{\sigma\sqrt{t}} \quad \text{and} \quad d_2 = \frac{\ln S/E + (r - .5\sigma^2)t}{\sigma\sqrt{t}}$$

Therefore

$$d_{1,2} = \frac{\ln S/E + (r + .5\sigma^2)t}{\sigma\sqrt{t}} = \frac{-.470004 \pm (.095 \pm .5\sigma^2)2.605}{\sigma\sqrt{2.605}} = \frac{-.22529 \pm 1.3025\sigma^2}{1.614\sigma}$$

One can use simultaneous equations to determine values of d_1 and d_2 that result in $2.25. For $\sigma = .439$, we calculate

$$d_1 = .040 \quad \text{and} \quad d_2 = -.668$$

The area under the normal curve for $d_1 = .4840$ and for $d_2 = .2521$. Hence

$$N(d_1) = 1 - .4840 = .5160; N(d_2) = .2521$$
$$\$11.25(.5160) - \$14.05(.2521) = \$2.26 \gtrless \$2.25$$

Of course, whether the value of σ is correct depends on how accurate the Black-Scholes model is. An analyst may want to compare σ as calculated with σ calculated on historical data. If there is a difference, is the market anticipating a change in the σ of holding-period returns? If so, what are the reasons?

Either reason may be true. The former, however, suggests that markets are inefficient or perhaps that convertibles are similar to dividend increases in that they carry information about the stock's underlying value. Although the latter reason suggests that institutional constraints may invite the use of a convertible, a high-grade debt instrument with warrants would serve the same function. Of course, once the warrants expired or were exercised, the debt remained; a successful conversion eliminates such debt.

A variation on the latter reason is the view that a large number of investors appear to demand an instrument with a fixed return that can rise in value if the underlying stock also increases in value. Because convertibles need not be and often are not the highest-grade fixed-income investment, their purchase involves certain sacrifices: for example, the interest rate is lower than for comparable nonconvertible securities. The same is true of warrants. Nothing is given away.

In Table 19-2 we present details of the 25-year convertible debenture of Allegheny Beverage Corporation. At the time of issue (September 1, 1985), the company marketed senior subordinated debentures at par with a coupon rate and hence a yield to maturity of 9.5 percent. The debenture issue could be converted to common stock at any time. **Conversion price** was set at $21.50 per $1,000 of face value. However, one had to convert the entire $1,000 debenture in order to receive

Table 19-2   Allegheny Beverage Corporation Convertible Debentures[a]

Type	Amount	Offering Price	Date Issued	Maturity Date	Coupon	YTM	Corporate YTM[b]
Sr. sub. debentures	$100 million	Par = $100	9-1-85	9-1-2010	9.5%	9.5%	11.64%

Moody's Rating	Call price	Conversion Price	Conversion Ratio	Market Price of Common on Date of Issue[d]
B$_2$	$106.50[c]	$21.50	46.51 shares per $1,000 debenture	$18 per share

[a] Offered August 29, 1985, through Smith, Barney, Harris Upham & Co.
[b] Average YTM of corporate bonds on August 30, 1985. YTM of Baa-rated corporate bonds was 12.4 percent (B$_2$ rating below Baa).
[c] Debentures could not be redeemed until September 1, 1988. Call price falls from that date until September 1, 1995, when it reaches $100. Annual mandatory sinking fund payments begin September 1, 1995, and are designed to retire 70 percent of issue by 2010.
[d] Allegheny was paying an annual dividend of 40 cents per share at the time of issue.

SOURCE: *Moody's Bond Survey* (September 9, 1985, pp. 2801 and 2828).

the stock. The **conversion ratio** was

$$\frac{\$1,000}{\$21.50} = 46.511628 \quad (46.51 \text{ shares of common per debenture})$$

When issued, Allegheny stock was trading at approximately $18 per share. Hence, the total conversion value of the debenture was $46.51 \times $18 = $837.18.

Obviously, no one would convert the debenture at that price. In the meantime, the investor would receive 9.5 percent (paid semiannually) per $1,000 of debenture. The opportunity cost—which is the option price—is a lower interest rate than would otherwise be earned if the debenture had not been convertible. How much lower? A crude comparison can be made with the YTM on nonconvertible debt instruments. At the time of issue, the YTM on corporate issues average 11.64 percent, with Baa issues averaging 12.4 percent. The B_2 rating on this debenture issue ranked it below Baa. It would have carried a higher yield to maturity, perhaps substantially higher, if its rating had precluded some institutional investors from purchasing the debenture.

On the other hand, risk-free U.S. Treasury securities of comparable maturity were trading at yield to maturity in excess of 10.5 percent. Suppose interest payments were risk-free and 10.5 percent was a representative risk-free rate at the time of issue. Accordingly, present value and hence market value of a risk-free security, assuming it remains outstanding until maturity, is

$$p.v. = \frac{\$95\left[1 - \left(1 + \dfrac{.105}{2}\right)^{-50}\right]}{.105} + \frac{\$1,000}{\left(1 + \dfrac{.105}{2}\right)^{50}}$$

$$= \$834.71 + \$77.43$$
$$= \$912.14 \approx \$912$$

If we assume the YTM of a B_2 subordinated debenture on the issue date is 13 percent—greater than 12.4 percent for Baa corporate debt—then

$$p.v. = \frac{\$95\left[1 - \left(1 + \dfrac{.13}{2}\right)^{-50}\right]}{.13} + \frac{\$1,000}{\left(1 + \dfrac{.13}{2}\right)^{50}}$$

$$= \$699.41 + \$42.91$$
$$= \$742.32 \approx \$742$$

We can now graphically portray the nature of the convertible option. In Figure 19-5, we show convertible value as a function of corporate (firm) value. On the issue date, a risk-free U.S. government security of comparable maturity with a comparable coupon rate has a market value of approximately $912. We crudely

Figure 19-5   Convertible Option—Convertible Debentures of Allegheny Beverage Corporation

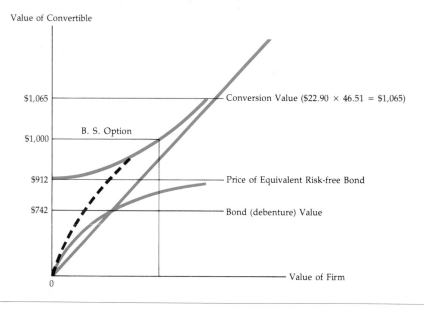

estimate bond value of the convertible debenture to be $742. Bond value rises as firm value rises (holding constant the maturity dates and the term structures of interest rates). As firm value rises, the debenture is also reevaluated and given a higher rating. In turn, comparable issues sell at lower yields to maturity. And given its coupon, market price of the debenture rises. However, debenture value falls if the firm's market value falls.

Because the issue is convertible to common stock, conversion value and offering price are known. The debenture is marketed at a premium over its conversion value and at an even greater premium over its investment value. (We can now understand why a convertible is a long-term but nevertheless complicated call option.) Using the graph of the Black-Scholes model, we expect debenture value to approximate conversion value as the stock's market price and hence the firm's value rises. Assuming the debenture remains outstanding for 25 years, the convertible is a very long call option. In this instance, beginning in 1995 (ten years after issuing the debenture) the company can retire some of the issue at a call premium of $106.50: $1,065 per $1,000 face value of debenture.

More important, if the stock's market price reaches $22.90, the bond's market price will approximate the call price of $1,065 ($22.90 × 46.51). If the stock's market price continued to rise, would the bond's price also rise? At $30 per share, the debenture would sell for approximately $1,395.30 (30 × 46.51).

The debenture would not sell substantially above the foregoing amount because the issuer could redeem it at the call price of $1,065. Hence, its value lies in the stock to which it can be converted. At a market price above $22.90, there is little to be gained because management could cancel the option by forcing conversion at any time.[17]

The downside risk of a convertible option differs considerably from the downside risk of a stock option. In the case of a convertible, the outlay is made and the option value approaches zero. Although this may ultimately happen to a convertible, the road to extinction does not follow the Black-Scholes path. If the stock's market price declines, so does the firm's value. If the value of the firm declines, the risk of default on debentures rises. If the risk of default on debentures rises, their market value as debt instruments declines. As chances of the market price rising to the conversion price become increasingly remote , option value falls toward zero (as suggested by the dotted line in Figure 19-5)[18]. However, debenture value begins to decline as it approaches the underlying bond (debenture) value. In a worst-case scenario—the firm is in default and the assets are insufficient to meet prior claims (a distinct possibility in the case of subordinated debentures)—debenture value will ultimately converge on zero.

Although details differ, a convertible preferred functions the same as a debenture: preferred shares are convertible to common shares. As noted in footnote 7 to Chapter 3 (which, of course, you read), prior to its breakup, AT&T had a $4 convertible preferred stock outstanding and carried on the books at a stated value of $50 per share. On August 29, 1982, this stock had an investment value of $36.90. The basis for this calculation was the yield on other AT&T preferreds, each rated "Aaa" and each yielding 10.84 at the time. Using this rate, we estimated market value at

$$\frac{\$4}{.1084} = \$36.90$$

However, market price of the stock was $58.75 at the time. We can now understand the reason for the discrepancy: preferred was convertible to common at a ratio of $50 of stated value to $47.50; that is

$$\frac{\$50}{\$47.50} = 1.052632 \quad (1.05 \text{ shares of common per share of preferred})$$

On that date, market price of the common stock was $55.25 per share. Thus, $55.25 \times 1.05 = \$58.01 < \$58.75$.

---

[17] One complication we ignore is the difference in income streams. Assuming that dividends of 40 cents per share at the time of issue remain unchanged, the investor who converts and holds the stock realizes only $18.604 (46.51 × .40) compared with $95 on the debenture. However, he or she also has an unrealized capital gain.

[18] As drawn, the Black-Scholes model appears to converge on the market price of the risk-free Treasury security. The option value is, of course, zero when the firm value is zero.

The preferred was selling very close to its conversion value; the option was *in the money* and could be called at $50 per share at any time. Hence, one would expect market price of the preferred to be close to its conversion value. Although it could not be estimated with certainty, AT&T's impending breakup in 1984 signaled that the issue would be called and converted. Indeed, the entire issue was called for redemption after September 30, 1983.[19]

THE STANDBY AGREEMENT AS A PUT OPTION

As we noted in Chapter 17, investment bankers are sometimes hired on a standby basis to purchase stock issued by a company to its existing stockholders. The standby arrangement guarantees that investment bankers will purchase the unsubscribed stock at the offering or exercise price, traditionally a price substantially below the stock's current market price. A company whose stock is selling at $50 per share may offer stockholders 5-for-1 rights at $40 per share: 1 right for each share owned but 5 rights to purchase a new share at $40. As a result, total shares increase by 20 percent. Assuming nothing else affects the stock's market price during the 30-day subscription period, for every 5 shares at $50 there is now an additional (sixth) share that brings in $40. Consequently, market price per share is now

$$\frac{\$50 \times 5 + \$40 \times 1}{5 + 1} = \$48.33$$

Although other factors could adversely affect market price of the shares, given the short exercise period the chances are small. The existing stockholders have an *in-the-money* call at the time of the offer and the company pays a fee to the investment bankers, who in turn write an *out-of-the money* (virtually risk-free) put. The put is purchased by the company in anticipation that a small number of shareholders will fail to exercise their rights (fail to sell them) for random and certainly not rational reasons.

Even though the company (understandably) wants to raise all the money it seeks, it may be less costly to set the subscription price closer to the market price. Suppose, for example, the company chose to offer the stock at $45 per share. When the rights expire, other factors being the same, the price falls to

$$\frac{\$50 \times 5 + \$45 \times 1}{5 + 1} = \$49.17$$

Suppose a 30-day put option on the stock at $45 is currently selling for $0.375 (3/8). Although the dilution will raise the option value, by how much is

---

[19] *Moody's 1983 Public Utility Manual*, Vol. I, p. 148.

moot since call value and hence put value are altered primarily by $ln\,S/E$. The $50 stock price will drop to approximately $49.17, or by 83 cents. The present value of this drop must be considered to estimate the option value. We next use a Black-Scholes model to estimate $N(d_1)$ and $N(d_2)$ for the call and add present value of the exercise price to determine the put value. Performing no calculations, we assume the value of such a put will rise by approximately the percentage change due to dilution; that is

$$\frac{\$50 - \$49.17}{\$50 - \$45} = .166 = 16.6\%$$

$$.375(1.166) = .437 = \left(\frac{7}{16}\right)$$

Although a crude approximation, it forms a basis for comparison and negotiation with investment bankers. By using current market value of the put, one at least has a basis for determining the price per share that should be charged for the standby commitment.[20]

THE LEVERAGED FIRM AS A CALL OPTION

When a company issues debt, it has written essentially a call option on its assets. However, in this instance, there is an upper limit on the call: the principal and unpaid interest on the debt. Moreover, the call is exercised only if the firm fails to meet its contractual obligations under the debt agreement. Finally, the lower value of the call option depends on the value of the firm's assets less the value of prior claims against them in bankruptcy. Although a "Aaa"-rated corporate bond is virtually risk-free of default, its value fluctuates as nominal yields on instruments of similar maturities adjust to changes in overall interest-rate levels. The price of a "C"-rated debt instrument—whose prospects for repayment of principal and interest are poor—depends on the value of the call option that underlies the assets to which it has a claim. If such assets have little or no value or if prior claims take precedent, the value of the call approximates zero—as does the value of the debt instrument.

SUMMARY

We concluded the chapter by suggesting certain extensions of the options framework. Warrants are relatively straightforward; convertibles are more complicated; treating standby arrangements with investment bankers as put options is

---

[20] Bear in mind that investment bankers write puts. They will, therefore, charge more as subscription price approximates current market price and chances of the stock falling below subscription price increase. Treating the standby arrangment as a put also permits one to compare the approximate cost of such financing with a conventionally negotiated or Rule 415 offering of the same securities.

relatively new; and viewing the leveraged firm as a call option adds even another dimension.

However, we began the chapter by analyzing the option contract as a tool for hedging—first under known outcomes with known probabilities and then treating market price of underlying stock on which conventional options are written as an observation on a random variable. Our discussion focused on the call option, which permits the buyer to deliver shares of stock to the writer of the call at a specific price termed the exercise price. The value of a call option—the price one is willing to pay and the writer must receive—is a function of several variables. Variance in stock price that affects variance in holding-period returns and length of time before the option expires are the driving forces behind option value. The greater the variance and the longer the time, the higher the value (price). Because in principle an options model permits one to hedge a portfolio perfectly and hence, using the hedge ratio, to earn a risk-free return from purchasing stock and writing calls on the basis of that ratio, value is also affected by the risk-free rate.

The Black-Scholes model was used as the basis for valuing call options. However, its calculus depends on continuous observations of the market price, continuous adjustment of the portfolio as the hedge ratio changes, the assumption that no dividends are paid on the stock, and the fact that the option cannot be exercised until maturity—a European rather than an American call option. Moreover, a key factor—the standard deviation of holding-period returns—is based empirically on past data and may not hold in the future. Although modification of the Black-Scholes model (to make it more realistic) has helped spawn an industry, the original achievement is nevertheless a major intellectual breakthrough in understanding financial arrangements directly or indirectly related to the call option.

Although less widely employed, the put option—which permits the buyer to sell stock to the writer at a specified price—is a mirror image of the call option and can, in theory, be calculated from the call value. Since the stock price cannot fall below zero but can rise to infinity, the value of puts is lower than the value of calls.

Bear in mind that although the option buyer has the right but not the obligation to exercise the option, the option writer must deliver (in the case of a call) or accept (in the case of a put) the underlying instrument at the exercise price. As we shall see in Chapter 20, futures contracts oblige both contractual parties to meet their obligations.

PROBLEMS AND QUESTIONS

1. Suppose an investor owns shares in Long-shot Crude Oil, Inc. Shares are currently selling for $30 and no dividends have been paid. Management has decided to drill in a new field. If successful, investors know the stock's market

price will reach $70. If unsuccessful, the stock's market price will fall to $10. The odds are .4 that the company will be successful and .6 that it will not.

a. Calculate the hedge ratio.

b. Using the hedge ratio to hedge his or her portfolio and the risk-free rate of 9 percent for the period, at what price will the investor write options, assuming $30 is the exercise price?

c. What is the value of the hedged portfolio?

d. What is the expected unhedged holding-period return?

e. What is the return on the hedged portfolio?

2. In Problem 1, if current market price is $50 instead of $30, what is the hedge ratio, assuming other values remain the same? At what price will investors write call options? Would differences in outcome probabilities affect the hedge ratio and the price at which investors would write options? Explain in detail.

3. "The greater the variance and the longer the time period before the option expires, the more valuable the option is." Explain.

4. Nathan Nasturtium is considering the purchase of a call option on the stock of XYZ Corporation. Based on the following information, use the Black-Scholes model to determine the value of the call assuming the stock pays no dividends:

$$\text{current market price of stock} = \$56.25$$
$$\text{exercise price} = \$58$$
$$\text{time remaining before option expires} = .3 \text{ years}$$
$$\text{risk-free rate} = .105$$
$$N(d_1) = .7838$$
$$N(d_2) = .7137$$

5. Using the Black-Scholes model, Pamela Panglossian wants to evaluate a call option on LMN Corporation that pays no dividends. She has the following information:

$$S = \$27$$
$$E = \$30$$
$$\ln S/E = -.105361$$
$$t = 1.0 \text{ year}$$
$$r = .095$$
$$\sigma = .25$$

Calculate the value of a call option.

6. In Problems 4 and 5, what are the respective values of the puts?

7. Discuss the primary criticisms of the Black-Scholes options model.

8. Suppose Longacre Corporation issues warrants that expire in five years. The stock's current market price is $10 and the warrants can be exercised at $18.

The risk-free rate (based on U.S. government securities maturing in five years) is 12.5 percent. The σ of past holding-period returns is .28 and $ln\ S/E$ is $-.587787$. Using the Black-Scholes model, estimate the value of the warrant.

9. Gavin Company is issuing convertible debentures on the following terms and convertible at any time to common stock of Gavin:

price to public	= $100 or $1,000
coupon rate	= 8.5%
call price	= $108
conversion price	= $25 per $1,000 of face value
maturity	= 20 years

On the day the convertibles were issued, market price of the common stock to which they are convertible was $20 per share. Yield to maturity on comparable issues of U.S. government securities was 10.5 percent. Corporate bonds of similar quality carried yields to maturity of 13 percent.

a. Calculate the conversion ratio.

b. Calculate the premium investors are paying for the privilege of converting the securities in relation to:

i. investment value of U.S. government securities of comparable quality.

ii. investment value of corporate debentures of similar quality.

10. ABC Corporation has warrants outstanding and the following information is relevant:

$$S = \$14$$
$$E = \$21$$
$$ln\ S/E = -.405465$$
$$r = .14$$
$$t = 2.75\ \text{years}$$
$$\sigma = .42$$

a. Using the Black-Scholes model, calculate the theoretical value of the warrant.

b. Suppose market price of the warrant is $4.50. Does this differ from your calculation in 10(a)? If so, how do you account for the difference?

SELECTED ADDITIONAL REFERENCES

Bhattacharya, Mihir. "Empirical Properties of the Black-Scholes Formula Under Ideal Conditions," *Journal of Financial and Quantitative Analysis*, Vol. 15 (December 1980, pp. 1081–1106).

Black, Fischer. "The Valuation of Options Contracts and Test of Market Efficiency," *Journal of Finance*, Vol. 27 (May 1972, pp. 399–417).

Black, Fischer and Myron Scholes. "The Pricing of Options and Other Corporate Liabilities," *Journal of Political Economy*, Vol. 81 (May–June 1973, pp. 637–59).

Block, Stanley and Timothy J. Gallagher. "The Use of Interest Rate Futures and Options by Corporate Financial Managers," *Financial Management*, Vol. 15 (August 1986, pp. 73–78).

Brennen, Michael and Eduardo S. Schwartz. "The Valuation of American Put Options," *Journal of Finance*, Vol. 32 (May 1977, pp. 449–62).

Brenner, Menachem, ed. *Option Pricing Theory and Applications* (Lexington, MA: Heath and Company, 1983).

Cox, John and Stephen A. Ross. "A Survey of Some New Results in Financial Option Pricing Policy," *Journal of Finance*, Vol. 31 (May 1976, pp. 383–402).

———— and ————. "The Valuation of Options for Alternative Stochastic Processes," *Journal of Financial Economics*, Vol. 3 (January–March, 1976, pp. 145–79).

Jarrow, Robert A. and Andrew Rudd. *Option Pricing Theory and Applications* (Homewood, IL: Richard D. Irwin, 1983).

Merton, Robert C. "The Rational Theory of Option Pricing," *Bell Journal of Economics*, Vol. 4 (Spring 1973, pp. 141–82).

Rendleman, Richard J. Jr. "Optimal Long-Run Investment Strategies," *Financial Management*, Vol. 10 (Spring 1981, pp. 61–77).

Roll, Richard. "An Analytic Valuation Formula for Unprotected American Call Options with Known Dividends," *Journal of Financial Economics*, Vol. 5 (November 1977, pp. 251–58).

Scholes, Myron. "Taxes and the Pricing of Options," *Journal of Finance*, Vol. 31 (May 1976, pp. 319–30).

Schwartz, Eduardo S. "The Valuation of Warrants: Implementing a New Approach," *Journal of Financial Economics*, Vol. 4 (January 1977, pp. 79–93).

Smith, Clifford W. Jr. "Option Pricing: A Review," *Journal of Financial Economics*, Vol. 3 (January–March 1976, pp. 3–51).

FINANCIAL
FUTURES AND
INTEREST-RATE
SWAPS

Although the options model developed in Chapter 19 may be viewed as a tool for mitigating risk, it is highly unlikely (for reasons already outlined) that one would purchase stocks and write options based solely on the hedge ratio calculated when employing the Black-Scholes options model. Within a broader and what ultimately may be a more important context, the option concept underlies many financial instruments—warrants and convertibles, for example—and practices, such as the standby arrangement on a rights offering. All these instruments and practices existed before the Black-Scholes model offered new insights.

Financial futures, however, have a different history. The problems involved in carrying commodities as inventories—particularly agricultural commodities, which have distinct seasonal patterns—helped bring about the futures markets in basic agricultural goods in the latter part of the nineteenth century. Futures markets were subsequently extended to other commodities, so that today they exist for such diverse goods as pork bellies and platinum. Those who use such commodities in production—a cereal manufacturer, for example, whose inventory needs include wheat, corn, oats, and so forth—can hedge the risk of price fluctuations by purchasing a futures contract for delivery of the commodity at a guaranteed price. Thus, if in November a cereal manufacturer anticipates the need for oats in March to replenish inventory, a March futures contract for delivery of oats at that time can be purchased at a specific price. Suppose the futures price for grain to be delivered in March is $1.27 per bushel. Of course, the market price in March could be higher or lower. The broker who wrote the contract loses money if oats must be purchased at a higher price in order to deliver them at $1.27, but makes money if the market price has fallen by March. In this instance, the *manufacturer is the hedger; the broker who guarantees the oats at $1.27 per bushel is the speculator. Such transactions are commonplace in the futures market.*[1]

Financial futures, including futures on foreign exchange, operate under the same basic principle: there is a demand for shifting risk and there are those willing to bear the risk. The growth of futures contracts in financial instruments and foreign exchange coincided with the increased variability in interest rates and stock prices, and in the movement from fixed to floating exchange rates that characterized the 1970s. Today futures are an integral part of financial markets. Whether they remain so or whether they are supplemented or replaced by other arrangements is anybody's guess. One possibility, the interest-rate swap, is considered later in the chapter.

THE FINANCIAL FUTURES CONTRACT

A financial futures contract is an agreement for the purchase or sale of a financial instrument to be delivered or received at a specified point in the future. The price is agreed on at the time the contract is consummated. In the case of a fixed-interest-rate security, the effect is to lock in price and interest rate on the date agreement is reached. In the case of foreign exchange, currency price is specified in advance in much the same way as price of oats to be delivered in the future is specified in advance.

Successful futures contracts require that the object of the contract be homogeneous. If one wishes to purchase a commodity—wheat, for example—he or she can enter into a futures contract on the Kansas City Board of Trade that specifies the commodity deliverable against the contract is number 2 soft red wheat. (Soft wheat is used for pastry; hard wheat is used for bread.) A 90-day T-bill contract traded on the International Monetary Market (IMM) is generally settled using a T-bill with 91 days to maturity. The T-bond contract traded on the Chicago Board of

---

[1] Rarely are the commodities actually delivered: each party usually enters into a reverse trade—with the buyer selling and the seller buying. Thus, if the market (spot) price of oats was $1.37 per bushel in March, the futures contract expiring at that time would also equal the market price less transaction costs. In a reverse trade, the buyer sells the contract at $1.37 and buys the oats at that price in the open market, making 10 cents per bushel on the contract and ensuring a net price of $1.27. The seller purchases the contract and loses 10 cents per bushel. If the market price had fallen to $1.17, the manufacturer would lose 10 cents on the contract but gain 10 cents on an open-market purchase. The speculator would gain 10 cents on the contract.

Trade (CBT) permits the seller of the contract to deliver any T-bond with a maturity of at least 15 years. The CBT assumes the bond has an 8-percent coupon, matures in 20 years, and is selling at par; adjustments are made for different coupon rates.

Unlike commodities, some financial futures can be settled in cash. (By definition, foreign exchange futures are settled in the currency specified in the contract.) Three-month time deposits denominated in Eurodollars—dollars on deposit outside the United States—can be settled in cash. More importantly, stock-index futures pegged to popular market averages must be settled in cash, because it is difficult to deliver averages even though some portfolios are indexed to them.

One aspect of futures contracts is universal: both parties to the contract are obligated either to deliver or to purchase the underlying instrument commodity or to make, if permitted or required, the cash settlement. Delivery can be avoided by reversing the trade: buying a futures contract to offset a sale or selling a futures contract to offset a purchase. In addition, when the contract is entered into, the buyer or seller must put up a percentage (margin) of the face value of the contract. As long as the contract is outstanding, the trader must maintain a specific amount of margin.

USING T-BILL FUTURES AS A HEDGE

To demonstrate the possibilities for using futures contracts as hedges, while at the same time elaborating on the preceding points, we offer the following illustration. In September, the treasurer of a manufacturing corporation anticipates his company will have \$10,000,000 available in December that can (for seasonal reasons) be invested in short-term securities for 90 days. He prefers to lock up the interest rate now rather than in December and finds a futures contract is available on T-bills. The current price of the contract is 91.80 and each contract is for \$1,000,000 worth of T-bills.

But what does the 91.80 mean? On investigation, the treasurer learns that T-bill contracts are quoted as the difference between 100 and the T-bill yield on a bank discount basis. Thus, $100.00 - 91.80$ yields a bank discount rate of 8.20 percent.[2]

---

[2] The 8.20 rate is for a 360-day year. The 90-day rate is .0205 ($8.20 \div 90/360$). The treasurer can calculate annual yield by finding the price of a 90-day bill:

$$\frac{100 - p}{100} = .0205$$

$$p = 97.95$$

Hence

$$\frac{365}{90} \cdot \frac{100 - 97.95}{97.95} \times 100 = 8.4879\%$$

This allows the treasurer to compare future-expected T-bill yields with other instruments not traded on a bank discount basis. (For further details, see Appendix 3-A.)

Further analysis reveals that T-bill prices can change by multiples of .01, or one basis point (1/100 of 1 percent). In other words, the dollar value of a single contract will change by at least $25 with each change of one basis point because

$$\$1,000,000 \times .0001 \times \frac{90}{360} = \$25$$

Consequently, a contract currently selling at 91.80 is equivalent to

(a)
$$100 - 91.80 \times \frac{90}{360} = 2.05$$

(b)
$$100 - 2.05 \times \frac{\$1,000,000}{100} = \$979,500$$

If the price should rise to 91.81, then

(a)
$$100 - 91.81 \times \frac{90}{360} = 2.0475$$

(b)
$$100 - 2.0475 \times \frac{\$1,000,000}{100} = \$979,525$$

Similarly, if the price should fall to 91.79, then

(a)
$$100 - 91.79 \times \frac{90}{360} = 2.0525$$

(b)
$$100 - 2.0525 \times \frac{\$1,000,000}{100} = \$979,475$$

In each case, (a) represents reduction of annual discount based on a 360-day year to a 90-day quarter (the discount is divided by four). In (b), quarterly discount is subtracted from 100 and then multiplied by the number of T-bills (face value assumed to be 100) required for a $1,000,000 contract ($1,000,000 ÷ 100 = 10,000). In each case there is a $25 change in the contract.

All futures contracts are established on margin. After all, the treasurer does not have $10,000,000 to invest today; this is why he wants to hedge. He must, however, put up an initial margin of $2,000 per contract. To hedge the entire $10,000,000 he must purchase 10 contracts, putting up an initial margin of $2,000 × 10 = $20,000.

Once the contracts are purchased, the margin must be maintained at $1,500 per contract. Known as **marking to the market**, the margin position is calculated at the end of every trading session. Because the treasurer purchases T-bill contracts at (let us assume) 91.80 or $979,500 per contract, if the price rose, the value of the contract would increase. Conversely, if the price fell, the value of the contract would decrease. The treasurer knows that if the contract is held to maturity, its price will ultimately approach the price of T-bills offered at that time. In the interim, however, he must be prepared to put up additional margin should the price fall. He may take in cash the gain in the margin should the price rise.

When trading futures contracts, maximum and minimum daily fluctuations are permitted; however, if one or the other limit is reached, trading ceases. In the case of T-bills, the limit is ± 60 basis points, or $\pm\$1,500$ (60 × $25) per contract. For example, suppose the T-bill market opened at 91.80 and in the course of a few hours rose to 92.40. In such circumstances, trading would cease and margin accounts would be settled for the day. In this simple scenario, the value of each contract rose by $1,500 (from $979,500 to $981,000) and the value of the margin rose by $1,500 (from $2,000 to $3,500). If the price had fallen by $1,500 (from $979,500 to $978,000), the value of the margin would have fallen by $1,500 (from $2,000 to $500). Once the account is initiated, the treasurer—obligated to maintain a margin of $1,500 per contract—must add $10,000 ($1,500 − $500) × 10 to the margin account if the price falls accordingly. The process of marking to the market in a futures account is time-consuming. Consequently, most treasurers—sensing that the opportunity cost of time is greater than that of money—are likely to leave more than sufficient margin in the account.

Trading in futures contracts expires at various times depending on the instrument. In the case of T-bills traded on the IMM, trading on maturing contracts generally terminates on Wednesday following the three-month Treasury-bill auction on Monday of the third week of the month, with delivery scheduled for Thursday of that week.

The treasurer, however, is unlikely to take delivery of securities. Rather, on the last trading day he will execute a reverse trade, in this case selling ten contracts at the final settlement price and using the proceeds to purchase newly issued T-bills. This procedure is generally less cumbersome and more efficient. In this instance, most participants in futures markets reverse their trades, with hedgers purchasing the underlying instrument in the open market. Suppose in December the final settlement price was 92.50, equivalent to the spot market price of newly issued 90-day T-bills. As shown in Table 20-1, the treasurer sells ten contracts to cover his position and purchases $10,000,000 in T-bills. In so doing, he has executed the perfect hedge: guaranteeing a yield in December that could have been earned in September if the funds had been available. Of course, if the price had fallen, the treasurer would have realized a loss on the contract, but would have made up the difference with a higher yield—a lower price on the purchase of the T-bills.

The hedge may be perfect, but it is not without cost: transaction costs in executing the initial contract and cover costs to close it. And the margin has an opportunity cost, as does management's time. Nevertheless, risk is shifted and unless one believes cash management should be a profit center for the corporation, the technique ensures a return on temporarily idle funds.[3]

---

[3] Suzanna Andrews. "Should Cash Management Be a Profit Center? *Institutional Investor*, Vol. XIX (July 1985, pp. 203–4).

Table 20-1   Hedging T-bills

September

Purchase ten September–December contracts on 90-day T-bills at 91.80 per contract = $979,500

December

Sell ten September–December contracts on 90-day T-bills at 92.50 per contract = $981,250

$$\text{profit per contract} = \$981,250 - \$979,500 = \$1,750$$
$$\text{total profit} = \$1,750 \times 10 = \$17,500$$

$$
\begin{array}{ll}
\text{buy } \$10,000,000 \text{ in 90-day T-bills at 92.50} = & \$9,812,500 \\
\text{less profit on futures} = & \underline{\quad 17,500} \\
\text{total invested} & = \$9,795,000
\end{array}
$$

$$\text{annual yield on bank discount basis} = \frac{10,000,000 - \$9,795,000}{\$10,000,000} \times \frac{360}{90} = .0820$$

CROSS HEDGING

Suppose that instead of anticipating $10,000,000 in idle funds in September, management expects to borrow $10,000,000 in December for 90 days. Suppose further that the company's borrowing rate is pegged to the three-month domestic certificate of deposit (CD). Although the differential is not fixed, it has varied from 1.5 to 2.5 percentage points above the 90-day CD rate. Because banks are unwilling to commit themselves in September to rates on loans to be made in December and because there is no futures market in bank loans, the treasurer cannot institute a perfect hedge.

However, the treasurer knows there is a futures market in domestic CDs similar in many respects to the futures market in T-bills. Each contract is for $1,000,000 and contract fluctuation is limited to 1 basis point ($25). Margin requirements are the same as those for T-bills: $2,000 initial margin and $1,500 maintenance. CD prices can fluctuate ± 80 basis points ($2,000). Delivery, however, is more complicated and the instrument delivered can vary from $2\frac{1}{2}$ to $3\frac{1}{2}$ months in maturity. Although final settlement can occur beginning the fifteenth day of the delivery month, it can occur up to the last trading day of that month.

Table 20-2   Using a CD Futures Contract to Hedge a Short-term Loan

September

Sell ten December contracts on 90-day CDs at 91.10 per contract = $977,750

December

Purchase ten December contracts on 90-day CDs at 89.50 = $973,750

$$\text{profit per contract} = \$977,750 - \$973,750 = \$ 4,000$$
$$\text{total profit} = \$ \quad 4,000 \times 10 \qquad = \$40,000$$

$$\text{current CD rate} = 100 - 89.50 = 10.50\%$$
$$\text{current borrowing rate} = 10.50 + 2.00 = 12.50\%$$

$$\text{borrow } \$10,000,000 - (.1250 \times \$10,000,000) \frac{360}{90} = \$9,687,500$$

$$\begin{array}{r} + \quad 40,000 \text{ profit on futures} \\ \hline \$9,727,500 \end{array}$$

$$\text{effective loan rate on bank discount basis} = \frac{\$10,000,000 - \$9,727,500}{\$10,000,000} \times \frac{360}{90} \times 100 = 10.90\%$$

Anticipating a rise in interest rates, the treasurer notes that futures contracts are currently selling at 91.90 or 8.90 percent on a bank-discount basis. If the treasurer could borrow today at that rate plus 2.00 percent, he would pay 10.90 percent interest on the loan. Anxious to lock up the rate, the treasurer sells—shorts ten CD contracts at 91.10. As anticipated, interest rates do rise and the price of December contracts falls to 89.50 at maturity.

In Table 20-2, we assume the treasurer liquidates his position by purchasing ten CD contracts on the last trading day at 89.50, yielding a CD rate of 10.50 (equivalent to the rate on new 90-day CDs at that time). The $40,000 profit he makes on the short position is used to reduce the cost of his loan—now 12.50 percent (10.50 + 2.00)— to 10.90 percent, the rate he wanted to ensure in September.

Apart from usual transaction costs, success of this hedge depends on the relationship between loan rates and domestic CDs. If this relationship changes or if the loan rate is pegged to the prime rate, the cross hedge becomes less than perfect.

THE RELATIONSHIP BETWEEN SPOT PRICES AND FUTURES PRICES

The foregoing illustrations suggest how one who wishes to hedge can use futures contracts for that purpose. Because a futures contract is held to maturity, the futures contract price converges on the spot (market) price of the commodity—in this case, the financial instrument in question. But what about the relationship between the spot price and the futures contract price prior to maturity? This is an intriguing question.

In an efficient market, the futures contract price should reflect the maximum-likelihood estimate of the spot price at the time the contract matures. If the spot price is expected to rise, the futures price would reflect that increase and be greater than the current spot price. Alternatively, if the spot price is expected to fall, the futures price would be less than the current spot price. If the spot price is expected to equal the current spot price, the spot price and the futures price would be equal. Thus, if

$$F = \text{futures contract price}$$
$$S^1 = \text{expected spot price (when futures contract expires)}$$
$$S = \text{spot price}$$

we might observe any relationship between F and S, so that $F \gtreqless S$.

To complicate matters further, one must allow for net carrying costs, C. For standard commodities, carrying costs can be considerable when one takes into account storage, insurance, interest on carrying the commodity, and loading/unloading. For financial instruments, storage costs are minimal. Instruments earn interest if owned; if borrowed, they incur borrowing costs. Opportunity costs of margin requirements and time/effort required in marking to the market offset carrying costs. On balance, net carrying costs for commodities are positive. Net carrying costs for financial instruments are probably lower and may approximate zero.

One must also recognize that speculators are selling the hedgers insurance against risk. As a group, they expect to earn a positive (normal) profit, P, that in competition is commensurate with profits earned elsewhere under comparable risk conditions. Therefore, the actual futures price observed could be biased downward in relation to the spot price.[4]

Thus, we observe only the futures price and the spot price. Suppose, for example, the spot price on a 91-day T-bill is 97.40 and the futures price on a 91-day contract is also 97.40. From the foregoing discussion, if you believe the market anticipates that the price and hence the yield on a T-bill of identical matu-

---

[4] John R. Hicks. *Value and Capital*, 2nd ed. (Oxford: Clarendon Press, 1950, Ch. 10, pp. 130–52).

rity issued in 91 days is the same as it is today, please write the author—he has a bridge over San Francisco Bay he would like to sell you.

In this instance, what the market really anticipates is that the price of a T-bill issued in 91 days will be less than the price of a T-bill of similar maturity issued today. Even assuming zero net carrying costs, the seller of the futures contract expects to pay less than 97.40 but will deliver new 91-day T-bills at that price to satisfy the obligation. Alternatively, the seller expects to settle the contract with a reverse trade at a lower price, thereby earning a profit on the transaction. It is always difficult to determine the normal profit rate. However, because $F - P < S + C$ is what one ordinarily expects to occur, if one observes that $F \geq S$ in the market, it implies that speculators anticipate the expected spot price, S^1, at the time the contract expires to be such that $S^1 = F - P$. After estimating carrying costs, $F \geq S + C$, then $S^1 = F - P - C$ and $S^1 + P + C = F \geq S$. Consequently, in this instance ($F = S = 97.40$), the market expects that $S^1 < S$.

Whether this outcome materializes is, of course, the essence of speculation. Net carrying costs can be approximated in advance; actual value for P, however, depends on what happens to the relationship between S^1 and S. Consequently, the futures contract price will converge on S^1, not S, and investors' expectations can be such that $S^1 \gtreqless S$ at the time the agreement is made.

DETERMINING THE HEDGE RATIO

As long as the face value of the securities to be hedged is equal to the face value of those used to hedge, one can approximate (less transactions costs and costs of marking to the market) a perfect hedge.[5] Our T-bill example illustrates this point. However, as our loan-commitment example suggests, most hedging must take place against an imperfect substitute—in this case the domestic CD.

Given the foregoing discussion of the relationship between the observed futures price and the observed spot price of an instrument, successful cross hedging depends on (1) futures being efficiently priced in each market and (2) futures being efficiently priced relative to one another. In the first instance, the futures price is the best estimate available of S^1. In the second instance, if there are two futures markets for two different instruments, A and B, then

$$\frac{F_A}{F_B} = \frac{S_A^1}{S_B^1}$$

If individual markets are efficient, arbitrageurs presumably would ensure efficiency between and among markets so that futures contracts would be efficiently priced,

---

[5] Peter W. Bacon and Richard E. Williams. "Interest Rate Futures, New Tools for the Financial Manager," *Financial Management*, Vol. 5 (Spring 1976, pp. 32–38).

both as to underlying instruments and any expected relationship among future spot prices: S_A^1, S_B^1, and so on.

Nevertheless, as our illustration of the loan contract and the CD suggests, where there is no futures market in one of the two instruments, the hedger assumes the relationship between CD price (rate) will be the same when the futures contract expires as when it was made. By implication, one is hedging on a one-to-one ratio: for every $1,000,000 loan, a $1,000,000 CD contract is sold. Although this strategy may be suboptimal for many real-world problems, it may be adequate for financial managers of nonfinancial firms.

What about portfolio managers? For example, suppose a commercial bank, an insurance company, or a pension fund holds long-term U.S. government securities as part of its portfolio and wishes to hedge the investment against price changes and hence yields. The techniques for doing so take us beyond the scope of this book;[6] however, a simple approach employed by Salomon Brothers (and other investment firms) consists of three basic steps:

1. Use simple regression analysis of past data to determine volatility of the yield instrument to be hedged relative to volatility of the futures contract. Suppose regression model analysis projects that for every 5-basis-point change in yield on 15-year Treasury bonds there is a 4-basis-point change in yield on a 12-month futures contract on 15-year Treasury bonds—a relative change in yield of 5-to-4, or 1.25-to-1.

2. Determine the price–value change per basis point of the securities and the futures contract. Suppose
   a. a one-basis point change in a futures contract results in a value change of .047 dollars;
   b. a one-basis-point change in yield on the securities results in a price change of .053 dollars.

3. Thus, the hedge ratio is

$$\text{hedge ratio} = \frac{\text{volatility of securities}}{\text{volatility of futures contract}}$$
$$= \frac{1.25 \times .053}{1.00 \times .047} = \frac{.06625}{.047} = 1.409574$$

Given the preceding relationship, for every dollar in securities owned one could sell $1.409574 in 12-month futures contracts in order to hedge the portfolio. Unlike the two earlier illustrations of hedging a future purchase of securities or a future

---

[6] Robert W. Kolb and Raymond Chiang. "Improving Hedging Performance Using Interest Rate Futures," *Financial Management*, Vol. 10 (Autumn 1981, pp. 72–79). See, also, Gerald D. Gay and Robert W. Kolb, *Interest Rate Futures: Concepts and Issues* (Richmond, VA: Robert F. Dame, 1981, pp. 237–364) and Robert W. Kolb, *Understanding Futures Markets* (Glenview, IL: Scott, Foresman and Company, 1985, pp. 54–84).

loan, this is an illustration of protecting a portfolio of assets (or at least one portion of it) from fluctuations in value. Suppose there are $10,000,000 worth of Treasury bonds in the portfolio that mature in 16 years. With a 12-month futures contract, upon maturity these bonds will be 15-year instruments. (Although such a perfect match may not be the case, the assumption simplifies the illustration.)

Suppose further that the bonds are currently selling at par with an 11.75-percent coupon, hence a 11.75 YTM. To protect the value and the yield, the manager sells futures contracts against the portfolio; the hedge ratio determines how many contracts are sold. For every dollar in T-bonds owned, the manager should sell 1.409574 futures contracts in T-bonds. Thus, $10,000,000 × 1.409574 = $14,095,740 in futures contracts. T-bond futures contracts are sold in $100,000 denominations. Consequently

$$\frac{\$14,095,740}{\$100,000} = 140.9574 \text{ or } 141 \text{ contracts}$$

Assume after two months that YTM on the T-bonds has risen to 11.95 percent, or 20 basis points. The price has fallen accordingly, so that 20 basis points × .053 = $1.06 per $100 of par value:

$$\frac{\$10,000,000}{\$100} = \$100,000 \times \$1.06 = \$106,000 \text{ loss}$$

Although the portfolio has declined by $106,000, the value of 141 futures contracts has fallen by approximately $106,000: for every 1.25 basis-point change in YTM on the bonds, there has been a 1.00-basis-point change in YTM on the futures contract. As a result

$$\frac{20}{1.25} \times .047 = \$.752 \text{ per } \$100 \text{ of par value}$$

As there are 141 contracts, sold at $100,000, the gain from reversing the trade is

$$\frac{\$100,000}{\$100} \times 141 \times \$.752 = \$106,032$$

The portfolio is a bit overhedged because the manager could not have sold fractions of a contract: 141 rather than 140.9574 contracts.[7] Assuming the empirical relationship continues to maturity, the gain or loss on the futures contract will offset the gain or loss on the securities. Similar computations can be made using T-bond futures as a cross hedge against corporate bonds in the portfolio. The general

---

[7] $100,000/$100 × 140.9574 × $.752 = $106,000.

weakness in these strategies does not lie in the computations; the problem is one that plagues all empirical work: past relationships may not hold in the future. In other words, the forces that gave rise to a 1.25-to 1.00-basis-point relationship between T-bonds and futures contracts may yield a different basis-point relationship and hence a different hedge ratio the following year. To be sure, the change may be modest and for practical purposes of little significance; nevertheless, empirical relationships are only as good as the analytical framework that explains them. Measuring what constitutes the relationship is not the same as explaining why the relationship exists.

STOCK-INDEX FUTURES

With respect to financial futures, the 1970s can be termed the decade of interest-rate and perhaps exchange-rate futures; however, in the 1980s they have had to share top billing with stock-index futures. Beginning on February 24, 1982, the Kansas City Board of Trade opened trading on the Value Line Stock Index. This trading quickly spread to other indexes. Shortly thereafter, the Chicago Mercantile Exchange opened trading on the S & P 500 and the New York Futures Exchange opened trading on the York Stock Exchange Composite Index. Others have been added, including a major market index listed on the Chicago Board of Trade.

Unlike other futures contracts, from their inception stock-index futures could be settled only in cash. In few other instruments (Eurodollar CDs, for example) is cash an acceptable means of settlement; otherwise, 90 percent of all futures contracts are settled by reverse trades. However, there is almost always the option of accepting or delivering the commodity per contract: 38,000 pounds of pork bellies, 100 tons of soybean meal, or $1,000,000 in Treasury bills. With stock-index futures, it is hard to deliver the portfolio. Although stock-index mutual funds that approximate averages do exist; such shares are bought and sold by the issuer; however, because there is no secondary market for the funds, cash is the only feasible means for settling futures contracts. All contracts are some multiple of the stock index. Concentrating on the S & P 500, which is perhaps the most widely used stock-index futures contract, the value of a contract is 500 times the index. Thus, on December 6, 1985, all June 1986 contracts were settled at 208.65 for valuation purposes—to determine margin and, when relevant, to determine cash settlement.[8] The value of a June 1986 contract on that date was 208.65 × 500 = $104,325.

---

[8] Settlement price is usually between the high and the low for the day (the high for that day was 211.25 and the low was 208.45) but need not be the average of the two. Settlement price relates to a period of time immediately preceding the close, when a large number of transactions often take place.

HEDGING WITH STOCK-INDEX FUTURES

A simple procedure for using stock-index futures as a hedge involves calculating the portfolio beta and using it to determine the hedge ratio. Thus

$$\text{hedge ratio} = \frac{\text{portfolio \$ value}}{\text{futures contract \$ value}} \times \text{weighted portfolio beta}$$

where

$$\beta_p = \sum_i^n = W_i \beta_i$$

In short, a portfolio beta is simply the weighted average of the betas of individual securities calculated against the index used for hedging—in this instance the S & P 500.

Assume a portfolio manager, witnessing a rising stock market but fearing a short-term sell-off, decides to hedge the portfolio by selling futures against the S & P 500. Assume further that the manager can sell three-month futures at 210. Thus, each futures contract (exclusive of transactions costs and margin) is sold for 210 × 500 = \$105,000. Market value of the stock portfolio is \$22,500,000 and portfolio beta is 1.26. To hedge, the portfolio manager sells

$$\text{hedge ratio} = \frac{\$22,500,000}{\$105,000} \times 1.26 = 270 \text{ contracts}$$

Suppose that after three months the S & P 500 has fallen to 195, so the value of each contract is now 195 × 500 = \$97,500. Reversing the trade, the portfolio manager purchases 270 futures contracts at this price as follows:

$$
\begin{aligned}
\text{sold 270 contracts} \times \$105,000 \quad &= \$28,350,000 \\
\text{purchased 270 contracts} \times \$97,500 &= \ 26,325,000 \\
\text{profit} \quad &= \$\ 2,025,000 \\
\text{decline in S \& P } \frac{210 - 195}{210} \quad &= .071429 \\
\text{decline in portfolio} \quad &= .071429 \times 1.26 = .09 \\
&= .09(\$22,500,000) \\
&= \$2,025,000
\end{aligned}
$$

Again, profit from the sale of futures contracts is offset by decline in portfolio value. If the index had risen, the loss on repurchase of futures contracts would have been offset by portfolio gain.

In the foregoing illustration, the number of futures contracts exactly equaled the portfolio value. In most cases, this does not occur. Because futures contracts cannot be purchased or sold in fractions, the portfolio may be overhedged or underhedged. Of greater importance, however, is beta coefficient stability. As noted earlier in the book, portfolio betas are relatively stable. Nevertheless, portfolio changes can occur, causing the portfolio to be improperly hedged.

OPTIONS ON FUTURES

Of course, one may not want to completely hedge the portfolio. After all, if the market moves positively, the portfolio manager may want to hedge against the downside risk but leave open the upside potential. One way to achieve this goal is through options on futures contracts. Options on T-bond futures contracts opened in October 1982; options on the S & P stock-index futures opened in January 1983. Other contracts have followed. We confine our attention to options on futures contracts for the S & P 500, our primary focus again being their efficiency as a hedging tool.

Exercise price of the S & P 500 futures option is established at about current contract price. Price is set by the exchange offering the option on the futures contract—in this instance, the Chicago Mercantile Exchange. Thus, most options are *at or near the money* when offered. This results in the immediate establishment of a positive value for both puts and calls. Consequently, on December 13, 1985, there appeared the following:[9]

March 1986	*S & P Futures Index*	*Calls*	*Puts*
Settlement price	210.15	—	—
Exercise (striking) price = 210	—	5.80	5.65

The March 1986 contract was settled on December 13, 1985, at 210.15. With an exercise price of 210 for March options, the puts and calls were nearly *at the money*. One purchases the option by paying 5.80 points for the call and 5.65 points for the put. The price of each option is the number of points multiplied by 500. Thus

$$\text{price of call} = 5.80 \times 500 = \$2,900$$
$$\text{price of put} = 5.65 \times 500 = \$2,825$$

In our illustration, the portfolio manager can sell 270 three-month futures contracts on the portfolio at an exercise (striking) price of 210. Let us assume that on

---

[9] *Wall Street Journal*, December 13, 1985, pp. 50 and 51.

December 13, 1985, the relationship between the spot price and the three-month futures contracts currently holds for our portfolio manager. One strategy to limit downside risk involves purchasing 270 puts at 210. Assume this is done and that after three months the index falls to 195. The options would have been exercised as follows:

$$
\begin{array}{ll}
\text{purchase 270 futures contracts at } 195 \times 500 = \$26,325,000 \\
\text{sell 270 futures contracts at } 210 \times 500 \quad = \$28,350,000 \\
\text{gross profit} \qquad\qquad\qquad\qquad\qquad\quad = \$\ 2,025,000 \\
\text{cost of options } 5.65 \times 500 \times 270 \qquad\quad = \$\quad 762,750 \\
\qquad\qquad\qquad\qquad\qquad\qquad\qquad\quad = \$\ 1,262,250
\end{array}
$$

Although there is a profit on exercising the options, the portfolio's market value has declined (as calculated earlier) by 9 percent or $2,025,000, resulting in a net loss of $762,750 ($2,025,000 − $1,262,250) or the cost of the option. If the index had risen to 225, portfolio value would have risen, so that

$$
\text{S \& P increase} \quad = \frac{225 - 210}{210} = .071429
$$

$$
\begin{array}{ll}
\text{portfolio increase} = .071429 \times 1.26 = .09 \\
\qquad\qquad\qquad\quad = 1.09(\$22,500,000) - \$22,500,000 \\
\qquad\qquad\qquad\quad = \$24,525,000 - \$22,500,000 \\
\qquad\qquad\qquad\quad = \$2,025,000
\end{array}
$$

However, portfolio profits must be reduced by cost of the options that would have been allowed to expire. Consequently, net profits are $1,262,250 ($2,025,000 − $762,750).

An alternative strategy involves writing 270 calls at 210. If the index had fallen to 195, portfolio's market value would have declined by $2,025,000. However, net loss would have been offset partly by the premium earned on writing 270 calls that would not have been exercised. Consequently

$$
\begin{array}{ll}
\text{gain on calls} = 5.80 \times \$500 \times 270 = \$\ \ 783,000 \\
\text{loss on portfolio} \qquad\qquad\qquad\ = (\$2,025,000) \\
\text{net loss} \qquad\qquad\qquad\qquad\quad = (\$1,242,000)
\end{array}
$$

If the index had risen to 225, the calls would have been exercised as follows:

$$
\begin{array}{ll}
\text{purchase 270 futures contracts at } 225 \times 500 = \ \$30,375,000 \\
\text{sell 270 futures contracts at } 210 \times 500 \quad = \ \$28,350,000 \\
\text{gross loss} \qquad\qquad\qquad\qquad\qquad\qquad = (\$\ 2,025,000) \\
\text{premium earned on writing calls} \qquad\quad = \$\quad 783,000 \\
\text{gain on portfolio} \qquad\qquad\qquad\qquad\ = \$\ 2,025,000 \\
\text{net profit} \qquad\qquad\qquad\qquad\qquad\ = \$\quad 783,000
\end{array}
$$

For those who wish to limit downside risk while maximizing potential gain on portfolio, purchasing puts is the better of the two strategies. Why not purchase puts on individual securities? The short answer is that it is more costly than using an index, assuming the portfolio beta is an accurate measure of systematic risk in relation to the index.

Unlike our earlier use of futures, the portfolio is not perfectly hedged. Moreover, outlay on a call option is nonrefundable (margin on a futures contract is refundable). For hedgers, initial margin requirements are $3,000 per contract and $1,500 to maintain margin. For 270 contracts, initial outlay is 270 × $3,000 = $810,000. Once the trade has been reversed, however, the margin is returned. Consequently, opportunity cost of the funds together with opportunity cost of **marking to the market** are lost. If opportunity cost was 4 percent per quarter on the funds used as margin and if the firm continued to maintain an average balance of $810,000 in the account, then $810,000 × .04 = $32,400. Of course, the amount could be higher or lower, depending on how the index moved. Moreover, those using futures contracts may not wish to completely hedge the portfolio, giving rise to both downside risk as well as upside potential. Fewer contracts require fewer total dollars tied up in margin.

Finally, both options and futures entail transactions costs. In the case of the latter, a reverse trade almost always takes place. In the case of the former, if the option expires there is only one transaction: the initial purchase or sale. It is possible, therefore, to incur higher transactions costs in the futures market.

INTEREST-RATE SWAPS

At times, tailor-made terms between two parties are more convenient than using organized markets to hedge risk. For example, suppose a firm has a portfolio of long-term assets and obtains much of its debt from short-term sources. The classic illustration of this type of institution is the savings and loan association (S & L), a major portion of whose portfolio has traditionally consisted of relatively long-term mortgages (some with fixed-interest rates) but whose primary funding sources are relatively short-term savings deposits. Although this condition of long-term fixed-rate assets and short-term variable-rate liabilities for S & Ls is changing, as long as the condition exists, a way to hedge against the financial squeeze inherent in this mix is to swap interest rates with a firm that has a portfolio of assets whose returns are variable but who has financed much of the debt component of its total capital from fixed-interest-rate securities.

As noted, many nonfinancial corporations finance some of their long-term assets from fixed-interest debt. As noted also, the instability that often characterizes modern financial markets has led to the use of variable-rate instruments.

Sometimes—particularly during periods of high inflation—the market demands such a premium for fixed-over variable-rate debt that firms are led to seek interest-rate swaps, which create a synthetic fixed-rate debt obligation at a lower rate than can be obtained in the capital markets.

Wait a minute! you are saying. In efficient markets, how can one firm obtain a lower fixed rate from another firm? The short answer is that it cannot. However, if markets are less than perfect, an interest-rate swap is a way to offset such imperfections.

Consider, for example, the first domestic interest-rate swap. In 1982, IT&T Financial Corporation entered into an agreement with the Student Loan Marketing Association (Sallie Mae) to swap interest rates.[10] Sallie Mae had issued $100 million worth of debentures maturing in seven years at 13.15-percent YTM. IT&T was rolling more than $100 million worth of commercial paper every 91 days at 50 basis points above the going Treasury-bill rate. Because of its status as a governmental entity, hence indirectly backed by the U.S. Treasury, Sallie Mae had a relative advantage over IT&T in obtaining longer-term funds at lower interest rates. Nevertheless, for short-term variable financing, IT&T had little or no disadvantage compared to Sallie Mae. Moreover, Sallie-Mae's portfolio consisted largely of floating-rate assets; whereas IT&T's portfolio consisted primarily of fixed-rate assets. What the two parties did was exchange interest rates on $100 million in debt. Sallie Mae agreed to pay IT&T's floating rate—50 basis points above the T-bill rate—and IT&T agreed to pay Sallie Mae's 13.15-percent fixed. Each party was responsible for the principal on its own obligations. Depending on the directions of short-term rates, monies exchanged hands periodically, with IT&T always paying the fixed rate. Thus was born the interest-rate swap in U.S. financial markets.[11]

The practice has rapidly spread through the business community, reaching $100 billion by the mid-1980s. Although complexities abound, particularly in international markets, the so-called *plain-vanilla swap* (a fixed-rate dollar loan is traded for a variable-rate dollar loan) remains the most common type of swap.[12] To illustrate (see Figure 20-1), suppose a commercial bank has $100 million in debentures outstanding with a 14-percent interest rate and a loan portfolio tied to the CD rate plus 2 percent. On the other hand, a major retailer has installment contracts at fixed-interest rates averaging 16 percent that will not be liquidated completely for several years. Meanwhile, the retailer can borrow short-term at the CD rate plus 2 percent. Through an intermediary, often an investment banking firm, the retailer

---

[10] Keith Wishon and Lorin S. Chevalier. "Interest Rate Swaps—Your Rate or Mine?, *Journal of Accountancy*, Vol. 63 (September 1985, pp. 63–64).

[11] Wishon and Chevalier, p. 63.

[12] Jan G. Loeys. "Interest Rate Swaps: A New Tool for Managing Risk," *Business Review of the Federal Reserve Bank of Philadelphia* (May–June 1985, pp. 17–25).

Figure 20-1   The Mechanics of an Interest-rate Swap

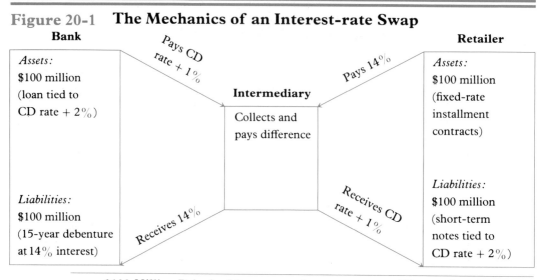

$100 Million Principal (payments for two years at different CD rates)

Date	CD (6-month rate)	Payments (1/2 CD rate + 1%)	Fixed Rate	Net Payment to Retailer	Net Payment to Bank
January	13.25%	$7,125,000	$7,000,000	$125,000	—
July	13.75%	$7,375,000	$7,000,000	$375,000	—
January	13.0%	$7,000,000	$7,000,000	0	0
July	12.5%	$6,750,000	$7,000,000	—	$250,000

and the commercial bank agree to an interest-rate swap on $100,000,000. Every six months the retailer agrees to pay the bank .5 of the 14-percent interest rate the bank must pay on the $100,000,000 in debentures: $7,000,000. In return, the bank agrees to pay the retailer the CD rate plus 1 percent.

In this swap, the bank ensures receipt of $14,000,000 per year to cover interest on the debentures. At the same time, the bank's interest rate will vary, rising with the rate it earns on the portfolio. Meanwhile, the retailer pays a fixed rate of 14 percent, 2 percent less than it earns on the contracts; its obligation is always $7,000,000 per six-month period. As a result, each firm comes closer to matching the return on its assets with the cost of its funds: each has hedged its position in order to reduce the impact of interest-rate changes on variability in earnings. For example, in 1984, through interest-rate swaps, Sears estimated that a 1-percent change in rates reduced variability in its earnings per share from 12 cents to 6 cents.[13]

Whether interest-rate swaps are a more efficient (less costly) means of reducing risk than futures depends on the circumstances. Negotiating a tailor-made contract satisfactory to both parties entails search costs often paid to an investment banker familiar with the nuances of capital structure and asset mix of many firms. Terminating such contracts prior to maturity and finding new parties also may be more expensive than using standardized futures contracts. On the other hand, a long-term swap between two satisfied parties may be less expensive than rolling over futures contracts every few months. To the extent that a standardized pattern for swaps is materializing, standardized contracts and a secondary market are not only feasible but appear to be developing.[14] Unlike some financial arrangements, interest-rate swaps do not depend on tax-law gimmickry. Therefore, their continued growth (or subsequent decline) depends on their effectiveness as compared with futures for hedging interest risk.

SUMMARY

In this chapter, we examined the role of financial futures as instruments for shifting risk. We also examined (briefly) interest-rate swaps as alternatives to financial futures. Long employed in commodities, extension of futures contracts to financial instruments is a relatively recent development. These "pork bellies in pinstripes," as they are sometimes called, can be used by financial managers to *lock in* interest rates on short-term investments and interest costs on short-term loans. Portfolio managers may use interest-rate futures, stock-index futures, and options on futures to hedge against risk; the techniques discussed are but a few among many strategies available, some having great complexity. Perhaps more important is the fact that many firms find it more efficient to hedge risk by matching (to the extent possible) maturities of assets to maturities of financing. When this is difficult to effect, interest-rate swaps are sometimes negotiated.

Continued growth of futures and swaps depends on the degree of volatility in financial markets. To the extent that interest rates become more stable, there is less reason to incur the costs involved in hedging. If volatility in financial markets continues to generate concern, one can anticipate further growth in futures, swaps, and perhaps some yet-to-be introduced arrangement for shifting risk from those who do not wish to bear it to those who do.

---

[13] Same as [10], p. 64.

[14] Same as [10], p. 65; same as [12], p. 22.

PROBLEMS AND QUESTIONS

1. A 90-day T-bill futures contract opens at 92.50. The low for the day was 92.45 and the high was 92.60. The contract was settled at 92.55.
   a. Calculate the market value of each contract.
   b. The day before, Sandra Sweets sold (short) a contract at 92.47 and placed the mandatory $2,000 margin with her broker. Based on the current settlement price, what happened to the margin in her account?

2. Augustus Heap, the new treasurer of Open Pit Sand and Gravel Corporation, expects to have $3,000,000 cash in 60 days that will not be needed for an additional 90 days. The current market price of 90-day T-bill futures contracts maturing in 60 days is 91.54. Anticipating a decline in interest rates:
   a. How may Heap use a futures contract to ensure the current rate—based on a price of 91.54—60 days from today?
   b. Suppose in 60 days the spot price of T-bills is 92.78. Why has Heap instituted a successful hedge? Explain in detail.

3. Having mastered the intricacies of hedging a return on short-term investments in T-bills, Heap decides to use T-bill futures contracts to hedge the short-term borrowing rate. The bank currently charges 12 percent, with interest deducted in advance using the 360-day year. A T-bill futures contract with the same maturity sells at 92.25.
   a. Suppose treasurer Heap wants to borrow $5,000,000 for Open Pit 90 days from today but at the current 12-percent rate. How may he use T-bills to accomplish this objective?
   b. Assume the spot price of T-bills is 91.50 in 90 days and the bank is charging 13.5 percent for short-term loans. Has Heap successfully hedged the original loan rate? Explain in detail.

4. "Generally, the futures price should be lower than the current spot price of the underlying security." Evaluate.

5. Suppose we learn from a regression model that for every 5-basis-point change in yield on a $12,000,000 corporate-bond portfolio there is a 3-basis-point change in yield on a 12-month futures contract on 15-year Treasury bonds. A futures contract change of 1 basis point results in a value change of $.056; a yield on securities change of 1 basis point results in a price change of $.073.
   a. Determine the hedge ratio.
   b. How many futures contracts are required to hedge the portfolio? Does one purchase or sell the contracts? Why?
   c. Using the ratio, would you expect the portfolio to be perfectly hedged? Explain in detail.

6. The S & P 500 stock futures index is 207.35, the value of a stock portfolio is $13,400,000, and the weighted beta is 1.13. Determine the hedge ratio for the portfolio.

7. On a given date there appeared the following:

Date	S & P Futures Index	Calls	Puts
Settlement price	207.35	—	—
Exercise (striking) price = 207	—	5.40	5.25

a. What is the price of each option?

b. If one desires to limit downside risk on the portfolio in problem 6, should one buy puts or write calls? Explain in detail.

8. A savings and loan association with a $100,000,000 portfolio of fixed-rate mortgages financed from short-term deposits tied to the CD rate negotiates an interest-rate swap with a large manufacturing company that has $100,000,000 in debentures outstanding. The S & L is earning 14 percent on the portfolio; the manufacturer must pay 12.5-percent interest on the debentures. The S & L is willing to pay the 12.5 percent if the manufacturer will pay the interest to the S & L at the CD rate plus 1 percent. The CD rate is currently 10 percent. Assuming an intermediary collects and disburses the payments, show the flow of funds to and from each firm. What does each party appear to gain from the exchange?

9. "Increased volatility in interest rates and stock prices will enhance the use of financial futures and swaps; reduced volatility will lessen their popularity." Evaluate.

SELECTED ADDITIONAL REFERENCES

Andrews, Suzanna. "Should Cash Management Be a Profit Center?" *Institutional Investor*, Vol. XIX (July 1985, pp. 203–4).

Bacon, Peter W. and Richard E. Williams. "Interest Rate Futures, New Tools for the Financial Manager," *Financial Management*, Vol. 5 (Spring 1976, pp. 32–38).

Block, Stanley and Timothy J. Gallagher. "The Use of Interest Rate Futures and Options by Corporate Financial Managers," *Financial Management*, Vol. 15 (Autumn 1986, pp. 73–78).

Bradford, Cornell and Kenneth French. "The Pricing of Stock Index Futures" (Center for the Study of Futures' Market: Columbia Business School, Working Paper Series, No. CSFM-43).

Khoury, Sarkis. *Speculative Markets* (New York: Macmillan 1984, Chs. 5–7).

Kolb, Robert W. *Interest Rate Futures: Concepts and Issues* (Richmond, VA: Robert F. Dame, 1981, pp. 237–364).

————— and Raymond Chiang. "Improving Hedging Performance Using Interest Rate Futures," *Financial Management*, Vol. 10 (Autumn 1981, pp. 72–79).

—————. *Understanding Futures Markets* (Glenview, IL: Scott, Foresman and Company, 1985).

Loeys, Jan. "Interest Rate Swaps: A New Tool for Managing Risk," *Business Review of the Federal Reserve Bank of Philadelphia* (May–June 1985, pp. 17–25).

Rendleman, Richard J. and Christopher J. Carabini. "The Efficiency of the Treasury Bill Futures Market," *Journal of Finance*, Vol. 34 (September 1979, pp. 895–914).

Smith, Clifford W. Jr., Charles W. Smithson, and Lee Macdonald Wakeman. "The Evolving Market for Swaps," *Midland Corporate Finance Journal*, Vol. 3 (Winter 1986, pp. 20–32).

Wishon, Keith and Lorin S. Chevalier. "Interest Rate Swaps—Your Rate or Mine?," *Journal of Accountancy*, Vol. 63 (September 1985, pp. 63–64).

21

MERGERS

Since 1897—when the first great wave of mergers began—the combining of two or more entities into a single organization has been an important factor in shaping the structure of American business. Consequently, no survey of finance is complete without treating the topic in some detail.

Preliminarily, we must point out that in financial parlance the term **merger** *has a broader meaning than in law. In corporate law, the generally accepted definition of merger is a union of two companies: A and B combine to form a third company, C, the new entity known in law as a* **consolidation***. Because in financial economics there is*

THE WALL STREET JOURNAL

"The merger has been approved in principle. The hang-up is over who is swallowing who."

no substantive difference between merger and consolidation, we use the terms interchangeably.

However, the term **combination** can refer to a merger, a consolidation, or to some other means whereby two or more firms pool their collective resources. A **joint venture**, for example, is an agreement between two or more companies to share the risks and rewards inherent in a specific project. Consider the several petroleum companies that jointly financed construction of the Trans-Alaska pipeline. At the time, two of the companies—British Petroleum and Standard Oil of Ohio (Sohio)—also effected a partial merger whereby British Petroleum would eventually control up to 54 percent of the common stock of Sohio.[1]

Even in the foregoing context the term merger is used broadly. Again, in legal parlance a merger is consummated when the acquiring company either purchases all the assets or the stock of the company to be acquired. If the acquiring company purchases the assets with cash, the acquired company now has cash as its only asset; its liabilities and stock remain outstanding. The acquired company can continue to exist as a newly formed third company or it may pay off its obligations, distribute the remaining funds to its stockholders as a liquidating dividend, and cease to exist as a corporate entity. If the acquiring company purchases all the stock of the acquired concern, the latter often ceases to exist.

To consummate a statutory merger: the acquiring company purchases all the stock of the acquired concern, the two companies must conform to the merger laws of the states in which they are incorporated, and approval by the stockholders of both companies is necessary. When assets only are purchased, the board of directors of the acquiring concern and the stockholders of the company whose assets are acquired must approve. When the acquiring concern purchases 100 percent of the acquired company's stock, it also assumes the latter's liabilities. When the transaction is complete, the acquired company—having no assets, liabilities, or equity—ceases to exist.

---

[1] Paul D. Phillips, John C. Groth, and Malcolm Richards. "*Financial Management*, Vol. 8 (Autumn 1979, pp. 7–16).

THE TAKEOVER

Although statutory mergers delight lawyers as they contemplate the fees involved, such protocols are not the only means by which companies acquire the stock of other companies. What if management or the board of directors of the company to be acquired does not wish to consummate the marriage? No problem: Go directly to the stockholders. Enter the **takeover** or, more accurately, the **hostile takeover**. The objective is the same—specifically, to acquire the company stock—but the means are different. Agreement among principal officers of two companies to recommend a merger to their respective boards and stockholders—cemented with cocktails, wine, and dinner (not to mention brandy and cigars) in an elegant setting—gives way to the late twentieth-century version of the "Gunfight at the O.K. Corral." Lawyers take a backseat to the corporate raider (corporate shark) and his or her investment banker. Names such as T. Boone Pickens, Carl Ichan, and Irv "the liquidator" Jacobs (among others) figure prominently on the list of corporate raiders. David G. Kay and the firm of Drexel Burnham Lambert figure prominently among investment bankers.[2]

In this instance, the weapon is not the Colt 45, but the **tender offer**. Appealing directly to the stockholders, a bid is made for their shares, which they (in turn) can tender to the buyer often at a figure as much as 20 percent more than the stock's current market price.[3] Thus the shootout begins.

However, management of the takeover target also has its methods (**shark repellents**) for preventing a takeover. If state law permits, the company has already included a *super majority approval provision* in its corporate charter. For a merger, instead of a majority of stock—just over 50 percent—the charter might require that as high as 80 percent of the shares vote in favor of the merger before it is approved. It

---

[2] Ford S. Worthy. "What's Next for the Raiders?" *Fortune*, Vol. 112 (November 11, 1985, pp. 20–24).

[3] Sometimes a two-tier system is employed. If the raider has acquired perhaps 5 percent of the stock in the open market prior to the tender offer, a bid may be made at one price for an additional 45 percent of the stock and at a lower price for shares tendered later. This encourages stockholders to tender their shares early to receive the higher price and to give the raider effective control of the company. See Oliver Hart, "Takeover Bids, the Free-Rider Problem, and the Theory of the Corporation," *Bell Journal of Economics*, Vol. 11 (Spring 1984, pp. 42–64).

also might stagger the terms of the board of directors, making it more difficult to immediately elect a majority once the stock is in hand. The company also may have included a *lockup provision* in the charter, requiring super majority approval to modify the corporate charter. There also may be a *fair merger price* provision in the charter, whereby price may be linked to earnings per share or to some unusually high multiple of the price–earnings ratio, which the bidder must pay to conclude the merger. However, because many states do not permit such provisions in a corporate charter, a company may have to reincorporate in a state where antitakeover provisions are permitted.

At a second defense level, management may call on the modern version of the cavalry—in this instance, the **white knight**. Enter another firm encouraged to bid for company shares. Better to be protected by a friendly takeover than to be devoured by a hostile raider.

Even if the battle is lost, top management at least does not find itself in the corporate equivalent of Boot Hill. (Those further down, however, may be visiting *outplacement counselors* as they prepare for a new career.) The **golden parachute**— several million dollars in severance pay—can tide one over for some time while contemplating a new beginning on the beaches of Maui.

Thus, a potpourri of strategies and counterstrategies have developed during the last few years. When Saul Steinberg made a bid to control Walt Disney Productions, Disney paid him and his group $325 million in **greenmail**—$12 above the market price—to prevent the takeover. Rather than submit to the takeover bid of T. Boone Pickens, Gulf Oil found a white knight in Standard Oil of California (Socal).[4]

Others prefer going private; this can be accomplished in two ways. A publicly held company can be purchased by a private concern. (In 1985, the Belzberg family of Canada acquired Scoville Inc. in this manner.) A more common approach is **leveraged buyout**, wherein a group of investors (including top management) borrow heavily to buy back the company's outstanding stock, thereby transforming the concern into a privately held but heavily leveraged corporation. In 1984, for example, 60 companies removed themselves from the market through leveraged buyouts.[5]

Nevertheless, both hostile and friendly takeovers continued to dominate the corporate scene throughout the mid-1980s. In each of the years 1984 and 1985, companies were merged whose assets had a book value of approximately $125 billion. This was more than double the book value of mergers in 1983, approximately double those in 1981 and 1982, and nearly four times the figures for 1979 and 1980.[6] In 1984 and 1985, billion-dollar mergers unheard of in 1980 were commonplace. As

---

[4] Anne B. Fosher. "Oops! My Company Is on the Block," *Fortune*, Vol. 110 (July 23, 1984, pp. 16–21).

[5] *Wall Street Journal*, August 12, 1985, p. 13.

[6] *New York Times*, December 29, 1985, Sec. 3, p. 1. As of this writing (mid-1987) and in the wake of insider trading scandals on Wall Street, Congress is holding hearings to determine the necessity of enacting restrictive legislation aimed at making takeovers more difficult.

examples, the 1984 Chevron-Gulf merger was valued at $13.2 billion, the 1985 Philip Morris acquisition of General Foods in excess of $5.6 billion, and the 1986 General Electric acquisition of RCA at approximately $6.3 billion.[7]

WHY MERGE?

Although recent combinations among American corporations have generated considerable attention in the popular press, behind the colorful figures and even more colorful language should lie an explanation or set of explanations. The basic principles of economics and principles of financial economics offer a starting point from which to rationalize business combinations in general—even though they may not fully explain recent experience.

In the context of basic economic principles, the merger of two companies (A and B) is justified if the value $AB >$ value of $A + B$. The term employed to express this inequality is **synergy**. A combination is synergistic (as the preceding equation suggests) if the value of the combined firms exceeds the sum of the values of the individual firms. This is sometimes called the $2 + 2 = 5$ effect.

In conventional economics, the source of the synergy could be **economies of scale or economies of scope**, each leading to lower production costs. The former term implies that the individual firms are not operating efficiently—the scale of enterprise is too small. The latter term suggests that perhaps in producing—but more likely in marketing—products, it may be more efficient to provide a range of goods rather than a single product. The salesperson representing a national manufacturer of food products may experience lower unit costs of marketing when, in making rounds, he or she offers a variety of goods to the wholesaler or to the retail chain. And sometimes the vertical integration of related products results in economies of production and marketing. Consider the classic illustration of a firm that has considerable research expertise uniting with a firm that has considerable marketing skills but produces a product or set of products undergoing rapid technological change.

To the extent such combinations lower production costs, they do so for technical reasons: the production function is altered toward greater output per unit of input. Firms so combined operate more efficiently than as individual entities and resource allocation within the firm is more efficient than resource allocation through the market. In addition, such a combination results in both social and private gains— lower prices and, in the short run at least, higher profits.

In contrast to technical economies inherent in the production function, there is also the possibility of **pecuniary economies**: the merger of two firms may result in

---

[7] Same as [6], p. 1. See, also, David Kirkpatrick, "Deals of the Year," *Fortune*, Vol. 113 (January 20, 1986, pp. 26–30).

a lower price for the resources used. In our discussion of the principles of financial economics, specifically those principles pertaining to cost of capital, we noted that cost of debt capital (hence weighted average cost of capital) is affected by firm size as well as by debt–equity ratios. In terms of the risk/reward trade-off, size is viewed as reducing risk. Consequently, if firm A combines with firm B and their bond rating rises from "A" to "Aa," clearly the combination has yielded a pecuniary economy that will be reflected in lower costs of capital and ultimately (in competitive-product markets) in lower prices for goods or services produced.

Although both technical and pecuniary economies are possible, even when they are not present the merger may be synergistic. Two firms might unite if their combination lowered transaction costs—costs of using the market. Even though the savings are pecuniary rather than technical, the synergy that may result stems not from lower prices for resources, but from the firm's superiority over the market as a means of allocating resources. As Oliver Williamson notes, "Transaction costs are the economic equivalent of friction in physical systems."[8] A firm reduces trans-action costs by allocating resources internally; the union of two firms can reduce such costs even further. Of course, one can carry the notion too far. A large firm with an unwieldy bureaucratic structure is difficult, costly, to manage. Thus, one may find that in the absence of technical or pecuniary economies, the gain from reducing transaction costs through acquisition may be more than offset by the additional costs of trying to manage the acquisition effectively. In such circumstances, the market is more efficient than the merger of the two firms.

Whatever the source of the economies, they must be viewed in a dynamic context. In the standard equilibrium model of economics and financial economics, technical and pecuniary economies play no role and transaction costs are generally ignored. Certainly, in long-run competitive equilibrium, the firm has already achieved operational as well as allocative efficiency inasmuch as price equals both marginal- and average-total cost. Because the model functions in a frictionless environment, transaction costs play no role in either the short or the long run.

In terms of financial economics, recall the discussion in Chapter 10, where we suggested it is possible to view the firm as a collection of assets, each with an unleveraged beta coefficient and the firm's unleveraged beta coefficient as the weighted average of the betas of individual assets. Of course, such a perspective presumes managers are homogeneous: the same assets in the hands of different managers perform the same way. In addition, the diversification that can result from conglomerate merger can be achieved by investors through portfolio diversification. Finally, although such institutional factors as tax deductibility of interest and bankruptcy costs may lead to an optimal capital structure, they are not unique to an individual firm.

---

[8] Oliver E. Williamson. *The Economic Institutions of Capitalism* (New York: The Free Press, 1985, p. 19).

Nevertheless, in Chapter 10, we chose not to employ the notion that a firm is a collection of assets, not because the view is devoid of insight, but because it lacks operational significance. Consequently, from the firm's perspective, if management of one company is superior to management of a second company, assets of the second company may be more valuable in the hands of the superior management.

Similarly, taxes can be a motivating force for one company and entry into the market a motivating force for another. Suppose a successful entrepreneur owns her own company. Although the company is incorporated, the stock is in her hands or the hands of her family and there is no ready market value. Aging and concerned about estate taxes, the entrepreneur decides to sell the company to a publicly held company for either cash or stock in that company. Consequently, when the grim reaper pays a visit, the heirs will have the liquidity necessary to meet the death duties imposed on the estate. The firm purchasing the company, on the other hand, may have a different motive. It may have found, through conventional capital budgeting analysis, that a merger would be more profitable than entering the market *de novo*.

Although the foregoing discussion suggests that two firms may have several different reasons for merging, long-run equilibrium analysis assumes those reasons away and hence is of no value in explaining the phenomenon.

Certainly firms and ultimately owners may benefit from mergers, but does society realize any benefits? The question is not trivial, for the combining of firms is an area in which public policy (through antitrust enforcement) has played a major but far from consistent role. Briefly, in determining what mergers are consistent with or at least not contrary to public interest, the issue of primary concern to public policy is monopoly power.[9] Does their merger lead to market domination by the combined firms? The 1968 and 1982 Department of Justice guidelines for approving mergers reflected attitudinal changes about combinations, with those of the Reagan administration (the 1982 guidelines) being more pro-merger oriented.[10] Thus a merger that may appear to genuinely benefit the parties involved may be prevented by agency enforcement or, if carried out, be challenged in court by the Department of Justice or the Federal Trade Commission. In the 1960s, for example, most horizontal mergers of companies in overlapping markets were challenged successfully. A similar result was obtained for most vertical mergers. What remained were conglomerate mergers—which dominated the period. In the 1980s—believing that only mergers clearly resulting in monopoly would be challenged—American firms (led by the oil companies) combined assets, as noted earlier, in record amounts.

---

[9] Public policy also has been concerned with size. Should public policy prohibit mergers because mergers result in large corporations? To what extent should size per se be a factor in preventing mergers? For a lucid, trenchant, and controversial analysis of merger policy, see Robert Bork, *The Antitrust Paradox* (New York: Basic Books, 1978, pp. 217–62.

[10] For commentary on the appropriateness of the Reagan guidelines, see Oliver Williamson, same as [8], pp. 98–102 and Thomas E. Kauper, "The 1982 Horizontal Merger Guidelines: of Collusion, Efficiency and Failure," *California Law Review*, Vol. 71 (March 1983, pp. 497–54).

THE TERMS OF THE MERGER

When two companies combine, they must agree that the merger offers both the buyer and the seller something of value. As our previous discussion suggests, that value may derive from several sources. As indicated, true synergy is possible. In addition, risk reduction for the buyer and its management (if not the stockholders) also is possible through conglomerate merger that results in greater diversification. Nevertheless, the buyer probably will have to offer the potential seller some of that expected gain in the form of a premium over the current market value of the seller's stock. This premium can best be understood in terms of the **Market Value Exchange Ratio**.

To illustrate, consider a standard statutory merger in which company A purchases company B by exchanging its shares for shares of company B and then dissolves company B. Such an exchange is tax free at the time it takes place because company B stockholders merely exchange their shares for company A shares. At the time of the merger, each company is in the following financial position:

	Company A	*Company B*
Current earnings	$45,000,000	$9,000,000
Shares outstanding	12,000,000	4,500,000
Earnings per share	$3.75	$2.00
Market price of stock	$56.25	$18.00
P/E ratio	$56.25/$3.75 = 15/1	$18.00/$2.00 = 9/1
Dividends per share	$1.25	$0.75
Payout ratio	$1.25/$3.75 = 1/3	$0.75/$2.00 = 3/8
Current yield	$1.25/$56.25 = .0\bar{2}	$0.75/$18.00 = .041\bar{6}

Examining the price-to-earnings ratio (the P/E ratio) reveals that investors place a higher premium on company A earnings relative to those of company B. The current yield on company A stock is lower than the current yield on company B stock. Given no further information—no unleveraged beta coefficients, no estimate of dividend growth, and so forth—we shall assume the market has priced each stock efficiently. The ratio of market prices for the two companies' shares is

$$\frac{\text{per-share market value of A}}{\text{per-share market value of B}} = \frac{\$56.25}{\$18} = \frac{3.125}{1}$$

Thus, a company A share is 3.125 times as valuable as a company B share. Viewed differently, a company B share is .32 as valuable (1 ÷ 3.125) as a company A share. If management of company A offered .32 shares of company A for every company B share, then:

$$\frac{\$56.25 \times .32}{\$18 \times 1} = \frac{18}{18} = \frac{1}{1}$$

In terms of per-share market value, there has been an even exchange of company shares.

Although company A management might make this offer, it is likely to be refused by company B shareholders. An owner of 100 shares of company B would receive 32 shares of company A and would immediately lose current income. Thus, dividends would fall because

shareholder in company B loses 100 × $0.75	$= -\$75$
shareholder in company B (with shares in company A) gains 32 × $1.25	$= +\$40$
loss in current income from exchange	$= -\$35$

The exchange may be even, but the shareholder is likely to view it as a loss. Indeed, to keep the shareholder even in terms of dividends, company A management would have to raise the dividends on all its shares to approximately $2.35 per share, so that $32 \times \$2.35 = \$75.20$.

Even if company A management raised the dividend, it might not entice company B shareholders to part with their stock. It might, however, sweeten the offer by paying a premium over the current market price of company B stock and increasing the dividend on company A stock so company B shareholders would receive the same cash flow from their shares in company A as they had received from their shares in company B. For example, suppose, company A management offers each company B shareholder .4 shares of company A for each share owned and increases the dividend from $1.25 to $1.88 per share. In terms of market value, company B shareholders earn a premium of

$$\frac{\$56.25 \times .4}{\$18} = \frac{1.25}{1}$$

In other words, company B shareholders gain 25 percent in terms of market value. As for dividends, owners of 100 shares in company B receive 40 new shares in company A, each paying $1.88, so that $40 \times \$1.88 = \$75.20$. Thus, dividends remain approximately the same.

When the companies merge, accounting figures will change, so that

	Company A	**Company B**	**A + B = A combined**
Current earnings	$45,000,000 +	$9,000,000 =	$54,000,000
Shares outstanding	12,000,000 +	.4(4,500,000) =	13,800,000
Earnings per share	$3.75	$2.00	$3.913
Dividends per share	$1.25	$0.75	$1.88
Payout ratio	$1.25/$3.75 = 1/3	$0.75/$2.00 = 3/8	$1.88/$3.913 = .48

Because the total number of shares in the merged companies are reduced, earnings per share of the combined companies rise. The exchange was based on a 25-percent premium over the ratio of current market values. For post-merger per-share earnings of company A to remain unchanged, $54,000,000 \div \$3.75 = 14,400,000$ shares must be issued. To obtain 14,400,000 shares, the exchange ratio must be

$$12,000,000 + 4,500,000x = 14,400,000$$
$$x = .5\overline{3}$$

Anything above this ratio would cause per-share earnings of the combined companies to be less than the $3.75 company A was earning prior to merger. Moreover, by increasing dividends, company A management has increased its payout ratio. If management had chosen to maintain the payout ratio at approximately $1/3$, dividends could have increased only to

$$\frac{\$3.913}{3} = \$1.3043$$

If company A management had raised the dividend to $1.30, company B share-holders—while still receiving a premium in terms of market value—would have lost current income. Again, assuming a 100-share ownership in company B, then

$$100 \times .75 = -\$75$$
$$40 \times 1.30 = \underline{+\ \ 52}$$
$$\text{Loss in current income} = -\$23$$

Of course, the market-value premium may be sufficient to entice company B shareholders to agree to merger even though their income would fall. This is a matter of negotiation between management of the two companies.

WHO BENEFITS AFTER THE MERGER?

Management of each company attempts to increase the wealth of its shareholders after merger has been completed. For shareholders of both companies to benefit, there must be synergy. Prior to merger

$$
\begin{aligned}
\text{total market value of A} &= 12,000,000 \times \$56.25 = \$675,000,000 \\
\text{total market value of B} &= \ \ 4,500,000 \times \ \ 18.00 = \underline{\ \ 81,000,000} \\
&= \$756,000,000
\end{aligned}
$$

If there are technical or pecuniary economies, if transactions costs are reduced, or if firm A management is more efficient than firm B management, the combined firm's total market value would rise. For example, suppose the market, for one or more of the foregoing reasons, continued to place a multiple of 15 times earnings on the combined firms—total market value of the *new* company A would be

$$15 \times \$3.913 \times 13,800,000 \text{ shares} = \$809,991,000$$

A company A stockholder owning 100 shares would experience a gain of

$$\$58.695 - \$56.25 \times 100 = \$244.50$$

A company B stockholder would give up $\$18 \times 100 = \$1,800$, having initially received $\$56.25 \times 40 = \$2,250$, which is now worth $\$58.695 \times 40 = \$2,347.80$. The owner of 100 shares in company A realizes a percentage gain of

$$\frac{\$2.445}{\$56.25} = .0435 \times 100 = 4.35\%$$

The owner of 100 shares in company B realizes a gain of

$$\frac{\$2,347.80 - \$1,800}{\$2,347.80} = \frac{\$547.80}{\$2,347.80} = .2333 \times 100 = 23.33\%$$

The preceding scenario represents only the gain from an increase in market price per share. If dividends had been raised to $1.88 cents per share, there would have been no gain for the former company B shareholders. However, company A shareholders would have gained

$$\frac{[\$2.445 + (\$1.88 - \$1.25)]100}{\$56.25 \times 100} = .0547 \times 100 = 5.47\%$$

Although both sets of shareholders gained from the merger, as one might expect from the premium paid, former company B shareholders benefitted more.

If management had chosen to maintain the payout ratio and to increase dividends only from $1.25 to $1.30 for the original 100-share stockholders in company A, the gain would have been

$$\frac{[\$2.445 + (\$1.30 - \$1.25)]100}{\$56.25 \times 100} = .0444 \times 100 = 4.44\%$$

Based on 100 shares, the former company B shareholders would have realized a gain of

$$\frac{\$2,347.80 - \$1,800 - \$23}{\$2,347.80} = .2235 \times 100 = 22.35\%$$

Although the result is less than under the former scenario, company B shareholders still benefit more compared with company A shareholders.[11]

However, suppose the market anticipated no synergy from the merger: because earnings are not to be expected to rise in the future, higher dividends are not justified. As a result, total market value of the combined firms equals the sum of the market values of each firm prior to merger: a total of $756,000,000. Although now only 13,800,000 shares are outstanding, market price per share falls to $756,000,000 ÷ 13,800,000 = $54.78. Now the price/earnings ratio is

$$\frac{P}{E} = \frac{54.78}{3.913} = 13.999 \equiv 14.00$$

which reflects company A acquisition of a company with a lower $\frac{P}{E}$ multiple but with no anticipated economies from the combination.

For the holder of 100 shares in company A

before merger 100 × $56.25 =		$5,625
after merger 100 × $54.78 =		$5,478
loss in market value	=	−$ 147

For the holder of 100 shares in company B

before merger 100 × $18 =		−$1,800
after merger 40 × $54.78 =		+$2,191.20
gain in market value	=	$ 391.20

In terms of market value, there has been a redistribution of wealth from company A shareholders to company B shareholders. Depending on whether the decline in the market value coincided with an increase in dividends from $1.25 to $1.88 or from $1.25 to $1.30, the redistribution would have been larger or smaller. A dividend increase from $1.25 to $1.88 would have added $63 to the income of 100-share stockholders in company A ($0.63 × 100) without materially affecting the income of company B stockholders. If dividends had risen only to $1.30, 100-share stockholders in company A would have received $5 in additional annual income ($.05 × 100), whereas 100-share stockholders in company B would have lost $23 in annual dividends.

---

[11] Because the $23 dividend loss is permanent, perhaps one should subtract the present value of that dividend as though the loss would continue for some years into the future. Assuming 14 percent is an appropriate discount rate over an infinite time horizon, the gain realized from the merger would be

$$\frac{\$2,347.80 - \$1,800 - \$23/.14}{\$2,347.80} = .1634 \times 100 = 16.34\%$$

There is still a relative gain for company B stockholders.

IS THE TARGET UNDERVALUED?

Although the foregoing analysis suggests that purchasing company stockholders may pay dearly for the merger, it is also possible that market price of the target company stock may be too low or (with due deference to the efficient market hypothesis) perceived to be too low. Consider the abortive attempt of General Aniline and Film Corporation (GAF) to acquire Union Carbide near the end of 1985.[12]

At the time, Union Carbide was drowning in litigation stemming from the death of at least 1,750 people alleged to have been caused by a chemical leak from its Bhopal, India plant. Moreover, the company had experienced operating losses during 1985. With such uncertainty surrounding its future, one would assume Union Carbide would not be a logical candidate for takeover. Or would it? In spite of significant problems, the company generated considerable cash flow and enjoyed a comparatively low debt ratio. When GAF management was considering its acquisition, Union Carbide was selling for $63 per share but its asset value was estimated at approximately $85 per share.

A company with such characteristics is termed a *cash cow*, which can be milked for its assets. And that was what GAF essentially planned to do. Typical of so many combinations at the time, instead of a statutory merger GAF would offer Carbide stockholders $68 per share (a $5 premium over the current market price). To finance this $4.13-billion *hostile purchase*, GAF would issue high-yield **junk bonds** and then sell certain Carbide assets (primarily the consumer products division) to retire the bonds issued.

However, whether Union Carbide was indeed a cash cow or a company selling at a discount from market value of its assets (because of uninsured damages it might have to pay the victims of the Bhopal tragedy) was a moot point. On the basis of expert legal advice, GAF concluded at the time that Carbide's tort exposure was not as great as current market price of its stock seemed to suggest.

Union Carbide management apparently held a similar view. If Carbide stockholders accepted the $68 per share offer and if GAF successfully floated the bonds and sold Carbide's consumer products division, GAF stockholders—not Carbide stockholders—would enjoy whatever value remained in other Carbide assets. Moreover, in a cash sale, stockholders of the selling company must pay a capital gains tax on the difference, if positive, between the price paid for the stock and the $68 received. Thus, if one had purchased shares at $38 and sold them at $68, the $30 gain would be subject to taxes. As a result, when GAF made the offer, Union Carbide recommended that stockholders not accept it. Indeed, Carbide countered

---

[12] Anthony Ramirez. "Restless GAF Is on the Prowl," *Fortune*, Vol. 113 (February 3, 1986, pp. 32–38). See, also, James B. Stewart and Daniel Hertzberg, "Landmark Victory," *Wall Street Journal* (January 13, 1986, pp. 1 and 12).

with a strategy in which it agreed to purchase 35 percent of its stock outstanding from tendering shareholders at $85 per share. Carbide would finance the purchase with cash and notes. The notes would not only serve the purpose of loading the company with debt, but would contain a convenant limiting the sale of assets. Consequently, Carbide would be more difficult to finance and thus a less-attractive purchase.

Notwithstanding, GAF was ready to purchase the notes issued to tendering stockholders and to nullify the restrictive clause on sale of assets. Moreover, GAF was now prepared to offer $74 per share for Carbide stock. In turn, Carbide revised its $85 per-share offer to include 55 percent of its stock, promising not only to issue more debt but to sell its consumer products division. GAF countered with an offer of $78 per share, for a total of $5.06 billion. GAF made this final appeal directly to Carbide's board as a friendly merger. When rejected, no new offer or hostile takeover at a higher price was attempted. GAF gave up on the ground that its stockholders would not benefit from a higher bid.

Although the period of time from the initial $68 per-share offer to GAF's announcement it would no longer pursue the merger lasted only 31 days (December 9, 1985, to January 8, 1986), Carbide considered turning the tables and purchasing GAF stock. Known as the **PacMan defense** against takeover, it was rejected by Carbide on the grounds that the market already placed a premium on GAF stock and that there would be no gain to Carbide shareholders from such a strategy.

Carbide also considered using a tactic known as the **poison pill**. In order to thwart the GAF offer, Carbide could have sold new stock to its shareholders at a deep discount from Carbide's current market price. This tactic would have increased the number of shares outstanding and would have forced GAF either to lower the offering price or to purchase the stock at a considerable premium over its market value and possibly its asset value. The board of directors rejected this strategy on the ground that it would appear as though management was trying to entrench itself.[13]

In GAF's aborted takeover attempt of Carbide, each company believed the market was undervaluing Carbide's shares by overreacting to the damages Carbide might have to pay as a result of the Bhopal litigation. The strategies employed by Carbide, however, caused GAF to abandon the takeover attempt on the ground that a price much more than $78 per share would overstate the value of the company to GAF shareholders. Because there was no apparent synergy, but only the possibility that the market undervalued Carbide's stock, a merger would take place only if each party had a different opinion of the degree to which the stock was undervalued. Within that range, bargaining would determine the ultimate outcome. Apparently Carbide considered GAF's offer inadequate; apparently GAF considered Carbide's position inflated.

---

[13] Same as [12], Stewart and Hertzberg, p. 1.

THE EMPIRICAL EVIDENCE

However interesting case studies are, modern research focuses on the general effects of mergers. Of particular interest to corporate finance are answers to the following basic questions: (1) Are mergers synergistic: do they create value? (2) If value is created now, is it divided between the parties to the merger? Although methodologies vary and in spite of technical or econometric problems in conducting research, some interesting answers to these questions emerge from the extensive literature in the field (see Selected Additional References at end of chapter). Jensen and Ruback published a useful summary of the evidence—at least into the early 1980s—which may or may not be modified in the 1990s as students of the subject examine more closely the merger mania that characterized the Reagan presidency.[14]

First of all, mergers do create value. Although estimates vary, on average market value of the shares of combined firms increases once the acquisition is completed.[15] However, the source of the increased value is difficult to isolate. Sometimes comparatively inefficient management is replaced by more efficient management. At other times there are tax savings realized through combination. Traditional sources of synergy—technical and pecuniary economies—as well as elimination of transaction costs can be factors. Nevertheless, to date it has been difficult to distinguish among alternative explanations for the gain; indeed, no single source may dominate the general results. Consequently, only case studies of individual mergers can add to an understanding of the specific synergistic source.

What about the socially unacceptable merger that may or may not be synergistic but that increases market value of the combined firms' shares because the merger results in monopoly power and hence monopoly profits?[16] Available evidence suggests that monopoly power does not appear to be a motivating factor, at least in recent years.[17] However, this does not imply that mergers will not be attacked. As a matter of public policy, size itself may be a reason for preventing a merger. For example, extremely large companies may wield excessive power in government because of the resources they control: they may have greater influence over the distribution of resources between public and private sectors of the economy as a single entity than as separate companies. Nevertheless, even if this is the case, scale economies in lobbying play no part in the kinds of studies we are summarizing—

---

[14] Michael C. Jensen and Richard S. Ruback. "The Market for Corporate Control, the Scientific Evidence," *Journal of Financial Economics*, Vol. 11 (April 1983, pp. 5–50).

[15] Jensen and Ruback, p. 22.

[16] If there are both synergy and monopoly profits, public policymakers must choose between greater efficiency and monopoly profit or reduced efficiency from not allowing the merger.

[17] B. Espen Eckbo. "Horizontal Mergers, Collusion and Stockholder Wealth," *Journal of Financial Economics*, Vol. 11 (April 1983, pp. 241–73). Robert Stillman. "Examining Antitrust Policy Toward Horizontal Mergers," *Journal of Financial Economics*, Vol. 11 (April 1983, pp. 225–40).

which focus on the narrower issue of market power, not clout in Washington or in the state capitols.

As to the second question of whether, if value is created now it is divided between the parties to the merger, the evidence suggests that the target enjoys more of the gain in value. In a typical pattern resulting in a successful acquisition, market price of the targeted company's stock begins to rise perhaps a month prior to the actual announcement. And when the acquisition takes place, market price of the stock may have risen by as much as 80 percent. Because in efficient markets most of the potential gain in the stock's price occurs prior to the acquisition announcement, those who purchase a targeted company's stock well in advance can realize substantial gains in a short time period. Hence, uncovering candidates for acquisition is a game Wall Streeters like to play. No doubt SEC lawyers experience many sleepless nights wondering (if not who) whether someone had inside information well in advance of the announcement date.

Shareholders of the target also are affected by the form of acquisition. Because they are associated with hostile takeovers and are sometimes countered by competing tenders, tender offers result in greater average returns to stockholders of the targeted company than when a friendly statutory merger occurs. Even if the acquisition fails, the targeted company's stock price remains high—at least for a while—because new suitors are expected. After all, what attracted one may also attract someone else. However, if no further attempts are made, the stock price of the potential target begins to drift downward toward its premerger price.

When we examine the results of research on shareholders of the acquiring corporation, the evidence is less impressive. Some studies suggest there is little positive impact on the price of the acquiring company's shares. Others studies report that returns are slightly negative as stock price drifts downward following acquisition.[18] There are several explanations for such results. First, it is difficult to separate the merger's impact from other factors that affect market price of the stock: although the target is removed, the acquiring corporation remains a going concern. Second, often the suitor is a larger company than the target; hence, gains expressed in percentages are relatively small when compared with those of the target. Third, on balance it is possible acquiring companies pay too much for the potential synergy. Most (if not all) of the gains go to the target's stockholders. For example, the Du Pont-Conoco merger created an additional market value of $2.4 billion; however, Conoco shareholders realized gains of about $3.2 billion whereas Du Pont (the suitor) incurred losses of almost $800 million.[19] On balance, it seems better to be courted than to do the courting.

---

[18] See, for example, Michael Bradley, Anand Desai, and E. Han Kim, "The Rationale Behind Interfirm Tender Offers: Information on Synergy," *Journal of Financial Economics*, Vol. 11 (April 1983, pp. 183–206).

[19] Same as [14], p. 25.

SUMMARY

Combining two firms into a single entity is a practice that has characterized American economic history since the late nineteenth century. Although merger mania waxes and wanes, the 1980s have seen considerable growth in merger activity. Institutional mechanisms by which acquisitions occur vary. One company may acquire the stock or the assets of another and may pay with cash or with its own stock. The acquired company may become a subsidiary of the acquiring firm or, on the other hand, may sell its assets for cash or stock and become a liquidated corporate shell. Alternatively, the acquired company can remain in business, using the cash to acquire other assets or using the stock as a basis for becoming a **holding company**. The form is often a matter of law, the substance a matter of economics. The preferred form of acquisition today is a cash purchase of the targeted company's stock, using bonds as a means of raising the cash. Once the company is acquired, certain assets are sold to pay off the debt and the remaining assets accrue to the acquiring company.

Synergy should exist at the heart of any merger of efficiently managed companies in efficient capital markets. Although the source of synergy varies, both pecuniary and technical economies are possible and transaction costs may also be reduced. In addition, where management of the acquiring firm is comparatively more efficient than management of the acquired firm, the combination should be more efficiently operated. Evidence on mergers suggests that on balance corporate combinations are synergistic; nevertheless, there is at present no identifiable general source of synergy. Consequently, case studies of individual mergers are useful in pinpointing gains in specific instances. Stockholders of merged companies also may gain because the combination results in monopoly power. There is, however, little evidence that monopoly is a primary motivation or result of recent corporate acquisitions.

Where synergy does exist, the shareholders of targeted companies appear on balance to be the relative gainers. The shareholders of suitors do not always lose in terms of market value; yet the bulk of potential synergy may accrue to those who own shares in the target.

In the final analysis, perhaps mergers may be viewed best as "a market in which alternative management teams compete for the right to manage corporate resources."[20] If true, competition should lead to tender offers whereby suitors pay up to present value of the potential synergy. In such circumstances, the suitors would earn a normal (not an excess) return on outlay, with most of the gain from the merger accruing, as evidence suggests, to the target.

---

[20] Same as [14], p. 6.

PROBLEMS AND QUESTIONS

1. Shark Corporation plans a hostile takeover of Dolphin Corporation. Given the following information:

	Shark Corporation	Dolphin Corporation
Present earnings	$12,000,000	$2,000,000
Shares outstanding	3,000,000	800,000
Price/Earnings ratio	12 to 1	7 to 1

a. Calculate earnings per share and market price per share for both companies.
b. Suppose Shark offers shareholders a 20-percent cash premium over the stock's current market price. What is the total price Shark would pay for Dolphin?
c. Assume Dolphin has no leverage in its capital structure but its net-asset market value per share is $26. Can Shark use junk bonds to finance the acquisition? Explain in detail.
d. Assume the tender offer is successful and the P/E ratio rises from 12 to 1 to 12.333 to 1. Is this outcome consistent with your answer to (c)?
e. Would you characterize the merger as synergistic? Explain in detail.

2. Sundial Corporation is considering a friendly merger with Moonbeam Corporation. Given the following information:

	Sundial Corporation	Moonbeam Corporation
Present earnings	$22,500,000	$13,500,000
Shares outstanding	7,500,000	5,625,000
Price per share	$36	$24
Payout ratio	45 percent	60 percent

a. Calculate the earnings per share, the price/earnings ratio, and the dividends per share for each company.
b. Suppose Sundial agrees to give Moonbeam shareholders .7 shares of Sundial stock for each share of Moonbeam. Based on current price per share, what does a 100-share owner of Moonbeam receive in value? Does he or she gain or lose in terms of current market price and dividends?
c. Following merger, the P/E ratio is 13 to 1. Calculate the change in value to Sundial shareholders and to former Moonbeam shareholders. To illustrate, use a 100-share owner of Moonbeam. Is there synergy? Is a former Moonbeam shareholder relatively better off than a Sundial shareholder? Explain in detail.

3. To prevent takeover by a raider, management of Bobsled Corporation decides to employ a leveraged buyout. Currently there is no debt in the company. There are 10,500,000 shares outstanding, each with a market price of $21.50, and the asset value per share is $28. A group of commercial banks will loan management 60 percent of the asset value. To entice its stockholders to sell, management tenders an offer at 15 percent above the stock's current market price. The remainder of buyout costs will be borne by management.

   a. How much will management pay for the shares outstanding?
   b. How much will be financed through the bank loan?
   c. How much money must management raise?
   d. Calculate the debt-to-total-capital ratio for Bobsled.

4. In problem 3, prior to the leveraged buyout Bobsled was earning $3.70 per share before taxes and was paying taxes at an average rate of .46. Assuming interest on the bank loan is .14, what is the return on equity management has invested? Would you characterize this return as satisfactory in light of the leverage assumed? Explain in detail.

5. Hawkeye Corporation is considering the following choices: (a) building a new plant at $55,000,000 with an after-tax cash flow of $10,375,000 per year for 15 years or (b) purchasing the stock of Butternut Corporation, which has just built a similar facility. Given the following information on Butternut:

Earnings per share (after taxes)	$3
Shares outstanding	3,200,000
Market price of stock	$28

In addition, Hawkeye's average cost of capital is 16 percent and 60 percent of Butternut's earnings are attributable to its new facility. The remainder of Butternut's assets have a per-share market value of $18.75. Using all the foregoing information, explain in detail why Hawkeye Corporation may be better off purchasing 100 percent of Butternut's stock at a 15-percent premium over its current market price than building new facilities. (Assume no monopoly power derives from the combination).

6. Management of Bramblebush Corporation believes that management of Sweetpea Corporation is inefficient. Bramblebush bases its judgment on the fact that Sweetpea, engaged in a similar business and having a similar leverage in its capital structure, has a lower price/earnings multiple, so that:

	Bramblebush Corporation	*Sweetpea Corporation*
Earnings per share (after taxes)	$4	$2.50
Shares outstanding	10,000,000	2,250,000
Price/Earnings ratio	12 to 1	8.5 to 1

Management of Bramblebush offers and Sweetpea accepts an exchange of one share of stock in Bramblebush for two shares in Sweetpea. Following the merger, market price of Bramblebush stock fluctuates between $47 and $48 per share. Does the market appear to agree with the Bramblebush assessment of Sweetpea's management? Why? Why not?

7. "Hostile takeovers serve a useful social function: they ensure that managerial inefficiencies are eliminated." Evaluate.

8. Define the following: (a) statutory merger, (b) combination, (c) joint venture, (d) junk bond.

9. "Empirical evidence showing that shareholders of target corporations benefit more from mergers—particularly hostile takeovers—than do shareholders of suitor corporations is consistent with the hypothesis that there exists a competitive market for the right to manage corporate resources." Evaluate.

SELECTED ADDITIONAL REFERENCES

Alexander, Gordon J., George Benson, and Joan Kampmeyer. "Investigating the Valuation Effects of Announcements of Voluntary Corporate Selloffs," *Journal of Finance*, Vol. 39 (June 1984, pp. 503–18).

Asquith, Paul. "Merger Bids, Uncertainty and Stockholder Returns," *Journal of Financial Economics*, Vol. 11 (April 1983, pp. 51–84).

Asquith, Paul, Robert Bruner, and David W. Mullins, Jr. "The Gains to Bidding Firms from Merger," *Journal of Financial Economics*, Vol. 11 (April 1983, pp. 121–40).

Bradley, Michael and L. Macdonald Wakeman. "The Wealth Effects of Targeted Share Repurchases," *Journal of Financial Economics*, Vol. 11 (April 1983, pp. 301–38).

Bradley, Michael, Anand Desai, and E. Hanlim. "The Rationale Behind Interfirm Tender Offers: Information on Synergy," *Journal of Financial Economics*, Vol. 11 (April 1983, pp. 183–206).

DeAngelo, Harry and Edward M. Rice. "Anti-takeover Charter Amendments and Stockholder Wealth," *Journal of Financial Economics*, Vol. 11 (April 1983, pp. 329–60).

Elgers, Pieter and John J. Clark. "Merger Types and Shareholder Returns: Additional Evidence," *Financial Management*, Vol. 9 (Summer 1980, pp. 66–72).

Eyer, Carol Ellen. "An Empirical Test of the Redistribution Effect in Pure Exchange Mergers," *Journal of Financial and Quantitative Analysis*, Vol. 18 (December 1983, pp. 547–72).

Hoffmeister, J. Ronald and Edward A. Dyl. "Predicting Outcomes of Cash Tender Offers," *Financial Management*, Vol. 10 (Winter 1981, pp. 50–58).

Jensen, Michael and Richard S. Ruback. "The Market for Corporate Control—the Scientific Evidence," *Journal of Financial Economics*, Vol. 11 (April 1982, pp. 5–50).

Keenan, Michael and Lawrence J. White, eds. *Mergers and Acquisitions: Current Problems in Perspective* (Lexington, MA: Heath, Lexington Books, 1982).

Langetieg, Terrence C., Robert A. Haugen, and Dean W. Wichern. "Merger and Stockholder Wealth," *Journal of Financial and Quantitative Analysis*, Vol. 15 pp. 689–717).

Lewellen, Wilbur G. and Michael G. Ferri. "Strategies for the Merger Game: Management and the Market," *Financial Management*, Vol. 12 (Winter 1983, pp. 25–35).

Linn, Scott C. and John J. McConnell. "An Empirical Investigation of the Impact of Anti-takeover Amendments on Common Stock Prices," *Journal of Financial Economics*, Vol. 11 (April 1983, pp. 361–99).

Miles, James A. and James D. Rosenfeld. "The Effect of Voluntary Spin-Off Announcements on Shareholder Wealth," *Journal of Finance*, Vol. 38 (December 1983, pp. 1597–1606).

Salter, Malcom S. and Wolf A. Weinhold. "Diversification via Acquisition: Creating Value," *Harvard Business Review* Vol. 56 (July–August 1978, pp. 166–76).

Schipper, Katherine and Rex Thompson. "Evidence on Capitalized Value of Merger Activity for Acquiring Firms," *Journal of Financial Economics*, Vol. 11 (April 1983, pp. 85–120).

Scott, James H. Jr. "On the Theory of Conglomerate Mergers," *Journal of Finance*, Vol. 32 (September 1977, pp. 1235–50).

Wansley, James W., William R. Lane, and Ho C. Yang. "Abnormal Returns to Acquired Firms by Type of Acquisition and Method of Payment," *Financial Management* Vol. 12 (Autumn 1983, pp. 16–22).

Wansley, James W., Rodney L. Roenfeldt, and Philip Cooley. "Abnormal Returns from Merger Profits," *Journal of Financial and Quantitative Analysis*, Vol. 18 (June 1983, pp. 149–62).

Williamson, Oliver E. *The Economic Institutions of Capitalism* (New York: The Free Press, 1985).

22

FINANCE IN AN INTERNATIONAL CONTEXT

Although characteristic, it is somewhat chauvinistic of Americans to view their economy as independent of the rest of the world. Yet, for nearly a quarter-century following the end of World War II, we could ignore the international context: America was the dominant force in the world. However, since that time the economies of most industrialized nations have become increasingly interdependent. For Americans, at times the awakening has been rude: witness the disruption that followed the height of OPEC's power in the 1970s. At other times, we have simply neglected to include international forces in the analysis of public-policy issues. Even in 1980, the debate over whether supply-side economics would generate sufficient savings to finance the deficits created by the Reagan tax-cut proposals was couched in terms of the U.S. domestic economy: either growth would or would not generate sufficient domestic savings over the longer run. Few dared to voice the view that whatever happened over time, sufficiently high interest rates would attract and maintain foreign capital to the United States (in at least the short run), thereby helping finance those deficits. This is, of course, exactly what happened.

Many U.S. business firms have been ahead of the general perception held by many Americans—at least those with roots in an older generation—for the multinational corporation is now commonplace and as much a feature of the economies of developed nations as it is of America. It is, in other words, a universal phenomenon. Consequently, many of our largest companies, as well as those of Western Europe and Japan, depend as much on world markets as on domestic markets for their sales and profits.

Our very real excuse for not focusing earlier on finance in an international context is that we believed it essential to develop the basic principles underlying the subject before extending them to an environment that has its own specialized vocabulary. Naturally, at times we consciously ignored our own prescriptions, such as in our discussions of futures markets and interest-rate swaps.

In this chapter, we remedy this "oversight" by offering an introduction to finance in an international context. Our focus (as it has been throughout this book) is on the firm: our discussion is at the micro level, leaving the aggregate issues to more specialized treatises on international finance. We shall, however, view international finance from both the supply and the demand sides—from the perspective of portfolio managers as well as managers of nonfinancial business firms.

INTERNATIONAL DIVERSIFICATION

Whether one is responsible for a portfolio of financial assets (for example, managers of pension funds) or a portfolio of real assets (for example, managers of nonfinancial corporations), diversification of assets reduces overall standard deviation of the portfolio. However, concentrating on domestic investments only can result in a less-than-efficient portfolio.

Consider the role of diversification in a portfolio of securities. Figure 22-1(a) and (b) reproduce graphs employed in Chapter 5. In this case, however, we have added international securities to domestic securities. The result, shown in Figure 22-1(a), is a reduction of the standard deviation of the total portfolio for a given number of securities. In terms of the Markowitz opportunity set in Figure 22-1(b), an investor can reach a higher level of indifference between risk and return, and enjoy a greater return relative to standard deviation of the portfolio. As the curve is drawn, the investor has all his or her funds in the market portfolio. A relatively more risk-averse investor would be on an indifference curve tangent to CML[1] at Q—with a lower return but also with lower risk. Nevertheless, the investor would divide his or her portfolio between risk-free securities and an internationally diversified market portfolio.

But what is the underlying rationale for the belief that international diversification reduces the standard deviation of a portfolio relative to what is obtained through domestic diversification only? Using the mathematics of covariance, our intuition suggests that random forces affecting returns on all securities result in lower coefficients of correlation for returns on international portfolios than for returns on domestic portfolios. There is a weaker correlation among returns on

Figure 22-1   **International Portfolio Diversification**

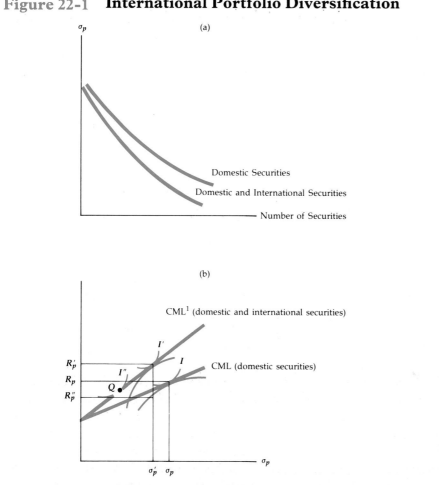

international portfolios for Japanese, Australian, Swiss, and American securities than among returns on domestic portfolios for securities within each country.

Although this notion is intuitively plausible, it is difficult to verify it empirically. Nevertheless, because many portfolio managers believe there is evidence that international diversification adds to return while it reduces portfolio variance, they act accordingly. Among early practitioners of international diversification, in 1980, First Chicago Investment Advisors (a subsidiary of First Chicago Corporation) developed what was labeled a Multiple Market Index—a portfolio that included international equity securities.[1] Indeed, approximately 20 percent of the portfolio was internationally based. It was estimated that for the same level of risk—measured by the standard deviation—an inflation-adjusted rate of return on the Multiple Market Index would be higher than on a typical pension-fund portfolio weighted 60 percent stocks/40 percent bonds. In terms of Figure 22-1(b) the difference in real terms, R'_p and R''_p, would be approximately .6 of 1 percent (60 basis points).[2]

Although this may seem a negligible difference, pension fund managers calculate their assets in billions of dollars. In that context, an internationally diversified portfolio employing investments other than stocks and bonds will add approximately $6,000,000 inflation-adjusted dollars per billion dollars of assets to the pension fund's income stream (.006 × $1,000,000,000).[3]

Assume a relationship between the MMI and a 60/40 stock/bond portfolio held for 25 years, with funds reinvested and compounded annually:

$$\$6,000,000 \frac{[(1 + .006)^{25} - 1]}{.006} = \$161,313,616$$

With a Multiple Markets Index, a billion-dollar portfolio would be worth an additional $161 million.

There are therefore, strong arguments for passively managed pension funds to invest beyond national borders: total return is higher for a given risk level and the portfolio is more efficient. Moreover, as financial markets throughout the world become increasingly integrated, they become more efficient. Portfolio diversification, of course, can take place whether or not the efficient market hypothesis holds. Nevertheless, the analysis that flows from the Capital Market Line, the Securities Market Line, and the characteristic line depends on efficient markets. To the extent such markets become increasingly integrated, the market portfolio for all investors becomes the internationally diversified market portfolio suggested in Figure 22-1(b)—with returns R''_p and σ'_p that all investors purchase. As the Capital

---

[1] Gary P. Brinson, Jeffrey J. Diermeier, and L. Randolf Hood. *Multiple Market Index* (Chicago: First Chicago Corporation, 1980). See, also, Gary P. Brinson, Jeffrey J. Diermeier, and Gary G. Schlarbaum, "A Composite Portfolio Benchmark for Pension Plans," *Financial Analysts Journal*, Vol. 42 (March–April 1986, pp. 15–24). Other components include: traded domestic equities of large and small companies, short-term money market instruments, venture capital, domestic fixed-income securities, and real estate. The portfolio is based on investable world wealth but tailored to specific parameters of a pension fund. For example, because pension funds pay no income taxes, the portfolio contains no tax-exempt issues of state and local governments.

For discussion of the aggregate data, see Roger G. Ibbotson and Lawrence B. Siegel, "The World Market Wealth Portfolio," *Journal of Portfolio Management*, Vol. 10 (Winter 1983, pp. 5–17). See, also, Gary Brinson. "Intelligently Setting a Portfolio Asset Mix," *Pension World*, Vol. 18 (March 1982, pp. 65–70); Roger G. Ibbotson and Gary P. Brinson, *Investment Markets Gaining the Performance Advantage* (New York: McGraw-Hill, 1987, pp. 251–79). For further analysis, see Robert H. Grauer and Nils H. Hakansson, "Gains from International Diversification: 1968–85 Returns on Portfolios of Stocks and Bonds," *Journal of Finance*, Vol. 42 (July 1987, pp. 721–39).

[2] Brinson, Diermeier, and Schlarbaum, pp. 20–21. The calculations on which the estimate is based cover the period 1960–1984.

[3] Only part of the increase is due to international diversification; some is due to addition of other investment vehicles.

Market Line suggests, separate individuals trade off return against risk at indifference curves I' and I''.

Although international diversification of a securities portfolio may be an intelligent investment strategy, what about international diversification of a real-assets portfolio? In short: Do multinational corporations do something for stockholders that stockholders cannot do for them? In Chapter 21 we outlined a portion of the rationale for believing that at times the firm may be more efficient than the market. Again, however, the context was national. Nevertheless, there is no reason to assume the rationale stops short at water's edge. Moreover, to the extent markets are not efficient internationally, multinational corporations may be useful vehicles through which stockholders can realize greater diversification than might otherwise be feasible.

The models adumbrated in this book, when applied internationally, are constrained in ways not considered when the models are applied in the domestic market context; however, most of these constraints are surmountable—but not cost free. For example, in international trade one must deal with different currencies. Exchange-rate risk, not present in the domestic market, may necessitate using a futures or forward market to shift the risk.

Another consideration is the political risk of government seizure of assets (plant/equipment) located in countries less hospitable to private enterprise. Even where takeover is no more than a remote possibility—such as in Western Europe, Japan, and much of the British Commonwealth—xenophobia generally lurks beneath the surface. Capital must often enter the host country as unobtrusively as possible. Nationals of the host country must constitute not only the work force but also much of the managerial personnel. Realistically, a low profile is often warranted—if not compelled.

Not to be forgotten is the issue of taxes. Generally, if a U.S. firm has a subsidiary or branch in another country, the branch income is reported annually on a U.S. tax form and U.S. tax rates apply, but in most cases subsidiary income is not reported until it reaches the U.S. as dividends paid the parent firm. There exists, therefore, the temptation to avoid taxes by reinvesting foreign profits in a foreign subsidiary. To render this potential tax haven less attractive, an American stockholder of 10 percent of a foreign subsidiary may be taxed on at least a portion of such earnings—whether reinvested or not. The rules are extremely complicated and beyond the scope of this book. However, the central point is that a multinational corporation owning a foreign subsidiary can reinvest those foreign earnings without being taxed—until they reach the U.S. as dividends paid the parent firm, when they are fully taxed. This compares with the general rule that 80 percent of dividends paid to one domestic corporation by another are exempt from taxation.

Although the rates and tax bases vary from country to country, foreign governments also tax earnings of American companies doing business abroad. However, under a complex set of rules, the United States government grants a federal income-tax credit for foreign taxes paid by a U.S. corporation. The principle, nevertheless is straightforward. Suppose a U.S. company earns $1,000,000 from a plant abroad. If its domestic tax rate is 34 percent, the company ordinarily would pay $340,000 in taxes on earnings. However, because the applicable foreign government taxes income at 25 percent, the U.S. company pays $250,000 to that government. Under the federal tax credit, the United States government receives $340,000 − $250,000 = $90,000 from the U.S. company. If the foreign tax rate is 50 percent, the foreign government receives $500,000 and the United States government receives nothing. However, the U.S. company receives no additional federal tax credit for the 16 percent difference in tax rates: the tax rate of the foreign government becomes the effective tax rate.

Note the foregoing applies only to income taxes—not to sales, property, or other taxes that may have been deductible had they been paid domestically to state governments. No federal tax credit is granted when such taxes are paid to foreign governments. At the same time, there are special (if somewhat complex) tax incentives for U.S. firms to locate plants in a less-developed country (LDC). Clearly, the tax considerations underlying the investment decision, including the investment form (wholly owned foreign subsidiary versus plant or branch), are complex—no doubt creating munificent fees for the lawyers involved as well as additional headaches (perhaps challenges) for those responsible for the internal accounting system.

Inasmuch as the thrust of our argument is that, at the level of the firm, the details rather than the substance of the principles of finance change when shifting from a domestic to an international context, the remainder of the chapter analyzes some of those changes.

EXCHANGE RATES

Perhaps the most pervasive risk underlying international markets is the change in value that occurs because of fluctuations in foreign exchange. Consider a portfolio manager holding fixed-income securities denominated in British pounds and valued at £5,000,000. If the pound is currently trading at $1.40—£1 = $1.40—U.S. dollar value of the securities is £5,000,000 × $1.40 = $7,000,000. Suppose that tomorrow the pound rises to $1.42—£1 = $1.42. In terms of U.S. dollars, market value of the securities has risen to £5,000,000 × $1.42 = $7,100,000. In the parlance of international finance, the pound has *appreciated* against the U.S. dollar: it takes more U.S. dollars to purchase one British pound. Alternatively, the U.S. dollar has *depreciated* against the British pound. In this instance, the value of pound-denominated securities in the portfolio rises because the British pound has appreciated against the U.S. dollar.

Consider a different example. Suppose a Canadian subsidiary of an American manufacturer has $4,000,000 in accounts receivable denominated in Canadian dollars. Assume Can$1 = $.75. In terms of U.S. dollars, the receivables are worth Can$4,000,000 × $.75 = $3,000,000.

Suppose that next month the Canadian dollar has depreciated (the U.S. dollar has appreciated), so that Can$1 = $.70. Consequently, if Can$4,000,000 in accounts receivable are still outstanding, they are now worth Can$4,000,000 × $.70 = $2,800,000.

Because exchange-rate risks affect profitability and (ultimately) market value of the firm or portfolio, it is critical that we understand the forces shaping exchange-rate fluctuations and how to hedge against them.[4]

FORWARD RATES

An interesting characteristic of the foreign-exchange market is the **forward rate** available for many currencies: an exchange rate agreed on now even though the currencies will not be exchanged until a later date. The forward rate contrasts with the *spot rate* at which a currency is currently trading. For example, on Monday, January 13, 1986, there was the following relationship between the U.S. dollar and the British pound.[5]

$$
\begin{aligned}
1 \text{ British pound} &= \$1.4450 \\
30\text{-day forward} &= 1.4390 \\
90\text{-day forward} &= 1.4285 \\
180\text{-day forward} &= 1.4130
\end{aligned}
$$

The first quotation is the spot rate for British pounds on January 13, 1986; the next three quotation are rates for British pounds guaranteed on that same date but payable 30, 90, and 180 days later—the forward rates at that time. The rates result from competition among foreign-exchange dealers and commercial banks, and represent trades not actual quotations. Although traders attempt to profit from buying and

---

[4] We ignore accounting procedures here in order to concentrate on the fact that it is market value that is ultimately affected. However, under Statement No. 52 of the Financial Accounting Standards Board, a company must determine whether it denominates its foreign subsidiary accounts in the currency of that country or in U.S. dollars. Various complex procedures govern whether a company can use local currency or U.S. dollars. If the company can use local currency, gains and losses due to exchange-rate differences are recognized in the equity portion of the owner's balance sheet. These gains and losses derive from revaluing assets and liabilities in terms of the exchange rate effective on the date of the financial statements. If the U.S. dollar is used for accounting purposes, some but not all gains and losses due to foreign-exchange fluctuations flow through the income statement. The result makes for an interesting puzzle for sharp securities analysts concerned with showing that the semi-strong form of the efficient market hypothesis is wrong. See Thomas I. Selling and George H. Sorter, "FASB Statement No. 52 and Its Implications for Financial Statement Analysis," *Financial Analysts Journal*, Vol. 39 (May–June 1983, pp. 64–69).

[5] *Wall Street Journal*, January 14, 1986, p. 59. The quotations are as of 3 PM Eastern Time and apply to commercial banks trading in amounts of $1,000,000 or more. The rates are also quoted in terms of U.S. dollars: $\frac{1}{1.4450} = .692042$. British pounds could have been purchased for one U.S. dollar on that date.

selling currencies, banks also enter these markets to service their customers engaged in international trade. In particular, importers of British goods are expected to settle in British pounds. If final payment takes place in 90 days, the importer that enters into a forward-exchange agreement is guaranteed the $1.4285 rate for each British pound purchased.

In addition, there are futures markets in some foreign currency exchange as well as options on futures. Regarding the British pound, on January 13, 1986, an importer—wanting a commitment for 60 days rather than for 30 or 90 days—could have purchased March futures, which settled at $1.4335 on that date.[6] The importer would, however, have had to purchase contracts in multiples of £25,000. It is interesting to note that at $1.4335, the rate was between the 30-day forward rate (which would have been transacted in February) and the 90-day forward rate (which would have been transacted in April). Both the forward rate and the futures rate suggested the British pound would depreciate against the U.S. dollar: In other words, it was selling at a discount to the dollar. If the forward rate had been higher than the current exchange rate for the pound, it would have been selling at a premium to the dollar.

From the discussion in Chapter 20, a futures price greater than the spot price is certainly possible. However, the futures price, F, is the market's estimate of the future spot price, S^1. The carrying costs, C, and the profit for risk bearing, P, must be included in the future price, so that $S^1 + C + P = F$. If $F > S$, then $S^1 + C + P > S$. In turn, this suggests that unless P and C are zero, then (in this instance) $S^1 < S$.

In the foreign exchange example cited earlier, however, $F < S$. What forces could give rise to this result?

SPOT AND FORWARD PRICES FOR EXCHANGE RATES—THE PURCHASING-POWER PARITY THEOREM

Regardless of its country of origin, currency serves the same general purpose: it is a unit of account, a medium of exchange, and a store of value. In perfectly competitive product markets and efficient financial markets, currencies of different countries should be priced in relation to each other so that the same basket of goods and services (less any transportation costs) may be priced the same regardless of the country in which it is purchased. Known as the **purchasing-power parity**

---

[6] *Wall Street Journal*, January 14, 1986, p. 50. On that date, the exercise price for an option on a March futures contract for £25,000 was $1.375 (137.5 cents); the settlement price was 6.55 cents per £. To buy the option, less commission, would have cost $1.4405 per £. See *WSJ*, p. 51.

theorem, this suggests that if the British pound is expected to fall in terms of the U.S. dollar, its price level in Britain is expected to rise in terms of the U.S. dollar. In terms of relative purchasing power, the currency depreciation is reflected in the lower anticipated exchange rate.

Although the purchasing-power parity theorem has intuitive appeal, it is at best a long-run explanation. Trade barriers, such as quotas and tariffs, and governmental intervention in the foreign-exchange market often result in a market basket of similar goods selling for different prices in different countries. Exchange rates do not adjust—at least in the short run.

SPOT AND FORWARD PRICES FOR EXCHANGE RATES—THE INTEREST-RATE PARITY THEOREM

The **interest-rate parity theorem** is an intuitively appealing argument for explaining the relationship between spot and forward prices. Because it is a short-run analysis, it is more suitable to the time horizon applicable to forward rates.

To illustrate, suppose we have a fungible (interchangeable) commodity, such as a risk-free security available in every country. One could hold U.S. dollars today or invest them in short-term U.S. government securities. Similarly, one could hold British pounds today or invest them in short-term British governmental securities. The forward price of dollars or pounds would be $S(1 + i) = F$, where F is forward price, S is spot price, and i equals the short-term risk-free interest rate. For dollars and pounds, the relationship would be

$$\$S(1 + i) = \$F$$
$$\frac{\$F}{\$S} = 1 + i_{\text{U.S.}}$$

and

$$\pounds S(1 + i) = \pounds F$$
$$\frac{\pounds F}{\pounds S} = 1 + i_{\text{U.K.}}$$

If the foreign-exchange markets are efficient, the two returns must equal one another, otherwise, arbitrage opportunities ensue. Consequently

$$\frac{1 + i_{\text{U.S.}}}{1 + i_{\text{U.K.}}} = \frac{\dfrac{\$F}{\$S}}{\dfrac{\pounds F}{\pounds S}} = \frac{(\$F)(\pounds S)}{(\pounds F)(\$S)} = \frac{F_{\$,\pounds}}{S_{\$,\pounds}} = \frac{\text{forward rate of pounds in \$U.S.}}{\text{spot rate of pounds in \$U.S.}}$$

More generally[7]

$$\frac{1 + i_{\text{U.S.}}}{1 + i_f} = \frac{F_{\$,f}}{S_{\$,f}} \tag{22-1}$$

where foreign currencies, f, are stated in \$U.S.

To establish an arbitrage opportunity, in addition to the usual criteria for efficient markets there must be no governmental intervention in the flow of funds across the borders of every nation involved, freely floating exchange rates without limits, and similar tax treatment of arbitrage profits in every participating country. Assuming these criteria, let us rewrite Equation 22-1 so that

$$\frac{1 + i_{\text{U.S.}}}{1 + i_f} - 1 = \frac{F_{\$,f}}{S_{\$,f}} - 1$$

Rearranging the terms and simplifying, we obtain

$$\frac{1 + i_{\text{U.S.}} - 1 - i_f}{1 + i_f} = \frac{F_{\$,f} - S_{\$,f}}{S_{\$,f}}$$

$$\frac{i_{\text{U.S.}} - i_f}{1 + i_F} = \frac{F_{\$,f} - S_{\$,f}}{S_{\$,f}} \tag{22-2}$$

Equation 22-2 represents an equilibrium between the spot prices and forward rates of foreign currencies in terms of the \$U.S. and the relatively risk-free rates of each participating country. Suppose, using the 90-day forward rate for the British pound, the relationship in terms of \$U.S. is

$$\frac{F_{\$,£} - S_{\$,£}}{S_{\$,£}} = \frac{1.425 - 1.4375}{1.4375} = -.008696$$

This implies that

$$\frac{i_{\text{U.S.}} - i_f}{1 + i_f} = -.008696$$

Suppose, however, that at the same time 90-day risk-free rates in the U.S. and the U.K. are .0275 and .0245 respectively, so that

$$\frac{.0275 - .0245}{1.0245} = .002928$$

The relative difference in 90-day rates favors the U.K., but the U.K. forward rate is

---

[7] We use the \$U.S. as the base. From the perspective of any country, the numerators of each fraction are the domestic interest rates and the forward rates for each foreign currency in terms of that country's domestic currency. The denominators are the foreign interest rates and the spot prices for each foreign currency in terms of that country's domestic currency (in this instance, the U.S.).

less than the spot rate. Intuitively, we would expect

$$\frac{F_{\$,f}}{S_{\$,f}} = \frac{1 + i_{\text{U.S.}}}{1 + i_f} \qquad (22\text{-}3)$$

Here, the forward rate for the British pound in terms of the \$U.S. should be

$$\frac{F_{\$,£}}{1.4375} = \frac{1.0275}{1.0245}$$

$$F_{\$,£} = \$1.4417$$

Thus, there exists an opportunity for arbitrage.

To capitalize on this opportunity, suppose a British arbitrageur owns the pound equivalent of 90-day risk-free U.K. securities, specifically:

1. owns $10,000/1.4375 = £6,956.52 in 90-day risk-free securities

2. sells the securities at current exchange rates and purchases $10,000 in U.S. Treasury securities; total earnings in \$U.S. are $10,000(1.0275) = $10,275

3. eliminates foreign-exchange risk by selling \$U.S. at the 90-day forward rate for delivery at that time; thus $10,275/1.425 = £7,210.53

4. remaining in U.K. securities would earn £6,956.52(1.0245) = £7,126.95

5. selling U.K. securities and buying U.S. securities would earn £7,210.53 − £7,126.95 = £83.58 in additional profits

The downward pressure generated by arbitrageurs from selling dollars in the forward market will cause the dollar to depreciate relative to the pound. In terms of the dollar, the price of the pound will rise until it reaches $1.4417.

Although it is an intuitively appealing explanation of the relationship between spot and forward currency rates, the interest-rate parity theorem tends to hold primarily (within the limits of transactions costs) when \$U.S. are compared with other major trading currencies, such as those of Western European countries and Japan. Although comparably risk-free securities exist and markets appear to be reasonably efficient in such countries, at times their governments intervene in the market and speculators, rather than arbitrageurs, may be a more potent force in determining the relationship between spot and forward rates at any given moment.

NONMARKET APPROACHES TO REDUCING EXCHANGE-RATE RISK

Other than employing forward exchange rates or futures markets in foreign exchange, firms may use nonmarket approaches to reducing exchange-rate risk. One such approach is **currency swap**. Suppose ABC Corporation has a London subsidiary to which it wants to transfer $1,000,000 in British pounds for 90 days. The spot rate for the pound is $1.38 and the 90-day forward rate is $1.36. If management uses the market to hedge the foreign exchange, it must simultaneously buy in the spot market and sell in the forward market. The transaction cost is the difference in the rates plus commission. Thus, ABC buys today at

$$\frac{\$1,000,000}{1.38} = £724,637.68$$

and agrees to deliver £724,637.68 × $1.36 = $985,507.25. The transaction, exclusive of commissions, costs ABC $1,000,000 − $985,507.25 = $14,492.75.

However, ABC's commercial bank may have anticipated the need for pounds in 90 days and has $1,000,000 in pound balances over and above its current requirements. Although the bank could presumably sell the pounds for 90-day delivery at the forward rate, thereby profiting on the transaction, it may offer ABC a forward rate of $1.375. In so doing, the bank avoids transactions costs and continues to serve a good customer.

Alternatively, ABC may be able to avoid the swap altogether. A British company, requiring $1,000,000 for 90 days for its U.S. subsidiary, may strike an agreement whereby it gives the British subsidiary of ABC £724,637.68 for 90 days and ABC gives the U.S. subsidiary of the British company $1,000,000 for 90 days. If the exchange is successful, at some future point the two companies might engage in a **parallel loan**. Under a parallel loan arrangement, ABC loans the U.S. subsidiary of the British company a specific amount of money in dollars for a specific period of time. The British company loans a comparable amount in pounds to the British subsidiary of ABC. Consequently, no foreign currency transactions are necessary.

Whether market or nonmarket techniques are employed, for most companies exchange-rate risks are a component of the business risk they face in less than perfect markets. The only question is the degree to which management wishes to limit its exposure. By operating in a variety of countries, multinational corporations tend to diversify that risk. However, a firm with the bulk of its sales in one or two foreign countries may use market or nonmarket techniques to reduce if not completely eliminate exchange-rate risks.

FINANCING INTERNATIONAL TRADE

As noted in Chapter 14, sales on open account—extension of trade credit—are widely used in the United States to facilitate the flow of commerce. In international trade, however, the traditional mechanism for financing goods is the **banker's acceptance**. For example, an importer of British woolens could buy directly from the British supplier, the supplier extending credit on account until the goods arrive.

Nevertheless, because of the length of time from purchase to receipt of goods, the necessity of doing business in two currencies, and perhaps the lack of familiarity with the credit rating of many buyers, most exporters turn to their banks for assistance.

The importer, a New York-based merchandiser of British woolens, obtains an agreement from its bank to provide, let us say, $1,000,000 in acceptance credit. The New York bank then notifies the seller or, more likely, the sellers' bank in London or Edinburgh that a **letter of credit** has been issued. This letter authorizes the seller (exporter) to draw a **time draft** on the New York bank, generally for the dollar (not pound) equivalent of the transaction. In addition, the letter of credit may contain certain conditions that must be met before the draft is accepted, such as inclusion of a document (bill of lading) certifying the goods have arrived. When the draft is presented to the New York bank with the appropriate documents, it is stamped *accepted* and endorsed by an appropriate bank officer. Thus is born the banker's acceptance.

The process does not end at this point. The seller (exporter) probably wants to collect the $1,000,000 and convert them to pounds—no doubt to cover the forward exchange-rate hedge transaction entered into when the exporter originally sold the woolens. Therefore, the exporter sells the acceptance—which may be due in 90 days—and may do so to the maker of the draft, the New York bank. The bank discounts the draft from its face value based on the going rate in the bankers' acceptance market. Assuming that rate is currently 13 percent and using the bank's 360-day year, we calculate the exporter receives

$$\$1,000,000 - (\$1,000,000 \times .13)\left(\frac{90}{360}\right)$$
$$\$1,000,000 - \$32,500 = \$967,500$$

The exporter may have these funds or their pound equivalent transferred immediately to its bank in the U.K.

Meanwhile, the New York bank may retain the acceptance until maturity, when it presents it to the importer for collection. In this case, the importer pays the bank $1,000,000 at maturity. Alternatively, the New York bank could sell the acceptance in the open market, rediscount it presumably at a higher price than $967,500 and thereby replenish its funds and earn a profit on the transaction. When the acceptance matures, the holder collects from the New York bank. At that time, of course, the bank receives the $1,000,000 from the importer. By substituting its credit for that of the importer, the New York bank—usually a large financial intermediary doing business on a worldwide basis—has developed an instrument for which there is an active secondary market. The bank charges a fee (commission) for accepting the draft and charges a separate fee for the letter. The draft itself is similar to a large time deposit or CD: the bank owes the holder $1,000,000 at maturity. Unlike other deposits, however, there are no reserve requirements; hence, it is less costly to maintain. Because all fees are up front, the acceptance is not likely to be prepaid. Thus, payment of the acceptance almost always coincides with maturity of the loan underlying it. Unfortunately, maturity of loans and the deposits used to finance acceptances are not always so well coordinated.

THE BANKER'S ACCEPTANCE MARKET

Although banker's acceptances are not federally insured, many investors regard them as high-quality paper in view of their low incidence of default. Borrowers, particularly importers who lack access to national or international money markets, may find the overall borrowing costs (including fees charged by the bank) are lower than if they borrowed directly from the bank.

The banker's acceptance market is over the counter and supported by approximately 30 dealers and a dozen brokers. The buyers are money-market mutual funds, insurance companies, pension funds, and other institutional investors. Only a few individuals participate directly in the market, where round lots have a face value of $5,000,000. Total size of the market increased from $7 billion in 1973 to $43 billion in 1979; in 1984 it reached $82 billion.[8] During this period, much of the growth was attributable to *third-country acceptances*: a less well-known bank in a foreign country accepts a time draft to facilitate credit for a U.S. importer.[9] However, rather than selling that acceptance at a huge discount, the foreign bank obtains credit by drawing a draft on a large U.S. bank and by agreeing to repay the U.S. bank when its own loan to the U.S. importer matures. Because the foreign bank is the borrower, transactions are between banks. Known as *refinance bills*, their secondary market is termed the interbank market.

CHANGES IN FINANCING INTERNATIONAL TRADE

As suggested in Chapter 15, competition has relegated the prime rate to a lesser benchmark on which to base short-term rates. Traditionally, banker's acceptances were the only source of below-prime-rate financing. Hence, there was a worldwide demand for U.S. dollar-denominated acceptances. Although the dollar still remains the medium in which acceptances are denominated, one does not have to use dollars from money center banks in the United States. There is always the Eurodollar

---

[8] Frederick H. Jensen and Patrick M. Parkinson. "Recent Developments in the Banker's Acceptance Market," *Federal Reserve Bulletin*, Vol. 72 (January 1986, pp. 4–8).

[9] Importers using regional U.S. banks often obtain acceptance credit through correspondents of such banks located in money centers (New York, Chicago, and others).

market and LIBOR rates (London Interbank Offered Rate). This alternative impacts the banker's acceptance market in two ways. First, foreign banks may issue their own dollar-denominated claims, such as Eurodollar CDs. Large Japanese banks have been especially successful in issuing CDs, thereby avoiding refinance costs with American banks. By the end of 1985, rate spreads between liabilities of large Japanese banks and large American banks had narrowed to within 5 basis points (.05 percent). Just a few years earlier, Japanese banks were paying as much as 50 to 60 basis points more. Apparently investors are becoming accustomed to dollar-denominated claims by at least some foreign banks.[10]

Second, nonfinancial corporations, particularly multinationals, can obtain short-term finance based on LIBOR from foreign banks and also may be able to avoid the acceptance market altogether or employ it less frequently. In addition, revolving credit facilities now offer such corporations the opportunity to borrow not only at LIBOR rates but also at domestic CD rates and at the prime rate. Banker's acceptance rates are seldom available under loan commitments to nonfinancial corporations; however, even if a corporation pays a fee for the commitment, the opportunity cost makes the corporation reluctant to borrow through acceptances when acceptances are not credited against the unused portion of the commitment. Competitive pressures from alternative sources have narrowed the spreads between LIBOR and the yield on prime banker's acceptances from more than 100 to 25 basis points.[11] Of course, as in the case of domestic borrowing, those engaged in international commerce but lacking access to a variety of credit instruments may yet find the acceptance less costly than a direct bank loan.

RAISING FUNDS IN INTERNATIONAL MARKETS— THE ROLE OF COMMERCIAL BANKING

As the last section suggests, the commercial banking system plays a major role in funding international trade. U.S. corporations, depending on the scope of their activities, may rely on foreign branches or affiliates of U.S. banks not only to finance exports/imports, but also as a source of short-term funds used for the same purposes as short-term finance is used for domestic purposes. In other words, the British division of a U.S. company may borrow funds through the London branch of its U.S. bank to help fund inventories and receivables. In addition, under the Edge Act, a U.S. bank is permitted to own stock in a foreign bank, which may be a wholly or partially owned subsidiary of the U.S. bank. Thus, whether branch or subsidiary, multinational corporations are well-served by their U.S. banks in the major trading

---

[10] Same as [8], p. 9.

[11] Same as [8], p. 10.

countries of Western Europe and Asia. Moreover, funding can be arranged in local currency or in Eurodollars.

Many companies also establish business relationships with foreign banks. There can be subtle political reasons for using a foreign bank, particularly if the foreign bank management has some governmental influence that may be useful in the future. And yet, the reason simply may be better terms. For example, European banks make longer-term loans than U.S. banks; consequently, foreign branches of U.S. banks may be precluded from or limited in making longer term loans. European banks are also merchant banks, and as such offer a wider range of services than most U.S. banks. As noted, however, U.S. banks are becoming more broadly based as laws that have constrained them are being replaced by more liberal legislation.

Finally, a procedural matter, foreign banks (particularly European banks) arrange loans somewhat differently than U.S. banks. Instead of monetizing the loan with a credit to the company's demand deposit, the European bank honors overdrafts. Thus, if a company has a $1,000,000 line of credit with a U.S. bank and chooses to use it, the company receives credit in its demand deposit up to that amount before it actually writes checks. If the company has a similar arrangement with a British bank, it may write the checks, overdrawing its account, and the British bank honors the overdraft, charging interest accordingly. Although some banks allow individual overdraft privileges on personal checking accounts up to a few thousand dollars, this practice is not yet common in the United States.

RAISING FUNDS IN INTERNATIONAL MARKETS—THE ROLE OF EUROBONDS

Although commercial bank participation in international finance is not new, use of foreign capital markets by U.S. companies to raise long-term debt is a relatively recent phenomenon. When U.S. companies raise money in international markets, they issue foreign bonds (**Eurobonds**); when such bonds are denominated in U.S. dollars, they are known as **Eurodollar bonds**. Thus, a Eurobond may be denominated in the currency of any foreign country. However, a distinguishing characteristic of the Eurobond is its availability to investors in several countries other than the country in whose currency it is denominated. Single currency denomination also distinguishes the Eurobond from a bond denominated in two or more currencies, with the investor able to choose the currency in which to receive interest and principal payments. When floated in multiple currencies, such an instrument is known as a *cocktail currency* issue.

The first U.S. dollar-denominated Eurobond was sold in 1957; the issuer was Petrofina, a Belgian petroleum company. During the 1960s, U.S. companies with foreign operations often financed the debt portions of such operations with Eurobonds. Nevertheless, in 1975, total overseas borrowing by U.S. firms accounted for only $300 million, or 1 percent of total borrowing. By 1984, overseas borrowing had risen to $20 billion, or 25 percent of total borrowing—most of it raised in U.S. dollar-denominated instruments, specifically Eurodollar bonds. In addition, firms with little or no exposure abroad were issuing Eurodollar bonds. In 1979, Portland General Electric Company (based in Portland, Oregon) issued the first public-utility Eurodollar bond. By 1985, 38 public-utility issues totaling $38 billion had been marketed.[12]

But why would U.S. firms without foreign subsidiaries employ foreign capital markets to issue long-term debt? The driving force should be a comparatively lower cost of capital—and there are factors that work in that direction. For example, because Eurodollar bonds pay interest annually rather than semiannually, a given coupon rate results in a lower YTM than for the same issue marketed at the same price in the United States. In addition, Eurobonds are bearer instruments; the holders simply clip coupons. Not only is interest paid once a year, but the onus is on the holders to obtain payment by presenting the coupon rather than the bond registrar issuing checks semiannually to the owners (as is the practice in the United States). Bearer bonds also have the advantage of anonymity. For foreigners seeking to avoid taxes in their native countries, such anonymity may be worth a small concession in yield.[13]

Moreover, the SEC has no jurisdiction over Eurodollar issues; hence, formal registration can be avoided. Of course, the issuer must adhere to foreign regulations, specifically regulations of the country in which the bonds are sold. These regulations appear to be less stringent and therefore less costly than the process employed in the United States, even allowing for Rule 415 flotations. Although bond-rating services are now employed to rate Eurodollar bonds as they rate domestic issues (an additional expense), at least among individual investors there appears only modest interest in these ratings. Individual investors rely more on the general reputation of the issuer; institutional investors, however, demand bond ratings before they commit funds. Initially, European debt markets were more oriented toward individual investors; more recently, institutions, particularly insurance companies and foreign central banks, have begun to play a more significant role in purchasing Eurodollar bonds.[14]

Eurodollar bond maturities are shorter than their U.S. counterparts: most mature in three to seven years, representing intermediate rather than long-term debt. Nevertheless, when real interest rates in the U.S. are comparatively high relative to those of the rest of the world, the issuer may want relatively short

---

[12] David S. Kidwell, M. Wayne Marr, and G. Rodney Thompson. "Eurodollar Bonds: Alternative Financing for United States Companies," *Financial Management*, Vol. 14 (Winter 1985, pp. 18–19).

[13] Prior to 1984, foreigners owning U.S. corporate issues were subject to a withholding tax; this was not true of Eurodollar bonds. In 1984, Congress repealed the tax, thereby making the two markets equally attractive with respect to U.S. tax laws.

[14] Same as [12], pp. 19–20.

maturities (at least for fixed-rate instruments). At the same time, high and rising real interest rates in the U.S. suggest—under the interest-rate parity theorem—that the dollar could be undervalued relative to foreign currencies. Consequently, a foreign investor might be willing to purchase a comparatively smaller dollar-denominated coupon issue, expecting to profit as the dollar appreciates against his or her currency. Because this opportunity is unavailable to the domestic purchaser of the debt, in these circumstances the issuer may be able to market securities at a lower interest cost to foreign investors than to domestic buyers.

Underwriting spreads, however, traditionally have been higher for Eurodollar bonds than for their U.S. counterparts. During the late 1970s, a company may have paid commissions of between 0.6 percent and 1.5 percent of total proceeds for a U.S. issue; for a Eurodollar bond, commissions would have been between 2 percent and 2.5 percent of total proceeds.[15] Part of the difference was due to lack of an integrated syndicate. Managers and underwriters tended to be separate—an underwriting group and a selling group—somewhat similar to the pattern that dominated U.S. markets during the early part of the twentieth century. With increased underwriting competition during the early 1980s, this pattern changed rapidly. The second factor resulting in lower commissions has been the increased institutionalization of the Eurobond market: it is less risky and therefore less costly to market an issue to a few large investors than to many small individual buyers. As a result, Eurodollar commissions now approximate those on U.S. issues.[16]

On balance, these factors have tended to provide U.S. companies a slight yield advantage in the Eurobond market as compared with domestic flotations. To a degree, the Eurobond markets have been segmented, allowing issuers to make effective use of them. Nevertheless, increased integration of world capital markets suggests this trend will not last; segmentation will disappear in such markets, and arbitrage opportunities presented by the interest-rate parity theorem will likely become more evanescent than in the past.[17]

RAISING FUNDS IN INTERNATIONAL MARKETS—OTHER SOURCES

U.S. companies, both domestic and multinational, may enter another country—often a third-world country—bringing expertise in such specific areas as steel production, energy generation, and oil production. It is not unusual for the U.S. company to obtain long-term loans from a development bank of the foreign country,

---

[15] Carol L. Courtadon. *The Competitive Structure of the Eurobond Underwriting Industry* (New York: New York University Graduate School of Business Administration, 1985, p. 6).

[16] Courtadon, p. 11.

[17] Courtadon, pp. 1–72, same as [12], pp. 18–27.

often a government-sponsored agency, to complete the project. The Inter-American Development Bank formed in 1959 by several Latin American countries is an example of an institution whose purpose is to make loans to facilitate local economic development.

Other agencies are designed to facilitate foreign import/export of goods and services. The United States Export-Import Bank, an independent agency of the federal government, was established in 1934 to loan money to foreign importers to help them purchase U.S. goods.

These and similar institutions throughout the world are generally public or quasi-public in nature. Although such loans form an integral part of international finance, generally they are not directly related to the thrust of daily operations. Their specific goals are domestic economic development and increased import/export of goods and services through aid to buyers otherwise unable to obtain credit. Consequently, management of profit-making enterprises tends to view these loans as supplemental sources employed when private and public objectives overlap.

As noted in earlier chapters, new stock issues are a relatively small component of external financing. U.S. corporations reinvest depreciation and a portion of earnings in new plant and equipment, following which they seek external debt sources. Some external debt sources contain warrants or are convertible to common stock; some are, in turn, issued as U.S. dollar-denominated Eurobonds.[18] Straight equity issues, however, are relatively rare. Nevertheless, there is no reason to assume that in integrated financial markets stock issues could not be sold in other countries. Indeed, modern communications systems link world markets on a 24-hour-a-day basis; only regulatory differences and ownership restrictions of specific countries ultimately prevent a U.S. corporation from employing underwriting syndicates to market new equity or debt issues in a world market for new issues.[19]

SUMMARY

The principles of finance are relevant to both an international and a domestic context. There is some evidence portfolio managers can add to return relative to risk involved: expand the efficiency frontier through international diversification. Takeover threats, unstable governments, and exchange-rate risks—if sufficiently random—may be offset by investing in financial assets of foreign countries, weighted by their relative contribution to total investable world wealth.

On the corporate side, there may exist—as there are in mergers—certain

---

[18] Courtadon, pp. 29–32.

[19] As an analogy, consider that a new domestic issue must not only conform to federal law but to laws of the individual states in which that security must be sold. Although over the years such laws have become more uniform—thereby facilitating sales in all 50 states—international uniformity may be more difficult to effect.

possibilities of resource allocation within the firm that may be more efficient than if carried out in the market. Differences in tax treatment, for example, may permit a corporation to exploit an investment opportunity abroad that an individual could not. In addition, that company may have access to foreign capital markets at lower effective costs. Thus, portfolio diversification may be even more complete if the portfolio contains shares of internationally diversified companies with access to investment opportunities at lower overall costs than if the portfolio directly invests in those real assets.

The most pervasive risk facing a company operating in international markets is the loss due to fluctuations in foreign-exchange rate. Most companies can hedge that risk by buying or selling currency in the forward or futures market. Because the forward market permits specific amounts tailored to individual need, it is more apt to be used by exporters and importers than the futures market. Companies with subsidiaries abroad must also face the reality that reported earnings will fluctuate with changes in exchange rates. Although this risk, too, can be hedged by employing forward or futures markets at a cost, sometimes the risk can be avoided by employing a currency swap or a parallel loan with a bank or other company.

Because foreign-exchange rates appreciate or depreciate against one another, economists have sought to explain the forces that bring about these changes. In perfect markets, a basket of goods should be priced the same (less transportation costs) regardless of the country of origin: exchange rates would adjust accordingly. Known as the purchasing-power parity theorem, it is at best a long-run explanation. Intuitively more appealing and more in accord with short-run experience in forward markets is the interest-rate parity theorem. In its basic form, short-term risk-free rates of the U.S. should have the same relationship with short-term risk-free rates of another country as the forward rate of that country's currency in U.S. dollars has to the spot rate. Thus

$$\frac{1 + i_{\text{U.S.}}}{1 + i_f} = \frac{F_{\$,f}}{S_{\$,f}}$$

Between two countries with comparable securities and allowing for transactions costs, this relationship holds reasonably well—although speculators with shorter holding periods may distort it, thereby providing others opportunities for arbitrage.

To finance international trade, the typical instrument employed is a banker's acceptance. An importer arranges for its bank to extend credit to an exporter by a letter of credit followed by a time draft accepted by the importer's bank. Once the goods are in the hands of the importer, the time draft becomes a banker's acceptance that can be held to maturity or sold in the banker's acceptance market. In effect, the bank has substituted its credit for that of the importer. The bank pays the note on maturity, a date that coincides with payment of the loan to the bank by the importer. Although U.S. dollar-denominated banker's acceptances are widely used, large companies can finance their imports or other needs through direct Eurodollar loans from foreign banks. Similarly, foreign banks can avoid refinancing their acceptances through U.S. banks by issuing their own acceptances denominated in Eurodollars.

Although traditionally commercial banks have financed international trade and made short-term loans, U.S. corporations—some without any involvement in international markets—increasingly turn directly to foreign capital markets to raise long-term debt. Known as Eurobonds (in the case of dollar-denominated instruments, Eurodollar bonds), these instruments presently represent a significant portion of borrowing by U.S. corporations. Some evidence suggests that capital markets have been segmented sufficiently to permit certain firms to issue instruments at lower YTMs than if the bonds had been marketed in the United States. Increasing integration of world financial markets, however, indicates that opportunities for arbitrage between these markets may be fleeting.

PROBLEMS AND QUESTIONS

1. Chauncey Chestnut, pension fund manager for Fifth National Bank of Wishbone Gulch, California, has attracted pension funds from large city banks through his ability to maximize returns relative to risk at the lowest possible cost to the client. His passively managed portfolios are fully diversified domestically. Of late, Chestnut has considered adding a diversified portfolio of international investments. Tracking the performance of such a portfolio relative to his present portfolio, he expects to achieve on average the following results for each holding period:

	Expected Return	*Variance*	*Covariance*
Domestic	.12	.03	− .00032
International	.16	.04	− .00032

Given the investable wealth appropriate to a pension fund, Chestnut estimates that 20 percent of the funds should be invested in the international fund and 80 percent in the domestic fund. If implemented, will this raise expected return and reduce variance of the combined portfolio? Explain in detail.

2. The 90-day risk-free rate for West German securities is .025. Comparable U.S. securities have a risk-free rate of .022. In terms of the U.S. dollar, the spot rate for the deutsche mark is .4066 and the 90-day forward rate is .4055. Under the interest-rate parity theorem, is the deutsche mark correctly priced? Explain in detail.

3. Against the U.S. dollar, the spot rate for the Swiss franc is .47. The 180-day risk-free rate on Swiss securities is .045; a similar rate on U.S. securities is .053. The

180-day forward rate for the Swiss franc against the U.S. dollar is .49. Show why an arbitrage opportunity exists. Ignoring transactions costs, how would a portfolio manager with $1,000,000 in U.S. Treasury securities alter her portfolio to take advantage of this opportunity?

4. As a portfolio manager, you notice the spot rate on the British pound is $1.36 and the 90-day forward rate is $1.38. The short-term risk-free 90-day interest rate for the U.K. is .03. The comparable rate for the U.S. is .04, and you hold $10,000,000 in 90-day T-bills at that rate. Should you sell those T-bills and invest in comparable U.K. instruments? Explain in detail.

5. Podunk Utility Corporation can raise funds in the Eurodollar bond market by selling $20,000,000 in bonds maturing in seven years at a coupon rate of 12-percent interest paid annually. The bonds would be marketed at par and the investment banker's spread would be 1.5 percent of proceeds. Alternatively, Podunk could place the issue privately in the United States at a 12.25-percent interest rate paid semiannually. There are no registration requirements in the Eurodollar bond market. Interest is tax deductible whether the bonds are marketed in Europe or placed privately in the U.S. Which approach offers the lower cost of debt capital? Explain in detail.

6. A U.S. exporter sells $125,000 in computer equipment to a British importer for delivery in 90 days. The two companies have enjoyed a successful business relationship in the past. As a result, the exporter will accept payment in British pounds on receipt of goods, the number of pounds to depend on the spot rate at that time. The 90-day forward rate for the pound is $1.43. How can the exporter employ the forward rate to help ensure receipt of the $125,000? Will the exporter actually receive the pound equivalent of $125,000 based on the forward rate? Explain.

7. In problem 6, suppose the British importer is unknown to the U.S. exporter. Through its bank in England, the importer has been financed with a dollar-denominated banker's acceptance of $125,000. The acceptance is received by the U.S. exporter, who immediately sells it through his or her American bank at the going rate of 11.5 percent. What are the net proceeds to the exporter?

8. What is a currency swap? What is a parallel loan? How can each be used as an alternative to the forward or futures market in foreign exchange?

SELECTED ADDITIONAL REFERENCES

Adler, Michael and Bernard Dumas. "Exposure to Currency Risk: Definition and Measurement," *Financial Management*, Vol. 13 (Summer 1984, pp. 42–50).
———— and ————. "International Portfolio Choice and Corporation Finance: A Synthesis," *Journal of Finance*, Vol. 38 (June 1983, pp. 925–84).

—— and ——. "The Exposure of Long-term Foreign Currency Bonds," *Journal of Financial and Quantitative Analysis*, Vol. 15 (November 1980, pp. 973–94).

Brinson, Gary P. "Intelligently Setting a Portfolio Asset Mix," *Pension world*, Vol. 18 (March 1982, pp. 65–70).

Brinson, Gary P., Jeffrey J. Diermeier, and L. Randolf Hood. *Multiple Market Index* (Chicago: First National Bank of Chicago, 1980).

——, ——, and Gary G. Schlarbaum. "A Composite Portfolio Benchmark for Pension Plans," *Financial Analysts Journal*, Vol. 42 (March–April 1986, pp. 15–24).

Chrystal, K. Alec. "A Guide to Foreign Exchange Markets," *Review of the Federal Reserve Bank of St. Louis*, Vol. 66 (March 1984, pp. 5–18).

Cornell, Bradford. "Inflation, Relative Price Changes and Exchange Rate Risk," *Financial Management*, Vol. 9 (Autumn 1980, pp. 30–34).

Courtadon, Carol L. *The Competitive Structure of the Eurobond Underwriting Industry* (New York: New York University Graduate School of Business Administration, 1985).

Dufey, Gunter and S. L. Srinivasulu. "The Case for Corporate Management of Foreign Exchange Risk," *Financial Management*, Vol. 12 (Winter 1983, pp. 54–62).

Errunza, Vihang R. and Lemma W. Senbet. "The Effects of International Operations on the Market Value of the Firm: Theory and Evidence," *Journal of Finance*, Vol. 36 (May 1981, pp. 401–18).

Fatemi, Ali M. "Shareholder Benefits From Corporate International Diversification," *Journal of Finance*, Vol. 39 (December 1984, pp. 1325–44).

Finnerty, Joseph E., Thomas Schneeweis, and Shantaram P. Hedge. "Interest Rates in the Eurobond Market," *Journal of Financial and Quantitative Analysis*, Vol. 15 (September 1980, pp. 743–55).

Fisher, F. C. III. *The Eurodollar Bond Market* (London: Euromoney Publications Limited, 1979).

Grabbe, J. Orlin. *International Financial Markets*, (New York: Elsevier Science Publishing, 1986).

Grauer, Robert R. and Nils H. Hakansson. "Gains from International Diversification: 1968–85 Returns on Portfolios of Stocks and Bonds," *Journal of Finance*, Vol. 42 (July 1987, pp. 721–39).

Ibbotson, Roger G. and Gary P. Brinson. *Investment Markets Gaining the Performance Advantage* (New York: McGraw-Hill, 1987, pp. 251–79).

Ibbotson, Roger G. and Laurence B. Siegel. "The World Market Wealth Portfolio," *Journal of Portfolio Management*, Vol. 10 (Winter 1983, pp. 5–17).

Jensen, Frederick H. and Patrick M. Parkinson. "Recent Developments in the Banker's Acceptance Market," *Federal Reserve Bulletin*, Vol. 72 (January 1986, pp. 1–12).

Kidwell, David S., M. Wayne Marr, and G. Rodney Thompson. "Eurodollar Bonds: Alternative Financing for U.S. Countries," *Financial Management*, Vol. 14 (Winter 1985, pp. 18–27).

Levy, Haim and Marshall Sarnat. "International Diversification of Investment Portfolios," *American Economic Review*, Vol. 60 (September 1970, pp. 668–75).

Rodriquez, Rita M. "Corporate Exchange Risk Management: Theme and Aberrations," *Journal of Finance*, Vol. 36 (May 1981, pp. 427–38).

Selling, Thomas I. and George H. Sorter. "FASB Statement No. 52 and Its Implications for Financial Statement Analysis," *Financial Analysts Journal*, Vol. 39 (May–June 1983, pp. 64–69).

Shapiro, Alan C. "International Capital Budgeting," *Midland Corporate Finance Journal*, Vol. 11 (Spring 1983, pp. 26–45).

Solnik, Bruno. "An Equilibrium Model of the International Capital Market," *Journal of Economic Theory*, Vol. 3 (August 1974, pp. 48–54).

———. "The International Pricing of Risk: An Empirical Investigation of the World Capital Market Structure," *Journal of Finance*, Vol. 29 (May 1974, pp. 365–78).

Stonehill, Arthur I. and Kare B. Dullum. *Internationalizing the Cost of Capital* (New York: John Wiley, 1982).

Stulz, Rene M. "A Model of International Asset Pricing," *Journal of Financial Economics*, Vol. 10 (December 1981, pp. 923–34).

23

EPILOGUE

It is, at this point, fitting that we summarize the central themes of the presentation:

First, and perhaps foremost: the analytical principles developed in this book apply both to portfolio management and to financial management. As intimated in Chapter 10, the theoretical revolutions begun by Markowitz and Tobin (portfolio management) and by Modigliani and Miller (financial management) can be viewed as *two sides of the same coin*. Compartmentalization of finance into portfolio theory and management and into corporate finance or financial management is still useful, particularly when one delves deeply into the process of managing financial assets as opposed to the process of managing real assets. We explored certain of these differences and, in keeping with the field's curricular format, emphasized financial management. Nevertheless, to be eclectic is to be flexible, both in terms of a career as well as in terms of the field's intellectual development: one should be equally at home facing the challenges of pension fund manager as of financial vice president of a chemical company.

Second: the fundamental valuation principle in finance is present value, or net present value. To be sure, we used percentage return on investment; however, for internal rate of return we emphasized the ambiguous results. Although holding period return proved a more useful measure, particularly as a measure of the cost of equity capital, a major component of its calculation—the market price of an investment at T_1—is the present value of expected cash flows from T_1 forward. Similarly, the market price of the same investment at T_0 is the present value of future cash flows from T_0 forward. What remains is the expected cash payment made to the investor between T_0 and T_1. Also, when management adds to the firm's market value by investing in plant and equipment, the expected net present value of future incremental cash flows, using the weighted average cost of capital as the discount rate, determines how much value is added. Consequently, even though it may be convenient to use return in the context of a ratio or a percentage (as when we developed Modern Portfolio Theory), present value provides the substantive components used to make this calculation.

Third: as suggested in the second central theme, present value, or net present value, is usually modified by *expected value*, emphasizing the risk inherent in nearly every investment decision. Coping analytically with risk is perhaps as difficult for managers as coping with it in practice. Thus, one of the most significant developments in financial theory is the explanation of how diversification results in a variance in return on a portfolio lower than the weighted average of the variances of returns on the securities comprising the portfolio. On this foundation, several scholars developed what has become known as the Capital Asset Pricing Model (CAPM), the major features of which we analyzed in Chapter 5. Built on efficient capital markets and comprised of risk-averse investors who hold diversified portfolios, the CAPM analysis leads to a single index model or characteristic line where the return on a financial instrument issued by any firm is a function of the firm's systematic risk as measured by its beta coefficient.

Fourth: the implications of CAPM are straightforward: management can make investment decisions that may alter variability of return on its portfolio of real assets. However, doing so will change the beta coefficient, and hence affect the stock's market price and the expected holding period return. Management also can alter the firm's capital structure by substituting debt for equity. Doing this also affects the firm's beta coefficient, and hence the expected return. Nevertheless, given the tax deductibility of interest, management can add value to the firm by employing some level of debt to finance assets. Beyond a critical level, the use of debt relative to equity will not add to the market value of the shares. Although it is difficult to pinpoint, as a rule of thumb, when a rising debt ratio causes a decline in a firm's credit rating and an increase in its cost of debt capital, total firm value may actually decline.

Fifth: the surface impression gained from our analytical discussion is that management can do nothing for the firm's stockholders they cannot do for themselves. In efficient markets, managerial decisions are reflected immediately in the stock's price and returns adjust accordingly. Because investors hold diversified portfolios in which only systematic risk drives expected returns, all management can do is move the company's stock up or down the securities market line. In addition, CAPM implies that the company is merely a collection of real assets, each with its own beta coefficient.

Sixth: our position is that a company is not merely a collection of assets (see Chapter 10). Even within the rigorous set of assumptions that underlie CAPM, the company serves a function. Specifically, in the economic theory of the firm, the production unit may organize resources more efficiently than the market and it is management's function to administer such resources. Moreover, because all managers are not created equal—at least they are not equally skilled—part of the rationale for mergers is the presumption that one management team may organize resources better than another. If the combination (the merger) is synergistic—if it increases total value of the merged firms—the shareholders benefit. Such benefits, however, may be somewhat elusive for the shareholders of the acquiring firm when compared to the benefits enjoyed by the shareholders of the acquired firm. Consequently, although CAPM offers useful insights into the value of managerial decisions on asset acquisitions and financial combinations, it is an incomplete explanation of the firm's market value. In other words, the return on assets or combination of assets is not independent of those who administer them.

Seventh: when we relax the assumption that capital markets are efficient—specifically, when we relax the implications of the rule of knowledge in the hypothesis—the role of a skilled financial manager is similar to that of a skilled securities analyst; it is to find underpriced investment opportunities. Moreover, just as a portfolio manager—anticipating a change in the yield relationship among classes of assets—re-weights the portfolio in order to profit from the expected change, so a financial manager alters the debt ratio in an effort to minimize the average cost of capital through time. Although these windows of opportunity may close rapidly, they are consistent with changing equilibrium conditions.

Nevertheless, financial theorists remain skeptical that market participants can anticipate equilibrium changes consistently. Yet, there are those who do indeed anticipate such changes correctly—just as there are those who toss a coin and come up with heads 15 consecutive times, who win lotteries, or who draw 13 cards of the same suit in a bridge game. Are they lucky or skillful? For games of chance, we know the answer; for portfolio managers or financial managers, we are less certain. When an athlete consistently outperforms the competition, we attribute the success to skill; we could say the same thing about a consistently successful manager. What remains elusive is the source of such skill. The point cannot be overemphasized. However, empirical tests of the efficient market hypothesis depend on econometric models that function on the basis of average relationships. Although there is room for clearly superior as well as inferior performance in the wings of probability distribution, econometric models attribute the results to chance. Yet the real world rewards or punishes those associated with such outcomes as though they are responsible for them.

Eighth: we know very little about many phenomena in finance. The constant payout ratio in the wake of fluctuating investment opportunities is only one example. Combining this phenomenon with financial theory, tax laws, and transactions costs provides a cogent argument for making dividends a cash distribution that cannot be profitably reinvested in the firm. Such a policy would result in fluctuating dividends—not a common practice. Scholarship in this area focuses on the information content of dividends. Management generally has an announced dividend policy—specifically, that dividends will be a constant percentage of earnings. By increasing dividends, management signals that company earnings are such that dividends can be sustained. Of course, in efficient markets, at the time the dividend increase is announced it already will be fully reflected in the stock's market price. Assuming the market values the information content inherent in a constant payout ratio, from management's perspective the independent variability in the holding period return and hence in the cost of equity capital will be marginally lower. Presumably this offsets higher transactions costs associated with raising external funds to finance capital budgets that otherwise would be partially financed from retained earnings.

Another example is the proliferation of financial instruments. Although in theory there are only debt and equity, in practice variations on debt and equity contracts abound. Witness the hybrid known as the convertible. In efficient markets, the trade-off between risk and return embodied in such variations is reflected in their respective yield differentials. As a result, financial theorists have little interest in the phenomenon. From an eclectic standpoint, however, one wants to know why there is such a proliferation. To date, there is no better answer than the institutional explanation that a variety of instruments serve the particular needs of a diverse and (over time) changing set of investors. For instance, we can trace the zero coupon bond to the desire of pension fund managers in highly volatile markets to lock up yields on at least a portion of their portfolios. In turn, the issuer receives the tax subsidy on the imputed interest even though there is no cash outlay until maturity. There are similar stories about other securities. Suffice it to say, the financial landscape is strewn with the wrecks of instruments that served the *ad hoc* needs of the issuer or met the peculiar economic conditions of the time.

A third and final example is the role liquidity plays in determining composition of assets and their financing. To the costs of financial distress must be added the costs of breaking up the firm not incorporated in the models used. In practice, maximization of stockholder wealth is tempered by realization that individuals have contracts with the firm. Employees often bear some costs, however small, when involuntary liquidation forces them to seek other positions. In some instances, of course, the uprooting is painful. Moreover, the ripple effects from the loss of a major employer create considerable havoc throughout the community. Externalities such as these can drive management, competition permitting, to invest more in permanent working capital and to employ less debt than is consistent with maximization of shareholder wealth.

Ninth: there is always the search for a better explanation. The Arbitrage Pricing Theory (APT), or some other model, may eventually replace CAPM. It will do so, of course, only if after substantial empirical testing it offers a more complete explanation of return on a security. Similarly, the revolution in the theory of options inaugurated by the Black-Scholes model may have implications that go beyond the narrow confines of the original notion. And there is always the hope for a testable theory that ties together the loose ends—a unified field theory of finance.

When and if that happens—a subject that over a generation ago was a body of detail in search of an explanation—we will have moved from an intellectually challenging discipline to a closed field of knowledge. The practitioner would possess a set of prescriptions for decision-making and the academic would either retool or, worse, become dean of the faculty. Fortunately for the academic, the need to consider either alternative appears some considerable distance into the future.

APPENDIX A
COMPOUND INTEREST
AND PRESENT VALUE

Because so many problems in finance make use of compound interest and present value formulas, it is useful to develop more formal proofs of certain more widely used techniques.[1]

---

[1] For a more detailed discussion, see Marjorie V. Butcher and Cecil J. Nesbitt, *Mathematics of Compound Interest* (Ann Arbor, MI: Ulrich's Books, 1971).

TOTAL VALUE OF AN ANNUITY

Total value S of an annuity a invested at rate r for n years is

$$S = a(1 + r)^{n-1} + a(1 + r)^{n-2} + a(1 + r)^{n-3} + \cdots + a(1 + r) + a \qquad \text{(A-1)}$$

If a is \$1,000 and n is 30, \$1,000 received at the end of the first year will compound annually at rate r for 29 years; \$1,000 received at the end of the second year will compound annually for 28 years; and so forth. The final \$1,000 will be received at the end of the thirtieth year and will not compound. If we multiply both sides of the equation by $1 + r$, we obtain

$$S(1 + r) = a(1 + r)^n + a(1 + r)^{n-1} + a(1 + r)^{n-2} + \cdots + a(1 + r)^2 + a(1 + r) \qquad \text{(A-2)}$$

If we subtract Equation A-1 from Equation A-2, we obtain

$$S(1 + r) - S = a(1 + r)^n - a$$
$$Sr = a[(1 + r)^n - 1]$$
$$S = \frac{a[(1 + r)^n - 1]}{r}$$

The foregoing expression is easily modified to allow the nominal rate of interest (r compounded m times per year) and the annuity a each to be broken into m finite payments of $\dfrac{a}{m}$ semiannually, quarterly, weekly, and so forth. Thus

$$S = \frac{\dfrac{a}{m}\left[\left(1 + \dfrac{r}{m}\right)^{mn} - 1\right]}{\dfrac{r}{m}}$$

because

$$\frac{a}{m} \div \frac{r}{m} = \frac{a}{m} \times \frac{m}{r} = \frac{a}{r}$$

$$S = \frac{a\left[\left(1 + \dfrac{r}{m}\right)^{mn} - 1\right]}{r}$$

PRESENT VALUE OF AN ANNUITY

Present value P (value today) of an annuity a received at the end of each year for n years and discounted at rate of interest r is obtained by the equation

$$P = \frac{a}{1+r} + \frac{a}{(1+r)^2} + \frac{a}{(1+r)^3} + \cdots + \frac{a}{(1+r)^n} \tag{A-3}$$

Again, if a is \$1,000 and n is 30, \$1,000 received at the end of the first year will be discounted at $(1+r)$; \$1,000 received at the end of the second year will be discounted at $(1+r)^2$; and so forth. If we multiply both sides of the equation by $\frac{1}{1+r}$, we obtain

$$\frac{P}{1+r} = \frac{a}{(1+r)^2} + \frac{a}{(1+r)^3} + \frac{a}{(1+r)^4} + \frac{a}{(1+r)^{n+1}} \tag{A-4}$$

If we subtract Equation A-4 from Equation A-3, we obtain

$$P - \frac{P}{(1+r)} = \frac{a}{(1+r)} - \frac{a}{(1+r)^{n+1}}$$

Multiplying both sides by $1 + r$ and simplifying, we find that

$$P(1+r) - P = a - a(1+r)^{-n}$$
$$Pr = a[1 - (1+r)^{-n}]$$
$$P = \frac{a[1 - (1+r)^{-n}]}{r} \tag{A-4-1}$$

As in the case of total value of an annuity, we can allow for finite divisions in a and r, so that

$$P = \frac{\frac{a}{m}\left[1 - \left(1 + \frac{r}{m}\right)^{-mn}\right]}{\frac{r}{m}}$$

$$P = \frac{a\left[1 - \left(1 + \frac{r}{m}\right)^{-mn}\right]}{r}$$

As

$$n \to \infty, \left(1 + \frac{r}{m}\right)^{-mn} \to 0, \text{ so that } P = \frac{a}{r} \tag{A-5}$$

PRESENT VALUES OF AN ANNUITY COMPOUNDED AT RATE g

Suppose a common stock has an annual dividend (paid at the end of the year) of a dollars, which is expected to grow at an annual compound rate of g for n years. Given the effective annual interest rate r, to calculate the present value P

$$P = \frac{a}{(1+r)} + \frac{a(1+g)}{(1+r)^2} + \frac{a(1+g)^2}{(1+r)^3} + \cdots + \frac{a(1+g)^{n-1}}{(1+r)^n}$$

$$P = \frac{a}{1+r}\left[1 + \frac{1+g}{1+r} + \left(\frac{1+g}{1+r}\right)^2 + \cdots + \left(\frac{1+g}{1+r}\right)^{n-1}\right] \qquad \text{(A-6)}$$

The bracketed expression is a geometric progression whose common ratio is $(1+g)/(1+r)$. If the first value in the progression is a (in this case 1) and if the common ratio is p, a general expression for the geometric progression is $a + ap + ap^2 + ap^3 + \cdots + ap^{n-1}$, where $a \neq 0$ and $p \neq 1$.

If S equals the sum of this geometric progression, $a + ap + ap^2 + ap^3 + \cdots + ap^{n-1} = S$. Multiplying both sides of the equation by $(p-1)$, we obtain

$$(p-1)[a + ap + ap^2 + ap^3 \cdots + ap^{n-1}] = (p-1)S$$
$$ap - a + ap^2 - ap + ap^3 - ap^2 + ap^4 - ap^3 + \cdots + ap^n - ap^{n-1} = (p-1)S$$
$$\frac{ap^n - a}{p-1} = S$$

Therefore

$$a + ap + ap^2 + ap^3 + \cdots + ap^{n-1} = \frac{ap^n - a}{p-1}$$

Substituting, using the terms in Equation A-6, we obtain

$$P = \frac{a}{1+r}\left[1 + \frac{1+g}{1+r} + \left(\frac{1+g}{1+r}\right)^2 + \cdots + \left(\frac{1+g}{1+r}\right)^{n-1}\right]$$

$$= \frac{a}{1+r}\frac{[(1+g)/(1+r)]^n - 1}{(1+g)/(1+r) - 1}$$

$$= \frac{a(1+r)^{-1}\{1 - [(1+g)/(1+r)]^n\}}{1 - [(1+g)/(1+r)]}$$

$$= \frac{a(1+r)^{-1}\{1 - [(1+g)/(1+r)]^n\}}{(r-g)/(1+r)}$$

$$= \frac{a\{1 - [(1+g)/(1+r)]^n\}}{r-g}$$

As in previous illustrations, one can allow for m finite annual time periods, so that

$$P = \frac{\dfrac{a}{m}\left\{1 - \left[\left(1 + \dfrac{g}{m}\right)\Big/\left(1 + \dfrac{r}{m}\right)\right]^{mn}\right\}}{\dfrac{r - g}{m}}$$

$$P = \frac{a\left\{1 - \left[\left(1 + \dfrac{g}{m}\right)\Big/\left(1 + \dfrac{r}{m}\right)\right]^{mn}\right\}}{r - g}$$

As long as $g < r$, as $n \to \infty$ the expression

$$\left[\left(1 + \frac{g}{m}\right)\Big/\left(1 + \frac{r}{m}\right)\right]^{mn} \to 0$$

and[2]

$$P = \frac{a}{r - g} \qquad\qquad\qquad \text{(A-7)}$$

Because of diminishing returns to capital in the long run (as $n \to \infty$), r will be greater than g. For the short run (where n is a finite number of years), g may be greater than r and the longer form of the equation is appropriate.

CONTINUOUS COMPOUNDING AND DISCOUNTING

Although r is the nominal annual rate of interest, the *effective* (annual) *rate i* is defined as

$$i = \left(1 + \frac{r}{m}\right)^m - 1$$

When m equals 1, $i = r$. As $m \to \infty$, then

$$i = \lim_{m \to \infty}\left[\left(1 + \frac{r}{m}\right)^m - 1\right]$$

$$i = \lim_{m \to \infty}\left(1 + \frac{r}{m}\right)^m - 1$$

---

[2] This version of the equation, when applied to common stocks, is associated with Gordon. See Myron J. Gordon, *The Investment, Financing, and Valuation of the Corporation* (Homewood, IL: Irwin, 1962, pp. 43–66).

By definition

$$e = \frac{\text{limit}}{m \to \infty} \left(1 + \frac{1}{m}\right)^m$$

where e is the base of the natural logarithms and is approximated by 2.71828.

Let $\dfrac{r}{m} = \dfrac{1}{m'}$

$$\left(1 + \frac{r}{m}\right)^m = \left(1 + \frac{1}{m'}\right)^{rm'} = \left[\left(1 + \frac{1}{m'}\right)^{m'}\right]^r$$

As $m \to \infty$, $m' \to \infty$; therefore

$$\frac{\text{limit}}{m \to \infty} \left[\left(1 + \frac{1}{m'}\right)^{m'}\right]^r = \frac{\text{limit}}{m \to \infty} \left[\left(1 + \frac{1}{m'}\right)^{m'}\right]^r$$

$$= \frac{\text{limit}}{m \to \infty} \left[\left(1 + \frac{1}{m'}\right)^{m'}\right]^r$$

$$= e^r$$

Consequently, as $m \to \infty$, $i = e^r - 1$.

The assumption that the annual interest payment is received continuously may be employed in calculating the future value of a sum certain as well as in calculating the present value of a future income stream. Suppose we invested $1,000 for two years at a nominal interest rate of 10 percent. Under the assumption that interest is paid annually $(m = 1)$, $1,000(1.10)^2 = $1,210$. If interest is paid continuously, $1,000(e^{.10})^2 = $1,221.40$.

Similarly, if we received $1,210 at the end of two years under the assumption that interest is paid annually, the present value becomes

$$\frac{\$1,210}{(1.10)^2} = \$1,000$$

If interest is paid continuously, then

$$\frac{\$1,221.40}{(e^{.10})^2} = \$1,000$$

If P equals present value, a equals future value, and t equals the number of years, under the assumption of continuous compounding

$$P = \frac{a}{(e)^{rt}} \tag{A-8}$$

$$P = ae^{-rt}$$

If we receive a_t dollars each year for n years into the future, the payment a_t at any point in time is a constant a_0, so that $a_t = a_0$. Because we are discounting continuously, we can use integral calculus to determine the present value of the payments, so that

$$P = \int_0^n a_t e^{-rt} dt \tag{A-9}$$

Note we have used Equation A-8 to discount each payment on the assumption the stream of payments begins immediately and we assume in Equation A-9 these payments continue for n time periods.

Similarly, if $a_t = a_0$ and we use the applicable rules of integral calculus

$$P = a_0 \int_0^n e^{-rt} dt$$

$$P = a_0 \left[\frac{-e^{-rt}}{r} \right] \Bigg|_0^n$$

$$P = a_0 \left[\frac{-e^{-rn}}{r} - \frac{-e^0}{r} \right]$$

$$P = a_0 \left[\frac{1 - e^{-rn}}{r} \right]$$

(Note that e^{-rn} replaces $(1 + r)^{-n}$ in Equation A-4-1.)
Similarly

$$\frac{\text{limit } P}{n \to \infty} = \frac{a_0}{r} \tag{A-10}$$

The result is the same as in Equation A-5, where $a = a_0$, so that

$$P = \frac{a}{r} = \frac{\text{limit } P}{n \to \infty} = \frac{a_0}{r}$$

When payment a_0 grows continuously at rate g for any time period t, $a_t = a_0 e^{gt}$, $0 \le t \le n$. Present value P of such a stream is given by the integral

$$P = \int_0^n a_t e^{-rt} dt$$

$$= a_0 \int_0^n e^{gt} e^{-rt} dt$$

$$= a_0 \int_0^n e^{-(r-g)t} dt$$

Using the rules of integral calculus, the solution to this equation is

$$P = a_0 \left[\frac{-e^{-(r-g)t}}{r-g} \right] \Bigg|_0^n$$

$$= a_0 \left[\frac{-e^{-(r-g)n}}{r-g} - \left(\frac{-e^0}{r-g} \right) \right]$$

$$= a_0 \left[\frac{1 - e^{-(r-g)n}}{r-g} \right]$$

$$\frac{\text{limit } P}{n \to \infty} = \frac{a_0}{r-g}, \text{ provided } r > g$$

The result compares with Equation A-7, where $a = a_0$.

APPENDIX B
PRESENT VALUE OF $1
RECEIVED AT THE END
OF THE YEAR

$$P = \frac{1}{(1 + r)^n}$$

Year	Present Value at 1%	Present Value at 2%	Present Value at 3%	Present Value at 4%	Present Value at 5%
1	0.990099	0.980392	0.970874	0.961538	0.952381
2	0.980296	0.961169	0.942596	0.924556	0.907030
3	0.970590	0.942322	0.915142	0.888996	0.863838
4	0.960980	0.923846	0.888487	0.854804	0.822703
5	0.951466	0.905731	0.862609	0.821927	0.783526
6	0.942045	0.887972	0.837484	0.790315	0.746216
7	0.932718	0.870560	0.813092	0.759918	0.710682
8	0.923483	0.853491	0.789409	0.730690	0.676840
9	0.914340	0.836756	0.766417	0.702587	0.644609
10	0.905287	0.820349	0.744094	0.675564	0.613914
11	0.896324	0.804263	0.722421	0.649581	0.584680
12	0.887449	0.788494	0.701380	0.624597	0.556838
13	0.878663	0.773033	0.680951	0.600574	0.530322
14	0.869963	0.757876	0.661118	0.577475	0.505068
15	0.861350	0.743015	0.641862	0.555265	0.481018
16	0.852821	0.728446	0.623167	0.533908	0.458112
17	0.844378	0.714163	0.605017	0.513373	0.436297
18	0.836017	0.700160	0.587395	0.493628	0.415521
19	0.827740	0.686431	0.570286	0.474643	0.395734
20	0.819545	0.672972	0.553676	0.456387	0.376890
21	0.811430	0.659777	0.537549	0.438834	0.358943
22	0.803396	0.646840	0.521893	0.421956	0.341850
23	0.795442	0.634157	0.506692	0.405727	0.325572
24	0.787566	0.621722	0.491934	0.390122	0.310068
25	0.779768	0.609532	0.477606	0.375117	0.295303

Year	Present Value at 6%	Present Value at 7%	Present Value at 8%	Present Value at 9%	Present Value at 10%
1	0.943396	0.934579	0.925926	0.917431	0.909091
2	0.889997	0.873439	0.857339	0.841680	0.826446
3	0.839619	0.816298	0.793832	0.772183	0.751315
4	0.792094	0.762895	0.735030	0.708425	0.683013
5	0.747258	0.712986	0.680583	0.649931	0.620921
6	0.704961	0.666342	0.630170	0.596267	0.564474
7	0.665057	0.622750	0.583490	0.547034	0.513158
8	0.627413	0.582009	0.540269	0.501866	0.466507
9	0.591899	0.543934	0.500249	0.460428	0.424098
10	0.558395	0.508349	0.463193	0.422411	0.385543
11	0.526788	0.475093	0.428883	0.387533	0.350494
12	0.496970	0.444012	0.397114	0.355535	0.318631
13	0.468839	0.414964	0.367698	0.326178	0.289664
14	0.442301	0.387817	0.340461	0.299246	0.263331
15	0.417265	0.362446	0.315242	0.274538	0.239392
16	0.393647	0.338734	0.291890	0.251870	0.217629
17	0.371365	0.316574	0.270269	0.231073	0.197845
18	0.350344	0.295864	0.250249	0.211994	0.179859
19	0.330513	0.276508	0.231712	0.194490	0.163508
20	0.311805	0.258419	0.214548	0.178431	0.148644
21	0.294156	0.241513	0.198656	0.163698	0.135130
22	0.277505	0.225713	0.183940	0.150182	0.122846
23	0.261798	0.210947	0.170315	0.137781	0.111678
24	0.246979	0.197146	0.157699	0.126405	0.101526
25	0.232999	0.184249	0.146018	0.115968	0.092296

Year	Present Value at 11%	Present Value at 12%	Present Value at 13%	Present Value at 14%	Present Value at 15%
1	0.900901	0.892857	0.884956	0.877193	0.869565
2	0.811622	0.797194	0.783147	0.769468	0.756144
3	0.731191	0.711780	0.693050	0.674972	0.657516
4	0.658731	0.635518	0.613319	0.592080	0.571753
5	0.593451	0.567427	0.542760	0.519369	0.497177
6	0.534641	0.506631	0.480319	0.455587	0.432328
7	0.481658	0.452349	0.425061	0.399637	0.375937
8	0.433926	0.403883	0.376160	0.350559	0.326902
9	0.390925	0.360610	0.332885	0.307508	0.284262
10	0.352184	0.321973	0.294588	0.269744	0.247185
11	0.317283	0.287476	0.260698	0.236617	0.214943
12	0.285841	0.256675	0.230706	0.207559	0.186907
13	0.257514	0.229174	0.204165	0.182069	0.162528
14	0.231995	0.204620	0.180677	0.159710	0.141329
15	0.209004	0.182696	0.159891	0.140096	0.122894
16	0.188292	0.163122	0.141496	0.122892	0.106865
17	0.169633	0.145644	0.125218	0.107800	0.092926
18	0.152822	0.130040	0.110812	0.094561	0.080805
19	0.137678	0.116107	0.098064	0.082948	0.070265
20	0.124034	0.103667	0.086782	0.072762	0.061100
21	0.111742	0.092560	0.076799	0.063826	0.053131
22	0.100669	0.082643	0.067963	0.055988	0.046201
23	0.090692	0.073788	0.060144	0.049112	0.040174
24	0.081705	0.065882	0.053225	0.043081	0.034934
25	0.073608	0.058823	0.047102	0.037790	0.030378

Year	Present Value at 16%	Present Value at 17%	Present Value at 18%	Present Value at 19%	Present Value at 20%
1	0.862069	0.854701	0.847458	0.840336	0.833333
2	0.743163	0.730514	0.718184	0.706165	0.694444
3	0.640658	0.624371	0.608631	0.593416	0.578704
4	0.552291	0.533650	0.515789	0.498669	0.482253
5	0.476113	0.456111	0.437109	0.419049	0.401878
6	0.410442	0.389839	0.370432	0.352142	0.334898
7	0.353830	0.333195	0.313925	0.295918	0.279082
8	0.305026	0.284782	0.266038	0.248670	0.232568
9	0.262953	0.243404	0.225456	0.208967	0.193807
10	0.226684	0.208037	0.191065	0.175602	0.161506
11	0.195417	0.177810	0.161919	0.147565	0.134588
12	0.168463	0.151974	0.137220	0.124004	0.112157
13	0.145227	0.129892	0.116288	0.104205	0.093464
14	0.125195	0.111019	0.098549	0.087567	0.077887
15	0.107927	0.094888	0.083516	0.073586	0.064905
16	0.093041	0.081101	0.070776	0.061837	0.054088
17	0.080207	0.069317	0.059980	0.051964	0.045073
18	0.069144	0.059245	0.050830	0.043667	0.037561
19	0.059607	0.050637	0.043077	0.036695	0.031301
20	0.051385	0.043280	0.036506	0.030836	0.026084
21	0.044298	0.036991	0.030937	0.025913	0.021737
22	0.038188	0.031616	0.026218	0.021775	0.018114
23	0.032921	0.027022	0.022218	0.018299	0.015095
24	0.028380	0.023096	0.018829	0.015377	0.012579
25	0.024465	0.019740	0.015957	0.012922	0.010483

Year	Present Value at 21%	Present Value at 22%	Present Value at 23%	Present Value at 24%	Present Value at 25%
1	0.826446	0.819672	0.813008	0.806452	0.800000
2	0.683013	0.671862	0.660982	0.650364	0.640000
3	0.564474	0.550707	0.537384	0.524487	0.512000
4	0.466507	0.451399	0.436898	0.422974	0.409600
5	0.385543	0.369999	0.355201	0.341108	0.327680
6	0.318631	0.303278	0.288781	0.275087	0.262144
7	0.263331	0.248589	0.234782	0.221844	0.209715
8	0.217629	0.203761	0.190879	0.178907	0.167772
9	0.179859	0.167017	0.155187	0.144280	0.134218
10	0.148644	0.136899	0.126168	0.116354	0.107374
11	0.122846	0.112213	0.102576	0.093834	0.085899
12	0.101526	0.091978	0.083395	0.075673	0.068719
13	0.083905	0.075391	0.067801	0.061026	0.054976
14	0.069343	0.061796	0.055122	0.049215	0.043980
15	0.057309	0.050653	0.044815	0.039689	0.035184
16	0.047362	0.041519	0.036435	0.032008	0.028147
17	0.039142	0.034032	0.029622	0.025813	0.022518
18	0.032349	0.027895	0.024083	0.020817	0.018014
19	0.026735	0.022865	0.019580	0.016788	0.014412
20	0.022095	0.018741	0.015918	0.013538	0.011529
21	0.018260	0.015362	0.012942	0.010918	0.009223
22	0.015091	0.012592	0.010522	0.008805	0.007379
23	0.012472	0.010321	0.008554	0.007101	0.005903
24	0.010307	0.008460	0.006955	0.005726	0.004722
25	0.008519	0.006934	0.005654	0.004618	0.003778

Year	Present Value at 26%	Present Value at 27%	Present Value at 28%	Present Value at 29%	Present Value at 30%
1	0.793651	0.787402	0.781250	0.775194	0.769231
2	0.629882	0.620001	0.610352	0.600925	0.591716
3	0.499906	0.488190	0.476837	0.465834	0.455166
4	0.396751	0.384402	0.372529	0.361111	0.350128
5	0.314882	0.302678	0.291038	0.279931	0.269329
6	0.249906	0.238329	0.227374	0.217001	0.207176
7	0.198338	0.187661	0.177636	0.168218	0.159366
8	0.157411	0.147765	0.138778	0.130401	0.122590
9	0.124930	0.116350	0.108420	0.101086	0.094300
10	0.099150	0.091614	0.084703	0.078362	0.072538
11	0.078691	0.072137	0.066174	0.060745	0.055799
12	0.062453	0.056801	0.051699	0.047089	0.042922
13	0.049566	0.044725	0.040390	0.036503	0.033017
14	0.039338	0.035217	0.031554	0.028297	0.025398
15	0.031221	0.027730	0.024652	0.021936	0.019537
16	0.024778	0.021834	0.019259	0.017005	0.015028
17	0.019665	0.017192	0.015046	0.013182	0.011560
18	0.015607	0.013537	0.011755	0.010218	0.008892
19	0.012387	0.010659	0.009184	0.007921	0.006840
20	0.009831	0.008393	0.007175	0.006141	0.005262
21	0.007802	0.006609	0.005605	0.004760	0.004048
22	0.006192	0.005204	0.004379	0.003690	0.003113
23	0.004914	0.004097	0.003421	0.002860	0.002395
24	0.003900	0.003226	0.002673	0.002217	0.001842
25	0.003096	0.002540	0.002088	0.001719	0.001417

Year	Present Value at 31%	Present Value at 32%	Present Value at 33%	Present Value at 34%	Present Value at 35%
1	0.763359	0.757576	0.751880	0.746269	0.740741
2	0.582717	0.573921	0.565323	0.556917	0.548697
3	0.444822	0.434789	0.425055	0.415610	0.406442
4	0.339559	0.329385	0.319590	0.310156	0.301068
5	0.259205	0.249534	0.240293	0.231460	0.223013
6	0.197866	0.189041	0.180672	0.172731	0.165195
7	0.151043	0.143213	0.135843	0.128904	0.122367
8	0.115300	0.108495	0.102138	0.096197	0.090642
9	0.088015	0.082193	0.076795	0.071789	0.067142
10	0.067187	0.062267	0.057741	0.053574	0.049735
11	0.051288	0.047172	0.043414	0.039980	0.036841
12	0.039151	0.035737	0.032642	0.029836	0.027289
13	0.029886	0.027073	0.024543	0.022266	0.020214
14	0.022814	0.020510	0.018453	0.016616	0.014974
15	0.017415	0.015538	0.013875	0.012400	0.011092
16	0.013294	0.011771	0.010432	0.009254	0.008216
17	0.010148	0.008917	0.007844	0.006906	0.006086
18	0.007747	0.006756	0.005898	0.005154	0.004508
19	0.005914	0.005118	0.004434	0.003846	0.003339
20	0.004514	0.003877	0.003334	0.002870	0.002474
21	0.003446	0.002937	0.002507	0.002142	0.001832
22	0.002630	0.002225	0.001885	0.001598	0.001357
23	0.002008	0.001686	0.001417	0.001193	0.001005
24	0.001533	0.001277	0.001066	0.000890	0.000745
25	0.001170	0.000968	0.000801	0.000664	0.000552

Year	Present Value at 36%	Present Value at 37%	Present Value at 38%	Present Value at 39%	Present Value at 40%
1	0.735294	0.729927	0.724638	0.719424	0.714286
2	0.540657	0.532793	0.525100	0.517572	0.510204
3	0.397542	0.388900	0.380507	0.372354	0.364432
4	0.292310	0.283869	0.275730	0.267880	0.260308
5	0.214934	0.207204	0.199804	0.192720	0.185934
6	0.158040	0.151243	0.144786	0.138647	0.132810
7	0.116206	0.110397	0.104917	0.099746	0.094865
8	0.085445	0.080582	0.076027	0.071760	0.067760
9	0.062827	0.058819	0.055092	0.051626	0.048400
10	0.046197	0.042933	0.039922	0.037141	0.034572
11	0.033968	0.031338	0.028929	0.026720	0.024694
12	0.024977	0.022875	0.020963	0.019223	0.017639
13	0.018365	0.016697	0.015190	0.013830	0.012599
14	0.013504	0.012187	0.011008	0.009949	0.008999
15	0.009929	0.008896	0.007977	0.007158	0.006428
16	0.007301	0.006493	0.005780	0.005149	0.004591
17	0.005368	0.004740	0.004188	0.003705	0.003280
18	0.003947	0.003460	0.003035	0.002665	0.002343
19	0.002902	0.002525	0.002199	0.001917	0.001673
20	0.002134	0.001843	0.001594	0.001379	0.001195
21	0.001569	0.001345	0.001155	0.000992	0.000854
22	0.001154	0.000982	0.000837	0.000714	0.000610
23	0.000848	0.000717	0.000606	0.000514	0.000436
24	0.000624	0.000523	0.000439	0.000370	0.000311
25	0.000459	0.000382	0.000318	0.000266	0.000222

SOURCE: Values for $P = \dfrac{1}{(1 + r)^n}$ were computer-generated. Consequently, values for the first year need not correspond exactly to values for the first year in Appendix C, which were computer-generated using $P = \dfrac{1 - (1 + r)^{-n}}{r}$.

APPENDIX C
PRESENT VALUE OF $1
RECEIVED EACH YEAR
FOR 20 YEARS

$$P = \frac{1 - (1 + r)^{-n}}{r}$$

Year	Present Value at 1%	Present Value at 2%	Present Value at 3%	Present Value at 4%	Present Value at 5%
1	0.990099	0.980392	0.970872	0.961538	0.952380
2	1.970392	1.941556	1.913468	1.886094	1.859407
3	2.940983	2.883878	2.828610	2.775088	2.723246
4	3.901964	3.807718	3.717099	3.629893	3.545947
5	4.853427	4.713449	4.579705	4.451820	4.329473
6	5.795473	5.601415	5.417190	5.242135	5.075687
7	6.728190	6.471980	6.230281	6.002052	5.786367
8	7.651675	7.325462	7.019691	6.732741	6.463207
9	8.566016	8.162218	7.786107	7.435328	7.107816
10	9.471303	8.982563	8.530202	8.110891	7.721727
11	10.367626	9.786826	9.252622	8.760472	8.306408
12	11.255074	10.575315	9.954001	9.385071	8.863244
13	12.133736	11.348350	10.634953	9.985642	9.393565
14	13.003695	12.106222	11.296072	10.563119	9.898633
15	13.865048	12.849238	11.937932	11.118382	10.379649
16	14.717872	13.577676	12.561101	11.652291	10.837761
17	15.562248	14.291842	13.166116	12.165663	11.274057
18	16.398270	14.991996	13.753511	12.659290	11.689578
19	17.226006	15.678430	14.323797	13.133933	12.085313
20	18.045546	16.351397	14.877473	13.590322	12.462202
21	18.856979	17.011175	15.415021	14.029155	12.821144
22	19.660366	17.658010	15.936913	14.451111	13.162994
23	20.455814	18.292166	16.443607	14.856836	13.488565
24	21.243376	18.913887	16.935539	15.246958	13.798634
25	22.023153	19.523418	17.413145	15.622075	14.093937

Year	Present Value at 6%	Present Value at 7%	Present Value at 8%	Present Value at 9%	Present Value at 10%
1	0.943395	0.934580	0.925926	0.917431	0.909091
2	1.833391	1.808019	1.783265	1.759112	1.735538
3	2.673010	2.624318	2.577098	2.531296	2.486852
4	3.465103	3.387214	3.312128	3.239721	3.169866
5	4.212361	4.100199	3.992711	3.889653	3.790787
6	4.917321	4.766542	4.622881	4.485920	4.355261
7	5.582377	5.389293	5.206372	5.032955	4.868420
8	6.209790	5.971302	5.746641	5.534822	5.334928
9	6.801688	6.515235	6.246890	5.995249	5.759025
10	7.360082	7.023585	6.710084	6.417660	6.144568
11	7.886870	7.498678	7.138966	6.805193	6.495062
12	8.383839	7.942690	7.536080	7.160728	6.813693
13	8.852677	8.357656	7.903778	7.486907	7.103357
14	9.294979	8.745472	8.244239	7.786153	7.366688
15	9.712243	9.107919	8.559482	8.060691	7.606080
16	10.105890	9.446652	8.851371	8.312561	7.823710
17	10.477254	9.763227	9.121640	8.543633	8.021554
18	10.827599	10.059091	9.371890	8.755628	8.201413
19	11.158111	10.335600	9.603601	8.950117	8.364921
20	11.469915	10.594018	9.818150	9.128548	8.513564
21	11.764071	10.835531	10.016805	9.292246	8.648695
22	12.041577	11.061244	10.200746	9.442428	8.771541
23	12.303373	11.272191	10.371061	9.580209	8.883219
24	12.550352	11.469337	10.528760	9.706614	8.984744
25	12.783351	11.653586	10.674778	9.822581	9.077041

Year	Present Value at 11%	Present Value at 12%	Present Value at 13%	Present Value at 14%	Present Value at 15%
1	0.900901	0.892857	0.884956	0.877193	0.869565
2	1.712523	1.690051	1.668102	1.646660	1.625709
3	2.443715	2.401831	2.361152	2.321632	2.283225
4	3.102446	3.037349	2.974471	2.913713	2.854978
5	3.695897	3.604776	3.517231	3.433081	3.352155
6	4.230538	4.111407	3.997549	3.888668	3.784483
7	4.712197	4.563757	4.422611	4.288305	4.160420
8	5.146123	4.967640	4.798770	4.638864	4.487322
9	5.537048	5.328250	5.131655	4.946372	4.771584
10	5.889233	5.650223	5.426243	5.216115	5.018769
11	6.206516	5.937699	5.686941	5.452734	5.233712
12	6.492357	6.194375	5.917647	5.660292	5.420619
13	6.749871	6.423549	6.121812	5.842361	5.583147
14	6.981865	6.628168	6.302488	6.002071	5.724476
15	7.190870	6.810864	6.462379	6.142168	5.847371
16	7.379162	6.973987	6.603875	6.265059	5.954236
17	7.548795	7.119630	6.729093	6.372859	6.047161
18	7.701617	7.249671	6.839905	6.467421	6.127966
19	7.839294	7.365777	6.937969	6.550369	6.198232
20	7.963328	7.469444	7.024752	6.623131	6.259332
21	8.075071	7.562003	7.101550	6.686956	6.312462
22	8.175739	7.644646	7.169513	6.742944	6.358663
23	8.266432	7.718434	7.229658	6.792057	6.398838
24	8.348137	7.784316	7.282883	6.835137	6.433772
25	8.421745	7.843140	7.329985	6.872927	6.464149

Year	Present Value at 16%	Present Value at 17%	Present Value at 18%	Present Value at 19%	Present Value at 20%
1	0.862069	0.854701	0.847458	0.840336	0.833333
2	1.605231	1.585214	1.565642	1.546502	1.527778
3	2.245889	2.209585	2.174273	2.139917	2.106482
4	2.798180	2.743235	2.690061	2.638586	2.588735
5	3.274293	3.199346	3.127171	3.057636	2.990612
6	3.684735	3.589185	3.497602	3.409778	3.325510
7	4.038565	3.922380	3.811527	3.705696	3.604592
8	4.343591	4.207162	4.077566	3.954366	3.837160
9	4.606544	4.450566	4.303021	4.163333	4.030966
10	4.833227	4.658603	4.494086	4.338935	4.192472
11	5.028644	4.836413	4.656005	4.486500	4.327060
12	5.197107	4.988388	4.793225	4.610505	4.439217
13	5.342333	5.118279	4.909513	4.714710	4.532681
14	5.467529	5.229299	5.008061	4.802277	4.610567
15	5.575456	5.324187	5.091578	4.875863	4.675473
16	5.668497	5.405288	5.162354	4.937700	4.729560
17	5.748704	5.474605	5.222334	4.989664	4.774633
18	5.817848	5.533851	5.273164	5.033331	4.812195
19	5.877455	5.584488	5.316241	5.070026	4.843496
20	5.928841	5.627767	5.352746	5.100863	4.869580
21	5.973139	5.664758	5.383684	5.126775	4.891316
22	6.011326	5.696374	5.409901	5.148551	4.909431
23	6.044247	5.723397	5.432120	5.166849	4.924525
24	6.072627	5.746493	5.450949	5.182226	4.937104
25	6.097092	5.766233	5.466906	5.195148	4.947587

Year	Present Value at 21%	Present Value at 22%	Present Value at 23%	Present Value at 24%	Present Value at 25%
1	0.826447	0.819672	0.813008	0.806452	0.800000
2	1.509460	1.491535	1.473990	1.456816	1.440000
3	2.073934	2.042242	2.011374	1.981303	1.952000
4	2.540442	2.493641	2.448272	2.404277	2.361600
5	2.925985	2.863640	2.803473	2.745385	2.689280
6	3.244616	3.166918	3.092255	3.020472	2.951424
7	3.507947	3.415507	3.327036	3.242316	3.161139
8	3.725576	3.619268	3.517915	3.421222	3.328911
9	3.905435	3.786285	3.673102	3.565502	3.463129
10	4.054079	3.923184	3.799270	3.681856	3.570503
11	4.176925	4.035398	3.901846	3.775691	3.656403
12	4.278450	4.127375	3.985240	3.851363	3.725122
13	4.362355	4.202766	4.053041	3.912390	3.780098
14	4.431699	4.264563	4.108163	3.961605	3.824078
15	4.489007	4.315215	4.152978	4.001294	3.859262
16	4.536370	4.356734	4.189414	4.033302	3.887410
17	4.575512	4.390765	4.219036	4.059114	3.909928
18	4.607861	4.418660	4.243118	4.079931	3.927943
19	4.634596	4.441525	4.262698	4.096718	3.942354
20	4.656691	4.460266	4.278616	4.110257	3.953883
21	4.674952	4.475628	4.291558	4.121175	3.963107
22	4.690042	4.488220	4.302080	4.129980	3.970485
23	4.702515	4.498541	4.310634	4.137081	3.976388
24	4.712822	4.507000	4.317589	4.142807	3.981111
25	4.721341	4.513935	4.323243	4.147425	3.984888

Year	Present Value at 26%	Present Value at 27%	Present Value at 28%	Present Value at 29%	Present Value at 30%
1	0.793651	0.787402	0.781250	0.775194	0.769231
2	1.423532	1.407403	1.391602	1.376119	1.360947
3	1.923439	1.895593	1.868439	1.841953	1.816113
4	2.320189	2.279994	2.240968	2.203064	2.166240
5	2.635071	2.582673	2.532006	2.482996	2.435570
6	2.884977	2.821002	2.759380	2.699996	2.642746
7	3.083315	3.008663	2.937016	2.868214	2.802112
8	3.240726	3.156428	3.075793	2.998616	2.924702
9	3.365656	3.272778	3.184213	3.099702	3.019001
10	3.464806	3.364392	3.268917	3.178064	3.091540
11	3.543497	3.436529	3.335091	3.238809	3.147338
12	3.605950	3.493330	3.386790	3.285898	3.190260
13	3.655516	3.538055	3.427180	3.322402	3.223277
14	3.694854	3.573272	3.458734	3.350699	3.248675
15	3.726075	3.601002	3.483386	3.372635	3.268211
16	3.750853	3.622836	3.502645	3.389640	3.283240
17	3.770518	3.640028	3.517692	3.402822	3.294800
18	3.786126	3.653566	3.529447	3.413040	3.303692
19	3.798512	3.664225	3.538630	3.420961	3.310532
20	3.808343	3.672618	3.545805	3.427102	3.315794
21	3.816145	3.679227	3.551410	3.431862	3.319842
22	3.822338	3.684431	3.555789	3.435552	3.322955
23	3.827252	3.688528	3.559210	3.438412	3.325350
24	3.831152	3.691755	3.561883	3.440630	3.327193
25	3.834248	3.694295	3.563971	3.442348	3.328610

Year	Present Value at 31%	Present Value at 32%	Present Value at 33%	Present Value at 34%	Present Value at 35%
1	0.763359	0.757576	0.751880	0.746269	0.740741
2	1.346076	1.331497	1.317203	1.303186	1.289438
3	1.790897	1.766286	1.742258	1.718795	1.695880
4	2.130456	2.095671	2.061848	2.028952	1.996948
5	2.389661	2.345205	2.302142	2.260412	2.219962
6	2.587528	2.534246	2.482813	2.433143	2.385157
7	2.738571	2.677459	2.618657	2.562047	2.507524
8	2.853871	2.785954	2.720794	2.658244	2.598166
9	2.941886	2.868147	2.797590	2.730033	2.665308
10	3.009073	2.930414	2.855331	2.783607	2.715043
11	3.060361	2.977587	2.898745	2.823587	2.751884
12	3.099512	3.013323	2.931387	2.853423	2.779173
13	3.129399	3.040396	2.955930	2.875689	2.799387
14	3.152213	3.060906	2.974384	2.892305	2.814361
15	3.169628	3.076444	2.988258	2.904706	2.825453
16	3.182922	3.088215	2.998691	2.913959	2.833669
17	3.193070	3.097133	3.006534	2.920865	2.839755
18	3.200817	3.103889	3.012432	2.926019	2.844263
19	3.206731	3.109006	3.016866	2.929865	2.847602
20	3.211245	3.112884	3.020200	2.932735	2.850075
21	3.214690	3.115821	3.022707	2.934877	2.851908
22	3.217321	3.118046	3.024592	2.936475	2.853265
23	3.219329	3.119732	3.026009	2.937668	2.854270
24	3.220862	3.121009	3.027074	2.938558	2.855015
25	3.222032	3.121977	3.027875	2.939223	2.855567

Year	Present Value at 36%	Present Value at 37%	Present Value at 38%	Present Value at 39%	Present Value at 40%
1	0.735294	0.729927	0.724638	0.719424	0.714286
2	1.275952	1.262720	1.249738	1.236996	1.224490
3	1.673494	1.651621	1.630245	1.609350	1.588921
4	1.965804	1.935490	1.905974	1.877230	1.849229
5	2.180739	2.142693	2.105778	2.069950	2.035164
6	2.338778	2.293936	2.250564	2.208597	2.167974
7	2.454984	2.404333	2.355481	2.308343	2.262839
8	2.540430	2.484915	2.431508	2.380103	2.330599
9	2.603257	2.543733	2.486600	2.431729	2.378999
10	2.649454	2.586667	2.526522	2.468870	2.413571
11	2.683422	2.618005	2.555451	2.495590	2.438265
12	2.708399	2.640879	2.576413	2.514813	2.455904
13	2.726763	2.657576	2.591604	2.528642	2.468503
14	2.740267	2.669764	2.602612	2.538592	2.477502
15	2.750197	2.678660	2.610588	2.545749	2.483930
16	2.757498	2.685153	2.616368	2.550899	2.488521
17	2.762866	2.689893	2.620557	2.554604	2.491801
18	2.766813	2.693352	2.623592	2.557269	2.494143
19	2.769716	2.295878	2.625791	2.559186	2.495817
20	2.771850	2.697721	2.627385	2.560566	2.497012
21	2.773419	2.699066	2.628540	2.561558	2.497866
22	2.774573	2.700048	2.629377	2.562272	2.498475
23	2.775421	2.700765	2.629983	2.562786	2.498911
24	2.776045	2.701288	2.630423	2.563155	2.499222
25	2.776504	2.701670	2.630741	2.563421	2.499444

SOURCE: Values for $P = \dfrac{1 - (1 + r)^{-n}}{r}$ were computer-generated. Consequently, values for the first year need not correspond exactly to values for the first year in Appendix B, which were computer-generated using $P = \dfrac{1}{(1 + r)^n}$.

APPENDIX D
AREAS UNDER THE
NORMAL CURVE[a]

$$z = \frac{x - E(x)}{\sigma}$$

z	.00	.01	.02	.03	.04	.05	.06	.07	.08	.09
0.0	.5000	.4960	.4920	.4880	.4840	.4801	.4761	.4721	.4681	.4641
0.1	.4602	.4562	.4522	.4483	.4443	.4404	.4364	.4325	.4286	.4247
0.2	.4207	.4168	.4129	.4090	.4052	.4013	.3974	.3936	.3897	.3859
0.3	.3821	.3783	.3745	.3707	.3669	.3632	.3594	.3557	.3520	.3483
0.4	.3446	.3409	.3372	.3336	.3300	.3264	.3228	.3192	.3156	.3121
0.5	.3085	.3050	.3015	.2981	.2946	.2912	.2877	.2843	.2810	.2776
0.6	.2743	.2709	.2676	.2643	.2611	.2578	.2546	.2514	.2483	.2451
0.7	.2420	.2389	.2358	.2327	.2296	.2266	.2236	.2206	.2177	.2148
0.8	.2119	.2090	.2061	.2033	.2005	.1977	.1949	.1922	.1894	.1867
0.9	.1841	.1814	.1788	.1762	.1736	.1711	.1685	.1660	.1635	.1611
1.0	.1587	.1562	.1539	.1515	.1492	.1469	.1446	.1423	.1401	.1379
1.1	.1357	.1335	.1314	.1292	.1271	.1251	.1230	.1210	.1190	.1170
1.2	.1151	.1131	.1112	.1093	.1075	.1056	.1038	.1020	.1003	.0985
1.3	.0968	.0951	.0934	.0918	.0901	.0885	.0869	.0853	.0838	.0823
1.4	.0808	.0793	.0778	.0764	.0749	.0735	.0721	.0708	.0694	.0681
1.5	.0668	.0655	.0643	.0630	.0618	.0606	.0594	.0582	.0571	.0559
1.6	.0548	.0537	.0526	.0516	.0505	.0495	.0485	.0475	.0465	.0455
1.7	.0446	.0436	.0427	.0418	.0409	.0401	.0392	.0384	.0375	.0367
1.8	.0359	.0351	.0344	.0336	.0329	.0322	.0314	.0307	.0301	.0294
1.9	.0287	.0281	.0274	.0268	.0262	.0256	.0250	.0244	.0239	.0233
2.0	.0228	.0222	.0217	.0212	.0207	.0202	.0197	.0192	.0188	.0183
2.1	.0179	.0174	.0170	.0166	.0162	.0158	.0154	.0150	.0146	.0143
2.2	.0139	.0136	.0132	.0129	.0125	.0122	.0119	.0116	.0113	.0110
2.3	.0107	.0104	.0102	.0099	.0096	.0094	.0091	.0089	.0087	.0084
2.4	.0082	.0080	.0078	.0075	.0073	.0071	.0069	.0068	.0066	.0064
2.5	.0062	.0060	.0059	.0057	.0055	.0054	.0052	.0051	.0049	.0048
2.6	.0047	.0045	.0044	.0043	.0041	.0040	.0039	.0038	.0037	.0036
2.7	.0035	.0034	.0033	.0032	.0031	.0030	.0029	.0028	.0027	.0026
2.8	.0026	.0025	.0024	.0023	.0023	.0022	.0021	.0021	.0020	.0019
2.9	.0019	.0018	.0018	.0017	.0016	.0016	.0015	.0015	.0014	.0014
3.0	.0013	.0013	.0013	.0012	.0012	.0011	.0011	.0011	.0010	.0010

[a] When x lies left of $E(x)$, the value of z is negative and the table measures the area left of x. When x lies right of $E(x)$, the value of z is positive and the table measures the area right of x.

APPENDIX E

FUNDAMENTALS OF

ACCOUNTING-BASED

FINANCIAL STATEMENTS

AND KEY RATIOS

VALUE IN ECONOMICS AND ACCOUNTING

To the economist, value is the current price an item will bring in the market. Value or price, as it pertains to production facilities or financial instruments, is the present value of future cash payments that derives from owning the production facilities or the financial instruments. Determination of present value is the subject of Chapter 3.

To the accountant, however, value is based (with certain exceptions) on the price or cost when the item is purchased. The primary exception is when current market value is less than *historical* or *original cost* of the item purchased. In certain instances, then, value is cost or market—whichever is lower.

Although modern financial theory is based on market value, the data used in many computations is based on the accounting approach to value. This is evident in the discussion of capital budgeting in Chapter 8 and even more palpable in the discussion of working capital in Chapters 13, 14, and 15. Consequently, one must have a basic understanding of how accounting information is derived and presented in order to function effectively in finance. What follows is an elementary presentation of accounting-based financial statements and key ratios for those students with little or no background in the subject.

THE BALANCE SHEET

The fundamental accounting equation is:

$$\text{assets} = \text{liabilities} + \text{owner's equity}$$

The firm's assets consist of those items necessary to produce the goods and services it markets. Liabilities and owner's equity reflect how such assets are financed. The former represent borrowing; the latter represent funds provided by the firm owner(s).

The equation is expressed formally in the **balance sheet** (statement of financial position) as of a certain point in time. Consider Table E-1, the balance sheet for

Table E-1   Balance Sheet—Golden Gate Manufacturing Corporation

Assets	End of Current Year	End of Previous Year
Current Assets		
Cash	$ 1,575,000	$ 750,000
Marketable securities at cost (market value: current year $13,500,000; previous year $12,800,000)	13,000,000	12,500,000
Accounts receivable (less allowance for bad debts: current year $210,000; previous year $200,000)	21,000,000	20,000,000
Inventories	16,100,000	14,800,000
Total Current Assets	$51,675,000	$48,050,000
Fixed Assets		
Land	$ 1,750,000	$ 1,750,000
Building	24,000,000	23,000,000
Machinery	20,000,000	17,000,000
Office equipment	1,250,000	1,000,000
	47,000,000	42,750,000
(*Less* Accumulated depreciation)	7,000,000	4,000,000
Net Fixed Assets	$40,000,000	$38,750,00
Prepayments and deferred charges	$ 1,000,000	$ 700,000
Intangibles (goodwill, patents, trademarks)	1,000,000	1,000,000
Total Assets	$93,675,000	$88,500,000

Golden Gate Manufacturing Corporation. There are two sets of figures: the first states the Company's financial position at the end of the current year and the second at the end of the previous year. Although the end of the year can coincide with the end of the calendar year—December 31—it can occur at any other time, such as June 30 or perhaps March 31. In other words, a firm's fiscal (accounting) year may correspond to the calendar year, but it need not; any date will do. The salient point is that the balance sheet indicates financial position as of a particular date.

The asset side of the balance sheet (Table E-1) is divided into current assets, fixed assets, prepayments and deferred charges, and intangibles. Current assets are assets that can be converted into cash within a reasonably short period of time—by convention, one year or the normal time between balance sheets.

Of the four categories included as **current assets**, cash represents cash on hand as well as bank accounts that function as money: accounts that serve to pay bills,

Table E-1 **Balance Sheet—Golden Gate Manufacturing Corporation (Continued)**

Liabilities	End of Current Year	End of Previous Year
Current Liabilities		
Accounts payable	$10,250,000	$ 9,500,000
Notes payable	8,100,000	8,250,000
Accrued expenses payable	1,500,000	1,250,000
Federal income taxes payable	750,000	700,000
Total Current Liabilities	$20,600,000	$19,700,000
Long-Term Liabilities		
First mortgage bonds (maturing in 20 years at 12.75% from end of current year)	$20,000,000	$20,000,000
Stockholders' Equity		
Capital stock		
Preferred stock: 9% cumulative $100 par value (authorized, issued, and outstanding—100,000 shares)	$10,000,000	$10,000,000
Common stock: $5 par value (authorized, issued, and outstanding—1,000,000 shares)	5,000,000	5,000,000
Capital surplus	15,000,000	15,000,000
Accumulated retained earnings	23,075,000	18,800,000
Total Stockholders' Equity	$53,075,000	$48,800,000
Total Liabilities and Stockholders' Equity	$93,675,000	$88,500,000

wages, and so forth. **Marketable securities** are usually short-term instruments such as U.S. Treasury bills, among other investments, which management has purchased with funds not immediately required in the business. When such funds are needed, these investments will have matured or will be sold. Although marketable securities are valued at original cost, their market value as of the date of the balance sheet is also noted.

Accounts receivable represent the amount of credit extended to customers. Given that these accounts will be paid, it is nevertheless customary to subtract an allowance for bad debts—valuing accounts receivable, for balance sheet purposes, after the allowance has been subtracted.

Manufacturing **inventories** consist of three subsets (not shown): raw materials, work in process, and finished goods on hand as of the balance sheet date.

If Golden Gate were a retail trade operation, inventories would consist of finished goods and probably would be the largest single category of assets. If Golden Gate were a public utility, inventories would consist primarily of fuel to generate power and would be a relatively small proportion of total assets. In accounting, the general rule is to value inventories at cost or at market value, whichever is lower. (Current assets are discussed in greater detail in Chapter 14.)

Fixed assets consist primarily of plant, land, machinery, and equipment—all **long-term assets**. In manufacturing, plant and machinery will be used to produce goods for several years into the future. Office equipment also will be used over several years. As a matter of preference, we use long-term rather than fixed; in law, **fixed assets** correspond to property attached to land and are termed *real property*. In a literal sense, the property is truly fixed. Equipment, however, may be moved from one location to another. Because both types of assets are useful for an extended time period, both can be labeled long-term assets.

For the student of finance, it is important to remember that such assets are valued at their original cost and that their original cost is recovered over a period of time through depreciation. (In Chapter 8, we discussed depreciation in considerable detail.) Bear in mind that each year the cost of the asset will be reduced by the amount of **depreciation** for that year. In Table E-1, Golden Gate increased its assets from the previous year by $4,250,000 ($47,000,000 − $42,750,000); accumulated depreciation on those assets rose from $4,000,000 to $7,000,000.

Depreciation can be described as a measure of the deterioration of a firm's assets from one year to the next as such assets are employed in producing goods and services. Although this notion of depreciation is accurate, it is not the same as accounting depreciation, where the useful life of an asset is determined—let us say ten years—and its cost less scrap value is recovered over that period.

Thus, if an asset costs $1,000,000 and is worthless at the end of ten years, one way of receiving the original cost is to depreciate the asset: $1,000,000 ÷ 10 = $100,000 in annual depreciation. At the end of six years, the accumulated depreciation would be $600,000 and the $1,000,000 asset would have a net value of $400,000 ($1,000,000 − $600,000). Because this net figure will probably bear no relationship to the market value or replacement cost of the asset, the net fixed-asset value of $40,000,000 at the end of Golden Gate's current year and $38,750,000 at the end of its previous year should not be interpreted as market value.

The other assets included are, first, *prepayments and deferred charges*, and second, intangibles. Prepayments are expenditures for services not yet rendered. For example, insurance premiums may be paid two years in advance: half the payment made each year and the balance sheet reduced accordingly. A deferred charge is similar to a prepayment. For instance, a firm may incur research and development costs in bringing a new product to market. The benefits generated by research and development costs (through increased sales) will last several years and such expenditures will be written off as part of the cost of the goods sold—but not in a single year. In this particular instance, prepaid expenses and deferred charges increased from one year to the next: more expenditures and prepayments were made than were written off during the year.

Finally, there are the intangibles, which may consist of patents, trademarks, exclusive franchises, and **goodwill**. Although this category suggests the firm is worth more than its assets, what value does one place on goodwill or, for that matter, a patent, trademark, or exclusive franchise? In economics, there is a ready answer: The difference between the firm's market value as a whole and the sum of the market values of its individual assets yields a measure of the value of the firm's intangibles. Because accountants generally eschew market value (unless it is lower than cost), intangibles are given a nominal value; some firms list the value of intangibles simply as $1. In the case of Golden Gate, we value intangibles at $1,000,000 for both the current year and the previous year. Apparently management believes the firm is worth more than the accounting value, if not the market value, of its assets.

The liabilities side of the balance sheet is divided into **current** and long-term liabilities. The former are payable within a year or less. **Accounts payable** represent credit extended to Golden Gate by its suppliers of raw materials and other items needed to produce goods; these accounts are often due within 30 days. If the money is owed to a bank or other financial intermediary, it is listed as notes payable and is evidenced by a promissory note. Golden Gate may have such other expenses as attorney fees and wages owed but not yet paid; these are listed as accrued expenses payable. Finally, depending on the tax laws in force at the time, a firm may accrue taxes prior to paying them. We have listed taxes as federal income taxes payable, owed but not yet paid. The same can be true of state and local taxes. Although other short-term funding sources or current liabilities are possible (see Chapter 15), these are the most common types.

Although long-term liabilities (discussed at length in Chapter 16) come from a variety of sources, they enjoy one common characteristic: they mature several years into the future. Golden Gate has employed only one type, a first **mortgage bond**, maturing (payable) 20 years from the end of the current year. If the end of the current year is 1989, in 2009 the company must pay the holders of these bonds (which are long-term promissory notes) $20,000,000. The first mortgage feature suggests the bondholders have a lien on the company's land and buildings, just as there is a lien on most privately owned homes: some bank holds the mortgage. Golden Gate must pay 12.75 percent interest each year on $20,000,000, or $2,550,000. Failure to do so could ultimately lead to bankruptcy and seizure of the assets on which the bondholders hold a mortgage.

As in the case of assets, book value of total liabilities need not be the same as their market value. For example, if Golden Gate currently must pay 13.5 percent to borrow $20,000,000, market value of the bonds would fall below $20,000,000 (how much below is discussed thoroughly in Chapter 3). Nevertheless, Golden Gate must still repay $20,000,000. Consequently, accounting or **book value** of the liabilities has greater significance than book value of the assets, as the figure represents what the firm owes its creditors.

The difference between the book value of assets and debt is the owner's equity. Because Golden Gate is a corporation, its owners are its shareholders. Consequently, in this instance, we use the term shareholders' equity. The shareholders' initial contribution is detailed in the capital stock account. Golden Gate has two types of stock outstanding, preferred and common. Preferred shareholders receive dividends ahead of common shareholders. And in the event the corporation is liquidated and the assets sold, preferred shareholders also may receive up to a specified amount, generally equal to the **par value** of the stock (in this case, $100 per share), before common shareholders receive any cash distributions. The preferred dividend is often a specific percentage of the par value. [Golden Gate pays preferred shareholders $9 per share (9% × $100) annually in dividends.]

By contract, common shareholders are residual owners without a specified dividend. The stock often has par value, in this instance $5, which serves no function except to suggest that when initially issued the shares had to be sold for at least $5 per share. In the case of Golden Gate, one might infer that the 1,000,000 common shares outstanding were sold at $20 per share—$5 per share ($5,000,000) represented by the common stock account and $15 per share ($15,000,000) represented by capital surplus. Through the same line of reasoning, one can infer that the 100,000 preferred shares outstanding were sold at $100 per share, as there is no capital surplus.

Note the words *authorized*, *issued*, and *outstanding*. The number of shares authorized is part of the charter of incorporation and generally can be augmented by vote of the shareholders. The number of shares sold is the number of shares issued. If the number of shares outstanding is less than the number of shares issued, the difference represents shares repurchased by the company and currently in its treasury. In the case of Golden Gate, we have assumed the number of preferred and common shares authorized, issued, and outstanding are 100,000 and 1,000,000, respectively.

The accumulated retained earnings account consists of after-tax profits not distributed as cash dividends as well as profits (after-tax gains) realized on the sale of assets: what the common shareholders have contributed to the firm over the years. In an accounting sense, accumulated retained earnings are part of the common shareholders' equity in the corporation.

THE INCOME STATEMENT

The *income statement*, or *statement of revenue and expenses*, can be linked to the balance sheet: it is a summary of operations for the current year and for the previous year. Focusing on the current year (see Table E-2), we find Golden Gate sold $132,500,000 worth of goods; however, it cost $100,050,000 to manufacture them. The cost of goods sold includes the costs of raw materials, labor, and the like associated directly with the manufacturing process. In addition, there was a

Table E-2   Income Statement—Golden Gate Manufacturing Corporation

	Current Year	Previous Year
Net Sales	$132,500,000	$129,400,000
(*Less* Cost of sales and operating expenses:		
Cost of goods sold	100,050,000	99,150,000
Depreciation	3,000,000	1,500,000
Selling and administrative expenses)	15,162,500	15,845,000
Operating Profit	$ 14,287,500	$ 12,905,000
Other Income	1,137,500	1,123,000
Earnings Before Interest and Taxes (EBIT)	$ 15,425,000	$ 14,028,000
(*Less* Interest on bonds)	2,550,000	2,550,000
Earnings Before Taxes	$ 12,875,000	$ 11,478,000
Provision for Income Taxes	5,150,000	4,591,200
Earnings After Taxes (EAT)	$ 7,725,000	$ 6,886,800
(*Less* Preferred stock dividends	900,000	900,000
Common stock dividends)	2,550,000	2,550,000
Retained Earnings	$ 4,275,000	$ 3,436,800

$3,000,000 depreciation expense, which corresponds exactly to the increase in the accumulated depreciation as shown in the balance sheet (Table E-1). Also, there were $15,162,500 in selling and administrative expenses associated with production and distribution of the items sold. Thus, profit from company operations was $14,287,500. Golden Gate earned other income of $1,137,500, of which the major portions probably came from various investments in short-term securities. Hence, total operating and nonoperating income was $15,425,000; we call this sum **Earnings Before Interest and Taxes (EBIT)**.

From EBIT must be deducted interest payments on the bonds, or $2,550,000. Because interest is tax deductible, the result is $12,875,000 in taxable income. We have assumed that Golden Gate pays federal income taxes of $5,150,000, or 40 percent of EBIT. This leaves **Earnings After Taxes (EAT)** of $7,225,000, of which $900,000 are specified dividends to preferred shareholders and $2,550,000 are cash dividends to common shareholders. The remainder are retained earnings of $4,275,000. This is exactly the increase from the previous year to the current year in the accumulated retained earnings account in the balance sheet (Table E-1).

Therefore, the balance sheet reflects financial position at a moment in time whereas the income statement reflects how financial position changed from the end of the previous year to the end of the current year.

STATEMENT OF SOURCES AND APPLICATION OF FUNDS

A more complete analysis of changes from one year to the next that links the income statement to the balance sheet is known as the statement of *sources and application of funds* or, simply, the *funds statement* (Table E-3).

Examining the statement, note that funds were provided by earnings after taxes and by depreciation. Concerning depreciation, it is important to remember that

Table E-3   Statement of Sources and Application of Funds (current year)—Golden Gate Manufacturing Corporation

Analysis of Sources and Application of Funds		
Funds Provided by:		
Earnings after taxes (EAT)	$7,725,000	
Depreciation	3,000,000	
Total		$10,725,000
Funds Used for:		
Preferred stock dividends	$ 900,000	
Common stock dividends	2,550,000	
Plant and equipment	4,250,000	
Prepayments	300,000	
Total		− 8,000,000
Increase in Net Working Capital		$2,725,000
Analysis of Changes in Net Working Capital		
Changes in Current Assets		
Cash	$ 825,000	
Marketable securities	500,000	
Accounts receivable	1,000,000	
Inventories	1,300,000	
Total		$3,625,000
(*Less* Changes in current liabilities:		
Accounts payable	$ 750,000	
Notes payable	− 150,000	
Accrued expenses	250,000	
Federal income taxes)	50,000	
Total		− 900,000
Increase in Net Working Capital		$2,725,000

it is a noncash yet tax-deductible expense. Because no monies are paid—as in the case of wages, salaries, and other such expenses—the cash is retained within the company and is available for use. The sum of EAT and depreciation ($10,275,000) represents the total funds available for use. Golden Gate used the funds not only for dividends but also for plant and equipment and for prepayments. However, the total ($8,000,000) left $2,725,000 unaccounted for. The explanation is that Golden Gate increased its **net working capital**.

Net Working Capital is defined as the difference between current assets and current liabilities. Examining these categories in Table E-3, we find there was an increase in each type of current asset in the total amount $3,625,000. Current liabilities also increased, except for notes payable (which were actually reduced). The net result was an increase of $900,000 that, when subtracted from current assets, produced a rise in net working capital of $2,725,000. In terms of accounting procedures, we now have a complete schedule of the funding sources generated during the current year and what was done with them.

RATIO ANALYSIS

The information contained in financial statements is useful in various ways to both financial practitioners and academics. One widely used tool is termed *ratio analysis*. Ratios are designed to measure, among other things, a firm's profitability and liquidity. Liquidity implies the firm's ability to meet its obligations as they come due. For such ratios to be useful, one must compare changes in them over time. To that end, intertemporal comparison systematically incorporates the vagaries of accounting principles—at least that is the hope.

LIQUIDITY RATIOS

Because book value of current assets and current liabilities is generally closer to their market value than to the market value of long-term assets and long-term debt, changes in these accounts over time may warrant closer scrutiny. For example, if net working capital fell year after year, this may signal that the firm is having difficulty meeting its obligations as they come due. One may want to further examine the extent of this decline.

The component of net working capital may be couched in ratio form, the result of which is known as the **current ratio**. Using the Golden Gate information, the current ratio is:

	Current Year		*Previous Year*	
current assets	$51,675,000	= 2.51	$48,050,000	= 2.44
current liabilities	$20,600,000		$19,700,000	

Because net working capital increased from one year to the next, so, too, did the current ratio. However, without several years' data to compare, there is no reason to attach special significance to the result.

The **quick-asset ratio** is a variation on the current ratio. Since the quick-asset ratio provides the ultimate measure of liquidity, it is also known as the **acid-test ratio**.

$$\frac{\text{cash} + \text{marketable securities} + \text{receivables}}{\text{current liabilities}}$$

The Golden Gate figures are:

Current Year	Previous Year
$\dfrac{\$35,575,000}{\$20,600,000} = 1.73$	$\dfrac{\$33,250,000}{\$19,700,000} = 1.69$

Because the numerator consists of cash or cash equivalents, the ratio determines whether current liabilities can be easily converted to cash. A ratio greater than 1.00 indicates they can.

Although there is no reason to assume Golden Gate is experiencing liquidity problems, when the foregoing calculations do raise such questions, it may be useful to probe more deeply. For example: Is the firm having difficulty collecting receivables? Is it taking longer to pay its bills? To answer the first question, we use the **receivables turnover ratio**, which is defined as

$$\frac{\text{annual credit sales}}{\text{receivables}}$$

Suppose 90 percent of Golden Gate's sales during the year were on credit. From the sales figures on the income statement (Table E-2) and the receivables figures on the balance sheet (Table E-1), we calculate:

Current Year	Previous Year
$\dfrac{.9 \times \$132,500,000}{\$21,000,000} = 5.68$	$\dfrac{.9 \times \$129,400,000}{\$20,000,000} = 5.82$

Dividing 365 days by the ratio, the result is the average number of days necessary to collect receivables. For Golden Gate, these figures are:

Current Year	Previous Year
$\dfrac{365}{5.68} = 64.26$ days	$\dfrac{365}{5.82} = 62.71$ days

A decline in turnover ratio over time suggests the firm is having increasing difficulty collecting its receivables and can be the source of a deteriorating working capital position. A similar calculation for purchases relative to accounts payable can be made. Although we list no purchase figures for Golden Gate, to the extent the ratio declined, the number of days required to liquidate obligations would rise. (For an alternative method of calculating receivables turnover, see Chapter 14.)

A deterioration in liquidity may also result from a decline in sales relative to inventories:

$$\frac{\text{sales}}{\text{inventories}}$$

Known as the **sales-inventory** or **inventory-turnover ratio** (cost of goods sold may be substituted for sales), its results for Golden Gate are:

Current Year	Previous Year
$\dfrac{\$132,500,000}{\$16,100,000} = 8.23$	$\dfrac{\$129,400,000}{\$14,800,000} = 8.74$

Again, a secular decline in the ratio suggests a buildup of inventories relative to sales and a deterioration in liquidity.

PROFITABILITY RATIOS

Profitability may be measured in relation to sales or to investment. **Gross-profit margin** is defined as:

$$\frac{\text{sales} - \text{cost of goods sold}}{\text{sales}}$$

For Golden Gate:

Current Year	Previous Year
$\dfrac{\$132,500,000 - \$100,050,000}{\$132,500,000} = 24.49\%$	$\dfrac{\$129,400,000 - \$99,150,000}{\$129,400,000} = 23.38\%$

The margin also may be calculated after taking into account all expenses:

$$\frac{\text{operating profit}}{\text{sales}}$$

For Golden Gate, these figures are:

Current Year	Previous Year
$\dfrac{\$14,287,500}{\$132,500,000} = 10.78\%$	$\dfrac{\$12,905,000}{\$129,400,000} = 9.97\%$

Finally, analysts often calculate earnings after taxes in relation to sales:

$$\frac{EAT}{\text{sales}}$$

For Golden Gate, the results are:

Current Year	Previous Year
$\dfrac{\$7,725,000}{\$132,500,000} = 5.83\%$	$\dfrac{\$6,886,800}{\$129,400,000} = 5.32\%$

The *profit-to-sales ratios*—at least the first two ratios—give one a sense of what it costs to generate a sales dollar and therefore what profit there is in each sales dollar. The third measure merely relates after-tax profits to sales. We shall use this measure again shortly.

None of the foregoing ratios speaks to the return investors earn on the book value of their contributions. One such measure for common shareholders is:

$$\frac{EAT - \text{preferred dividends}}{\text{par value} + \text{capital surplus} + \text{retained earnings}}$$

For Golden Gate, the results are:

Current Year	Previous Year
$\dfrac{\$7,725,000 - \$900,000}{\$43,075,000} = 15.84\%$	$\dfrac{\$6,886,800 - \$900,000}{\$38,800,000} = 15.43\%$

Book value of shareholders' equity for a **nonfinancial business** firm such as a manufacturer rarely equals market value. Although the latter is of primary interest to us in this book, the financial statements of publicly held companies are widely circulated. The foregoing ratio is often used as a measure of performance and on occasion we refer to it or to its components. (See, for example, Chapter 6.)

Debtholders and preferred common shareholders contribute to the corporation's productive assets. Consequently, a measure of the total accounting return on such assets is:

$$\frac{EBIT}{\text{total assets}}$$

For Golden Gate, the relevant computations are:

Current Year	Previous Year
$\dfrac{\$15,425,000}{\$93,675,000} = 16.47\%$	$\dfrac{\$14,028,000}{\$88,500,000} = 15.85\%$

From the common shareholders' perspective, the residual owners of all assets, the ratio can be rewritten so that:

$$\frac{EAT}{\text{total assets}}$$

Again, for Golden Gate:

Current Year	Previous Year
$\dfrac{\$7,725,000}{\$93,675,000} = 8.25\%$	$\dfrac{\$6,886,800}{\$88,500,000} = 7.78\%$

The immediately preceding ratio and the EAT-to-sales ratio are related in the following way:

$$\frac{EAT}{\text{sales}} \times \frac{\text{sales}}{\text{assets}} = \frac{EAT}{\text{assets}}$$

The multiplier is the *asset-turnover ratio*. For Golden Gate, the results are:

Current Year	Previous Year
$\dfrac{\$132,500,000}{\$93,675,000} = 1.414$	$\dfrac{\$129,400,000}{\$88,500,000} = 1.46$

As the name suggests, the turnover ratio measures how rapidly assets are turned into sales. What is important about the foregoing relationship is that a relatively high turnover of assets and a relatively low profit per unit of sales may combine in one company to produce the same EAT-to-sales ratio as the opposite relationship does in another company. For example, assets of a retail grocery chain primarily consist of inventories rapidly turned over into sales. Its turnover ratio might be as high as

8 to 1, in which case the retail trade operation could earn as little as 1.25 percent on sales and still earn a 10-percent after-tax return on assets. Thus, $8 \times .0125 = .10 \times 100 = 10$ percent.

On the other hand, a manufacturing concern (such as Golden Gate) or a public utility would have a substantial investment in fixed assets and, therefore, a comparatively lower turnover ratio. Such entities must earn more per unit of sales to realize the same after-tax return on assets as the retail grocery chain. To enjoy a 10-percent after-tax return on assets with a turnover ratio of 1.5 would require

$$1.5x = .10$$
$$x = .0667 = 6.67\%$$

return on sales.

CAPITALIZATION RATIOS

In the text, particularly in Chapters 6 and 7, we employ what are known as **capitalization ratios**. Although conceptually the values used in computing capitalization ratios are market values, the context is that of the balance sheet. In this appendix, we use accounting figures to compute the ratios. The first such ratio is the **debt ratio**, defined as:

$$\frac{\text{book value of long-term debt}}{\text{book value of long-term debt} + \text{book value of shareholders' equity}}$$

There is some controversy over treatment of preferred stock. Although it is lawfully equity, management may treat preferred shareholders as debtholders, ensuring that their dividends are paid when due (just as bond interest must be paid when due). However, for purposes of this presentation, we shall follow the equally lawful practice of treating preferred shareholders as owners. For Golden Gate, the figures are:

Current Year	Previous Year
$\dfrac{\$20,000,000}{\$73,075,000} = 27.37\%$	$\dfrac{\$20,000,000}{\$68,800,000} = 29.07\%$

The complement to the debt ratio is the equity ratio. The denominator remains the same but the numerator is the book value of the shareholders' equity:

$$\frac{\text{book value of shareholders' equity}}{\text{book value of long-term debt} + \text{book value of shareholders' equity}}$$

For Golden Gate, the values are:

Current Year	Previous Year
$\dfrac{\$53,075,000}{\$73,075,000} = 72.63\%$	$\dfrac{\$48,800,000}{\$68,800,000} = 70.93\%$

Since the two ratios are complements, their sum is 100 percent or 1.00.

Finally, there is the **debt-to-equity** ratio:

$$\frac{\text{book value of long-term debt}}{\text{book value of shareholders' equity}}$$

For Golden Gate, the figures are:

Current Year	Previous Year
$\dfrac{\$20,000,000}{\$53,075,000} = 37.68\%$	$\dfrac{\$20,000,000}{\$48,800,000} = 40.98\%$

Because we make considerable use of debt-to-equity ratios in Chapters 6 and 7, we do not elaborate further in this appendix. However, we note that short-term debt has been excluded, thereby following the assumption that these sources primarily fund current assets. Although a case can be made for including short-term debt in debt-to-equity ratios, we have raised the issue in a different context (see Chapter 13). In any event, what is presented here is consistent with practice.

MISCELLANEOUS RATIOS

Several ratios employed in practice serve specific functions. One such ratio, which is pertinent to our discussion in Chapter 11, is the *payout ratio*—the ratio of common-stock dividends to after-tax earnings:

$$\frac{\text{common-stock dividends}}{EAT}$$

For Golden Gate, the ratio is:

Current Year	Previous Year
$\dfrac{\$2,550,000}{\$7,725,000} = 33.01\%$	$\dfrac{\$2,550,000}{\$6,886,800} = 37.03\%$

Publicly held companies usually have a policy that maintains dividends at a specified percentage of earnings. Although we have made no specific assumption concerning Golden Gate's dividend policy, management is unlikely to raise or lower the dividend unless it believes the dividend can be maintained or that it cannot be sustained in the forseeable future.

Another set of ratios revolves around a firm's ability to meet its long-term debt obligations. Although conceivably a part of the general collection of ratios used to measure liquidity, long-term debt may warrant special consideration. The simplest ratio is **times interest earned**—the ratio of EBIT to interest payments:

$$\frac{EBIT}{interest}$$

For Golden Gate, the results are:

Current Year	*Previous Year*
$\dfrac{\$15,425,000}{\$2,550,000} = 6.05$	$\dfrac{\$14,028,000}{\$2,550,000} = 5.50$

One interprets the foregoing ratio to mean that EBIT are five to six times greater than interest on the debt. As long as funding sources are relatively simple, *times interest earned* can be an indicator of the firm's ability to meet this obligation as it comes due. Yet, even then there is no guarantee of sufficient funds to pay the interest. Although from earlier discussions of net working capital, the current ratio, and the quick asset ratio, we know Golden Gate has sufficient liquid assets to meet the interest payments, this sufficiency is not evident in the times-interest-earned formula.

In a more complex *financial* or **capital structure**, one must consider the relative standing of each funding source. To illustrate, suppose a firm has an EBIT of $20,000,000, a $3,000,000 interest payment on mortgage bonds, and a $2,000,000 interest payment on an unsecured long-term note for funds borrowed from an insurance company. In the event the firm is liquidated and its assets sold, the bondholders participate before the insurance company: mortgage bond claims are *senior* to note claims, as a note is *junior* to a mortgage bond. Times interest earned for the senior securities would be:

$$\frac{\$20,000,000}{\$3,000,000} = 6.67$$

Because interest on the note has a junior claim, interest on the mortgage bonds must be paid first and the times-interest-earned ratio for the note would be:

$$\frac{\$20,000,000}{\$3,000,000 + \$2,000,000} = 4.00$$

Suppose further that the company must repay $1,000,000 each year in principal. Given that the repayment of principal comes from earnings after taxes and that the firm is in the 40-percent tax bracket, it must generate $1,666,667 before taxes to repay $1,000,000 in principal after taxes. If T is the tax rate:

$$EBIT\,(1 - T) = \$1,000,000$$
$$EBIT = \frac{\$1,000,000}{1 - T}$$

In terms of the times-interest-earned formula, coverage for the note is:

$$\frac{\$20,000,000}{\$3,000,000 + \$2,000,000 + \$1,000,000 \div (1 - .4)} = 3.0$$

CLOSING COMMENTS

This appendix only introduces you to accounting-based financial statements and key ratios; underlying these statements and ratios is a set of accounts the development of which warrants separate treatment. However, familiarizing yourself with this material will facilitate your study of the principles of finance.

One should maintain a healthy skepticism for the figures generated. Even when you make intertemporal comparisons, rapid changes in price level may further distort results based on historical or original rather than current cost. Moreover, rapid rise in inflation causes real value of the debt burden to fall: the principal will be repaid in inflationary (cheaper) dollars. Deflation causes the opposite result.

In addition, seasonal factors may create a misleading impression about the firm's liquidity. For example, if its balance sheet is at the seasonal ebb, the firm will have invested more of its funds in marketable securities and less in inventories. Further, its short-term borrowing will be less than at the seasonal peak. Consequently, net working capital and liquidity ratios will appear more sanguine than might otherwise be the case.

Nevertheless, the accounting framework and the information produced by the system of accounts form the base for financial managerial decisions. And although the analytical techniques developed in this book may require modification of that base, to modify it correctly one must first know how the information was derived.

APPENDIX F
PERTINENT FEATURES
OF THE TAX REFORM
ACT OF 1986[1]

---

[1] For more details, see U.S. Congress, House of Representatives, *Tax Reform Act of 1986 Conference Report to Accompany H.R. 3838* (Washington: U.S. Government Printing Office, 1986, 2 Volumes). For an excellent summary and comparison with previous tax law written in less arcane language, see *The Price Waterhouse Guide to the New Tax Law* (New York: Bantam Books, 1986).

The corporate tax rates are

Corporation Rates

Taxable Income	Effective July 1, 1987	Old Rate
0 – $ 25,000	15%	15%
$25,000–$ 50,000	15%	18%
$50,000–$ 75,000	25%	30%
$75,000–$100,000	34%	40%
over $100,000	34%	46%

Furthermore, all taxable income between $100,000 and $335,000 is subject to a 5-percent surtax: an effective income-tax rate of 39 percent. In addition, there are no longer preferential tax rates for capital gains.

Income Tax Rates Effective January 1, 1988

Married Taxpayer Filing Jointly		Unmarried Taxpayer	
Taxable Income	Rate	Taxable Income	Rate
0–$29,750	15%	0–$17,850	15%
over $29,750	28%	over $17,850	28%

Taxpayers with taxable incomes more than a certain level lose the benefit of the 15-percent tax rate on lower income amounts: an additional 5-percent tax applies to taxable income between $71,900 and $149,250 for married couples; for an unmarried taxpayer, the additional 5-percent tax applies to taxable income between $43,150 and $89,560. Within this latter income range, the effective marginal rate becomes 33 percent.

Income from unincorporated business enterprises is part of the income of individual proprietors or partners, and as such taxed at rates applicable to them as individuals. Marking a major break with past legislation, the Tax Reform Act of 1986 makes the effective maximum individual rate lower than the effective maximum corporate rate: exclusive of the surtax, 28 percent and 34 percent respectively. As in the case of corporations, individuals no longer enjoy special preferential rates on capital gains.

DEPRECIATION ON PROPERTIES USED FOR BUSINESS PURPOSES

The Accelerated Cost Recovery System (ACRS), discussed in Chapter 8, was modified in the Tax Reform Act of 1986; eight classes of depreciable assets have been created based on established class life or midpoint of the Asset Depreciation Range (ADR).[2] Depending on the classification, the method of depreciation is straight-line, 200 percent (double-declining balance), or 150 percent of straight-line depreciation. Unless specifically exempted, all property falls into one or more ADRs as a basis for depreciation. The classifications currently in effect are:

Class	Type of Depreciation	Description of Property
1	3-year 200% class	Property with ADR midpoints of 4 years or less (excluding automobiles and light trucks).
2	5-year 200% class	Property with ADR midpoints of more than 4 but fewer than 10 years: automobiles; light trucks; certain qualified technological equipment; computer-based telephones; central office equipment; research and experimentation property; geothermal-, oceanthermal-, solar-, and wind-energy properties; and biomass properties that qualify as small-power production facilities.
3	7-year 200% class	Property with ADR midpoints of 10 years but fewer than 16 years: single-purpose agricultural or horticultural structures and property with ADR midpoints not classified elsewhere.
4	10-year 200% class	Property with ADR midpoints of 16 years but fewer than 20 years.
5	15-year 150% class	Property with ADR midpoints of 20 years but fewer than 25 years: sewage treatment plants; telephone distribution plants and comparable equipment used for two-way exchange of voice and data communications.
6	20-year 150% class	Property with ADR midpoints of 25 years or more: municipal sewers (excluding real property with an ADR midpoint of 27.5 years or more).
7	27.5-year straight-line class	Residential rental property (including manufactured homes that are rental property).
8	31.5-year straight-line class	Nonresidential real property; real property with ADR midpoints of 27.5 years or more or with no ADR midpoint.

---

[2] For background to the ADR, see Commerce Clearing House, *Standard Federal Tax Reports 1983 Depreciation Guide*, Vol. 70 (May 26, 1983, p. 10).

APPENDIX G
USING A FINANCIAL
CALCULATOR

Several companies—among them Hewlett-Packard, Texas Instruments, and Sharp—manufacture specialized financial calculators that efficiently solve many basic problems in finance. Any one is an inexpensive substitute for a computer when the data base is small. For most problems presented in this text and for numerous real-world applications, financial calculators are especially practical: they perform algebraic functions commonly employed in the field, and they are small and easily portable. Technological advances have brought down the price (of most of them) to under $100 and falling. In addition, some are equipped with tapes for hard copy. Although this necessarily augments size and cost, it permits one to process larger amounts of data.

INTERNAL RATE OF RETURN AND
NET PRESENT VALUE

In footnote [22] of Chapter 3, you were shown how to calculate Internal Rate of Return (IRR). More generally, one ordinarily calculates IRR and Net Present Value (NPV) using one set of entries. Although keystrokes differ with the calculator used, the following format displays the process involved:

Keystrokes	Display
1. Press appropriate keys to clear all registers; choose number of decimal places desired.	1. 0.00
2. Key in cash-outlay change sign to $-$ (minus) and enter into register that accepts cash flow zero (CF_0).	2. $-CF_0$
3. Enter each successive cash flow for T_1 through T_n into appropriate register (CF_j).	3. CF_j for cash flows T_1 through T_n displayed successively as they are entered.
4. Enter cost of capital in appropriate register (generally labeled i not r).	4. Rate for i.
5. Press key or combination of keys that computes NPV.	5. Value for NPV.
6. Press key or combination of keys that computes IRR.	6. Value for IRR.

Programs usually handle even as well as uneven cash flows and positive as well as negative cash flows. Results are based on cost of capital compounded annually. If there are multiple rates of return, you will not know it: only one rate appears in the display.

Because we argue that NPV is preferred to IRR (see Chapter 8), the primary weakness in preprogrammed packages is the assumption that interest is compounded annually. If necessary, one can finesse this problem by calculating cost of capital or any interest rate i to the degree of precision desired. For example, suppose one wanted to determine NPV for the following set of cash flows using a 15-percent cost of capital:

Outlay	CF_1	CF_2	CF_3
$1,890,000	$850,000	$1,175,000	$575,000

Employing the procedure for calculating NPV outlined earlier: NPV = $115,671.08.

However, suppose one had reason to determine NPV when cost of capital was compounded continuously. To do so, one need only employ the power function and the storage registers. If the calculator contains e as a separate function, use e. If there is no separate function for e, use 2.71828 and the general power function y^x. Assuming no separate function for e, the procedure is as follows:

Keystroke	Display
1. Enter 2.71828	1. 2.71828
2. Using the power function, raise 2.71828 to .15 power.	2. 1.161834
3. Using a storage register, store 1.161834.	3. No change.
4. Enter CF_1.	4. 850,000
5. Recall 1.161834 from storage.	5. 1.161834
6. Use the division key to determine the PV of CF_1.	6. 731,601.85
7. Store 731,601.85 in another storage register.	7. 731,601.85

Repeat strokes 1 through 7 for CF_2 and CF_3, so that

$$2.71828^{2 \times .15} = 1.349859$$
$$2.71828^{3 \times .15} = 1.568312$$

and

$$\text{PV for } CF_2 = 870,461.59$$
$$\text{PV for } CF_3 = 366,636.30$$

To determine NPV:

Keystroke	Display
1. Recall CF_1 from memory and enter.	1. 731,601.85
2. Recall CF_2 from memory, press addition key, and enter result.	2. 1,602,063.44
3. Recall CF_3 from memory, press addition key, and enter result.	3. 1,968,699.74
4. Key in CF_0 (1,890,000) and press subtraction key. Display is NPV.	4. 78,699.74

YIELD TO MATURITY (BOND)

Certain financial computations are so widely used that they routinely are programmed into many financial calculators. Yield to Maturity (YTM) is one such computation. Because the YTM function (initially discussed in Chapter 3) is stored in the calculator's permanent memory, all one must do is enter the appropriate data into the calculator and press the function or functions that determine YTM.

For example, suppose on December 1, 1987, you purchased Aged-in-the-Wood Ginger Ale Corporation's $8\frac{3}{4}$ bonds maturing June 1, 2007, at 91. A general procedure for determining YTM is:

Keystroke	*Display*
1. Clear all registers. Use specified keys to display number of decimals desired (assume six).	1. 0.000000
2. Using appropriate register, enter purchase price as percent of 100.	2. 91.000000
3. Enter coupon rate in appropriate register.	3. 8.750000
4. Enter purchase date (December 1, 1987) as 12.011987.	4. 12.011987
5. Key in settlement data (June 1, 2007) as 6.012007.	5. 6.012007
6. Press appropriate keys to determine YTM (9.783399%).	6. 9.783399

These examples suggest the uses to which calculators—specifically those preprogrammed to meet the special needs of finance scholars and practitioners—can be put. Some models are programmable, permitting development of more sophisticated versions of standard models that complement the basic financial calculator and are limited only by available memory and user ingenuity.

---

* There are no problems in Chapters 1 and 23; because of the need for graphs, no answers are provided for problems in Chapter 2 (see *Instructor's Manual to Accompany Principles of Corporate Finance*).

CHAPTER 3

1. (a) $5,360.10, (b) $5,606.76, (c) $5,694.99, (d) $5,695.98.
3. (a) $13,347.70, (b) $13,182.32.
5. (a) 12.5% (b) $28.00.
7. $30,166.70
9. $18.18
11. 15%
13. $177,520.83
15. YTM on first bond $= 12.1667\%$; YTM on second bond $= 2.7144\%$.

CHAPTER 4

1. The odds are one in eight that three heads will appear and three in eight that two heads and a tail or two tails and a head will appear.
3. (a) One would expect to observe one head and one tail on half the tosses.
   (b) 400 times
   (c) .707
5. No; the actuarially fair bet is $500, not $400. Because only the second person declined the bet, we do not know whether the first or third persons also would have accepted the bet if the wager was $500.
7. (a) $\mu = 15\%$, $\sigma = 2.9326\%$
   (b) The financial officer was suggesting that distribution is symmetrical and could be normally distributed.
9. (a) 2.228 in 100, (b) infinitesimal, (c) 10.125%, (d) 99.87 in 100, (e) 97.72 in 100.

CHAPTER 5

1. (a) $\bar{R}_p = E(R_p) = 9\%$, $\sigma_p = 2.06\%$
   (b) $\bar{R}_p = E(R_p) = 9.2\%$, $\sigma_p = 2.41\%$

(c) Compared with .261772, an equally weighted portfolio has a lower coefficient of variation .229067 and preferred by a risk-averse investor.

3. $\bar{R}_x = E(R_x) = 14.4\%$

5. (a)

Portfolio	*Coefficient of Variation*
A	0.80
B	0.64
C	0.67
D	1.00

   (b) Portfolio B is preferred by a risk-averse investor. D is the inferior portfolio.

7. (a) $\beta_{jm} = 1.00$, $\beta_{km} = 1.25$;
      $\bar{R}_j = E(R_j) = 12\%$, $\bar{R}_k = E(R_k) = 14\%$
   (b) Because the covariance of the risk-free rate with the market portfolio is zero, the beta coefficient for the risk-free rate is zero.

9. (a) $\sigma_p = 13.0384\%$,
   (b) $\sigma_p = 11.5382\%$. Since the return is the same and the standard deviation is lower, one more security would be added to the portfolio.

11. $\bar{R}_p = E(R_p) = 18.5\%$
    $\sigma_p = 10\%$

CHAPTER 6

1. At a marginal tax rate of 10%, the after-tax cost of debt capital is 10.62%. At a marginal tax rate of 20%, the after-tax cost of debt capital is 9.44%. In the 20% tax bracket, Stalled Computer would issue preferred stock rather than debt.

3. 17%

5. Book value per share $= \$24.88$; return on book value is 29.54%.

7. (a) HPR $= .160648$, (b) $E(R_{xyz}) = 15.23\%$.

CHAPTER 7

1. $k_e' = 19.25\%$, $k_o = 17\%$. For an explanation, examine the assumptions underlying the M & M Hypothesis as adumbrated in this chapter.

3. (a) $k_o = 13.8\%$,
   (b) $k_o = 15.0\%$. Because $k_o = k_e$—the cost of unleveraged equity—the results are consistent with the M & M Hypothesis.

5. Zero. There is no gain from leverage.

7. The answer is yes; the explanation is based on the assumptions underlying the hypothesis. When the tax and bankruptcy assumptions are relaxed, an optimal capital structure—or at least a minimum debt-to-total-capital ratio—emerges as a basis for financing new capital projects.

9. Examine the assumptions underlying both. Because each set of assumptions suggests there is no optimal capital structure, neither is consistent with reality.

11. Bankruptcy costs represent the loss of wealth associated with financial failure and the liquidation of assets in bankruptcy court. Agency costs are those associated with monitoring management decisions that may affect the firm's liquidity. To reduce agency costs, restrictive covenants are often made a part of the indenture underlying debt securities and of the preferred stock contract. Because agency costs increase the cost of equity, the average cost of capital eventually rises with leverage.

CHAPTER 8

1. 23.38%

3. 36.51% and -246.51%

5. NPV = $31,480. Because the NPV is positive and the reinvestment rate equals the cost of capital, the project is acceptable. Under NPV, the reinvestment rate implicit in the calculations is the cost of capital.

7.

Project A	Project B
NPV = $ 130.43	NPV = $ 181.47
TV = $1,495.00	TV = $1,562.50

Both approaches yield the same result. Hence, project B is preferable to project A.

9. (a) *IRR for project A* = 52.03%; *IRR for project B* = 54.77%.
   (b) 54.03% > 15% and 54.77% > than 15%. Consequently, both projects are acceptable.
   (c) *NPV of project A* = $72,658.01; *NPV of project B* = $142,483.77. Because NPV of each project is positive, both projects are acceptable.
   (d) An additional $90,000 outlay on project B yields an additional NPV of $69,825.76. Unless there is a dollar constraint on the budget, project B is preferable to project A.

11. Just as a bond returns principal representing the original investment, so a capital investment returns the original investment through depreciation. In calculating NPV or return on either, the time when principal or depreciation is

received affects the final outcome. For the same reason, one should include as part of the project investment any noncash expense returned.

13. (a) 2.25 years; (b) average return on investment $= 48\%$, average return on average investment $= 24\%$; (c) \$13,881.54; (d) 23.59%.

15. If neither explicitly includes inflation in the cash flows, both may understate the return or net present value. In the case of the former, the internal rate of return would be higher if after-tax cash flows rose because of inflation. In the case of the latter, the average cost of capital would include an anticipated rate of inflation in the cost of debt and equity. Consequently, NPV would be understated.

17. In 10 years, the replacement cost of the asset would be

$$\$300,000(1.09)^{10} = \$710,209.10$$

Management should not be deterred from making the investment. Depreciation merely recovers the original cost of the asset. When it comes time to replace it, management will examine the outlay's NPV at that time to determine whether it is acceptable.

CHAPTER 9

1. (a) **Expected Cash Flows**

\$ 400,000
2,250,000
4,200,000
4,750,000
2,400,000
\$14,000,000

σ of expected cash flows $= \$5,700,877$

(b) 2.46 σs

(c) \$24,378,116

(d) If cash flows are uncorrelated through time, $\sigma = \$9,086,491.78$; if cash flows are perfectly correlated through time, $\sigma = \$18,071,013$.

(e) If cash flows are uncorrelated through time, the probability that NPV < 0 is .38% or 38 in 10,000; if cash flows are correlated through time, the probability rises to .0885 or 8.85 in 100.

(f) Correlation through time has raised the odds that NPV will be zero or less from 38 in 10,000 to 8.85 in 100.

3.

Outlay	NPV to T_o	PV of Abandonment	
$10,000,000	$17,130,437 + $4,752,609	= $21,913,046	
$20,000,000	$21,304,348 + $6,956,522	= $28,260,870	

There is no reason to change strategies. The inclusion of abandonment value raises the net present value of the $20,000,000 outlay.

5. The risk-averter is concerned with whether the actual outcome is x percent above or x percent below the expected net present value. Happiness is above the expected outcome; misery is below it.

7. The corporate executive had the following in mind. If the project is so large that a single outcome would place the firm in severe financial distress, one may want to examine further the chances of that outcome materializing: reexamine the simulations under which the probability distribution was generated.

CHAPTER 10

1. $k_e = .1496 = $ cost of unleveraged equity; $k'_e = .16325 = $ cost of leveraged equity.

3. $k'_e = .159838$ when beta on debt is zero; $k'_e = .156181$ when beta on debt is .3.

5. $\beta_{ju} = .928$

7. (a) .1702 (b) .168283 (c) .163057.

9. (a) $k_e = k_0 = .2$ and company market value is $48,000,000.
   (b) Market value of the stock rises from $24.00 to $24.53 per share.

CHAPTER 11

1. (a) last year, $1.50; this year, $2.00; next year, $1.75.
   (b) If dividends are a signal, management should not increase them to $2 even if the payout ratio declines. The signal telegraphs that management does not expect the earnings level to remain at $8.00 per share next year.

3. (a) $D_1 = 0.75 per share; $P_1 = 22.25 per share; $M_1 = -235,955$ shares retired.
   (b) $D_1 = 4.50; $P_1 = 18.50; $M_1 = 324,000$ new shares issued.
   (c) No. As spelled out in chapter text, shareholder wealth remains unchanged in either case.

5. The stock price should fall by 75 cents. On that day, the stock goes ex-dividend. Those who purchased the shares on the 15th will receive the dividend; those who purchased the shares on the 16th will not receive the dividend.

7. A cash dividend may contain information: presumably management increases dividends on the assumption that it expects to maintain the dividend. Because management usually has a policy of paying out a stated percentage of earnings as dividends, the increase signals that management expects to maintain a rise in earnings for the foreseeable future. A stock split or dividend, however, simply increases the number of shares outstanding. However, given what it knows about the company's future earnings, a tender offer may signal management's belief that the stock is underpriced.

CHAPTER 12

1. (a) NPV = $96,129 and IRR = 25.83%. Discounting for a total of 17 years— January 1, 1979, through December 31, 1995—leaves the payback period, nevertheless, unchanged.

   (b) If the project began on January 1, 1980, and terminated December 31, 1996, the values would be the same as 1(a).

3. (a) $242,454, (b) $181,020, (c) $55,973, (d) $117,407.

5. (a) Given the assumptions made, there would be no perceptible change in the stock's price. Only if the number of shares had been reduced and the average cost of capital had fallen would the market price per share have changed.

   (b) It appears that changes in debt have a relatively small influence on the firm's total market value and hence on the price per share.

7. (a) 14.68%, (b) 5.27%, (c) 11.86%, (d) 13.85%.

CHAPTER 13

1. The expected return in firms X and Y should be .1705.

3. To the extent independent variability or standard deviation of the return on any firm declines as the firm adds current assets relative to total assets, management experiences a lower unleveraged beta.

5. Under the absolute priority theory of reorganization, claims are settled as if the firm were being liquidated. Under the relative priority theory of reorganization, all security holders sacrifice, with junior security holders sacrificing relatively more than senior holders.

7. Although several plans are feasible, the court will probably use $100,000,000 as the valuation figure. Consequently, the firm is insolvent and stockholders would be eliminated from the reorganization.

CHAPTER 14

1. (a) EOQ = 200; TIC = $400,000.
   (b) When demand rises by 10%, EOQ rises to 210 and TIC rises to $419,523.81. When demand falls by 10%, EOQ drops to 190 and TIC to $379,473.68. Each represents an approximate 5% change.
   (c) A buffer stock of 10 units is adequate to meet the maximum increase in demand. If demand should fall to 190 units, management would not order additional units.

3. (a) $70,710.61
   (b) $100,000
   (c) Because Widget receives its expenditures in advance but may pay out cash monthly, recalculating the EOQ yields the same results as 3(a) and (b)—but as monthly rather than quarterly cash balances. The efficacy of the model depends on paying bills at a constant rate.

5. With a $12,000 variance, daily cash balances should be $1,271.32. With an $8,000 variance, daily cash balances should be $1,110.60.

7. (See *Instructor's Manual.*)

9. (a) $32,594.99
   (b) No, they are related. Credit and collection costs rise with the bad-debt ratio.

CHAPTER 15

1. $k_i = 13.57\%$ (Last National Bank); $k_i = 14.39\%$ (next to Last National Bank).

3. $k_i = 13.40\%$

5. $k_i = 17.74\%$

7. $k_i = 13.97\%$

9. Annual payments = $205,726:

Year	Annual Payment	=	Interest at 14%	Principal Payment	Balance
0					$800,000.00
1	$ 205,726	=	$112,000.00	$ 93,726.00	706,274.00
2	205,726	=	98,878.36	106,847.64	599,426.36
3	205,726	=	83,919.69	121,806.31	477,620.05
4	205,726	=	66,866.80	138,859.19	338,760.86
5	205,726	=	47,426.52	158,299.48	186,461.38
6	205,726	=	25,264.59	180,461.38	0
	$1,234,356	=	$434,355.96	$800,000.00	

CHAPTER 16

1. (a) *Fixed-income bond:*

   price = $1,000 or the face value; 50,000 bonds would be issued.

   Zero-coupon bond:

   price = $131.367; 380,613 bonds would be issued

   (b) The treasurer must weigh the fact that in the event of a decline in interest rates the company is locked into zero-coupon bonds against the advantage of tax-deductible interest imputed annually with no drain on cash until maturity.

3. Book value per share = $32.867

   $$\frac{\text{market value}}{\text{book value}} = .761$$

5. Under cumulative voting, one would need 1,400,001 shares to elect a majority (seven) directors. If the rule were one-share-one-vote, 1,400,001 shares would be needed to elect the entire board.

7. (See *Instructor's Manual.*)

9. (a) 4,000,000 shares

   (b) As there will be one new share for every three outstanding, three presumptive rights are required to purchase one share.

   (c) Cumulative rights:

   $$\frac{\$21 - \$15}{3 + 1} = \$1.50 = \text{value of the presumptive right}$$

CHAPTER 17

1. (a) $74,362,000, (b) 10.644%.

3. (a) $850,000

   (b) Underwritten $r = 10.36\%$; shelf-registered $r = 10.32\%$. There is a four basis-point savings.

5. Briefly, there is a presumption that shelf-registered stock *overhangs* the market and may be issued at any time. However, such stock is unlikely to be sold unless management believes the funds will be invested profitably (management could be right or wrong). In efficient markets, expectations would be fully discounted. There should be no consistent pattern concerning market price of the stock of companies with shelf-registered shares.

7. If the stock is offered through one syndicate only, there may be a tendency to

underprice the issue so as to ensure acceptance. Competing bids would be expected to eliminate any inefficiencies.

A rights offering purposely underprices the stock. Although management may want to make a rights offering, some companies lack a sufficient number of shareholders to use this procedure effectively.

CHAPTER 18

1. NLA = $1,619,346.18. Because NLA is positive, the company should lease.

3. *25-percent tax bracket:*
   Present value of the service contract is $1,894,721.51. Present value of the additional lease payments is $2,022,359.74. Unless it found the present value of future service payments less than either alternative, the company would prefer the service contract.

   45-percent tax bracket:
   Present value of the service contract is $1,715,496.91. Present value of the additional lease payments is $1,532,400.45. In this case, unless it found the present value of future service payments less than either alternative, the company would make the additional lease payments.

5. The NLA without the purchase option is $43,735.36. The purchase option adds $12,541.98 to the contract. The company would lease and take the purchase option.

7. There is no clear-cut answer. If inflation is fully anticipated, it is corporated in the asset price. Unanticipated inflation gives rise to gains. Most unanticipated gains, however, accrue to real property—particularly to the land component of commercial real estate.

9. NLA = $40,932.63. Present value of additional lease payments for service is $49,898.05. Present value of a service contract if the asset is purchased is $49,795.69. There is virtually no net advantage to purchasing the asset and buying the service contract rather than making the additional lease payments. Present value of the purchase option is $14,728.65. Hence, Dry Hole should lease the asset, accept the purchase option, and make the additional lease payments for service.

CHAPTER 19

1. (a) $\frac{3}{4}$(buy 3 shares and write 4 calls), (b) $15.619, (c) $92.476, (d) 140% (e) 9.0%.

3. As the text suggests, the greater the variance the greater the chances for a large

gain. The chances for a large gain improve the longer the option has to run. Hence, the greater the variance and the longer the time period until expiration, the more valuable the option.

5. $2.56

7. Briefly, the model implies that the option is exercised at maturity. Dividends and taxes are not included. The stock trades continuously and the hedge ratio is adjusted continuously. The natural logarithms of prices are normally distributed. The model requires a measure of variance, but past variance may not be an adequare measure of future variance.

9. (a) The conversion ratio is $1,000 \div 25 = 40$ shares of common stock for each debenture.
   (b) (i) $1,000 - $834.125 = $165.875 premium over U.S. Treasury securities.
       (ii) $1,000 - $681.726 = $318.274 premium over comparable corporate bonds.

CHAPTER 20

1. (a) *open,* $981,250; *low,* $981,125; *high,* $981,500; *settle,* $981.375.
   (b) Sandra has lost $200 in margin and is down to $1,800.

3. (a) Sell five T-bill contracts at 92.25 ($922,500 yield) on a bank discount basis of 7.75%.
   (b) The loan costs 12.75% on a bank discount basis. The spread between the T-bill rate and the loan rate has widened. The cross hedge has been less than perfect.

5. (a) 2.176964
   (b) 231.236 contracts
   (c) No; this is a cross hedge, and the relationship between corporate bonds and Treasury futures may change.

7. (a) *price of call* $= 5.40 \times 500 = $2,700$; *price of put* $= 5.25 \times 500 = $2,625$.
   (b) The preferable strategy is to buy the put: the price is guaranteed. Should the market decline, losses may be recouped by exercising the put at the agreed price covering the contracts at the lower price. All that is lost is the option cost. When one writes a call and the market declines, all that is gained is the option price.

9. Interest-rate volatility encourages financial managers to hedge. There are, however, two sets of costs involved: direct costs of the futures contracts and reduction in the potential for gains due to volatility. As volatility lessens, the potential for both short-term gains and losses decreases. Consequently, managers are less likely to incur the direct costs of using futures contracts.

CHAPTER 21

1. (a) For Shark, EPS is $4 and market price is $48 per share. For Dolphin, EPS is $2.50 and market price is $17.50 per share.

   (b) $16,800,000

   (c) Yes; at $26 per share, Dolphin's net asset value is $20,800,000. Borrowing $16,800,000, the resulting net asset value is $4,000,000. Junk bonds could finance the acquisition. Subsequently, the assets could be sold to liquidate the debt.

   (d) Yes; because $4,000,000 ÷ 3,000,000 = $1.33; $48.00 + $1.33 = $49.33/$4.00 = 12.33 to 1.

   (e) The increase in market value comes from the remaining net asset value. Although the market recognizes this, it does not assume Shark will do anything more with the assets than will Dolphin's management. No other economies seem to have resulted from the merger. Hence, there is no synergy.

3. (a) $259,612,500, (b) $176,400,000, (c) $83,212,500, (d) 60%.

5. The NPV of the new facilities is $2,845,358. The value of the merger is $10,720,000. The firm's value would be higher from merger than from building a new plant.

7. The issue is hotly debated. Where value of the firm's assets is greater than value of the firm's securities, the market may perceive management inefficiencies that might be eliminated by a takeover. However, some takeovers may result in monopoly power: others may achieve economies of scale or scope.

9. As the chapter suggests, shareholders of the target corporation (on balance) tend to benefit more than shareholders of the acquiring corporation.

CHAPTER 22

1. The expected holding-period return rises from .12 to .128 and the variance declines from .03 to .020698 as a result of international diversification.

3. The interest-rate parity theorem suggests that the Swiss franc should sell at .47360 rather than .49. The portfolio manager should take the following steps:

   Sell $1,000,000 in U.S. Treasury securities and purchase $1,000,000 ÷ .47 = 2,127,659.57 Swiss francs.

   Invest the funds in Swiss securities at 2,127,659.57(1.045) = 2,223,404.25.

   Immediately sell 2,223,405.25 Swiss francs at the forward rate, so that 2,223,405.25 × .49 = $1,089,468.08.

Investment in U.S. securities would have earned $1,000,000(1.053) = $1,053,000. Less transactions costs, the profit is:

$$\begin{array}{r} \$1,089,468.08 \\ \underline{1,053,000.00} \\ \$ \quad 36,468.08 \end{array}$$

5. With the Eurobond, the cost to maturity is 12.33 percent. With the private placement, the cost to maturity is 12.25 percent. It remains less expensive to place the bonds privately in the U.S.

7. $121,484.375

APPENDIX I

THE GREAT MELTDOWN OF 1987

In 1929 it was *The Great Crash*. In the vocabulary of the nuclear age, the 1987 stock-market plunge may be just as vividly termed *The Great Meltdown*. Whatever the appellation, on October 28, 1929, the Dow Jones Industrial Average (DJIA) fell a record 12.8 percent in a single day. On October 19, 1987, the DJIA eclipsed that mark, falling 508 points, or 22.6 percent—the largest decline ever experienced on one trading day.[1] The 1929 debacle ushered in the Great Depression; what will follow the 1987 collapse is, at this writing, essentially moot. A larger and stronger economy, with built-in safeguards in the banking system not present in 1929, suggests that the aftermath should be less devastating.

Nevertheless, the market plunge of 1987 serves to remind us of the limitations of the financial models employed in this book. Whether we use the CAPM, the APT, or the M & M cost-of-capital or valuation models, nothing contained in them suggests why the collapse took place and, as important, why it took place when it did. The pundits will remind us that the twin deficits in the balance of trade and in the federal budget were inconsistent with the record levels to which stock prices had soared; maybe, but this component of the information set has been available for some time. More substantive is the argument that futures and options markets permit one to buy puts or sell futures on portfolios partially or completely indexed to a market average (an insurance strategy in *program trading*; see pages 583–87). In a declining market, this process creates an enormous reservoir of potential panic for those writing the puts or buying the futures contracts—and doing so on smaller margins than are required for purchasing the underlying stocks.

Although publication deadlines do not permit enumeration of and expansion on additional factors that likely have contributed to and that should help explain the collapse, be assured there will be ample analyses available in the near future. Meanwhile, one is reminded again of the premier lesson of the Efficient Market Hypothesis (EMH): *As yet there is no systematic way to anticipate shifts in equilibrium conditions* (page 642). Yet, some apparently did so.[2] Were they lucky or skillful? Only time will tell.

---

[1] *Wall Street Journal*, October 20, 1987, p. 1.

[2] *Wall Street Journal*, October 20, 1987, p. 22.

GLOSSARY OF FINANCIAL TERMS

Abandonment Value: The amount that can be realized from selling or liquidating a project before its useful life has ended.

Absolute Priority: In bankruptcy, a legal principle in which senior claims must be fully satisfied before junior claims can receive anything. The principle is applied to liquidation and (presumably) to reorganization of a corporation.

Accelerated Cost Recovery System (ACRS): Depreciation schedules adopted under the Economic Tax Recovery Act of 1981 that permitted recovery of an asset's original cost over a period less than the asset's useful life. (See Appendix F for depreciation schedules in force in 1988.)

Accelerated Depreciation: Depreciation that writes off an asset's cost faster than under the straight-line method. (See Chapter 8 for greater detail.)

Accounts Payable: Accounts that arise primarily from a firm's purchase of goods on credit.

Accounts Receivable: Accounts that arise primarily from a firm's sale of merchandise or services on credit rather than for cash.

Accretion: The addition of value over time as contrasted with amortization, which reduces an amount over time. For example, a bond sold at a discount will accrete to par over the life of the instrument.

Accrual: Short-term liabilities that continue to recur. Examples include accrued wages, accrued taxes, and accrued interest.

Accrued Interest: Interest earned but not yet due and payable: interest due from the last payment date to the present. When a bond is sold, the buyer is responsible for the accrued interest owed the seller.

Acid-test Ratio: Synonymous with *quick ratio*. Inventories are subtracted from current assets and the residual divided by current liabilities. Alternatively, the acid-test ratio is the sum of cash, marketable securities, and receivables on the corporate books divided by current liabilities.

Acquiring Firm: In a merger, the firm that purchases another company acquires it. The firm that is purchased is an acquired company or firm.

Adjustment Bonds: Also known as *income bonds*, these instruments pay interest only if earned. The interest payments may or may not be cumulative.

Advance Factoring: The factor (lender) of accounts receivable provides the firm a loan against such receivables prior to their collection.

After-tax Yield: The yield earned on an investment after income taxes are deducted.

Agency Costs: The costs associated with monitoring company management to ensure compliance with contractual agreements contained in its debt and preferred-stock contracts. Such costs ultimately are borne by the firm's common stockholders.

Agent: One who acts on behalf of another, called the *principal*. For example, a broker is an agent for a stockholder wishing to sell his or her company shares.

Aging Schedule: In analyzing accounts receivable, used to determine how long such accounts have been outstanding. From the aging schedule, one can determine how many accounts receivable are not past due, how many are one month past due and so on.

Alpha: In portfolio theory, the alpha of a security is the risk-adjusted expected or realized return over and above what would be expected or realized from a fully diversified or market portfolio of securities. In principle, when excess return on a market portfolio is zero, alpha for the security should be zero. Excess return, expected or actual, is the difference between expected return or actual return on the security or portfolio and expected or actual risk-free rate of interest.

American (U.S.) Option: A put or call that can be exercised at any time prior to expiration (a European option can be exercised only at expiration of the option and not before).

Amortization: The gradual extinguishment of an amount or value over time. In the case of a loan, installment payments of equal amounts are made over the life of the loan. Although size of the payment may be constant, it will include both principal and interest. In accounting, the term includes such practices as depreciation of long-term assets, depletion of natural resources, and writing off intangible assets (for example, goodwill). Prepaid expenses, such as insurance premiums paid in advance, are also amortized over time. A bond premium is amortized over the life of the bond.

Annual Report: The report issued to stockholders that summarizes operational results in a series of financial statements. Additional detailed information is filed with the Securities and Exchange Commission (SEC) in a 10K report.

Annuity: Series of equal payments for a specified number of time periods, often years. When cash payment occurs at the end of that time period, the term *ordinary annuity* is sometimes used.

Arbitrage: Technically, the simultaneous purchase or sale of a security or commodity in one market and the sale or purchase of the same or equivalent security or commodity, usually in another market, so as to equalize their prices in the two markets. The term has been extended to include such practices as swapping of similar debt issues based on anticipated changes in price spreads. The term also has been employed in financial theory to suggest that in perfect markets with no income taxes the shares of a leveraged firm cannot sell at a premium over the shares of a similar but unleveraged firm.

Arbitrage Pricing Theory (APT): A theory of returns on securities developed by Stephen Ross. The essence of APT is that return on any security, assuming investors hold fully diversified portfolios, is a function of a few variables. If return on a security is inconsistent with return on other securities for the same variable, an opportunity exists to arbitrage that security by purchasing or selling it.

Arrearages: An overdue payment or set of payments. The term is commonly employed to describe unpaid cash dividends on cumulative preferred stock.

Asked Price: The price at which a dealer or specialist in a particular security is willing to sell to a potential buyer.

Authorized Stock: The maximum number of shares a corporation may issue under the terms of its charter. The charter may be amended to increase the number of shares authorized.

Baby Bonds: Bonds issued in $100 rather than conventional $1,000 denominations.

Balance Sheet: The financial statement of a firm or individual that summarizes accounting or book value based on historical cost of assets, liabilities, and net worth (ownership equity) at a point in time. The balance sheet conforms to this equation: asset = liabilities + net worth.

Balloon Payment: A large final payment on a loan. The ultimate balloon payment, payment of the entire principal at maturity, is the conventional procedure for bonds as opposed to installment loans, which contain a balloon payment at the end but lower-level payments in other years.

Banker's Acceptance: An instrument generally used to finance exports and imports; represents the unconditional obligation of the accepting or guaranteeing bank.

Bankruptcy: A legal concept under which a firm, unable to pay its debts, seeks court protection in order to liquidate its assets to satisfy creditors' claims. The concept also can apply to individuals. (See *Reorganization*.)

Basis Point: .01 percent. A bond whose yield to maturity is 12.45 percent has a 30-basis-point differential over a bond whose yield to maturity is 12.15 percent.

Bear Market: A market in which securities prices are falling or are expected to fall.

Bearer Security: A security concerning which the primary evidence of ownership is possession. Most securities today are registered with a registrar, often a commercial bank, designated by the issuer.

Benefit-Cost Ratio: The ratio of an investment's present value to its initial outlay. In the private sector, the benefit–cost ratio is the profitability index.

Beta: Measure of a security's systematic risk. A security's theoretical beta is the product of the coefficient of correlation between the return on that security and the market portfolio times the standard deviation of return on the market portfolio and the standard deviation of return on the security's return. This product is divided by the market variance to determine beta. In statistical terms

$$\beta_{jm} = \frac{r_{jm}\sigma_j\sigma_m}{\sigma_m^2} = \frac{\text{COV}_{jm}}{\sigma_m^2}$$

Beta coefficients can be expected (*ex ante*) or actual (*ex post*). The latter is the slope of a regression between the actual return on a security or portfolio of securities and the actual return on the market portfolio.

Bid: The price a dealer or specialist will pay for a particular security.

Bill of Lading: A document that establishes ownership of goods in transit.

Black-Scholes Option Model: A model (discussed in Chapter 19) in which the theoretical value of a call option is an algebraic function of the stock's market price, the present value of its exercise price, and two normal-probability density functions, $N(d_1)$ and $N(d_2)$. $N(d_1)$ is the hedge ratio.

Blue-chip Company: A large and well-known corporation; usually a household name such as General Motors, IBM, and the like.

Blue-sky Laws: State laws (as opposed to federal laws) pertaining to the terms and conditions under which new securities may be distributed or sold within a particular state. Blue-sky laws may be more restrictive than federal laws, and may actually prohibit the sale of what are deemed risky securities even though the risks are known to potential investors.

Bond: An interest-bearing debt certificate evidenced by a written contract whereby the issuer agrees to pay the lender a fixed principal (the sum borrowed) at the end of a specified period of time, generally in excess of ten years. In the interim, the lender receives semiannual interest payments for the use of the funds, Bonds are often secured by specific collateral. The term however, may be applied to any debt instrument.

Bond Rating: The evaluation of a bond's probability of default. Although the classification schemes used by the two major rating agencies—Moody's and Standard & Poor's—differ, each has a top and bottom rating with gradations in-between.

Book Value: The value of a security or a firm as shown on the corporate books. The book value of common stock equals the sum of the par or stated value, the capital or paid-in surplus, and the retained earnings. Book value per share is the sum of these three accounts divided by the number of shares outstanding.

Break-even Analysis: An analytical technique for determining the relationship between costs and revenues. The break-even point is the dollar amount of sales at which total costs equal total revenues.

Broker: An agent for an individual who is the buyer or seller of real estate or financial assets. One can be a stockbroker, real-estate broker, mortgage broker, and so forth. This contrasts with a dealer, who is a principal buyer and seller for his or her own account and not for someone else. In some areas of finance, one may be a broker-dealer. A stock-exchange specialist buys and sells for his or her own account as a principal or dealer, while acting as a broker for other brokers' orders from the public.

Bull Market: A market in which the prices of securities are rising or are expected to rise.

Business Risk: The risk inherent in the nature of a business venture. Although business risks can be viewed in terms of financing solely from equity, when debt is used financial risk of failure to meet principal and interest on the debt instruments issued must be added.

Call Option: An option to purchase an asset at a given price on or before a specific expiration date. A European call can be exercised only on the expiration date.

Call Premium: The difference between the price at which a company can call its bonds or debentures and the par value of those bonds on debentures.

Call Price: The price at which a bond or other debt instrument may be called before maturity. Preferred stock also may have a call price even though there is no maturity date.

Call Provision: The stipulation in a debt or preferred-stock agreement permitting the issuer to repurchase or call in the outstanding securities at a price specified in the indenture or contract.

Capital: In finance, all funding sources: all debt and equity used by a firm to purchase what in economic theory is termed *real capital*—primarily plant and equipment, but also inventory.

Capital Asset: A general term for any asset on which a return may be earned. Long-term assets of a nonfinancial corporation are capital assets of that corporation; securities that comprise its capital or financial structure are capital assets in the portfolios of financial institutions or individuals.

Capital Asset Pricing Model (CAPM): The theory of what determines the price and return on a capital asset. In its simplest form, assuming all investors hold diversified portfolios, the return on a capital asset equals the risk-free rate plus the beta coefficient of the asset times the excess return on the market portfolio.

Capital Budget: The schedule of investment projects (usually prepared annually). The preparation process is known as capital budgeting.

Capital Gain or Loss: The difference between an asset's purchase price and its current market price represents an unrealized capital gain or loss. The difference between an asset's purchase price and its sale price is a realized capital gain or loss.

Capital Lease: Financing an asset through a lease arrangement, rather than purchasing and funding the acquisition with debt or equity. A capital lease is also known as a *financial lease*.

Capital Market: In finance, the market for funds, particularly long-term funds. A capital market is also known as a *financial market*. When short-term funds are raised, however firms acquire them in a *money market*.

Capital Market Line (CML): The mathematical relationship between the return on some combination of both the market portfolio and a portfolio of risk-free securities in relation to the standard deviation of that portfolio.

Capital Rationing: When funds are scarce relative to the number of profitable investment opportunities in the capital budget, a firm must choose among projects: it must ration the available capital.

Capital Structure: The mix of securities types and maturities of debt and equity— employed in financing assets is termed the capital structure of the firm. Some practitioners distinguish capital structure from financial structure, the latter including both short-term and long-term funding sources.

Capitalization Rate: The discount rate used to determine present value of future cash flows.

Capitalization Ratios: A series of ratios relating debt to equity, debt to total capital, and equity to total capital. Book value or market value may be employed in computing capitalization ratios. (See Chapters 6 and 7 and Appendix E for examples of how capitalization ratios are used in finance.)

Cash Budget: A forecast of sources and uses of cash over a period of time, often a year, divided into monthly projections to allow for seasonal factors.

Cash Cycle: The length of time necessarily required from purchase of raw materials to conversion to cash or accounts receivable generated from sale of the final product. Cash cycle is also called *operating cycle*.

Cash Flow: The dollars a firm or individual realizes from an investment. Cash inflows less cash outflows for expenses associated with the investment represent net cash flows from the investment. After-tax cash flows are profits after deductions for taxes for noncash expenses, primarily depreciation.

Certainty Equivalent: An amount certain due at some point in time is equal in desirability or utility to an amount at risk due at the same point in time. An investor may be indifferent between receiving an amount certain ($40) a year from today and an even chance of receiving $0 or $100 a year from today.

Certificate of Deposit (CD): A time deposit issued by a bank, evidenced by a certificate stating interest rate paid, face value due at maturity, and date of maturity.

Characteristic Line: A line (calculated *ex post* using regression techniques or specified *ex ante* as an equation) that measures the relationship between return on an asset and return on the market portfolio. The slope of the characteristic line is the beta coefficient.

Chattel Mortgage: A mortgage on personal property such as equipment, as opposed to real property such as real estate.

Clientele Effect: A pattern of stock ownership based on particular policies, specifically dividend policy. Investors in high tax brackets, for example, may form a clientele for stocks with few or no dividends but with expectation of a relatively high capital gain.

Closed-end Mortgage: A mortgage against which no new debt can be issued. This contrasts with an open-end mortgage, against which an unlimited amount of debt can be issued.

Coefficient of Variation: The standard deviation of a variable divided by its expected value. The coefficient of variation of cash flows from an investment equals the standard deviation of cash flows divided by expected value.

Collateral: Assets pledged to secure a loan. If no collateral is pledged, the debt is unsecured.

Collateral Trust Bonds: Bonds secured by other financial assets, usually common stock. Collateral trust bonds contrast with mortgage bonds, which are secured by real property, specifically plant and land.

Collection Period: The period from the date of a product's sale to the receipt of cash from the customer.

Collect on Delivery (COD): A sale for which payment must be made when the goods are delivered to the buyer.

Combination: In finance, any means whereby two or more firms pool their collective resources (See *Merger* and *Joint Venture.*)

Commercial Bank: An institution whose primary source of funds (other than stock) are demand deposits (checking accounts) and time deposits, including passbook savings accounts. Most commercial bank funds are invested in short-term loans to business firms.

Commercial Finance Companies: Nonbanking organizations that make loans to businese firms, often loans on equipment purchased on an installment basis. Commercial finance companies obtain capital from the sale of stocks and bonds as well as through short-term bank loans.

Commercial Paper: Unsecured notes of corporations. To avoid registration with the SEC under the Securities Act of 1933, commercial paper must mature no later than 270 days from date of issue.

Commitment Fee: The fee paid to a lender in order to obtain a formal line of credit.

Common Stock: Ownership shares in a corporation for which no dividend is specified. Owners of common stock are the residual claimants to all company earnings and assets.

Compensating Balance: A noninterest bearing deposit that must be maintained by corporations as part of a loan agreement with a bank. A 10-percent compensating balance on a $1,000,000 loan requires the firm to maintain $100,000 on deposit at the lender bank.

Competitive Bidding: In corporation finance, a procedure requiring certain companies (primarily public utilities) to submit new securities offerings registered under the Securities Act of 1933 to sealed bids by competing investment banking syndicates. Competitive bidding is also used by federal, state, and local governments when offering new debt issues to the public.

Composition: An agreement whereby a firm's creditors will accept less than the full amount due on a debt obligation.

Compound Interest: The reinvestment of each interest payment in order to earn interest on the interest already paid.

Concentration Banking: A system in which firms make payments to a regional collection center to which regional banks deposit funds in various firms' accounts. Such funds or portions thereof may then be transferred to the principal bank of a corporation.

Conditional Sales Contract: A sale, often of equipment, in which title does not pass to the purchaser until the final installment is paid.

Conglomerate Merger: The merger of two companies producing totally unrelated products. In law, the term also includes mergers of firms producing the same product but competing in different markets. (See *Horizontal* and *Vertical Merger*.)

Consolidation: The joining of two or more corporations (A and B) to form a third corporation (C).

Continuous Compounding: As interest is compounded in successively smaller fixed intervals, compounding eventually becomes continuous:

$$\left(1 + \frac{r}{m}\right)^{mn} \to e^{rn} \to (2.71828)^{rn}$$

Controller: The corporate financial officer responsible for budgeting, internal cost accounting, and controls.

Conversion Premium: The difference between a convertible's market value and its conversion value.

Conversion Price: The par or stated value of a debt instrument or preferred stock divided by the number of common shares into which it is converted. For example, if a $1,000 bond is convertible into 25 common shares, its conversion price is $40($1,000/25).

Conversion Ratio: The number of shares for which a debt instrument or preferred stock can be exchanged.

Convertible Security: A bond, debenture, or preferred stock that generally can be converted into common shares.

Corporation: A state-chartered business firm whose owners or stockholders ordinarily are not personally liable for the company's debts.

Correlation Coefficient: Measure of fit between two or more variables. If the correlation coefficient between the returns on two securities is $+1$, the returns are positively and perfectly correlated. If the coefficient of correlation is -1, the returns are negatively and perfectly correlated. If the coefficient of correlation is zero, there is no relationship between the returns.

Cost of Capital: The return security holders expect to earn on their investment. The cost of capital for a particular security equals the opportunity cost or alternative return on an investment of comparable risk.

Cost of Goods Sold: The costs associated with the production of the goods for which revenue has been received. Such costs generally include labor, raw materials, and allocation of overhead directly associated with manufacture of the goods.

Cost to Maturity: The cost of a debt instrument viewed from the perspective of the issuer as opposed to the yield to maturity seen through the eyes of the security holder. The difference is due to flotation costs, including investment banker's compensation or spread.

Coupon: The stated interest payment on a debt instrument. The term is a carryover from the period in which all debt instruments actually had interest coupons on them that the owner clipped every six months, returning them (through a bank) to the issuer for payment of interest.

Covariance: The measure of co-movement between two variables, such as the covariance between return on a security and return on a market portfolio. It can be defined as the correlation between two variables multiplied by the standard deviation of each variable:

$$\text{COV}_{jk} = r_{jk}\sigma_j\sigma_k$$

Covenant: In a debt contract, a firm's promise to abide by the provisions of the contract: to meet interest, principal, and sinking-fund payments when due. A restrictive covenant constrains the firm during the life of the debt contract. A limitation on dividends is an example of a restrictive covenant.

Cover: In the futures market, connotes an offsetting transaction. One covers a short- or net-sale position by purchasing an identical contract. Similarly, one covers a long- or net-purchase position by selling an identical contract.

Covered Option: Call options sold or written by an investor against stocks actually held in the investor's portfolio.

Cross-hedging: In the futures market, use of a futures contract as an instrument to hedge against another. For example, in September a firm expecting to invest $10,000,000 in commercial paper in December purchases futures on December Treasury bills, hoping that the differential between current yields on T-bills and commercial paper will be the same in December. (See *Hedging*.)

Cum Dividend: Literally, with dividend. One purchasing a stock cum dividend receives the recently declared divided payment.

Cum Rights: Literally, with rights. One purchasing a stock cum rights receives the option to purchase a specific number of shares at a given price.

Cumulative Preferred Stock: Preferred stock is superior to common stock with respect to dividend payments. When preferred stock is cumulative, dividends may not be paid on common stock until all dividends (past and present) on preferred have been paid.

Cumulative Voting: A stockholder may cast all of his or her votes for one director. The total number of votes that may be cast equals the number of shares owned times the number of directors to be elected.

Currency Swap: A firm that requires U.S. dollars for a specific period may swap, for example, British pounds sterling for U.S. dollars with another firm requiring pounds sterling. The two firms avoid the transactions costs of using the foreign exchange market.

Current Asset: An asset that ordinarily will be converted into cash within a year. Cash also is a current asset.

Current Liability: Liability that ordinarily must be paid within a year.

Current Ratio: A measure of liquidity in which current assets are divided by current liabilities.

Current Yield (bond): The annual interest payment divided by the current bond price as contrasted with yield to maturity, which is computed using both the repayment of principal and the fact that interest is paid semiannually.

Cutoff Rate: In capital budgeting, the cutoff rate is the minimum rate acceptable on investment opportunities. (See *Hurdle Rate.*)

Debenture: A long-term debt instrument secured only by the full faith and credit of the issuer. No other specific collateral is pledged as security.

Debt: The general term for borrowing. The instruments issued by suppliers of funds — creditors—include notes, debentures, bonds, or mortgages. Those to whom the instruments are issued are debtors. Users of borrowed funds refer to such funds as debt capital.

Debt Capacity: The amount of debt or debt-like instruments (such as lease) that management believes it can safely handle. Externally, the debt capacity may be limited by the debt ratio consonant with a specific credit rating (such as "A"-rated corporation).

Debt Ratio: One of the capitalization ratios in which, by convention, the numerator is the book value or market value of long-term debt and the denominator is the sum of the book value or market value of long-term debt and equity.

Debt-to-Equity Ratio: One of the capitalization ratios in which the numerator is the book value or market value of long-term debt and the denominator is the book value or market value of equity.

Decision Tree: In risk-analysis of capital budgeting, a graphical representation used to depict the relationship between probabilities of occurrences and outcomes through time.

Deep Discount Bond: A bond (or debenture) with a stated interest or coupon rate deliberately below the market interest rate at the time of issue. To yield current market rate, the bond must sell at a substantial discount from its face value. (See *Original-issue Discount Bond.*)

Default: The failure to fulfill a contractual obligation; most commonly, the failure to pay interest on debt as it comes due. When this failure occurs, the debtor is in default and the entire principal must be paid. Failure to do so usually means the debtor will declare bankruptcy.

Deferred Taxes: A balance-sheet liability that represents additional federal income taxes due in the future.

Degree of Financial Leverage (DFL): Measures the responsiveness of percentage changes in earnings per share (EPS) to changes in earnings before interest and taxes (EBIT). Mathematically, where $In \equiv$ interest payments:

$$DFL = \frac{EBIT}{EBIT - In}$$

Degree of Operating and Financial Leverage (DOFL): Sometimes known as the degree of combined leverage, measures the responsiveness of earnings per share to both operating and financial leverage. Mathematically, where *In* represents interest:

$$DOFL = \frac{x(p - v)}{x(p - v) - F - In}$$

Degree of Operating Leverage (DOL): Measures the responsiveness of percentage changes in EBIT to percentage changes in sales. Mathematically, the DOL can be calculated from output x, price p, average variable cost v, and total fixed costs, F:

$$DOL = \frac{x(p - v)}{x(p - v) - F}$$

Demand Deposit: Checking accounts of individuals, businesses, or other entities held at commercial banks.

Depreciable Life: For tax purposes, the normal period over which the cost of an asset may be recovered.

Depreciation: In accounting, depreciation represents the recovery (through expense charges against revenue) of the cost of an asset over its estimated useful life. Accounting depreciation may differ from depreciation for tax purposes; it also may differ from economic depreciation (recovery of the replacement cost of an asset over its useful life).

Devaluation: The process whereby the currency price of one country is reduced in terms of the currency price of another country. An *official devaluation* is affected by the central government of a country; a *market devaluation* occurs when the price of one currency falls in terms of another. For example, when the value of the pound rises from $2.10 to $2.30, there is a corresponding devaluation of the U.S. dollar in terms of the British pound.

Development Bank: A bank that is often sponsored by a government whose primary purpose is to make intermediate and long-term loans to support economic development of a country.

Dilution: Reduction in earnings per share caused by conversion or exercise of warrants or debentures.

Direct Placement: The sale of securities by the issuer to the ultimate purchaser without the underwriting services of an investment banker. Direct placement also is associated with private placement. However, the latter usually defines a sale to a few individuals or institutions, thereby avoiding registration of the issue with the SEC. Although a company can directly place securities with its public stockholders, it must first register them under the Securities Act of 1933.

Discount: Narrowly defined, the difference between face value and market price of a debt instrument. Treasury bills, commercial paper, or zero coupon bonds with no stated interest payment are marketed at a discount.

Discounting: In this book, the process of determining present value of a future stream of income or cash flows. Also used to describe the process whereby a bank deducts interest on a loan in advance. Actually, the bank is discounting the note, thereby giving the borrower less than the principal amount of the loan. The difference between the principal and what is actually received is the discount interest.

Discount Rate: The rate used to calculate present value of future cash flows or income. Thus, for a constant income stream a for n years in the future

$$\text{present value} = \frac{a[1 - (1 + r)^{-n}]}{r}$$

where r is the discount rate.

Disinflation: Deceleration of the inflation rate. If the price level is rising 6 percent a year and falls to 3 percent a year, the inflation rate has decelerated.

Diversifiable Risk: The part of the risk that can be eliminated by diversifying into a portfolio of investments. Also known as *unsystematic* or *company-specific risk.*

Divestiture: The sale by a firm of certain assets or an entire division. Divestiture may be voluntary or court-ordered following a suit brought under one or more sections of the Clayton or Sherman antitrust statutes.

Dividend: A payment to stockholders either in cash or stock. If cash, the dividend represents a distribution of company assets. If stock, the dividend represents an increase in the number of shares outstanding.

Dividend Payout: Dividends per share divided by earnings per share. If a company earns $6 per share and pays $2.40 in dividends, the dividend payout is

$$\frac{\$2.40}{\$6.00} = .40 = 40\%$$

Dividend per Share: The total dividends divided by the number of shares outstanding. If a company pays $10,300,000 in dividends on 2,060,000 shares, the dividend per share is

$$\frac{\$10,300,000}{2,060,000} = \$5$$

Dividend Valuation Model: The model postulates that the current market price, p, of a stock is the present value of its future dividends. If $D \equiv$ current dividends, $g \equiv$ dividend growth rate, $r \equiv$ discount rate, and $n \equiv$ number of years dividends are expected to grow:

$$p = \frac{D\left[1 - \left(\dfrac{1+g}{1+r}\right)^n\right]}{r - g}$$

Dividend Yield: The dividend per share divided by the market price per share. If the current dividend is $2 per share and the market price of the stock is $40 per share, the dividend yield is

$$\frac{\$2}{\$40} = .05 = 5\%$$

Divisional Cost of Capital: The marginal cost of new capital for a particular division of a company rather than for the company as a whole.

Draft: A written order to pay. A check drawn on a demand deposit is a draft.

Dutch Auction: A competitive bidding technique in which the lowest price required to sell the entire securities offering becomes the price at which the securities are sold.

Earnings After Taxes (EAT): Net income available to stockholders after all expenses and income taxes are deducted. If preferred stock is outstanding, preferred dividends also must be deducted; the remainder is available to common stockholders.

Earnings Before Interest and Taxes (EBIT): Earnings before interest on debt and income taxes are deducted. Also used interchangeably with *net operating income* (NOI). When interest is deducted, EBIT becomes *earnings before taxes* (EBT).

Earnings per Share: The total earnings available to stockholders divided by the average number of shares outstanding for the period over which earnings are calculated.

Economic Life: The length of time over which an asset will add to the firm's profitability. Although the term *useful life* is sometimes used in place of economic life, an asset can still add to profitability yet be technologically obsolete. A substitute may, therefore, prove even more profitable.

Economic Order Quantity (EOQ): A model designed to compute the optimal order quantity that minimizes the firm's total cost of inventory. When applied to cash management, EOQ represents the optimum number of securities that must be converted to cash to meet the transactions demand for cash:

$$EOQ = Q = \sqrt{\frac{2DA}{C}}$$

where $D \equiv$ total demand for materials or cash, $A \equiv$ acquisition or ordering costs in the case of inventory and transactions costs in the sale of securities, and $C \equiv$ carrying costs in the case of inventory or opportunity costs of cash management.

Economies of Scale: Economies associated with the most efficient size of plant or facility.

Economies of Scope: Economies derived from producing or marketing a series of products in the same plant or with the same sales force.

Effective Date of Registration: The date on which a security may be offered publicly. Generally occurs 20 days after the registration statement is filed in accordance with the provisions of the Securities Act of 1933.

Efficient Capital Markets: Capital or securities markets characterized by the free flow of information and where investors have homogeneous expectations about risk and return. Investors also have identical time horizons and make choices based on risk and return. Return is measured by the mean or average return expected from an asset or portfolio of assets. Risk is measured by the variance or standard deviation in those returns. All investors maximize the utility of their terminal wealth.

Efficient Frontier: In portfolio theory, the curve that represents portfolios available to an investor from which the investor must accept more risk as measured by standard deviation to achieve a higher expected return. Portfolios on the efficient frontier are said to be *efficient portfolios*.

Electronic DTC: A depository transfer check sent via telecommunications between banks to effect a uniform one-day clearing time.

Equipment Trust Certificate: An instrument used to finance railroad rolling stock, aircraft, and sometimes trucks. Equipment trust certificates are sold to investors and pay for approximately 75 percent of the equipment purchase price. The transportation company makes the 25-percent down payment; the 75-percent debt is paid off over time. The company takes title to the equipment only when the debt has been completely retired. Thus, the transportation company is treated as a lessee making lease payments that eventually retire the certificates.

Equity: The ownership interest in a business. When the firm is incorporated, equity refers to one or more classes of owners—the usual division being between preferred stockholders who receive a stated dividend and common stockholders who are residual owners. Equity also refers to the net-worth portion of the balance sheet containing stock, capital surplus, and retained earnings.

Equity Ratio: One of the capitalization ratios in which the numerator is the book value or market value of equity (stock in the case of a corporation) and the denominator is the sum of the book value or market value of long-term debt plus equity.

Eurobond: A bond sold in a country other than the country in whose currency the bond is denominated. A Eurodollar bond is a bond sold outside the United States but denominated in U.S. dollars.

Eurodollars: U.S. dollar deposits in banks outside the United States: in Europe or anywhere else in the world.

European Option: An option that can be exercised only on its expiration date, as opposed to U.S. option, which can be exercised on or before its expiration date.

Exchange Rate: The ratio of one currency's value relative to another: the rate at which one currency may be exchanged for another. A currency may appreciate—become more expensive—relative to another currency. Alternatively, a currency may depreciate—become less expensive—relative to another currency.

Ex-dividend: The date on which purchasers of the stock will not receive the quarterly dividend: on that date, the stock sells ex-dividend.

Exempt Securities: Securities not subject to registration under the Securities Act of 1933. Usually small corporate issues and issues of government-sponsored agencies and municipalities.

Exercise Price: The dollar amount that a company must pay out for a share of stock, usually common stock, when a stockholder exercises a warrant or an option. In the parlance of option theory, the exercise price is sometimes known as the *option* or *strike price*.

Expected Net Present Value (NPV): The anticipated net present value of an investment. Conceptually, it is the mean or maximum-likelihood estimate of a probability distribution of cash flows.

Expected Return: The anticipated return on an investment. Conceptually the mean or maximum-likelihood estimate of a probability distribution of possible returns.

Expected Value: The weighted average of all possible outcomes, where the weights are the probabilities assigned to such outcomes. Expected value is the maximum-likelihood estimate or mean of the probability distribution of expected values.

Ex-rights: A stock without the right to purchase new shares from the issuing company at a special subscription price sells ex-rights. If such a right comes with the stock, it is said to sell cum-rights. During a rights offering, there is a limited period within which a stock sells cum-rights; when the period ends, the stock sells ex-rights.

Extra Dividend: A dividend in the form of cash or stock paid in addition to the regular or usual dividend paid by the company.

Face Value: In a debt instrument, the amount due at maturity. Usually represents the amount actually borrowed.

Factor: One who buys or sells accounts receivable. A factor is often a subsidiary of a commercial bank or is a commercial finance company. To factor accounts receivable is to sell them to a factor.

Federal Funds Rate: The interest rate charged by banks lending excess reserves to other banks on a short-term basis.

Federal Reserve System: The central banking system of the United States.

Field Warehouse: A secured area in which inventory used as collateral for an inventory loan is housed. Under the supervision of a field warehouser, the borrower may remove the inventory only with the lender's permission.

Finance: The money resources available to governments, business firms, or individuals.

Financial Distress: A condition in which cash flows are inadequate or marginally adequate to meet cash expenses as they come due. In an extreme case, such inadequacy may result in bankruptcy.

Financial Intermediaries: Financial institutions—the most important of which are insurance companies, banks, savings and loan associations, and other deposit-type institutions. The primary function of a financial intermediary is to channel funds from sources, mostly households, to users, largely such nonfinancial business firms as manufacturers, utilities, and governments. (See *Nonfinancial Business Firm*).

Financial Lease (Finance Lease): The long-term noncancellable lease of a real asset, often equipment. The lessee commits to a series of fixed payments that, for practical purposes, covers the useful life of the asset. The asset is, therefore, financed through lease payments rather than through purchase accompanied by issuance of debt. Until the Tax Reform Act of 1986, there were special tax provisions for the Financial Lease.

Financial Leverage: The relationship between borrowed funds and shareholders' equity as summarized in the debt-to-equity ratio. Although it legally is equity, preferred stock ordinarily is included with debt. [See *Degree of Financial Leverage (DFL)*.]

Financial Management: The acquisition, management, and financing of company resources through the use of money.

Financial Manager: One who raises funds by issuing securities and invests them primarily in the real assets of a nonfinancial business firm.

Financial Plan: A plan based on cash-flow projections that specifies inflows and outflows of cash required to meet operating expenses and that delineates capital-budgeting decisions attendant to implementing the firm's objectives over a certain period of time.

Financial Risk: The risk that a firm will default on interest payments when they are due. Because failure to pay interest can result in bankruptcy and financial loss to stockholders, common and preferred, cost-of-equity capital rises with financial leverage. The financial risk due to use of debt is different from the basic business risk due to cost of unleveraged equity.

Fisher Effect: The relationship between nominal and real interest rates. The nominal rate is the algebraic sum of the real rate and the rate of expected inflation. The real rate is presumed free of the risk of default. When this is not the case, a premium for the risk of default must be added to the risk-free real rate when determining the real rate on corporate bonds.

Fixed Assets: The physical facilities used to produce goods and services: primarily plant, land, and equipment. (Also known as *long-term assets*. See Appendix E.)

Fixed-asset Turnover: The ratio of sales divided by fixed assets. Indicates volume of sales a firm will generate relative to its fixed assets.

Fixed-charge Coverage: The ratio of earnings before interest and taxes divided by interest. In accounting terminology, the ratio measures a firm's ability to meet interest payments as they come due. To the denominator may be added such other cash payments associated with total debt burden as lease payments and sinking-fund obligations that must be met in cash.

Fixed Costs: A firm's expenses independent of output or sales volumes.

Float: The amount payable on checks already written but not yet deducted from the accounts on which they are drawn.

Flotation Costs: The costs incurred in issuing securities. Flotation costs represent the difference between what the public pays for the securities and what the company receives as proceeds. They include the investment banker's spread and other costs associated with selling the issue.

Foreign Exchange Rate: See *Exchange Rate.*

Forward Rate: The forward rate of exchange is an exchange rate agreed on today concerning specific currencies to be delivered in the future. It is similar to a futures contract, except that the amounts exchanged are not standardized.

Funding: The process by which short-term debt is replaced with long-term securities, either debt or stock.

Futures Contract: A contract to deliver or accept delivery of a standard amount of a specific commodity or financial instrument at some future point and at a price determined at the time the contract was made.

General Lien: A claim against all assets of a given type. A public utility may issue bonds with a general lien on all its generating facilities.

Geometric Mean: Technically defined as the nth root of the product of n numbers. Used to calculate average rate of return over a period of time. Thus, if the holding period return on a stock is 25 percent from T_0 to T_1 and -5 percent from T_1 to T_2, the average rate of return from T_0 to T_2 is

$$\sqrt{(1.25)(1 - .05)} - 1 = .089725 = .09 = 9\%$$

Going Private: A process whereby a firm, usually its management, buys out the publicly held shares of the company to prevent takeover by another firm.

Going Public: A company that offers its stock for the first time to any investor through a public offering in conformity with regulations of the Securities and Exchange Commission under the Securities Act of 1933.

Golden Parachute: The provisions in employment contracts of top management for severance pay should they lose their job as the result of takeover.

Goodwill: The difference between a firm's market value as a going concern and its book value.

Greenmail: A premium paid by a targeted company to the entity and/or individual attempting to take over the company in exchange for the shares.

Gross Profit Margin: The ratio of net sales less costs of goods sold to net sales: the percent of each sales dollar remaining after accounting for the cost of producing such goods.

Growth Rate: The rate g at which cash dividends are expected to grow. In terms of the dividend model—used to estimate a stock's present intrinsic value—g is the long-term growth rate.

Growth Stock: In the short run, a stock for which superior investment opportunities abound. Because the expected rate of return is substantially higher than the expected real growth in the economy, the market price of the stock is expected to appreciate faster than the market as a whole.

Hedge Ratio: In options, the ratio of the number of options written relative to the number of shares owned that ensures a risk-free return on the funds invested. (See Black–Scholes model, Chapter 19). In futures, the ratio of the volatility of securities to the volatility of futures contracts. (See Chapter 20.)

Hedging: For the firm, matching the maturity of assets with the maturity of liabilities. The term is also associated with the futures markets. For example, if one holds a Tresury bill that matures in six months, one could sell a six-month futures contract on the security. Because the contract specifies the price to be paid for the security when delivered in six months, the seller is hedging by shifting the risk of price fluctuations. (See *Cross-hedging*.)

Holding Company: A company that owns the majority or all the stock of one or more other companies. These *other companies* are subsidiaries of the holding company.

Holding Period Return (HPR): The ratio of the difference between market price of a capital asset at the end of the time period and at the beginning of the time period—$P_1 - P_0$ plus dividend D_1 divided by market price at the beginning of the period:

$$HPR = \frac{P_1 - P_0 + D_1}{P_0}$$

The holding period return calculated may be the expected return or the actual return. Since P_1 could actually be less than P_0 and D_1 could be zero or too small to offset $P_1 < P_0$, the actual holding period return may be negative.

Horizontal Combination: The union of two or more firms engaged in similar lines of business and operating in overlapping markets: for example, two petroleum companies that sell their products in the same market.

Hurdle Rate: In capital budgeting, the minimum acceptable rate of return. The hurdle rate for a firm should be the marginal cost of new capital given the firm's capital structure and dividend policy: internal rate of return r should exceed weighted average cost of capital k_0, for all projects. Alternatively, net present value NPV discounted at k_0 should be positive. Consequently, the hurdle rate on an accept-or-reject basis should be k_0.

Income Bond (debenture): A bond (debenture) on which interest is paid only if earned.

Incremental Cash Flows: The additional cash flows a firm receives from investing in a project.

Incremental Cost of Capital: The marginal cost of new capital required holding the capital structure constant. It is the weighted average cost of new capital from each source.

Indenture: The contract portion of a bond that specifies obligations of the debtor during the period in which the bond is outstanding.

Independent Investment Projects: In capital budgeting, projects whose cash flows are unrelated: the adoption of one project does not affect the internal rate of return or net present value of another project.

Index: The measure of present value relative to base year. The S & P 500 uses a value of 10 for stocks in the index for the base years 1941–1943. If a subsequent year's index were 180, it would be interpreted as an 18-fold increase in value over the base years 1941–1943.

Index Fund: A portfolio of securities weighted in accordance with a market portfolio represented by an index.

Indifference Curve: A curve joining outcomes equally satisfying to an individual. A set of indifference curves shows how an investor can move from a lower level of satisfaction to a higher level. In finance, an investor trades off risk against return seeking to allocate funds so as to obtain the highest level of satisfaction: to reach the highest indifference curve.

Inflation Premium: The additional premium investors demand as part of their return to compensate for expected inflation.

Insider: One who has access to information that, if generally known, would materially affect market price of an investment, often a common stock. Trading on inside information violates regulations issued under the Securities Exchange Act of 1934.

Insolvent: A company (or individual) either unable to meet obligations as they come due or whose liabilities exceed market value of its (his or her) assets.

Installment Loan: A loan in which monthly payments amortize both principal and interest over the life of the loan. Interest, however, is often paid on the original principal and does not decline as principal is reduced.

Interest: The rate paid on money borrowed or on money lent. The stated rate of interest is the percent of face value of the loan that must be paid periodically. Thus, if a firm borrows $1,000 at 11 percent, the stated rate of interest is $110 per year. If interest is paid quarterly, however, the effective rate of interest is

$$\left(1 + \frac{.11}{4}\right)^4 - 1 \times 100 = 11.4621\%$$

Interest-rate Futures: Futures contracts on interest-bearing financial instruments.

Interest-rate Parity Theorem: The theorem holding that short-term interest rates in two countries have the same ratio as the forward rate of one country in terms of another has to the spot rate of that country to the other. (See Chapter 22.)

Interest Rate Swap: An agreement by two firms to pay the interest on one another's debt. A company with assets whose returns in the short run vary with interest rates but whose liabilities consist of fixed-interest payments on long-term debt may swap payments with a company whose returns are fixed over a long time period but that is financed in part by a short-term loan with interest rates that change as the loan is renewed.

Intermediation: The process by which savings are accumulated in financial institutions and then lent or invested in the securities of businesses and governments.

Internally Generated Funds: The cash flows that can be used to pay dividends to stockholders or reinvested in the firm. Cash flows from operations consist primarily and often exclusively of profits after taxes and depreciation.

Internal Rate of Return: The rate that equates present value of future cash flows to outlay on the project and makes net present value of the project equal to zero.

In the Money: An option in which market price is greater in the case of a call or less in the case of a put than exercise or strike price.

Intrinsic Value: The value associated with present value of future payments on a common stock. If a securities analyst determines that a stock's intrinsic value is greater than its market price, this is a signal to purchase the stock.

Inventory: The goods and materials used in the production process (raw materials) or the stock of finished goods available for delivery or sale.

Inventory Turnover Ratio: The ratio of sales or cost of goods sold for the year to end-of-the-year inventory. (Also known as *sales inventory ratio*. See Appendix E.)

Investment Banking: Intermediation between those who need funds and those who supply them. Investment bankers provide this service. (See *Underwriting*.)

Investment Company: A financial intermediary that pools investors' funds to purchase financial instruments: stocks and corporate bonds; long-term government securities; or money-market instruments, including commercial paper and treasury bills. Investment companies are of two types: closed-end (a specific number of shares outstanding) and open-end or mutual funds (the number of company shares is unlimited).

Investment Market Line (IML): In this text, a term used exclusively to connote the relationship between expected return and β on all investable wealth. [See *Securities Market Line (SML)*.]

Investment Tax Credit (ITC): A tax credit instituted to encourage business firms to invest in plant and equipment. It represents a deduction from taxes and not from taxable income. The Investment Tax Credit was repealed by the Tax Reform Act of 1986.

Joint Venture: An agreement between two or more firms to enter into a partnership for developing a specific project, such as the Alaska Pipeline. (See *Combination*.)

Junior Securities: In the event of liquidation of the firm, securities that rank below other securities. Unsecured debt, for example, is usually junior to secured debt.

Junk Bonds: High-yield bonds whose quality ratings render them ineligible for purchase by most institutional investors. They may be issued by new companies making their first public offering or they may be issued by established companies to raise funds with which to purchase shares in other companies. In the latter case, if the takeover is successful, the company purchasing shares of the target company may sell certain of its assets to retire the issue.

Lease: A contract enabling the user (lessee) to hold property (often equipment or real estate) for a specified period of time in exchange for making periodic payments to the owner (lessor).

Letter of Credit: An instrument used primarily in international trade. Issued by a bank, a letter of credit authorizes an exporter to draw a time draft on the issuing bank. The letter of credit specifies the draft will be accepted once appropriate documents are received showing the goods exported have been received by the importer. Once approved, the time draft authorized by the letter is a banker's acceptance.

Letter Stock: Privately placed stock whereby a letter is delivered to the owner stating that the stock was purchased for invesment and not for short-term resale. To be offered publicly, letter stock must subsequently be registered under the Securities Act of 1933.

Leverage: A general term used to describe the variability in earnings that changes in sales can cause as a result of fixed costs (operating leverage) or interest costs (financial leverage). [See *Degree of Financial Leverage (DFL)*, *Degree of Operating Leverage (DOL)*, and *Degree of Operating and Financial Leverage (DFFL)*.]

Leveraged Buyout: A process by which investors, often company management, borrow heavily to buy out the shares of the company in order to prevent a takeover. (See *Going Private*.)

Leveraged Lease: A special type of financial lease in which the lessor provides only 10-to-20 percent of the funds necessary to acquire the asset and borrows the remainder. However, the lessor (being in a high tax bracket) can take full advantage of the deductibility of depreciation and interest.

Lien: A creditor's legal right to obtain a debtor's property being used as collateral for a loan. The creditor may exercise the lien if the debtor fails to pay interest or principal on the loan when due. The debtor will probably respond by petitioning a federal court for protection under the bankruptcy laws.

Limited Partnership: A business form (structure) in which general partners are personally liable for the business debts but other (limited) partners are not.

Line of Credit: A prearranged unsecured loan arrangement with a bank or other financial institution whereby the client can borrow up to a certain amount or to the limit of the line of credit.

Liquidation: The process by which a firm is dissolved through sale of its assets. The liquidation may be voluntary or may result from bankruptcy proceedings.

Liquidity: In finance, the term has two meanings: a firm's ability to meet its financial obligations as they come due or the investors' ability to sell assets on short notice at current market value. An active secondary or trading market offers liquidity to investors.

Liquidity Ratio: A ratio that measures a firm's ability to meet its short-term obligations. The ratio of current assets to current liabilities is a measure of liquidity, as is the ratio of current assets minus inventories to current liabilities (quick ratio).

Listed Security: A security that for trading purposes is listed on an exchange, such as the New York Stock Exchange.

Loan Commitment: (See *Revolving Loan Commitment*.)

Lock Box: A check collection system whereby a commercial bank monitors a post-office box to which payments are made by one of its customers. The bank deposits the checks immediately, thereby minimizing the time between receipt of the checks and charge to the customer's account.

London Interbank Offered (Offering) Rate (LIBOR): The interest rate charged one another by banks on short-term Eurodollar deposits.

Long Position: Describes a position in which one holds or owns a security or commodity.

Long-term Debt (liabilities): Debt that, by convention, has a maturity in excess of one year. Some writers distinguish among short-term, intermediate-term, and long-term debt. If so: short-term debt matures in less than one year; intermediate-term debt matures in one to five years (possibly as long as ten years); and long-term debt matures in ten years or longer.

Majority Voting: A voting system under which each director is voted on individually (as opposed to cumulative voting, where a stockholder has as many votes as there are directors to be elected and may cast all votes for one director).

Margin: The percentage of the purchase price required by the Federal Reserve when purchasing securities (primarily stock), the balance can be borrowed from a bank or broker.

Marginal Cost (revenue): The additional cost (revenue) generated by the sale of one more unit of a product.

Marginal Cost of Capital: The incremental cost of additional funds raised. The average cost of capital employed in capital budgeting is the weighted average of the marginal costs of different funding sources: the marginal cost of debt (preferred and common stock) at the time the funds are raised.

Marginal Efficiency of Investment: (See *Internal Rate of Return and Yield.*)

Marginal Tax Rate: The income-tax rate paid on additional income. When applicable, it may be the sum of both federal and state tax rates. It is the rate employed in capital budgeting to determine after-tax cash flows.

Marketable Security: A security, usually a short-term debt instrument, that is readily convertible to cash with little or no loss of principal.

Market Portfolio: The portfolio containing all investable wealth.

Market Rate of Discount: The rate at which the market discounts expected future returns on an investment.

Market Value Exchange Ratio: In a merger, it is the ratio of the market value of the offer made by the acquiring firm to the market value of the target firm. To induce target shareholders to tender their shares, the number of shares offered (exchanged) to target shareholders is usually greater than justified by the exchange ratio.

Marking to the Market: In the context of the futures market, a term used to describe whether an investor must put up additional margin on a contract.

Matching Principle: A guideline for working-capital management holding that current assets should be financed from current liabilities.

Maturity: The length of time before a debt instrument can be redeemed at par or face value.

Maturity Factoring: An arrangement whereby a factor collects accounts receivable for a company and guarantees payment to the company at maturity.

Merger: The combination of two or more firms in which only one survives. (See *Combination.*)

Modigliani and Miller (M & M) Hypothesis: Under strict assumptions, Modigliani and Miller postulate that a firm's average cost of capital is independent of its capital structure and equal to the cost of an unleveraged capital structure.

Money Market: The market for such short-term securities as commercial paper and Treasury bills. Maturities of the instruments traded are less than a year.

Money Market Fund: An investment portfolio consisting of money market instruments. Individuals who are unable to purchase such instruments separately because of large minimum denominations participate indirectly by owning shares in these funds.

Monte Carlo Simulation: A method for calculating the probability distribution of possible project outcomes.

Mortgage Bond: A corporate bond backed by a mortgage on specific real property: land and/or buildings.

Multinational Corporation: A corporation with production and distribution facilities in foreign countries.

Multiple Internal Rates of Return: In capital budgeting, when the sign of after-tax cash flows changes from positive to negative or from negative to positive, there may be more than one solution to the equation: more than one rate of return.

Mutual Fund: An investment company with an unlimited number of authorized shares. Proceeds from the sale of its shares are invested in financial instruments. The mutual fund stands ready to repurchase its shares at their net asset value: at the market value of the securities divided by the number of shares outstanding.

Mutually Exclusive Investments: In capital budgeting, projects that are perfect substitutes for each other (for example, two machines to serve the same purpose); the adoption of one precludes the adoption of the other.

Negative Pledge Clause: The clause in a debt contract whereby the borrower agrees not to give other lenders an exclusive lien on any of its assets. Alternatively, the borrower pledges not to issue debt with priority over outstanding debt. A debenture contract may contain a negative pledge clause preventing issuance of mortgage bonds secured by real property.

Negotiable Order of Withdrawal (NOW) Account: A savings account that functions as a checking account.

Negotiated Underwriting: An offering in which the issuer secures underwriting of its securities by negotiation rather than through competitive bidding or through a shelf registration and subsequenct sale of part or all of the issue to the lowest bidder.

Net Lease: A lease in which the lessee promises to insure and maintain the equipment.

Net Leasing Advantage: A mathematical calculation employed to determine whether a firm should finance an asset through leasing rather than purchasing it through conventional debt financing.

Net Present Value: The present value of future after-tax cash flows minus capital investment outlay.

Net Profit: The profit after taxes from which stockholders receive dividends.

Net Working Capital: Current assets minus current liabilities.

Net Worth: Book value of a company's common stock, capital surplus, and retained earnings. When divided by the number of shares outstanding, the result is book value per share.

Nominal Interest Rate: The interest rate unadjusted for inflation and risk of default. If the nominal rate is the yield on a U. S. government security, risk of default is presumed to be zero.

Nondiversifiable Risk: That part of a security's risk that cannot be reduced by diversification. It is also known as *systematic risk*.

Nonfinancial Business Firm: A firm that engages primarily in the manufacture and/or distribution of goods and services to others: manufacturers, wholesalers, and retailers. Also included are public utilities and transportation companies. (See *Financial Intermediary*.)

Nonrefundable Debt: Debt that may not be called in and replaced by another debt issue.

Normal Curve: Symmetrical bell-shaped distribution central to the study of applied statistics. The curve is completely described by its mean and standard deviation.

Note: Unsecured corporate notes usually maturing in 10 years or less, but occasionally maturing from 10 to 15 years. In the case of U.S. securities, a note is a debt instrument maturing in 1 to 10 years.

Note Payable: A written promise to pay a specified amount to a creditor on or before a stated due date.

Operating Cycle: (See *Cash Cycle*.)

Operating Lease: A lease whereby the lessee makes periodic payments to the lessor with no intention of eventually owning the asset. (See *Finance Lease*.)

Operating Leverage: (See *Degree of Operating Leverage*.)

Operating Loss: The loss incurred when operational expenses exceed operating income: there is no taxable income.

Operating Profit: Sales less expenses (but not less interest and taxes). If there are no accounting adjustments, operating profits equal earnings before interest and taxes (EBIT).

Opportunity Cost: A foregone opportunity. The opportunity cost of purchasing one type of security is the loss of return on investment alternatives.

Option Writer: One who agrees (for a fee) to sell a security to the buyer of a call option at the exercise price or to buy a security from the purchaser of a put option at a specified price. The writer is known as the maker of the option.

Organized Security Exchange: A formal exchange either registered or exempted from registration by the Securities and Exchange Commission. Exchanges have a physical floor and rules by which securities are traded. (See *Over-the-Counter Securities Markets*.)

Original-issue Discount Bonds: Bonds or debentures sold at a discount from par or face value because their stated rate of interest is below the going yield on debt instruments of comparable quality and maturity. (See *Zero Coupon Bonds*.)

Over-the Counter (OTC) Securities Markets: A network of securities dealers, connected by a communications system of telephones and computer terminals, that provides quotations on outstanding securities. OTC is one part of the secondary securities market. (See *Organized Security Exchange*.)

PacMan Defense: In mergers, an attempt by the targeted firm to take over the company making the tender offer. (See *Takeover* and *Tender Offer*.)

Parallel Loan: An agreement between two companies domiciled in different countries to make loans to each other's subsidiaries in order to avoid foreign-exchange transactions costs. A British firm may loan the British subsidiary of a U.S. company the pound equivalent of $10,000,000 while the U.S. company loans the U.S. subsidiary of the British company an identical amount for an identical period.

Par (Stated) Value: An arbitrary value assigned to a stock; it can be a nominal amount, such as $1, or no par. Par value represents the minimum that must be received when the stock is sold. Par value on bonds represents the principal borrowed and due at maturity (usually $1,000).

Payback Period: The number of years required to return an asset's original investment from cash inflows: from after-tax profits plus depreciation.

Pecuniary Economies: Financial economies realized from the combination of two or more firms, such as lower material costs and lower borrowing costs due to greater size. (See *Technical Economies.*)

Perpetuity: A stream of equal cash payments expected to continue forever.

Poison Pill: A tactic employed by the target of a merger to make itself less attractive to the raider. The target may sell additional shares to its stockholders at a deep discount, thereby forcing the raider to lower its price. Alternatively, the target may issue debt in order to retire shares, thereby increasing its leverage. (See *Shark Repellent.*)

Portfolio Manager: One who invests primarily in financial instruments issued by nonfinancial business firms, governments, and, in the case of households, mortgages and other related loans.

Preauthorized Debt (check): A debt (check) that does not require authorization of the person on whose account it is drawn.

Preemptive Right: A stockholder's right to purchase new shares of company stock before the shares are offered to the general public. In practice, the preemptive right is often waived.

Preferred Stock: A stock with prior but often limited claims on income and assets over claims of common stock. The claims are junior, however, to the claims of all debtholders.

Present Value: The value today of a specific set of future payments.

Primary Market: The market for new issues, as opposed to the secondary or trading markets for outstanding securities.

Prime Rate: Traditionally, the rate charged by banks to their best customers.

Principal: The amount a borrower must repay at a specific point in the future.

Private Placement: (See *Direct Placement.*)

Prospectus: The document summarizing the information contained in a registration statement filed with the Securities and Exchange Commission. Prior to a public offering, a preliminary prospectus (absent price and underwriting spread) is circulated by investment bankers among interested investors. The final prospectus, containing price and underwriting spread, must be distributed to purchasers of the newly offered securities.

Public Offering: A securities offering registered with the Securities and Exchange Commission for distribution to the general public rather than to a few investors. (See *Direct Placement.*)

Purchase Money Mortgage: A mortgage secured to purchase the asset used as collateral for the loan.

Purchasing-power Parity Theorem: Currencies of different countries should be priced relative to one another so that the same market basket of goods could be purchased for the same amount of money regardless of the country.

Put Option: An option to sell a security at a specified (exercise) price, as opposed to a call option to buy a security at a specified (exercise) price.

Quick Ratio: (See *Acid Test Ratio.*)

Raider: One who specializes in purchasing shares of a company either to take it over or to extract a premium from the company for shares held. (See *Greenmail* and *Takeover*.)

Rate of Return: The return on an investment. Expected rate of return is the anticipated return; actual return is the amount realized.

Real Assets: Plant, equipment, and inventory, as opposed to financial assets, which are claims on real assets.

Realized Rate of Return: The actual or *ex-post* return on an investment is the realized return on an investment, as opposed to the expected or *ex-ante* return.

Real Rate of Interest: The nominal or observed rate of interest adjusted for risk of default and expected inflation.

Receivable Turnover Ratio: The rate at which receivables are turned into cash. It is the ratio of annual credit sales to accounts receivable. (See Appendix E.)

Red-herring Prospectus: A preliminary prospectus. (See *Prospectus*.)

Refinancing: A term used to describe replacing one issue of preferred stock with another. Refinancing is similar to re-funding debt, except the latter must be re-funded or retired at maturity. Although debt may be re-funded before maturity in order to obtain a lower rate of interest, in general a company refinances preferred stock so as to pay a lower dividend.

Re-funding: The process by which a maturing debt security is replaced by a new debt-security issue.

Registration Statement: A statement filed by an issuer with the Securities and Exchange Commission containing all financial information necessary to make a public offering of securities.

Reorganization: A formal procedure under Chapter 11 of the Bankruptcy Reform Act of 1978 whereby a firm is revitalized rather than liquidated. Assets may be sold to reduce the debt in the capital structure.

Repurchase Agreement (repo): The sale of government securities by a bank or securities firm to an individual or corporation under an agreement to repurchase the securities at a specified price within a short period of time, perhaps a few days or even overnight.

Required Rate of Return: The minimum rate of return necessary to purchase a security or to make a real capital investment.

Retained Earnings: On a corporate balance sheet, the accumulation of reported earnings less dividends.

Revolving Loan Commitment: A commercial bank's guarantee that a specific amount of credit will be available to a firm for a specific period of time. The firm pays a commitment fee on any unused portion of the credit. The loan commitment often carries a variable rate tied to the 90- or 180-day certificate rate of deposit (CD) rate.

Rights Offering: A procedure whereby a corporation offers its shareholders the right to purchase new shares in the company at a price less than the going market price.

Risk: The uncertainty associated with any investment outcome. At a basic level, risk is measured by the standard deviation (variance) of the probability distribution of holding period returns in relation to the expected holding period return.

Risk-free Rate: A certain return: an expected holding period return with no variance. In principle, the return should be both free of the risk of default and of purchasing power. A

Treasury bill maturing within a short period of time, no longer than three months, is the most widely used proxy for a risk-free rate.

Risk Premium: The difference between expected rate of return on a risky asset and on a risk-free asset.

Rule 415: (See *Shelf Registration.*)

Sale Leaseback: An arrangement whereby a firm sells an asset to another firm and leases back the asset over an extended period of time.

Secondary Market: The market for trading in securities outstanding. Such securities may be traded over the counter through a network of securities dealers linked by telephone and computer terminals or on the floor of a securities exchange.

Secured Loan: A loan for which specific property has been pledged as collateral.

Securities and Exchange Commission (SEC): The federal regulatory agency that oversees the administration of federal securities legislation pertaining to both primary and secondary securities markets.

Security Market Line (SML): A graphical representation depicting the relationship between expected return on securities and their systematic risk or beta coefficients.

Senior Securities: Securities that, in the event of bankruptcy, rank above junior securities. For example, first mortgage bonds rank above debentures and debentures are senior to preferred stock. If there is no secured debt in the capital structure, unsecured debt is senior to all other securities.

Shareholder Wealth Maximization: The firm's objective is to maximize shareholder wealth by maximizing market value of its shares.

Shark Repellents: Any technique designed to make it difficult for one firm to take over another firm. For example, a corporate charter may contain a super-majority approval provision (perhaps 80 percent of shares outstanding) to consummate a merger. (See Chapter 21 for details.)

Shelf Registration: Sanctioned in 1983, a procedure whereby an eligible corporation can register a specific amount of securities for a public offering but may sell them in whole or in part at any time during a two-year period. Shelf-registered securities need not be sold immediately following the registration statement, which was the case prior to institution of this procedure.

Short Position: Describes a position in which one has sold securities, futures contracts, or has written options without owning the securities underlying them.

Short-term Debt: By convention, debt that matures in less than one year.

Sight Draft: Literally, an order to pay on sight: a customer must pay before receiving certain goods.

Sinking Fund: A required annual payment made to retire an issue of debt or preferred stock.

Specialist: In an organized exchange, a securities dealer who buys and sells for his or her own account in an attempt to maintain a fair and orderly market.

Spot Price: The current or going market price of a commodity or security as opposed to its forward or futures price.

Standard Deviation: A statistical term for measurement of variability in a probability distribution of values. The expected or mean value of that distribution, $\pm$ three standard deviations, encompasses almost all the area under a normal curve. The symbol for the standard deviation is the script form of the Greek letter sigma, σ.

Stand-by Agreement: An agreement between a company and its investment bankers whereby the latter agree to purchase the unsubscribed portion of shares offered to existing stockholders. (See *Rights Offering* and *Preemptive Right*.)

Stochastic: Changes in stock prices from transaction to transaction approximate a random or stochastic process.

Stock Dividend: The issuance of stock in lieu of or sometimes in addition to a cash dividend. A 3-percent stock dividend yields the owner of 100 shares an additional 3 shares.

Stock Split: The issuance of a specific number of new shares for each share outstanding. A two-for-one stock split implies the firm will issue two new shares for each share outstanding.

Subordinated Debt: A debt instrument (usually a debenture) whose claims, in the event of bankruptcy, can only be met after the claims of all other creditors are met. Subordinated debt is the most junior of all securities.

Syndicate: A group of investment bankers formed specifically to purchase for resale a securities issue.

Synergy: If the combination of two firms, A and B, is such that $Value_{AB} > Value_{A+B}$, the combination is said to produce synergy. Synergy is sometimes known as the $2 + 2 = 5$ effect.

Systematic Risk: (See *Nondiversifiable Risk*.)

Takeover: The purchase offer made by one firm to the stockholders of another firm without approval of the management or directors of the target firm. Also known as a *hostile takeover*. (See *Tender Offer*.)

Target Firm: The firm sought to be acquired in a takeover.

Technical Economies: The economies associated with greater physical output per unit of input. (See *Economies of Scale*. Contrast with *Pecuniary Economies*.)

Tender Offer: A bid made by one firm directly to the shareholders of another firm to tender their stock, often at a premium above the going market price. (See *Takeover*.)

Term Loans: Loans with maturities generally between one and ten years. Payments on principal are often amortized over the life of the loan.

Term Structure: The relationship between yield and maturity and length of maturity for bonds or debentures of comparable quality rating.

Third Market: The over-the-counter market for securities registered on the New York Stock Exchange, or possibly on another exchange.

Time Draft: A draft that must be paid at a future date. When accepted by a bank, a time draft becomes a banker's acceptance.

Times Interest Earned: Earnings before interest and taxes (EBIT) divided by interest charges.

Trade Credit: Credit that arises between firms when one firm sells goods to the other but permits the buyer to pay at the end of a specific period of time, often 30 days,

Transactions (transacting) Costs: The costs associated with buying and selling financial assets or real assets. In a more general context, they are the costs avoided when a firm organizes resources internally rather than through markets.

Treasury Bills: Short-term securities issued by the U.S. government that mature in less than one year. Treasury bills are often proxies for the risk-free rate.

Trustee: One who holds legal title to property and administers it for a beneficiary.

Uncertainty: In statistics, a situation in which the probabilities are subjective. In finance, *uncertainty* is used interchangeably with *risk*.

Underwriting: A process whereby a group of investment bankers agree to purchase an issue of new securities at a specific price guaranteed the issuer. The investment bankers then reoffer the securities to investors at a higher price.

Underwriting Spread: The difference between the selling price of a new security offering and what the offering firm receives. The spread represents the commission earned by the investment bankers for assuming the risk of marketing the issue.

Unsystematic Risk: (See *Diversifiable Risk*.)

Utility: In finance, the algebraic or graphical representations of the satisfaction one derives from risk-taking as a function of expected wealth.

Valuation: The process of determining an asset's value based on its expected cash flows and discounted at a return commensurate with the risks involved in receiving such cash flows.

Variable Rate Securities: Financial instruments on which the interest or dividend paid varies over time.

Variance: The standard deviation squared: σ^2. (See *Standard Deviation*.)

Warrant: The right to purchase shares at a specified price. For example, a company may offer debentures with detachable warrants that permit warrant holders to purchase one share of stock for each warrant issued at an exercise price above the market price.

Watered Stock: A stock originally sold at a price below its par value.

Weighted Average Cost of Capital (WACC): The cost of individual funding sources weighted by the proportion of respective market values to total market value of the company.

White Knight: A friendly investor encouraged by management to bid on its company in order to prevent a hostile takeover. (See *Takeover*.)

Working Capital: A firm's current assets and current liabilities. (See *Net Working Capital*.)

Yield: The return on a security in the form of cash payments. For expository purposes, the yield is often described as a ratio or percentage.

Yield to Maturity (YTM): The cash return on a debt security expressed as a percentage and based on the assumption the security is held to maturity.

Zero Balance Account: A demand deposit that contains no balance and to which the firm transfers funds to meet all checks drawn against it. If there is a balance at the end of the day, it is transferred to the firm's concentration account located in a major city.

Zero Beta Portfolio: An investment portfolio consisting of investments, each of which has a zero beta or a securities portfolio whose weighted betas average zero.

Zero Coupon Bond: A long-term debt instrument purchased for less than face value that pays no interest but repays the face amount at maturity. (See *Original-issue Discount Bonds*.)

INDEX

DATE DUE

APR 14 '97			
APR 15 '97			

PRESENT VALUE OF $1

RECEIVED EACH YEAR FOR 20 YEARS

$$P = \frac{1 - (1 + r)^{-n}}{r}$$

Year	Present Value at 1%	Present Value at 2%	Present Value at 3%	Present Value at 4%	Present Value at 5%	Present Value at 6%	Present Value at 7%	Present Value at 8%	Present Value at 9%	Present Value at 10%
1	0.990099	0.980392	0.970872	0.961538	0.952380	0.943395	0.934580	0.925926	0.917431	0.909091
2	1.970296	1.941556	1.913468	1.886094	1.859407	1.833391	1.808019	1.783265	1.759112	1.735538
3	2.940983	2.883878	2.828610	2.775088	2.723246	2.673010	2.624318	2.577098	2.531296	2.486852
4	3.901964	3.807718	3.717099	3.629893	3.545947	3.465103	3.387214	3.312128	3.239721	3.169866
5	4.853427	4.713449	4.579705	4.451820	4.329473	4.212361	4.100199	3.992711	3.889653	3.790787
6	5.795473	5.601415	5.417190	5.242135	5.075687	4.917321	4.766542	4.622881	4.485920	4.355261
7	6.728190	6.471980	6.230281	6.002052	5.786367	5.582377	5.389293	5.206372	5.032955	4.868420
8	7.651675	7.325462	7.019691	6.732741	6.463207	6.209790	5.971302	5.746641	5.534822	5.334928
9	8.566016	8.162218	7.786107	7.435328	7.107816	6.801688	6.515235	6.246890	5.995249	5.759025
10	9.471303	8.982563	8.530202	8.110891	7.721727	7.360082	7.023585	6.710084	6.417660	6.144568
11	10.367626	9.786826	9.252622	8.760472	8.306408	7.886870	7.498678	7.138966	6.805193	6.495062
12	11.255074	10.575315	9.954001	9.385071	8.863244	8.383839	7.942690	7.536080	7.160728	6.813693
13	12.133736	11.348350	10.634953	9.985642	9.393565	8.852677	8.357656	7.903778	7.486907	7.103357
14	13.003695	12.106222	11.296072	10.563119	9.898633	9.294979	8.745472	8.244239	7.786153	7.366688
15	13.865048	12.849238	11.937932	11.118382	10.379649	9.712243	9.107919	8.559482	8.060691	7.606080
16	14.717872	13.577676	12.561101	11.652291	10.837761	10.105890	9.446652	8.851371	8.312561	7.823710
17	15.562248	14.291842	13.166116	12.165663	11.274057	10.477254	9.763227	9.121640	8.543633	8.021554
18	16.398270	14.991996	13.753511	12.659290	11.689578	10.827599	10.059091	9.371890	8.755628	8.201413
19	17.226006	15.678430	14.323797	13.133933	12.085313	11.158111	10.335600	9.603601	8.950117	8.364921
20	18.045546	16.351397	14.877473	13.590322	12.462202	11.469915	10.594018	9.818150	9.128548	8.513564
21	18.856979	17.011175	15.415021	14.029155	12.821144	11.764071	10.835531	10.016805	9.292246	8.648695
22	19.660366	17.658010	15.936913	14.451111	13.162994	12.041577	11.061244	10.200746	9.442428	8.771541
23	20.455814	18.292166	16.443607	14.856836	13.488565	12.303373	11.272191	10.371061	9.580209	8.883219
24	21.243376	18.913887	16.935539	15.246958	13.798634	12.550352	11.469337	10.528760	9.706614	8.984744
25	22.023153	19.523418	17.413145	15.622075	14.093937	12.783351	11.653586	10.674778	9.822581	9.077041

Year	Present Value at 11%	Present Value at 12%	Present Value at 13%	Present Value at 14%	Present Value at 15%	Present Value at 16%	Present Value at 17%	Present Value at 18%	Present Value at 19%	Present Value at 20%
1	0.900901	0.892857	0.884956	0.877193	0.869565	0.862069	0.854701	0.847458	0.840336	0.833333
2	1.712523	1.690051	1.668102	1.646660	1.625709	1.605231	1.585214	1.565642	1.546502	1.527778
3	2.443715	2.401831	2.361152	2.321632	2.283225	2.245889	2.209585	2.174273	2.139917	2.106482
4	3.102446	3.037349	2.974471	2.913713	2.854978	2.798180	2.743235	2.690061	2.638586	2.588735
5	3.695897	3.604776	3.517231	3.433081	3.352155	3.274293	3.199346	3.127171	3.057636	2.990612
6	4.230538	4.111407	3.997549	3.888668	3.784483	3.684735	3.589185	3.497602	3.409778	3.325510
7	4.712191	4.563757	4.422611	4.288305	4.160420	4.038565	3.922380	3.811527	3.705696	3.604592
8	5.146123	4.967640	4.798770	4.638864	4.487322	4.343591	4.207162	4.077566	3.954366	3.837160
9	5.537048	5.328250	5.131655	4.946372	4.771584	4.606544	4.450566	4.303021	4.163333	4.030966
10	5.889233	5.650223	5.426243	5.216115	5.018769	4.833227	4.658603	4.494086	4.338935	4.192472
11	6.206516	5.937699	5.686941	5.452734	5.233712	5.028644	4.836413	4.656005	4.486500	4.327060
12	6.492357	6.194375	5.917647	5.660292	5.420619	5.197107	4.988388	4.793205	4.610505	4.439217
13	6.749871	6.423549	6.121812	5.842361	5.583147	5.342333	5.118279	4.909513	4.714710	4.532681
14	6.981865	6.628168	6.302488	6.002071	5.724476	5.467529	5.229299	5.008061	4.802277	4.610567
15	7.190870	6.810864	6.462379	6.142168	5.847371	5.575456	5.324187	5.091578	4.875863	4.675473
16	7.379162	6.973987	6.603875	6.265059	5.954236	5.668497	5.405288	5.162354	4.937700	4.729560
17	7.548795	7.119630	6.729093	6.372859	6.047161	5.748704	5.474605	5.222334	4.989664	4.774633
18	7.701617	7.249671	6.839905	6.467421	6.127966	5.817848	5.533851	5.273164	5.033331	4.812195
19	7.839294	7.365777	6.937969	6.550369	6.198232	5.877455	5.584488	5.316241	5.070026	4.843496
20	7.963328	7.469444	7.024752	6.623131	6.259332	5.928841	5.627767	5.352746	5.100863	4.869580
21	8.075071	7.562003	7.101550	6.686956	6.312462	5.973139	5.664758	5.383684	5.126775	4.891316
22	8.175739	7.644646	7.169513	6.742944	6.358663	6.011326	5.696374	5.409901	5.148551	4.909431
23	8.266432	7.718434	7.229658	6.792057	6.398838	6.044247	5.723397	5.432120	5.166849	4.924525
24	8.348137	7.784316	7.282883	6.835137	6.433772	6.072627	5.746493	5.450949	5.182226	4.937104
25	8.421745	7.843140	7.329985	6.872927	6.464149	6.097092	5.766233	5.466906	5.195148	4.947587

SOURCE: Values for $P = \frac{1 - (1 + r)^{-n}}{r}$ were computer-generated. Consequently, values for the first year need not correspond exactly to values for the first year in Appendix B, which were computer-generated using $P = \frac{1}{(1 + r)^{n}}$.